Leadership Handbooks

OF

Practical Theology

Leadership Handbooks

OF

Practical Theology

VOLUME ONE
Word & Worship

GENERAL EDITOR
James D. Berkley

BAKER BOOK HOUSE
Grand Rapids, Michigan 49516

*In honor of the men
who introduced me to
the meaning of pastoral ministry:*

*Mark L. Koehler
Robert B. Munger
Sonny Salsbury
H. Hollis Allen*

Leadership Handbooks of Practical Theology, Volume 1: Word and Worship

© 1992 by Christianity Today, Inc.
Chapter 5, "The Basic Form of the Sermon," is adapted from *The Witness of Preaching* by Thomas G. Long, with permission from Westminster/John Knox Press. © 1989 Thomas G. Long.

Copublished by Christianity Today, Inc., and Baker Book House Company. Distributed by Baker Book House Company.

Second printing, September 1994

Printed in the United States of America

Library of Congress Cataloging-in-Publication Data

Leadership handbooks of practical theology / general editor,
    James D. Berkley.
       p.   cm.
    Includes bibliographical references.
    Contents: v. 1. Word & worship.
    ISBN 0-8010-1033-0 (v. 1)
    1. Theology, Practical—Handbooks, manuals, etc.
I. Berkley, James D., 1950–
BV3.L33   1992
253—dc20   92-21971

Contents

Introduction   xv
Contributors   xvii

PART I: Preaching
  Introduction   1

  1. **The Purpose of Preaching:**
     Its Biblical and Historical Background   3
     Edmund P. Clowney
        Evangelistic Preaching   10
        Prophetic Preaching   12
        Pastoral Preaching   16

  2. **Understanding and Applying the Text**   19
     Robertson McQuilkin
        Interpreting Historical Passages   22
        Interpreting Psalms and Proverbs   24
        Interpreting Job and Ecclesiastes   28
        Interpreting the Prophets   30
        Interpreting the Gospels   31
        Interpreting the Epistles   32
        Interpreting Apocalyptic Passages   34

  3. **Denominational Preaching Traditions and Distinctives**   37
     John Bishop
        Renaissance and Reformation Preaching   40
        Seventeenth- and Eighteenth-Century Preaching   42
        Nineteenth- and Twentieth-Century Preaching   47
        Cross-cultural Preaching   48

4. Planning Preaching 51
Stuart Briscoe
Preaching the Lectionary 54
Preaching Book Series 56
Preaching Topical Sermons 60
Preaching and the Calendar 61
Guest Preachers 62

5. The Basic Form of the Sermon 65
Thomas Long
The Children's Sermon 68
Women in the Pulpit 70
African-American Preaching 75
Trends in Homiletics 76
Preaching on Radio or Television 78

6. Preparing a Sermon 81
Dan Baumann
Staying Spiritually Fresh 84
The Pastor's Library 86
Using Bible-Study Software 91
Imagination and Creativity in Preaching 92
Titles and Introductions 93
Conclusions 94
Invitations 96

7. Sermon Illustrations 99
Michael P. Green
Managing Sermon Illustrations 102
Pulpit Plagiarism 104
Storytelling 109
Pulpit Humor 110

8. Working from Applications to Action 113
David Mains

9. Sermon Delivery 119
Ralph L. Lewis
Preaching Without Notes 122
Preaching from a Manuscript 124
Before and After You Preach 128
Preaching as if One-on-One 129
Emotion in Preaching 130
Persuasion Versus Manipulation 132
Adapting to the Congregation 133
Surveying Sermon Response 134

PART II: Worship
Introduction 137

10. The Purpose and Meaning of Worship 139
Ralph P. Martin
The Use of the Bible in Worship 142
Anglican Worship 144
Lutheran Worship 148
Reformed Worship 149
Free Church Worship 151
Pentecostal and Charismatic Worship 152
Worship in the African-American Church 153

11. Prayer 157
C. John Weborg
Invocations 160
Prayers of Confession 162
The Pastoral Prayer 166
The Prayer Meeting 167
Prayer Vigils 168

12. Planning Worship 171
Howard Stevenson
The Time and Day of Worship 174
Services Not on Sunday Morning 176
The Church Year 180
Holy Days and Holidays 181
Observing National Holidays 182
Preparing Church Bulletins 184
Announcements 185
The Call to Worship 186
The Public Reading of Scripture 187
Creeds and Confessions 189
Public Sharing of Concerns 190
Passing the Peace 191
Proclamation of the Word 192
The Offering 194
Benedictions 195

13. Leading the Worship of God 197
Ronald B. Allen
Drawing Out a Timid Congregation 200
Including Youth and Children in Worship 202
Pastoral Care in Worship 206
Worship Leaders and Ushers 207

14. Special Church Services   209
James L. Christensen
Celebrating the Advent Season   212
Lent and Holy Week   214
Ordination and Installation of a Minister   218
Reception of New Members   219
The Church as a Healing Community   221
Revival Services   222
Outdoor Worship Services   223
Fine Arts Festivals   225
Radio Services   226
Televised Services   227

15. Special Services in the Community   229
Edward G. Dobson
Baccalaureate Services   232
Military Chapel Services   234
Hospital Chapel Services   236

16. Balancing Tradition and Innovation   239
Paul Anderson
Contemporary Worship   242
Art in Worship   244
Symbolism in Worship   249
Vestments   250
Choral Readings   251
Drama in Church   253
Dance as Worship   254
Multimedia in Worship   255
Worship for People with Disabilities   257
Architecture, Acoustics, and Lighting   258

PART III: Music
Introduction   261

17. The Purpose of Christian Music   263
Gordon L. Borror
Performance or Offering?   266
Dealing with Conflicting Musical Tastes   268

18. Planning a Music Program   273
Gordon L. Borror
Selecting and Purchasing Music   276
Obeying Copyright Law   278

19. Overseeing a Music Program   283
Garth Bolinder

Working with Organists and Pianists   286
Should Church Musicians Be Paid?   288
Purchasing Musical Instruments   291
Maintaining Pianos and Organs   293

20. Keys to Congregational Singing   295
Howard Stevenson
Selecting a Hymnal   298
Introducing New Music   300

21. Directing Choral Music   305
Mary Hopper
Leading Children's Choirs   308
Leading Youth Choirs   310

22. Directing Instrumental Groups   317
Daniel A. Sommerville
Directing Handbell Choirs   322

23. Concerts and Special Events   327
George H. Dupere
Coordinating Special Music   330
Using Electronics   332

PART IV: The Lord's Supper
Introduction   337

24. The Purpose of the Lord's Supper   339
Ralph P. Martin
The Lord's Supper: How Often?   344

25. Planning the Lord's Supper   349
William H. Willimon

26. The Administration of the Lord's Supper   357
Harry Boonstra
Preparing People to Partake   360
Communion for Shut-ins   362

PART V: Baptism
Introduction   367

27. The Purpose of Baptism   369
Geoffrey W. Bromiley
Baptism or Dedication?   372
Modes of Baptism   374

Baptism: Private or in Worship?   378

28. **Preparing People for Baptism**   381
William H. Willimon
Infant Baptisms and Dedications   384
Preparations for Adult Baptisms   386
Difficult Requests for Baptism   390

29. **Performing Baptisms**   393
Calvin C. Ratz
The Role of Godparents   396
The Congregation's Role in Baptism   398
Baptism Follow-up   402

30. **Confirmation**   405
Paul Anderson

PART VI: Weddings
Introduction   411

31. **The Purpose of a Marriage Ceremony**   413
Douglas M. Cecil
Divorce and Remarriage   416
Dealing with Matters of Etiquette   418

32. **Planning a Wedding Ceremony**   423
Donald Wilson Stake
Writing Vows   426
The Wedding Sermon   428
Wedding Music   432
Wedding Innovations   433
The Blessing of a Civil Marriage   435
The Renewal of Marriage Vows   436

33. **Performing Wedding Ceremonies**   439
James D. Berkley
The Wedding Rehearsal   442
The Role of Wedding Hostess   444
The Role of Wedding Musicians   449

34. **Handling Wedding Details**   451
Edd Breeden
Working with Photographers and Florists   454
Rehearsal Dinners and Receptions   456

PART VII: Funerals
Introduction 461

35. The Purpose of Funerals 463
James Christensen
    Cremation or Burial? 468

36. Planning Funeral Services 471
Robert Blair
    The Eulogy 474
    The Funeral Sermon 476
    Music for Funerals 480
    The Committal Service 482
    Military Rites 483

37. Pastoral Responsibilities for Funerals 485
Douglas M. Cecil
    Working with Funeral Directors 490

38. Handling the Hard Deaths 493
Roger F. Miller
    Funerals for Strangers and Nonbelievers 496

Introduction

R esponding to the need for a comprehensive and up-to-
date reference work for pastoral ministry, LEADERSHIP,
a practical journal for church leaders (published by
Christianity Today, Inc.), teamed with Baker Book House to develop a
set of three *Leadership Handbooks of Practical Theology* to cover the
full spectrum of ministry practice. This first volume, with nearly two
hundred articles by a hundred writers, speaks specifically about *Word
& Worship*—the priestly, prophetic, and sacramental responsibilities
of a parish minister. Coming volumes on *Outreach & Care*, along with
Leadership & Administration, will round out the series.

How to Use This Book

While many of you will want to read this series from cover to cover
to augment a systematic understanding of the practice of ministry,
others may reach for this volume seeking specific reference information. Since articles are arranged topically rather than alphabetically,
a word on the book's logic will help you understand how to find the
appropriate articles. Here is a suggested method:

• *Turn to the table of contents.* This, of course, is a comprehensive
listing of the articles in this volume. The titles have been kept simple
and direct to indicate the subject matter covered in the articles.

• *Note the seven main sections.* Parts I through VII—Preaching,
Worship, Music, the Lord's Supper, Baptism, Weddings, and Funerals—denote the main subject areas handled in this volume. Questions

of ministry practice that fall within these areas are likely to be covered within the various sections.

• *Look for a main essay that matches your subject.* Each section is divided into several chapters anchored by a main essay. The chapters also include a number of briefer articles (sidebars). The title of a main essay shows the subject covered in the chapter, and there are 38 chapter essays to cover the full sweep of subjects.

• *Check the brief articles accompanying the chapter essays.* The sidebars to the main essays cluster in the subject area the essay addresses. Each one briefly touches on a specific aspect of practical ministry, offering background, insight, and ideas. If you haven't found an essay that meets your specific need, you will probably find one of the 147 sidebars speaks directly to it.

• *Take a trial run.* Let's say you want to teach new members about your worship service, and the subject of benedictions comes up. You turn to the table of contents and find "Part II—Worship." In that section are seven chapters, and "Planning Worship" appears to have items of the kind you need. In fact, you see the sidebar titled, appropriately enough, "Benedictions."

If you don't find such an obvious match, you may want to search the table of contents again, keeping in mind that a given subject may be under a title different from one you would give it, or it may be placed "logically" in another section. While no generic logic exists in human minds to make a classification system such as this universally clear, it is intended that you will find the table of contents not unlike a self-evident filing system.

User Friendly

You will find the writer's name at the end of each article, and information about the writers is located in the "Contributors" section in the front of the book.

A listing of "Resources" follows most main essays. This listing combines reference materials from notes in the text and suggested bibliographic references for further reading and investigation.

The *Leadership Handbooks of Practical Theology* are compiled with the belief that parish pastors earnestly seek to understand and deepen their practice of ministry, making themselves better able to minister to the many needs of their congregations and the world. It is with a love for ministry that the handbooks are written, and it is with a prayer for even greater effectiveness that they are published. As this volume and the successive *Leadership Handbooks of Practical Theology* are employed among the myriad demands of modern ministry, may they become trusted and valuable friends.

Contributors

General Editor
James D. Berkley

Consulting Editor
Paul E. Engle

Executive Editor
Marshall B. Shelley

Senior Copy Editor
Gary Wilde

Editorial Administrator
Bonnie Rice

Assistant Copy Editor
Noel A. Calhoun III

Editorial Assistant
Cynthia Thomas

Acquisitions Editor
J. Isamu Yamamoto

Writers

Ronald B. Allen, Th.D., Dallas Theological Seminary. Professor of Hebrew Scriptures, Western Seminary, Portland, Oregon.

Gregory Asimakoupoulos, M.Div., North Park Theological Seminary. Pastor, Crossroads Covenant Church, Concord, California.

Paul Anderson, M.Div. Lutheran Divinity School. Senior Pastor, Trinity Lutheran Church, San Pedro, California.

Larry D. Ballenger, D.Min., San Francisco Theological Seminary. Associate Pastor, Irvine Presbyterian Church, Irvine, California.

Scott G. Bauer, M.Div., Fuller Theological Seminary. Executive Director of Ministries, The Church on the Way, Van Nuys, California.

Dan Baumann, Th.D., Boston University School of Theology. Senior Pastor, First Baptist Church, Geneva, Illinois.

Nancy D. Becker, M.Div., Union Theological Seminary (New York). Pastor, Ogden Dunes Community Church, Ogden Dunes, Indiana.

James D. Berkley, D.Min., Fuller Theological Seminary. Editor, YOUR CHURCH, Carol Stream, Illinois.

Perry H. Biddle, Jr., D.Min., Vanderbilt University. Minister and author, Old Hickory, Tennessee.

John Bishop, Ph.D., Drew University. Retired Methodist minister and lecturer, Philadelphia, Pennsylvania.

Robert Blair, M.A., Pepperdine University. Retired minister, Church of Christ in Hollywood, Los Angeles, California.

Stephen A. Bly, M.Div., Fuller Theological Seminary. Pastor, Winchester Community Church, Winchester, Idaho.

Garth Bolinder, M.Div., North Park Theological Seminary. Pastor, Hillcrest Covenant Church, Prairie Village, Kansas.

Harry Boonstra, Ph.D., Loyola University (Chicago). Theological Librarian, Calvin College and Seminary, Grand Rapids, Michigan.

Paul D. Borden, Ph.D., University of Denver. Executive Vice President and Academic Dean, Denver Seminary, Denver, Colorado.

Gordon L. Borror, M.A., California State University at Los Angeles. Assistant Professor of Church Music, Western Conservative Baptist Seminary, Portland, Oregon.

Edd Breeden, M.Div., Fuller Theological Seminary. Senior Pastor, First Presbyterian Church, Santa Cruz, California.

Emily R. Brink, Ph.D., Northwestern University. Music and Liturgy Editor, CRC Publications, Grand Rapids, Michigan.

Stuart Briscoe, D.D., Trinity Evangelical Divinity School. Senior Pastor, Elmbrook Church, Waukesha, Wisconsin.

Geoffrey W. Bromiley, D.Litt., University of Edinburgh. Senior Professor (retired), Fuller Theological Seminary, Pasadena, California.

Donald J. Bruggink, Ph.D., University of Edinburgh. Professor of Historical Theology, Western Theological Seminary, Holland, Michigan.

Jamie Buckingham, M.Div. Southwestern Baptist Theological Seminary. Former Editor-in-Chief of *Ministries Today* and Editor-at-Large of *Charisma*, Palm Bay, Florida. Deceased.

Samuel L. Canine, Ph.D., Bowling Green State University. Professor of Pastoral Ministries, Dallas Theological Seminary, Dallas Texas.

C. Harry Causey, M.Mu., Florida State University. Director, The National Christian Choir of Washington, D.C., and President, Music Revelation, Rockville, Maryland.

Douglas M. Cecil, D.Min., Dallas Theological Seminary. Assistant Professor of Field Education, Dallas Theological Seminary, Dallas, Texas.

James L. Christensen, D.D., Phillips University. Christian Church Minister, retired.

Edmund Clowney, S.T.M., Yale Divinity School. Adjunct Professor of Practical Theology, Westminster Theological Seminary in California, Escondido, California.

Richard J. Coleman, Th.M., Princeton Theological Seminary. Pastor, First Congregational Church, Plympton, Massachusetts.

John Crosby, M.Div., Gordon-Conwell Theological Seminary. Senior Pastor, Christ Presbyterian Church, Edina, Minnesota.

Arthur DeKruyter, Th.M., Princeton Theological Seminary. Senior Pastor, Christ Church of Oak Brook, Oak Brook, Illinois.

Edward G. Dobson, Ed.D., University of Virginia. Senior Minister, Calvary Church, Grand Rapids, Michigan.

Edwin Duncan, M.S., University of Utah. Director, The Wesley Bell Ringers, Christ United Methodist Church, Salt Lake City, Utah.

George H. Dupere, D.M.A., Arizona State University. Associate Minis-

ter: Music and Worship, Camelback Bible Church, Paradise Valley, Arizona.

James A. Edgren, D.Min., Wesley Theological Seminary. Chaplain U.S. Army, Retired. Director, Commission on Chaplains, National Association of Evangelicals, Washington, D.C.

Larry D. Ellis, B.S., University of Oklahoma. Minister of Worship and Music, Meadow Hills Baptist Church, Aurora, Colorado.

Howard A. Eyrich, D.Min., Western Conservative Baptist Seminary. Executive Director, Center for Biblical Counseling and Education, and Assistant Professor of Practical Theology, Covenant Theological Seminary, Saint Louis, Missouri.

Leighton Ford, M.Div., Columbia Theological Seminary. President, Leighton Ford Ministries, Charlotte, North Carolina.

Connie Fortunato, B.A., Wheaton College (Illinois). Director of Children's Music Ministry, Twin Lakes Baptist Church, Aptos, California.

Joseph Galema, D.M.A., University of Michigan. Director of Cadet Chapel Music Activities and Protestant Cadet Chapel Organist, United States Air Force Academy, Colorado.

Mark Galli, M.Div., Fuller Theological Seminary. Associate Editor, LEADERSHIP journal and CHRISTIAN HISTORY, Carol Stream, Illinois.

Timothy George, Th.D., Harvard University. Dean, Beeson Divinity

School, Samford University, Birmingham, Alabama.

Henry V. Gerike, M.Div., Concordia Seminary. Director of Choral Activities, Concordia Seminary, Saint Louis, Missouri.

Cinda Warner Gorman, D.Min., San Francisco Theological Seminary. Co-pastor, Westwood First Presbyterian Church, Cincinnati, Ohio.

Reg Grant, Th.D., Dallas Theological Seminary. Associate Professor of Pastoral Ministries, Dallas Theological Seminary, Dallas, Texas.

Michael P. Green, Ph.D., University of North Texas. Professor, Moody Graduate School, Chicago, Illinois.

John Guest, D.Litt., Geneva College. John Guest Evangelistic Team, Sewickley, Pennsylvania.

Donald Guthrie, Ph.D., University of London. President, London Bible College, Northwood, England.

Jack W. Hayford, B.Th. LIFE Bible College. Senior Pastor, The Church on the Way, Van Nuys, California.

Jerry Hayner, D.Min., Southern Baptist Seminary. Pastor, Forest Hills Baptist Church, Raleigh, North Carolina.

E. V. Hill, D.D., California Graduate School of Theology. Pastor, Mount Zion Missionary Baptist Church, Los Angeles, California.

Mary Hopper, D.M.A., University of Iowa. Associate Professor of Music,

Wheaton Conservatory of Music, Wheaton (Illinois) College.

David Allan Hubbard, Ph.D., St. Andrews University, Scotland. President, Fuller Theological Seminary, Pasadena, California.

Kent Hughes, D.Min., Trinity Evangelical Divinity School. Senior Pastor, College Church in Wheaton, Illinois.

Darrell Johnson, M.Div., Fuller Theological Seminary. Pastor, Fremont Presbyterian Church, Sacramento, California.

Douglas F. Kelly, Ph.D., University of Edinburgh. Professor of Systematic Theology, Reformed Theological Seminary, Jackson, Mississippi.

D. James Kennedy, Ph.D., New York University, New York City. Senior Minister, Coral Ridge Presbyterian Church, Fort Lauderdale, Florida.

John Killinger, Ph.D., University of Kentucky. Distinguished Professor of Religion and Culture, Samford University, Birmingham, Alabama.

Craig Brian Larson, B.S., Illinois State University. Assemblies of God Minister and Associate Editor, LEADERSHIP, Carol Stream, Illinois.

Ann A. Letson, M.Div., Louisville Presbyterian Theological Seminary. Director of Clinical-Pastoral Education, Alliant Health System, Louisville, Kentucky.

Ralph Lewis, Ph.D., University of Michigan. Professor of Preaching,

Asbury Theological Seminary, Wilmore, Kentucky.

Thomas G. Long, Ph.D., Princeton Theological Seminary. Francis Landey Patton Professor of Preaching and Worship, Princeton Theological Seminary, Princeton, New Jersey.

Grant Lovejoy, Ph.D., Southwestern Baptist Theological Seminary. Assistant Professor of Preaching, Southwestern Baptist Theological Seminary, Fort Worth, Texas.

Gordon MacDonald, M.Div., Denver Seminary. Pastor, Trinity Baptist Church, New York, New York.

Don Maddox, M.Div., Princeton Theological Seminary. Interim Pastor, First Presbyterian Church of Granada Hills, Northridge, California.

David Mains, D.D., Roberts Wesleyan College. Director, Chapel of the Air, Wheaton, Illinois.

Karen Mains, Author and lecturer, West Chicago, Illinois.

James E. Martin, Ph.D. Trinity Theological Seminary. Senior Pastor, Mt. Olivet Baptist Church, Portland, Oregon.

Ralph P. Martin, Ph.D., King's College, University of London. Professor of Biblical Studies, The University of Sheffield, England.

James Earl Massey, Ph.D., Asbury Theological Seminary. Dean, School of Theology, Anderson University School of Theology, Anderson, Indiana.

William B. McClain, D.Min., Boston University. Professor of Preaching and Worship, Wesley Theological Seminary, Washington, D.C.

Donald W. McCullough, Ph.D., University of Edinburgh. Pastor, Solana Beach Presbyterian Church, Solana Beach, California.

Robertson McQuilken, M.Div., Fuller Theological Seminary. Chancellor, Columbia Bible College and Seminary, Columbia, South Carolina.

Robert P. Meye, D.Theol., Basel University. Associate Provost for Church Relations and Christian Community, Fuller Theological Seminary, Pasadena, California.

Shawn Micheal. Studio Manager, Martech/Martinsound, Alhambra, California.

Calvin Miller, D.Min., Northwestern Baptist Theological Seminary. Professor of Communications and Ministry Studies, Southwestern Baptist Theological Seminary, Ft. Worth, Texas.

C. John Miller, Ph.D., University of the Pacific. Executive Director, World Harvest Mission, Jenkintown, Pennsylvania.

Roger F. Miller, M.Div., Lexington Theological Seminary. Pastor, First Christian Church, Muscatine, Iowa.

Robert H. Mounce, Ph.D., University of Aberdeen. President Emeritus, Whitworth College, Spokane, Washington.

Larry Moyer, Th.M., Dallas Theological Seminary. Executive Direc-

xxii   **Contributors**

tor, EvanTell, Inc., Dallas, Texas.

David Neff, M.Div., Andrews University. Managing Editor, CHRISTIANITY TODAY, Carol Stream, Illinois.

Lloyd J. Ogilvie, Th.M., Garrett Theological Seminary. Pastor, First Presbyterian Church of Hollywood, California.

Steve Pederson, Ph.D., University of Iowa. Drama Director, Willow Creek Community Church, South Barrington, Illinois.

Richard M. Peek, D.S.M., Union Theological Seminary (New York). Minister of Music, Covenant Presbyterian Church, Charlotte, North Carolina.

William Phemister, D.M.A., Peabody Conservatory. Professor of Piano, Wheaton Conservatory of Music, Wheaton (Illinois) College.

Dave Philips, D.Min., Fuller Theological Seminary. Pastor, Desert Hills Presbyterian Church, Carefree, Arizona.

E. Lee Phillips, D.Min., Vanderbilt Divinity School. Minister at large, Atlanta, Georgia.

Timothy R. Phillips, Ph.D., Vanderbilt University. Assistant Professor of Systematic and Historical Theology, Wheaton College Graduate School, Wheaton, Illinois.

Paul W. Powell, B.D., Southwestern Baptist Theological Seminary. President, Annuity Board of the Southern Baptist Convention, Dallas, Texas.

Timothy J. Ralston, Th.D., Dallas Theological Seminary. Instructor in Pastoral Ministries, Dallas Theological Seminary, Dallas, Texas.

Calvin Ratz, M.A., Syracuse University. Senior Pastor, Brightmoor Tabernacle, Southfield, Michigan.

Donald P. Regier, Th.M., Dallas Theological Seminary. Associate Professor of Christian Education, Dallas Theological Seminary, Dallas Texas.

Ramesh Richard, Th.D., Dallas Theological Seminary. Professor of Pastoral Ministries and World Missions, Lecturer in Systematic Theology, Dallas Theological Seminary, Dallas, Texas.

Lawrence C. Roff, D.Min., Westminster Theological Seminary. Pastor, Covenant Presbyterian Church, Steubenville, Ohio.

Douglas J. Rumford, D.Min., Fuller Theological Seminary. Pastor, First Presbyterian Church of Fresno, California.

Sonny Salsbury, B.A., Pasadena College. Executive Director, Camp Ghormley, Rimrock, Washington.

Robert N. Schaper, Ph.D., School of Theology of Claremont. Professor of Preaching Arts, Fuller Theological Seminary, Pasadena, California.

Douglas G. Scott, S.T.M., General Theological Seminary. Rector, Saint Martin's Church, Radnor, Pennsylvania.

Bruce L. Shelley, Ph.D., University of Iowa. Professor of Church History, Denver Seminary, Denver, Colorado.

David Sherbino, D.Min., Fuller Theological Seminary. Professor of Pastoral Studies, Ontario Theological Seminary, Toronto, Ontario.

Marguerite Shuster, Ph.D., Fuller Theological Seminary. Pastor, Knox Presbyterian Church, Pasadena, California.

Daniel A. Sommerville, D.Mus., Northwestern University. Minister of Music, Wheaton (Illinois) Bible Church and Orchestra Director, Wheaton College.

Byron Spradlin, M.Div., Western Conservative Baptist Seminary. Senior Pastor, New Hope Community Church, Rancho Cucamonga, California.

Donald Wilson Stake, B.D., Princeton Theological Seminary. Pastor, Union Presbyterian Church, Schenectady, New York.

Michael Stauffer, M.F.A., Northwestern University. Associate Professor of Theater/Communications, Wheaton (Illinois) College.

Ray C. Stedman, D.D., Talbot Theological Seminary. Retired pastor, Grants Pass, Oregon.

R. Paul Stevens, D.Min., Fuller Theological Seminary. Associate Dean, Regent College, Vancouver, British Columbia.

Howard Stevenson, D.M.A., University of Southern California. Minister of Music, Worship, and Creative Arts, First Evangelical Free Church, Fullerton, California.

Douglas Stuart, Ph.D., Harvard University. Professor of Old Testament and Chair of the Division of Biblical Studies, Gordon-Conwell Theological Seminary, South Hamilton, Massachusetts.

Joni Eareckson Tada, H.H.D., Gordon College. President of Joni and Friends, Agoura Hills, California.

Virginia Vagt, M.B.A., Northern Illinois University. Research Consultant, Malvern, Pennsylvania.

Timothy S. Warren, Ph.D., Ohio State University. Associate Professor of Pastoral Ministries, Dallas Theological Seminary, Dallas, Texas.

Diane Wawrejko, M.F.A., Arizona State University. Creative Arts Ministry, Naperville (Illinois) Vineyard and Teacher with Von Heidecke Ballet Company, Chicago, Illinois.

C. John Weborg, Ph.D., Northwestern University. Professor of Theology, North Park Theological Seminary, Chicago, Illinois.

Scott Wenig, M.Div. Denver Seminary. Preaching Pastor, Bear Valley Baptist Church, Denver, Colorado.

Dale Wheeler, Th.D., Dallas Theological Seminary. Professor of Biblical Languages and Bible, Multnomah School of the Bible, and Professor of Hebrew, Multnomah Graduate School of Ministry, Portland, Oregon.

David W. Wiersbe, M.A., Northern Illinois University. Pastor, Hope Evangelical Free Church, Roscoe, Illinois.

William Willimon, S.T.D., Emory University. Dean of the Chapel, Duke University, Durham, North Carolina.

Ralph F. Wilson, D.Min., Fuller Theological Seminary. Pastor, Church of the Live Oaks, Rocklin, California.

John W. Yates II, D.Min., Fuller Theological Seminary. Rector, The Falls Church (Episcopal), Falls Church, Virginia.

Part I:

Preaching

The ministry of the Word—what privilege compares to it? Or what responsibility?

The charge to "rightly divide the Word of God" ought to make the stoutest pastor's heart quake—and sing, as well. Lives are at stake. The kingdom of God. Eternal destinies. Preaching—empowered by the Spirit—gives to one person the ability to change the world, even as he or she transforms the worlds of those who hear. So it's a grand and an awesome task to mount the steps of the pulpit.

But isn't that odd? After all, only words are preached, and only mortals preach them. True, but they become immensely important words as mere mortals speak with God's power about *the* Word.

If preaching were but public speaking, if proclamation were no more than newscasting, then there would be little reason to read a book such as this, little cause to get excited about improvement. Preaching, however, remains a lifelong, engaging quest for those who realize its consequences, and thus the drive for continual improvement.

Here, you will find ideas, inspiration, and nourishment for your quest. Preachers have opened their hearts to write about what they care about most: faithful and effective preaching.

The Purpose of Preaching: Its Biblical and Historical Background

D o you not know what a passion for sermons has burst in upon the minds of Christians nowadays? Preachers are held in special honor, not only among the masses, but among them of the household of faith."

You may wonder about that comment. Television preachers do have a following, but scarcely special honor with the public! The comment, however, was made some time ago—about A.D. 380, in fact. It was made by the patron saint of preachers, John of Antioch, surnamed Chrysostom (Golden Mouth) by admiring posterity. His words are from an eloquent passage in which he warns the preacher against the desire for praise (Schaff 1894, 73). Good preachers, he points out, can be devoured by this monster, since they are expected to do better every time, while poor preachers nurse their private despair before audiences wilted in boredom.

Chrysostom knew the temptations of praise. Trained in Greek rhetoric, he drew crowds who, like a claque in the theater, would join in noisy shouts of acclamation and applause. Their clapping distressed him; he often preached against it, sometimes with such eloquence that his rhetoric was drowned in louder applause. On the other hand, he was also booed, for he never ceased to condemn the luxury and worldliness of the Christian populations of Antioch and Constantinople, the cities where he ministered. His prophetic boldness earned him death in exile.

Chrysostom was not the last Christian preacher to reach great crowds with Scripture. Billy Graham's audiences have been more vast by far. Must we not suppose, however, that modernity is slowly but surely bringing the centuries of preaching to an end? Others since Voltaire's time have boasted that if twelve men were able to establish Christianity, one is capable of destroying it. Many more have administered the last rites for preaching.

Are the doomsayers at last being justified? Ours is a visual age, dealing in images, not words. Even images must now flash by at frenetic speeds. Young people blinded by strobe lights and deafened by rock video cannot be expected to listen to talking heads. Perhaps Chrysostom, in his day, could compete with the theater, but his culture still had a taste for words. The church, it is said, cannot resist pop culture; it must join it. Let it replace preaching with theater and be delivered, not only from clericalism, but also from the whole Gutenberg regiment of marching words.

Proclamation's Rationale

This call for surrender is neither new nor convincing. Human beings are wired for language. They may find it difficult to listen, but certainly they will not stop talking. Preaching, however, is not just another outlet for the human desire to talk, given an opportunity. Mr. Talkative is not a hero in Bunyan's *Pilgrim's Progress*. Rather, the rationale for preaching is the fact that God has revealed himself and his will for us in words, the inspired words of the Bible.

To be sure, God has also revealed himself in his works; we sing, "How Great Thou Art!" as we see the boiling glory of a cumulus cloud, or the blurring beat of a hummingbird's wings. But the one we address is not to be found in the cloud or the bird, nor can our sin-darkened eyes find joy in his glory until we find faith through his Word. The living God is the God who speaks, who addresses us personally and calls us to stand before him and hear his words.

Israel saw no image when God spoke from Sinai (Deut. 4:15); God gave Moses no image, but rather two tablets of stone engraved with the words of his covenant. The priests were to teach the people the words of God's law; they were to be written on their doorposts and gates; indeed, bound on their foreheads and wrists to shape their thoughts and control their actions (Deut. 6:8, 9).

The Lord who made his covenant in words continued to reveal himself in words. He gave Moses songs to put on their lips (Deut. 31:19). He promised to raise up other prophets like Moses and at last to bring the final Prophet (Deut. 18:18). The seasons of God's saving deeds are matched by the seasons of his revealed words. Both point forward to Jesus Christ.

God's Old Testament revelation promises both judgment and blessing. The prophets of the Old Testament call to remembrance the sins of the people and predict destruction (Hab. 1:5). They are also messengers of hope, declaring that God purposes good at last (Jer. 29:11). Ezekiel sees the severity of the judgment. He surveys the people, not as an assembled congregation, but as dry bones scattered on the valley floor. Yet when he prophesies in the Spirit, the bones come together, are covered with flesh, and become a living host. So desperate was their condition that only the Word of God could renew them. So great are the promises preached by the prophets that only God can make good on them.

The final theme of the prophets is that God himself must come to deliver his people. The shepherds have failed; the sheep are scattered. It is God who must be their Shepherd and gather his flock (Ezek. 34:11–16). The kings have failed, the enemy has prevailed; God himself must put on his helmet of salvation and his breastplate of righteousness and come to save his own (Isa. 59:15–18).

When God comes, the old order will explode with the glory of his appearing. The meanest pot in Jerusalem will be like a temple vessel, and the weakest citizen will be like King David. What will the King be like in that day? He will be as the Angel of the Lord among them (Zech. 12:8). The coming of the Lord is joined in the prophets to the coming of the Messiah; the child to be born will bear the divine name, "Wonderful Counselor, Mighty God, Everlasting Father, Prince of Peace" (Isa. 9:6).

Proclamation's Biblical Integrity

New Testament preaching can be understood only in terms of the fulfillment of the Old Testament promises. John the Baptist proclaimed the coming of the Lord. His was the voice crying in the wilderness, "In the desert prepare the way for the Lord" (Isa. 40:3; Matthew 3:3). The coming One is so exalted that John was not worthy to lace his sandals. John baptized the penitent to prepare for his coming, but how dare he baptize Jesus when he came? What John did not understand was that Jesus came as Servant as well as Lord, that he came first, not to bring the promised judgment, but to bear the judgment on the Cross for the sins of his people.

Did the coming of the Incarnate Word bring to an end the need for preaching? Did the presence of the Lord and the acts of the Lord remove the need for the Word of the Lord? Not in the least. Jesus himself was a preacher and teacher. Further, Jesus prepared and commissioned his disciples to take up the message of his person, his work, and his teaching.

It has been said that Jesus left no book, only a fellowship, but that ignores the claims of the New Testament. Jesus sent the Holy Spirit to bring to the remembrance of his disciples all that he did and said (John 14:26; 16:13). The Spirit was his gift from the throne of glory; in that power the apostles proclaimed the saving lordship of the risen King, and in that power the apostles and prophets laid the foundation of the church in the written Scriptures of the New Testament (Eph. 2:20; 3:5).

The apostolic witness presented the living Lord whom they had seen and known. In Jesus they saw the glory of God, not only on the Mount of Transfiguration, but also in the fishing boat and on the Cross. They presented their witness, however, in words: God-given words of truth and power. Luke describes how the Word of God spread and prevailed (Acts 6:7; 12:24; 13:49; 19:20).

Apostolic Preaching

Apostolic preaching was first of all proclamation—the announcement of the coming of Jesus Christ, his death, Resurrection, and Ascension, and his coming again to judge. Christ is enthroned at the Father's right hand; all power is his. Luke's record of Paul's preaching at Antioch in Asia Minor shows the heart of the message (Acts 13:16–41). Paul traces the history of Israel to its climax in the Resurrection of the Son of David, to which he is witness.

Proclamation demands response; there is forgiveness for those who trust in Christ. The righteousness that could never be attained by striving to keep the law of Moses is the gift of God through Christ's provision. In addressing cultured Greeks on Mars Hill, Paul begins with the God they admit they do not know: the Creator of heaven and earth, not the gilded idols housed on the Acropolis just above him as he speaks. He then leads to Christ, shown to be the Judge of the nations by his Resurrection from the dead.

Apostolic preaching shapes the New Testament. We are admonished and encouraged to life that adorns the gospel, but gospel proclamation comes first. The Epistles of Paul and Peter lead to a repeated *therefore:* "Therefore, I urge you, brothers, in view of God's mercy, to offer your bodies as living sacrifices . . ." (Rom. 12:1).

Early Church Fathers

The thrust of the apostles' style of preaching was soon blunted after their death. Proclamation faded from preaching and was replaced by pious exhortation. The church father Origen (185–254) brought classical learning to the exposition of Scripture, but he seems to have been embarrassed by the details of the Old Testament, much as the Greek philosophers had been embarrassed by the pagan myths. Like them, he used the allegorical method to draw ethical principles from the text. When the Book of Exodus gives a recipe for anointing oil, there must be a deeper meaning. "If these words . . . contain no hidden mystery, are they not unworthy of God?" (Origen 1971, 40). Origen distinguished the historical meaning of the text from the moral and mystical meaning. Through arbitrary allegories, Origen could, indeed, make a text mean anything he chose.

Yet he did not despise the words of Scripture, but preached through Leviticus word by word. "Holy Scripture never uses any word haphazard and without a purpose" (Origen 1971, 47). He sought Christ and the church in the Old Testament; mystical devotion to Christ rises everywhere in his allegorical exposition of the Song of Songs.

Yet in Origen's writings the apostolic proclamation of the gospel was diverted. No longer does God's redemption in the Old Testament drive us forward to the fulfillment of all the promises in the finished work of Christ. Rather, the Scripture has become a treasury of words, loosed at times even from the sentences where they are found, so that Origen applies *his* doctrine, not what the Bible says.

Chrysostom (347–407) made less use of allegory and presented even more forcefully the ethical imperatives of the Christian faith. Yet, for all of his faithfulness and eloquence, the clear gospel message of apostolic preaching was not heralded.

With Augustine (354–430), a new beginning was made. While his preaching showed his mastery of Latin rhetoric, his content brought forward again the grace of God's salvation. Augustine rejoiced in the deity of God the Son, and the wonder of God's royal grace. The hard-won orthodoxy of the church flowered in the devotional power of his preaching:

And now, with what words shall we praise the love of God? What thanks shall we give? He so loved us that for our sakes He, through whom time was made, was made in time; and He, older by eternity than the world itself, was younger in age than many of his servants in the world; He, who made man, was made man; He was given existence by a mother whom He brought into existence; He was carried in hands which He formed; He was nursed at breasts which He filled; He cried like a babe in the manger in speechless infancy—this Word without which human eloquence is speechless! (Fant and Pinson 1971, 137).

It might seem that Augustine had surmounted the doctrinal aberrations of Origen and the moralistic teaching of Chrysostom to point the church back to the apostolic gospel. Yet it was a legalistic message that prevailed and set the tone for the Middle Ages. Leo the Great (d. 461) continued the tradition of sonorous prose, but "reinterpreted the legacy from Augustine in a moralistic way . . ." (Brilioth 1965, 62).

The major trend, however, was the elaboration of the liturgy of the Mass, so that preaching was crowded out of the service of worship. Increasingly, preaching was reserved for fast days and for special occasions. It was practiced more in the monastic orders than by parish priests. The Crusades gave new impetus to preaching, but to preaching linked with indulgences promised to those who would battle for the Holy Land.

Medieval Revival

The revival of learning in medieval scholasticism brought a renewal of preaching in the universities and in the mendicant orders (the Dominican "preaching friars"). University preaching was in Latin, guided by many manuals that applied Aristotelian logic to the sermon. The format called for a unified message based on a biblical text and structured with theme and divisions. The body of the sermon developed the divisions with confirming quotations from other Scriptures or the Fathers, and led to a brief conclusion.

The rigor of scholastic outlining guarded clarity and unity in preaching, but the medieval handbooks went far beyond showing the use of sermon outlines. They prescribed in minute detail every imaginable device of sermon crafting. They showed how to relate the ABCs of point one to the DEFs of point two and the GHIs of point three, all with rhyming endings. Bits of their pedantry have lived on in academic preachers laboring for the salvation of their sermons.

Rhetorical expertise was not lacking in Luther's day. Tetzel hawked indulgences with panache to fund the building of St. Peter's in Rome. What was missing from late medieval preaching was the gospel. Luther, too, was a master communicator in strong, sometimes earthy, German, but he preached what the Bible says about salvation through faith alone. The artist Cranach painted Luther preaching: on the left, the congregation; on the right, Luther in the pulpit; in the middle, Christ crucified.

Luther preached from about 1509 until three days before his death in February 1546. On Sundays he preached sometimes three or four times. In Wittenberg there was preaching on the catechism on Monday and Tuesday, and on Bible books the other days, often with Luther as the preacher. So, too, in Geneva Calvin expounded the Bible every morning; in Berne, crowds were drawn to the preaching of Zwingli.

The Reformation opened a flood of preaching and teaching in the Scriptures. The spread of printing made possible the distribution of sermons; not only the Bible, but also preaching in print, swept across northern Europe.

The Reformers made the preaching of the Word central in worship; the sacraments were not to be separated from the preached Word. The contrast between the cathedral of Chartres and a congregational church in colonial New England marks the shift from dramatic mystery to gospel proclamation. The soaring pillars of Chartres raise a vast canopy over the nave that leads to the screen and the altar, where the drama takes place. In the New England building, the Puritan tradition has put the pulpit in the center, bearing the open Bible.

After the Reformation

In the centuries since the Reformation, preaching has at times retained orthodoxy but lost passion, and at other times turned to angry tirades or feathery ear-tickling. Yet the stream of biblical exposition and proclamation has not dried up. Rather, the missionary movement of evangelical Christianity has carried the gospel around the globe. Today preaching is international, with styles as different as the cultures they reflect. Yet the preaching and teaching of the missionary pioneers still echoes in thatched shelters on the African plains or in the huge metropolitan churches of Korea.

Missionary and evangelistic preaching has its own annals. Columba confronted the Druids in Scotland centuries before John Wesley took to the fields in England or George Whitfield's voice carried two city blocks to touch Benjamin Franklin (in his pocketbook at least) in Philadelphia (Moffett 1930, 167, 169).

In America a lineage of evangelists has brought gospel preaching to great crowds. Times of revival, as well as of missionary expansion, have been nurtured in prayer and preaching. The preaching of Jonathan Edwards (1703–1758) contributed to the Great Awakening; the profundity of his mind was immersed in Scripture and fired by the unction of the Spirit. He preached in the Puritan fashion: his carefully organized discourses expounded the text of Scripture, addressing the will and emotions as well as the intellect, to reach the hearer's heart.

Preaching sparked the revivals that swept Wales and transformed its life in the nineteenth and early twentieth centuries. Edward Matthews (1813–1892) held congregations spellbound as he took them with the shepherd seeking his lost sheep. His eloquence traversed hill and dale, crossed torrents, and crashed through thickets, finding but a trace of wool on a bramble bush, until at last he could hoist the sheep on his shoulders and shout, "She is found!"

The congregation shouted with him, "Glory be to God!" (Dargan and Turnbull 1974, 2:504). No doubt the people thrilled to hear the musical cadences of the Welsh language, rising to a *hwyl* that turned prose to poetry and song. Yet God's instrument in the Welsh revival of 1904–1905 was not a trained and eloquent preacher, but Evan Roberts, a miner and blacksmith, who called for repentance, surrender, and public confession of Christ.

Questions of Culture

The endless varieties of preaching show God's use of many servants in many situations, but servants they were, not the masters of the Word of God. The great divide in preaching is between those who serve the Word and those who merely use it.

Charles Haddon Spurgeon is an example of truly serving the Word. While his words were often eloquent, vivid with images and burning in appeal, his power lay in the Scriptures that had gripped his heart. Spurgeon did not apologize for boldly proclaiming a biblical concept that was distasteful to his contemporaries: the blood of Christ. "This much we are resolved on," he wrote, "we will be true to our convictions concerning the sacrifice of our Lord Jesus; for if we give up this, what is there left? God will not do anything by us if we are false to the Cross. . . . God give us to be faithful witnesses to the blood of the Lamb in the midst of this ungodly world!" (Dargan and Turnbull 1974, 2:540f).

Can the power of the gospel shape preaching in the fragmented world of ethnic cultures jostling into the twenty-first century? Cultural diversity in preaching styles will but enhance the gospel message, for it will bring to light more of the biblical descriptions of

---

Evangelistic Preaching

In some ways evangelistic preaching is easier than other kinds of preaching, and in other ways it is more difficult. In either case, it is extremely rewarding because God uses the proclamation of the gospel in evangelistic preaching to bring lost people into his eternal kingdom.

The Differences

What sets evangelistic preaching apart? Evangelistic preaching is taking the truth of a portion of Scripture and explaining it to a non-Christian audience. The following three distinctions further define it:

• *A sharper aim or purpose.* The purpose is to present the gospel clearly, with the intent of seeing the hearer come to faith in Christ. So specific is the purpose that the congregation can sense one's intention. Such a sermon is not prepared for believers, but rather prepared for and given to the unsaved.

• *A sharper focus on the audience.* In evangelistic preaching we speak to only one segment of people—the lost. Therefore, we cannot assume they know the Bible. It's good to avoid statements such as, "In Genesis 3 . . ." We cannot expect a friendly attitude toward us or our subject, nor should we expect even interest in what we're going to say. We should assume they're not interested and seek to win them through the message.

• *Less textual digging.* Unlike speaking to believers, when we explain biblical passages to an unsaved audience, we should mention only what is crucial to understanding the text. For example, in preaching to nonbelievers from Ephesians 2:1–10, it's more important to *elaborate* on the phrase "by grace you have been saved" and just *summarize* as simply as possible the phrase "and seated us with him in the heavenly realms in Christ Jesus."

preaching.

The New Testament speaks of preaching as *proclamati* ald's trumpet announcing the Lord who came and is comin *teaching*, explaining the meaning of the finished work of instructing believers in the issues of faith and life; and as *encourage* *ment*, lifting up hands that hang down; but also as *warning* and *re-* *buke*, humbling pride and confronting rebellion. Preaching reasons, commands, guides, entreats, counsels, and illumines; it evokes the response of repentance, faith, and praise. Always it leads to Christ, the living Word. No one preacher can touch all the stops on the console of Scripture, but the medley of universal proclamation will discover fresh harmonies of beauty and power.

Another question is raised by cultural diversity, however. We have learned to be critical of our own cultural assumptions. We do not interpret the Bible apart from a grid with which we begin. Does that

---

The Evangelistic Sermon

• *It has simple organization.* It has been said that some preachers are too much like Christopher Columbus in their sermons. When they start out, we're not sure where they're going; when they arrive, we're not sure where they are; and when they return, we're not sure where they've been.

When we preach evangelistically, the audience must be able to follow our logic. The simplest evangelistic messages are the most effective.

• *It is life-revealing.* The nonbeliever should feel we're reading his or her diary. As we explain the Scriptures, that person should think, *Yes, that's what it says.* As we apply it to life, he or she will say, *Yes, that's me.*

• *It is relatively short.* Mark Twain supposedly said that few sinners are saved after the first twenty minutes of a sermon. Although Twain likely exaggerated, an evangelistic sermon should be at most thirty minutes long. Brevity enhances di-rectness and causes people to think the preacher is someone who has something to say, says it, and sits down.

• *It is highly illustrative.* To be reached, the unsaved person must know we not only understand the Bible, but life as well. Jesus, the Master Communicator, knew the importance of stories, which gain attention, add interest to the message, enliven the hearers, and drive home truth.

• *It contains humor.* Humor relaxes an often-unrelaxed audience. It also conveys to the nonbeliever that the speaker is a wholesome person who knows how to laugh, not someone raised in a jar of sour pickles.

The evangelistic preacher, whose job it is to herald the one message a lost person must hear to be saved, must take his or her assignment seriously—first on one's knees, next in the study, and then before a lost people whom God loves.

—*Larry Moyer*

grid form the bars of a prison from which we cannot escape? Do we find in the Bible only what our cultural bias disposes us to find?

Curiously, the mind-set of our age would confound itself by answering yes. If all truth is relative to culture, then that very statement is foolish, since declaring *truth* to be relative is declaring that the truth we were speaking of does not exist. Once we lose the norm of what Francis Schaeffer felt compelled to call "true truth," we lose the authority of gospel preaching. The gospel claims to be God's revelation, not human invention. If all religions are equally true, the Christian gospel is uniquely false, for it declares that Jesus Christ alone is the Way, the Truth, and the Life. The theologians who now proclaim the "myth of Christian uniqueness" are quite aware of this; to recognize all religions, they must find Christian orthodoxy intolerably in-

Prophetic Preaching

Preaching is boldly proclaiming to the unbelieving world the Good News of what God has done in Jesus Christ. Preaching is meant, as well, to edify and exhort those who do believe. But, in addition, preaching involves saying clearly and with force what God expects of people and what he plans to do in time, proclaiming truth to both the saved and the unsaved concerning God's will for their lives.

This, I believe to be prophetic preaching, as it was in Ezekiel 37:7a.

Certainly prophetic preaching is a delicate matter that must be handled with the utmost care and prayer. People can be shaken by prophetic preaching, and they may react uncharacteristically. Any prophet worth his salt was tormented at times. And prophetic preaching puts the preacher out on a precarious limb.

To say "Thus saith the Lord" is to be accountable, and the test of such prophetic preaching is that it comes true.

Who Preaches Prophetically?

I do not believe prophetic preaching to be a permanent gift. It is unlikely that any particular preacher should *only* preach prophetically. God has other functions for the preacher, other messages, other gifts. The prophetic is but one kind of preaching.

But each of us who preaches ought to declare prophetically what the Holy Spirit of God reveals to us in our spirit. To avoid the difficult, to shirk the leadings of the Spirit, to preach only to curry the favor of the crowd—these temptations ought to fall before the overwhelming responsibility of speaking God's words after him. We must confront our world with the gospel; we must warn and reprove the world with God's Word. We are after all the mouthpiece of

tolerant (Hick and Knitter 1989, 44, 45).

The preaching of God's revealed truth requires that we stand under the Word of God, especially in the atmosphere of contemporary pluralism. Human culture is never self-sufficient. When the Creator is denied, some idol is enshrined at the religious core of knowing and doing. The Christian preacher exposes the idols on today's Acropolis and uncovers again the altar dedicated "to the unknown God." The great threat facing preaching in America is not first its dilution with pop psychology, nor even its dabbling in entertainment; it is the threat to the gospel message itself by the undercutting of the authority of what the Bible says.

Only God's Word can give significance to human life and deliver culture from despotism or despair. To be sure, we seek the meaning of

---

the Almighty.

Common Problems

One danger, of course, is sensationalism. It isn't difficult to get wound up in "prophetic preaching" that reflects more our own notions than God's will. We might take sensationalistic turns that lead us into fanciful excursions or worse. We can stumble over the difficulty of preaching God's future and not our own fantasies.

Another problem is getting caught up in the trivial. We wisely want to avoid the plight of being considered merely a fortune teller of sorts, dealing with relatively trivial specifics, such as whether a person is going to get a job or find a fortune.

On a higher plane, but no less problematic, is the business of preaching about such things as the exact date of Jesus' return or other specifics of biblical prophecy that theologians have disputed for centuries. Rare is the expositor with the insight denied all other preachers for two millennia!

True Prophetic Preaching

The kind of prophetic preaching I believe in gives God's answers to problems facing a people as well as individuals. God does not leave his people without hope, without a word from heaven. God speaks through preachers to help individuals set their course or change their paths, and he uses prophetic preaching to warn, encourage, and direct whole people groups in his ways.

Prophetic preaching necessarily involves warnings of God's displeasure, of his wrath and withering majesty that cannot be compromised. Prophetic preaching will never minimize his judgment or his blessings. Prophetic preaching—a *forth*telling as well as a *fore*telling— is truly meant to "disturb the comfortable as well as comfort the disturbed."

Like Israel, the believers today should be able to ask in belief the question "Is there a word from the Lord?" and receive from the prophetic preacher an unabashed answer.

—*E. V. Hill*

the Bible's words in the cultural setting of the passage: its literary form, its historical and social context. But the Bible, through its sometimes bewildering diversity, records one great story of redemption that leads to our great God and Savior, Jesus Christ. Preaching becomes significant by grasping the meaning of the text in its biblical setting and by applying that meaning to the situation of those who hear. Cultural sensitivity enables us to transmit the message so that it both communicates and confronts as God's own Word.

Fidelity to God's Word does not bind us to traditions, even to orthodox traditions. But preaching that temporizes truth to gain a hearing loses converting power—the power of the preacher to declare, "Hear the Word of the Lord!"

The Service of Preaching

If the power of preaching is the power of God's Word, then God's calling to preach is a calling to ministry, to service in the Word. The apostles, knowing that call, would not leave the prayerful service of the Word to serve tables. Seven others, endued with the Spirit, were chosen to management roles in the apostolic church.

The preacher may wonder if even apostles could carry off today so narrow a definition of their role. Have not religious sociologists demonstrated that ministers assign the greatest importance to that which least occupies their professional time—preaching? In reality they are managers, project developers, fund-raisers, counselors, hospital chaplains, even plant superintendents.

One reassurance is that the ministry of the Word is not limited to sermon preparation, nor even to the authoritative teaching of the Word that is the minister's special calling. At a hospital bed, in marriage counseling, with a breakfast prayer group, the Word of God is also ministered. Since ministers are called to aid the saints in developing their gifts, their calling must be seen, not as a monopoly on teaching, nor as a lordship over the congregation, but as servanthood: the service of a pastor to the flock, a pastor who finds in Christ the model of the Shepherd who gave his life for the sheep. The paradox of gospel service does not discard a structure of authority in the church, but it makes that authority a license to serve, to seek the things of others, to support, to give the days and years of life, and, if necessary, life itself.

To appreciate the richness and the fellowship of the ministry of the Word will answer in part the dilemma of the preacher. There is much more to ministering the Word than preaching sermons. Yet that offers only a partial answer. The other part remains: the priority of the minister of the gospel is ministering the gospel. It is the Word that equips for ministry, and it is the Word that is ministered: "All Scripture is

God-breathed and is useful for teaching, rebuking, correcting, and training in righteousness, so that the man of God may be thoroughly equipped for every good work" (2 Tim. 3:16, 17).

The passage states the function as well as the equipment of the one who is "the man of God" in this special sense of one called to minister the Word. Wisdom in ministering the Word is the Spirit's gift, granting insight into the Scriptures and into human need.

The scribe of the kingdom (Matt. 13:52) brings forth treasures from all the Scriptures. Never before has a student of the Word been so lavishly equipped in the tools of study. Computer-assisted research produces the riches of Scripture at the tap of a "search" key. Recent commentaries continue to cull the centuries of scholarly reflection on Bible passages. The thrill of discovery at finding Christ in the Scriptures awaits the interpreter at every turn.

Yet wisdom is more than Bible information, or even scriptural insight. It is an understanding of the Word refracted through obedience and deepened in meditation and prayer. Jesus promised to send prophets, wise men, and teachers who would be flogged, pursued, and murdered in their service of the Word (Matt. 23:34). The minister who never cries "Who is sufficient for these things?" does not understand Christ's calling. To be entrusted with the very oracles of God, to shepherd and feed the flock of Christ, to stand before an amused or hostile world with the folly of the gospel—this is not to choose a profession; it is to choose the Crucified.

—Edmund P. Clowney

Resources

Blackwood, A. 1947. The Protestant pulpit. New York: Abingdon-Cokesbury.

Brilioth, Y. 1965. A brief history of preaching. Philadelphia: Fortress.

Chrysostom, 1894. On the priesthood. In *Nicene and post-Nicene Fathers, vol. 8*, ed. P. Schaff. New York: Christian Literature.

Dargan, E., and R. Turnbull. 1974. A history of preaching. Grand Rapids: Baker.

Fant, C., and W. Pinson, eds., 1971. Twenty centuries of great preaching, vol. 1: Biblical sermons to Savonarola, A.D. 27–1498. Waco, Tex.: Word.

Hick, J., and P. Knitter. 1987. The myth of Christian uniqueness: Toward a pluralistic theology of religions. Maryknoll, N.Y.: Orbis.

Moffett, H. 1930. Autobiography of Benjamin Franklin. New York: Macmillan.

Origen, 1971. The first homily on the Song of Songs. In *Twenty centuries of great preaching, vol. 1: Biblical sermons to Savonarola, A.D. 27–1498*, ed. C. Fant and W. Pinson. Waco, Tex.: Word.

Pastoral Preaching

A familiar adage says that preaching should "comfort the afflicted and afflict the comfortable." People typically think of pastoral preaching as doing the first—comforting the afflicted. Afflicting the comfortable? That's prophetic preaching. People also commonly distinguish pastoral preaching from evangelistic preaching. Evangelistic preaching saves the lost; pastoral preaching nurtures the saved.

Pastoral preaching, however, is more than these common notions allow. After all, *pastor* is the Latin word for *shepherd*. Pastoral preaching is preaching done as an undershepherd of God's flock. The shepherding motif has several implications for the way pastoral preaching is understood and practiced.

Pastor as Shepherd

Pastoral preaching presumes the preacher has an ongoing, caring relationship with the flock. Experts in medicine and psychology may offer help, but they lack the unique caring relationship that pastors have with parishioners.

Love for the flock produces a concern for the long-term health and strength of the flock. Pastoral preaching thus aims to feed the flock a balanced diet from God's Word. It tries to declare "the whole counsel of God" over time. Doing so requires careful sermon planning or the use of a lectionary.

Pastoral preaching views sermons as one of many experiences that shepherd and flock share. Pastoral preachers understand that the New Testament pictures them as sheep as well as shepherds. They identify with the congregation and resist overstating their pastoral authority. The preacher speaks for, as well as to, the church.

Preaching to Needs

Pastoral preaching tends to wounded members of the flock. By addressing felt needs, pastoral preaching heightens the relevance of sermons, which in turn attracts hearers who might otherwise ignore Christianity. Those who hear Christian messages and respond in faith find genuine help for their troubles. They discover that God works to strengthen people for the living of their days.

The potential pitfalls of this approach are numerous. Letting human needs dictate all sermon subjects can inadvertently convey that God exists solely to help people get what they want out of life, when in fact he often frustrates human wants. Also, "needs" have sometimes been defined too narrowly; people need a moral-ethical framework and solid doctrine. Scripturally informed pastoral preaching guards against losing the holiness of God in the forgiveness of God.

When God comforts, he typically corrects or challenges as well. Healthy pastoral preaching does the same. It is not hesitant to assert the claim of God as well as the comfort of God. It speaks timely words of judgment without falling into judgmentalism. Without a scriptural word of judgment, irresponsible behavior goes unchecked and church discipline ceases to exist.

Sound pastoral preaching also resists some counselors' use of the Bible as a mere resource—a kind of grab bag from which one picks and chooses. The Bible is more than just one counseling resource among many; it is the pre-eminent source. Furthermore, the Bible is a source of truth as well as help. In fact, if it is not truth, it cannot help. Pastoral preaching is biblical preaching.

Protecting the Flock

Pastoral preaching accepts the responsibility of protecting the flock. It promotes sound teaching and refutes those who err. It seeks to reclaim and restore the wayward. In this sense, pastoral preaching may include "prophetic-type" messages of rebuke and sharp warning. Such pastoral rebukes differ from other prophetic preaching because the pastoral preacher doesn't expect to shake the dust off his feet and move on.

Pastoral preaching offers an exciting challenge for all who attempt it. Those engaged in shepherding can draw encouragement from realizing that the flock is God's, and the Great Shepherd himself watches over it.

—Grant Lovejoy

2

Understanding and Applying the Text

The first and fundamental task of preaching is to determine what the Bible author meant and what that meaning means today. To put it another way, the twofold task of the interpreter is to determine (1) the meaning the author intended to communicate, and (2) the response God desires from the preacher and the hearers. The two are intimately related. What the text says to God's people today must be based on—and flow directly from—what it said to God's people originally, or the sermon is no longer an authoritative word from God.

Our task, then, is not to dazzle people with ideas that no one could ever imagine were hidden away behind the text. Rather, we must demonstrate how they, too, can read the Bible with understanding and apply it to their own lives with integrity.

Before Interpreting: What Size Text?

The length of text we choose depends somewhat on the text itself but also on the depth to which we wish to examine the text. In any event, we must resist the temptation to choose a passage too long for the allotted sermon time, or the listener will feel either overwhelmed (if we try to cram in all the good stuff) or incomplete (if the we don't do justice to the whole text). If the passage is too long for adequate coverage in a single message, it's far better to create a short series of sermons.

In preaching through consecutive passages of Scripture, seeking to determine the next section that can be handled in the time allotted, we can look for a major change in the flow of thought and choose a unit of thought for which the Bible author provides a beginning and an ending. A change in events is easy to identify, but a change in thought is sometimes more subtle. If there is a major shift in thought only at the beginning and end of an extended passage, we need to interpret the whole passage as a cohesive unit. To analyze only part of the section will often lead us away from the author's intended meaning. So, when the unit of thought is too long for a single sermon, we should clearly bridge to the next episode in a to-be-continued series. At the very least, if we choose to use only part of what the author treated as a whole, we must be true to the meaning of the whole in treating the part.

Once we have chosen the passage or passages to be treated, the two basic tasks of interpretation and application begin.

Task #1: What Did the Author Mean?

Probably no preacher today would use the medieval procedure of deriving four distinct meanings from each text: literal, allegorical, moral, and prophetic. Yet most of us have occasionally yielded to hermeneutical temptation, "adjusting" a passage to make a particular point. The task of the honest interpreter, however, is to determine the single meaning intended by the author.

A common error is to leave the audience with the impression that our application of the text is what the author meant to communicate in the first place, when actually it is not. In such cases, we must clearly distinguish for the hearers what the Bible author intended to communicate, apart from the implication we are drawing from that instruction, principle, or event. We need to do this first task of identifying the single meaning of the author in full view of the hearers: "This is what the Bible author said, and God's authority is behind it; we must trust and obey. Now, friends, it seems to me that this truth applies to our lives today in the following way . . . "

We can follow standard guidelines or procedures as we seek to understand the human-communication aspect of the text. These are summarized here in four steps:

1. Examine the external context. What is the original historical, physical, and cultural setting? We can get this background from Bible dictionaries, encyclopedias, handbooks, atlases, and, especially, critical (as distinguished from devotional) commentaries. We unlock most passages more readily by knowing what kind of person was speaking, and on what sort of occasion.

Studying the cultural context is especially helpful in trying to understand what the author meant. Two cautions are necessary, however. First, we must not read into the text our present understandings. For example, in defining *salt*, it won't do to go to an encyclopedia and note all the characteristics of salt identified by the scientist and apply these with ingenuity to the text. We must study, rather, what the people of Jesus' day used salt for, how *they* understood "You are the salt of the earth" (Matt. 5:13).

A second caution is that we must not let modern cultural perspectives modify the meaning of the ancient text. For example, just because our age tends to look more leniently on homosexual relationships, we may not make Paul say that only *promiscuous* homosexual relationships are against nature, when he clearly identified all homosexual activity as depraved behavior (see Rom. 1:26ff).

2. Examine the internal context. This principle of interpretation is so important that one might almost say internal context is king, both in relation to our study of textual words and textual thoughts.

● *Words.* Context *is* king in understanding the meaning of individual words. Are there words in the text that are important theologically, or equivocal in their meaning? We cannot avoid the rigor of a careful word study for each of them if we will understand the passage. How is the word used in the rest of Scripture and in other contemporary literature? Scripture uses critical words, such as *world* and *flesh*, in many different ways. Such words demand a thorough investigation before preaching about them.

Having examined all the possible meanings of the word, ultimately the meaning we assign it must fit the context. We must not force on it some meaning that is not demanded by this particular context, or— unthinkable—tell our people that it means *several* things.

For example, in a critical passage concerning the Christian life in 2 Corinthians 3:18, is Paul saying that we steadfastly *keep our attention fixed on* Christ as the basis of our spiritual growth or that we *reflect* the glorious likeness of Christ? Some translations choose one, some the other. Either interpretation is theologically true, but that does not release the preacher to choose the one that makes the point he or she would like to make. One must trace the flow of thought in the larger context and in the text itself to determine which of the two meanings Paul had in mind.

● *Thoughts.* Context is not only king for the meaning of words; it is just as essential in the task of analyzing the flow of thought. Those who have the linguistic tools to trace grammatical constructions can use them. Those who don't ought not use that fact as an excuse to bypass this critical step of careful exegesis. They can discern the structure or thought flow in a good translation and check their understandings with a trusted critical commentary.

The meaning derived from the text must be in conformity with the structure of the text itself. For example, in Philippians 1:11 ("filled with the fruit of righteousness that comes through Jesus Christ"), is it the *righteousness* that comes through Jesus Christ, or the *fruit?* In translation, the structure of this sentence may make the answer ambiguous, but a critical commentary will reveal that the cases in the Greek text demand that it is the fruit Paul had in mind. Therefore, it is not legitimate to use this passage to teach the truth of how our righteousness comes through Christ.

3. *Examine the entire context.* After we thoroughly examine the background of the text, the key words, and the structure or flow of thought in the passage chosen for exposition, we focus on the larger

---

Interpreting Historical Passages

In our hard-data and spreadsheet-oriented society, stories rarely are used to communicate truth or instruct us about the foundational principles of our society. Instead, they often serve only as supplemental anecdotes.

In contrast, biblical writers often used stories to communicate truth, without providing explanatory essays. More Scripture is written in narrative than in any other form. To understand stories, however, we must study them with different assumptions than we bring to the logical, well-reasoned arguments in Romans or Galatians.

Interpretive Assumptions

First, we should assume that inspired stories have all the characteristics of any good story. They must be studied as stories, dealing with the narrative as a unit. After all, no parent would read only the middle of a bedtime story to a child as though it were the entire story.

Second, we must view the narratives as literature, not history. The stories of the Bible are true and do record history, but that is not their primary purpose. Each writer developed theological arguments by putting stories together in certain ways. Therefore, a topical arrangement was more important than a chronological one.

Third, the exegetical idea of each story in the Bible is unique. Although Noah, Abraham, Moses, David, and Ruth were people of faith while Cain, Esau, Achan, and Jezebel were the unfaithful, the Holy Spirit and the human authors were more creative than we think. When the events change, so should the preaching theme and application.

Fourth, accept the characters in narratives as real people who at times did great things and at other times failed miserably, as we see with David the adulterer or Peter the coward.

Interpretive Techniques

Narrative passages tend to be long, so a chart of a passage enables us to see it as a whole. Here's how to fill in a chart:

• List the characters. Include all major and minor players, as well as crowds and groups.

context. Context is still king, so we cannot study the meaning of a passage in isolation. Meaning must fit and flow from the context of the entire chapter and the entire book. In fact, many preachers make it a practice to read the entire context, even the entire book, many times before beginning the detailed analysis of the passage chosen for exposition, getting a feel for the author's broad flow of thought.

To use a text out of context to make a point we wish to make is to undercut the authority of Scripture. Our point may be quite biblical, but the approach can lead us and our hearers into using the authority of a Bible text to validate a purely human idea or even a false concept.

• Note the literary devices. Rhetorical structures like repetition, chiasm, and other patterns may be important. They help distinguish between primary and secondary portions. Also be sure to ascertain the tone of the story to determine the author's point of view.

• Observe the action. Note the design of the story and pay careful attention to what occurs and what does not occur. Is the story recounted in a straightforward manner or with flashback? Is it told in first or third person? Is the emphasis on plot, action, character development, or a combination of these?

• Frame the scenes, noting different settings, and then find the plot. Look for disequilibrium, then reversal, and, last, resolution.

• Study the dialogue, especially when dialogue is repeated (or repeated with slight variations).

• Pay attention to the narrator, who, in biblical stories, knows motives, sees all, hears all. When the narrator intrudes with information you would not otherwise know, it's likely to be significant.

Interpretive Results

This concluding three-step process should result in fresh, biblically sound sermon ideas:

1. *Write a summary sentence* of each paragraph that accurately reflects what has occurred.

2. Then, *write a sentence summarizing the action* in the entire narrative—your "what sentence." Withhold interpretive ideas from this sentence. You want to determine exactly what has occurred before wrestling with meaning.

3. Finally, *write out your exegetical idea.* First, write the subject of the exegetical idea in the form of a question. For 1 Samuel 3:1–4:1a, the question might be: "Why does God honor Samuel by causing all of Israel to recognize him as God's prophet?" Next, answer the question in the complement: "Because Samuel honored God's words to him by delivering a message of judgment to Eli."

Check this interpretation against your chart and your "what sentence." If agreement occurs, rewrite the exegetical idea as a declarative sentence, such as: "God honors Samuel by establishing him as prophet because Samuel honored God's word to him by delivering a message of judgment."

You now have the idea of the story and you are ready to put your interpretive results to work developing homiletical possibilities.

—*Paul Borden*

4. Watch for figurative language. We must consistently withstand two dangerous temptations when working with figurative language: (1) the temptation to impose on the biblical analogy some point of comparison that fits our contemporary frame of reference, and (2) the temptation to make several comparisons from a single figure of speech. Sticking to two basic rules will help counter these tendencies.

The first rule for discovering what the author intended to communicate through figurative language is to remember that such language is totally immersed in the ancient culture. We must discover the point of comparison the readers *of that day* would have understood, not what might come to mind today, particularly what might come to a gifted pastoral imagination!

For example, commentators have crafted strange interpretations of Christ's statement about believers at his return (that it would be like vultures converging on a carcass, Matt. 24:28). We today would

---

Interpreting Psalms and Proverbs

Proverbs and Psalms share two crucial features. First, since they were both compiled for God's covenant people, the sayings were not offered as means of salvation but as advice on how the redeemed should behave. Second, both books are almost entirely poetry. Therefore, we must consider the special function of imagery, sound, and linguistic balance as we approach interpretation. Also, unlike Job and Ecclesiastes, Psalms and Proverbs can be taught and preached piecemeal. Neither book contains a plot, a story-line, or a dramatic scenario.

Interpreting the Psalms

The best way to read a psalm is to be sensitive to its mood. For example, you will find complaint, adoration, and thanksgiving to be common motifs.

Complaints usually begin with a call for help (Hear! Save!), an ad-dress to Yahweh (O Lord), and a poetic, often highly figurative, description of the predicament (Dogs surround me; my heart melts like wax; my feet sink in mire). In addition, to spur God to action, a psalmist may protest innocence or confess sin, appeal to the past (My fathers called to you, and you answered them), declare trust (My hope is in you), or make a vow (I will offer thanks before the congregation).

Hymns of adoration are addressed to the congregation or to the Lord, and usually contain a call to worship (Praise! Sing! Enter!), a mention of Yahweh's name (Sing to the Lord!), an address to the group summoned to praise (O heavenly beings, and all nations), and a reason for the praise (for the Lord has done great things).

Songs of thanksgiving voice the praise of those who have received forgiveness, healing, or rescue. They

be much more comfortable if he had said, "like filings converging on a magnet." But we have let our western, literalistic way of thinking intrude. The task of the preacher in unlocking figurative language is to get into the mind-set of the people who originally wrote and read it.

The second rule for handling figurative language is to recognize that there is normally only one point of comparison, to be determined by the context. *Figurative language* includes allegories (such as Christ's use of the vine and the branches or the four soils) in which many points of comparison are intended. We know that because the author in the context says so. But if the parable or the metaphor is not explained, we must look for only a single point of comparison.

Death, for example, is used in Scripture to refer to the spiritual state of a person before salvation, after salvation, and in at least three other ways. We are not free to conjure all the analogies that might be made with physical death, but must look for the single point of refer-

---

normally include an expression of thanks (I will bless the Lord), an account of the predicament (Day and night, your hand was heavy upon me), a picture of the rescue (He drew me from the pit), the payment of the vow (I have told the news of deliverance), and a word of instruction to the congregation (Many are the pangs of the wicked, but steadfast love surrounds one who trusts the Lord).

Catching the mood and thrust of such psalm-types is the key to discovering their use in Israel's life. That discovery, in turn, gives us clues for their use in contemporary preaching, liturgy, and music.

Interpreting Proverbs

The first nine chapters of Proverbs contain *sustained speeches* on various topics from avoiding bad companions and adulterous relationships to seeking wisdom as a reliable, experienced teacher. Study each speech as a self-contained homily that carries a consistent theme from beginning to end. Excerpting popular passages from them may bend their argument and muffle their meaning.

You can handle the collection of *shorter sayings*, almost always two-liners (in 10:1–22:16), in two ways: (1) topically, by combining a number of sayings on the same subject and building them into a sermon or lesson, or (2) individually, by expounding the meaning, setting, and application of a single saying.

The *words of the wise* in 22:17–24:34 often come in clusters as a series of admonitions buttressed by a list of reasons. Similarly, in chapters 25–29, several proverbs on the same subject appear in sequence. Finally, the alphabetical poem on the excellent woman (31:10–31) lists her virtues and accomplishments from *aleph* to *taw* (like our A to Z) and should be treated as a whole. All these cases are illustrations of the basic rule of interpretation for Proverbs: the form, order, and tone of the text all dictate how we are to understand and preach its message.

—David Allan Hubbard

ence the author had in mind. To be "dead to sin" should not be taken
to mean "as totally incapable of response as a corpse," any more than
it should be taken to mean foul smelling or anything else physical
death entails.

We must constantly ask ourselves: *What does this particular context
show to be the point of comparison intended by the author?* A parable
should not be made to teach money management or labor relationships when those details of Christ's made-up story are irrelevant to
the single point of comparison that is clear from the context.

Task #2: What Response Does God Desire?

The twofold task of the preacher derives from the nature of the
Book. It was authored by human beings, so the first task is to use the
basic tools of understanding human communication to get at the
meaning intended by the author.

The Bible is more than human in origin, however. It was inspired
by God and thus is *God's* Word and self-revelation. Therefore the second task is to derive from the meaning of the text what response of
trust and obedience *God* desires from his people today. This can be
done in two ways.

1. Utilize the unity of all Scripture. That there is a single Author
behind the authors means, among other things, that the Bible speaks
with one voice. This unity of Scripture means that the Bible is the best
commentary on itself, and each teaching of Scripture must be set in
the context of *all* the Bible says on that subject and related subjects.

For example, it will not do to take a text like "whatever you ask will
be done" and treat the promise as a blank check, guaranteed to be
honored by the bank of heaven no matter who the asker is, what is
asked, and why it is asked. Any teaching on prayer must be consonant
with all the Bible says about prayer.

In utilizing the unity of Scripture, we need to avoid two common
errors that violate the authority of Scripture:

• *Majoring on minors.* This occurs when we make obscure passages, uncertain interpretations, or minor biblical emphases prevail
over clearer passages or broader biblical teaching. When an uncertain
teaching is made to prevail over far clearer revelation, it is the interpreter or the interpretation that has become authoritative.

• *Making unwarranted deductions.* Deduction is legitimate, but we
violate the authority of Scripture when we treat a deduction as infal-
lible truth or—worse—when we turn deduction against other clear
teachings of Scripture. Logical deduction then becomes an extrabibli-
cal philosophical position that has been used to subvert the plain
intent of the biblical author.

God's sovereignty, for example, sometimes has been extended logically beyond clear biblical teaching in such a way as to undercut the complementary biblical teaching about human responsibility. The opposite error pushes logically beyond what Scripture says about human responsibility toward some kind of self-determination. Unfortunately, it is much easier to go to a consistent extreme than to stay at the center of biblical tension.

2. Appropriately apply the text. In making application of a text there are two stages of inquiry: Is this audience the one to which this passage is addressed? What specific response does God desire of us?

My thesis is that every teaching of Scripture is addressed to all people of all ages, unless the Bible itself in some way limits the audience. Otherwise, Scripture is no longer the authority, but the person who chooses which text is intended for us.

Scripture, itself, may limit the audience in various ways, however. For example, much of Old Testament teaching is restricted, according to New Testament revelation, to the nation Israel.

The response God desires is faith and obedience. Because it is *God's* Word, we trust it. All of it. But obedience is another matter. If the passage is addressed to us and is didactic or, especially, imperative, we readily understand how we are to respond. There are more than six hundred such commands in the New Testament alone! Yet most of our behavior is governed by *principles* enunciated in Scripture. Consider at least three ways principles come through to us from Scripture:

• Principles may be stated as such in Scripture. Here's an example: "Love your neighbor as yourself." Such a principal must be applied to the current situation, or the preacher falls short of the mandate to proclaim God's will for his people.

• Principles may be derived from a command or pattern of commands. The statement "whoever looks on a woman with desire has already violated the law against immorality," taken with many related teachings and commands, produces the law of sexual purity, of abstention before marriage and fidelity in marriage in both mind and body. If we fail to apply this passage to the contemporary context, we have failed. For example, pornography is not mentioned in Scripture but is a major contemporary violation of the principle.

• Principles may be drawn from historical events. Yet this is true only if the implication of those events is explicated in Scripture. If the Bible fails to comment on an event or the action of some person, not telling us whether it is good or bad, desirable or undesirable behavior, we may not use an historical event as a requirement or principle for obedience today. Just because some form of communal living was practiced in the early church, for example, does not mandate that pattern for all believers of every time and place. This means that narrative or historical passages may be used as the basis for a sermon, but only as illustrative, not as normative.

To the extent the story illustrates clear biblical truth—either positively or negatively—to that extent we should feel free to draw from it. But to use historical passages to teach truth when the Bible offers no interpretation of the event is to open a Pandora's box of uncontrolled "interpretation." Joseph's flight from the seducing wife of Potiphar, for example, is a powerful illustration of pervasive biblical truth on the subject of sexual purity, integrity toward God, and successfully meeting temptation. It will not do, however, to take Joseph's despotic rule, in which he used natural calamity to enslave the whole population, as a basis for legitimating such behavior. We certainly ought to preach from narrative passages, but always under the control of direct, clear biblical teaching.

The first interpretive task, then, is to use all the principles for understanding human communication to identify the meaning intended by the author. The second task is to apply that Word with integrity, discovering whether the passage is intended for our obedience today and clearly applying that truth to the contemporary context. Approaching the text this way, we may earn heaven's seal of approval as good workers who understand and apply the Word of God faithfully.

—*Robertson McQuilkin*

Resources

McQuilkin, R. 1992. Understanding and applying the Bible. Chicago: Moody.

Ramm, B. 1970. Protestant biblical interpretation. Grand Rapids, Mich.: Baker.

Virkler, H. 1981. Hermeneutics: Principles and processes of biblical interpretation. Grand Rapids: Baker.

Zuck, R. 1991. Basic Bible interpretation. Wheaton, Ill.: Victor.

Interpreting Job and Ecclesiastes

Since the overall approach to understanding both Job and Ecclesiastes is the same, we can suggest three broad interpretive guidelines. First, seek to grasp the thrust of the entire book and interpret it as a whole. We get in trouble if we use isolated texts to make points unrelated to the whole message.

Second, get a feel for the kinds of issues in Hebrew society that spawned these writings, especially the conflict between traditional doctrine and the authors' experiences: dealing with God's apparent freedom to allow undeserved suffering for reasons undisclosed to the sufferer (Job); finding meaning in a world tightly controlled by God's sovereignty but marked by instances of baffling injustice (Ecclesiastes).

Third, note how Job and Ecclesiastes employ *experience* to counter conventional wisdom. The lessons, illustrations, and arguments are drawn from real life, relentlessly attacking the academic oversimplifications of their fellow teachers.

Interpreting Job

Despite similarities, the books call for their own specific methods of investigation. Here are some suggestions for Job:

Compare the beginning and ending. Both are prose accounts of life in the land of Uz. The first is a story of deprivation; the second, of restoration. In the beginning Satan visits the courts of heaven; in the ending neither the Adversary nor the court is mentioned. Thus, Yahweh ultimately takes full responsibility for Job's predicament.

Catch the power and pathos of the poetic section. This is the heart of the book (chapters 3–41). The vivid word pictures and the pounding repetition highlight Job's plight and intensify his quarrel with the "friends" and with the Lord.

Recognize the triangular nature of the arguments (chapters 4–27). The arguments are dialogues between Job and each friend, but often parts of Job's speeches are addressed to Yahweh. Like the complaints of the Psalms, they imply that God is present and ultimately responsible for the unfolding events.

Feel the suspense created by Elihu's intrusion (chapters 32–37). He seems to appear from nowhere with a twofold role: he anticipates Yahweh's speeches by describing the divine majesty; he postpones the final solution—Yahweh's voice from the whirlwind.

Accept Job's experience of Yahweh as an encounter, not an explanation. Avoid deriving complex theological explanations for the problem of suffering from a book that does not attempt to offer them. Yahweh's demonstration of complete sovereignty was enough to spark Job's humility and trust.

Interpreting Ecclesiastes

Test the various translations of the theme word. The Hebrew *hebel* has been translated: vanity, futility, absurdity, brevity, or mystery. The last is my preference.

Weigh the relative emphases given to the two major themes. There is the "vanity verdict" (see 1:2; 12:8, etc.) and the "alternative conclusion" (about finding joy in life's simple gifts like food, drink, work, and love). Ask yourself: *Which is the dominant and which the secondary theme in the book?*

Distinguish between the preacher's two main types of argumentation. We find: (1) demonstrations of his theme of vanity (1:4–2:26; 3:1–4:16; 5:13–6:12; 8:10–9:12), and (2) collections of words of advice (5:1–12; 7:1–8:9; 9:13–12:8). By alternating these approaches, the preacher sets up a rhythm between his major themes: what's wrong with life (the demonstrations) and how to cope with it (the words of advice).

Ponder the double role Ecclesiastes seems to play in the Canon. Not only does the book serve to correct the extremes of oversimplification in the wisdom teachers, it also helps prepare us for Jesus' fuller revelation by posing questions whose full answers are found in him alone.

—*David Allan Hubbard*

Interpreting the Prophets

The prophetical books are easily misinterpreted, because prophetic literature is so different from what today's culture expects. Two interpretation flaws appear regularly in misguided attempts at understanding:

• *Ancient-modern nation confusion.* Because no specific modern nation is mentioned in the Bible, attempts to link prophecy with particular current events are almost invariably incorrect, as history shows. The church, not any state, is the true Israel (Gal. 3:29).

• *Genre confusion.* Prophecy must not be spiritualized—removed from the historical truth to which it speaks. Nor should it be personalized—treated subjectively, as if its meaning were found in a self-centered application. We cannot ask of prophetical literature, "What does this tell me about myself?" since God did not inspire the prophets to preach about private needs but about a greater picture—his all-encompassing plan of redemption. The prophets can help us lose our modern, unbiblical preoccupation with self.

Attention to History

All sixteen Old Testament prophets preached during a monumental 300-year period (760–460 B.C.), during which Israel and Judah were reduced from independent nations to a single, pitiful, remnant state (Judah), one tiny district in the huge Persian empire. Why? Because a long history of disobedience to God's covenant required the unleashing of its curses.

This was an era of dramatic change, and God's prophets spoke to its significance for his overall plan of redemption. Were his ancient promises of greatness void? Was there any hope for the future? Would the era of curse be supplanted by blessing? Prophetic preaching is mainly about historical developments, and no interpretation of its message that ignores historical context can hope to be accurate.

Remember the Covenant

Prophets were covenant messengers of the long-established terms of God's relationship to his people. They were reminders, not innovators. The Mosaic covenant (Exod. 20–Deut. 33) contained a perspective of blessing-curse-blessing (cf. Lev. 26 and Deut. 28–33) and prophetic revelation is comprehensible only within this scope.

The first era of blessing was prosperous life in the Promised Land. Then, as a result of covenant breaking, came the curse era of conquest and exile, starting for northern Israel with the Assyrian conquest of 722, and for Judah with the Babylonian conquest of Jerusalem in 587. The second era of blessing is the age of the new covenant, undeserved, but granted by God's grace. In speaking of the second era of blessing, the prophets predict the church age, our own "last days" initiated by Christ, and how its blessings are not only greater than those of the first era, but eternal for those who know God's redemption.

Analyzing Oracles

Nearly all prophetic teaching is in the form of oracles, self-contained verbal revelations from God, spoken or sung publicly in order to explain what God was doing in history and why. We must carefully identify the beginning and end of an oracle and be sure that we understand its characteristic terminology. We must patiently analyze the oracle's historical and literary context, understanding its place in the book in question as well as its place in the scope of history.

We must also diligently scrutinize its form and structure. Most prophetic oracles are poetry, and all employ multiple figures of speech. Some are visionary, and their symbolism—understood by the prophet and his audience—must be identified accurately and not subjectively for a modern audience unused to such symbolism. All oracles must be interpreted faithfully within the biblical-theological context of the whole of revelation, since understanding redemptive history is essential to conveying accurately what the prophets were inspired to say. People need to know the big picture if they are to orient their lives properly. They need to hear us preach the prophets accurately.

—Douglas Stuart

Interpreting the Gospels

"Sir, we would see Jesus." This crucial request is not well-honored by simply repeating a narrative unit from the Gospels, and much less by simply embellishing it. Faithful proclamation happens when we hear and interpret the gospel in the Gospels, so that persons once again hear and obey Jesus' call to follow him and live as true children of the kingdom of God. In faithful preaching, then, the original Proclaimer—Jesus—becomes the proclaimed.

Proclaiming the Proclaimer

What procedures can help us faithfully proclaim the Proclaimer as we preach from the Gospels? In addition to using all of the resources available to help us understand and interpret this portion of the Scriptures, we can follow some key steps:

• *Select the texts prayerfully.* We must exercise great care in selecting preaching texts. They should not be chosen willy-nilly, based on how we feel on a Monday morning. We may be led to offer a series of sermons interpreting an entire gospel, or to preach on critical gospel themes, or to show how the gospel speaks to the lives of Christians today. Careful study and prayer hatch effective preaching plans.

• *Study the context thoroughly.* A given textual unit—and its message—should always be viewed in the full context of the fourfold gospel witness, the New Testament witness as a whole, and the Old Testament background. Each of these contexts provides a vital perspective on the whole narrative and its component parts.

As the Spirit of God inspired the

Evangelists to proclaim Jesus through the medium of a full narrative account, so proclamation through a narrative unit, which possesses its own integrity, is best done with a substantial knowledge of its larger narrative framework. This approach falls in line with the ancient and biblical recognition that Scripture is the best interpreter of Scripture. Our hearers grow in their interpretive skills as we provide a window into this important hermeneutical principle.

• *Seek cultural understanding.* Study the environmental, geographical, historical, cultural, and religious elements coloring the text. Awareness of cultural factors helps us illuminate specific words, customs, religious practices, and popular ideologies. In his earthly ministry, Jesus walked in the midst of the world, its people, and its history; therefore, we can hardly understand the gospel narrative of Jesus apart from some understanding of the scene of his incarnate ministry.

• *Respect the literary genre.* It's wise to pay attention to the literary devices in which a gospel narrative is cast, especially as we interpret specific narrative units and parables. We shouldn't allow details to run away with the story, but rather should search for the center, the overriding theme that runs through the heart of the story.

• *Determine the key theological issues.* What universal matters of faith and practice arise in a given unit? These should be communicated in a sermon with contemporary illustrations that make impact today.

• *Make valid applications.* Ask how the Evangelist's message to the faithful in his own time speaks to today's congregation, a congregation with certain needs that are unique when compared to those of the first gospel readers. We should frame the sermon in clear, strong points and well-chosen words that reflect and honor the illuminating and empowering work of the Holy Spirit.

We must always ask ourselves when preaching from the Gospels: *Is my text so presented that Jesus is truly proclaimed in the power of the Spirit of God?* Preaching from the Gospels is a special privilege calling for special interpretive care. It is fortunate that we can still truly hear and faithfully proclaim the Proclaimer in spite of the separation of time and circumstance.

—Robert P. Meye

Interpreting the Epistles

The New Testament letters are full of difficult passages. It is no simple matter to grasp, let alone pass on, their meaning. Yet they contain such an abundance of truth that no constructive preaching should neglect them. The following considerations can help us avoid some common interpretive mistakes.

Survey the Background

We must begin with at least some knowledge of the background of the entire epistle. These are historical letters, written centuries ago for particular situations. To ignore the original reason for the writing, while concentrating on present application, runs the serious risk of misinterpreting the text. So we gather the basic facts: who the writer is, what we know about him (if anything) from elsewhere in the New Testament, and what is the main purpose of the letter. We are then in a position to consider any particular statement or passage within the whole letter.

Know Text and Context

Now we must select either a single text or a continuous passage for exegesis and eventual sermon preparation. If we really want to let the text speak for itself, we are more likely to fail with a single text than with an extended passage, since no single statement in the epistles was intended to stand on its own. It's certainly tempting to use a short text or verse as a mere hook upon which to hang the development of a broad theme, but this is not a good way to handle the epistles. Yet, if a single text is to form the basis of our exposition, we must carefully consider the surrounding context.

The best interpretive approach is to deal with an extended passage, while avoiding extremely long passages that introduce too many themes for hearers to cope with in a single sermon. For this reason, the epistles naturally lend themselves to series treatment, in which the general flow of the argument within a whole letter can be explored. We become immersed in an epistle when working on a series, and this comes through to hearers as we preach.

Apply the Text

Although our circumstances are different from those of the original readers, God's truth is eternal. Therefore, we approach the epistles with the assumption that they are intensely relevant to our age. The preacher must simply find and make plain the relevant applications. Of course, there is a golden rule here: Preach unto others only as you have "preached" unto yourself! No passage, whether plain or obscure, will ever mean much to our hearers if we have not already applied it to our own lives.

Avoid Temptations

Since we are dealing with the Word of God, whomever the human writer of the letter happens to be, we must approach each text with a listening ear; we must let it speak to us. Of all parts of the New Testament, epistle texts seem to lend themselves to the imposition of our own meanings. But we must avoid this tendency at all costs. Though it's tempting to use a text to justify what we want to believe, our aim is to discover what the text actually says to us.

Another temptation, especially when dealing with Paul's letters, is to skate over the more weighty passages in the mistaken belief that our hearers are incapable of absorbing them. However, it is these weighty passages that form the basis of much of our Christian doctrine. We must be ready to explain, in lucid language, all the truth-gems we can mine from the treasure chest of God's revelation.

—Donald Guthrie

Interpreting Apocalyptic Passages

Every literary work must be interpreted in a manner consistent with the genre in which it is written. For example, poetry follows rules appropriate to poetry. Narrative, being more literal, calls for a different approach. It follows that apocalyptic, as a specific literary genre, must be understood on its own terms.

Apocalyptic Defined

But what is apocalyptic literature? Several hundred years before Christ, the prophetic voice had grown silent. Earlier confidence that God would work out his plan within the course of history gave way to a restlessness that called for God's immediate and decisive intervention into history. Thus arose a body of literature now referred to as apocalyptic (from *apokalupsis,* the first word in the Book of Revelation, meaning "disclosure"). Apocalyptic writings abounded in the 300-year period leading up to about A.D. 100. Although apocalyptic passages appear throughout Scripture, Daniel and Revelation are normally considered as the two canonical apocalyptic books.

Apocalyptic literature makes extensive use of vivid and often bizarre symbols. One of Daniel's beasts had four heads and four wings like a bird, and looked like a leopard (Dan. 7:6). John pictures demonic locusts with lion's teeth and women's hair (Rev. 9:7–8). So readers of apocalyptic must definitely understand that they are dealing with a distinct kind of literature. Failure at this point leads to interpretations as grotesque as the images of the book!

Interpretation Principles

Here are some basic principles to keep in mind when reading apocalyptic passages:

• Pay close attention to indications within the text itself as to how to understand specific symbols. For example, the first chapter of Revelation identifies stars as angels and lampstands as churches (Rev. 1:20). Later, we learn that the great prostitute is a city (Rev. 17:18), and the seven heads of the beast she rides are simultaneously seven hills and seven kings (Rev. 17:9).

• Resist the assumption that a literal interpretation is always more faithful than a figurative one. It is, only if the author is writing in nonfigurative language. We have no trouble accepting such obviously figurative passages as Psalm 98:8, in which rivers clap their hands and mountains sing together for joy. But many popular writers would convince us that the New Jerusalem will be a gigantic, 1,400-mile cubed city that descends from heaven (Rev. 21:10,16). Rather, we should ask ourselves what the author intends, in this richly symbolic Book of Revelation, by giving us the dimensions of a cube. Is it not probable that he had in mind some relationship to the inner shrine of the temple, the place of the Divine Presence (1 Kings 6:20)?

• While not ignoring the details, always look for the larger themes. We'll never appreciate the forest if we concentrate on minute inspection of each tree. Primarily, Revelation is a triumphant declaration of God's final victory over Satan. It encourages believers to remain faithful in the terrible times that precede the end.

• Interpret apocalyptic from within its own historical and cultural setting. While the principles it enshrines relate to the consummation of history, it was written first of all for its immediate audience. John the Seer did not enter a time warp, visit the present age, and then return to describe as best he could what would happen twenty centuries later. He did not see actual helicopters (the locusts of Rev. 7:9–10) or watch television (the worldwide viewers of Rev. 11:9).

He saw what he described in the visions that make up his book. Although this type of language falls strangely upon modern ears, it was commonly understood by first-century believers.

—Robert H. Mounce

3

Denominational Preaching Traditions and Distinctives

With its preaching," said P. T. Forsyth, "Christianity stands or falls because it is the declaration of a Gospel." His words ring true when we recognize that times of revival in the church have always been heralded by the renewal of the preacher's influence. And in almost every denomination's statement of the nature and purpose of the church, preaching is not only first in order but first in significance.

Arthur A. Cowan entitled his Warrick Lectures for 1954, "The Primacy of Preaching Today," and in it he said, "It is the preacher's task to declare the Word of God, to give focus to the various elements of worship, and gather them up around their center."

Let us look at how the various strains of Christendom have approached the sermon by tracing the practice of preaching through these different strains and by discovering the place the sermon occupies in the service, and what it is meant to accomplish.

Lutheran Preaching

Martin Luther's one aim was to present the gospel by expounding the Bible. His expositions appealed to the heart and the will as well as to the intellect. "He is the best preacher who can preach in a plain, childlike, popular and simple way," said Luther. "In my preaching I take pains to treat a verse of Scripture, to stick to it and so to instruct the people that they can say, 'That's what the sermon was all about.' "

Spurgeon said of Luther, "Nobody doubted that he believed what

37

he spoke. He spoke with thunder because there was lightning in his path."

At Easter 1519, Luther began a continual exegesis of the Gospels and Genesis. A year later he began a collection of sermons on the appointed lessons for the day. Doctrine drawn from the Scriptures was combined in a fruitful unity with practical application to the needs of his hearers. He considered preaching the most important part of worship, but insisted that it must be rooted in and derive its authority from the Bible.

A. E. Garvie said of Luther: "While he retained the allegorical method of exposition, his sense of reality and his intimacy with the very core of the truth of the Scriptures freed him from bondage to it. As regards form, there was no endeavor to give the sermons organic unity but, as in the ancient homily, the passage was expounded verse by verse. In his language, nature spoke rather than art. It was simple, fresh, abounding, strong and manly. It was he who put the sermon in Protestantism in the place held by the Mass in Roman Catholicism and made preaching the most potent influence in the churches of the Reformation" (Garvie, 1958). Lutherans have retained a liturgical setting for their preaching, and the sermon topic is determined by one of the lessons appointed for the day.

Presbyterian and Reformed Preaching

In these churches the liturgical element may be lacking, but the exegetical and prophetic elements usually come through strongly. Since John Calvin expounded the books of the Bible in continuous order, both Old and New Testaments, the influence of the Old Testament has been a distinguishing mark of Presbyterian preaching. Calvin was the great expositor; two thousand of his sermons were taken down by a stenographer. It is as an expositor that he became a prophet. He stood in the pulpit, as he himself said, "As a trumpet to recall to God and his obedience the people that were his."

He stressed the preacher's duty to craft his words to the understanding of his hearers, to speak to their condition. Beza said of Calvin's preaching, "Every word weighed a pound."

Scotland felt the influence of Calvin in the fiery preaching of John Knox. Calvin's gift of clear exposition was also handed on to the Puritans in England to preachers such as William Perkins and Thomas Goodwin.

The preaching services in the Reformed tradition gave little place to the liturgical element. The hymns, lessons, and prayers were made subservient to the sermon, arranged to reflect and illumine the preacher's theme. The British Puritans, and the Presbyterians, Congregationalists, and Baptists were men of the Bible, the whole Bible, and nothing but the Bible. They were at one with the Reformed churches of the continent in giving prominence to the ministry of the Word. Ministers preached not only on Sundays, but also gave weekday lectures. There were fast days and thanksgiving days, so ministers would preach as many as six sermons in a week!

Through Barth and Brunner, the Reformed tradition of the German-speaking part of the church took up the expository legacy of Calvin and brought theology and preaching into a closer union than at any time since the Reformation. Dr. H. H. Farmer, a Presbyterian, entitled his Warrick Lectures "The Servant of the Word" and said that "the central and distinctive trend in contemporary theology was the rediscovery of the significance of preaching." The sermon is a spoken sacrament and the sacrament is an acted sermon.

Anglican Preaching

Modern Anglican worship highly honors the Word of God, incorporating readings from each major section of the Bible in each eucharistic service. Great care is given in providing lessons from Old and New Testaments in morning and evening prayer. A place is given to the preaching of the Word, but that was not always the case.

For instance, Richard Hooker, in his *Ecclesiastical Polity*, resisted the Puritan demand for a sermon at every service. He agreed that the hearing of the Word is an essential part of worship but argued that the reading of Scripture by itself without a sermon is a proclamation of the Word. For Anglicans today, however, the Sunday Eucharist almost always now includes a sermon (though sometimes quite brief).

R. H. Fuller, in *What Is Liturgical Preaching?* argues that preaching should be liturgical, for this corresponds to *paraklesis*, or exhortation, in the New Testament. Its purpose is to lead up to the act of Communion. His idea of preaching is that it is an exposition of the liturgy, not only an exposition of Scripture.

Canon Charles Smyth, in *The Art of Preaching: A Practical Survey of Preaching in the Church of England, 1747–1939*, claims the character of the sermon in Anglicanism was changed by John Tillotson in the seventeenth century so that it lost its heroic note and became a moral essay, the vehicle of a sober, utilitarian ethic rather than a proclamation of the gospel. From that time onwards, the homiletical essay has remained an acceptable style for some Anglicans, though it can have significant defects when consistently used in place of textual exposition. Nevertheless, it may be prophetic if the preacher has a message for his own time and hearers.

In the first part of the nineteenth century, two preachers lifted the homiletical essay to its highest level—J. H. Newman and F. W. Robertson. Among the Anglican preachers of the last two centuries, we find a noble line of prophets, such as R. W. Church, H. Scott Holland, H. H. Henson, William Temple, and Phillips Brooks.

Methodist Preaching

In contrast to the moral essay that was once so prominent in Anglicanism, the preaching of the early Methodists stands out as a movement that called for profound and specific personal response from its hearers. From this time onwards, the evangelistic sermon began to occupy a special place of honor in the Protestant tradition. Indicative of the high regard in which Methodists hold the office of preaching, the standard sermons of John Wesley have almost reached canonical

Renaissance and Reformation Preaching

The Protestant Reformers reclaimed the centrality of preaching in Christian worship. Forerunners of the Reformation, such as John Hus in Prague and Savanarola in Florence, had moved large masses of people through their powerful preaching. The Reformers continued this tradition by using their sermons to exposit the Word as well as to contribute to worship. They then passed on their skills with timely advice to the preachers who would follow them.

Preaching as Exposition

Zwingli was the first Reformer to introduce systematic expository preaching into regular services of worship. Instead of using "canned" sermons, he preached straight through the Gospel of Matthew when he became the "people's priest" at the famous Great Minster church in Zurich. Calvin followed this model as well. When he returned to Geneva in 1541 after three years of forced exile, he picked up his sermons at the very text where he had stopped in 1538!

Luther, too, believed the preacher should be a *bonus textualis*—a good one with the text—well-versed in the Scriptures. He excoriated those "lazy, no good" preachers who got all their material from others and from homiletical helps and sermon books, without praying, reading, and searching the Scriptures for themselves.

Preaching as Worship

Article Seven of the *Augsburg Confessions* (1530) defined the church as the assembly of saints where the gospel is purely preached and the sacraments rightly administered. In the act of preaching, God speaks directly to his people. For this reason Luther quaintly described the church as "not a pen house, but a mouth house." Preaching was to be an act of worship.

Since, as the *Second Helvetic Confession* (1566) put it, "the preaching of the Word of God is the Word of

status as required reading for all Methodist preachers, clerical and lay.

Since Wesley's preaching took place mostly in the open air because Anglican pulpits were barred to him, it usually had no connection with a liturgy. Wesley's sermons were clearly biblical, but he had a tendency to read the whole Bible in light of the Pauline gospel, as did Luther with his concentration on the doctrines of the Atonement, sin, and grace. In proclaiming the gospel of salvation, the sermon became a social and political factor of the first order by, paradoxically, concerning itself almost solely with the individual. "Dost *thou* not hear the Savior calling *thee* to repent and turn?" This personal address, the wooing note, was a sharp contrast to the homiletical essay with its

---

God," the sermon became a central focus of Protestant worship. The proclamation of the Word was laced in the context of the praise and prayer of the congregation. Ideally, preaching was accompanied by the celebration of the Lord's Supper, the "visible words" of God being displayed in the sacrament, while the preacher declared the written Word audibly for all to hear. In all of this, the hearers were to look beyond the preacher to Christ.

Preaching as Art

Both Luther and Calvin had lots of advice for aspiring preachers. According to Luther, a good preacher should "be able to teach well, in a correct and orderly fashion. Next, he should have a good head. Third, he should be able to speak well. Fourth, he should have a good voice. Fifth, he should have a good memory. Sixth, he should know when to stop. Seventh, he should know his stuff and be diligent. Eighth, he should stake his body and life, possessions and honor on what he says. Ninth, he should be willing to let everyone vex and poke fun at him" (Knaake 1833, vol. 6, no. 6793).

To aid in training skillful preachers, Luther published collections of his own sermons and distributed them to unlearned clergy in order to improve the quality of their preaching.

John Calvin said preachers were "like a father dividing the bread into small pieces to feed his children." The purpose of preaching was to be edification. "What is required is not merely a voluble tongue, for we see many whose easy fluency contains nothing that can edify." The pastor must not "fly about among the subtleties of frivolous curiosity: or be a 'questionarian' " (Torrance 1965, 225, 361). As such advice was followed, preaching would become an epiphany of the presence of God, as the Holy Spirit illuminated the mind and made the preached words the occasion of the voice of God.

—*Timothy George*

References

Knaake, J., et al, eds. 1833 ff. Tischreden. D. Martin Luthers Werke. Kritische Gesamtausgabe, vol. 6. Weimar, Germany: Böhlau.

Torrance, D., and T. Torrance. 1965. Calvin's New Testament commentaries. Grand Rapids: Eerdmans.

often impersonal tone. Personal, challenging Methodist preaching brought a new freshness, a convincing power to the sermon.

In the preface to his standard sermons, Wesley wrote, "I design plain truth for plain people. I labor to avoid all words not easy to understand." That is why the common people heard him gladly. At the Conference of 1746, Wesley answered the question "What sermons do we find by experience to be attended with the greatest blessing?" by saying, "Such as are more close, convincing, practical. Such as have most of Christ, the Priest, the Atonement. Such as urge the hei-

Seventeenth- and Eighteenth-Century Preaching

Throughout both the seventeenth and eighteenth centuries, sermons shaped understanding as decisively as television does today. In Protestant circles, they were heard up to seven times a week, making preaching the center of community life. Yet pastors faced serious obstacles: a legally captive audience, a church calendar that could prescribe the same texts year after year, and intense political scrutiny. The resulting sermons, shaped by contemporary aesthetic and literary tastes, could sometimes be tedious and derelict.

Building Disciples

Effectively barred from power at the turn of the century, the Puritans directed preaching toward training a godly laity. Their sermons typically had a threefold structure: (1) the principal doctrine, (2) supporting biblical arguments, and (3) application. Preaching climaxed with the individual standing before the holy God, fleeing to God's free mercy in Christ, demonstrating gratitude through obedience.

As Baxter remarks: "It is no small matter to . . . deliver a message of salvation or damnation, as from a living God. . . . It is no easy matter to speak so plain, that the ignorant may understand us; and so seriously that the deadest hearts may feel us . . ." (Baxter 1860, 128).

This preaching could produce committed disciples. Only a few preachers, however, approached the ideal. Legalistic harangues or mere Bible-quoting sessions frequently held sway.

Cultural Influences

The seventeenth century's deadly religious and political conflicts were reflected culturally through a Baroque aesthetic that pointed to an eternal world beyond Creation. The Baroque's homiletic equivalent, witty or metaphysical oratory, was widely followed. The text was explicated word-by-word and supplemented with insights from classical and patristic writers. Literary devices helped illustrate and wittily extract the text's meaning.

For example, use of the rhetorical paradox could provoke a sense of wonder at God's loving condescension: "The *Word, by whom all things were made,* to come to be

nousness of men living in contempt or ignorance of Him." He pressed home the truth that when he preached, he pleaded for a verdict. This explains the frequent entry in his journal, "I offered Christ."

In the minutes of the Twelfth Conference, Question 36 is, "What is the best general method of preaching?" The answer: (1) To invite, (2) to convince, (3) to offer Christ, (4) to build up, and to do this in some measure in every sermon.

Wesley's sermons were effective from both the ethical and the evangelical standpoint. He combined a passion for saving souls with a

---

made itselfe. . . . What . . . the *Word* an *infant?* The *Word* and not able to speak a word?" (Andrewes 1629, 47–48). Once the text's meaning was displayed, the sermon was complete. It had defined the landmarks for parishioners in their pilgrimage to another world.

By the latter half of the century, however, the empirical sciences thwarted Baroque preaching. The Enlightenment had redefined the cultural assumptions; Creation must be explained only in terms of natural causes. With science spawning the industrial revolution, the eighteenth century was fundamentally optimistic regarding humanity and society.

A new style of preaching originated, reflecting the rational cosmos of Neoclassicism. Science's discovery of a cosmos working with mechanical precision revealed a Moral Governor who was "good to all and his tender mercies are over all his works" (Tillotson 1695, 7:1–103) Before long, Neoclassicism had exchanged Christianity for moralism. Preaching ceased to be an encounter with a holy God.

Outdoor Preaching

Rationalism had effectively curtailed the church's influence. Evangelistic field-preaching constituted the most important counterattack throughout the eighteenth century, as George Whitefield and John Wesley reclaimed the countrysides and urban centers for the gospel. Inevitably, their sermons focused on sin, God's grace in Jesus Christ, conversion, and sanctification.

But field-preaching had an additional requirement: the text must capture the audience's immediate concerns. The message must be intelligible to the simplest; it must demand an immediate response. Here the field-preachers excelled. They would preach despite the rain, the ridicule, and the rotten eggs. The result was a religious revolution. A Whitefield line sums up their challenge to us: "Prosperity lulls the soul, and I fear Christians are spoiled by it" (Whitefield 1797, 214).

—*Timothy R. Phillips*

References

Andrewes, L. 1629. XCVI sermons. London.

Baxter, R. 1860. The reformed pastor. London.

Tillotson, J. 1695–1704. Sermons, 14 vols. London.

Whitefield, G. 1797. Eighteen sermons preached by the late George Whitefield. Newburyport: Blunt.

passion for educating them in righteousness. His was a social gospel as well as a gospel for the individual. This has been characteristic of Methodism ever since, combining the warmed heart with the enlightened mind, the personal appeal with practical counsel.

Pentecostal Preaching

"The preaching event is a living, breathing, flesh and blood experience of the ministry of the Holy Spirit," says James Forbes in his Beecher Lectures of 1988. He speaks of the ebb and flow of the ministry of the Spirit in the history of the church. In this approach Pentecostals and charismatics, as well as mainline Christians, face a common problem. Many find it difficult to know with certainty that the Spirit shapes our personal and religious experience. Spirit-anointed preaching, therefore, begins with a preacher who is a godly person and who recognizes that first and foremost he or she is to preach the Good News in a way that is timely and relevant to the needs of the people.

Pentecostal preaching is typically characterized by great freedom of delivery. It will contain material that is encouraging and constructive. According to Sam Shoemaker, we need to pray "to get loose under the Holy Spirit that God may say fresh and exciting things to us, so that our preaching may have fire in it."

Pentecostal preachers favor a simple style of speech, profusely illustrated from experience, a strong emotional stress, and an appeal for decision. Though such preaching may occasionally lack some of the structural precision found in other denominational sermons, Pentecostals will claim that only strong, emotional preaching can reach and touch the poor and the underprivileged. The warmth of the fellowship is mediated in preaching, which comes in the form of testimony as well as in text.

"Anointed preaching carries the hearer beyond the limited benefit of the preacher's personality and rhetorical skill," says James Earl Massey. Such preaching "makes the preacher an agent of grace; gives him a new power to point beyond himself and to allow the beyondness of God to break through with immediacy and authority in his words."

African-American Preaching

In the worship of African-American churches, the sermon is the focal point toward which all else leads and from which all else follows. The agonies and ecstasies of the sermon must be *experienced*. They are difficult to describe in prose for they are more like poetry. "Preacher and congregation are caught up in a common bond of suffering, and a release of the Scripture and the preacher's interpretation of it becomes, for all who are present, a living recital of their own despair and hope" (Duke, 1980).

All this is conveyed through a combination of word and chant in which preacher and people are totally involved. The pitch of excitement rises with the rising of the preacher's voice, and encouragement is given to him by volleys of "Amen" and "Praise the Lord" from the congregation.

The African-American church of an earlier generation met the genuine needs of an enslaved people, and the sermon gave them strength for another week. It relieved their pain for a moment by pointing to the finitude of this world and the ultimate, infinite reality of heaven. Now that emphasis is often supplemented with a healthy theology of hope for the present, and justice, not only in the future, but also in the here and now. Blackness, community, power—these are the images presented in the sermon, giving people a sense of pride in their race, based on the fact that they are a people loved by a God who particularly cares for the oppressed.

In African-American churches, the preacher becomes the agent of contact with divine will and holy Word. He or she is understood to be a charismatic figure. This explains the preacher's authority among the people. The preacher is free to deal with any aspect of life. He or she is expected to bring a word from the Lord for the living of these days. There is usually an altar call, an invitation to discipleship. Preaching is forceful and emotional, making the Bible come alive.

Roman Catholic Preaching

Renewed emphasis on the power of God revealed in the reading and the preaching of the Word has become an important part of Roman Catholic worship since the Second Vatican Council, which ended in 1965. Protestant textbooks on homiletics are studied by Catholic seminary teachers and their students.

Jesuit theologian Father Walter J. Burghardt, in the preface to his book *Preaching, the Art and the Craft*, quotes a Catholic scholar as saying in 1963, "Today preaching is strictly orthodox, but it is often vapid and lacking in vitality. It no longer seems to make converts or to lead to sanctity those who already have the faith." He goes on to say that since the seventies, his own preaching has increasingly reflected: (1) a return to the Bible for homiletic inspiration and counsel, (2) a deepened awareness of the link between liturgy, Scripture, and the homily, (3) a focus on imagination rather than just clarity, and (4) an anguished concern that the faith find expression in the struggle for social justice.

Though the church had at one time eliminated the Hebrew Scriptures from the Mass for about a thousand years, it now incorporates an Old Testament lesson every Sunday. Today the people hear three lessons and a sermon every Sunday (just as Luther desired!).

Transdenominational Concerns

It has been said that every sermon should seem like twenty minutes even if it is actually longer. In earlier days the sermon could occupy an hour or more, as the presence of an hour glass in the pulpit revealed. Today, there is a demand for short sermons. We are told that the attention span of the modern congregation, accustomed to snippets of news and commentary on television, is quite short.

"The demand for short sermons on the part of Christian people," said P. T. Forsyth, "is one of the most fatal influences at work to destroy preaching in the true sense of the word. How can a man preach if he feels throughout that the people set a watch on his lips? A Christianity of short sermons is a Christianity of short fibre" (Forsyth, 1907). On the contrary, a sermon should last as long as the preacher needs to deliver his or her soul.

The scope of preaching must not be limited by a too narrow view of its function. It should include both teaching and exhortation. Sometimes preaching has been the preparation for and the supplement to worship offered in prayer and sacrament. Sometimes preaching is mainly instructive, being an exposition of Scripture or some doctrine. Sometimes it is a direct appeal to the will to secure a verdict. That is why John Newman said that definiteness is the life of preaching. This quality is supremely necessary in what has been called the ministry of conquest, that is, preaching that aims at conversion. A really live sermon, then, no matter the denomination of the preacher, is "a speech concluding with a motion."

—John Bishop

Resources

Cowan, A. 1955. The primacy of preaching today. London: Hodder and Stoughton.

Duke, R. 1980. The sermon as God's Word. Nashville: Abingdon.

Garvie, A. 1958. The Christian preacher. Edinburgh: T. and T. Clark.

Farmer, H. 1941. The servant of the Word. London: Nisbet.

Forsyth. P. 1907. Positive preaching and the modern mind. London: Hodder and Stoughton.

Smyth, C. 1940. The art of preaching. London: S.P.C.K.

Nineteenth- and Twentieth-Century Preaching

Christian preaching has always had two distinguishable concerns: the extension of the Christian witness and the enrichment of the Christian community. Two kinds of preaching have emerged: evangelistic preaching and pastoral preaching—*kerygma* and *homilia*.

Revivalistic Preaching

Before television came in the 1950s, revivalistic preaching of the American frontier and biblical exposition in Bible conference circles shaped preaching in Protestant pulpits.

Revivalistic preaching tends to be otherworldly, individualistic, suspicious of learning, and unconcerned about style. While most people would not consider it appealing today, this was not always so. On the American frontier, revivalistic preaching spoke to the democratic, independent spirit of common people.

Camp meeting preaching offered people salvation in a simple, emotional, and usually entertaining style. One of the better known of the frontier preachers was circuit-riding Peter Cartwright, who insisted that uneducated evangelists like himself were setting the frontier on fire, while other learned preachers were trying to light matches.

Black preachers were as quick as whites to paint eternity in sharp emotional tones. "Slave religion," as scholars call it, was probably a blend of West African and southern evangelical elements. When free from white control, preaching served

an almost exclusive role in offering blacks integrity and hope.

Biblical Exposition

"Expository preaching" is a product of three generations of itinerant Bible teachers. It focused on taking a portion of Scripture and explaining what it means and how it applies to the believer's personal life. It is nearly always rational, orderly, and pious.

The years after the Civil War marked the birth of the "Bible School Movement" and the expository style of preaching. The founding of Bible schools and camping centers brought the systematic devotional study of the Bible. When speakers at these conferences—usually pastors of urban churches or popular Bible school teachers—took to the airwaves in the 1930s, they created a style of preaching that was often indistinguishable from Bible teaching.

Resistance to theological liberalism also deepened commitment to expository preaching, especially outside of the South. It was the preacher's way of "equipping the saints."

The Effects of Counseling

After the Second World War, two significant developments united to reshape preaching in America: the growth of counseling as a pastoral skill and the cultural influence of television.

The trailblazer in counseling through preaching was Harry Emerson Fosdick, who developed modernist views and communicated them during the crowning portion of his career at the prestigious Riverside Church in New York City. He called his style of preaching "pastoral counseling on a group scale." Others called it "life-situation preaching."

Fosdick began with a need or issue in human life, surrounded it with Scripture, and then crafted his manuscript. He wanted preaching to be "a co-operative dialogue in which the congregation's objections, doubts, and confirmations are fairly stated, and dealt with."

Critics were quick to point out the dangers in such preaching. Since its primary sources were newspapers and weekly magazines, the sermon had the character of "an editorial comment with a mild religious flavor." Whatever its flaws, life-situation preaching continued to spread.

The Influence of Television

Television's influence paralleled the impact of counseling. By 1960 preachers faced congregations who were watching television daily and were shaped by that experience. Unfortunately, television is a pictorial event that mirrors culture without critiquing it.

Moreover, television is a medium of entertainment, promising to relieve stress and fill an hour with an interesting, vicarious experience. Although some people expect the sermon to do the same, preachers have had to make sure the call to commitment and the price of discipleship do not get lost in spectacle.

—*Bruce L. Shelley*

Cross-Cultural Preaching

Cross-cultural preaching is and will be more and more in demand as our world becomes progressively culturally diverse. Our cities are ever increasing in population with the people of the world. Most come having been exposed to various religions and sundry practices of Christianity. They don't fit snugly into the Christian stereotype, and even the stereotype today is hardly singular. Churches are filled with dissimilar people with multiple experiences and expectations.

Some people also arrive at church with preacher heroes—someone in the past who preached in a way they yet want to rediscover, and they search in vain to find a duplicate in their new world. Tragically, many preachers try to imitate people's heroes. Though these imitators may become popular, they often lose their authenticity. Though they entertain, there are few spiritual victories.

Success for a Reason

Peter, in preaching the first sermon after the Pentecost, preached to a cross-cultural crowd as the Scriptures attest: ". . . Jews from every nation under heaven" (Acts 2:5b). Obviously he spoke effectively to the people of many nations and tongues, for "about three thousand were added to their number that day" (Acts 2:41).

Billy Graham in our century has possibly preached to more cultures and classes of people than anyone in the history of Christianity. His sermons translate equally well for the cultivated and the street-smart, the churched and the pagan of Britain and of Russia, of the Far East as well as the Midwest.

I believe both Peter and Billy have been successful for the following reasons:

• *They pray.* The conveyance of the message to the ears of people depends upon voice and language, but the conveyance of the message to the heart depends upon the Holy Spirit's response to our prayers. Cross-cultural barriers can look overwhelming from a purely communications standpoint. But the God who made cultures knows how to pierce them effectively with his message and through his messengers to the cultures.

• *They keep it simple.* For the most part, people have at most but an elementary understanding of the Word of God. Therefore, the more simple and unencumbered the message, the more effective it can be. It may not be impressive, but it is much more likely to be received.

Translating is a difficult task, but it is made easier as we stick to the basic, powerful message. And cultural translation from one way of looking at the world to another, even apart from language, goes more smoothly the more basic the theme.

The slow, simple delivery of the Word of God may well soak into the soul like a slow, soaking rain is absorbed into soil without runoff or waste.

—E. V. Hill

4

Planning Preaching

The best-laid plans of mice and men are apt to go awry," wrote Robert Burns, the Scottish poet, after his plow turned over the nest of a tiny field mouse. He was right, of course. But does that mean we should abandon planning and simply go with the flow? Alice's friend, the Cheshire Cat, apparently thought so:

"Would you tell me, please, which way I ought to go from here?"

"That depends a good deal on where you want to go," said the cat.

"I don't care where . . . ," said Alice.

"Then it doesn't matter which way you go," said the cat.

". . . so long as I get somewhere," Alice added as an explanation.

Normally in a choice between cat and mouse I would choose to be the cat, but in this instance I go with the mouse. Like airline pilots with flight plans and football coaches with game plans, this preacher favors a preaching plan even though it may go awry. Better to have a clear sense of what I am trying to achieve, even if it doesn't always work out, than to take a deep breath and open my mouth with the idea of seeing where I might finish!

But not all preachers agree. Charles Haddon Spurgeon, the nineteenth-century "prince of preachers," did not like to plan his preaching ahead of time, and he advised his students against it, too. He recognized that a planned preaching schedule could become a fetter, in that the events of the day, the importance of the moment, and the circumstances of the hour might not mesh with the planned preaching in terms of relevance and effectiveness.

As a young man, Spurgeon had heard a series of sermons on He-

brews that affected him so adversely that he "wished frequently that
the Hebrews had kept the epistle to themselves, for it sadly bored one
poor Gentile lad" (Spurgeon 1972, 95). He apparently determined not
to inflict others with similar treatment. Even so, Spurgeon admitted
that "Matthew Henry, John Newton, and a host of others" would not
agree with him.

What Is Planned Preaching?

A young pastor once startled his congregation by announcing,
"When I stood up before you this morning, only the Lord and I knew
what I was going to say. Now the Lord only knows!" In all probability
he had failed to prepare adequately. He may even have believed that
preparation is not only unnecessary but also evidence of lack of faith.
Didn't Jesus say, "Do not worry about what to say or how to say it. At
that time you will be given what to say" (Matt. 10:19–20)? Yes, he did
say that, but he was not training pastors for preaching to congregations; he was preparing disciples for arrest and questioning under
torture—two experiences with some similarities but really quite
different!

At the most basic level, *planned preaching* means preparing in ad-
vance what you intend to say, before opening your mouth. This does
not preclude the possibility of spontaneity or thinking on your feet.
Neither does it conflict with beliefs in Jesus' promise that "the Holy
Spirit will remind you of everything I have said to you" (John 14:26).
Even the Holy Spirit only *reminds* us of what is already *in* the mind.
So, this promise actually makes a case for preparation rather than
dissuading us from doing it.

No preacher would expect to communicate the whole of divine revelation in one sermon, though some have come perilously close to
trying. But most pastors do wish to say, like Paul, "I have not hesitated to proclaim to you *the whole will of God*" (Acts 20:27). To do this
they would need to know the ground they had covered to date, with a
view to filling up what was lacking in the future. In other words, both
they and their congregation would benefit greatly from extended
planning over a period of time.

What Are the Advantages?

Planned preaching posts benefits for several parties:
• *Advantages for the congregation.* In the same way that healthy
bodies require a diet made up of the various food groups, a healthy
congregation needs a balanced diet of God's Word. All pastors are
human and have their own preferences, priorities, prejudices, and
problems, which show up in their preaching. Their congregation may,

as a result, lack certain biblical nutrients.

For example, I have always had a problem with prophetic preaching because, when I was growing up, I heard many "expositions" of eschatology, as dogmatic as they were fanciful, that over the years have been proved totally wrong. So I have tended to avoid this aspect of biblical truth. On the other hand, my natural inclinations and business training have produced a preference for the logical reasonings of Paul's epistles rather than the poetic utterances of David's psalms. So if I am not careful, I can subject the congregation to an overdose of some truths and a starvation diet of others. It is the recognition of this possibility that leads me to plan carefully.

When a congregation knows the Scripture that will be expounded on a given Sunday, people can read and study it in advance to great profit. A group of young businessmen do this regularly in my home church, and then, as they explained it to me, they come to see if I get it right! There is also greater incentive for the congregation to invite friends or relatives to attend a worship service if they are aware that the subject matter is of particular relevance and interest to the one they wish to invite.

• *Advantages for the preacher.* A good sermon, like fine wine, excellent cheese, and most people, needs time to mature. Once the sermon idea has been conceived, the preacher has a lot of work to do before stepping into the pulpit with it. The Scripture must be exegeted, the train of thought developed, factual information verified, and illustrations collected before the writing of an outline or manuscript begins.

All this requires quality work immersed in quiet meditation and prayer. And there's the rub! While senior pastors of very large churches (who often specialize in preaching and who have multiple staff members to assist them) are usually given time to do all these things, the majority of pastors who work in small churches may not have similar privileges. They are expected, understandably, to be involved in a multitude of activities that are so time and energy consuming that thoughtful, quality preparation time is practically nonexistent, and Saturday night may find them desperately trying to hatch the next morning's sermon.

Some of the resultant tension can be relieved by planning a series of messages well ahead of time. Then the preacher will be able to think about an already-determined topic while dealing with must-do-today activities. Driving to the hospital, he can listen to a relevant tape; visiting a sick person, she can recognize an illustration; lunching with a businessman, he can pick his friend's brain for some helpful information; while fixing the copy machine, she can be meditating on the passage from which she will preach. This is hardly quality preparation time, but until congregational pressures or expectations change—or help appears in the form of added staff—it will have to do, and it will be infinitely better than the nerve-wracking Saturday-night scramble.

The preacher will, of course, need to block out time for the planning, and if this is not readily available, a specific request should be made to the church leadership for an opportunity to engage in this significant work. At the same time, the preacher should recognize—and, if necessary, help his or her church leadership to see—that quiet, unhurried preparation time is as much a priority as anything else. It should figure largely in the apportionment of a pastor's time.

Eugene Peterson, the veteran Presbyterian pastor, said: "The trick, of course, is to get to the calendar before anyone else does. I mark out the time for prayer, for reading, for leisure, for the silence and solitude out of which creative work—prayer, preaching, and listening—can issue" (Peterson 1989, 32).

Preaching the Lectionary

Using a lectionary can help a busy preacher in at least three ways. First, because the lectionary sets out the biblical themes for each Sunday's worship, the preacher, along with other worship leaders, can coordinate plans for worship well in advance. Rather than build services around only the sermon, worship planners can also use the anthems, hymns, prayers, and other elements of worship to develop the themes in the readings.

Second, this coordinated-planning benefit can extend beyond worship into Christian education. Since the lectionary is organized around the major events in Jesus' life and ministry, it can serve to expose church members to the key elements of the gospel message.

Third, an ecumenical lectionary supports our working with other preachers on sermon ideas. Many clergy study groups meet weekly for discussion of the upcoming lectionary texts. Such fellowship provides the soil in which creative preaching blossoms.

Provide Balance

How do you decide, though, which of the lectionary readings to choose? The most common practice is to preach from the Gospel reading. This has the advantage of leading the congregation through the key passages in the four Gospels every three years, but it can appear to relegate the other portions of the Bible to inferior status.

It is better to vary the choice of preaching texts, exposing the congregation to a wide variety of biblical materials. Some preachers focus upon the Gospel texts during Christmas and Easter, moving to the other readings for the rest of the year. This does provide some balance, but we need to be careful not to deprive our congregations of those Old Testament and epistolary texts that provide background for the Christ-

● *Advantages for church workers.* Everyone will benefit if the worship service displays significant cohesion and purpose. The worship experience is an opportunity to come before the Lord to hear his Word. This means preparation to hear the Word and opportunity to respond to the Word should be central to every service. For the service to be prepared adequately, advance notice of the topic is essential. Then the musicians can practice or compose suitable music, and worship leaders can develop appropriate readings, prayers, and drama and arrange for testimonies and other elements of the service. If worship leaders are expected to prepare in this way, obviously a few weeks' lead time is invaluable.

We have found it helpful occasionally to prepare discussion materials that supplement the sermon and personal-devotional materials that help apply the Word preached. These have been used both in

---

mas and Easter events.

Sustain Continuity

Congregations need not only balance in the selection of preaching texts, they also need continuity, an understanding of how a particular text fits into its larger context. In other words, to hear a preacher address a text from Matthew one week and a text from Genesis the next week, followed by a text from James the third week, can make for an unnecessarily choppy exposure to God's Word. The hearers may never grasp how that text from Matthew, for example, fits into the larger themes and patterns of Matthew's gospel.

The need for continuity, then, is in tension with the need for balance, but it is not impossible for the preacher to give attention to both. *The Common Lectionary* often provides continuous readings from the Old Testament or the Epistles (several weeks, for example, devoted to readings from 2 Samuel), and this presents the possibility of preaching a short series on a particular

book. Such a series would be long enough to give the hearers a sense of continuity, but not so long as to upset the overall balance among types of texts they will encounter.

Respond to Circumstances

Extraordinary pastoral and community events—the death of a President, the closing of the local mill, the outbreak of war—must receive treatment from the pulpit on short notice. In these cases, we should consider the lectionary to be a guide, not a shackle.

If the readings for a given Sunday simply do not speak to the current pressing need in the community, we go elsewhere in Scripture. On the other hand, it is not good to make this move too quickly. We should always hold the events and crises of the day in the light of the church's regular, patterned reading of Scripture. Often the lectionary passages will speak with more unexpected power and wisdom than the seemingly "obvious text" we might select to match the occasion.
—Thomas G. Long

midweek services and on Sunday mornings or evenings. Obviously, for this to happen, "to be forewarned is to be forearmed."

What Should Characterize Planned Preaching?

Preachers should always be concerned about validity, vitality, and variety, both in planning and presentation.

●*Validity.* The validity of preaching is determined by the degree to which it is an exposition of divine truth as opposed to an explanation of human opinion. Some preachers regard exposition as relentless verse-by-verse progress through rough biblical terrain, so they avoid it. They prefer to use biblical texts in much the same way NASA's shuttle blasts off from Florida and eventually lands in California.

Preaching Book Series

The chief theological question of all time, according to writer Annie Dillard, is: "What in the Sam Hill is going on here anyway?" As preachers, we must answer that question from the pages of Scripture, using both Old and New Testaments.

We can do it well by preaching through whole books (or major parts of books) in a series of messages. In series preaching, the biblical text can make its own point about "what's going on here" as it exposes the powerful springs of action in human behavior.

Benefits of Series Preaching

Preaching in series offers some distinct advantages: it develops a biblically informed congregation that is aware of the panoramic way revelation unfolds; it provides a planned preaching year with consistent transitions from week to week; and it builds a solid teaching ministry from the pulpit, fulfilling Christ's command in the Great Com-

mission (see Matt. 28:19–20).

Also, when preaching through a book, you will be less vulnerable to majoring on your favorite theological hobby horses. In addition, when topics of judgment or sin appear in the text, they will arise naturally, and you thus will avoid the accusation that you had someone or something specific in mind to criticize on a particular Sunday.

Developing a Series Outline

Begin your outline development by thoroughly studying a selected book (or major portion), looking for key themes. It's best to do an exegetical outline first, and then look for connections and transitions among the major text blocks. The main headings in your outline will then provide grist for the creative sermon titles in your series.

Because Scripture is marvelously varied—some portions biography, some carefully crafted logic, some wildly dramatic and vision-

Both the sermon and the shuttle have starting points and finishing points far removed from each other, linked only by rapid orbiting at great distance from the subject.

But, as John Stott explained, exposition "refers to the content of the sermon (biblical truth) rather than its style (a running commentary). To expound Scripture is to bring out of the text what is there and expose it to view. The expositor pries open what appears to be closed, makes plain what is obscure, unravels what is knotted, and unfolds what is tightly packed" (Stott 1982, 125–126).

The preaching plan, then, should start with a commitment to ensure that hearers will be exposed to significant segments of Scripture. Looking back over a previous year, I see my preaching was based on passages from Genesis, Leviticus, Deuteronomy, Psalms, Proverbs,

---

ary—a preacher has a wide range of material to apply to the problems and needs in the congregation. For example, a series on one of the books of the Psalms will speak to different emotional make-ups among the people. A careful explanation of the New Covenant (perhaps from 2 Corinthians 2–6 or John 13–17 or Romans 5–8) will do wonders in releasing parishioners from a legalistic Christianity or low self-esteem.

Some Do's and Dont's

Knowing the benefits of this kind of preaching has inspired me to use it regularly. But I've had to keep a few basic guidelines in mind, such as:

• Devote the first sermon in a series to an overview of the entire book. This gives listeners a grasp of your direction and an overall context for the points you will be making.

• Master the whole book or section before attempting to preach through it. You'll avoid coming to a "surprising" passage, in the middle of your series, that contradicts something you said earlier.

• Focus on one major theme in each passage. You won't be able to deal with everything in a book, but you can hit the high points and drive them home with impact.

• Let the text speak for itself. Avoid imposing extraneous material upon the clear thrust of the passage. Save your creativity for illustrative material that clearly ties the text to modern living.

• Don't preach through books during the summer months. With many people on vacation or coming and going for various reasons, it's hard to maintain continuity.

• Don't make the series too long. Book series should not be so long and drawn out that people lose the thread of development—or even worse, lose interest. You can break long books into several series, interspersing briefer textual or topical studies.

• Don't let it get boring. Use humor and illustrations that keep tying the text to life. A judicious use of humor, without descending to joke telling or mere entertainment, can make all the difference in the effectiveness of your series sermons.

—*Ray Stedman*

Isaiah, Matthew, John, Acts, Romans, Galatians, Thessalonians, 1 Peter, and Revelation (to name a few) and that my succeeding plans took me into Hebrews.

• *Vitality.* There is a direct correlation between the vitality of the preaching and the interest of the hearer and speaker in the material being covered. Not all preaching is as lacking in vitality as that of the seventeenth-century cleric, Dr. South. I read somewhere that on one occasion, he put his complete congregation to sleep—including the king—so he interrupted his sermon to say, "Lord Lauderdale, rouse yourself. You snore so loudly that you will wake the king." My guess is that the subject and the subject's subject were of no interest to the sovereign.

Good planning will take into account the interests, the needs, and the situations of the hearers. So, for instance, I titled my Deuteronomy expositions "Enjoying the Good Life" and tried to show how God gave his ancient people a "good land" full of "good things" that they were to enjoy. Then I went on to show how they and we should behave in such blessed circumstances.

In Thessalonians, I discovered a dominant theme of encouragement (the word is mentioned nine times), so my theme was "The Awesome Power of a Little Encouragement." Everybody is interested in that. I was also concerned that the congregation should understand holiness, even though I knew it would not be on the top of anyone's felt-need list. But once I was able to show that "knowledge of the Holy One is understanding," the people were eager to examine various Scriptures, so that in understanding God in his holiness, they might have a solid basis for fuller life in all its dimensions.

When I had to deal with the subject of stewardship, I encouraged the congregation to explore Scripture with me to see how stewardship includes such timely subjects as ecology (the stewardship of creation), time management (stewardship of time), and financial planning (stewardship of money).

•*Variety.* The Bible contains biography and history, poetry and pithy sayings. It was written by kings and courtiers, shepherds and farmers, from the heart of Judaism and the centers of paganism, in prison cell and royal palace, in order to encourage or rebuke, in Greek or in Hebrew. It is prophetic, evangelistic, didactic, and apocalyptic. This variety should be reflected, because variety is the spice of preaching.

There are also many kinds of sermons—and I don't mean long, medium, and short. Include some narrative sermons and some inductive presentations. Add a major biographical study. Incorporate an apologetic thrust. Unfold a teaching section, and do a series answering oft-asked questions. Then, to spice up the variety, occasionally change the order of service so that the emphasis on the sermon changes slightly and captures the congregation's attention.

What Is the Procedure?

Preachers who minister in liturgical churches have a ready-made preaching plan presented to them in the shape of the lectionary, which outlines readings from Scripture for each Sunday. These are designed to cover the major doctrines of the church. While this approach can become stereotyped, some preachers from nonliturgical traditions have utilized the approach on occasion. For those who do not use this type of plan, the following procedures will be helpful:

● *Develop a planning calendar.* Make a note of:

— Special Christian events (Christmas, Easter, Pentecost, etc.).

— Special cultural events (Independence Day, Memorial Day, Mother's Day, etc.).

— Special church events (Covenant Sunday, Missions Festival, Communion, baptisms, etc.).

— Special personal events (pastor's vacation, study leave, mission trip, etc.).

● *Block off periods of time for preaching through series.* Determine to what extent you need to feature the events listed above. Look also to see if the period immediately before or after the event should be used to emphasize the event.

For example, you could use the period between Easter and Pentecost to explore what happened in the early church during that period. The Advent season could be spent studying the reasons Christ gave for his Coming. The two or three weeks after a missions festival could concentrate on practical matters related to the preparation and support of missionaries.

● *Determine the remaining time gaps and identify uninterrupted slots for sermon series.* These periods of varying duration will fit various sermon topics, some of which require longer attention than others. For example, an exposition of Romans would take longer than a series on stewardship. At least most congregations would hope so, anyway!

● *Remember to maintain the variety of subject matter and approach.* If there are morning and evening services, it is best to plan different subject matter and style for each.

Don't feel you have to develop a detailed plan a complete year in advance, but it would be helpful to know what the general outline of ministry will be. And, of course, feel free to break into the plan if an event of major significance or broad interest occurs. Timely preaching is effective preaching.

—Stuart Briscoe

Resources

Perry, L. 1965. A manual for biblical preaching. Grand Rapids: Baker.

Peterson, E. 1989. The contemplative pastor. Carol Stream, Ill.: Christianity Today, Inc.

Spurgeon, C. 1972. Lectures to my students. Grand Rapids: Zondervan.

Stott, J. 1982. Between two worlds. Grand Rapids: Eerdmans.

Preaching Topical Sermons

Though homileticians of an earlier era distinguished sharply between textual and topical sermons, the distinction is no longer helpful. Nearly everyone now agrees that preaching must be a proclamation of the Word of God revealed in Scripture. All Christian preaching will therefore be textual.

But how is the text selected? Some sermons begin with a text (from the lectionary or a pre-planned sermon series) and move toward a theme. Other sermons, however, begin with a theme and move toward a text. We call these "topical" because the topic governs the choice of biblical passage.

Reasons for Topical Preaching

• *Seasonal needs.* Both the calendar of the church year (Advent, Christmas, Lent, Easter, Pentecost) and the calendar of popular culture (New Year's Day, Mother's Day, Father's Day, Memorial Day, Independence Day, Labor Day) enjoin the treatment of certain themes on a given Sunday.

• *Special concerns in the congregation.* A stewardship drive, a building campaign, a community tragedy, a programmatic emphasis (the creation of fellowship groups, say, or the development of a new Christian education program)—all become occasions for topical sermons.

• *Ethical issues.* The Bible does not address directly many of our current ethical problems. But can we ignore the dilemma of a single woman considering an abortion, or the agony of a family wondering whether to "pull the plug" on an ailing relative? Facing circumstances like these, the preacher will quite properly begin with a theme and then move to a text that illuminates it.

• *Modern biblical illiteracy.* Non-Christians don't have a burning interest in the Pentateuch or the Minor Prophets, but they *do* want to know: "How to Have a Happy Marriage." And they would like help "Dealing with Stress." Preaching that reaches beyond the walls of the sanctuary will occasionally address such topics.

Guidelines

• *Proclaim the text, not personal ideas.* We must be stern with ourselves, ruthlessly suppressing the urge to offer opinions and insights that, however clever, do not flow from the biblical passage being proclaimed.

• *Make the connection to the text obvious.* The more controversial the theme, the more obvious should be the sermon's relation to the text. When wading into the troubled waters of ethical conflict, be certain your feet stay on solid rock. Make it as clear as possible that you are expounding an authoritative text. If your hearers don't like what comes through, they will be forced to argue with the Bible instead of you.

• *Be fair with controversial topics.* Assume good will on all sides. Most arguments over serious matters occur because the issues are complex. You lose nothing and gain much by being charitable—even to those with whom you disagree. It's demeaning to the gospel to caricature opponents unfairly, turning all prochoice advocates, for example, into eager baby killers. We preach not only *to* the congregation but *for*

the congregation. When we express fairly the truth of opposing positions, our hearers feel their side has been heard.

• *Allow adequate preparation time.* Topical preaching demands plenty of time for biblical exegesis. It requires more lead time than lectionary preaching, for instance. This is because we may get into a text and discover it doesn't say what we thought it did! It's always wrong to cajole a previously announced theme out of an unwilling text. If we discover that a text doesn't really deal with our topic, we must select a different text. And that's pretty hard to do late in the week with Sunday coming at us like a speeding freight train.

—*Donald W. McCullough*

Preaching and the Calendar

National holidays and the church holy days that are set aside in the annual Christian calendar provide worthwhile homiletical resources. Why? Because there is a natural rhythm inherent in all of life, repeated in cycles—the course of planets, the seasons, the stages of human development, all of which progress from beginning to end and then begin again. This is true spiritually as well, a fact that has long been celebrated in our Judeo-Christian tradition.

Before Christ, the Jews had developed their own annual observances, centering on the Sabbath and the major festivals of Passover, Pentecost, and Tabernacles. These celebrations established the rhythmic character of Judaism, insuring the regular teaching of God's pivot-

al truths and actions. It was only natural that early Christians would gradually develop their own cyclical celebrations.

Preaching after Christ

Preaching the church year helps us focus upon the major aspects of our Christian faith by following in the footsteps of Christ. Certain days in the Christian year are fixed by date: Christmas (December 25), Epiphany (January 6), Transfiguration (August 6), All Saints (November 1), and the various days for saints. Other days are movable: Easter (the first Sunday following the first full moon after the spring equinox of March 21), Ascension (40 days after Easter), Pentecost (50 days after Easter), Trinity Sunday (the

Sunday following Pentecost), Advent Sunday (the Sunday nearest St. Andrew's Day), Ash Wednesday (46 days before Easter).

Themes associated with the days and seasons provide rich preaching inspiration. For instance:

• *Advent* refers to the coming of the Lord in history, in one's life, and in the future when Christ returns. It is the season of personal examination and preparation.

• *Epiphany* celebrates the visit of the Magi. It reminds us of the worldwide message of the gospel and our obligation to proclaim it.

• *Lent* comprises the 40 days (excluding Sundays) prior to Easter. Lent commemorates Christ's period of temptation and fasting in the wilderness, calling us to examine our lives for sin and to seek cleansing.

• *Pentecost* reminds us of the powerful manifestation of the Spirit to the church and challenges us to open up personally to the Spirit-filled life.

The major moments in Christ's life offer particularly powerful preaching opportunities, as each moment has its equivalent in the life of a believer. For instance, Christ's birth and our regeneration, his baptism and our baptism, his temptation and ours, his transfiguration and our sanctification, his death and ours, his resurrection and our hope of eternal life, his ascension and our present inclusion with him at the right hand of God. As the local church celebrates these days year in and year out, a sense of familiarity and anticipation builds among the people who treasure these traditions. The great truths of the church year become a part of us.

Preaching for Our Culture

So, too, with national days. We should avoid letting the secular culture set our preaching agendas, but some of the themes associated with certain persons and moments in our national history do lend themselves to valid Christian respect. For example:

• *President's Day.* We remember that Washington and Lincoln clearly modeled for us dedication, integrity, sacrifice, personal discipline, and commitment to justice and freedom.

• *Mother's Day and Father's Day.* We can lift up the importance and value of strong family relationships and the honoring of our parents.

• *Veterans Day and Memorial Day.* We recognize that laying down our lives for the sake of others is commendable, and we can appropriately honor those who have done so.

• *Labor Day.* We can sincerely thank God for the blessing of work, for our witness in our work, and for the gracious, God-ordained gift of rest from work.

—*John W. Yates II*

Guest Preachers

"When the cat's away, the mice will play." Most of us have heard that statement applied to the phenomenon of church members taking leaves of absence while their minister is away. But since the work of the church transcends the personality or ability of any particular pastor, even in a pastor's absence, members should continue to grow spiritually. What can a pastor do to help a congregation prepare for, and respond favorably to, its guest speakers?

Who Supplies the Pulpit?

Some churches have the luxury of employing staff ministers who do quite well in the pulpit. Others have former pastors in their membership who are available for such responsibilities. In some cases, gifted lay persons can offer "view from the pew" messages that congregations need to hear.

In urban areas, many of us have access to seminary or college personnel who relish the opportunity to present God's Word in the local church. Area bishops, directors of missions, or other denominational officials often have a list of available preachers who are retired or whose responsibilities are not targeted toward a single church. Some who minister in and through parachurch organizations such as Inter-Varsity, Campus Crusade, Fellowship of Christian Athletes, or Gideons International will gladly offer themselves for pulpit supply.

What Should They Know?

It is disconcerting for a visiting minister to find upon arrival that he or she will be speaking on the same topic or Scripture the pastor addressed the previous Sunday. Those responsible for pulpit supply should attempt to share with the guest speaker any pertinent information regarding topics. For example, our church provides an up-to-date profile on the church's work, which includes a statement of philosophy of ministry, as well as a thumbnail sketch of current ministries. This information can give guest speakers insight into needs of the church that could be addressed in a sermon.

Sometimes sermon topic suggestions for the pulpit guest can be made. Obviously, that has to be done well ahead of time to enable the speaker to prepare adequately. Many guest ministers have "sugar sticks" (otherwise known as favorite sermons) they like to preach when they are filling a pulpit. Often those sermons are effective, but it is helpful to provide a pulpit guest some boundaries to work within. That way the preacher will better be able to "scratch where the parishioners itch"—or at least where the pastor *thinks* they itch.

What Other Arrangements?

Send your guest speaker a bulletin that outlines the worship service. On it, highlight and comment on each item of the guest speaker's responsibility. Will he or she just preach the sermon? Or is the guest to provide an invocation, other prayers, Scripture readings, and benediction?

It's best to state clearly the financial arrangements with the pulpit guest *before* the event and to provide the honorarium on that same Sunday, rather than sending it later. The going rate for mileage should be offered those coming from out of town. Hotel or motel accommodations must be planned ahead of time, and a host family or individual should be secured for a lunch or dinner engagement as required.

Finally, be sure to promote the guest speaker's coming ministry and encourage a positive response. The Sunday a guest preacher speaks need not be a down Sunday; your guest can provide fresh guidance and God-glorifying inspiration while you are away.

—Jerry Hayner

5

The Basic Form
of the Sermon

Sermon form is a curious beast. In many ways, a sermon's form, or structure, is its least noticed feature. Most hearers would be puzzled to be asked, "What was the form of the sermon you just heard?" Ask them about what the preacher said or about their own responses, and they can usually come up with an answer, but the form of a sermon slips by them as undetected as the meter of a hymn.

Despite the fact that it passes by relatively unnoticed, form is absolutely vital to the meaning and effect of a sermon. Like the silent shifting of gears in a car's automatic transmission, sermon form translates the potential energy of the sermon into productive movement, while remaining itself quietly out of view. Form is as important to the flow and direction of a sermon as are the banks of a river to the movement of its currents.

In artistic creations (and sermons are artistic creations of a sort), form and content cannot be easily distinguished. Think of Michelangelo's *David*. What is *form* and what is *content* in that magnificent sculpture? Or see the blurring of form and content in the fluid grace of the youthful Willie Mays as he glided almost magically across center field tracking a hard-hit line drive (an aesthetic event as well as an athletic achievement).

Instead of thinking of sermon form and content as separate realities, it is far more accurate to speak of the form *of* the content. A sermon's form, although often largely unperceived by the hearers, provides shape and energy to the sermon and thus becomes itself a

65

vital force in how a sermon makes meaning. Since a sermon may assume many possible shapes and designs, the question for the preacher is how to create a form for a particular sermon that best embodies its message and aims.

The Traditional Approach

The classical way to plan the form of any message—sermon or other—has been to create an outline, a schematic diagram of the parts and order of the message. Developing an outline, it is said, forces the preacher to make choices, not only about what will be said when but also about the logical connections among the various pieces of the sermon. Once a good outline has been produced, the preacher can simply flesh out the parts to create the finished sermon.

How is a good outline created? Let us examine a representative sermon outline and explore the means by which it was fashioned. Here is one preacher's fairly typical sermon outline, this one for a sermon based on Psalm 19:1–14.

Title: How Does God Speak to Us?

    I. God speaks through nature (19:1–6)
        A. In the silent processes of life
        B. In the cosmic wonder of the universe

   II. God speaks through the divine Word (19:7–11)
        A. In the Bible
        B. In the preaching and teaching of God's people

 III. God speaks in our life experiences (19:12–14)
        A. In our sense of failure and sin
        B. In our hunger to be faithful

Why did the preacher come up with this form and not some other? In this instance the structure of the text itself was a guide, since the preacher saw how the sections of the sermon could match divisions that can be made in the text. Even so, the outline was created by the preacher and not by the text; nothing dictates that it must be divided just this way. The preacher was aided by the flow of the text, but finally this sermon structure came—as all sermon forms do—through a creative act of the preacher's imagination.

But how can we know whether or not this outline is a good one? Homileticians have always been concerned about this question, of course, and over the years have developed a catalog of virtues by which sermon outlines could be tested. For instance:

• *Unity*. Each major point should support the main proposition.

- *Order.* The major division should be of equal importance.
- *Movement.* Each major division should carry the thought forward by saying something distinguishable from what has gone before.
- *Proportion.* The major divisions should be stated in parallel construction.
- *Climax.* The major divisions should be arranged in an ascending scale of impact.

If we apply these criteria to the foregoing sermon outline, the results are fairly encouraging. Lately, however, homileticians have developed some serious doubts about this business of creating sermon forms through outlines. Outlines are a good way of organizing *material,* but when we create a sermon, we are not primarily asking, "What is the most orderly way for this material to fit together?" We are, rather, asking, "How can people best *hear* the material in this sermon?" A sermon form should be a plan not only just for shaping information but also for the experience of listening.

Questioning the Tradition

Disenchanted with traditional outlining, many homileticians have begun searching for alternative means to create apt sermon forms. Fred Craddock, in his landmark essay *As One Without Authority* (Abingdon), proposed that sermons be shaped according to the same process of creative discovery employed by preachers in their exegetical work. When preachers study biblical texts, he said, they do not know in advance what those texts mean; they must search for meanings, putting clues together until meanings emerge at the end. Sermons, therefore, ought to recreate imaginatively this inductive quest, so that the listeners can share the preacher's experience of illumination.

What does this inductive sermon form look like in actual practice? Instead of being composed of points (I, II, III), a sermon would consist of a series of small segments, or movements, building cumulatively toward a climatic "Aha!" The problem being solved in the sermon is always the question, "What does this biblical text mean for us today?" That question hangs in the air at the beginning, and the sermon rolls along the pathway of discovery, gathering clues, until it finally arrives at the place where the listeners are prepared to make a decision for themselves about the claim of the text upon their lives.

A different sort of problem-solving form has been suggested by Eugene Lowry in his book *The Homiletical Plot* (John Knox). For Lowry, any "felt need" on the part of the hearers—whether originating in the biblical text, a theological doctrine, or a situation in life—can serve as the organizing task. Lowry believes sermons should begin by describing this problem, dilemma, or bind so clearly that the hearers feel "ambiguity" and desire its resolution.

For example, a preacher who begins a sermon by saying, "Today I want to talk about love" is, in Lowry's view, "dull," because no suspense has been created at the sermon's beginning.

Far better, he says, is the opening line: "Our problem is that so many times we extend our hand in love only to bring it back bruised and broken. To love is to risk rejection." What makes that introduction better is that it creates imbalance; it generates conflict by raising an experiential problem about love to the level of awareness. The listeners, he maintains, will want so much to see that conflict resolved that they will listen to the rest of the sermon to discover how it all comes out.

The job of the remainder of the sermon, claims Lowry, is "the resolution of that particular central ambiguity." Sermons, he claims, should be designed around five basic movements, or stages: (1) upsetting the equilibrium, (2) analyzing the discrepancy, (3) disclosing the clue to resolution, (4) experiencing the gospel, and (5) anticipating consequences for the future.

The Children's Sermon

Although it *is* difficult to proclaim the gospel to children, it can be done, and it can be done well.

Common Failings

Why do some children's sermons fail?

• *Rambling.* With children, time is of the essence. A good children's sermon gets directly to the point and then leaves it before the children lose interest.

• *Moralism.* Christianity certainly has its standards and expectations, but the time and place to be moralistic with children is not during Sunday worship. Children's sermons should enable children to experience God's goodness and the caring of God's people. Children need to feel this more than they need to be advised about their behavior.

• *Humanism.* Humanism tends to confuse the gospel with the wisdom of the ages or parental advice—something easy to do. No matter how it is dressed, worldly wisdom will always be advice about merely how to get along in the world.

• *Excessive teaching.* Although every good sermon should contain at least a little sound teaching, children's sermons frequently slide into more than just a little. It is easier to teach because children have so much to learn, but proclamation of God's good news needs to take precedence over mere teaching.

In Search of Better Ways

There are many effective ways to proclaim the gospel to children:

• *Variety.* No one type of presentation stands above the others. Striving to be creative and being

A third homiletician, David Buttrick, has perhaps given the most sustained attention to the relationship between sermon form and the issue of how sermons work to mold faith in the consciousness of the hearers. His ideas about good sermon form are based on a simple analogy: The human mind works something like a camera. Everything out there in the world is streaming through the lens of human consciousness, but, as every photographer knows, not everything can be captured on film. The photographer must pick something on which to focus, thereby creating both foreground and background.

As the preacher presents one idea after another, the hearers are busily snapping away with their mental cameras. Now, when the sermon is finished, what do the hearers have? If the sermon is poorly constructed, all they have is a cluttered box of random snapshots. If the sermon is well-formed, however, they will have something like a filmstrip, a series of pictures that possess a lively sense of movement from one to the next and work together to produce coherent understanding.

---

unafraid to try something different will avoid mediocrity.

- *Simplicity and directness.* Keeping it simple and direct for children may seem obvious, but so often the reverse happens. When speakers are not sure where they are headed, they tend to take detours while getting there. Another temptation is to try to do too much, to complicate what begins as a simple idea.

- *Targeting.* Children are not all alike; age especially makes a difference. Therefore, target a sermon for a particular age group. Even if the other age groups are only grazed, at least one group receives special attention on a given Sunday. A targeted sermon also says to children that the speaker cares enough to enter into their world.

- *Open-endedness.* Children can think. There is no need neither to beat them over the head with the obvious nor to tidy up all the loose ends and give them a complete package. Children can be given something to work out for themselves.

A good storyteller, for example, knows the most effective story is one where the meaning does not have to be spelled out. The story carries its message best when listeners find their own stories within the one being told.

- *Proclamation by participation.* How true it is that people learn by doing! For children, the ratio is something like 60 percent retention of what they do, 30 percent of what they see, and 10 percent of what they hear. If this ratio is accurate, then proclamation by participation should be a primary goal.

An effective children's sermon is as rare as a truly great adult sermon, but children's sermons need not be a chore at best or a madcap zoo at worst. When targets are set high, striving will make speakers better proclaimers, not only to the children but to all the family of God.

— *Richard J. Coleman*

Sermons, then, are "a movement of language from one idea to another," and because of this, Buttrick likes to call the individual ideas or units of the sermon *moves*. Because of his understanding of how human consciousness works, Buttrick insists that these moves must be built according to a single blueprint. Every move is required to possess three indispensable parts: (1) opening statement, (2) development, and (3) closure.

Buttrick is persuaded that, given the diminishing attention spans of contemporary people, about four minutes is the most people will devote to a single idea, so each move must complete its work within that limit. A well-designed twenty-minute sermon, then, consists of an ordered sequence of no more than five or six of these three-part, precision-designed moves.

Homileticians like Craddock, Lowry, and Buttrick have gone a long

Women in the Pulpit

On July 31, 1763, James Boswell reported to the great Dr. Samuel Johnson that he had just been to a Quaker meeting where he had heard a woman preach. To this piece of intelligence Johnson responded with his famous remark: "Sir, a woman's preaching is like a dog's walking on his hinder legs. It is not done well; but you are surprised to find it done at all."

Johnson's judgment appears dated in this generation. No one who has heard mixed groups of seminarians in preaching classes could reasonably judge a woman's preaching inferior to that of her male contemporaries. Differences *among* men and *among* women are far greater on every score than differences *between* men and women.

Both have the same tasks: to pay attention to the text, to make sense, to be clear, to be themselves, and, by all means, to be both inclusive and varied in their language, illustrations, and structure—if they don't want to lose big chunks of the congregation to irritation or boredom.

Pros and Cons

Women do at least as well as men in terms of basic verbal skills, but some may show a bit more perceptiveness about human interaction and feeling. If their somewhat different experiences in life give them an alternate slant on a familiar text, that can be good: Most of us have heard the usual perspectives often enough to have become resistant to them. Women can affirm such differences as gifts to be used gladly.

Nonetheless, despite these possible advantages, women still have

way toward restoring creativity and excitement in sermon form. There are also problems, however, in some of their suggestions about sermon form. To begin with, any scheme that purports to be able to lead a group of people to the place where they exclaim, "Aha! I have discovered a surprising new truth!" must reckon with the fact that human creativity is fragile and unpredictable. People do not always respond the way we expect them to.

A deeper issue for the problem-solving form comes from the fact that these forms usually *do* work to create listener interest. However, if a congregation is treated week after week only to the problem-solving design, it is inevitably grasping that the purpose of the gospel is merely to resolve personal problems.

And do ideas really get formed in human consciousness the way Buttrick claims they do? He wants every move to state the idea, to

---

trouble being heard. The mechanical part of the problem—the voice itself—is the least of it. Good professional training can make an astounding difference in the resonance and clarity of one's speaking voice. Women preachers can find help for their voices.

The larger problem, however, comes with the double bind that people don't want women preachers to be masculine but tend to consider supposedly feminine traits incompatible with the authority of the pulpit. Consider just a few differences in labeling of men and women. The naive male seminary intern is "an earnest young man" to be respected; the naive female intern is "a sweet young thing" to be discounted. The man whose voice breaks with emotion in the pulpit is a person who feels deeply; the woman is merely emotional, "as women are." The man is a real leader, while the woman is pushy and insists on her own way. And so on. All a woman can do about such perceptions is try to steer a steady course between extremes.

The End of Novelty

The good news is that congregations are often remarkably eager to love and admire their pastors. When they come to know and respect her, they begin to forget gender. But that takes time, time not available to the visitor who simply cannot yet get past the sheer novelty of a woman preacher. Even today, people tell me frequently that they have never before heard a woman preach. That is where the really tough barrier lies, a barrier that will remain until women in the pulpit are no longer considered a novelty.

That day will arrive, as illustrated by the story of a 5-year-old girl. Her grandmother reported that she was playing wedding with her dolls. The punch line of the story did not come when she had the minister ask the man if he took the woman to be "his *awful* wedded wife." No, the punch line came when Grandma asked if the little girl wanted to be the bride, and she responded firmly, "No, I'm the minister."

—Marguerite Shuster

develop the idea, and then to restate the idea. Less direct, more poetic ways of coming to understanding get washed away. We must also seriously question whether a sermon is only a string of ideas. Some moments in good sermons are like the congregational singing of "A Mighty Fortress" at a funeral. It would seriously miss the mark to ask, "What is the main idea in singing this hymn?"

As the debate among homileticians about sermon form continues, it has become increasingly clear that a sermon's form should grow out of the shape of the gospel being proclaimed as well as out of the listening patterns of those who will hear the sermon.

Finding a Satisfactory Sermon Form

How does the preacher find, or create, a good form for a given sermon? Good sermon form is an artistic achievement, and no universally accepted and always-reliable process exists for creating a satisfactory sermon form. What follows, however, are three suggested steps designed to raise the central questions that form must address.

● *Start with the focus and function.* Begin creating a sermon form with the focus and the function. A *focus statement* is a concise description of the central, controlling, and unifying theme of the sermon. In short, this is what the whole sermon will be about. A *function statement* is a description of what the preacher hopes the sermon will create or cause to happen for the hearers. Everything the sermon needs to accomplish the focus and function should be included in the structure, and anything that does not help us to achieve these aims is extraneous and should be weeded out.

For example, consider the focus and function statements for a sermon on Romans 8:28–39:

Focus: Because we have seen in Jesus Christ that God is *for* us, we can be confident that God loves and cares for us even when our experience seems to deny it.

Function: To reassure and give hope to troubled hearers in the midst of, not apart from, their distress.

Together, this focus and this function constitute the claim of this sermon on Romans 8. Now the preacher asks, "How can the claim be presented in such a way that the listeners can hear it?"

● *Divide these larger tasks into smaller components.* Focus and function statements express the overall tasks of the sermon, and these tasks can only be done bit by bit, over time, through the sermon. Thus the preacher will break them down into a set of smaller undertakings.

Our example focus statement indicates that the sermon will say that, "because we have seen in Jesus Christ that God is *for* us, we can be confident that God loves and cares for us even when our experience seems to deny it." If the sermon as a whole does in fact say this, along the way the following tasks are necessary:

a. Say where and how we have seen in Jesus Christ that God is for us.
b. Name and describe experiences that seem to deny God's love and care.
c. Describe clearly how what we have seen in Jesus Christ is able to create present confidence in God's love and care.

Our example function statement indicates that the sermon intends "to reassure and give hope to troubled hearers in the midst of, not apart from, their distress." If the sermon as a whole is to accomplish this, then along the way it must:

d. Provide reassurance, based upon God's continuing love and care, to troubled hearers.
e. Evoke a sense of hope for people who struggle with situations that seem to have no future.
f. And perhaps call into question all shallow reassurances that do not deal honestly with suffering.

• *Decide the sequence in which these tasks should be done.* Decisions about sermon sequence are made almost exclusively on the basis of the needs and capacities of the listeners. Should one begin by describing the biblical text, and then show how that text speaks to our experience? Or will they hear the text better if the preacher begins with a description of human need and then shows how the text speaks to it? But if human need prefaces the sermon, will people hear the text only as an "answer" to what is already present rather than a new way of seeing life altogether?

Returning to the example sermon, one preacher may decide the best sequence is as follows (using the letters a–f from above):

1. Start with the experience of the hearers.
   b. Name and describe experiences that seem to deny God's love and care.
2. Give the "typical" religious responses to these experiences and describe how these are insufficient.
   f. Call into question all shallow reassurances that do not deal honestly with the kind of experiences described in (b).
3. Say how the text gives a deeper response to suffering.
   c. Describe clearly how what we have seen in Jesus Christ is able to create present confidence in God's love and care and is different form the shallow reassurances of (f).
   a. Say where and how we have seen in Jesus Christ that God is for us.
4. Move to what this deeper response means for our living.
   e. Say how (c) and (a) evoke a sense of hope for people who struggle with situations that seem to have no future.
   d. Say how the hope described in (e) provides reassurance, based on God's continuing love and care, to troubled hearers.

This form has taken the set of six tasks and organized them into a sequence that will allow each to be accomplished at the right moment in the sermon. To use this form, the preacher must clearly decide that the place to begin is with the felt need of human crisis and that the remainder of the sermon should be a careful working through the gospel response to that crisis.

This is not the only way, though, to order these tasks. Here is another preacher's design:

1. Start with the ways the Christian community has responded to suffering.
   f. Call into question all shallow reassurances that do not deal honestly with suffering.
   a. Say where and how we have seen in Jesus Christ that God is for us, indicating how this points toward a deeper response to suffering than we have seen in (f).
   c_1. Describe clearly how what we have seen in Jesus Christ (a) is able to create present confidence in God's love and care.
2. Ask whether even this deeper response can face up to our immediate experience of suffering.
   b. Name and describe experiences that seem to deny God's love and care.
   c_2. Return to the description of the relation between what we have seen in Jesus Christ and our present confidence in God's love and care, this time relating what is said directly to the experiences named in (b).
3. Reflect on what this deeper response means for our living.
   d. Provide reassurance, based upon God's continuing love and care, to troubled hearers.
   e. Evoke a sense of hope for people who struggle with situations that seem to have no future.

Both of these forms for the sermon are good ones. The first sermon form presented the human dilemma and allowed the claim of the text to emerge as a response. The second sermon form sets up the text's claim early and then tested it against human experience. One can imagine a third structure in which the preacher would raise the question of human suffering (b), move to descriptions of how Christian people have learned to live in the face of such events (d) and (e), and then ask, "What gives faithful people hope and trust in the midst of all that seems to deny God's care?" (a) and (c). In this form, the full claim of the text would not come until the very end of the sermon.

A Matter of Discernment

Deciding which form to employ is a matter of discernment on the part of the preacher. If the sermon is to be an act of Christian proclamation, the hearers must not be passive. They should participate with the preacher in the creation of the event of proclamation, and the preacher should choose the sermon form that best allows the hearers to exercise their ministry of active and creative listening.

—Thomas Long

Resources

Buttrick, D. 1987. Homiletic: Moves and structures. Philadelphia: Fortress.

Craddock, F. 1971. As one without authority. Nashville: Abingdon.

Craddock, F. 1985. Preaching. Nashville: Abingdon.

Long, T. 1989. The witness of preaching. Louisville: Westminster/John Knox.

Lowry, E. 1980. The homiletical plot: The sermon as narrative art form. Atlanta: John Knox

Lowry, E. 1985. Doing time in the pulpit: The relationship between narrative and preaching. Nashville: Abingdon.

African-American Preaching

In the African-American church, Sunday morning in Savannah is just like Sunday morning in Atlanta or New York or New Orleans or Oakland. It's Sunday, and that's the time to *have* church. And that means somebody preaching the Word. In the black worship tradition, preaching is not just a homily or comments on current events or didactic statements on doctrine; it is also delivering the Word with preparation and power and passion.

Why do people still come to clapboard churches in Mississippi and gather in rented school buildings in new subdivisions and newly integrated suburbs of Maryland until they can build a church? They come to hear the Word—to *have church*. But that Word is to be delivered in a special way, and when it is, the people leave and say, "We *had* church today!"

Characteristics

What are some of the characteristics of preaching in this tradition?

• Black preaching is, almost without exception, biblical. It takes the biblical message and stories, and weaves them in such a way that they come alive and relate to the needs, feelings, and existential situations of those gathered in the congregation. Thus, black preaching often gives imaginative details in its dramatic telling of the gospel stories.

• Black preaching is generally poetic rather than rigorously logical. Many metaphors are used, and nouns, adjectives, and adjectival clauses predominate, rather than verbs and verb forms. These words create a picturesque message on the canvas of the mind. A good deal of description and imagery is used. The black preacher is convinced that preaching is primarily an art form rather than a debate, and, therefore, one is more likely to plead out of passion than argue out of logic.

• Black preaching is a dialogue that does not occur *after* but *during* the sermon. It is a call-and-response style of communication coming out of the African tradition. The congregation is encouraged and expected to participate in the act and art of preaching with verbal and body response. The sermon gives voice to the congregation's message. Preaching in the black tradition is cooperation between the pulpit and the pew.

• Black preaching is declarative rather than suggestive. There is little room for equivocation and sophistry. The question is not whether God exists. That is a philosophical question. God does exist. The approach is more like the style of the Hebrew prophets and the apostles, rather than the Greek orators and philosophers. The question for the black preacher is: Now that God exists, what difference does it make in my life, in my situation, in society?

• Black preaching slowly and deliberately builds to a climax and celebration. The preacher is expected to allow time for both the mind and the emotions to react in a natural process, so the people can respond and reflect on what has been said, and anticipate what is coming next. Timing is important. The preacher measures the delivery to maximize comprehension and effect.

• Black preaching is didactic as well as inspiring. It seeks to inform as well as lift. It seeks to discern the action of God in history as it relates to the existential dilemma of those gathered. It seeks to speak to the human condition, to lend healing to the hurts of the souls of those gathered, and to bring a "balm of Gilead" to the convulsions of the spirit.

Nothing substitutes for proclamation. The people come expecting to hear a Word from the Lord. And when that Word is preached with passion, preparation, and power— cutting a path through the wilderness of despair and offering grace and hope to those who are bruised, underloved, confused, or thirsting— people leave, saying, "We *had* church today!"

— *William B. McClain*

Trends in Homiletics

Does preaching change over the years? Yes, the practice of preaching undergoes constant and, in some ways, astonishingly rapid development. The basic goals and purposes of preaching endure, of course, but, because preaching is an oral art, it is deeply influenced by its cultural context and shaped by the needs and capacities of each new generation of listeners.

The sermons of only a few decades ago (not to mention those of earlier centuries) now sound quaint to our ears and are strikingly dissimilar to contemporary sermons in terms of style, length, and content.

Four Determinants

What will preaching be like in the coming years? What forces are gathering to shape the sermons of the next generation of preachers? Here are four major areas of influence on the future of preaching:

• *Biblical scholarship.* As we reap the benefits of the newer forms of biblical scholarship, especially literary and rhetorical approaches to the Bible, the connection between biblical texts and sermons will become richer and more imaginative. Instead of viewing texts simply as vessels containing theological ideas, preachers will see the biblical materials as rhetorical acts, as poetic expressions of theological truth, as art forms capable of regenerating themselves in the art of the sermon.

Preachers will give more attention to the ways texts employ symbols and evocative language. They will be more aware of the elements of plot and character in narratives and recognize more fully the creative interaction between text and reader.

• *Communication studies.* In various ways, preaching has always been listener oriented and influenced by the rhetorical science of the day, but older homileticians tended to understand the hearers uniformly, as versions of some "ideal listener."

Increasingly, however, we are learning that people do not all hear the same message alike. Variables, such as age, personality type, cultural background, developmental level, and gender subtly tune the act of listening. Preachers will become more aware of these differences among hearers, even in a seemingly homogeneous congregation, and will respond by creating sermons that vary in structure, style, and subject matter. As we learn more about how people think and process information, and how images work in human consciousness, we will design sermons with language and structure capable of addressing these communication realities.

• *Social concern.* Preaching in the coming decades will grow more responsive to the crises in human society. The fragility of the ecological environment, the increasing ideological pluralism of our time, the economic imbalances among nations, the threats of war and disease—all of these and other issues will demand the attention of the responsible preacher. Congregations will need and want help in thinking through these issues from a theological point of view, and any preaching that steers clear of the crucial social problems of the age will be seen as irrelevant.

• *Teaching ministry.* When preachers know their congregations have heard the gospel many times over, the problem becomes how to make old news new again. Thus, for the past two decades, homiletics has focused upon story preaching and other indirect means of communication, seeking to invigorate those who have "heard it all before."

It is now apparent, though, that preachers address congregations that often don't know much about the Bible or the basic concepts of the Christian faith. Christians need to have a working knowledge of the faith. They need to know the essential biblical stories, and they must possess a useful theological vocabulary in order to function capably as people of faith. Thus, preachers will give increased attention to education and to the building up of the Christian community.

—Thomas G. Long

Preaching on Radio or Television

Although preachers deal primarily with one commodity—the written Word that reveals the Living Word—their ordinary method of transmission is the spoken word. Sermons must be designed to "grab people by the ears." Though written words can be absorbed by the human brain at a much speedier rate than spoken ones, illiteracy has always been one of the great problems facing human populations. Therefore, God decreed early on that "faith comes by hearing." Jesus came preaching, not writing, and it is still the spoken word that does most of the work of witnessing today.

But what does the preacher whose words will be transmitted out of the sanctuary and over radio and television frequencies need to know? What adjustments must a preacher make when the message travels through electronic media rather than going directly from pulpit to pew? Here are a few suggestions:

• *Gear up for greater formality.* The strictly in-house worship event is the gathering of a spiritual family, a warm fellowship in which people have grown close to one another. Sudden, informal changes in program format and an easygoing conversational style present few problems in such an environment. Broadcasting, however, calls for stricter timing, an even flow in the order of service, and a bit more formality in the presentation of the message. The media audience looks on at a distance. Drastic breaks in continuity can lead to serious disruptions of concentration.

Verbal liberties that we may take in an evening or midweek service must be guarded against in the delivery of the broadcast or televised sermon. The free use of idiomatic and vernacular expressions that may add "personality" to a private service translate poorly over the air. We may get by with sentences ending in prepositions in the first venue, because the entire service is less restrained. But to the electronic audience, the old motto applies: A preposition is the wrong word to end a sentence with.

• *Use attention-getters liberally.* Because listeners at home usually are bombarded with constant distractions, media preachers must use frequent attention-getters to keep interest focussed on the message. While such awakeners may not be necessary in face-to-face communication, the unseen audience finds them helpful.

For example, one might use a pungently humorous line such as "A lie is an abomination unto the Lord and a very present help in time of trouble." Any use of short, dramatic anecdotal material will help renew attention.

• *Bring the audience into the action.* Taking a cue from the newscaster, preachers do well to make frequent use of the present tense and action verbs, rather than casting the entire sermon in the past tense. The time lag between the occurrence of news and its reporting on the air is usually small, especially in contrast to the print media. Media audiences have been programmed to expect messages that are current and dynamic—and none is more up to the minute or exciting than the gospel.

• *Treat the clock with utmost re-*

spect. The nemesis of the commercial broadcaster—the clock—must not be ignored by ministers whose sermons are prepared with the media audience in mind. A full church service, with two or three taped segments edited in, will typically allow no more than 27 or 28 minutes for the sermon itself. Running over may be of little consequence in off-the-record worship, but it can prove disastrous to the precisely timed format of broadcasting.

—*D. James Kennedy*

6

Preparing a Sermon

Quality preaching does not happen by accident. It is the result of hard work, creative thinking, careful research, and a dependence upon the Holy Spirit. In other words, there is no short cut to homiletical excellence.

Those who want to preach well need to reserve large chunks of time for sermon preparation, because it takes time, time, time. Harry Emerson Fosdick spent one hour in preparation for every minute of delivered sermon. Bill Hybels, pastor of the well-known Willow Creek Community Church in suburban Chicago, does approximately the same, and it shows!

Some preachers may complain about the stranglehold of administration, but many of them might well admit that they just don't enjoy studying. For them, administrative detail is a convenient scapegoat. Yet, as Chuck Swindoll once said, "Every time I say yes during the week, I say no to the congregation that gathers on Sunday morning." So time should be carved out early in the week, with attention given to at least these seven essential steps.

Step One: Preparing the Preacher

All of life is preparation for preaching. In more ways than we dare admit, the strength of a public ministry is predicated upon the quality of the individual's interior life. A regular devotional time tunes the heart to God and immerses the mind in the truths of Scripture. If Christ is an infrequently sought friend in private, it is most likely that his touch on the preacher's public life will be superficial.

Wide reading is also indispensable. The reading fare of effective preachers usually includes biography, history, contemporary social and psychological studies, and a range of secular magazines such as *Time*, *Newsweek*, and *U. S. News and World Report*. Of course, the informed preacher reads a quality daily newspaper, too. No pulpit speaker can allow cultural ignorance to set in.

Step Two: Choosing the Subject and Text

Which comes first—the subject or the text? Actually, there is no rule to follow; either may come first, or they may be chosen simultaneously. If we follow the lectionary, much of textual choice-making will be resolved immediately. The text has been essentially determined in advance. For others, however, the question can become a weekly anxiety.

Advanced planning can help relieve much of that anxiety. Some preachers plan at least three months in advance. For others, the process may include a year or more. It goes something like this: The preacher (perhaps in conjunction with pastoral staff and/or laity) takes a retreat away from the office to get the big picture. He or she conducts a review of past sermons, exposing segments of Scripture that have not been studied, theological truths that have not been shared, and life situations that have not been addressed. These areas are duly noted. Then, a study of the congregation is undertaken. Reviewing the church directory (preferably a recent pictorial directory) helps suggest current needs facing the people.

Understanding what has recently been preached and what the congregation needs leads to the selection of critical themes. For example, Chuck Swindoll decided he and his congregation had been too bound by "manmade restrictions and legalistic regulations" (Swindoll 1990, xiii). In response, he shared a sermon series, based primarily on the book of Romans, entitled *The Grace Awakening*. The themes are obvious in the titles he chose:
1. Grace: It's *Really* Amazing!
2. The Free Gift
3. Isn't Grace Risky?
4. Undeserving, Yet Unconditionally Loved
5. Squaring Off Against Legalism
6. Emancipated? Then Live Like It!
7. Guiding Others to Freedom
8. The Grace to Let Others Be
9. Graciously Disagreeing and Pressing On
10. Grace: Up Close and Personal
11. Are You Really a Minister of Grace?
12. A Marriage Oiled by Grace
13. The Charming Joy of Grace Giving
14. Grace: It's *Really* Accepting

We can learn at least two things by reviewing these fourteen sermon titles. First, notice that Swindoll breaks his theme into bite-sized pieces. Grace is too large a subject to cover in a single sermon. He divides grace and provides fourteen separate facets of that diamond of a subject. Each chosen facet is large enough to merit an individual sermon and yet small enough to be covered thoroughly.

Second, he expresses themes in the language of today rather than in the language of the text. Thus, he avoids surrounding his sermons with the air of antiquity. Sermons ought to be based on Scripture for authority, of course, but be expressed in contemporary terms. Good preaching exists at the intersection of the eternal Word and everyday life. Swindoll's titles illustrate this well.

When we choose a neglected part of the Bible for an expository sermon, the unfolding text dictates the subjects to be studied as they occur sequentially in the Scripture portion. For example, I shared a series from the book of 1 John:

1 John 1:1–10—"Honesty: The Basis of Fellowship"
1 John 2:1–14—"Must We Love All Christians?"
1 John 2:15–27—"When the World Is in the Church"
1 John 2:28–3:10—"His Second Coming Makes a Difference Now"
1 John 3:11–24—"When Love Gets Serious, It Sacrifices"
1 John 4:1–6—"When the Doorbell Rings"
1 John 4:7–21—"How to Overcome Fear"

My process of development went like this: (1) Our people needed a study series that would enhance fellowship within the congregation; (2) I chose 1 John because fellowship is a controlling theme of the book; (3) seven key themes emerged from exegetical study of the text; (4) I found ways to express those themes in terms that were true both to the Scripture and to the congregation's present experience.

Planned preaching takes into account the need for a balanced biblical diet (Old *and* New Testament; law *and* grace; gospels *and* epistles, etc.). Here are questions to ask each week as sermon planning unfolds:

1. What do the people need to hear this week?
2. What parts of God's Word need to be expounded now?
3. What has God laid upon my heart?

Step Three: Studying the Text

Three main tasks confront us as we turn to our text. These are, in order:

● *Read the Scripture in different translations.* Multiple versions with their distinctive nuances cast helpful light on the teaching of the text.

● *Exhaust your ideas on the subject.* All your life God has been teaching you about himself. Record these insights. Dependence too early on commentaries produces scissors-and-paste preaching. Sermons never were intended to be the secondhand sharing of what others say. Phillips Brooks, more than a century ago, reminded us that "preaching is truth through personality" (Brooks 1969, 5). Let the distinctive marks of your personality, and the ways God has worked with you, come through. You are God's gift to the congregation. What you think and feel is important as a witness to what God is doing in one of his people.

● *Glean from the commentaries.* Give preference to exegetical and critical works. Devotional commentaries have their place, but consult them only after you have a firm understanding of the text etymologically, grammatically, and culturally. More than one reader has smiled at G. Campbell Morgan's counsel to preachers: Buy fifty exegetical commentaries for every devotional commentary purchased. Then, Morgan proceeded to write scores of devotional commentaries. Yet

---

Staying Spiritually Fresh

Every preacher knows the problem of handling the perennial need to be spiritually fit to preach. Since we are persons first and preachers second, we need to manage personal factors along with professional concerns.

Spiritual freshness involves first a sense of promise in what we have been called to do. This, in turn, conditions the way we approach our work and generates a love for that work of preaching. An acutely felt sense of promise in our work harnesses interest and energies in a way nothing else can.

Second, spiritual freshness involves a sense of God being involved in what we do. A sense of God's involvement grants a center of understanding out of which fresh courage and creativity result. The focussed action of preaching is then both personal and fresh.

Means to the End

To gain a sense of promise and involvement with God we must:

● *Give God our attention in prayer.* True prayer is attentiveness to God. The basic concern here is not asking but being attentive, opening ourselves to meet with God in a willed encounter—on God's terms.

Ours is a day when so much has been reduced to capsule form in order to lower the demands upon our eyes, minds, and time. We need to realize, then, that what first attracts us does not always deeply engage us. Spiritual freshness is sustained as we let God engage us, and the attentive action of prayer allows such engagement.

● *Meditate on spiritual meanings.* Meditation should flow from prayer, allowing ourselves to react thoughtfully on how the inner and the outer

the sentiment behind Morgan's counsel is worthy. Serious grappling with the meaning of the text is the preacher's greatest responsibility. After such study, we surely will be filled with our own "devotional" responses and suggestions.

Joel Gregory, the gifted preacher-expositor at First Baptist Church, Dallas, uses an exegetical notebook for this segment of preparation. He devotes one page to each verse under consideration. On each page he records his inductive findings; insights from dictionaries, lexicons and concordances; comparisons found in a study of various translations; and insights from analytical commentaries.

In light of the crucial step of studying, it's clear that one of a preacher's wisest investments is a high-quality library. When preaching an expository series through a Bible book, consider investing in a half dozen of the best exegetical commentaries on that section of Scripture. The process of understanding a text may be painstaking, but it is a worthy enterprise. God has not promised to honor our cleverness, our illustrations, our applications, or our alliterative outlines. He has, how-

---

world relate. By pondering our experience, we can focus ourselves to live by the meanings that generate growth in godliness. Meditation opens us to wonder, which involves more than mere thoughtfulness can discover on its own.

Meditation and prayer go together. Meditation keeps prayer thoughtful, and prayer sanctifies our thinking, claiming it always for God's use.

● *Worship God.* Many of us who must so often guide others in worship sometimes fail to worship as we do. We regulate the ritual, yet fall short of a lively response to God in our own heart. We who preach must remember that our own praise to God should find other forms in addition to that of the sermon we prepare and offer.

● *Dialogue with others.* Human contacts often can become events of discernment and disclosure out of which blessing issues. Honest and open interaction with others can open new springs of creativity within us, especially when any blockages within us are sensed and dealt with properly.

● *Read depth material.* Reading that informs, sensitizes us to truth, and stirs us to seek God will help us preach with freshness and fitness.

Scripture comes first, of course, but a steady, solid program of reading helps us relate the wisdom of Scripture to our own life and the lives of those we serve. For instance, John Wesley moved beyond religious formalism after encountering the writing of William Law, and Martin Luther King's insight into nonviolent noncooperation with evil took shape after reading E. Stanley Jones's book about Mahatma Gandhi.

If we "work as if it all depends on [us]," to repeat Augustine's oft-quoted advice, "and pray as if it all depends on God," then spiritual freshness will be the result.

—James Earl Massey

ever, promised to honor his Word (Isa. 55:11). We must, therefore, know its meaning so that it can be shared with clarity and conviction.

Step Four: Shaping the Material

This is the task of taking all the available material and deciding what to include in the sermon—and what to exclude. Joel Gregory prepares three to five times more material than he will use for preaching. He says, "If you say all you know, you don't know enough." Then he adds, "The art of exposition is the art of elimination" (Baumann 1990, 6, 7). If you share all you know, you are running close to shallow. For example, don't parade Greek syntax and grammar before the congregation; people need your textual conclusions, not necessarily a rehearsal of the exegetical process.

The Pastor's Library

Annie Dillard underscored the importance of one's library, explaining that the reader must be "careful of what he reads, for that is what he will write. He is careful of what he learns, because that is what he will know." This is especially true for those in ministry, because their libraries are a penetrating revelation of their minds and hearts.

Effective ministers have always been great readers, from the arch bibliophile Charles Spurgeon to Alexander Whyte, who advised, "Sell your bed, if need be, to buy books," to D. Martyn Lloyd-Jones, who, on vacation at the beach, sat reading heavy theology while his children played in the surf.

A Select Library

Is a vast library necessary, then, for ministerial effectiveness? The answer is a measured no, because what is essential is a *select* library. Jonathan Edwards, for example, did quite well with his four hundred volumes. An adequate, working library develops from two emphases: balance and quality.

Those beginning to build a library must begin with the basics: a study Bible; a concordance, such as *Strong's Exhaustive Concordance to the Bible* (Abingdon, 1967); a topical concordance, such as *Nave's Topical Bible* (Moody, 1970); a Bible dictionary, such as *The New Bible Dictionary* (Eerdmans, 1982); a New Testament word study, such as *Vine's Expository Dictionary of New Testament Words* for English readers (Zondervan, 1985); a dictionary of church history, such as *The New International Dictionary of the Christian Church* (Zondervan, 1978) or *The Oxford Dictionary of the Christian Church* (Oxford University Press, 1974); a one volume theology, such as Millard Erickson's *Christian Theology* (Baker, 1985); a dictionary of practical theology, such as *The Evangelical Dictionary of Theology* (Baker, 1984); and a book of cross-references, such as *The Treasury of Scripture Knowl-*

In the process of shaping the material, you will develop and hone five sermon components: form, illustrations, applications, conclusions, and introduction.

● *Form.* Too many sermons resemble the earth as described in Genesis 1:2: "formless and empty, darkness . . . over the surface of the deep." Yet listeners deserve to be treated with respect. Therefore, the preacher owes them a semblance of order, form, and movement.

Every sermon should have movement. In most instances there should be an outline (even in biographical or first-person sermons). The outline should be crisp, clear, and contemporary. Although sometimes outlines are expressed in alliterative terms, this isn't necessary, and often it can feel forced.

A sermon from 1 Corinthians 10:13 on "Victory over Temptation" might have the following outline:

---

edge (Nelson, 1992). You can then augment this essential core of books with their multivolume counterparts and other works on theology, history, vocabulary, apologetics, pastoral theology, and devotion.

As to commentaries? The best advice is not to purchase sets unless you need to have something on the shelves immediately that covers the entire Bible. If so, *The Tyndale Old Testament Commentaries* (24 volumes, Eerdmans) and *The Tyndale New Testament Commentaries* (20 volumes, Eerdmans) would make an excellent beginning.

Several annotated bibliographies of books on the Bible and theology help insure balance and quality—when we consult them comparatively. An older but still-helpful volume is Charles Spurgeon's *Commenting and Commentaries* (Banner of Truth Trust, 1969). Next, Cyril J. Barber's *The Minister's Library* (Moody, 1985, 1987) provides incisive help. Also informative are the two volumes entitled *Old Testament Books for Pastor and Teachers* (Westminster, 1977) by Brevard S. Childs and *New Testament Books for Pastors and Teachers*

(Westminster, 1984) by Ralph P. Martin. Finally, an *Annotated Bibliography on the Bible and Church* (Alumni Association of Trinity Evangelical Divinity School, 1986), edited by Douglas Moo, provides the candid assessment of an entire seminary faculty.

Accumulating a Library

We can find many of the essential volumes at reasonable prices through local bookstores and catalogues. However, we're wise not to neglect the rich resource of used books. There are scores of fine second-hand sources for Christian books in the United States and Great Britain. Most Christian college librarians will gladly supply a list of such sources.

It is not how many books we read, but how *well* we read. A person who reads widely but not well deserves to be pitied rather than praised. As Thomas Hobbes said, "If I read as many books as most men do, I would be as dull-witted as they are." Let's read well—to God's glory.

—*Kent Hughes*

I. Temptation is common to all (13a)

II. God's faithfulness is promised to all (13b)

III. Victory is possible for all (13c)

Or "The Father Waits" from Luke 15:11–24 might be outlined:

I. I want my way (11–13)

II. I want (14–20)

III. I am wanted (20b–24)

Note that the points are succinct, stated in contemporary language, and true to the text. Since most people honor logic and clarity, they appreciate effort expended on developing a lucid sermon structure. We should always try to let the passage determine the structure, rather than imposing a structure artificially on the passage.

• *Illustrations.* Well-chosen illustrations are absolutely imperative in a contemporary sermon. They make abstract truth concrete. They make sermons interesting. And, they allow us to repeat ourselves without sounding redundant.

Here are some guidelines to remember: (1) Illustrations should express truth that is typical—"This could also happen to me." (2) Every major point deserves an illustration. (3) Illustrations are best when committed to memory. The effective use of illustration demands eye contact and total involvement. (4) Illustrations should be short. They are a means, not the end. (5) They should be to the point. A good illustration out of context is a bad illustration.

• *Applications.* Few preachers do better with applications than Chuck Swindoll, pastor of First Evangelical Free Church in Fullerton, California. He puts wheels on his messages. Swindoll believes applications should be brief enough to be remembered, clear enough to be written down, and realistic enough to be achieved.

Elucidate a subject, and you may have taught. Preaching, however, is concerned with the transformation of people. Therefore, every sermon is an opportunity to invite people to *do something.* Thus, applications are the preacher's responsibility; they become suggestions for the congregation to consider.

Every good sermon is a volley between the past (what the text said) and the present (how it is applied today). A sermon without application is a dissertation on ancient history—and no more. We must wrestle with every text until it yields one or more applications, and then our job is to make the applications clear and possible.

• *Conclusion.* Because the conclusion is the final impression made by the preacher, it deserves to be clear-cut and memorable. Who could forget Peter Marshall's graphic conclusion to a sermon on Elijah: "If God be God, worship him. But if Baal be god, worship him and go to hell. Let us pray" (Baumann 1972, 145)?

Recapitulation is a valid form of conclusion, but it needs to be more than a mere rehashing of what the people have already heard.

We must add fresh language or a story that grabs people.

● *Introduction.* The last item to be prepared is the introduction, because we need to know the entire sermon before we have sufficient clues to develop the introduction. We must introduce all that follows, and this can be prepared only when we are clear about the body of content we'll be presenting.

An effective introduction, like a good golf shot off the tee, is not a luxury; it is an imperative. A poor start is almost impossible to overcome. The best introductions are short, to the point, and interesting. They hook the listeners and invite them to get interested in what will follow. Many preachers prefer to start where people are (with a recent news event or a contemporary story) and then bring the congregation to the text.

A well-chosen illustration often works best. In a sermon on prayer, I began with a story about my son Steve, who was six at the time. He was praying at bedtime: "Lord, thank you for this world; bless Mom and Dad, and Lynn; bless Kevin, and Billy, Jimmy, Stuart, Joel, Glenn, Papa and Nana Baumann, Papa and Nana Jones . . ." Then he started praying for the same people a second time, and then a third time.

Finally I quietly interjected an amen.

Steve opened his eyes, and they were aflame. He looked me straight in the eyes and said, "Daddy, I wasn't finished yet; besides, I wasn't talking to you." He had caught the essence of prayer—talking to God. The sermon was off and running!

Step Five: Writing the Sermon

Ideally, we write our sermons in full to develop our skill of expression, logic, and balance. This also helps us overcome a tendency toward repetition and triteness.

Sue Nichols reminds us: "When amateur communicators say the first thing that comes to mind, their material pours out in long, wordy sentences with featherweight verbs and trite, obvious sentiments. . . . A skilled communicator dams up the initial flow. He curtails it until he can sort out his precise message, until he can phrase it with strength and release it in an altered but more powerful form" (Nichols 1963, 26).

Caution: Sermons are not oral essays. All sermon writing should be done with the ear in mind. Oral style differs from written style. An essay can be read and reread. People hear a sermon only once, so it must picture the truth in in a way that does not require going back to "read" it again.

Carl Lundquist, the late president of Bethel College and Seminary, St. Paul, Minnesota, once delivered a powerful sermon that didn't have a complete sentence in it for at least ten minutes. It was marvelous for the ear, but an English teacher would have failed the student who turned in a similar piece as an essay. This difference between prose writing and sermon writing cannot be overstated.

Some will choose to take limited notes into the pulpit rather than a manuscript. The key is to do what leads to your most effective communication. Some need a manuscript in front of them when the sermon is delivered, most have notes, and a few brave souls preach without notes. We all must find what best suits us and our style.

Step Six: Soaking in the Material

If the sermon is completed before the weekend—say, Thursday—Friday and Saturday remain available for the "soaking" process. The more a preacher is immersed in the sermon, the more it becomes a part of the preacher. It can then come *through*, not *over*, the pulpiteer.

If practicing the sermon before a mirror, in the pulpit with an empty sanctuary, or at home makes delivery more effective, then we should do it regularly. Afterward, we can bathe the sermon in prayer. Unless God is in it, it is a hollow endeavor, done only in the flesh. There will be sound, but no unction.

Step Seven: Preaching the Word

When we enter the pulpit with a certain amount of fear, it causes our faces to color, our voices to have timber, and our spirits to lean on the Lord.

Years ago as a teen, I was asked to speak in a small suburban church near Chicago. I was petrified, and it showed. After the service the pastor admonished me, "All fear is sin. You need to trust the Lord."

He was dead wrong. All really effective preachers of the gospel have some fear. Show me a preacher who has no fear, and I will show you a preacher who is trusting in personal power rather than God's power. We must preach the Word in dependence upon the living Christ. The same Spirit who inspired the text will fill and use us.

An author of the finest ministerial manual ever written wrote to a younger herald of God, "Preach the Word; be prepared in season and out of season; correct, rebuke and encourage—with great patience and careful instruction" (2 Tim. 4:2).

—Dan Baumann

Resources
Baumann, D. 1972. An introduction to contemporary preaching. Grand Rapids: Baker.
Baumann, D. 1990. Joel Gregory: Reviving the starved. Lecture at Rom Lectureship, 8 November, at Trinity Evangelical Divinity School, Deerfield, Illinois.
Brooks, P. Reprint 1969. Lectures on preaching. Grand Rapids: Baker.
Nichols, S. 1963. Words on target. Richmond: John Knox.
Swindoll, C. 1990. Grace awakening. Dallas: Word.

Using Bible-Study Software

Using a computer for sermon preparation will not solve all of your exegetical and homiletical challenges, but Bible-study software can definitely lighten your burden. These programs provide split-second retrieval of information that would otherwise require hours of page turning.

Software Features

Along with the advantage of doing word searches at incredible speed, virtually every software program now has ultracomplex search capabilities. This means you can look for several words at the same time and find the verses where they appear together, where any of them appear singly, or where some and not the others appear. Most programs also allow you to attach personal notes to verses, create your own list of verses for specific topics to be retrieved later, and send your results into your word processor. These are all features you should expect and ask for when buying a computer Bible.

Three other features you should require in your computer Bible are:

• A topical Bible, such as *Nave's Topical Bible* (a real timesaver for those topical sermons or doctrinal notes for the classroom).

• A cross-reference system (to help you quickly rabbit-trail through related passages).

• Multiple versions of the Bible that will appear on the screen simultaneously in synchronized windows (*i.e.*, scroll one, scroll all). Multiple versions will let you not only look at different lines of translation side by side but also will give you ideas about how to communicate the translation you finally choose.

A few programs will actually display the biblical languages and allow you to do lexical and grammatical searches in those languages. Most pastors and teachers will probably want to purchase a program with this capability. In addition, some specialized programs let you:

• Search for illustrations for your sermons.

• Prepare multilingual documents.

• Look up words in a Bible dictionary.

• View the synoptic gospels in parallel passages.

• Chase down words and phrases in nonbiblical Greek works and the writings of the church fathers.

User Cautions

Computer programs have built-in, purely "mathematical" rules of interpretation. If you neglect sound hermeneutical procedures, these programs may produce exegetical fallacies for you—and do it at lightening speed. For example, if you search for all the biblical occurrences of *murder, slay, assassinate,* and even *kill,* you still miss Genesis 9:6 ("Whoever sheds the blood . . ." NIV), and end up with an incomplete theology of *murder.* Topical, synonym, and cross-reference capabilities in software programs will help, though not eliminate, these kinds of problems.

The greatest potential for abuse

is with the *Strong's Concordance* feature many programs offer. Be aware that Strong's dictionary is not the best reference and that using it is not the same as looking at the original-language text.

While the Strong's information can be helpful for getting into the lexicon, the speed with which it retrieves information and the authoritative feel with which it presents the results can lead to misuse. One can be impressed by the fact that different Greek words lie behind the same English phrase, but human interpreters must still draw their own conclusions about what these parallels mean in the various contexts concerned.

In short, computer-based Bible-study software can make research much easier. What it *can't* do is cogitate, compose, and communicate. That's our job.

—*Dale M. Wheeler*

Imagination and Creativity in Preaching

What bunglers we are, A. J. Gossip used to say, that we have the most exciting tale in the world to preach about and cannot manage to interest the very people who will sit spellbound for two or three hours in an opera or a movie! He was right. There is no excuse for boring, pedestrian preaching—not when we are talking about Jesus Christ and the kingdom of God.

But how do we avoid being boring and pedestrian?

The trick is to be imaginative and creative, to keep restating and reapplying the gospel in terms that are always fresh, intriguing, and relevant. Considering how many sermons most preachers deliver in a lifetime, it's easy to understand how sermons fall into formulas and patterns, and thus become predictable. But predictability kills interest. The antidote to predictability is to preach on the growing edge of one's own awareness, always embodying the most recent insights in newly discovered images and metaphors.

The Importance of Seeing

Eudora Welty, the well-known novelist and short-story writer, said that the aspiring writer must do three things in order to succeed: (1) learn to see; (2) learn to listen; and (3) find a voice. By finding a voice, she meant developing a character who would tell the story. But that came last. The most important things were learning to see and learning to listen. There are plenty of stories around us everywhere if we can only get our antennae up and become aware of them.

The same rules apply to good preaching. Preachers who are sensitively tuned to the world around them constantly live in the excitement of the gospel as it interfaces with life. They see the whimsy in certain remarks, the pathos in some situations, the beauty in the natural environment, the impishness in children, the tenderness in lovers, the glory of the elderly—and they make their sermons breathe with references to all of them.

Since these preachers know that biblical faith is basically *incarnational*—that it has to do with the way God's Spirit is related to flesh and blood, rock and bone—they keep their preaching lively and meaningful by always extending the Incarnation in their sermons and never failing to relate dogma to daily human existence.

The Necessity of Notebooks

"Note it now; think about it later." That was Flannery O'Connor's dictum for herself; it is also a good one for preachers. Since they fail to log them at the time when they get them, many preachers lose 80 percent of their good ideas and illustrations. We don't have to be geniuses

to be creative preachers; we only have to work at storing the materials that come our way and then draw on the storehouse as we need them.

The great pianist Paderewski would often rehearse a single bar of music forty or fifty times until he had mastered it. Once, when he played for Queen Victoria, she said, "Mr. Paderewski, you are a genius!"

"That may well be," said Paderewski, "but before I was a genius, I was a drudge."

Imagination begins in drudgery, in the slow, painstaking discipline necessary to accumulate books of material that is fresh, piquant, and powerful. Then, when we have seen and listened—and have it down in our books—we will be ready to preach with creativity and genius.

—John Killinger

Titles and Introductions

The sermon title is one of the first ways people in the pew experience a sermon, and it may be the single largest impression they take from the service. A title can pique interest, set the tone for the sermon, deliver the message in brief, and accomplish a number of other tasks in just a few words on a church sign or newspaper announcement. For some people, the title will determine whether they elect to hear the sermon at all!

Good Titles

In selecting a title, the direct approach often works best. If the message is about lying, then that's what the title can be. If it's about faith in God, make that the title. We ought

not be tempted to believe we must make complex that which should be simple.

The title should reflect the tone of the message. A flippant title hardly dignifies a somber message. The title, while we want it to be fresh and effective, must be as spiritually and biblically respectable as the sermon.

The title, whenever possible, also should lean toward positive rather than negative or ambiguous expressions. The hearer may well benefit more from the positive "God Is" than the provocative "Is There a God?"

Gospel preachers are wise to keep their ears and eyes open in search of possible title ideas. Many good ideas emerge from conversations with church members. Pastors can glean titles from recurring themes in people's conversation, the burdens church members mention, and the questions they pose. Another fruitful field for title ideas is the Bible, itself.

Used carefully, secular books and periodicals can yield interesting titles that have the advantage of being fresh on people's minds. Contemporary titles can appear to lend preaching a sense of immediacy and relevance, although the Bible hardly needs pop culture to be relevant. We must exercise care, however. As gospel preachers, let's not believe that by borrowing an exotic title from secular society we are improving a message.

Good Beginnings

Once we have selected the title, our responsibility turns toward beginning the sermon effectively, the role of the sermon introduction. We want the introduction to give definition to the title and to relate its relevance to people's lives, people who may not be attuned to the message without an arresting introduction.

The introduction opens the door, allowing people to enter into the experience of the sermon. If the opened doorway looks inviting, people will want to enter into the sermon message. If, however, the doorway is easily ignored, the congregation may tune out the rest of the sermon.

The key to introductions is to so present the question the sermon will address that people simply are compelled to follow along. One of the ways to do this is to convince people that the questions covered by the sermon are important to their lives. The Spirit of the Lord ultimately does this convincing, but we can be the means the Spirit uses by bringing to our introductions biblical and contemporary examples that speak to real needs and concerns. We cannot assume people will naturally be listening to the Word of God in our sermons; we must arrest their attention from a world filled with blaring substitutes.

As we begin our sermons, the introduction should cause the hearers to see their personal needs and anticipate God's solutions as the sermon unfolds. Hungry people want to be fed, but the introduction must gain their attention and convince them there's food to be found.

—*E. V. Hill*

Conclusions

The conclusion is the sermon's finale. It completes the sermon, integrating varied strands, reviewing the central proposition, and inviting the audience to life response. It is the final opportunity to make a powerful case for the value of the sermon in the life of the hearers. Here the preacher "returns home," reviewing the central proposition to refocus the thoughts of the congregation. As the final movement within the sermon, the conclusion should crescendo to a climax.

Weak Conclusions

Rather than blossoming with impact, however, some conclusions seem to wither, causing the entire sermon to die on the vine. This can happen when the preacher uses any of several ill-advised approaches:

• *Stopping because "time is up."* We may win a popularity vote with this method, but our pulpit work will not be finished, and our sermons will not experience closure.

• *Enticing with false conclusions.* Conversely, we definitely will lose that popularity vote if we frequently miscue the audience about when we are going to finish. This is done by prematurely closing our Bible or using "lastly"—and lasting a long while before actually sitting down.

• *Incorporating multiple conclusions.* This technique resembles the aeronautical "touch and go," as uncomfortable as a pilot landing and taking off several times at the same airport. Hearers may begin to suffer sermon vertigo.

• *Introducing fresh thoughts.* If we really want to hear our congregations cry for liberation, we can bring brand new ideas into our conclusions. That makes the people unable to guess that at any moment we hope to stop.

• *Making the conclusion longer than the sermon points.* We can actually manage to veto the main points of a message by making the conclusion longer than any one of them, or all combined.

• *Introducing the conclusion too early.* By giving the conclusion early in the message, we fail to preserve the sermon's suspense, which should lead to the final thrust at the end.

Strong Conclusions

Two features will be evident in an effective conclusion: *cohesion* and *resolution.* Cohesion means that for the first time, the congregation hears, briefly summarized, everything we have been elaborating. Through resolution, the hearers begin to sense that a destination has been reached. In terms of persuasion, we grasp the attention of the hearers for a prompt arrival at this declared destination. How? By illustratively riveting them to the explicit or implicit appeal for change that flows from the text. Plain, precise, realistic language will help keep hearers from missing the point.

The congregation should not leave the preaching event with uncertainty about what God wants them to be and do. In a persuasive conclusion, a preacher, to use G. Campbell Morgan's phrase, "storms the citadel of the will." Preachers may use the following ingredients of an effective conclusion:

• *A clear statement of the central proposition.* We may also include a brief summary of the main points.

• *Applications and implications woven with practical suggestions for obedience.* The hearers may be wondering: *What is this speaker trying to get me to do?* Don't leave them wondering. Tell them plainly, and explore with them how it can work.

• *A final story that illustrates the central proposition.* If the anecdote pragmatically tests the theme of the sermon in the laboratory of life or defines the proper applicational boundaries of your central proposition, by all means use it.

In every sermon, we must put our final appeal into the hands of the Holy Spirit. Through his power, we expect to see the character and conduct changes that God's Word calls forth in our people.

—*Ramesh P. Richard*

Invitations

While in South Africa one time, I saw Africans, Europeans, and Asians surge forward to stand together at the cross following an invitation. How do we give an effective invitation like the one they responded to?

We Must Be Honest

First, we must be *honest before God*. The gospel message is both an announcement and a command: It tells what God has done and calls people to respond. Since God is making his appeal through us, we are to speak his message faithfully, present his call, trust him with the response, and give him the glory.

Second, we must be *honest with ourselves*. None of us has completely pure motives. The only reason we have to ask people to commit their lives to Christ is that God is calling them.

Third, we must be *honest with the listeners*. The Scriptures use many metaphors to describe the step of faith: coming, following, kneeling, opening, receiving, turning. An invitation is a symbolic expression of that spiritual reality. We need to explain that:

- Their response to an invitation is an outward expression of an inward decision.
- There are many ways they can express their commitment to Christ.
- Jesus is the alternative, not just an additive to life.
- They must not put off God's call.

An honest invitation will say with tenderness but seriousness, "Now is the day of salvation."

More Than One Method

How do various Christians give an invitation?

- The simple, straightforward appeal to walk to the front during the singing of a hymn is often effective.
- Some preachers begin the invitation with their opening prayer and repeat it throughout the message as the truth is applied, asking such questions as, "Is this you? Has God been speaking to you about this and this? Are you sensing that God is calling you?"
- Others ask people to stand one at a time and openly say, "Jesus is my Lord" after an invitation.
- At some evangelistic luncheons or dinners, those who have invited Christ into their lives after an invitation are asked to include their names and addresses on blank three-by-five cards as an indication of their decision.
- English evangelists sometimes use an "after-meeting." They dismiss the congregation but invite interested people to remain for an explanation of how to make a Christian commitment.
- In some Lutheran churches, people are invited to kneel at the altar or to take the pastor's hand as they leave and quietly say, "I will."

There is no one way to extend the invitation, but in every situation there is surely some way.

Some Do's and Don'ts

In giving the invitation, *do* pick up the feelings of those in the throes of decision. Empathize with their fear of embarrassment, of not being able to follow through, of what others will say. Hear the inner voice that tells them this is too hard, or they can wait. *Don't* berate or threaten.

Don't ask them *only* to raise their hand, then *only* to stand, and then *only* to come forward. We must not trick people or make them feel used. *Do* make the meaning of the invitation clear.

It's not wrong to give an invitation with several prongs: salvation, rededication, renewal. *Don't*, however, overexplain and confuse.

Do give people time to think and pray. Sometimes those moments seem agonizingly slow, but be patient. When there is no response, don't prolong the invitation until the audience groans inwardly for someone to come forward so you'll stop.

Do give the invitation with conviction, courage, urgency, expectancy. But *don't* try to replace the Holy Spirit.

To find balance isn't easy. Therefore, we must ask God to speak *to* us as well as *through* us.

—*Leighton Ford*

7

Sermon Illustrations

The fun house is a favorite attraction at the amusement park, especially for the fearless. First, the lights turn off. Then the walkway twists and turns. Hot and cold air blows. A wall suddenly gives way, and, with a brief flash of light, things appear from nowhere. Everything seems unpredictable—loud sounds, absolute silence, rooms that tilt, rooms that spin, rooms with no doors. Then a clock strikes 12:00, and the floor shakes and collapses, sliding everyone down to the exit. The mind-boggling, confusing event is suddenly over.

How many sermons are like a trip to the fun house? The congregational adventurers never really know what is happening, or why. We preachers, however, are called to make the sermon something other than a trip in the dark, full of the unexpected for our hearers. Thankfully, we can light up the darkness with our wise use of illustrations.

How Will My Illustrations Help?

When Henry Ford first began mass marketing his famous Model A automobiles, they were well-known for coming in any color you wanted —so long as it was black. We all know any automobile manufacturer who would offer cars today only in black would be out of business by tomorrow. Color does not insure a better-designed or more reliable car, but it does make for a more interesting one.

Good biblical preaching is built on God's Word, and sermon illustrations are like added color. Although they are no substitute for careful study and exposition of the text, illustrations do make a sermon's presentation more interesting. In addition, like a flashing red light in one's rear-view mirror, they can arrest attention; they ignite a response as quickly as a lightening bolt in a drought-stricken land.

Illustrations have been compared to lights, footlights, windows, doors, and even fishhooks. Their versatility is amazing. Because illustrations can arouse an audience and focus attention, they are useful in introducing a sermon or a key point. We spend hours preparing points that our hearers must understand in a few minutes. With illustrations that clarify and amplify, we can repeat a key concept without becoming boring and transform abstract theological terms into concrete, understandable truths. Since no one will respond to an appeal that isn't believed, illustrations help us show the truthfulness and relevance of our points.

Finally, because illustrations have the ability to penetrate emotional, intellectual, and volitional barriers, they are able to persuade and motivate hearers to apply the truth being taught. Yet, whatever function a specific illustration performs, it should do its task without distorting, confusing, or supplanting the truth being illustrated.

Where Will I Find Illustrations?

Most speakers agree that the best illustrations are those developed personally by the speaker. Here are some ideas that may help in this task.

• *Commit yourself to gathering illustrations.* Those who develop excellent illustrations are like hunters stalking their prey or artists laboring over a creation. Extreme analogies? Perhaps, but they do convey the commitment it takes to find and develop good illustrations.

• *Decide on a simple way to record potential illustrative material.* Many speakers carry 3 × 5 cards or a small, spiral-bound memobook in their pockets to record potential illustrations. When I read a copy of a magazine I will not be keeping, I tear out the page with something I want and immediately write on the top of the page where it should be filed. Photocopy machines make collecting illustrations from books quite easy. I keep a card in any book I read and write on the card the pages for photocopying and the topic the illustration should be filed under. When finished, I give the book and card to an assistant, who makes the copies and files them.

• *Learn how to develop an illustration.* This assumes we can precisely state the idea we want to illustrate. A widely used technique for coming up with ideas is brainstorming or free-association thinking. We set before us a large sheet of paper, recording ideas as they germinate and thinking about a number of things that might open up an illustration.

For example, with a specific sermon point that needs illustrating, we can think about personal life experiences, history, literature we've read, relationships we've had or observed within our families, church, or community (Lewis 1983, 127). Some people like to record their ideas in an outline format; others use interconnected balloons or line structures that look like trees. None of these methods is better than the others. We simply need to choose some way to record ideas that develop, so that later we can evaluate them and begin to fashion illustrations out of some of them. When the ideas stop, we can begin to sort through them. Often a good illustration will emerge in rough form.

● *Use a wide variety of sources of illustrations.* Consider these prime sources: the Bible itself (check *Nave's Topical Bible*), biographies, hymn stories, general literature, magazines (especially current-events magazines such as *Time, Newsweek,* and *U.S. News & World Report,* as well as magazines read by members of the congregation such as *Forbes* and *The Wall Street Journal*), movies, and published sermons. Look for illustration sources in areas that are not a part of common knowledge, such as Aesop's Fables or the writings of the church fathers and great theologians.

For example, Calvin said, "It is better to limp in the way than to run with swiftness out of it" (*Institutes 6:3*). During any Olympic year, this image-laden statement can be related to a widely publicized race and turned into a graphic, relevant, and memorable illustration.

One source of illustrations that many overlook is the local newspaper. It usually is filled with the raw material for relevant illustrations. Reference resources available in most libraries can be of great service, too. Become familiar with *Public Affairs Information Service, New York Times Index, The Annual Register of World Events, Facts on File,* and *Famous First Facts,* for instance. The reference librarian will be glad to help locate these and other free sources of raw material for illustrations.

Most published books of illustrations lack the extensive indexing that would make them readily usable. In addition, the quality of illustrations in such books varies so widely that usually it is wiser to review the book personally before purchasing it. Also, edited volumes of illustrations from many sources offer a variety of styles, unlike the books of illustrations that come from a single great preacher—whose preaching style may not complement yours.

Another illustration source is the congregation itself. In most ministries exist people who read widely and possess the ability to find good illustrative material. When their knowledge of one's preaching style is joined with a little training and a long-term sermon plan, these resource people can become effective illustration finders. We can make a monthly or quarterly meeting with them a time of fun as well as spiritual nourishment, and we will reap the benefits of their loving labor.

Will My Illustrations Be Effective?

Three words summarize the process of shaping an effective illustration: revise, revise, and revise. No preacher is so good that he or she gets a new illustration right the first time. Good illustrations will be reworked many times before they are ready to be used in a specific sermon. The final version usually bears only a faint resemblance to the first. Such is the labor of illustrating.

Along with the standard advice to revise thoroughly and shape

---

Managing Sermon Illustrations

Waiting until we are in the process of preparing a sermon to look for a great illustration is a mistake, because usually the search will be in vain. The solution is to create an effective storage-and-retrieval system for speaking material, a system much like a library.

Filing Sermon Illustrations

Key principle: Any storage-and-retrieval system should be simple and portable. The first major decision should be choosing a standard size of paper. Typewriter paper can be too large for sermon purposes, while most index cards are too small. I recommend three-holed paper that measures 9½ x 6 inches. It works well in a binder and also holds a lot of information, yet folded vertically, it can fit into a suit pocket or most Bibles.

Next, as you find good material, you can copy or staple them onto the paper and then put them into a binder by category, coding that binder by its theme. Before long, your binder will be full of illustrations, quotes, and outlines. Major themes, such as "relationships," will emerge. When twenty to thirty items are stored in that category, it's a good idea to separate them by creating a more specific category, such as "love."

At the top of each page, mark the theme of the illustration and the page number in the notebook. When you use an illustration, note the location and date at the bottom of the page. This procedure makes it possible for every entry to be coded and later noted. It also makes it easy to avoid repeating the illustration during a return engagement.

As you can imagine, illustrations will soon fill the "love" binder, coded L. Love entries tend to fall into two categories: family-oriented love and more general love. Create, then, two new notebooks: one marked FL, meaning family love, and the other GL, meaning general love. The changeover is simple, because you add only one letter to the original code, leaving the page numbers

each illustration for its intended context, a few other guidelines will help prevent weak or ineffective illustrations:

- Be concise. The parable of the Prodigal Son required only 498 words. Enough said.
- Make sure the illustration fits the sermon point and that the connection is clear. We cannot assume background knowledge on the part of the audience. In a society that is increasingly biblically illiterate as well as culturally illiterate, it is difficult to underestimate an audience's lack of background knowledge. It's good to avoid using any illustration that needs extensive explaining. We want to make the point of the illustration as explicit as Nathan did with David: "You are the man" (2 Sam. 12:7a).

---

the same. As the notebooks continue to grow, before long the FL (family love) notebook is ready for a split into MFL (marriage-family love) and PFL (parental-family love).

Transplanting Illustrations

I've learned that I should always be in search of powerful quotes and good stories even if I have no idea how I can currently use them. When I find a good illustration that I'm not sure how to classify, I put it into what I call a "tomato book" (from my wife's tomato transplanting). Out of the tomato books have grown scores of sermon illustrations. Many of my best quotes and stories found their application long after I had heard and filed the tidbit.

I have another book simply called "Travel." There I keep copies of about two to three hundred of my best material. I can use these items in almost any situation. This book travels with me constantly, and I guard it with my life.

Using a Computer

A number of computer programs permit cross-referencing. I use the "Agenda" program by Lotus Software. In seconds, it can find in my database every item that includes the key word I am researching.

To keep all of one's material in a computer isn't necessary. I enter only a title or a one-sentence identification of items, the notebook in which it can be found, and one or more key words that identify the subject.

For example, a book entry might read: "*Leadership Is an Art*, DePree, leadership, management, people development, mentoring." Or a reference to a quote: "Quote from *Practicing the Presence of God*, Brother Lawrence: 'I turn my little omelette in the pan for the love of God ...' work, purpose, mission." I add the notebook and page where I can find a fuller version of the quote.

Any system of compiling illustrations becomes a reflection of personal style. What is important is that one's system be simple, quickly usable, reflective of personal thinking and style, and up-to-date. Beyond that, all it needs is regular attention.

—Gordon MacDonald

- Choose illustrations that live where your audience lives. It's easy to forget the needs and concerns of older members of our congregations. Older ministers may become out of touch with what a teenager wrestles with, what a young family must struggle with, and how challenging it is to raise children. We must resist these tendencies as we find illustrations that grab our congregations.

- Make illustrations the supporting material for an argument, not the argument itself. We shouldn't use an illustration unless the point really does need illustrating. Mechanistic rules about how many illustrations to use are almost pointless, unless we preach to machines!

- Use quotations with great care. If the congregation clearly recognizes a quote's relevance and authority, fine. Otherwise, it is probably better to say it in our own words.

There is a difference between the affect a statement has when in

Pulpit Plagiarism

If plagiarism is an occasional problem for writers, it is a weekly problem for preachers.

In the strictest sense of the word, everyone plagiarizes. After all, as Solomon once said, there's not much new under the sun. But to give credit for every single idea would break the flow of a sermon. While courtesy calls for gratefulness, effectiveness places some limits. How then do we know when to give credit in the midst of the sermons we preach?

What Is Plagiarism?

All preachers have a way of picking up cute phrases, vivid word images, clever bits of dialogue, and even snappy one-liners. Such snatches are below the threshold that requires attribution. But there is a level that enters the forbidden zone of plagiarism in preaching. It happens when we take credit for something valuable that is not genuinely ours.

Professional writers have strict guidelines concerning plagiarism. One definition is found in *A Handbook to Literature* by Thrall and Hibbard (Odyssey, 1960): "Literary theft. A writer who steals the plot of some obscure, forgotten story and uses it as new in a story of his own is a plagiarist. Plagiarism is more noticeable when it involves stealing of language than when substance only is borrowed. From flagrant exhibition of stealing both thought and language, plagiarism shades off into less serious things such as unconscious borrowing, borrowing of minor elements, and mere imitation."

Writers and musicians know that while they can copyright words and notes, they cannot copyright an idea. It is in this area that the blacks and whites blend to gray, and each preacher must determine the difference between what is illegal, legal

print and how it sounds orally—the difference between reading and listening. Passages that move us often do so because of all that we have read in the book up to that point. In oral communication we will not read the full context of a quotation, and thus the insight and force of a quotation may be lost on the hearers.

Remember, too, that since the sermon is a message of truth, it is not the place to compromise integrity. Footnotes don't belong in a sermon, although they may belong in a manuscript printed for distribution. Whether speaking or writing, however, we must be careful to give credit where credit is due.

- Avoid embarrassing parishioners. For example, I'm careful not to destroy the confidence of those I have ministered to by using their experiences for illustrations. This is especially true of my own family and those I counsel. Most people would consider the use of their per-

---

but unethical, or permitted.

Giving Credit Gracefully

The question is not whether we use material that originates with others. Of course we do. The question is how to give credit properly.

We can give credit without distracting people from the message of the sermon. It is easy to say, "I have learned something from So-and-so this week while studying our text." Now I am free to take off on whatever tangent I wish. At the same time, I have pointed people back to the genesis of an idea. If they return to the spring to drink, they, too, may come up with original thoughts, just as I did.

Giving credit often strengthens the message. It lets people know we are reading—and listening. It adds authenticity. Giving credit, instead of distracting from a sermon, often leads listeners into the situation. They wait eagerly to hear what we have gleaned from others. Courtesy demands a certain amount of credit, and ethics demands we not retell

a story as if it happened to us, unless it really did.

Honesty and Courtesy

The springs inside us that flow with eternal truth sometimes get clogged with debris. Our pumps, then, can be primed by others' sermons, written, taped, or heard in person. A preacher once joked, "When better sermons are written, I'll preach them."

Stimulation from other preachers can be good, but perhaps the greatest argument against preaching someone else's material is this: If it is not our own, if we have not experienced the truth we are preaching, how can it minister life to others? We need to do much more than purely plagiarize. We must grapple, ourselves, with the meaning that others have illuminated.

Here is a good rule to follow: Everything we say is free, and we expect nothing in return. Everything we borrow we try to credit, because God has a way of blessing honesty.
—*Jamie Buckingham*

sonal experience as an illustration a betrayal of confidence, even if reported without identifying facts.

• Avoid using poetry. Poems rarely are effective in sermons anymore. Perhaps at the turn of the century, congregations enjoyed poetry, but such is not the case with contemporary audiences. People today enjoy little exposure to a form of communication that previous generations cherished. Thus, when hearing a poem, folks often pause in their listening, concluding that the preacher is speaking to someone else.

• Be careful with humor. Humor can be a distraction; it can hurt those it uses for its point or appear sacrilegious. It also can reach behind the veneer of culture and defensiveness to reveal sin and sinful attitudes. Like a live hand grenade, handle it with caution or risk great damage. Of course, never use sarcasm in the pulpit. There will always be a remnant that takes you literally, to their horror.

• Get the facts straight. Nothing can destroy credibility faster than wrong facts or fictionalized details. This point is especially critical when we use illustrations based on science or statistics.

For example, a book on illustrating sermons confuses the two basic concepts of mass and weight in an illustration. In his book about illustrating sermons, a famous preacher retells the story of a dying woman who volunteered to let researchers record her brain waves at death. The story states that when dying she was praying, and her brain "registered more than fifty-five times the power used by a fifty-kilowatt (radio) station." When a preacher tells me that a dying woman's brain was using 2,750,000 watts of power, I wonder if he is competent to read the Bible with any degree of trustworthiness.

In a society undergoing rapid social change, statistical descriptions of that society are often out of date by the time they get published. In addition, predictions based on current trends almost guarantee errors. The reason is simple: Most predictions are based on a linear projection of the present trend, while most trends are anything but linear.

There is an old saying that statistics don't lie, but statisticians do. Unless we are absolutely sure of the reliability and correct interpretation of a statistic, we are wise not to use it. Since many preachers have little background in science or mathematics, we can make horrifying statements that simply are not true and that are recognized as such by our listeners trained in these areas. Then, not only does the illustration fail, but our authority and the reliability of the message both suffer.

We can use historical and descriptive statistics that are properly referenced and come from reliable sources. Timeless statistics, such as the size of the universe as a reflection of the majesty of God, will benefit our hearers, as well as predictive statistics that are properly researched (such as census projections prepared by the government).

How Can I File Illustrations?

Several methods of filing illustrations have enjoyed widespread use. One method is to use a "commonplace book." This is a large notebook or scrapbook into which illustrations and other useful items are placed. Eventually the pages and volumes are numbered, and an index developed. Another approach is to use a looseleaf Bible and jot illustrations next to the passages they illustrate. Others use various kinds of index-card systems. Computer data bases are becoming popular, since they offer the added potential for extensive cross-referencing and quick retrieval.

To be fast enough for usefulness, a computer-storage system needs a hard disk and a relatively fast processor. (Some older computers require more time than we would use if we retrieved our illustrations from a card file by hand.) A number of data bases can be used for filing illustrations. The basic requirements are the ability to hold several thousand illustrations, do extensive cross-referencing, keep Bible references in order, revise existing illustrations (including a note for when and where used), and add new illustrations.

Wise preachers file illustrations under broad headings, since most illustrations fit several specific applications or can be modified to do so easily. This rule for filing keeps material available at the broadest appropriate levels. In addition, the use of broad headings lends consistency and logic to the file and avoids the kind of highly specialized heading that sounds good at the moment but ultimately becomes nonretrievable.

The first word of a heading should be a noun rather than a modifying word, such as an adverb or adjective. For example, an illustration on choosing happiness in the midst of a severe trial should not be filed under "Choosing Happiness" but under either "Happiness," "Choices," or "Decisions," with a cross-reference under the heading "Trials" and the notation "See: Choices, for Happiness."

Some categories, such as "Evangelism," "Children," and "Church," tend to become large. The use of standard subheadings can be helpful here. To some degree such standardizations are arbitrary, but once we get used to them, we find they save time. Some useful subheadings are: application of; benefit of; example of; definition/description of; humorous; lack of; motive for; necessity of; purpose for; requirements for; results/consequences of; response to; source of; value of (Green 1989). No subheading should be used when the illustration is general in nature.

Many illustrations can illustrate not only different aspects of one topic but different topics. In addition, some illustrations directly refer to other topics. In these cases, cross-referencing helps us retrieve the illustration when needed. When the cross-reference is not unique to the illustration at hand, but instead reflects some kind of logical relationship between the two topics, the cross-referencing should be done with a topic-to-topic cross-reference card for both topics. The cross-referencing can be to a general topic or to a specific subtopic. When a cross-reference is unique to an illustration, make up a cross-reference card to file under the other topic. Cross-referencing of the topic-to-topic kind should be noted in the index-of-topics list.

The vast majority of illustrations should be filed under a topic, not a particular passage, since we will preach a topic many times to a group but will probably preach a specific passage only once. Thus, filing illustrations under specific passages makes them inaccessible, unless we happen to look under that passage. There are two exceptions to this rule. The first occurs when an illustration is so specific that it is useful only with one verse in the entire Bible. The second occurs when a topic would not come to mind when preparing a message on a verse that lends itself to the illustration. A prepared list of illustration topics for filing saves a great deal of time and can allow others to file for you (Green 1991).

The greatest Illustration was the Word Incarnate, and we must keep in mind that the written Word is the ultimate basis of our sermon's authority, not a powerful illustration.

—Michael P. Green

Resources

Banks, L. 1902. Windows for sermons. New York: Funk and Wagnalls.

Barnhouse, D. 1967. Let me illustrate. Westwood, N.J.: Revell.

Broadus, J. 1979. On the preparation and delivery of sermons, fourth ed. New York: Harper & Row.

Green, M. 1989. Illustrations for biblical preaching. Grand Rapids: Baker.

Green, M. 1991. Green's filing systems. Grand Rapids: Baker.

Hostetler, M. 1989. Illustrating the sermon. Grand Rapids: Zondervan.

Jeffs, H. 1909. The art of sermon illustration. London: James Clarke & Co.

Lewis, R., and G. Lewis. 1983. Inductive preaching. Westchester, Ill.: Crossway.

Macpherson, I. 1964. The art of illustrating sermons. New York: Abingdon.

Sangster, W. 1978. The craft of sermon illustration. England: Pickering and Inglis.

Storytelling

Well-told stories wield power; they actually can change people's lives. I've found that the same principles yarn spinners use to make characters appealing and heighten suspense can aid preaching.

Bible stories, we soon discover, are a great resource for illustrations. The Bible is packed with stories, adventures, mysteries, romances. It brims with heroes, villains, suspense. Through these stories, people can gain personal insights from events and characters in the Bible.

Characterization

In order to spotlight characters in a Bible story or modern-day sermon illustration, we must know them. This thinking takes time, because people are complex. But if we don't do it, we end up with cardboard figures who are indistinguishable and boring.

One way to bring biblical characters alive is to find contemporary parallels, such as describing King Jeroboam as the consummate one-minute manager, high on the list of corporate headhunters.

Another way to vitalize characters is to concentrate on the universal elements of their personalities: ambition, loss, romance, unfulfilled desires, success, stress, and so on.

Bible characters also become more relevant when we unveil their possible thoughts and motivations. Listeners identify with the Bible character when they can identify with the character's struggles.

Action and Plot

When we recount a Bible story in a message, we obviously neither write the plot nor alter it. But learning what makes for a good plot can attune us to the crescendos and decrescendos of a story, so we can reserve the highest intensity for the climax.

The key to understanding a story's plot, and where the climax falls, is identifying the conflict. Sometimes, feeling pressure from the clock, we are tempted to rush the beginning of the story to get to the climax and make the point. But to slight the conflict is to defuse the climax, leaving an emotional dud.

Since conflict sparks interest, it is good to begin a story with a conflict. Don't typically launch a story with an eloquent description of a person, landscape, or background events; unload that cargo as the plot progresses.

In preparing to tell a story, consider: What problems is this person trying to solve? What adversity is there to overcome?

Dialogue

Of the methods for enlivening a character, dialogue is perhaps the most powerful. Some fiction writers advise that dialogue should make up one-third of a novel. Some of the most memorable words in the Bible come from dialogue.

Using dialogue in sermon stories helps in several ways. First, dialogue invites immediacy. The storyteller gathers the listeners and characters into the same room and allows the listeners to eavesdrop on each conversation.

Second, dialogue heightens emotion. Which has more drama, to say, "Elijah sat down under the broom tree and felt depressed," or "Elijah sat down under the broom tree and said, 'I have had enough, Lord. Take my life; I am no better than my ancestors' "?

Third, dialogue reveals the person. We learn much about Naomi through her own words: "Don't call me Naomi. Call me Mara, because the Almighty has made my life very bitter. I went away full, but the Lord has brought me back empty."

Telling a story well requires extra preparation, but that extra time will help people experience the story in a powerful way.

—*Craig Brian Larson*

Pulpit Humor

A letter to the editor of a Christian magazine pronounced: "The Christian life is essentially serious. This is a vale of tears. Humor has no place in the pulpit or the Sunday school." I expect the writer would have found more supporters of his position in the last century than today. It seems the twentieth century has rediscovered comedy.

Biblical scholars have even pointed out how the prophets and Jesus himself used humor. Well-known preachers regularly use humor effectively, and most hearers of sermons today would wonder why a preacher who shows a fine sense of humor away from the pulpit might choose to show none of it while preaching.

It pays not to underestimate the value of humor. Humor builds rapport between the preacher and the congregation; it holds attention, gives perspective to life, eases interpersonal tensions. Most church members recognize a sense of humor as a sign of emotional health and goodwill. In addition, by holding and focusing attention, humor can enhance the hearer's retention

of a preacher's message. As young seminarians are often reminded: It is not necessary to be dull in order to be devout. Here are tips to consider as we seek to decrease the dullness quotient in our sermons.

Using Humor Effectively

• *Know the congregation.* Congregations vary in their capacity to appreciate humor. Some groups relish it; others barely endure it. Response to humor is usually better at the later worship service than at an early service. People also laugh more freely in settings in which their personal chuckles do not stand out, so large crowds or smaller groups seated in a tight cluster will feel more freedom to laugh aloud than will a congregation scattered throughout a large room.

• *Build on your unique ability.* Humor has to seem natural if it is to work. Build on the kinds of humor you normally use away from the pulpit, whether that is joke telling, understatement, hyperbole, apt metaphors and similes, word plays, or satire. Since you have your own special brand of humor, don't attempt to be funny exactly the way someone else is.

● *Keep humor the servant of your sermons.* Humor that interrupts the flow of a sermon is like a fidgety flower girl at a wedding—cute, but a distraction. Cultivate witticisms, word plays, apt metaphors, and the like as quick alternatives to lengthy jokes. The speed with which a preacher gets into and out of the humor affects how much it derails the train of thought.

Avoiding Humor's Pitfalls

● *Resist disparaging humor.* Never use put-downs or stereotyping unless they are aimed at you or a group of which you are a part. Some so-called humor is nothing more than a thin veil cast over a dagger of hostility. A laugh that costs us listeners—and credibility—is much too costly.

● *Use humor sparingly.* If people view a preacher primarily as an entertainer, they take his or her statements less seriously. Humor, like a tasty garnish, should never be offered as the main course.

● *Don't advertise humor.* Avoid saying, "Let me tell you the funniest story." The surprise element is crucial to humor's effect.

● *Never explain or repeat humor.* The effect depends on the hearers' discovering the humor for themselves. If a joke falls flat, move on quickly.

● *Avoid using humor at a sermon's conclusion.* Laughter at this time will likely release emotional energy that should have been channeled into responses of faith and commitment.

Humor is not the remedy for all sermonic ills. When poorly used, it can even hinder a sermon's impact. But when used wisely, humor can make a sermon sing.

—Grant Lovejoy

8

Working from
Applications to Action

Application may be the most difficult—and neglected—part of preaching. But a sermon is meant to encourage the *doing* of the Word, not just the hearing of it.

When lay people say they heard a preacher, and comment, "Oh, he was good!" they usually can describe the sermon's subject with varying degrees of accuracy. If they are asked, however, "And what did he want you to do or to stop doing?" they are on a desert journey without water. Most people cannot remember, perhaps because the preacher never made it clear.

The major component necessary for better preaching is the imperative, the call for specific action arising from the sermon text.

After choosing a text, a preacher needs to look for two things: the subject and the response being called for. These two elements need to be identified before anything else in the passage, because the success of preaching hinges on imparting not only the meaning but the imperative of a text.

Scribes or Preachers?

In Christ's preaching, to what did the multitudes respond? After the Sermon on the Mount, Scripture records: "When Jesus had finished saying these things, the crowds were amazed at his teaching, because he taught as one who had authority, and not as their teachers of the law" (Matt. 7:28–29). There is a grand difference between a scribe (teacher of the law) and a preacher. The following kinds of comments infest sermons with *the scribes' disease:*

113

"Here's what so-and-so writes about these verses."

"A related passage that sheds some light on this one is . . ."

"Those who want to dig deeper into God's truth would do well to probe this passage further."

Scribes tend to be fascinated with information. By contrast, preachers, like Christ, are more action oriented. For them, the word *sermon* means thrust. "It's a thrust from the sword of the Spirit," writes Simon Blocker in *The Secret of Pulpit Power.* "And the preacher knows whether or not his thrust has been driven home."

Sometimes people say they like certain preachers because they found that speaker interesting, clever, able to project personality into his or her sermon. But preachers weren't meant to be entertainers. The bottom line shouldn't be: "The preacher wasn't boring, and I enjoyed listening to her."

People may leave a scribe's service pumped full of interesting new information. They can say how one verse relates to another, or how the ethics of the Decalogue foreshadow the completion of the Beatitudes. But what a shame for them to leave church services unaware of what they are to do or to stop doing!

If someone wants to know how to play music, it does little good for a music teacher to talk about the lives of famous composers, or to compare in detail the various instruments in the orchestra, or review how violins are made. It may make the music teacher sound learned and wise, but this person needs to be told, "Lesson one is on how to hold your flute. Between now and when we meet next week, I want you to practice holding it like this."

Most Christians do not need more information or "deeper truths"; they have not processed a fraction of the ones they already know. Profundity is not the crying need, but rather simplicity coupled with directness: "Here's what my text is about, and it is calling us to do this."

Preaching needs to communicate specific responses to genuine needs felt by real people. People respond favorably to such down-to-earth preaching anchored in their world. They don't particularly want more ideas. They aren't enamored with brilliant analysis or formal essays. Preachers can't assume listeners have a great love for theology or a vast reservoir of biblical knowledge.

The question that should always be asked is: What practical suggestions can I give to help people respond to what is said? That is a watershed question. If that question is adequately addressed, listeners will appreciate what they hear. And they will be helped by it.

Bridges to Behavior

There are ways to make sure we are communicating. I have tried various methods, such as brainstorming my sermons on Wednesday nights with a random group of parishioners invited to my home, or holding a pastor's class after Sunday worship to discuss the sermon. The people who have most shaped my sermons have not been ministers but parishioners gracious enough not only to listen but also to critique what they heard.

In discussing my sermons with listeners, I've found it doesn't take long before they agree that the subject is relevant and the response called for in the passage is legitimate, but they also admit they need help with the "how to's." That is what the serious Christian comes to a sermon to hear.

"Don't say any more about the subject," people have told me. "I already agree with the biblical challenge to respond. Tell me how to pull it off! Can't you use your time building a bridge for me to get into this coveted new land?"

As preachers, we must build practical bridges. We need to list the first steps necessary to respond to what Scripture requires. And, we need to walk people over those bridges, step by step, to get them to that point.

For example, when Billy Graham preaches about conversion—being born again—he challenges his hearers to follow Christ. That's his desired response. Now, how are they to do this? What is his bridge?

"What I want you to do," he tells them, "is to get up from where you are sitting and to walk down here to the front." He knows trained counselors are ready to talk with these people and lead them to Christ. It's a good bridge—"Here's how to do what I've been telling you about."

A number of other bridges lend themselves to evangelistic sermons. The traditional invitation is only one of many possibilities.

Some people find an immediate public response intimidating. They intend to respond—the Word has done its work — but making such a sudden decision and walking in front of all those people seems out of the question. They need bridges less threatening in a congregational setting, such as:

• The pastor's phone number printed in the bulletin with specific hours he or she will be at the phone with the sole purpose of taking calls from those wanting to investigate the implications of becoming a Christian.

• Cards on which the inquirers can write their phone number so the preacher can call them. People can place the cards in the offering plate or give the card to the preacher at the door.

• A meeting after the service, sometimes over lunch, for any who want to continue working toward a decision.

• Inexpensive books these people can either borrow or buy after the service. When they sign one out or pay for it, they leave a record of their interest or possible decision, which can be used for follow-up.

People will rarely seek out a bookstore to find a recommended book, but at a church book table, they eagerly snatch up books on consignment from local bookstores.

• A challenge to talk with a Christian of their choice about any decision they have made. Most know a mature believer whom they trust. We can offer to arrange such a meeting if they have no such acquaintances. They may find talking to a lay person less intimidating than speaking with a pastor.

• Cassette tapes for those who have made decisions. Again, as they sign up, the church gets their names for follow-up. Cassettes can help new believers affirm their decisions. Although neither books nor cassettes provide all a new believer needs, telling people to take this step is a safe bridge to the action we ultimately desire: growth through involvement with other Christians.

Each of these alternatives builds a bridge to action. People can walk away from a service knowing something concrete to do if they have made a decision. They have their first steps outlined for them.

More Bridges

The use of bridges, however, is not limited to evangelistic sermons. Every sermon can benefit from suggested steps to action. Since the type of bridge depends on the response intended by the text, countless possibilities are available. To determine what bridge to use for a particular sermon, you might ask: What response does the text demand, and how can I best move the people toward that response?

When preaching on prayer, for example, I might want people to learn to pray thankfully. I could say, "When you pray, be thankful." But leaving it at that would leave most listeners at a loss: Thankful for what? And how do I pray thankfully?

I can provide a bridge, such as asking my listeners to take a few minutes later that day to write out ten things they were thankful for. The next day they are to write out ten more, not repeating any from the first day, and on the third day ten more, until the week is up and they have a list of seventy blessings. When they return with their list the following week, I can talk about it some more. By that next Sunday, they are ready to hear more, because they have acted on the first sermon.

For sermons on addiction to pornographic materials, I have asked my congregation if during the next week, they are willing to throw away questionable mail before opening it—to destroy that hidden stash of unseemly materials, to avoid particular book racks, magazines, and theater marquees. Since pornography can be an addiction, I asked them to consider one additional step they could take to break its hold. The bridge is meant to take them from knowing what is bad to determining what to do in response.

I have also suggested a simple graph for people to chart their day-to-day battle with a bad habit. People can choose the behavior they want to plot, such as fighting immorality.

A sermon by John Huffman at the Congress on Biblical Exposition offers another bridge. His bridge is simple: Get into an accountability group. He described how he had done it, and what it meant to him and his preaching. He shared his weakness and his need for counsel. His sermon provides an idea of what he wanted his listeners to do and how to do it.

Bridges take many forms. An Episcopal priest once finished a fine Good Friday sermon about the Cross by displaying a crucifix and suggesting that his listeners obtain one to help them remember the richness of propitiation and redemption—those big theological words that mean so little apart from the Cross. For them, contemplating a crucifix could move them beyond theological language to worship their Lord, whose agony a crucifix strongly portrays.

Supply a short list of Scriptures to be memorized; print a card with the sermon theme for people to carry in their wallets; suggest they evaluate a certain television show for its secular or Christian message; put a question in the bulletin for people to discuss over Sunday dinner—the bridges are varied. The common denominator is their specific practicality. Bridges can be done immediately as a way to put the sermon's message to work.

Why Build Bridges?

If we fail to tell our listeners what to do, if we don't construct good bridges for them, we simply cannot expect them to figure out applications for themselves. We need not worry about sounding "Mickey Mouse." The specifics, the how to's, the practicalities belong in great exposition every bit as much as in Sunday school handouts.

When approaching a text with the idea of building bridges to action, first, zero in on the text's subject. Second, extract from the Scripture the response being called for. Third, construct a bridge that will help people get from where they are to where this text teaches they should be. Help people respond to the challenge of the passage.

According to a 1985 poll, 42 percent of the adults in America attend religious services in a typical week. If four in ten adults leave their preaching services saying, "I know what God wants me to do, and I have been given a reasonable way to begin the process. I'm going to do it!"—if this can be accomplished Sunday after Sunday—then our preaching will fulfill its purpose, and God's Word will equip his people to begin doing his will.

—*David Mains*

9

Sermon Delivery

During my fifty years of preaching and teaching preachers, I have heard and critiqued more than 20,000 talks and sermons. I have also seen delivery become nearly a forgotten factor in ministerial training. Yet my experience has convinced me that delivery will become even more important for effective twenty-first-century communication than it was when Aristotle included it as one of his five canons of speech.

Delivery History

In the history of rhetoric there has been a constant, pendulum-like shifting of opinion about what constitutes the best delivery style. In other words, delivery has been something of a loose cannon among the other four classic canons of rhetoric:

- *Invention* determines our selection of the sources and materials that will most effectively convey personal, visual, and shared experience.
- *Arrangement* provides hearers with a mix of examples from the Bible and contemporary life that leads them along toward our sermon's crucial call to life response.
- *Style* is oral, direct, and personal, incorporating those elements most attractive and convincing to our listeners.
- *Memory* frees us to keep our eyes on our hearers rather than on our manuscript. (For every effective sermon reader, many think they are.)

Finally, there's *delivery*.

119

The first four canons have served as long-time guides. But *delivery* has tended to point preachers all over the map, depending on where, when, and on whom it is modeled. Good delivery has been viewed as everything from "improvised impromptu" to stuffy decrees read from the manuscript; from the rough, flamboyant, spread-eagle gyrations of a Billy Sunday to the silky smooth appeals of certain television evangelists.

In the late nineteenth century, delivery was practically everything when it came to the study and practice of rhetoric. The elocutionary experts taught speakers how to say anything (or nothing!) in a nice way, stressing pedantic, specific, and exaggerated movements. For the first six weeks of a public-speaking course, students practiced rising from their seats, walking with mincing, dainty steps to the speaker's stand, and curtsying while gesturing with a broad sweep of the arm—always allowing the wrist to lead the gesture. The student then returned to his or her seat. Such was Speech 101 in any university at the turn of the last century.

During that era of American history, our nation's population, often deprived of formal education, flocked to popular lectures in Chautauquas, churches, and town halls across America. They listened and marveled as speakers such as Russell Conwell, William Jennings Bryan, Josh Billings, and a host of others used polished delivery to impress them with a wide variety of messages. Specific facial gestures and body movements were rehearsed and exaggerated. Much preaching of that day followed this ideal.

A century later we've perhaps swung to the other extreme. Almost nothing related to delivery has been written since the 1940s. John A. Broadus, in 1870, wrote a classic book that has had unprecedented influence in the training of preachers. The three revisions of his *Preparation and Delivery of Sermons* have retained three whole chapters on delivery. But the fading of Broadus during recent decades has meant the waning of attention to sermon delivery.

Yet it is more difficult to hold an audience's attention today than it has ever been in human history. Whereas the nineteenth century offered occasional Chautauqua lectures, a hundred years later we have cable television with dozens of channels offering constant warmth, wit, personality, and persuasion from a seemingly endless stream of sophisticated professional communicators. Every sermon preached next Sunday will be compared, at least subconsciously, to the skilled media performances the parishioners watched during the week.

If that competition isn't enough, consider what the communication experts have discovered in our century: body and facial expressions count for as much as 58 percent of a speaker's impact; voice and tone account for 39 percent of the impact; and our words account for a mere 3 percent of our persuasive speaking power. If these figures are anywhere near reality, we can no longer afford to spend our energies on words alone.

Delivery Effectiveness

Those who are convinced delivery is important may wish to engage in some self-evaluation. Preachers can begin to guage the effectiveness of their delivery by asking themselves nine crucial questions:

1. *Am I direct?* Delivery involves bodily action, intensity or earnestness, personal presence, content, material, and a straightforward style. Each of these elements can contribute warmth and personal impact to a message. Yet it is the eyes and the voice that most significantly determine the level of directness.

• Eyes. Television ruined the day, if it ever existed, when the speaker could preach like Charles Wesley, with eyes closed for extended periods. Today some experts insist that we need eye contact 85 percent of the time, even while reading such mundane materials as the minutes of the last meeting. What gives anyone the impression our sermons and Scripture readings demand any less directness?

Even children detect fright or flight when a speaker crops out hearers by looking six inches above their heads, appearing to read off the back wall. We must look at the people. Preachers need to see individuals to speak to individual needs.

One layman made a huge contribution to my preaching directness. He'd heard my sermons regularly for seven years. As a patent lawyer for a Fortune 500 company before he was selected to be vice president, he knew speaking and he knew people. One day he drew me aside to say quietly, "When you get to the end of your sermons, why do you always look down before you summarize or challenge us? Why don't you keep looking at us when you tell us what you want us to do?" That changed my preaching. I learned to get the first and the last few minutes of the sermon in mind so my eye contact could be constant.

If pews could vote, we'd realize that most people in the church are tired of being read to. We should make our delivery direct with constant eye contact. Broadus says, "Plunge in, trembling knees and all."

• Voice. The best preaching voice is never heard, because it never calls attention to itself. Golden, round tones scraping the bottom of the barrel convey a staged effort rather than genuine sincerity. Expanded conversational tones are best for today's preachers. We need to be as direct with the congregation as if we were talking to one person in private.

Avoid high pitch. Too often the untrained voice returns to a basic pitch one fourth below its *highest* possible pitch, resulting in a nagging, irritating screech. Ideally, voice pitch should fluctuate up and down from one-third above one's *lowest* pitch.

One way to do this is to breathe deeply with rhythmic use of the diaphragm. Project a full-bodied tone. Baritone and contralto speaking levels are more pleasant to the listening ear than soprano and tenor levels.

2. *Am I personal?* Persons and their stories are much more interesting to our hearers than any of our ideas or concepts. Haven't we all awakened in church when the preacher put a face or a person's name on a theological truth? The Relating God relates to us.

The 2,920 persons in the Bible serve for more than filler. Even evil finds a face in human biographies—in Lot's wife, in Pharaoh, in Judas, in Ananias and Sapphira, and in Herod who was "eaten by worms and died." Arguments don't persuade us nearly as well as people do.

3. *Am I earnest?* Does what I'm saying seem vital to me? Emphatic words, strong sentences, short paragraphs, vivid pictures—all these contribute to the congregation's recognition that we are earnest.

Jesus and Paul both conveyed emotion when they spoke. That doesn't make them illogical, but sometimes they were *non*logical. For ex-

---

Preaching Without Notes

It was Sunday morning, and the manuscript was lost. Adventure or crisis? I was forced to ask myself: *If I can't remember what I want to say in this sermon, how can I expect my listeners to remember what I've said?*

This preaching adventure happened early in my ministry when I once laid my Bible and sermon manuscript on top of the car—and drove off, the Bible and manuscript scattering in the wind. When I arrived to lead worship, I panicked at the thought of preaching without a manuscript. Yet, in the twenty-five minutes that followed, my life as a preacher was transformed dramatically.

I found I was able to remember most of what I'd labored to write after all, I was delighted at being in dialogue with my congregation, and I experienced a greater freedom in communicating than I'd ever known. The response from the congregation was overwhelming. Their preacher had lost his manuscript and found his audience.

Steps to Note-free Preaching

Any effective sermon takes months to prepare, and preaching without notes takes more, not less, preparation. Here are the steps I suggest:

● *Prepare a yearly preaching guide.* Each summer, take time to outline the title, text, and potential themes of the September-through-July sermons. In a file folder for each title, place ideas, illustrations, anecdotes, stories, quotes, and Scripture references that you might utilize.

● *Outline carefully.* As you prepare specific messages, jot key

ample, Jesus left the logical, cognitive realm when he made his universal appeal to our human emotion: "Come to me, all who are weary and burdened, and I will give you rest. Take my yoke upon you, and learn from me; for I am gentle and humble in heart, and you will find rest for your souls. For my yoke is easy, and my burden is light" (Matt. 11:28–30). You look in vain for heavy logic here. Deep emotion rides the crest of these words. He touches our human life. He shares our universal need of rest. And we reach out to him. Our emotion needs to show through our delivery.

Beware, however, the tendency to raise your vocal pitch when you share your deep feelings. We keep our hands closer to our bodies; we breathe in shorter breaths; we use shorter strokes in our gestures when we are emotional.

4. *Do I share my personal experience?* Cold, authoritative decrees tend to raise questions and hackles. Today people respect the pastor who shares about his or her faith journey as a real fellow human being.

---

points under the headings of introduction, body of thought, and conclusion. The points under the body of thought section should follow a progression and contain the essential thrust of the biblical text and the theme you're trying to communicate.

• *Write the sermon anyway.* Yes, even though you will actually deliver the sermon note free, you must still write it out completely first. Write it in the tone of a letter to a friend, as a one-to-one dialogue. Include Bible references, illustrations, and real-life anecdotes under each point of the body of thought.

• *Polish what you've written.* Imagine your sermon is answering a question just asked by a parishioner. How would you frame your answer? Remember, you're not writing a chapter of a book to be read; you are giving a *verbal* response. Write as you would speak.

• *Practice aloud.* Toward the end of the week, set aside several hours to read the sermon aloud at least six times, memorizing only Scripture verses or brief quotes verbatim. Then set the manuscript aside and talk it out. I like to pace back and forth as I do this. On the day of preaching the sermon, spend at least an hour reading and talking through the manuscript again.

• *Trust the Lord completely.* Enter the pulpit assured that you will remember what you have prepared. As you become caught up in a dialogue with your people, you will be amazed by the surge of excitement and gusto you feel.

J. B. Phillips said that translating the Book of Acts into contemporary English was like rewiring an old house with the current turned on. That is how I feel when I preach without reading a manuscript or using notes—it's electric! I'm plugged in, and the Spirit can flow through me unimpeded to illuminate the hearts and minds of my listeners.

—*Lloyd John Ogilvie*

Effective delivery requires more than demanding authority with a loud voice. While "Jesus taught them as one having authority and not as the scribes," he did so with the quiet confidence of shared experience rather than with pronouncements of decrees, even though the latter approach might have appealed to a power-structured society. Yet "the Son of Man did not come to be served, but to serve, and to give his life as a ransom for many" (Matt. 20:28). If we share from our own personal experience, our delivery will carry more power and authority than a thousand generic pronouncements.

5. *Do I use oral style?* The Bible is written in an oral style, and good preaching will likewise couch its ideas. This simply means that when we preach, we must be sure that we sound like a speaker rather than a reader. Our sermon may be written out, but it must be spoken as a

---

Preaching from a Manuscript

The use of a manuscript can be dangerous because it can lead to insufferable boredom when a preacher reads instead of proclaims. Not all dangerous things should be avoided, however. Medicine, matches, and other good things can be dangerous, which simply means they should be used properly. Here, then, are some guidelines.

From Manuscript to Sermon

1. *Write in an oral style.* Don't compose prose to please an editor of *Pulpit Digest.* The manuscript should be for your eyes only. Don't be afraid of sentences that are incomplete or that end in a preposition.

2. *Speak it as you write it.* Paragraph by paragraph, preach it aloud. Listen for how it *sounds*. Does it flow? Is there rhythm?

3. *Preach the message not the manuscript.* There is no such thing as a written sermon; a manuscript is simply a tool for use during the event of preaching. Absorb the con-

tent so fully that you can proclaim it with conviction and passion. Don't read it!

4. *Learn the text.* Be so familiar with the manuscript that you need it only to refresh your memory. Read it through several times on Saturday evening and twice on Sunday morning.

5. *Don't try to memorize the prose.* Master ideas and general structure, but don't attempt to remember every word. The concentration needed leaves little freedom to think about pacing and to observe congregational reactions and other things necessary for good speaking.

Some Practical Tips

1. *Use half-sheets (5½" × 8½").* This size fits easily into most Bibles without folding and takes less space on the pulpit. More important, the human eye can take in a span of about five inches; a single glance, therefore, can reveal an entire line.

2. *Single space between lines.* The

conversational event. (Of course, we should practice *writing* in oral style, too.) Conversations, when seen as transcripts on paper, look grammatically horrifying—filled with sentence fragments, run-ons, stops and starts. Yet this *is* the way we talk.

Consider the characteristics of oral style over written style: Instantly intelligible, more eagerness, energy, directness, and personal feeling; more vividness and suspense; more rhythm and movement; more illustrations and questions; more personal pronouns, contractions, verbs, and connectives; fewer Latin terms and more Anglo-Saxon terms; more comparison, contrast, and repetition; more direct discourse; more active voice and less passive voice.

No preacher incorporates all these elements in a given paragraph. But the more oral elements a sermon includes, the more interesting,

---

eye should be able to take in as much as possible in one glance.

3. *Double space between paragraphs.* This keeps the eye from getting lost in a sea of words. Keep paragraphs short with plenty of daylight around them.

4. *Experiment with indentation.* Perhaps illustrations should be indented and quotations indented even further. Since this gives the eye variety, the overall print pattern of each page aids the memory.

5. *Underline or shade key words and phrases in each paragraph.* A well-written paragraph will have a central idea with a *few* important words. When the eye glances down, underlined or shaded words jump out, and usually the whole paragraph can be remembered. Use different colors for different elements of the sermon (for example, red for key words, yellow to indicate quotations, and blue to signify illustrations).

6. *Do not staple.* Fastened pages must be turned, and that's hard to do unobtrusively. Loose pages can be slid easily across the pulpit. The major enemies of this method are open windows and vigorous air-conditioning systems. When drafts threaten, slip the edge of the manuscript under your Bible.

7. *Always double-check page sequence before the worship service.* Having pages out of order is a nightmare. Therefore, number your pages and then check and double-check them. If tragedy strikes, don't stall; look down and get the problem straightened out as quickly as possible.

Why a Manuscript?

The advantages of using a manuscript outweigh the disadvantages. Writing helps *clarify thinking*. The struggle to put ideas on paper forces the preacher to find the right words, shows weak transitions, exposes flaws in logic. Writing *sharpens the use of words*. It's usually easier to see cliches and jargon than to hear them in the act of preaching. Writing *makes possible the use of metaphors, similes, and active verbs*. Few speakers have the genius to invent such things extemporaneously, but using a manuscript can inspire many of us.

—Don McCullough

vital, individual, and persuasive it will be.

6. *Am I more than merely cognitive?* The cognitive aspects of life are lionized by our left-brain logic in our traditional educational systems. Analysis, abstraction, theory, and theology cut a wide swath in our ministerial training. Yet, the overload of left-brain accents during the week leave many people starved for the chance to relate meaningfully to others and to God. Therefore, church services must minister more relationally.

Since the Bible and all of human life revolve around relationships, the contemporary person cannot be satisfied with a partial gospel accent that focuses only on the cognitive, analytical, theological, or theoretical. The human, relational element must be part of our sermons and our delivery. In other words, our preaching, if it's going to be life changing, must appeal to listeners' senses as well as their logic. Our appeals to the head must be supported by appeals to the heart.

Despite their immersion in our primarily left-brain educational systems, people today respond favorably to visual and relational right-brain approaches. In our time, television makes more converts to a right-brain approach every day, since the American public reads less and watches more. That means the traditional, no-nonsense left-brain, cognitive approach fades among common people.

How does all this tie in to a preacher's delivery? It means that now, perhaps more than at any time in the history of preaching, the impact of what we say depends on *how we say it.* If we are going to communicate the gospel of relationship and emotion, our congregations need to see and feel that message in our delivery.

The James-Lange theory of emotion suggests that acting out an emotion tends to make us feel that emotion. For example, if we act timid and fearful, we tend to begin feeling frightened. Project a full-bodied, confident image, and we tend to feel more confident. We must let the demeanor of our delivery reflect our message.

Then there is the matter of our body movements. They function in one of three ways: to suggest, to emphasize, or to describe. Most of us instinctively use our hands to describe a circular stairway or the fish that got away, but we need to incorporate appropriate gestures for a broad range of preaching purposes.

Men particularly, seem to demand more than a left-brain, logical style of preaching. Why won't Daddy go to church? Probably he is already drowning in a sea of words. Mom may be impressed by the preacher's vocabulary, but Dad needs more. He needs pictures, action. He needs to visualize it. Our delivery can help him do that.

7. *Am I inductive?* Examples from the Bible, history, and life can lead us cumulatively to accept concepts and suggestions for changing behavior. Our exhortations gain power as this kind of evidence accumulates. We reach desired conclusions with much less resistance.

About 90 percent of the Bible is presented inductively. Persons, examples, and events lead us to conceptual conclusions. Of course, the Bible contains some hortatory elements. But from Genesis to Revelation, exhortation is swathed in personal narratives and real-life examples. So when we organize a sermon inductively, the delivery becomes more natural, people listen more attentively, and the sermon makes greater impact.

8. *What are my hearers telling me?* Check crowd movement and attention. Top speakers arrest listeners' movements. When E. Stanley Jones spoke in our chapel, he held the crowd virtually motionless as he shared examples from his book on conversions. Two days later a retired preacher plodded along at 55 words per minute, and I saw about two hundred crowd movements per minute. If you watch for instant feedback, you can adjust your delivery accordingly to keep the people listening.

9. *Do people see Jesus when I preach?* Do I lift up myself? Or Jesus? Enough said.

Delivery Remedies

What does the preacher with insufficient instruction in sermon delivery do? Is it too late? It's never too late to begin to sharpen sermon delivery. Here are some suggestions:

• Record your sermons on videotape and look for ways to improve your delivery on your own. When teachers are no longer available, you may need to tutor yourself.

• Ask someone to help you. Perhaps you could share tapes and critiques with pastor friends. All of us have pet idiosyncrasies and provincialisms of which we are unaware. But we can sharpen our diction, fix bad grammar, and transform awkward movements with the help of an objective observer who points out these foibles.

• Take a public-speaking course at a local college.

• Find a continuing-education seminar with accent on speech.

• Enroll in a sales or communication seminar for businesspeople.

• Join a speech club such as Toastmasters to work on your delivery.

• Take note of effective delivery styles of television personalities.

Each of the five ancient canons of speech remains vital for our preaching today. Yet the last canon—delivery—determines the effectiveness and success of the first four. If we ignore its importance, our twenty minutes of poor delivery can easily negate our twenty hours of good sermon preparation.

—Ralph L. Lewis

Before and After You Preach

What occurs during the time you spend before and after you preach? How do you do your best to let God do his best through you before you head into the pulpit? And what do you need to do to remain focused on God after the service?

These questions aren't about sermon preparation, but about personal preparation, about getting ready to be a conduit for God's Word and winding down after performing that task on Sunday morning.

Before You Preach

1. *Rest well the night before.* The preacher's house should be the dullest place in town on Saturday evening. The pulpit demands tremendous physical, mental, emotional, and spiritual energy. Getting to bed early is an important part of preparing to preach.

2. *Rise early enough for a meaningful time of prayer.* If you've studied, outlined, and written a sermon as though it all depends on your diligent work, pray as though it all depends on God's mighty power.

3. *Review the sermon.* Preach through the message at least twice, giving particular attention to those sections that still aren't fixed in your memory.

4. *Eat a good breakfast.* Preaching demands much from the body as well as the spirit. Eat enough to sustain you through the morning. Those with multiple worship services may need a midmorning snack to gain some energy. (Pineapple juice makes a good pick-me-up and does wonders for the throat.)

5. *Scan the morning newspaper.* Read the headlines of the front page to discover whether any tragedy of note has befallen the nation or community. It would be embarrassing and pastorally irresponsible, for example, to enter the pulpit without knowledge that the President had been assassinated or war declared.

6. *Get to the sanctuary early enough to check details.* Is the sound system set properly? Are the flowers centered? Have hymnals been placed in the chancel chairs? You don't want to be needlessly distracted during worship, let alone during the sermon. Others probably have responsibility for these particulars, but a few minutes of double-checking can ease tension during the service.

7. *Pray with leaders.* Prayer before worship centers the heart and mind on God. By praying with others, you not only model leadership that is dependent on God, but you also show that worship is an act of the whole fellowship of believers and therefore everyone's responsibility.

8. *Expect problems.* Rarely does a worship service happen without a glitch. Something annoying will usually occur. By expecting problems, you will be less upset when they happen.

9. *Worship with the congregation.* You have prepared yourself, your sermon, and the sanctuary. Now relax. Don't use the hymns and prayers as time to think about the sermon. Join the people in praise, confession, and intercession.

After You Preach

1. *Before going home, make a list of the things that need following-up the next week.* It's worth taking a few minutes at your desk to put in writing the concerns that have come to mind during the service. This will free your mind for a more relaxing afternoon.

2. *Let go of the sermon.* You're still too close to your own preaching to be objective about it, and you're too tired to receive criticism with an open spirit. It's a good idea to trust the power of the gospel to do its work in people's lives.

3. *Allow yourself to come down emotionally.* The adrenalin has been pumping all morning; you've been charged up by preaching and leading worship. But what goes up must come down. There's nothing sinful about depression on Sunday afternoon; it's part of a natural biological and psychological cycle. If you don't fight it, you will get out of it sooner.

—Don McCullough

Preaching As If One-on-One

What would it have been like to stand in the valley and hear Jesus there on the hillside, this Divine Archer with words for arrows? He pauses and takes aim at someone—at *me!* How could he speak to so many, yet make me feel as if he had singled me out personally, addressed me individually?

I never get the impression from Jesus' preaching that he intended to impress the crowds with his rhetorical skill. Rather, the Lord often engaged his audiences in a conversation with one-on-one flavor. Any lively conversation like that will have at least four aspects: seeing, speaking, listening, and responding.

See

WHEN I LOOK, LET ME TRULY SEE says a popular wall poster. The first step in effective one-on-one communication isn't speaking; it's truly seeing. There is a difference between looking at someone and really seeing him or her. Just looking doesn't require eye contact; we can slide by with a glance. But seeing a man, a woman, or a child establishes contact—a bridge that is nearly tangible. To really see someone says we care that they understand, that they actually hear for themselves rather than merely listen to what we have to say.

How long should we "see" someone? Consider this rule of thumb: The minimum is as long as it takes to have the person *see you back.* The maximum is not so long as to make someone uncomfortable.

Speak

Once communicators have "seen" their communication partners, they can begin speaking, maintaining intimacy in their voices even if they have to speak loudly. It's a rare church that is not equipped with microphones and speakers, but even with these aids, we must take care not to let the size of the congregation draw us into a one-sided shouting match.

People do dislike being shouted at. They long for the dignity of a personal visit. The great storytellers—Bill Cosby and Garrison Keillor are two of the best—rarely shout at us, unless they are parodying a bad preacher. Rather, they emphasize their points with a vocal variety that adds color and texture not only to volume but to rate, pitch, and tone as well. So as we speak, we need to allow our voices to take on the varied expression that might characterize an enthusiastic conversation with a friend.

Listen

Not listening is one of the most arrogant mistakes we can commit. It assumes every thought we express rings with such clarity and elegance that the scholar and the 6-year-old alike would, on a single hearing, echo an understanding Amen.

Recall how often the Lord Jesus repeated himself or restated his ideas. Why? Because he "listened" to his audience and knew when they needed clarification. He listened for different silences: "Yes, I see; you've touched my heart" or, "I'm lost, let's start over!"

Listening means attending to the nonverbal responses of the congregation's members. It means watching for knitted brows, smiles, folded arms—or half-closed eyes. As we tune in to subtle signs of understanding or confusion, of excitement or sadness or joy, we will know whether or not we are getting through.

Respond

Hearing our audiences frees us to respond appropriately. If hearers seem confused, we can try restate- -ment. If they are convicted, a pause may allow time for the truth to take root. If we find them joyful or excited, we can quicken the pace slightly to keep the tempo moving.

Responding appropriately creates a dynamic communication loop with our listeners. They become involved, having been enlisted as partners in a potentially life-changing conversation.

—Reg Grant

Emotion in Preaching

The emotional aspects of preaching can be bewildering. Conscientious preachers want to avoid manipulating people emotionally, yet because they know that, as Ralph Lewis writes in *Persuasive Preaching Today*, "emotions are the highway for human motivation," they seek to include emotion in their messages.

If sermons are to move the whole person, they must necessarily touch the emotions as well as the intellect. The best sermons aim not only to present something for hearers to *know* and *do*, but something for them to *feel* as well.

Abuses of Emotion in Preaching

Preachers who become preoccupied with getting an immediate, tangible response to the sermon may abuse emotion by valuing feeling for its own sake instead of seeing it as one means of persuasion. If they know how to excite people's feelings, they may ratchet emotions higher and higher until they produce some visible response.

Yet excessively emotional appeals often lead to a postdecision backlash. Those who responded in a moment of high feeling may later conclude that emotion overcame their better judgment. Then excessive emotion has done a disservice.

Preachers also misuse emotion when they pretend to have a depth of feeling that they do not actually experience. Such deception makes sermonic appeals dishonest. On the other hand, when preachers declare the gospel with little or no emotional appeal, they may leave the impression that the gospel is unimportant. Passionless intellectualism tragically caricatures Christian preaching.

Legitimate Use of Emotion

The preacher's own depth of feeling is the key to proper emotional appeals in preaching. The Roman rhetorician Quintilian rightly insisted that "the prime essential for stirring the emotions of others is . . . first to feel those emotions oneself." Preachers need either to preach on subjects about which they feel deeply or learn to feel deeply about the subjects they address. Prayerful meditation on the Scripture text and the congregation's needs gives the Holy Spirit opportunity to fire our zeal for the task.

Several principles can serve as guidelines for letting genuine emotions play their role in effective preaching:

● Plan worship that engages the whole person. Expressive forms of worship provide fertile soil for emotional appeals in the sermon.

● Balance emotional appeals based on threat (fear) with emotional appeals based on promise (faith). Both are biblical. Study how the sermon text combines the two. Fear appeals are more powerful but are subject to the law of diminishing returns.

● Respect the hearers' emotional thresholds. Though failing to provide adequate emotional appeal leaves hearers unmoved, pushing people beyond their comfort zones produces defensiveness.

● Lay an informational base upon which to make emotional appeals. As Ralph Lewis writes, "A convinced mind must precede a committed heart." Emotion is a complement to thought, not a substitute for it.

● Understand that tapping into a hidden reservoir of emotion may produce an intensity of response that surprises both the preacher and the person responding. Issues that carry a load of guilt and shame with them are especially prone to be explosive. Doing individual pastoral reconnaissance can help preachers address such sensitive topics with skill in the pulpit.

● Employ sensory language that engages hearers' imagination. Offer vivid images and concrete examples. Use metaphors of sex, blood, and death carefully, since they are extraordinarily potent in creating emotional intensity. Help hearers tap into memories that cause their values and desires to surface. Explain how those desires are best fulfilled in a response of faith.

● Build on conflict's capacity to

arouse emotion by presenting sharply contrasting alternatives when appropriate.

Remember, even with our most powerful and emotional appeals to truth, we must leave room for hearers to reject the appeal. If they are not free to say no, their yes becomes meaningless.

—Grant Lovejoy

Persuasion Versus Manipulation

The line between manipulation and persuasion is easier to identify than to define. When Elmer Gantry preached to defraud the good people of Cato, Missouri, it was manipulation. When Martin Luther King declared "I have a dream," he elevated persuasion to new heights. What's the difference?

Manipulative Insecurity

Manipulation in ministry occurs whenever the emphasis shifts from the power of God to that of the speaker. Focusing on visible results, for example, quickly devalues the audience, who become objects to be altered rather than persons of dignity made in the image of God.

While manipulation can happen in isolated acts, it is most dangerous when it becomes an ongoing pattern of dealing with others. Over time, unhealthy communication reveals certain clear danger signals:

• *Resistance to criticism.* Those who manipulate resist true dialogue, presenting their positions as God-given, overstepping healthy boundaries in their need to assert authority. Manipulative leaders prefer docile sheep to free agents who might take issue with them.

• *Extreme judgmentalism.* Manipulators display intolerance of those who question the values of the speaker. Beware the speaker who constantly "proof-texts," insisting on unique interpretations without presenting alternatives.

• *Negativity, fear, and shaming.* Manipulation and persuasion produce entirely different emotional atmospheres. Heightening the fear of disaster or ostracism is a tool of manipulation; subtle (or not so subtle) shaming marks an attempt to establish control.

• *Calls for immediate response.* Hearers must take action *now*, without consideration of the timing of the Holy Spirit or the individual's need to think things through.

• *Demands for never-ending performance.* Hearers are never doing enough. As preacher Bill Hybels chillingly pointed out, most unhealthy sermons could be summarized by "Do more, pray more, confess more, give more."

Manipulation occurs in settings deficient in relationship, indifferent to mutuality and love. In the play "My Fair Lady," Henry Higgins callously manipulates young Eliza, transforming her appearance without regard to her soul. Yet, when Higgins realizes that he has established a relationship with another human being, he is no longer satisfied with outer conformity. Only as Eliza refuses to be manipulated further is she free to be persuaded rather than recreated in the image of the speaker.

Persuasive Integrity

How does the Christian of integrity communicate persuasively without falling into manipulative practices? Recognizing our temptation to gain power and success, we begin to reestablish the priority of God-centered communication. The Christian message receives power not from gimmicks or emotionalism but from the Holy Spirit working through the clear message of the gospel. Paul said, "I was determined to know nothing but Christ, and the power of his resurrection" (Phil. 3:10). When we trust God to transform lives, we are free to love without regard to response, reputation, or personal authority.

Authentic persuaders become transparent to their listeners, not to gain sympathy but to establish common ground. As much as possible, the speaker employs language that says *we*. Through credible examples that avoid the fantastic or emotionally wrenching, the Christian persuader connects truth to specific situations. Humble acknowledgement that only God can change lives reminds both speaker and audience where to place ultimate trust. The speaker uses Scripture carefully, encouraging people to develop insights of their own. Those who seek to persuade with integrity value the people to whom they communicate and seek to know them.

The task of sharing the gospel of Christ is awesome, and the temptation to perform, to "be successful," is great. Only constant acknowledgement of dependence on God's transforming power can help us avoid the trap of manipulating those whom God loves.

—John Crosby

Adapting to the Congregation

The gospel is the gospel. What the living God has done in coming to the world through Jesus Christ does not change from era to era and culture to culture. But given the geography, history, and politics of the places we serve, the challenge to the preacher is this: How do I announce the Good News in ways that connect—here? Having served churches in three disparate locations—Los Angeles, Manila, and Sacramento—I found preachers have to adapt to the context in order to communicate.

Assessing the Context

Many preachers can assess the context intuitively, but here are three ways to get started immediately upon arriving at a new ministry:

• *Learn the history of the city.* Who were the first settlers? Why did they come here? What were their dreams? They set in motion a trajectory that still holds sway over the city.

• *Absorb the topics of local discourse.* Read the newspapers and the local tabloids. Listen to the radio talk shows. Pay attention to the conversations at the beauty parlor or barber shop. What are the "in" words? What issues keep getting the headlines? Letters to the editor and radio call-in conversations provide good windows into popular opinion.

Also, study the ads: What appeals to people in the area?

• *Join a community group*—Rotary, PTA, Little League, Chamber of Commerce. What are the concerns people discuss in these groups? How do folks articulate their concerns? What basic presumption about life do these concerns reflect?

Three Examples

From the communities where I pastored, here is what I found:

• *Los Angeles*. Bright lights. Sandy beaches. Passionate love for the automobile. Crowded freeways. Ethnic diversity. Hollywood. The operative word is *life*. One cannot help getting swept up in the quest for all the gusto.

So preaching enthusiastically announces life, authentic life in Jesus Christ. Preaching holds him up as abundant life in its fullness. And preaching confronts the unreality—the illusion—of what Los Angeles calls real life. Preaching exposes the myth of a fulfilling life apart from God.

• *Manila*. Lush greenery. Heat. Humidity. Crowds. Massive poverty. The key task for most people is simply to survive. Only a few have the time to reflect philosophically.

So preaching compassionately announces *hope:* The God who comes to us in Jesus Christ cares,

comforts us, and works changes. Preaching holds up Christ as the Liberator, not from meaninglessness, as in Los Angeles, but from sin manifested in unjust social systems. Here preaching announces Jesus' "gospel of the kingdom," a new order that not only brings forgiveness and eternal life, but also calls for justice, bread, housing, and healing.

• *Sacramento*. Clean. Orderly. Laid-back. Trees. Pluralism. Arrogance (decisions made here in the capital of California set the pace for the rest of the nation). Yet, insecurity (we do not have a major-league football or baseball team). Confrontational (people can treat pastors the way they do legislators). The operative word is *power*.

So preaching graciously, but firmly, announces *truth:* We are not gods; we do not control the world. We do not even control our own lives! Preaching holds up Christ as Lord, as the One who has the last word.

A popular statement in Sacramento is "No one is going to tell me how to live my life!" To which I graciously respond, "That is a dangerous statement when 'no one' includes the One who died for you on the Cross." Preaching in this context turns regularly to parables, which sneak behind defenses and debunk the prevailing ideologies.

—*Darrell Johnson*

Surveying Sermon Response

When surveys are carefully planned and analyzed, they not only provide comments on how to improve your sermon, but they also tell you what people gained from it. I recommend a written, one-page, anonymous survey focused on a specific sermon. Here is a sample:

Sermon Survey

The pastor is seeking feedback from people within the congregation. Please take a few minutes to complete this survey. Thank you.

1. Overall, how would you rate today's sermon?
☐ Excellent ☐ Good
☐ Fair ☐ Poor

2. How would you compare today's sermon to most of the pastor's sermons?
☐ Better ☐ About the same
☐ Poorer
If today's sermon seemed better or poorer than usual, why?

3. What are the main points you remember from today's sermon?

4. What, if anything, did you gain from the sermon?

5. What, if anything, did you think was weak about the sermon?

6. Do you think today's sermon will change your life in any concrete way?
☐ Definitely yes
☐ Probably yes
☐ Maybe
☐ Probably no
If yes, what do you think will change?

7. If you could tell the pastor one positive thing about his/her sermons, what would it be?

8. If you could give the pastor one suggestion about sermon content or delivery, what would it be?

9. Please add other comments you may have about today's sermon or other sermons.

10. Are you:
☐ Male ☐ Female

11. Your age: ☐ Under 30
☐ 30 to 50 ☐ Over 50

12. How long have you attended this church?
☐ Less than 1 year
☐ 1–3 years
☐ More than 3 years

Suggested Procedures

Number of surveys: Regardless of your church's size, fewer than twenty returns may not be enough feedback, and more than fifty is not necessary to get representative opinions.

Distribution: Pick personable and trustworthy people to distribute the survey. I suggest distributors approach individuals as they leave the sanctuary, asking if they would like to help the pastor by taking a few minutes to complete a survey on today's sermon. It will be most accurate and helpful if people complete the survey at that time.

Surveys should be distributed among young and old, women and men, leaders and nonleaders, and new and long-term members. Distributors can personally collect the surveys or tell people where to place them when they have finished. A cardboard box nearby marked SURVEYS would ensure anonymity. It is important that distributors thank people for their time.

Analyzing the results: While you may want only to read the survey forms, tabulating the answers provides a better understanding of what the feedback really means.

Some Tips

• Use a blank survey to record your tabulations and analysis.

• If you see major differences in the way people answer based on age, sex, or length of time at your church, you may want to tabulate each group separately.

• Survey a cross section of church members on at least three or four Sundays.

• For questions 1, 2a, and 6a, compare the percentages for each answer with the answers to your next sermon survey. A spread of more than 10 percentage points indicates a difference in your congregation's receptivity to these two types of sermons.

• For the remaining questions, count the number of times a response is repeated. These comments represent the typical response to your sermons. Don't place too much weight on a single complaint. Remember, one response represents only one person's view, not the church's as a whole.

• Talk over the results with trusted fellow leaders. It's always helpful to have more than one interpretation of survey results.

—*Virginia Vagt*

Part II

Worship

In the Old Testament, the proper posture for worship was to fall on one's face before the King. That was utterly appropriate in that day. Worship leaders today, however, don't particularly care to fall on their faces in front of their people because of ill-prepared or poorly conceived worship leadership. In so public a forum, with so much expected, they want to offer—and deliver—only their best.

To do that best, so that congregations can worship their best, worship leaders must understand Christian worship intimately. What *is* true worship? How are the people of God best led to express their praise for him? What is appropriate and inappropriate? How have we come by the means of worship we typically employ, and where do we go from here?

Worship certainly has much to do with heart, but a better prepared mind best directs that heart. The writings in this section feed the mind intent on offering the best to God in worship. They help us conceptualize what worship is meant to be, plan for effective worship, and realize those best-laid plans. Articles in this section deal with the worship leader as well as the worship task.

Here, then, is counsel for today's priests, who dare—with their people—to approach the throne of the Almighty God to fulfill the chief end of mankind: to glorify God and enjoy him forever.

10

The Purpose and Meaning of Worship

Worship is a noble word. Yet, like any familiar word we use, it is open to misunderstanding and abuse. We may need to rescue this critical term from some popular misperceptions and restore it to its pristine beauty and significance.

Defining Worship

Two great dangers face those who seek to understand worship in its true biblical essence. First, we face the great enemy, overfamiliarity. We may have become so tied to a regular round of church meetings that we understand worship to refer to any religious or social exercise done on church premises. Second, we face the peril of defining the quality of worship solely by reference to our feelings.

To avoid both these dangers we must at least recognize that an encounter with God in his holy character transcends the dynamics of ordinary meetings among human beings, whether at the church building, or not. And we must also recognize that such an encounter may very well be painful, entailing a call to sacrifice, self-examination, repentance, and amendment of life: "It is a dreadful thing to fall into the hands of the living God" (Heb. 10:31). Worship is therefore not always immediately painless and pleasant, and it is never casual, thoughtless, or flippant.

To be sure, we are meant to *enjoy* the worship of God just as we are called to revel in life itself as God's good gift to us. "Man's chief end is to glorify God and to enjoy him forever" runs the old catechism. But observe the sequence. First we are called to *glorify*, that is, honor and reverence God, and find our center in him. Enjoyment and pleasure will then flow as a direct consequence of this. Such feelings are not goals we set for ourselves. Rather they will likely come to us as a by-product, a spin-off from the original intent of putting God first and foremost.

All of this is simply to say that we must not presume to be "buddy-buddy" with the God of the Bible. When we approach worship, we approach the One who is a consuming fire (Heb. 12:28–29) and whose eyes are too pure to behold evil (Hab. 1:13). Yet this process of self-scrutiny leading to an acknowledgement of our need of pardon and restoration is the step we must take on the road to intimate communion with God (1 John 1:9), who calls us back in love (Hosea 14:1). Moreover, God has himself opened the way to such access by what Christ the Lord did for us on the Cross and is doing on our behalf in his priestly ministry of intercession (Heb. 7:25; 10:21).

Our worship, then, enlivened by the Holy Spirit, connects us with the God of our salvation whose character is spelled out as *holy love*. God is holy; hence the call to reverence and awe. Yet, he is love; hence the assured merciful welcome. God's mercy is ready to receive us for Christ's sake and in Christ's person, who is the perfect worshiper (Heb. 2:11–12). It is he who joins us with himself to the Father in reconciliation and family oneness: "Here am I, and the children God has given me" (Heb. 10:13b). In this way Jesus acts as bridge builder, uniting God's people with God himself.

In light of this discussion, we are now in a position to offer a definition of worship that goes beyond the classic formulation of Evelyn Underhill, for example, that worship is "the response of the creature to the Eternal" or "an acknowledgement of God as transcendent." Both definitions suffer the unfortunate tendency of making God too remote and aloof. They fail to show how worship impacts on real life in this world. A more comprehensive definition might run like this: Worship is the dramatic celebration of God in his supreme worth in such a manner that his worthiness becomes the norm and inspiration of human living.

Expanding on a Theme

Having ventured a definition, let's expand on it by noting several theological characteristics of true, biblical worship:

1. True worship is God directed. Naturally, interactions among human beings take place in worship services, and people get certain psychological needs met in worship. However, the theocentric quality of worship stresses that it is an exercise of the human spirit directed primarily to God (see John 4:24). Worshipers embark on the enterprise not simply to satisfy their needs, to make themselves feel better, or to minister to their aesthetic tastes and social well-being. Rather they worship in order to express and articulate the greatness of their God, as bidden by the Israelite Psalmists: "Ascribe to the Lord the glory due his name" (Ps. 96:8).

2. *True worship focuses on divine worthiness.* Because the Lord is great, he is "most worthy to be praised" (Ps. 96:4). Worship derives from the Anglo-Saxon word for "worth-ship" and focuses on what is deserving of human attention, admiration, and appreciation. To worship God is to ascribe to him the honor and adulation that are most appropriate to who and what he is. It lifts up the wonderful superiority of all his works in creation and in the unfolding drama of salvation history that runs through both the Hebrew and Christian Scriptures. Thus, God's nature, best understood as a blend of holiness (Isa. 6:1–9) and love (1 John 4:8, 16), sets the standard as the object of Christian worship. Put another way, the God whose name we celebrate is altogether worthy of praise for what he has done in creation (Rev. 4:11) and in redemption (Rev. 5:12–14).

3. *True worship recognizes God's holiness at all times.* "Exalt the Lord our God and worship at his holy mountain" is the summons of Psalm 99:9, with this reason given: "For the Lord our God is holy." The holiness of God is at the heart of the Christian idea of worship, with the double effect of awakening in us both a lively sense of our creaturely dependence and a stark recollection of our frailty (Isa. 6:1–9; Luke 5:8). Yet, on the positive side, the holiness of God can bid us draw near, since the divine character is attractive and gracious (Heb. 4:14–16).

The men and women of Scripture's story invariably felt initial discomfort and unease when they became aware of the divine presence. Recall Abraham's trepidation during his colloquy with Yahweh (Gen. 18:17). Job was overwhelmed by an awesome theophany (Job 42:5–6), and Moses surely trembled at the place of fiery revelation (Exod. 3:5). These same feelings no doubt descended upon Peter at the lakeside (Luke 5:8), upon Paul at the moment of his conversion (Acts 9:4), and upon John as he sensed a numinous presence in exile (Rev. 1:17). Yet these experiences prepared the biblical personalities to appreciate God's tender mercy and pardoning grace (Ps. 130:3–4).

4. *True worship exerts a claim on the worshiper.* In light of this consideration that God's holy yet grace-filled character is the norm, we can understand how worship demands that worshipers offer their best. True worship yields a human response that is thoughtful, costly, and offered with a worthiness corresponding to the worth of God. The Old Testament rituals and rites heavily accentuate this need for the

devotees' preparation, as the entire Book of Leviticus makes clear. David "will not offer burnt offerings to the Lord" that cost nothing (2 Sam. 24:24). And Joshua admonishes the people, "You cannot serve the Lord" (Jos. 24:19) when their easygoing, idolatrous ways had led them to lose their vision of Yahweh as a holy and jealous God who requires a wholehearted dedication to his name.

5. *True worship requires utter seriousness.* Put into modern terms, the foregoing Bible passages stress the seriousness of our worship. We cannot worship in the true sense if our attitude is slipshod and flippant—not to say frivolous—and our approach to God is offhand and routine. Here is a vital principle at stake: Worship is not something we attend in a detached way as spectators on the sidelines; it is an exercise that should involve our whole selves, engaging our complete interest and participation. Attention is called for, not merely attendance.

The Use of the Bible in Worship

"The Word of God comes to the people of God in a way that determines their worship." So reads the constitution of one Protestant tradition, articulating the relationship between the public reading of the Bible and the acts of worship. The Word of God comes to us and shapes the tone, manner, and depth of our adoration, confession, and praise.

The Word Performs

"The Word of God comes to the people of God. . . ." As the writer of Hebrews says, the Word is "living and active" (4:12). It makes things happen. It not only *in*forms, it *per*forms.

Do not human words have this creative quality? Walk into a crowded room and yell "Fire!" and watch what happens as a result of uttering that little word. If our human words perform, how much more the Word of the Living God:

● "In the beginning . . . God said, 'Let there be light' . . . and there was" (Gen. 1:1, 3).

● Jesus "got up, rebuked the wind and said to the waves, 'Quiet! Be still!' Then the wind died down and it was completely calm" (Mark 4:39).

The living Word of the living God makes things happen. A verse of Charles Wesley's "O for a Thousand Tongues to Sing" says it so well: "He speaks, and listening to his voice, new life the dead receive; the mournful, broken hearts rejoice; the humble poor believe." We who lead worship need to recover a confidence in the creative power of God's Word.

Worship Is Responding

". . . in a way that determines their worship." Worship is *response*. We humans, at the center of our beings, have longings that strive up-

Complementing the Cognitive with the Aesthetic

The church has occasionally been guilty of viewing the assembled company of worshipers as a body of inert and largely passive auditors. Set in serried rows and ranks, the people come together in an auditoriumlike environment to hear God's Word read and explained. It may be argued that such an ambience has both merit and deficiency. On the plus side, the insistence on worship as an encounter with the divine Word—meant to be received, understood, and applied—highlights the initiative of God and the role of worshipers as God's obedient servants who are blessed as they hear and do God's will (Luke 10:27–28).

On the downside, such a seating arrangement and such an understanding of worship fails to engage entire persons as emotional, active beings as well as cognitive respondents. Using our uplifted hands and

---

ward. But without the Living One speaking a self-revealing Word, we only grope in the dark, aching in frustration and ambivalence.

Worship that brings us into wholeness is response to God's self-revelation, which is why the psalmists consistently put it the way they do: "Come, let us worship the Lord, for . . .", "for the Lord is good."

C. S. Lewis observed that the Living Word, Jesus Christ, produced only three effects on the people who met him: hatred, terror, or adoration. You never find anyone expressing mild approval. Given the inherent nature of the Word, no response at all is out of the question; we either try to hide, try to get rid of the revelation, or worship. Therefore, we who lead worship help the people of God do their work by, in every way possible, speaking God's Word.

The Word in Worship

The portion of the Word read as a call to worship sets the tone for what follows, freeing people to worship in spirit and truth. The Word spoken before the prayer of confession frees people to believe that God will receive our honest admissions of sin (see Isa. 43:25).

The Word spoken before the prayers of intercession frees people to believe that the God revealed in Jesus of Nazareth really does want to receive and embrace their fears, sorrows, and longings (see Isa. 46:3–4; Matt. 11:28).

The Word spoken as the benediction frees people to go back to their normal routines of life with a greater awareness of God's presence and call to obedient service (see Num. 6:24–26; Isa. 43:10; 49:14–16; 2 Cor. 13:14; Eph. 3:20–21; 1 Thess. 5:24; 2 Thess. 3:16; Heb. 13:20–21; Jude 24–25).

"The Word of God comes to the people of God in a way that determines their worship." Let God's Word loose among the people of God and watch what happens.

—*Darrell Johnson*

arms in praise, celebrating God in sacred mime and dance, or viewing colorful art images can broaden our appreciation of the story of salvation that we want to rehearse and reenact in worship. Thus it is claimed by modern proponents of free expression and spontaneous group praise that worship is fully satisfying only when it calls into play the full range of human senses in word and action. In other words, aesthetic values should be equally appreciated along with the spoken Word and a cerebral response.

Obviously there will be some tension created if these polarities of worship are regarded as mutually exclusive and pressed to do battle with one another. Somehow we have to hold in balance the emphasis on the cognitive and the sensory (engaging the five senses), and recall

---

Anglican Worship

The political, ecclesiastical, theological, and liturgical events that combined to bring about the Anglican tradition are important and complex. Anglican worship, by definition, is the tradition that was formed from the emergence of the national Church of England in the 16th century, marked by the first *Book of Common Prayer* written by Thomas Cranmer. The text was introduced into the parish churches of England on Pentecost—June 9, 1549.

An English History

The *Book of Common Prayer* reflects an English Reformation, even though the Church of England maintains an apostolic succession like that of the Roman Catholic Church. Thomas Cranmer was strongly influenced by Zwingli, Luther, and other Reformers. And though Bishop Gardiner, a Roman Catholic prelate, found the 1549 *Prayer Book* acceptable, it proved the kiss of death, resulting in the book's revision in 1552. This revised text

formed the basis of changes since that time.

Cranmer, a liturgist of amazing gift and ability, skillfully utilized existing resources: the Sarum rite (the worship form for the cathedral at Salisbury), the work of Spanish Cardinal Quignonez, and the "Consultations" of the Bishop of Cologne, Nicholas von Wied.

The form of the *Prayer Book* has remained virtually unchanged. It includes a church calendar, the service of Morning and Evening Prayer ("Matins" and "Evensong"), Holy Communion, and services of Baptism, Confirmation, Matrimony, Prayer for the Sick, and Burial. Services added later were the Psalter and Ordinal (ordination of deacon, priest, and bishop).

Prayer Shared with Laity

The special contribution of this work is the place of Morning and Evening Prayer. The medieval church had the "Seven Hours" to mark the devotional life of the faithful, but this was virtually exclusive

that our being made in the image of God is wonderfully complex and intricate (Ps. 139:14–16).

Balancing Form and Freedom

This reminder leads us to the complicated issue of set forms versus the freedom of the Spirit. But do they really exclude each other? In reality there should be no conflict between the two ways of practicing worship. Both styles have much to offer, yet each way of worship stands in need of the complementary role and contribution of the other.

Adopting set forms of worship ensures that there will be fidelity to

to the clergy, particularly the monastics. Cranmer attempted to bring the daily office into common church life through Morning and Evening Prayer. The forms for these services were not greatly different from the various liturgical sources for the Roman Church.

The *Prayer Book* presents a Eucharist that is divided into a Service of the Word and a Service of the Upper Room. There is to be a homily preached for the Sunday service, and the calendar follows the Christian Year.

The profound departure from the Roman church lay in the placing of the *Prayer Book* in the hands of the laity in their language. This is behind the name, *Book of Common Prayer*, for it was to be the means whereby all could join the worship of God, especially in prayer. The worship of the church was to be for the whole church, and not just the ordained (though the responsibility of leadership for corporate worship was carefully ordered).

It must be admitted, however, that Anglican worship did not actually accomplish this completely, and until recently was visibly dominated by the clergy.

Liturgy: Episcopalian Strength

Cranmer began a tradition of worship that is theologically broad and literarily beautiful, and Anglicans continue it today. The central commitment to a *Prayer Book* liturgy has been the strength of the Episcopal church.

Within this context exists a variety of practice. There are "low" churches, in which Protestant influence is most obvious, including Morning Prayer and the sermon as the regular service and only a few actions commonly regarded as more Roman (sign of the cross, genuflecting, chanting, and incense). There are also "high" or Anglo-Catholic churches, in which the Mass would include everything in a Roman Catholic church except the Pope.

The influence of the *The Book of Common Prayer* on virtually all the traditions in the English-speaking world is enormous. It is evidenced in many churches in marriages, funerals, baptisms, and often the Eucharist, all of which are filled with phrases or whole sections originating in Cranmer's work.

—*Robert N. Schaper*

the historic "shape" of the gospel, expressing prominently the major evangelical themes of creation, humankind's need, and its redemption in this world and beyond. The heritage of the past is thus preserved by a liturgy that draws on church history and experience down through the ages.

A prearranged order of service places firm control on the subjective tastes and fancies of the minister, and delivers the congregation from his or her more glaring foibles. It gives some flexibility for creative thinking and planning, but sets boundaries within which the truest worship of God, worthy of the historic gospel, can be offered.

Of course, there always lurks the danger of letting our worn language convey archaic and fossilized idioms that have lost their meaning. But recognizing and valuing the legacy of the past need not entail such a pitfall.

In complementary ways, we can make room for the present activity of the Spirit, whose role is to lead the worshiping church into a deepening apprehension of God's truth and to make the gospel contemporary. It follows that there will be space in worship for what is spontaneous and suited to the needs of the present hour. "Do not quench the Spirit" (1 Thess. 5:19) is Paul's word of caution in circumstances that suggest an attempt to limit the Spirit's operation or squelch some of his gifts. Liturgies *can* have this dampening effect, though their right use need not lead to such a suffocating of the Spirit. Moreover, there is always a need to be alive to what the Spirit is saying to the churches in our times and to fashion our prayers, confessions, hymns, and proclamations to speak relevantly to our contemporaries, without betraying the ancient message of God's truth.

Practicing Fellowship-in-Worship

We distinguish between the Christian's private and family devotional life and his or her sharing in the public worship of God as an act of corporate fellowship. In the latter sense, worship is by definition a communal enterprise that is much more than the sum of individual practices of prayer, meditation, and Scripture study. The extra dimension stems from the enrichment of the assembled congregation at worship.

The church is more than a convenient meeting place for men and women whose individual interests and religious experience draw them together but who remain separate and detached from one another. The worship of the church pulsates with a "common life" (*koinonia*) that flows through the body of Christ and in which individuals participate through their baptism by one Spirit into one body (1 Cor. 12:13).

To conceptualize worshipers as isolated units, each worshiping in a self-contained compartment, however closely associated, is really to mistake what the New Testament means by the church. The ideal set forth in the pages of the New Testament is that of fellowship-in-worship. Recovery of the wholeness of the church's life as "life together" in Christ, to use Bonhoeffer's phrase, would go a long way toward setting our worship, as a corporate exercise, on a more stable foundation. It would help deliver many modern congregations from ministerial monopoly, with one person conducting a virtuoso performance in front of assembled spectators. It would also confront the overemphasis on narrow individualism—the kind that disfigured the Corinthian assembly, in which *koinonia* had tragically broken down.

The classic description of the Christian *synaxis*, the gathering for worship, divides the service into two parts corresponding to "word" and "sacrament." The "liturgy of the Word" is followed by the "liturgy of the Upper Room." The former offers the gospel to the general public congregation; the latter feeds the baptized faithful.

This model has stood the test of time and has done much to conserve the liturgical heritage of past centuries. Yet it often still operates within the framework of the merely rational and severely didactic. Admittedly the eucharistic climax of such a service offers visual contact with the realities behind the bread and the wine. Yet it still remains the case that worshipers are there to be instructed, taught, edified, and prepared to contemplate the heavenly mysteries of the Communion table.

What may be needed to make the circle complete is a vision of worship as related to life and society. The ministry of intercession, whereby the prayers of God's people reach out to lift up the world to him, has always had an honored, if somewhat obscure, place in the history of the worship liturgy. We need to recover its importance, for it carries with it a reminder that while worship is directed primarily to God, it fits and equips God's church to be the agent by which his will is done on earth.

Relating Worship to Real Life

Our last prescription must therefore call the church to relate its worship to real life, for worship serves an ancillary function of preparing the assembled company to accept its role as Christ's servants and stewards over the entire range of human existence. In the high moments of public praise and prayer and communion with God, we discover our full personhood, since we see ourselves "under the aspect of God," whose name and presence we invoke and enjoy. Worship does indeed transcend the barriers of time and space, bringing us into touch with heaven's reality and fulfillment, as the author of Hebrews knew well (Heb. 12:22–24). It permits us to see within the veil; it brings to life in our temporal experience what truly belongs to the eternal state where God is "all in all," and his will is done perfectly.

Barth's wonderful description of worship as "the most momentous, the most urgent, the most glorious action" is exactly the case. But it carries the corresponding summons that out of this vision and awareness of heavenly joys and perfections, we should see our present life and lot. That is why Paul could glide so effortlessly from his statement on "spiritual worship" (Rom. 12:1) into a series of the most practical, down-to-earth applications of what that worship means in everyday life.

—Ralph P. Martin

Lutheran Worship

The foundation for all worship in the Lutheran church is justification by grace through faith, as expressed in Ephesians 2:8–9: "For it is by grace you have been saved, through faith—and this not from yourselves, it is the gift of God—not by works, so that no one can boast."

Article IV of the *Augsburg Confession*, the article on which the church stands or falls, expresses it quite clearly: "We cannot obtain forgiveness of sin and righteousness before God by our own merits, works, or satisfactions, but we receive forgiveness of sin and become righteous before God by grace, for Christ's sake, through faith, when we believe that Christ suffered for us and that for his sake our sin is forgiven and righteousness and eternal life are given to us."

Receiving Through Worship

For Lutherans, worship means first of all being a receiver—a recipient of God's grace and mercy through the forgiveness of sins for the sake of Christ. Being a receiver

thus implies a Giver, who is God, the Initiator of all worship. True worship is Divine Service, God coming to us through his means of grace —the Word and the Sacraments.

To receive God's grace and mercy calls for a response. In a 1522 sermon on Matthew 21:1–9, Luther reminded his hearers: "We cannot give God anything but praise and thanks, for everything else we receive from Him, be it grace, words, works, Gospel, faith, and all things" (*What Luther Says*, p. 1545). That response of thanks and praise is evident in the vocations of daily lives and as believers gather to offer worship to God in and through Christ Jesus—in Divine Service, their service of thanksgiving and praise.

Lutheran Form of Worship

Although they have been accused of abolishing the Mass, Lutheran confessors have responded: "We do not abolish the Mass but religiously keep and defend it. In our churches Mass is celebrated every Sunday and on other festivals" (*Apology of the*

Augsburg Confession, Art. XXIV). Lutherans also value the worship forms inherited from many cultures and peoples. Ceremonies from all ages of the church—the use of the church year, vestments, altars, candles, the sign of the cross, the lectionary (appointed Scripture readings)—are retained as well, as is the rich heritage of congregational, choral, and instrumental music.

Because of the Sacrament of Holy Baptism, by which God claims men, women, and children as his own and makes them part of his family, Lutheran worship is corporate. That corporateness is expressed as believers speak to one another in psalms, hymns, and the canticles of the liturgy. They are strengthened in that corporateness, that body of Christ, as they receive his body and blood in the Sacrament of the Altar.

The Divine Service

Large parts of the liturgical forms Lutherans adopt in their Divine Service are direct quotations of Scripture or paraphrases. Lutherans generally use the following outline from *Lutheran Worship* or *Lutheran Book of Worship* for the Divine Service:

Invocation: "In the Name of the Father . . ."
Confession of Sin and Absolution
Introit (Psalm) or Entrance Hymn
Kyrie: "Lord, have mercy . . ."
Hymn of Praise
Prayer (Collect) of the Day
Old Testament Reading
Psalm
Epistle
Alleluia Verse
Gospel
Sermon
Hymn of the Day
Nicene Creed
Prayers
Offering
Preface: "The Lord be with you . . ." "Lift up your hearts . . ."
Sanctus: "Holy, Holy, Holy, Lord, God of power and might . . ."
Prayer
Words of Institution
Lord's Prayer
Agnus Dei: "Lamb of God. . ."
Reception of the Sacrament of the Altar
Blessing
Canticle: "Lord, now you let your servant . . . " or "Thank the Lord and sing his praise . . ."
Prayer
Benediction

—*Henry V. Gerike*

Reformed Worship

The Reformed tradition is formed by a conviction that all of life is worship and the whole world belongs to God. Reformed worship is best understood in the context of a strong history of daily family worship, encouragement of education and intellectual development, and rigorous seminary programs. The emphasis on education also reflects a tradition of worship that is highly word oriented, intellectual in approach, and led by an ordained minister.

In North America, neither the Reformed groups of European continental origins nor the Presbyterians of English and Scottish origins developed a prescribed liturgy. Presbyterians adopted "directories for worship" that provided outlines and guidelines, not specific contents. The Reformed groups were even less prescriptive. Consequently, forms of worship varied considerably among different Reformed groups.

Yet some Reformed distinctives can be described briefly in terms of John Calvin's list of three requirements for public worship: the preaching of God's Word; prayers, both spoken and sung; and the administration of the Sacraments. Later he included the giving of alms as well.

Three Requirements

• *Preaching.* Reformed worship has always had at its center the exposition of God's Word. No visual symbols were to detract from the preaching; indeed, the main visual element in the plain sanctuaries was the large pulpit Bible. Exegetical preaching was most characteristic, and preaching included not only exposition but application. For many, going to church was "going to sermon." While still the centerpiece of Reformed worship, the sermon today is often balanced by a growing emphasis on other liturgical acts of the congregation.

• *Prayers.* By prayers, Calvin meant the spoken and sung acts of the people. Spoken prayers, usually offered by the minister, were largely extemporaneous and often lengthy and didactic.

Sung prayers formed the essential "service book" of the Reformed churches. Perhaps most distinctive was the commitment to unaccompanied and unison singing of the Psalms and a few other portions of Scripture. The Reformation gave the people their voice, and the one great gift of the Reformed tradition to church music was the *Genevan Psalter* (1562).

Such singing remained unchallenged for two centuries, but eventually organ accompaniment was introduced in the Netherlands. In North America, one group after another left exclusive psalmody, first producing psalter-hymnals, and then hymnals. Today, although psalmody is returning with remarkable vigor, hymnody remains more characteristic of Reformed worship.

• *Sacraments.* The Reformed tradition recognizes two sacraments, baptism and the Lord's Supper. Baptism, available also to infants, was considered part of public worship. The mode for baptism was optional, though sprinkling was typical.

Calvin desired weekly celebration of the Lord's Supper, but quarterly Communion became the pattern. The emphasis was strongly penitential. In the most severe groups, members seldom, if ever, communed because of their keen sense of unworthiness. Influence from the liturgical movement of the twentieth century has brought more frequent celebration and greater emphasis on nourishment for the believer, rather than only the remembrance of the Cross.

New Influences

A few small denominations have conserved most of these worship features and continue largely isolated from the larger communions of which they were once a part. Meanwhile, other denominations with Reformed roots are reclaiming their heritage, often through ecumenical dialogue. Reformed worship today is increasingly participatory, with more visual and symbolic richness than earlier. Individual Reformed congregations are also varying their services more than ever before, with influences from the highly liturgical, evangelical, and/or charismatic traditions blending with the rich Reformed heritage passed on from the Reformation.

—Emily R. Brink

Free Church Worship

Worship in the free church stems from the beliefs and practices of the sixteenth-century Puritans and Separatists who broke away from the Anglican Church in opposition to liturgical use of *The Book of Common Prayer*. The early free church forerunners brought about a nonepiscopal type of church government and stressed worshiping according to one's conscience, with freedom and spontaneity.

Two New Testament texts have decisively influenced free church practice through the centuries, in both theory and practice: "God is Spirit, and his worshipers must worship in spirit and in truth" (John 4:24) and "Where two or three come together in my name, there am I with them" (Matt. 18:20).

Theory

Free church worshipers stand for the *spiritual* quality of worship, placing little or no reliance on external forms, such as elaborate ceremony or ritual. They tend to distrust a set pattern of worship that could put boundaries on the Spirit's free movement. If God is Spirit, those who approach him should seek to be led by the Spirit and be open to his gracious prompting and control. Printed prayers and a rigid structure to be followed week after week do not seem to lend themselves to such a point of view.

The idea of the church, in the free church tradition, can be summed up in one phrase, based on the Matthew 18:20 text: *the gathered community.* And it is God who brings the church together, not human clerics. The church comes together freely, primarily to hear God's Word read and proclaimed. The ministry of the Word takes precedence as the preeminent sacrament of worship, with the other means of grace (baptism and the Lord's Table) regarded as acts of witness and reminders of the gospel message.

Practice

Free church theology results in a decidedly different look in worship, compared to the worship practices of liturgical traditions. Church interiors typically have a central pulpit, raised and honored in the architecture (as opposed to a central Communion table). This pulpit speaks of the primacy of preaching, which conveys God's truth to be understood and obeyed.

The congregation participates in worship chiefly by assenting to extemporary prayers and expository preaching. The key is to maintain each worshiper's freedom to be open to the Spirit's leading.

Fellowship is also prized—the mutual fellowship and edification of each believer-priest. The socializing effect of believers' unity in Christ has traditionally strengthened the idea of a separation of the church from the world and the state's control. Yet the free church has often led in social reform by exercising its witness in a prophetic role as society's critic. Hence the Nonconformist conscience in Britain and the U.S. in the nineteenth century led to many humanizing changes in social structures.

Strengths and Weaknesses

Free church worship at its best calls the liturgical traditions to remember the authority of Scripture, the central role of preaching as communicating God's Word to every generation, and the individual's worth before God. However, the free church can fail to offer Christians an opportunity to worship God in "the beauty of holiness." Because it tends to value simplicity and rationality above visual artistry or the mystical, the free church may limit such inroads to deeper spirituality for many people. For example, the free church tradition must be careful, in its excellent emphasis on preaching, not to devalue the place of the Eucharist in true Christian worship.

—*Ralph P. Martin*

Pentecostal and Charismatic Worship

Our primary mission is to worship God, our Creator, and to offer eternal praise with thanksgiving for his personal forgiveness and redemption of our sins through Jesus Christ. The Pentecostal and charismatic prescription for worship maintains this focus and adds to it the conviction of God's present desire to reveal himself to worshipers for the purpose of transforming them and presenting the gifts of the Holy Spirit to empower ministry.

Pentecostal refers to the outpouring of God's Spirit on the day of Pentecost (Acts 2). "Tongues of fire sat upon each one," each one was "filled with the Holy Spirit," and each one "began to speak with other tongues." The Upper Room demonstrates the possibility of God's personal interaction in the life of the worshiper and further presents an expectation of God's power for ministry.

Charismatic is the anglicized rendering for *gifts* of the Holy Spirit. Here the very word *charismatic* declares the openness of the worshiper to both receive gifts and to minister them to others (1 Pet. 4:10). Pentecostals and charismatics expect God to "show up" as they worship (Matt. 18:20). They seek his presence, not out of an unfounded hope but because he has promised in his Word to reveal himself as they worship (Ps. 22:3).

God's Casual Presence?

This pursuit of God's presence can be misperceived as being either overly emotional, or casual and without substance. Worshipers who are expecting personal transformation often display a degree of passion less familiar in other Christian traditions. The degree of informality, however, is not based on an absence of reverence for God's holiness but is rather a reflection of the worshipers' conviction that God is available to work personally in one's life.

Pentecostal/charismatic worship has its roots in the period following the First World War, when growth and freedom of American society influenced the shaping of an open, joyous worship form in Pentecostal churches. Contemporary Pentecostal worship forms underwent radical sensitization to the culture in the late 60s and early 70s, when charismatic renewal and the revival of the Jesus People added large numbers of young people to the church.

The introduction of nontraditional worship instruments like guitars, synthesizers, and drums, all a part of a pop-culture sound, accompanied this rapid influx of young people. This has fundamentally altered worship forms even beyond traditional Pentecostal/charismatic churches.

Physical Expression in Worship

Demonstrative physical forms of worship are prominent in Pentecostal/charismatic churches. Romans 12:1 exhorts believers to "offer your bodies as living sacrifices, holy and pleasing to God—which is your spiritual worship." The Psalms offer a worship guide that includes songs, spoken praise, upraised hands, and even dance.

Often the "song of the Lord," a free-form blending of voices in spontaneous songs, will be sung by a congregation "with my spirit," or "with my mind" (1 Cor. 14:15). In these gatherings the manifestation of prophecy, tongues, and interpretation of tongues, along with gifts of healing and miracles, are frequent.

Universal Characteristics

The worship forms of Pentecostal/charismatic churches vary as widely as their church polity. Some are historic Pentecostal denominational churches, that have long-established traditions and rather conservative worship forms. Others are new and independent charismatic churches without benefit of liturgical roots. Still others are charismatic churches within other denominations, mixing both a liturgical and charismatic worship style.

Wherever church life is vital and advancing, however, the same characteristics are universally found: an expectation that God will work, a passionate pursuit of the fullness of the Lord's presence, and a readiness to minister the gifts of the Holy Spirit by worshipers committed to being filled.

—Scott G. Bauer

Worship in the African-American Church

Worship in the black church hinges on a strong faith in the love and sovereign power of Almighty God. Because of the injustice and inhumane treatment they suffered in America, blacks have seen a connection between themselves and God's oppressed people, who suffered similar oppression in Egypt. In coming together for worship, blacks express their faith in God to unite them and heal them as a people.

Music and Singing

American blacks developed their church music as their special method of dealing with life in the midst of the poor economic and social conditions they experienced during the second half of the 1800s. The songs sung by the slaves while they suffered under the hands of their hard taskmasters expressed their longings for deliverance and their hope for a better day. The slaves used music as their vehicle for building courage and a strong faith in God. Once they became free, it was only natural that this powerful art would accompany them into the church and be preserved as a major influence.

Black gospel music has become the most well-known and popular form of music in the black church, with its joyful message of salvation and inspiration. The name "black gospel" brings to mind Sunday morning worship services with a pulsating Hammond organ and a soul-stirring, energetic choir. The congregation often sings with the choir. It is common to hear such audible responses as "Amen," "Yes Lord," "Sing it," "All right now," and other similar phrases during singing. Some people may stand, sway with the music, clap, weep silently, or even dance. These responses show the music has touched the depths of the soul.

Music in the black church is intensely creative. Musicians often play without written music, inventing runs and chords as they go. The spiritual atmosphere usually dictates the type, intensity, and length of a song (or the entire worship service), with the fluctuating volume levels lifting the congregation into higher realms of praise.

The choruses of many gospel songs may be sung over and over again without boring the congregation. Out of each repetition evolves a higher emotional experience. Sometimes new verses and tunes will be created and added to a song while it is being sung. To those unfamiliar with black culture, such worship may seem disorderly. However, full participation of the group is the goal.

Other Aspects

Several prayers may grace the worship. These usually include the pastor's prayer for the congregation, a prayer for healing, an offering prayer, a sermon prayer, and a believer's prayer.

Baptism and the Lord's Supper are the two most common ordinances. In most churches, the Lord's Supper is served once per month, usually on the first Sunday.

In the typical black church, the sermon will almost always be preceded by a song. The preacher, knowing the power of music, relies upon it to get the congregation in the mood for what is about to be spoken from God's Word. The congregation usually continues its vocal responses (begun during the time of singing) while the pastor is preaching. The preacher expects this.

Involved Worship

Blacks have learned through experience that true worship must involve each person as well as God himself. Worship on Sunday morning is a time of unrehearsed celebration, in which one's name, age, color, and occupation doesn't matter. All are one, and all have the same objective. Those who have no voice in the outside world can speak, leap for joy, and sing and shout, because they are worshipping God—the impartial God, the Champion of the oppressed.

—James E. Martin

11

Prayer

Let us pray" is an invitation to do something. It contrasts with "Shall we pray?" or "Will you pray with me?" by being more than a mere inquiry. When congregations hear those latter two questions, they have a right to ask, "Well, shall we?" or "Indeed, will I?" But because prayer is intrinsic to public worship, not optional, the invitation to pray—Let us!—takes on the tone of a heavenly directive.

The one who extends this invitation is a host who prepares for the invited guests. If those who lead the people in their praying are conscious of this host-guest relationship, they will not be casual in preparation, "off the cuff" in language used, or "spur of the moment" in developing the prayer's content. These leaders of public prayer will find themselves standing in a tradition that reaches far back into New Testament history.

The History of Public Praying

● *The deacon as historical forerunner.* The one who leads congregational praying—the host of this event—has an antecedent in the office of the deacon in the early church, showing that the leader of the people at prayer need not be clergy. The deacon was not a presbyter (or priest), but a special servant of the bishop attending the needs of people. Originally designated simply as one serving at the table, the deacon became the "floor manager" of the assembly and had specific responsibility for leading the intercessions following the sermon and

157

the dismissal of those preparing to be baptized. Since the deacon directed the outreach mission of the church and coordinated the pastoral works of charity, he or she knew best what the needs were and how to bring them to prayer.

Thus, the deacon, the host of the assembly at prayer, was the link between the people and the world, between the people and the times in which they lived, and among the people and their needs as a congregation. The knowledge of the way things were going, most notably embodied in the deacon, was the way the world, the times, and the needs gained access to the Christian ears and hearts—and eventually the hands—that could help. Through the prayers of the people of God, the world and the times were put in relation to God. In keeping with patristic thought, prayer was understood to have been one of the primary ways the world was preserved so that all people might have an opportunity to hear the gospel and confess Jesus Christ as Lord.

• *Today's prayer leader as successor to the deacon.* He or she who is the host in the assembly of people at prayer, whether clergy or lay, is the successor to this historic deacon's role. Since it was the deacon who announced the needs for prayer and made the assignments of charity for the needy, it is this deacon who became the model of leadership at public prayer.

No doubt the litany, a form of antiphonal praying, got its start here. The deacon might have suggested several needs under certain categories (for example, the sick, the imprisoned, those in authority). At the end of each category, the people might have responded with something like, "Lord, have mercy" (*Kyrie Eleison*) or "Lord, hear our prayer," a later expression.

Roots of this form of praying can be found in Scripture as, for example, the repeated response in Psalm 136, "His love endures forever." Other scriptural examples could include the cry "Spare your people, O Lord," in Joel 2:17, and the repeated phrase "Let them give thanks to the Lord for his unfailing love and his wonderful deeds for men," in Psalm 107. The publican's cry, "God have mercy on me a sinner" (Luke 18:13) had a fixed liturgical character already in its scriptural setting.

• *Form as leading to freedom.* What began *ex tempora*—out of the times—likely had a somewhat impromptu character, dealing in the immediacy of fresh news and needs. But the deacon who led the people in their prayers also prayed out of a tradition that supplied memorable phrases (*Kyrie Eleison*, "Lord have mercy;" *Maranatha*, "Our Lord come"); confessional statements ("Jesus is Lord!"); entire prayers (the Lord's Prayer, which Tertullian called the epitome of Christian teaching, and the prayers of Paul); Psalms; and, of course, the stories of Jesus' ministry.

Early on, the *Didache* gave a form of worship for the celebration of the Lord's Supper, including a prayer of thanksgiving to be said after receiving the Eucharist. Such forms release a language into the living stream of tradition, and while language may not necessarily be repeated verbatim, it is repeated in terms of themes and motifs. Thus, while improvisation is done impromptu, it is not done in scorn of the tradition that sets its boundaries.

• *Jesus as exemplar.* When the disciples asked Jesus to teach them how to pray, he did not. No technique was offered. He simply taught them a prayer, the one we call the Lord's Prayer. We can assume, then, that we can learn to pray by learning prayers. Isaiah had said the Lord had given him "an instructed tongue, to know the word that sustains the weary" (Isa. 50:4a). Leaders of people at prayer can have their tongues instructed by reading the Scriptures and by praying the classic prayers found in such books as *The Lutheran Book of Worship* or the *Book of Common Prayer* of the Episcopal Church. One not only learns the prayer, one lives the prayer and finds the prayer even begins to pray the person, if one may speak that way. For example:

> Almighty and everlasting God, you are always more ready to hear than we are to pray, and to give more than we either desire or deserve: Pour upon us the abundance of your mercy, forgiving those things of which our conscience is afraid, and giving us those good things for which we are not worthy to ask, except through the merits and mediation of Jesus Christ Our Savior; who lives and reigns with you and the Holy Spirit, one God forever and ever. Amen. (*Book of Common Prayer*, 234)

The one who leads the people in prayer puts words into their mouths, feelings into their hearts, and thoughts into their heads. Under most circumstances this might be considered an invasion of privacy or a form of mind control, so prayer leaders need to be schooled in prayer so that the stewardship of this responsibility is carried out with integrity and with a minimum projection of personal ideology and needs. The mind of the people is to become captive to Christ, not the leader.

Two Forms of Public Praying

• *The collect.* Prayer leaders need to know how to construct their own public prayers. For example, often a worship service in a free church begins with an invocation. Such a prayer in the nonliturgical churches has its roots in the traditional collect. A collect, while a brief prayer, has a definite structure: (1) an address to God, (2) a relative clause referring to some characteristic of God, (3) a petition, (4) a result clause, and (5) a concluding doxology. Using this form, leaders of worship can craft prayers, classic in form and substance yet extempore in idiom and motif. Here is one of my own, with the respective parts numbered:

[1] Gracious God, [2] you hate nothing you have made and grudge existence to no one. [3] Fill us with such knowledge of your Word and love of your truth [4] that we may both discern and do what your Word teaches and truth demands of us, [5] through Jesus Christ our Lord, who lives and rules with you and the Holy Spirit, one God forever. Amen.

More recently, the worship books of the major traditions, both liturgical and nonliturgical, have substituted "Prayer for the Day" for the collect. Not only is the expression more intelligible upon seeing it, it puts integration front and center: What is prayed in this prayer sets the theme for the entire service. It serves as the plumb line to test the unity of all of the component parts of the service.

• *The pastoral prayer, or prayers of the people.* In the nonliturgical churches, the main form of prayer has been called the "pastoral prayer." Traditionally, it has been a comprehensive prayer that includes confession, thanksgiving, and petitions, offered by the pastor, usually following the reading of the Scriptures.

The practice of one comprehensive prayer seems to have emerged

---

Invocations

The invocation is the opening prayer of a worship service. It requests God's blessing and calls worshipers to recognize the presence of God among them. An effective invocation helps people begin their worship with holy anticipation, thinking, *What does God have in store for this hour today?* As you pray, the worshiper's attention turns from self, the creature, to the mystery and majesty of the Creator.

Tone and Direction

When a judge enters the courtroom, a voice calls out, "All rise," and an almost tangible attitude of respect descends upon the room. In the same way, your invocation calls out, "Let us lift up our hearts; the Lord God Almighty is in our midst." Such a statement ushers expectant worshipers into the presence of an active, approachable Creator, imploring, "Do something mighty in us, Lord." Therefore, invocations should not sound chummy or overly familiar: "Good morning, Lord" or "We just wanna thank you."

An invocation has purpose; it requests something. Thus, it leads worshipers in a definite direction by having something to achieve. Peeling back the layers of lassitude and lethargy accumulated during the week, it exposes worshipers to the glory and grace of an infinite God who is intimately concerned with their lives.

Invocations often ask God to prod, lure, guide, touch, center, shape, direct, or edify. They begin with lines such as: "O God, who knows us better than we know ourselves," "O God of this day and every day," "Holy,

out of the Puritan reforms rooted more in the Congregational than in the Presbyterian tradition. Hughes Oliphant Old, a critic of this form of prayer, says it: (1) made one unbearably long prayer, tolerable only to the most mature Christians; (2) disturbed the ancient order by putting the prayer between the Scripture reading and the sermon; (3) diminished the specifically intercessory character of prayer by conflating many types of prayer; and (4) made the prayer too dependent on the personal gifts and skills of the pastor (Old 1984, 101). Nevertheless, vast segments of the Protestant churches retain little other praying than the pastoral prayer during their services of worship, though a brief invocation may open the service and an offertory prayer bless the offering.

In the mainline churches of free church orientation, however, a shift is taking place. The pastoral prayer is being reconsidered and reconfigured into the more classical form of "the prayers of the people," led either by clergy or laity. Structured in dialogue form, but not exclusive of spontaneity, it is placed following the sermon.

Thus, the pastoral prayer (or prayers of the people) is returning to

---

holy, holy, Lord, God of Hosts." The worshiper stands face to face with the God who has done—and continues to do—mighty things.

Themes and Words

Like all other worship prayers, invocations fit into an order of worship with a theme and direction determined by the liturgical year, the national year, biblical emphases, or local events. When wrapped in the worship theme, invocations blend cohesively, emphasize the main objective, and gain greater weight by virtue of their association with an overall purpose. Suggestive of things to come, they are forerunners of themes that will unfold in the service.

How should you word your invocations? Try to use the clearest, most compelling language you can muster, while maintaining the essential dignity of your task. For example, a Christmas invocation could begin: "O God of self-disclosure, who in Bethlehem's manger fulfilled all prophecy, fulfill your will in us today as we worship and pray." For a worship service centered on the family, consider: "Holy God, who planted us in families to bring us to maturity and teach us to love, so enter this family of faith today, that through our worship, we may be led into good works for all the family of this needy earth."

Remember that an invocation is an introducer, not the high point of worship. It is a prayer that ushers worshipers into the presence of the Most High God. As worship leader you are a facilitator with the Holy Spirit in high transactions of the soul. Let every word count as you point to the way that is life, the love that is forever, the truth that cannot be vanquished, the God who bids us come.

—*E. Lee Phillips*

its classic place, namely, after the sermon as a response to the Word, as a prelude to going forth unto the world's people, for whose preservation and salvation the people of God continue to pray. Such a position also places this season of prayer nearer to the Holy Communion and to the offertory.

How to Lead Public Praying

• *A significant contrast.* Leading public prayer is not the same activity as praying when someone asks, "Will you lead in prayer?" This request usually has something to do with getting a meeting started. Such praying is usually off-the-cuff. Not only is this prayer offered in haste and without preparation, it is one person's prayer alone. It has little to do with leading others in praying.

Prayers of Confession

Properly done, the confession of sin followed by the assurance of pardon can be a comforting and exhilarating element of worship. Coming into the awesome presence of God naturally produces a sense of humility. The recognition of unworthiness in the presence of holiness prompts us to pause in repentance. Since we are spiritually tainted, we need to be cleansed and forgiven before entering into the presence of the holy God.

Like the publican in our Lord's parable, we come with a humble heart and declare, "Lord, be merciful to me a sinner." Yet, the fact that we are sinners who need to be forgiven should not detract from a positive affirmation of God's grace. To feel cleansed of guilt for irreparable and persistent sin is the unique experience of all who stand in the shadow of the Cross. To arise from one's knees (spiritually, if not physically) a new creature, healed and

reconciled, is cause for rejoicing. When this takes place early in the worship service, it prepares us for the special presence of God in the rest of our worship actions.

Confessing Appropriately

The prayer of confession need not be long or detailed. It can be a silent prayer inwardly voiced by each individual worshiper, or it may be a corporate prayer expressed aloud, either in unison or by the liturgist on behalf of all. If it is done corporately, we need to keep the terms generic. After all, everyone has not committed the same specific sins in a given period of time. All, however, can confess our pride, selfishness, and ungodly thoughts. Also, since this is a *personal* prayer for forgiveness, based on confession of known and recognized sins in individual lives, it isn't appropriate to use this prayer to make people feel guilty of

By contrast, leading public prayer in Christian worship is precisely that: leading the people, not just in prayer, but in praying. "Let us pray" helps define the task's true character. The pronoun *us* is plural, including the leader and the people. The leader acts representatively, enabling others to pray in and through the prayer offered on their behalf. Such prayers are not substitutes for the prayers of the people, not replacements for their prayers, but rather the vehicles of their prayers.

There is every reason to announce, "Let us pray," and then go to work, to the hard work of a "face to face" with God. In the presence of God we then come face to face with ourselves, the ministry of our church, and the needy world. Again, we do not lead in prayer; we lead the people in praying.

- *An essential conviction.* How does one lead the people in praying?

---

specific social sins about which *we* may have strong personal feelings.

Varieties of Confessions

Prayers of confession find their place in all of the printed liturgies of the historic church. Consider this classic liturgical confession:

> Almighty and most merciful Father, we have erred and strayed from thy ways like lost sheep. We have followed too much the devices and desires of our own hearts. We have offended against thy holy laws. We have left undone those things which we ought to have done, and we have done those things which we ought not to have done. But thou, O Lord, have mercy upon us. Restore us who come with penitent spirit according to thy promises declared unto mankind in Christ Jesus, our Lord. And grant that we may hereafter live a godly and righteous life; to the glory of thy holy Name.

A prayer of confession may also be sung by the choir or a soloist. Here are a few anthems that could be used in this way:

- "At Thy Feet We Humbly Kneel"—J. S. Bach
- "Create in Me a Clean Heart, O God"—Mueller
- "Create in Me a Clean Heart, O God"—Hopson
- "I Lay My Sins on Jesus"—W. Engelbrekt

Many traditional hymns as well as contemporary songs work well to bring a confessional element to worship. For example:

- "Pass Me Not, O Gentle Saviour"
- "Just as I Am, Kind and Merciful God"
- "Dear Lord and Father of Mankind"

Musical settings of Psalm 51 are especially appropriate.

It's challenging to be especially fresh and creative in the early part of the worship service as we bring the people together for cleansing and renewal. But starting with confession to their Lord will free worshipers to express the depth of their adoration for him.

—*Arthur DeKruyter*

First, by being convinced of the importance of the task. There have been preachers known for their prayers as well as their sermons. Ernest Fremont Tittle of First Methodist Church, Evanston, Illinois, wrote an essay on the pastoral prayer, arguing that pastors needed to prepare their prayers with as much rigor as they composed their sermons. After-worship conversations had convinced him that often his prayers had had more impact than his preaching (Tittle 1951, 10–11).

Roger Hazelton argued that the glorification of the sermon, so central to Protestantism and so high on the pastor's agenda, may have produced better sermons but spelled disaster for the pastoral prayer (Hazelton 1943, 2). Harry Emerson Fosdick advised his colleagues to remember that extempore spontaneity is not the only alternative to printed liturgies. Thoughtful, skillful preparation of the prayers is always an option (Fosdick 1959, 8).

● *A look at creativity.* The prayers of the people can be led in a variety of ways, but all of the ways assume significant preparation. Since praying is the work of the people, the leader must find creative ways to enable the people to do just that—to pray.

Again, a set of categories did emerge in church history to guide the people's intercessions, and eventually these became part of the classic litany. The categories that seemed to guide the praying were prayers for: (1) the church, (2) the salvation of the world, (3) deliverance of the poor, (4) growth in human and Christian virtues, (5) the needs of individuals and groups of people, and (6) the commemoration of the dead and grace to persevere to the end (Mitchell 1985, 66, 137–138; Mazziotta 1984, 16).

Such praying remains nonparochial by keeping church and world in relation. It takes personal interest in the needs of people, keeping present experience connected with the blessed hope. If we learn the basic elements of this form, we can be freed to lead the prayers, knowing that such praying will balance church and world, the personal and the communal, the present and the future. The form, then, is a plumb line for inclusiveness, not a straitjacket imposed on one's creativity.

As to enabling all to pray, the leader has several options. He or she may present several petitions within the aforementioned categories, allowing enough time for the people to pray for each petition in silence. When a more fixed form of the litany is to be used, the leader can say something like, "Let us pray for our world: For peace in Northern Ireland; for healing and justice in South Africa; for a just settlement of political and religious issues in the Middle East, let us pray to the Lord."

The people can answer, "Lord, in your mercy, hear our prayer." And so it continues.

People can even be encouraged to add their own petitions in each category, saying, "For [people respond with needs], let us pray to the Lord." The response would be the same. For variety, people can sing the response, using a simple and familiar musical line.

Another option is to announce the petitions and invite people to offer prayers aloud, one by one, for each of the concerns. (This requires time and some sensitivity, because some personalities tend to dominate such occasions.)

Yet another method enables each to pray *audibly*, yet all to pray in common. The one leading the prayer invites the people to voice their prayers simultaneously, once needs are announced. This method has about it an appealing, powerful auditory element, as each in his or her own words prays for the needs of others in sounds not uniform, not in unison, but in unity of spirit and prayer.

Whichever form of intercession is employed, the leader can conclude the time of prayer with a brief collect, perhaps inviting people, with the words used in the ancient church, "boldly to pray the prayer our Savior Christ taught us," leading into the Lord's Prayer.

Resources for Public Praying

The worship or liturgical books of the various traditions are repositories of classic prayers. The following books make fine additions to the worship leader's bookshelf:

- *A Guide to Prayer* (Nashville: The Upper Room)
- *Book of Common Prayer* (New York: The Seabury Press) (Episcopal)
- *Book of Worship* (New York: Office for Church Life and Leadership of the United Church of Christ)
- *The Lutheran Book of Worship* (Minneapolis: Augsburg Publishing House)
- *The Service for the Lord's Day: Supplemental Liturgical Resource 1* (Philadelphia: Westminster Press) (Presbyterian)
- *Thankful Praise* (St. Louis: CBP Press) (Disciples of Christ)

Having been led in praying, let us be led by what we have prayed into discernment, direction, and duty.

—*C. John Weborg*

Resources

Book of common prayer. New York: Seabury.

Erickson, C. 1989. Participation in worship. Louisville: Westminster-John Knox.

Fosdick, H. 1959. A book of public prayers. New York: Harper and Brothers.

Hazelton, R. 1943. The root and flower of prayer. New York: Macmillan.

Mazziotta, R., C.S.C. 1984. We pray to the Lord. Notre Dame: Ave Maria.

Mitchell, L. 1985. Praying that shapes believing. Chicago, et al.: Winston.

Old, H. 1984. Guides to the Reformed tradition. Atlanta: John Knox.

Tittle, E. 1951. A book of pastoral prayers. New York and Nashville: Abingdon-Cokesbury.

The Pastoral Prayer

The pastoral prayer is the most important prayer in the services of all but the liturgical churches (in which the eucharistic prayer takes preeminence). As direct communication with God, it is the heart of worship. C. H. Spurgeon said that if he had time for only the sermon or the pastoral prayer in a service, the pastoral prayer would remain.

Where and By Whom

In free church traditions, the pastoral prayer comes early in the service to help prepare people for the hearing of the sermon; in Reformed and liturgical churches, it usually comes after the sermon as a response to the preached Word.

Although laity lead this prayer in some congregations, normally the pastor gives this prayer. In it the pastor acts as priest for the people, as Moses did in Israel's history. Because of their training and generally better command of language, pastors can articulate the praises and petitions that people may feel but may be hesitant or unable to express.

In any event, although the pastor usually says the prayer, it should be a prayer *of the people*, one to which they can state a hearty "Amen!"

The Classic Structure

The pastoral prayer is the most complete prayer in the service and usually includes all the parts of prayer:

It begins with praise of God for who he is. This might not be more than a phrase or sentence, and it of-ten is incorporated into the address, for example: "Eternal and glorious heavenly Father . . ."

Then the prayer moves on to thanksgiving, remembering what God has done for us, and then comes confession (unless done earlier), emphasizing how we have abused or taken for granted his goodness.

Next this prayer turns to petition and intercession, which are nearly indistinguishable in the pastoral prayer. Here all concerns—within or outside the congregation—are mentioned, usually according to the following categories:

• The universal church and all its members.
• Those in authority, from the President to the local city council.
• The welfare of the world—political, social, and even environmental.
• Missionaries.
• The church and its leaders: denominational officers, pastors, deacons, and elders.
• Members and friends of the congregation.

Specific concerns often arise out of specific requests, which people volunteer just before the prayer in some churches. In a bidding prayer, one variation of the pastoral prayer, the pastor mentions a subject and then pauses for people to pray silently.

Theme

Given its scope and meaning, the pastoral prayer should be prepared as well as, if not better than, the sermon. To some that means writing the prayer out word for word; for others it means thinking carefully ahead of time about what will be said.

In either case, choosing and developing a theme is vital to holding the attention of the people and securing their "Amen" to the prayer. The theme may be based on the sermon; for example, accompanying a sermon on grace can be a prayer that praises and thanks God for his grace, confesses our taking that grace for granted, and asks that his healing and reconciling grace touch people's lives.

The theme may also be structured around the liturgical season or even a secular holiday—appropriately baptized! Although the theme can be generic—crafted on the goodness of God and the needs of his people—a pastoral prayer often is most effective when it is built thoughtfully upon a specific theme.

— *Mark Galli*

The Prayer Meeting

Some so-called prayer meetings today are not really meetings *for prayer*. Typically, the pastor leads a service that focuses on lengthy Bible study, relegating a brief period for actual prayer. The sense of purpose is often weak. Unity is minimal.

So what can a pastor do to revitalize the local prayer meeting?

Recalling the New Testament Prayer Meeting

A limited survey of the New Testament reveals three broad principles to keep in mind:

● *New Testament gatherings gave priority to prayer.* Luke's gospel begins with "all the assembled worshipers" concentrating on praying outside the temple (Luke 1:10). In Acts the believers were "continually devoting themselves to prayer" (Acts 1:14 NASB). There is no hint of a Bible-study format or a sermon dominating these gatherings.

● *New Testament prayer meetings were highly participatory.* The post-Ascension prayer meeting described in Acts 1:14 involved "all" who were present. No one was a mere observer. Similarly, Luke stresses that after Pentecost, prayer gatherings included all the new converts (Acts 2:41–42; 4:23–24).

● *New Testament "pray-ers" met in unity.* The congregants were "in one accord" about the purpose of their prayer meetings. For example, in Matthew 18:15–20, Jesus taught that the act of agreeing had church discipline as its purpose. After the Ascension the disciples became of one mind in asking for the coming of the Holy Spirit (see Acts 1:13–14; 4:23–24).

Renewing Today's Prayer Meeting

The key to undertaking a process of renewal in our prayer meetings is to educate and introduce new changes gradually. We could use the forty-minute "Bible Hour" in the typical prayer meeting to study prayer for a period of three months, basing our teaching on Luke-Acts and Matthew 18:15–20.

At the conclusion of this study,

regular members of the gathering can develop for themselves a definition of *prayer meeting* that emphasizes the prominence of prayer, the participatory nature of the prayer gathering, and the importance of seeking one-mindedness. From there, the meeting format can be reshaped to look something like this:

• *Opening.* Ten minutes (or less) to concentrate on building a common purpose.

• *Singing.* A hymn or chorus related to spiritual renewal.

• *Thanksgiving.* Ten minutes devoted to giving thanks for past answers to prayer.

• *Praying for ministry renewal.* Ten minutes given to local program and mission concerns.

• *Praying for personal problems.* Fifteen minutes devoted to health, financial, and family concerns.

• *Closing.* A hymn or chorus related to commitment.

Innovating to Meet Needs

Traditional forms of the prayer meeting are not sacred, so churches can innovate to meet special needs. One church, for instance, scheduled a two-hour meeting on Sunday evenings from 5:00 to 7:00. The first hour is given exclusively to seeking grace for personal revival and missionary outreach into the community. The second hour is spent building unity through confessing sins and weaknesses, and engaging each member in a radical commitment to kingdom service.

Another congregation found many members could meet together for prayer on Wednesdays from 5 to 6 A.M. Now about a hundred people gather with a pastor for an hour that is broken into ten segments of six minutes each that alternate between private and public prayer.

It's true that our prayer-meeting practice may need some overhauling. But we can be sure the believers will still gather to pray — often in large numbers — if our prayer meetings have clear purpose and are grounded in the biblical mandate to "pray without ceasing."

—C. John Miller

Prayer Vigils

The prayer vigil is centuries old, but it can still open the door to a new dimension of prayer, allowing a fresh breeze of the Spirit to blow across your congregation.

Benefits

"Can't we just pray at home?" some might ask when a church proposes a prayer vigil. Not if they want the unique advantages of a vigil. The special feeling of praying in the sanctuary lifts this hour above people's sometimes-discouraging experiences of prayer at home, where there might be many distractions and interruptions. When they come to the quiet sanctuary, they seem to sense God's presence.

Benefits endure as well. A vigil teaches people to intercede for one another. Prayer vigils often renew a Christian's desire to pray at home. Christians also find a new longing to spend time before the Lord.

Prayer Resources

Some people hesitate to commit themselves for a lengthy time, such as an hour, because they feel inadequate at prayer; they don't want to set themselves up to fail like the disciples in the Garden.

To allay those fears, a church can offer suggestions on what to do during a prayer vigil. Here are a few:

• Bring things to help you talk with God: your Bible, a hymnal, the church directory, and the church's current prayer list.

• Be yourself. Talk to God as you would talk to your best friend.

• Get comfortable. The stiffer you feel, the more formal your relationship will be. Sitting is fine. If kneeling helps, do it.

• Try praying out loud, though not loud enough to disturb others. Being able to hear yourself pray improves your concentration, and you'll find your mind doesn't wander as easily.

• Don't feel you have to do all the talking. Discuss something with the Lord, and then be silent. Sometimes God uses the times of listening to implant his answers in our minds. Gradually you'll find prayer can be a conversation.

An Hour of Prayer

The following suggestions help people fill their prayer time meaningfully. People's times may differ, but if they are given times and instructions such as these, they can get started.

Preparation (one minute): Ask God to help you spend this time profitably with him.

Confession (four minutes): Spend a moment going over with him recent sins that weigh on you. Ask for his cleansing, accept it by faith, and thank him for it.

Praise and thanksgiving (nine minutes): Sing your adoration to the Lord using a hymnal or choruses you know. As your heart begins to adore him, you'll sense his presence more deeply.

Petition (nine minutes): Pray about life's difficulties. Use this time to talk over with the Lord your own struggles.

Intercession (nine minutes): Pray for friends, loved ones, relatives, neighbors, fellow workers. Don't just read a list of names to God, but talk to him about their lives and needs.

Prayer for the church (twelve minutes): Pray for your pastor and church leaders. Intercede for the Sunday school children and the youth, the families, the singles, the widows, the sick, the shut-ins.

Prayer for the nation (eight minutes): Pray that God will guide our public officials and those who serve our communities. Pray for righteousness in government and a public policy sensitive to true justice.

Prayer for other nations (eight minutes): Pray for the work of Christ throughout the world. Intercede for unreached peoples. Pray for missionaries, for Third World pastors and churches, for the people of God who are suffering persecution. Pray for peace.

As people see how they actually can pray for an hour, they're more willing to risk it. After one successful experience, they'll be eager to sign up the next time.

— *Ralph F. Wilson*

12

Planning Worship

W orship is the adoration and praise of that which delights us," writes John Piper. "We praise what we enjoy, because praise completes the enjoyment. We worship God for the pleasure to be had in him."

The challenge in worship, however, is to discover continual enjoyment in an oft-repeated exercise. How can we combat the propensity to let the heaven-directed activity of worship fall into dullness and routine? How can we do justice to this exalted calling when it falls to us to plan and lead it week after week, year after year?

For worship leaders, Sunday seems to come every three days. It's like a voracious animal that consumes all our efforts and then wants more. Trying to find freshness and newness in worship constantly challenges us. Here are some of the procedures I have found helpful as I plan a worship service.

Finding the Focal Point

It's good to center worship around a theme — a focal point or central idea that gives the service sequence and depth. Sometimes the theme is supplied by the season of the year: Advent or Lent or Easter or Thanksgiving. Other times a special church emphasis, such as a missions month or family Sunday, suggests worship themes.

Of course, the sermon topic is a natural focal point. If the topic happens to be "God's Faithfulness" or "The Love of God" or "God's

Sovereignty," it is not difficult to blend the hymns, anthems, and the spoken word with the sermon.

The pastor and the worship leader need to communicate regularly about sermon plans. For instance, in memos and conversations, my pastor and I discuss sermon title, passage of Scripture, central thought, key words or phrases that might be repeated or underscored in the message, songs and hymn texts that have come to mind in his planning and preparation, and other worship ideas or suggestions.

Sometimes it's asking too much to know this detailed information weeks and months in advance. Also, it's not easy to highlight every sermon subject. (I recall a three-week sermon series from Ecclesiastes that focused on various characteristics of "The Foolish Man.") It's also difficult to coordinate worship and sermon when the preacher exposits Scripture verse by verse.

Consequently, over the years I've discovered the worship portion of the service doesn't have to be connected with the sermon; it can have a life of its own. This has been a liberating concept. When that's the case, I often let the theme of the choir anthem become the theme of worship, and I fit the other parts of worship into it.

In any case, when we focus on one theme, people can come to the end of the worship time drawn together and to God.

Listing the Worship Resources

After determining the focal point of worship, try taking a yellow pad to list all the available resources for that theme. When I do that, I first turn to four or five hymn books I keep by my desk. I go to the topical index and the Scripture-reference index, and I list all the hymns that might contribute to the worship theme. It matters not whether the song is known to our congregation, because a hymn can be used in several ways. It can be paraphrased in prayer, read by the congregation, recited by the leader, sung to another tune in the same meter, used as a solo, or played by an instrumental musician.

Next, list all the appropriate worship choruses. The interjection of these memorized and more personal songs often adds a delightful note of spontaneity and freshness. I keep a list of song titles at hand to avoid having to go through ten or a dozen of the latest spiral-bound booklets.

Then, read the Scripture text in several translations, versions, and paraphrases. I also use a topical Bible and a concordance, both of which help me locate related passages that can be used in prayer or during transitions in worship. Related readings and poems provide still another helpful source of fresh language.

Finally, review the various means of presenting these items: the spoken word, the choir, a pipe organ, people who can read interpretively, soloists and instrumentalists, a readers group, handbells, children's choirs, and the whole congregation.

This exercise with the yellow pad almost always will produce more material than we ever could use in one service, but the process of listing these resources helps stoke creativity.

Exploring All the Possibilities

As you plan corporate worship week after week, one principle to constantly remember is this: The higher the predictability, the lower the impact. Therefore, try to look at each element of worship from different angles to see how it might be approached freshly or arranged in creative combinations with other elements.

For instance, with a Scripture reading I ask myself: *How can this passage make a special impact on these people who routinely sit in this room Sunday after Sunday? Does it always have to be read as a monologue? Can it be read responsively by two people? Can it be sung? Can it be read dramatically by a practiced readers team? Is this a conversation between one, two, four people? Is there a crowd involved that the choir could represent? Can the prophet shout or call from some distant vantage point in the room? Can different people in the congregation stand and proclaim God's Word from where they are?*

Once when we read the Parable of the Sower, we had four different voices each take one soil and read that portion and its interpretation. Another time the choir shouted, "Hosanna to the Son of David!" during a reading for Palm Sunday. Another time still, a "prophet" declared from somewhere in the organ chambers, "Prepare ye the way of the Lord; make straight in the desert a highway for our God!"

The text can be taken directly from a particular Bible translation or rewritten as a contemporary paraphrase. Or combine a variety of passages into a mosaic of Scripture. You can also weave together Scripture and music by interspersing hymn stanzas among portions of the Psalms, for instance.

Likewise, use prayer creatively. Although normally one person prays publicly in a service, sometimes several people can lead in prayer, one after the other, in turn praying prayers of adoration, confession, intercession, petition, and thanksgiving.

Still another idea: guided silent prayer. Or how about two, three, or four different places in one service for prayer? Or try taking a hymn that has just been sung and "pray the hymn," using the words of the hymn as the basis for the organization and content of a spoken prayer. All the elements of worship lend themselves to creative treatment.

After this exploration, begin to design a sequence of events that has logic and flow. When I do this, I am reminded of the difference between a streamlined passenger train and a freight train. A freight train is just a number of cars of all descriptions, linked together but with gaps between. From within a streamlined passenger train, on the other hand, people experience the cars as clearly connected. Passengers easily walk from one car to another even as the train is moving at high speeds. Make worship like a streamlined passenger train—intellectually, emotionally, and spiritually continuous. That type of service, I believe, engages people most meaningfully.

As I think about the placement of various events in the drama of worship, several key principles emerge.

Focusing Attention

I have learned to appreciate a plan that I inherited when I came to First Evangelical Free Church in Fullerton in 1980. Just before we begin worship, our people are warmly greeting and talking to one

---

The Time and Day of Worship

If the eleventh commandment is "Thou shalt worship the Lord thy God at 11:00 A.M. on Sunday," the twelfth commandment must be "Thou shalt finish worshiping the Lord thy God at 12:00 noon sharp." Or so it seems.

While Sunday morning is an appropriate time to worship God, it is certainly not the only time to worship. The Scriptures imply that the early church met on Sundays *and* on the rest of the week (Acts 2:46).

Advantages and Disadvantages

Here are some of the advantages of offering alternative times and days for worship:

• *The ability to vary services.* Not everyone is comfortable in a traditional worship service, nor is everyone comfortable in a contemporary service. If a church is committed to one style of ministry, some people will be left out. By having multiple services that are different, a church reaches out to new people groups.

• *A choice of times and formats.* Multiple services enable people to decide when and how they will worship. For example, at our church "Saturday Night" is contemporary and nontraditional. Sunday morning is traditional, with the focus on teaching. Sunday night is informal, with extended exposition of the Bible. I repeat the Sunday night sermon on Wednesday night and encourage people to come back either Sunday night or Wednesday night, but not both.

• *The prudent use of facilities.* When a church grows beyond the confines of its worship space, one solution is to build a bigger room. However, adding multiple services enables the church to continue growing without putting major dollars into bricks and mortar. A sanctuary that seats 200 can, in a typical week, easily accommodate 800 to 1,000

another, both in and out of the sanctuary. Though there is organ music, it is not, as in many churches, a signal for silence in the pews.

A few minutes before the stated beginning time, one of our pastoral staff comes to the platform to greet people, underscore some announcements, and then encourage people to examine the bulletin, open their hymnals, and collect their thoughts for worship. Then the organist draws the veil of quietness with thirty to forty-five seconds of musical accompaniment, perhaps employing a hymn that will be used, a related musical thought, or a short praise chorus.

Worship then can begin, but again, in a variety of ways. Sometimes we open quietly with the singing of a simple chorus, sometimes majestically with brass and timpani, sometimes formally, sometimes informally, sometimes with an anthem, sometimes with a reading or a Scripture passage. But in any case, the mind and spirit are focused on the occasion at hand: worship.

---

people in various services.

The greatest disadvantage of holding alternative services is a perceived lack of unity or oneness among the membership. Alternative services tend to create separate congregations using the same facility.

For example, our "Saturday Night" is, in reality, a separate church. The two Sunday morning services are really two separate churches. Churches need to explore ways to overcome this, such as renting a larger facility to bring all the separate "congregations" together for a worship and praise service at regular intervals.

How It Can Work

Our church has two traditional Sunday morning services of worship, and we're adding a third. Several years ago we started the Saturday night service that, for lack of a better name, we called "Saturday Night." This offering is anything but traditional. We use a live band that plays contemporary music. We employ drama. Dressed in blue jeans and sitting on a bar stool (renamed a church stool), I give a talk, and at the end I answer questions from the audience.

Such a format draws people. We average over 600 in attendance, and more than 50 percent are unchurched, so their only exposure to church is "Saturday Night." The service has become a haven for the hurting and abused, a place of healing for people with bad religious experiences, and a place of safety for skeptics and seekers. It is radically different than any service on Sunday.

Offering alternative services is not easy. Preaching in multiple services demands much of preachers. Churches have to recruit volunteers for each additional service. Service people (child-care workers, ushers, parking lot directors, musicians, greeters) burn out quickly. Yet, for many churches the great benefit of reaching out to entirely new groups of seekers offsets the burden of added work.

—*Edward G. Dobson*

Once we positioned one of our soloists six to eight rows back in the congregation and gave her a cordless lapel mike. At a preplanned point, she started to sing while seated, without accompaniment, without music in hand, "Brethren, we have met to worship." After singing a phrase or two, she stood and continued singing as quiet support from the organ joined her. She slowly moved down the aisle to the steps and faced her brothers and sisters, encouraging them in song to "love God supremely" and "pray with expectation as we preach the living Word." As the song came to a close, she moved back to her seat, singing as she sat down, repeating, now a cappella, "Brethren, we have met to worship / To adore the Lord, our God." All was quiet; no one dared breathe; we were brought face to face with the supreme privilege and responsibility of worship.

Services Not on Sunday Morning

"I like the Sunday night service better than the Sunday morning worship because it's more relaxed and less formal." So said a church member, and others echoed the comment.

"My favorite event of the week is the Wednesday evening dinner and prayer groups," said another.

Traditionally, churches have met on Sunday mornings for their major worship services. In all likelihood, that tradition will continue. But what are some alternatives for those congregations wanting to continue or add regular meeting times other than Sunday morning?

Sunday Nights

In many locations the standard Sunday evening worship service has fallen upon hard times. Churches that draw people from broad surrounding areas find those members reluctant to travel to the church building twice on Sunday. For this and other reasons, some churches have settled on implementing specialized ministries for Sunday evening, either in the church facilities, in home groups, or in various community locations.

Single adults, college students, youth, and other homogeneous segments of society are the recipients of such target ministries, which emphasize informality and mutual support-oriented agendas. Usually participants enjoy a light snack and enter into significant conversation and sharing of personal concerns.

Other churches emphasize Christian education, using a short-term seminar approach. Four- to six-week topical courses on such matters as family life, ethics, parenting, or doctrine draw interested members for limited slots of time they can fit into busy work and family schedules. The advantage? Participants need commit only to a limited number of sessions. Specific events and topics can be promoted so as to maximize their potential and secure individual response.

Remembering Content and Flow

After we focus people's attention, the rest of the service can develop in countless ways, but with two overriding principles guiding the planning: logical content and emotional flow.

We want the content of the songs, readings, and prayers to contribute to the chosen theme. The task is to present a drama that unfolds in a reasonable sequence and helps us reflect on God—who he is and our relationship to him.

It is good for people to discover why a certain hymn was chosen, what it contributes to the theme, why it was placed just there in the order of service, and how it relates to the Scripture just read or the prayer that will follow. Sometimes the pastor or worship leader can

---

What about a more traditional Sunday evening worship service? For the most part, these will be attended by members of the church, not by those who are in need of evangelization. This usually commends a less formal worship style geared to Christian fellowship, music, expository Bible teaching, and congregational prayer. A service of this type should deepen believers' spiritual lives.

Midweek Opportunities

Another traditional event for many churches has been the Wednesday night prayer meeting. But now many congregations gather for a time of Bible study and prayer either on Wednesday night, on another weekday evening, or on an early midweek morning (say, 7 A.M.). Congregants share prayer requests, perhaps hear a short devotional by the pastor or lay leader, and then spend time in prayer. Occasionally, these meetings offer group members opportunity for sharing with one another about the ways God is working or leading in their lives. Some churches also invite members to come forward for prayer and anointing with oil for healing in body and spirit.

A growing number of churches have discovered the midweek dinner and prayer service. People can stop at the church facility on their way home from school or work and enjoy dinner with their Christian friends before worshiping or studying the Bible with them. After the dinner, to get the maximum benefit out of the evening, some churches hold their Sunday school teacher training sessions, committee meetings, children's choir, and other discipleship programs. Churches that have family life centers (with a gymnasium and game rooms) usually have a family night, focusing on fellowship and recreation.

The key is to keep our approach to regular, non-Sunday morning meetings creative and flexible. We must be open to the changing needs of our congregation and community, and listen to the suggestions of those who see unmet needs. Then we can proceed with confidence in Christ's ability to produce spiritual fruit.

—*Jerry Hayner*

supply that connection; other times we assume the worshipers will discern it.

At the beginning of a service, the goal is to establish the supremacy of God as the object of our worship. The thrust is God-directed, corporate worship. The pronouns of songs here usually will be "we," "us," and "our." Later in the service, occasions often arise for more personal expressions. Then congregational songs often will use "I," "me," and "my," drawing people to focus on their particular and individual relationships with God. This part of the service may be quieter and more reflective.

Emotional development is important. The service should not proceed in an emotional monotone; it should develop with a variety of intensity. If everything is quiet, somber, or reflective, the service may tend to feel listless. If everything is triumphant, with one grand climax after another, people may quickly tire.

We also want to avoid jarring emotional shifts. Continuity of worship means a natural flow from one part to another. Otherwise, the jerking from one mood to the next will distract people from worship.

Even the smallest details can be distracting. For example, when I intend to follow a prayer with a song, I usually try to think of a refrain or chorus that most people know by heart. Then, instead of interrupting the prayerful atmosphere with an abrupt, "Please turn to hymn number 492," I have the organist simply begin playing chord progressions to establish a key, and I start singing, "I love you, Lord, and I lift my voice. . . ." With a small cue or motion, I invite the congregation to join in.

Keeping It Personal

Unless we guard against it, worship can become mere performance, an impersonal presentation of words and songs. To counter this danger, we need to remember that, above all else, our worship must be authentic and personal.

We can sometimes lead worship from the floor of the sanctuary. That helps overcome the separation of leaders and congregation that the platform can foster. Or have people come from out of the pews to lead a portion of the service. Engage the congregation in some way.

As an example of this method, our pastor once was preaching a series on Great Questions — things asked by Jesus and asked about him. One week the question was, "Who is the greatest in the kingdom of heaven?" Jesus, of course, used a child to make his point.

I led some songs from the piano, and after about fifteen minutes, I had three children come forward. We talked about what Jesus thought of children, and I asked one of the girls to read the Scripture. I spoke briefly about some qualities of children that we never want to lose touch with: trust and the willingness to let others help. I also said we never want to lose the songs of childhood. Then the kids and I sang "Jesus Loves Me." A little touch like that helps make the service more personal.

Encouraging Participation

Sometimes people come to church and feel like they're watching worship instead of actually worshiping. We counter this spectatorism by giving people plenty of opportunities to participate — through singing, reading, and praying — and by using nonprofessionals for different parts of the service.

If a person stands from the pews to read a proclamation, in a sense everyone does it. Any time we move the participation away from the pulpit and professional staff, worship becomes less a show than a common undertaking of leaders and people.

We do the same when we involve people's hearts as well as their heads. I'm convinced there are too few points of genuine inspiration in most of our lives. I'll always remember the words of one man who asked to sing in our choir. "You know why I want to sing in the choir?" he began. "I'm an engineer, and I work with things I can measure, weigh, and feel. I'm inclined to take my spiritual life in much the same way — an inventory of knowledge and a cerebral concept of my Christian life. I need to learn to express the emotion of the gospel."

He was onto a great truth: We have an inner need to experience worship, not just to watch it.

Worshiping a Creative God, Forever

We seek variety, not for its own sake or because we want to put on a good show, but because we serve a God of infinite variety. We want to catch a glimpse of his face and his character from every possible angle. Each new revelation of truth and beauty, and every expression of love and concern, helps us understand him more.

Worship is the ceaseless activity of heaven; one day, it will be our eternal activity. The practice of worship here on earth is perhaps our most significant preparation for the life to come.

—Howard Stevenson

Resources

Causey, C. 1983. Open the doors to creativity in worship. Rockville, Md.: Music Revelation Press.

Hustad, D. 1980. Jubilate! Church music in the evangelical tradition. Carol Stream, Ill.: Hope.

Schaper, R. 1984. In his presence: Appreciating your worship tradition. Nashville: Thomas Nelson.

The Church Year

In the beginning, God created the church calendar, making the world in six days and resting on the seventh. That basic idea, that different times each have their own purpose, is what stands behind the idea of the church year.

In the Old Testament, it's clear the Jewish year revolved around three principal religious feasts: Passover, Pentecost, and Tabernacles. It did not take the Christian church long to celebrate Easter, adding Lent to prepare for this great event. After Christmas emerged as a special day, Christians soon observed Advent before it. Today, the church year has filled out to include Advent, Christmas, Epiphany, Lent and Holy Week, Easter, and Pentecost.

Reasons for the Seasons

The reasons for abiding by the church year are many, two of which stand out:

First, the church insures that the major events of the biblical story of redemption are remembered annually: the birth and Second Coming of Christ (Advent), the death of Christ (Lent and Holy Week), the Resurrection (Easter), and the coming of Holy Spirit and the birth of the church (Pentecost).

Second, observing the church year reminds us that Christians live by our own table. Regardless of the attention given to the secular calendar, the church year remains a symbol that God is in charge of time, that he redeems the world according to his schedule, and that we

even mark time differently when we enter his church.

Colorful and Meaningful

Each season has its own meaning, and therefore each can be celebrated uniquely. One of the ways churches do that is by highlighting certain colors during each season.

Here are the meanings and colors associated with each season of the church year:

• *Advent.* Advent is Latin for "coming." The four Sundays preceding Christmas are designed to help us prepare for Christ's Second Coming by reminding us of what preceeded his first coming. Purple is the color highlighted, representing repentance as Christians prepare for Christ.

• *Christmas.* This season celebrates Jesus' birth and extends from Christmas day to Epiphany (January 6). White is the color for this occasion, as it is the color for Christ.

• *Epiphany.* This word means "to shine forth." This season lasts from January 6, the day of the coming of the Magi, to Ash Wednesday. It extols Christ's giving light to the whole world, which the Magi represent. The liturgical color is green, symbolizing the growth of the church throughout the world.

• *Lent.* These forty days (not counting Sundays) before Easter are a time to ponder Jesus' forty days in the wilderness. It is a season of reflection, prayer, repentance, and fasting. It begins with Ash Wednesday and culminates with Holy Week.

Like Advent, its color, if any, is purple, reflecting repentance.

• *Easter.* This eight-week season celebrates the Resurrection. Although Christians contemplate the Resurrection every Sunday, this season gives Christ's Resurrection special prominence. Its color is also white. On the fortieth day after Easter Sunday, the Ascension of Christ is honored as well.

• *Pentecost.* During this season the church celebrates the coming of the Holy Spirit and the birth of the church. Since we live in this era of salvation history, it is appropriately the longest season, lasting until Advent. Fiery red is the color for Pentecost Sunday — baptism of fire — and green, representing growth in the Spirit, for the rest of the season. The Sunday after Pentecost Sunday is Trinity Sunday, in which the nature of God is recalled as a way of summing up all that has occurred from Advent through Pentecost.

— Mark Galli

Holy Days and Holidays

The purpose of every special Sunday service of worship, whether an ordinary or a holiday service, should be to set us in the presence of Almighty God, giving us the opportunity for praise and prayer and for renewing our faith and commitment.

Integrity and Accommodation

Two principles should guide us when we consider how to worship on Sunday mornings during special occasions.

The first principle is *integrity.* Worship is always the worship of God. No matter what the occasion is or what is happening in the community, we gather to offer homage to the Most High God. Nothing should distract us from this purpose.

The second principle is *accommodation.* Every worship service is imperfect, a fumbling attempt to frame praise. Because this is true, it is important to accommodate people's natural, human inclinations as springboards to worship. Liturgies based on seasons, holidays, patriotic events, and other special occasions are invaluable aids to the spirit of praise.

Following the Church Calendar

There is nothing new in following the church calendar. As far back as Christians can recall, we've celebrated the days and seasons of the church year.

• *Christmas.* Following the four prepatory Sundays of Advent is Christmas, when Christians pull out all the stops to celebrate the birth of their Lord. The use of an Advent wreath with appropriate readings each Sunday, thoughtful decoration of the sanctuary with appropriate symbols of the faith, and special services on Christmas Eve enhance the meaning and joy of this exciting time.

• *Easter.* This is the day to celebrate Christ's victory over evil and death. First, however, we must move through the time of reflection beginning on Ash Wednesday and climaxing with Holy Week. During

Holy Week observances, the Maundy Thursday service is a special time to remember the inauguration of the Lord's Supper, and Good Friday is when we vividly recall the sufferings and crucifixion of Christ. Then we will be prepared for renewal and affirmation on Easter.

• *Pentecost.* Fifty days after Easter and ten days following Christ's Ascension is Pentecost, when Christians celebrate the coming of God the Spirit. At this occasion, people can remember the promise of the gospel, that the divine Spirit is at work in the world, bringing all things to God's intended conclusion.

• *All Saints' Day.* On November 1, many Christians honor the memory of God's saints who have preceded us in the faith. This occasion can emphasize such themes as the perseverance of the saints, the priesthood of all believers, the communion of saints, and the role of Christians in the work of the kingdom.

A Host of Secular Occasions

If the liturgies point unwaveringly to God's glory, the interests and enthusiasms of the secular world can be appropriated and incorporated into Christian worship. In each case, the principles of integrity and accomodation again apply.

• *Valentine's Day.* This day is a sensible time to talk about the true nature of love, distinguishing between the *eros* love of popular tradition and the *agape* love of the Christian gospel.

• *Mother's Day and Father's Day.* These days of tribute offer similar opportunities to focus on the significance of love. It is important that all of the liturgy be compatible with the Christian faith and point the worshipers toward God.

• *Independence Day.* This event, which can so easily become a trumpet-blowing, flag-waving occasion without reference to the Transcendent One, may be sensitively channeled into a worship experience that transforms our nationalism. This day can be an opportunity to confess our sins as a nation and thank God for the many blessings we enjoy as citizens.

• *Thanksgiving.* This holiday belongs not just to the church but also to the nation as a whole. Because it is entwined with the nation's history, it is a wonderful occasion for inviting members of other faiths to worship with us.

— John Killinger

Observing National Holidays

Not only does Sunday seem to come every three days amidst the duties of the busy minister, but seasonal events and national holidays keep coming around on a regular basis, too. We gladly accept the challenge to lead our congregations in celebrating the joyful message of "He is risen indeed!" and of "Peace on earth to people of good will!" But what should our attitude be toward apparently "secular" observances such as Memorial Day, Fourth of July, Labor Day, or Mother's Day?

Not of This World

If we grant the basic premise that our *spiritual* ministry in worship, discipling, instruction, and even evangelism is far removed from affairs of state and national pride, then we solve the problem rather easily. The answer is simply to avoid anything that would resemble equating spiritual ministry with national celebration. In this view, the church and her mission is purest and strongest when she is entirely separate from national events that might dilute, distract, or stain the unique role she plays in the world— that of being involved solely in matters of the spirit.

Thus, some would exclude such national hymns as "America, the Beautiful," "My Country, 'Tis of Thee," or "The Star-Spangled Banner" from the hymnal and most certainly avoid them in a service devoted to the worship of God. Americanism, patriotic fervor, and national pride, though perhaps commendable, are not synonymous with being a follower of Jesus Christ. Our Lord took the coin of the realm in his hand and clearly pronounced the division of allegiance in saying, "Render to Caesar the things that are Caesar's, and render to God the things that are God's."

In the World

On the other hand, we are "in the world." We are citizens of a country that needs the loyalty of its strongest members, those who obey the laws, pray for leaders, and seek to live peacefully with their neighbors. These things, too, can be found in the exhortations of Scripture. Many would argue that duty to country is actually a means of submitting to God, since Paul said, "The authorities that exist have been established by God" (Rom. 13:1b).

A Memorial Day concert or a Fourth of July service may attract a holiday crowd because people are free and are looking for an unusual event to highlight the day. Patriotic holidays, national occasions of remembrance and thanks are commendable in their role and in our role as citizens. But it seems particularly difficult to predicate the Christian message on those bases.

The danger of appropriating popular and patriotic occasions comes in making the crossover "into the world" without maintaining some sort of separation in our thinking. We are in safest territory when we keep the goals of good citizenship and of good Christianity clearly defined and separated. Being a good Christian may require being a good American, but still to preserve strong reservations, deep convictions, and fervent concerns for our country. To be a good American, however, is not necessarily to be a good Christian.

Leslie Brandt in *Psalms Now* (Concordia) has captured this tension in two sentences of his paraphrase based on Psalm 137:

How grateful we are, O God,
   for our great country,
   for the blessing You lavish
   upon our land!
How concerned we are, O God,
   that our very nation may become our god
   and that we worship the gifts
   rather than the Giver!
          —Howard Stevenson

Preparing Church Bulletins

All you want to do is pray, praise, and preach, but every week there is that folded and stuffed brochure that announces everything from your sermon title to a pie-throwing contest with the junior high group. What can you do about the church bulletin?

The only thing you can't do is ignore it.

Remember the Purpose

A bulletin serves as a billboard for visitors, friends, and relatives. Therefore, make sure it contains the church name, address, and phone number, as well as the names and phone numbers of key staff members. List the times of your services.

It's also a worship aid that allows the entire congregation to know what occurs next, and thus it insures a smoother flowing worship. Further, it's a "things to do" list for the church family, a printed record of coming events and projects. And it's a letter to the congregation to communicate important past events and information.

Strive for Quality

If you can afford it, have a photo or a pen-and-ink drawing of the church on the cover. If that's impossible, develop a church logo for the cover. Try to stay away from stock photo bulletins, since they tend to make all churches look the same.

Spend time with the bulletin layout. Reading a church bulletin should be easy on the eyes. Creative use of balance, white space, and various type styles can make the difference between a bulletin that is read and one that is ignored.

Proofread every detail for possible mistakes. It is best for at least two people to double-check it for errors. You really don't want the third hymn to be "O for a Thousand Tongues to Sin." Finally, purge the bulletin of vocabulary that is only intelligible to committed regulars.

Space Considerations

Edit every announcement. Not every chairperson of the church potluck is a good writer. If space is a problem, print only the necessary facts. Even the order of worship can often be tightened up. (For instance, do "Offering" and "Offertory Prayer" need to be on two separate lines?)

Leave some items for the church newsletter or bulletin board. Keep asking, *Does this really need to be in the bulletin*? If space is a serious problem, instead of a full cover, use a small logo in the upper left-hand corner. Then begin your worship order on the outside of the bulletin, thus freeing inside space for other information.

If space remains a problem, consider going to a trifold bulletin. Using longer paper can add two pages to the available space. As much as possible, use inserts only for forms that need to be filled out and turned in or for extremely important events. Bulletin clutter detracts from the effect of important announcements and distracts worshipers.

Steer clear of the use of smaller type to gain space. In fact, it is a good idea to provide a large-print edition for members of your congregation who might need one. Copy machines that enlarge make such bulletins relatively simple to produce.

Since the church bulletin is one of the first impressions visitors have of your church and one they likely will take with them, it definitely is worth a little extra effort.

— Stephen A. Bly

Announcements

Congregations need to be *informed* about, and *involved* in, what is going on. To accomplish these important objectives, we must communicate effectively. The prime time to communicate is in the worship service, simply because most people are in attendance at that time.

The problem is that announcements concerning relatively mundane matters do not always contribute to a sense of worship. It is difficult to concentrate on the holiness of God if you are being exhorted to do something about the dinginess of the men's room!

On the other hand, because worship and service are inextricably linked together, there is no necessary conflict between being encouraged to volunteer to teach fifth-graders in Sunday school and praising the One who clearly has their interests at heart. So we must carefully think through our use of announcements and their place in worship.

Guidelines for Announcements

• *What should I include in the announcements?*

1. Information concerning specific, forthcoming events of general interest to the congregation.

2. Information relating to congregational life when there is a need for the congregation, as a whole, to know (for example, announcements about a death, board decisions, financial matters).

3. Information concerning opportunities for ministry.

• *What should I* not *include in the announcements?*

1. Matters relating to a relatively small group in the congregation that meets separately.

2. Impromptu announcements (for example: "There is a Cadillac in the parking lot, registration ALM 812, with its lights on" or, "Mrs. Smith's twins have just thrown up on the nursery carpet").

3. Intricate details of illness and impending surgeries (for example, no mention of hernias and gall bladders).

• *When should I schedule the announcements?*

1. At a point where they fit most appropriately into the theme of the service. Some ministers give all the announcements *before* the service begins. The problem, of course, is that late arrivals miss out. Sometimes people listen more carefully to announcements given at the *end* of the service, immediately before the benediction, particularly if they relate to the theme of the service.

2. At a point when they are least likely to intrude on the atmosphere of worship. Wherever we place them,

we must take care not to give the impression that the announcements are more important than praise, prayer, and preaching.

● *How can I make the announcements really work?*

1. By using video or overhead projectors to enhance the attention of the congregation. An announcement concerning children's camp could be illustrated with slides from the previous year's experience. An outreach ministry could spring to life through pictures of people the ministry is reaching.

2. By using drama. Used sparingly, drama can attract attention and get the message across. An an-nouncement about a women's conference could be made by a woman going through a purse, frantically looking for the ticket she has lost, all the time describing what she fears she is missing.

3. By creative use of bulletins. Your bulletins can give "teasers" that will lead people to inquire further for details: "Would you like to go to the Holy Land? Check at the information desk for details."

4. By brief interviews about a proposed event. These interviews can lead to the answers being given for common questions in people's minds.

—*Stuart Briscoe*

The Call to Worship

From the time of Adam and Eve, the inclination of people who are aware of the majesty and awesomeness of God has been to hide from his presence. Sinners have feared to stand in the presence of the holy God.

The Invitation from God

If God was approached at all, unworthy-feeling persons brought appeasing gifts and sacrifices to win a hearing. Smoking mountains and shaking earth, burning bush and whirlwind, manna from heaven and plagues of judgment—all spoke of the awesome God who called individuals to be holy, even as he was holy. Who would dare to approach him? In fact, even God's chosen ones were warned to keep a distance from the mountain of his presence.

The surprising grace of the God of Scripture meets us in the unexpected invitation of God to approach him with boldness and confidence. This call to worship was instituted in the Old Testament and codified in the ceremonial laws relating to tabernacle and temple worship. The call is a recognition and affirmation of one of the cardinal revelations of Scripture: God is the One who initiates the relationship between the Creator and creature. In grace and mercy he reaches down to us; we do not call him.

The Beginning of Worship

Our God calls us, and this is where worship begins. Most properly, therefore, the call to worship is a Word from God, a Scripture text that reflects his desire that we corporately come into his presence. He sets the tone. The dignity and weight of the worship experience depends on God's presence. No other meeting on earth is comparable. Those who lead in worship should be careful to communicate the magnitude of what is about to happen between God and his people by carefully preparing the call to worship.

In the narrower sense, the ordained person most properly calls God's people together, with words such as: "Come, let us worship and bow down. Let us kneel before the Lord our God, for he is our Maker and we are the people of his pasture and the sheep of his hand." In a more extended and representative sense, the choir or other musicians in leadership may sing the call. Many appropriate anthems can be used for this purpose, such as:

- "Sing It Again and Again"—Ron Soderwall
- "Sing and Rejoice"—Will James
- "O Praise God in His Holiness"—Lowell Mason
- "Now Let Us All Praise God and Sing"—Gordon Young

There are books of choral music such as:

- *Choral Fanfares* by Alfred Rock Maier Company.
- *Four Festival Introits* by Coronet Press

The congregation may also participate in the call by singing words of God's invitation in the hymns of the church:

- "Come We that Love the Lord"
- "Clap Your Hands, All You People"
- "Sing a New Song to the Lord"
- "Make a Joyful Noise unto the Lord"
- "O Worship the King"
- "Let the Whole Creation Cry"

In our generation, which has made so many things common, God's holiness and essential transcendence may be forgotten. Parishioners may consider worship to be a right, coming to services with little forethought or preparation. In such cases, worship services become little more than religious exercises, spiritual pep rallies centered on reviving languishing commitments to the church program.

Yet how serious it is to call people into the very presence of God! With a meaningful, weighty call to worship, we can help our people awaken to the holy moment when worship begins, when God graciously chooses to meet with his people for Communion, dialogue, and renewed covenant.

—Arthur DeKruyter

The Public Reading of Scripture

Christians read Scripture in worship partly because of the examples of Jesus and the early church, who continued a long-established Jewish practice. But primarily they read out of their conviction that they must stay in touch with God's authoritative written Word, the life source of every believer. Scripture reading in worship is both a *voicing of* God's Word and a *listening to* God's Word.

At least three practical questions arise with regard to public Scripture reading: How do we choose the Bible passage to be read? What alternatives in format are there? How can we learn to read more meaningfully?

Selecting Passages

Worship planners who do not use a lectionary will want to choose passages carefully. Some suggestions:

• Choose passages relatively simple in style, language, and concepts, especially if the congregation will be asked to read them aloud. Don't let the length become burdensome.

• Use familiar texts and devotional texts often, balancing the use of Old and New Testaments. They create a spirit of warmth and gratitude.

• Choose passages with an eye to the theme of the service. You will usually select passages that complement the sermon text. Yet, matching Scripture texts with hymns and songs can also be meaningful. Other elements of worship may also suggest appropriate texts.

• Consider using a variety of translations. Worship planners might well use the majestic, much-loved King James Version of Psalm 23, for instance, while utilizing newer translations for less familiar portions of Scriptures.

Choosing Options

Frequently, one person reads Scripture to the congregation. Scripture reading may, however, be done by the worshipers in unison. Unison reading works well to emphasize experiences in which the whole congregation shares.

Another approach asks worshipers to read Scripture responsively, as litanies. Many hymnals include selections for such readings. Responsive readings may involve alternate reading between pastor and congregation or choir and congregation, or even more complicated patterns. Responsive reading works especially well with dialogue.

For dramatic effect, place a reader out of the congregation's sight, perhaps in a choir loft, and have him or her read the Scripture as "a voice from on high."

Reading Meaningfully

A student once asked me after a chapel service: "Why do musicians read Scripture better than preachers do?" There was enough truth in the question to make it sting. Why indeed? Perhaps, for musicians, the whole message must come through the reading, while we preachers focus more on our soon-to-follow sermonic comments than on the reading itself. Yet all worship leaders can learn to read Scripture more meaningfully by practicing some basic principles:

• Try to convey the attitude of the passage as well as its words. Get into the spirit of the writer by careful study of the passage, and then imagine yourself in the writer's place.

• Read interpretively, emphasizing key nouns and verbs. Vary pitch, rate, and volume to convey the emotional tone of the passage. Use pauses before key statements to build suspense, or after key statements to let the truth sink in.

• Group words into natural phrases, so the reading will sound as if the passage were being spoken. Many readers find it helpful to mark pauses or special emphases they will use as they read.

• Read without interruption,

comment, or exhortation. If explanation seems necessary, give it before the reading. Then let the passage speak for itself.

Finally, rely on God's promise to honor his Word (see Isa. 55:10–11). This should give sufficient encouragement to any and all who lead in the public reading of Scripture.

—Grant Lovejoy

Creeds and Confessions

Churches have used various creeds or confessions as part of their worship services since the early centuries. Reciting in unison what the congregation believes reflects ancient biblical practice. The *Shema* (Deut. 6:4–5) was recited by the Old Testament believer as well as by contemporary Jews. The first Christian confession was most certainly "Jesus is Lord" (1 Cor. 12:3; Rom. 10:9).

History of Creeds

The early church apparently expanded into baptism the practice of a public statement of great truths of the faith. The Ethiopian eunuch publicly professed faith in Christ before Philip baptized him, according to some ancient texts of Acts 8:36–38. Jesus clearly taught the doctrine of the Holy Trinity in connection with baptism (Matt. 28:19). The Apostle's Creed developed from the Trinitarian statement of faith professed by those baptized in second- and third-century Roman congregations.

Somewhat later, the Nicene-Constantinopolitan Creed was formed in the heat of fierce religious and political controversy in the fourth century. Church leaders from all parts of the known world reaffirmed the full deity of Jesus Christ and of the Holy Spirit against influential heretics. As centuries passed, other creeds were composed to expound upon and protect against error.

By the early Middle Ages, congregations were regularly reciting a creed during worship, usually after the sermon and immediately preceding Communion. The Nicene Creed tended to be used with the Lord's Supper, and the Apostle's Creed with baptism.

Although the Protestant Reformation rejected many elements of medieval Catholic theology and worship, nearly all Protestants continued using traditional creeds in their services until the triumph of British Puritanism in the mid-seventeenth century. The Puritan "Regulative Principle" ("All that is not specifically required or warranted by Scripture is forbidden in Christian worship and practice.") eliminated the use of any creed, the Lord's Prayer, organs, and the concept of the church year as relics of the Roman church. Such practices were believed to be contrary to the purity and simplicity of New Testament worship.

Two Streams

Protestant worship can be divided roughly into two main streams: continental (French and Dutch Calvinist, German Lutheran, and the Church of England) and Puritan (pre-twentieth-century Presbyterians, Baptists, free church and, in certain respects, Pentecostal/charismatics). Whereas the continental tradition has historically recited creeds in worship, not until recently has the Puritan tradition begun to do so.

The continental tradition typically confesses its creed following the sermon as a corporate offering to God. Twentieth-century Presbyterians and other evangelicals of the Puritan tradition often repeat a creed preceding the sermon, as a declaration of the faith's content and to set the tone for what is to follow.

Today many evangelical congregations, including those in the Puritan tradition, use creeds in worship for various reasons. It deepens the grasp of eternal truth, for, as people recite the creed, it becomes a part of them. Creeds can also reach out evangelistically to unbelieving visitors, testify to the essential unity with Christians of other ages and denominations, and help to safeguard the most fundamental beliefs over the ages.

Congregations have much choice in the use of creeds. Often parts of denominational confessions are used instead of creeds; sometimes children's catechisms are incorporated. The creed ought to reflect the sermon, season, or worship theme. Careful planning for the inclusion of creeds and confessions in harmony with Scripture and Christian tradition helps to insure fresh yet historic vitality in modern worship.

—*Douglas F. Kelly*

Public Sharing of Concerns

Somewhere between a worship service that is planned to the minutest detail and one that is utterly fluid lies a flexibility to the Spirit of God that recognizes both advanced planning and spontaneity can bring glory to God. Perhaps nowhere is this continuum more evident than in the desire to share the concerns of the people in the main worship service.

It seems so self-evident: a caring body of believers surely will want to be open to each other to the extent that anyone is free to share a joy, a sorrow, or a prayer request at any time so that the brothers and sisters may rejoice, weep, and bear with those who are feeling concerns.

But therein lies a tricky road to navigate—between extremes that present rigid formalism on one side and ill-considered, homemade theology on the other. Depending on tradition and leadership, a congregation may want to explore one or more of several options:

• Offer cards for prayer requests in the sanctuary narthex where worshipers may place concerns for pastors to lift up later in the service. Often ushers bring these forward prior to the announcements and pastoral prayer.

• During a "concerns of the church" or "body life" segment of worship, the leader may describe an area of pastoral concern to focus upon that morning, such as health needs, economics, family, and so on. People then speak their concerns to the congregation.

• With an ear to the ground for the concerns of the congregation, the pastor might call upon a member to prepare a lay witness or testimony that particularly underscores a need.

Assuring a Proper Manner

One problem with sharing times is that they can degenerate into trivialities or extended descriptions of ailments. One way to handle this is to work with the people who have a story to tell but may not be skilled at articulating it. If particular people tend to miss the point week after week, the pastor or other church leader can meet with them individually and privately to ask them to write out what they intend to say. Then the leader and the person sharing can meet prior to the service to go through the sharing experience.

Some churches ask persons who understand the process to model the kinds of sharing that build the church body. Congregations soon discover the dynamics of healthy sharing when they experience it. Even an audio tape of especially well-handled sharing can both instruct and inspire those who don't have experience in speaking their needs in public.

Still other churches structure the sharing time by tapping and preparing a person to give a "lay witness." This brief talk offers a word of testimony of God's work in the person's life, particularly as he or she has been touched by a ministry of the church. While a lay witness shouldn't come across as "canned" or too professional, it can be delivered in a way that uplifts and encourages the congregation—while avoiding some of the unknowns of completely unstructured sharing.

Whatever the procedure used, the worship leader must be sensitive to the need for worship to be responsive and caring while at the same time conforming to the tradition and directive of the Spirit.

—Larry D. Ballenger

Passing the Peace

Passing the peace in a liturgical service follows the confession of sin by the congregation and the declaration of forgiveness by the minister. Everyone rises to their feet, and the minister turns and greets the people with arms outstretched toward them, saying, "The peace of the Lord be always with you." The congregation responds in unison, "And also with you."

The pastor then says, "Let us greet one another with the peace of the Lord." With that, the pastor begins to move out into the congregation and greets individuals in a personal manner with the same words already used corporately. Similarly, people in the congregation greet one another with those words.

The History

A look at some statements from early church leaders can help us see how this tradition developed to its present form.

• *Paul.* "Greet one another with a kiss of love. Peace to all of you who are in Christ" (1 Pet. 5:14).

Paul also gave similar injunctions in such passages as Romans 16:16, 1 Corinthians 16:20, 2 Corinthians 13:12, and 1 Thessalonians 5:26.

With the Jews it had been the custom for a disciple to kiss his rabbi on the cheek and to lay his hands upon the rabbi's shoulder. This practice, or something similar known as "the kiss," became incorporated into the worship of the early church.

● *Tertullian.* "What prayer is complete from which the holy kiss is divorced? What kind of sacrifice is that from which men depart without the peace?" (*De Oratione 18*). Here the "holy kiss" was equated with "the peace" and was apparently a standard part of the Communion service.

● *Augustine.* "They demonstrated their inward peace by the outward kiss" (*De Amicitia 6*). The kiss was usually given after catechumens had been dismissed (before the Eucharist) and only church members remained.

● *Justin Martyr.* "When we have ceased from prayer, we salute one another with a kiss." The kiss was preceded by a prayer "for the gift of peace and of unfeigned love, undefiled by hypocrisy or deceit . . ." (from Cyril of Jerusalem, *Catechetical Lectures 25.5.3*)

● *Athenagoras.* Insisting that the kiss be given with care, he pronounced: "If there be mixed with it the least defilement of thought, it excludes us from eternal life" (*Legatio Christians 32*).

From the fourth through the thirteenth centuries, the kiss was confined to those of the same sex. Eventually, substitutes were introduced. For instance, wooden or metal tablets with pictures of the crucifixion on them were first kissed by the priest and then passed to the congregation. Each believer kissed the tablet and handed it on to his or her neighbor. Many Orthodox churches still use this method.

Benefits

As a corporate act of worship, the peace takes the vertical dimension of our gracious relationship with God and personalizes it in a horizontal, face-to-face expression of love among his people.

When this is done, several benefits unfold: (1) a warm sense of community pervades the congregation, (2) visitors begin to feel included, (3) believers experience a fellowship that goes deeper than a mere social hello, and (4) family members find opportunity for expressions of reconciliation.

One well-known church has used the peace at the beginning of worship, immediately following the opening hymn. As the time of greeting begins to quiet down, the choir starts leading in praise songs. Worshipers, still on their feet, feel moved naturally to redirect their focus to divine adoration—as it springs from the joy of fellowship.

—*John Guest*

Proclamation of the Word

Each Sunday preachers step into the pulpit as God's heralds to proclaim his message. But why is preaching a standard part of our worship? This special proclamation and teaching activity has a long heritage.

Preaching in History

The sermon in worship developed late in Judaism as an addition to the public reading of Scripture at annual feasts. The preacher's role was assumed only by occasional prophets, who challenged the people to covenant obedience. During the Babylonian captivity, the Jewish exiles replaced the traditions of temple sacrifice with the synagogue study of Scripture. The language shift from Hebrew to Aramaic (and later to Greek) required translation explanations after the Scripture readings. Eventually, invitations were extended for exhortations from resident or visiting scholars (see Acts 13:15). The "sermon" had appeared as a focus for the gathered people of God.

The early church continued the synagogue practice, adding the Eucharist (Acts 20:7–12). Before the Reformation the Eucharist dominated church gatherings, with a sermon usually preceding this central celebration. But the Reformers established the sermon's dominance, sometimes to the virtual exclusion of the Eucharist, a trend amplified by the Puritans. In America, the frontier camp meeting shifted the meeting climax to the sermon's invitation to personal response, an influence felt in all subsequent Protestant practice.

Preaching Today

The sermon has come to dominate modern worship. Since the sermon forms the single most time-consuming act, it's tempting to disparage all else as "preliminaries." If we gather only to learn, perhaps this would be acceptable. However, we also gather to praise God, especially if we have designated this a *worship* service.

Liturgical services permanently fix the placement of the sermon, while free church worship planners must wrestle with the purpose and placement of the sermon relative to the other events. Where there is choice, one basic rule ought to guide our planning: The sermon precedes the event it complements. It prepares the congregation for its next corporate act. Since most modern sermons call us to Christlike behavior (an *ethical* purpose), they naturally *follow* our major acts of adoration, commissioning us to serve and guiding our activity until we meet again.

Alternatively, a sermon may focus on God's person or work as an object of praise. This type of sermon directs our grateful response (a *doxological* purpose). It should *precede* our time of focused adoration.

On some occasions the sermon contains both purposes—ethical and doxological—directing us to consider each element equally: first God's character or work, and then our behavior. Here the sermon may be divided into these separate units, with each delivered prior to the element for which it has prepared us. For example, a sermon focused on God is followed by adoration. Then the service ends with a message oriented to behavioral change.

Alternatives to Preaching

Christian worship requires that we know God's person and work, not that we necessarily hear a sermon. But when the sermon is absent from an occasional worship service because of special time restraints, its place must be taken by another presentation of the Word, such as:

- Scripture itself, through effective reading, readers' theater, or dramatic presentation of biblical characters and events.
- Visual arts and technologies

(especially audio-visual).

- Biblically centered music lyrics.
- Personal testimony, illustrating the truth of God's Word in action.

Such alternatives work best when combined. In any case, when the sermon is absent, the Word must still be present to lift our praise beyond human experience.

—Timothy J. Ralston

The Offering

The offering is, perhaps, the most fundamental act of Christian worship. It's certainly one of the oldest, having been part of Israel's worship from earliest times. Upon entering Canaan, the people were told to offer the firstborn of their livestock as a thanksgiving (Ex. 13:11–12), and, according to Justin Martyr, the collection of money was a part of early Christian worship.

The offering is first that part of the service where people formally dedicate themselves—"offer" themselves—to God anew. Since how we spend money is close to who we are, the giving of money has become the key symbol of "offering ourselves as a living sacrifice."

A Variety of Offerings

There are three principle ways in which churches give opportunity for people to offer their gifts:

- *Offering box.* Some churches place boxes at the back of the church so that people can simply deposit their offerings as they enter or leave. This answers the objections of those who think the passing of plates mere-

ly a way to collect money from a captive audience. The offering box also emphasizes the individual offering his or her gifts to God.

- *Passing the plate.* Most churches pass offering plates or bags among people in the pews. Since the passing of the plates is preceded or concluded with a public prayer of dedication, this method emphasizes public thanksgiving and dedication, and more consciously ties the spiritual and physical aspects of faith.
- *Placing on the table.* Upon occasion (perhaps on stewardship Sunday or soon after) members of the congregation can individually walk forward and place their offerings in offering plates placed at the front of the sanctuary. This takes a greater step of faithfulness, requiring people to walk forward.

Attention to Details

If the church decides to pass the plate—the usual procedure—a number of decisions must be made.

- *What to do with guests.* Some churches announce that visitors, as guests, needn't feel obliged to give.

Others think that since the offering is founded in thanksgiving and aimed toward God, no one is a guest, so all should be invited to express thanks and dedication.

• *What to do before and after.* Pastors are wise to craft how they announce the offering, making sure to highlight not the duty of "having to give" but the privilege of giving thanks in this way. Some make use of Paul's encouragement: "Each one of you must give as you have made up your mind, not reluctantly or under compulsion, for God loves the cheerful giver." Since this form of offering emphasizes the public and corporate nature of the act, a prayer of thanksgiving and dedication usually accompanies it.

• *What the people do.* While the ushers collect the offering, the congregation can simply sit in silence, using the time to pray and reflect on ways they can dedicate them-selves anew to God. Sometimes the choir or a soloist will sing, not as a way to entertain people during a lull in the service but as a song-offering to God. Often the organist plays quietly, concluding the piece soon after the ushers are ready to come forward, but not stopping abruptly (which would signal that, in fact, the organ was mere filler.

• *Where to put the plates.* After the plates are passed, they can simply be taken out of the sanctuary. Most churches think it better, however, to bring them forward as an act of public thanksgiving and commitment, with the congregation joining in a hymn of praise, usually some form of the doxology. Often the plates are placed on the Communion table, showing publicly the tie between the spiritual and physical, and reminding the worshipers of the Incarnation of our Lord.

—*Mark Galli*

Benedictions

Pronouncing the benediction is a privilege, a priestly function of high responsibility. As the final element of a worship service, the benediction offers the minister the opportunity to be warmly, yet authoritatively, pastoral. Through it, the pastor speaks God's affectionate words of blessing over the congregation.

The word *benediction* comes from the Latin *benedico*, which means "to speak well" or "to speak words of good omen." It is a blessing, meant to bring good. Its opposite is *malediction* or curse, which sends evil. For the Hebrew, the power of the spoken word was great. A word was more than a symbol; it carried the power to achieve an end. Thus, to give a child a name was to give the child an attribute; to reveal your name to a stranger was to make yourself vulnerable to a curse. The Hebrews didn't delineate between speaking and doing, for speaking could accomplish much in its own right. A blessing, therefore, was much more than the sum of kind words; it actively brought good.

In the New Testament, the Greek word for *benediction* is *eulogia* (from which we get *eulogy*), literally meaning "good words." Closely related is the verb *eulogeo*, to bless, in the sense of calling down God's providence upon another. While the Hebrew sense inferred mostly material blessings, the New Testament usage added images of spiritual good.

Benedictions Misunderstood

To better understand what benedictions are, it is helpful to understand what they are not:

• *Prayers*. A prayer speaks to God. A benediction speaks for God. Notice the party being addressed in a benediction: "The Lord bless *you* and keep *you* . . ." The *you* here is the congregation. The minister is giving them something good from God, not speaking to God in prayer.

• *Sermonettes*. While a benediction addresses the congregation, it is a favor given to them, not something asked of them. The benediction is not the place to recap sermon points or make a final plea. A brief charge before the benediction can accomplish that purpose. The benediction is meant to be a warm and loving gift, not a burden.

• *Wishful thinking*. Greeting cards offer sentiments akin to candy in a vending machine. Benedictions offer the power of God at work through the pastor. *God* is blessing the people—actively giving them something good—in the benediction.

A Matter of Attitude

A pastor's demeanor often speaks as loudly as the words. Here are ways to help people receive the full impact of the benediction:

• *Move toward the people*. Pastors usually remove themselves from behind pulpits and rails, and stand close to the people at the front of the sanctuary. This symbolizes closeness and immediacy.

• *Lift your hands*. The symbol of blessing is laying hands on one's head. Since pastors cannot do that physically with an entire congregation, they can do it symbolically by lifting their hands high—palms toward the congregation—as if gently touching each worshiper.

• *Speak to persons*. Pronounce the benediction with active eye contact. Choose individuals in many parts of the sanctuary, and focus a moment on each. Say the words of the benediction tenderly, warmly, personally, yet decisively, as you would if you were speaking them to a dear friend in parting.

• *Let your face speak*. Sometimes a look can communicate more eloquently than words. Your eyes and your smile will reinforce the sincerity and affection of God's words for your people.

Classic Benedictions

The most enduring benedictions come to us from Scripture. From Numbers 6:24–26 comes the trinitarian blessing: "The Lord bless you and keep you; the Lord make his face shine upon you and be gracious to you; the Lord turn his face toward you and give you peace."

The New Testament gives us many benedictions, the most common being another trinitarian formulation in 2 Corinthians 13:14: "May the grace of the Lord Jesus Christ, and the love of God, and the fellowship of the Holy Spirit be with you all." Benedictions grace the endings of other Pauline letters (Rom. 15:13; 1 Cor. 16:23; Gal. 6:18; Eph. 6:23–24; Phil. 4:23; 1 Thes. 5:23, 28; 2 Tim. 4:22) and can be found elsewhere in the New Testament (Heb. 13:20–21; Rev. 22:21).

—*James D. Berkley*

13

Leading the Worship of God

There was a day long ago when a woman led the redeemed in a new song. The spray of water could still be felt in the hot desert air. The noise of horses' hooves, the braying of donkeys, the crying of babies commingled with the laughter of men and women in the joyful din of deliverance. And then there was the sound of music. Miriam, the sister of Moses and Aaron, and other women took up their instruments and lifted their voices in song. And so they led the people in the worship of Yahweh, for he had saved his people from the armies of Egypt. They sang these words: "Sing to the Lord, for he is highly exalted. The horse and its rider he has hurled into the sea" (Exod. 15:21).

On a grand, still-future day, angels in heaven will sing in honor of the Lamb. John the mystic, in his futuristic vision of that day, heard choirs of angels that beggar the imagination, in numbers that are beyond comprehension, sing these words of praise: "Worthy is the Lamb, who was slain, to receive power and wealth and wisdom and strength and honor and glory and praise!" (Rev. 5:12).

Between these grand events of God's salvation of Israel at the beginning of her history and the exaltation of the Lamb at the end of our history, we may find ourselves also leading in the worship of God. And who, we may ask, are we to join in this company? What does it take to lead in his holy worship? If I do not worship in spirit and truth, how may I lead others rightly?

As we consider these and similar questions, three impressive realities center upon us. The true worship of God makes these demands upon the worship leader:

(1) A necessary infusion of the sense of God's presence.

(2) A compelling desire to respond to his actions.

(3) A determined intention to reflect on his wonders.

God's Presence

To worship God, one must first be awash with a sense of his presence. It is never enough merely to know *about* God; we must know God. The Trinitarian God of Holy Scripture is not conjured up like a snake from a charmer's basket. He is ever present and ever real. One who leads in God's worship must first be filled with a sense of his nearness.

This means the leader in worship may not begin his or her work cold. "Preparation precedes presentation"—we have said this with reference to preaching. But it also is necessary for leading in worship. Fumbling through a hymnal or grasping for an overhead five minutes before the service is folly. Even when it "works," it is wrong. If an ill-prepared worship leader leaves the worship service thinking, *Well, that went well enough,* he or she is mistaken. The worship of God is not just something to muddle through. It is an act of response to the living God, based on an intense relationship with him.

Further, the worship of God, as is the case of all other aspects of the Christian life, is not something done simply under one's own power. All true worship of God is Spirit empowered. The Holy Spirit gives us the desire to worship God, when in our own flesh we may not feel like worshiping. The Holy Spirit makes our worship true, by directing our thoughts and hearts, by moving through our words and actions. The Spirit of God makes our worship possible, gives it its power, and frames its direction. So, in the worship of God, we are enabled *by God* to do our task rightly! This comes from a sense of oneness with him.

And how may one develop this oneness with God? By the classic spiritual disciplines, particularly the reading of Scripture and involvement in prayer. To pray rightly in the congregation, we must first pray rightly in our own private moments. To lead the congregation in conversation with the Father, we must first be on regular speaking terms with majesty. So the leader of worship must be a person of prayer. I suspect all will agree.

The leader of worship must also be a person of the Word. Again, I assume agreement, but the practice of both prayer and personal Bible reading are more easily agreed to than done regularly. Among the Scriptures we who lead worship might determine to read again and again are the books of Leviticus, Isaiah and the Psalms—each for a different reason.

Bible Reading for Preparation

Leviticus? Yes, and Isaiah and the Psalms as well.

How many times has any of us desired to read through the Bible in a year, only to find our best intentions coming to a grinding halt somewhere in Leviticus? For many, that book gives rise to a personal application of the statement: "Thus endeth the reading of the Scripture."

To be sure, Leviticus is not as exciting a read as *The Chronicles of Narnia*. All that talk of rite, ritual, and regulation is numbing to the modern reader. A tenth of an ephah of this and a quarter hin of that, talk of kidneys, loins, and fat, and of burning and incense—all these things come to us from a world so removed that it seems to be another planet.

Yet the important connecting point in Leviticus is this: Yahweh is holy. That is, he is transcendent, other, distant, remote; he is altogether removed from all that he has made. The Hebrew word (*qadosh*) emphasizes the utter uniqueness of the God of Scriptures. All true worship of God, in a sense, begins with God's holiness. That is, it is only when we begin to grasp how unexpected it is that we may worship God that true worship may begin to happen.

Leviticus reminds us in innumerable ways that all humanity is sinful. People sin in thought, word, and deed. Women and men, the aged and the very young—all participate in the universal human condition of sin. Sin creates a vast gulf between God and people.

Then God comes near. Then the Holy One stoops low. Then the King of Glory bends close. And he speaks. And his words to ancient Israel formed the regulations of Leviticus given through his spokesman Moses.

At the time of this revelation, the people who understood listened gladly. The rites and regulations were no burden. They were the stipulations that would lead a sinful woman to peace with God. These were the laws (the truth) that would bring a sinful man to a sense of comfort in the midst of a growing recognition of God's holiness.

As dense and detailed as the book seems to be, its riches are profound. Sinful people may find forgiveness and deliverance. People may come near to God and sense his presence. They just need to come in the way that he has prescribed. Had God said to do a strange contortion of a dance while holding one foot, to wade across a river, and then to sing an acrostic hymn backwards, godly people would have learned to do these things. Gladly.

What he did say had to do with sacrifice and offering. That God spoke at all was a mark of his grace. That he spoke with detail and demand is a sign of his majesty. That he promised a payoff of fellowship and communion with himself is demonstration of his mercy.

As modern worship leaders, we will benefit from rereading Leviticus regularly. We do not need to read Leviticus for detail, for we are not priests. We can read simply for impressions, for the sense of things. We read recognizing we are believers in the same Yahweh of our forebears in Hebrew culture.

This book, in all its heavy detail, hammers away on the need for sinful people to come to God on his terms. Long thought by Christians to be an instrument of God's heavy hand, the Book of Leviticus is better to be seen as an instrument of his great grace. Merely by doing what God demanded, with an attitude of repentance and a spirit of renewal, the sinful person could find the guilt lifted away, with only joy remaining.

Isaiah is another book that calls for our regular reading and study. Not every chapter, of course, is equally productive for worship leaders.

Drawing Out a Timid Congregation

Many people want to display their joy and praise more openly in worship. It's not that they have a diminishing respect for the mind; they simply have an increasing need to experience their faith more expressively.

Expressive Worship

Not everyone is comfortable with more expressive worship. Some are concerned that emotional display will lead to unseemly behavior. Others believe expressive worship is unworthy of thoughtful Christians. But there is value in worshiping God with both head and heart:

• *It nurtures humility.* Many times emotional reserve is but a fearful quest to retain control of one's life. Expressive worship cultivates a willingness to be taught by and to submit to the Holy Spirit.

• *It creates a climate of warmth and acceptance.* When an expressive atmosphere is developed, the spirit of fellowship is cultivated, creating a climate for evangelism.

• *It fosters commitment.* Rather than encouraging people to be placid observers, expressive worship demands participation and, therefore, commitment.

Four Dimensions

Encourage people to do four things, each of which helps them engage in worship:

1. *Personalize their praise.* Sometimes even the praise of devout Christians becomes merely a recitation of theological truths, but when they personalize their praise, their worship will be more meaningful and their praise more heartfelt.

2. *Verbalize their thoughts.* Let people hear the sound of their voices early in the worship. When they respond to the leader's "Good morning" or greet one another at the beginning of service, they learn that speech is a part of worship.

3. *Mobilize their bodies.* People can express their praise in a physi-

Lengthy chapters of Isaiah are directed as angry indictments against nations that have long ago felt the wrath of the divine hand. But certainly one who discovers the riches of Isaiah at chapter 6 will finally discover as well chapter 40. There, as in Leviticus, a stunning counterpoint is made of God's great transcendence (vv. 25, 26) and his imminence (vv. 27, 28). He who is beyond all comparison is also indescribably near. His nearness can fill one, enmesh one, overwhelm one. When the sense of his nearness is a factor in the spiritual life of the worship leader, that person is truly ready to lead others in the worship of God.

Perhaps all know the importance of the Book of Psalms in the history of the worship of Israel. But many may still not have discovered the role the Psalms may play in forming the character and informing the sensibilities of the worship leader today.

---

cal way by using their hands and arms. Some people feel comfortable lifting their arms in adoration. Other congregations might clap to a spiritual or hold hands in prayer.

4. *Energize their love.* Christians gather not as individuals praising God, but as a community. Help people to recognize one another's presence and reach out in feeling.

Begetting a Response

Although people want freedom to express themselves in worship, they often find it intimidating. The worship leader can do several things to help ease their discomfort and encourage greater participation:

• *Remember the purpose of worship.* God wants his people to engage their emotions in worship, but not merely for the sake of being emotional. Therefore, anything done in worship should have a firm biblical base.

• *Acknowledge their fears.* Since people are anxious about trying new things, especially in a group, I sometimes will say to the congregation, "No one's going to scream or shriek.

Let's praise the Lord, but we can do it without hollering." A statement like that relieves people's fears of somebody going berserk.

• *Soften self-consciousness.* Most people are self-conscious when they participate in something new. Anything a worship leader can do to lessen that feeling, such as playing music, will enhance the experience.

• *Don't overwhelm people with the new.* Whenever people are stretched to experience a new dimension of worship, they should immediately be brought back to something familiar.

• *Touch a variety of emotions.* Naturally, some people are more comfortable with some forms of emotion than others. Which emotion is touched is less important than that the heart is engaged in the worship of God.

• *Treat people with respect.* Most people come to worship because they care about the Lord and they want to show him they care. Affirm such presence and faith, especially when leading people toward more expressive worship.

— *Jack Hayford*

It is said that in the New Testament we finally discover the extent of the grace of God on our behalf in the story of Jesus the Messiah. But in the Book of Psalms, we feel the rich grace of God. Here is where we experience his *hesed*, his loyal love or everlasting mercy. In the Psalms of lament we learn that it is permissible to hurt deeply and to express that hurt to God and man. In the Psalms of praise we learn that it is mandatory to respond fully in praise to God for who he is and for what he does. We learn that the word *hallelujah* is not simply a spiritual filler in song or prayer. It is the command to God's people to rejoice, to praise, and to enjoy him forever.

These three books—Leviticus, Isaiah, and the Psalms—each for different reasons, inform worship leaders of the enormousness of their task—and the possibility of doing it well in the service of God.

God's Actions

To worship God, we also discover an inner compulsion to exult in him, to say yes and amen, to acknowledge all he has done. In addition

---

Including Youth and Children in Worship

Corey was 8 years old, and he'd never been to "big church" before. Now he was sitting quietly in the third pew, flanked by his grandparents, as the service came to a close. Did he feel he had been a part of what had gone on during the hour? The adults certainly felt God had been with them in their worship. But did the style, order, content, and language of the worship service magnify or obscure the Lord for this 8-year-old visitor?

If Corey, along with other children and youth, truly did feel a part of that worship hour, it was probably because the service was characterized by several of the following:

• *Children led worship, too.* In addition to an anthem offered by the Joyful Noise Choir, which sounded really good and was sung with enthusiasm, 12-year-old Zeke Han-

sen read the morning's Scripture. Also, junior higher Mary MacKenzie gave a portion of the announcements. Cheery, colorful banners made by the kids decorated the sanctuary.

• *Worship leaders affirmed the children.* When the pastor invited all the "young disciples" to come forward and sit on the steps for a brief object lesson, Corey hesitated. But the pastor's invitation was so earnest and the response of many other kids so immediate and energetic that he felt reassured. As he sat on the steps looking back at his grandma and grandpa, he couldn't help noticing the smiles on so many faces in the congregation. They all seemed very interested in Corey and the other kids up there.

• *Children understood the language.* Corey found the children's

to a sense of God's nearness—to believe oneself to be awash with a sense of the Divine—there is also the necessity in worship to celebrate God's goodness and the benefits he has brought into our life.

For the Christian, the central aspect of the celebration of the actions of God is the Person and work of the Lord Jesus Christ. He is the Lamb slain from before the foundations of the earth. He is the one whose Coming was promised in the Hebrew Scriptures, whose life and work form the centerpiece of the New Testament, and whose coming again is the hope of believers through the ages. Our worship rightly centers on him. The celebration of the Lord's Table is the pivotal act by which we honor him.

The Christian also celebrates the innumerable actions of God on behalf of his people. These include the actions described in Scripture, those that transpired throughout history, and those experienced by his people today as he acts in kind providence and intervenes in answer to prayer, as he energizes and encourages, empowers and enables the peoples of his church throughout the world. Each of the gracious acts of God is a provocation to wonder, a call to celebration.

---

sermon interesting and understandable (he loved the model sailboat the pastor had used for an object lesson). During the rest of the service as well, everyone, including the pastor, used language that each young person could grasp.

• *Joy filled the room, during and after.* The genuine enthusiasm Corey noticed throughout the service did not get turned off when the last amen was pronounced. The pastors and the people in the congregation were just as sincere and warm after the service as they were before it. And one more thing—several funny things were said during the service, and everybody laughed. Corey like that a lot.

• *Musical variety held interest.* Corey loves music. He really enjoyed the handbell ringers and noticed that some songs were accompanied by organ, others by piano, drums, and guitars. One of the songs everybody sang together was introduced by a story telling how it came to be written. That caught Corey's attention.

• *The preacher told a good story.* The pastor knew the value of parables—not only the ones Jesus told, but also modern-day parables. The sermon featured a story from the *Chronicles of Narnia* by C. S. Lewis. It helped Corey understand the point and kindled an interest in reading those books as well. Corey found that parables are fictional stories that help us understand a true story better.

Jesus said, ". . . unless you change and become like little children, you will never enter the kingdom of heaven" (Matt. 18:3). As we plan our corporate worship experiences, let's take a moment to see them through children's eyes, not only for all the Coreys, but for our own sakes as well.

—*Sonny Salsbury*

God's Wonders

To worship God in spirit and in truth, we engage not only senses and feelings, but also mind and heart in a unified effort. Is this not the intention of the words of the great Shema? These words and their setting (Deut. 6:19) call upon the believing person to hear and obey, to love and respond, to know and to respect, to teach and to act. The whole person of the believer, in all his or her being, is to be engaged in the response of wonder to the God of glory.

Here we celebrate God for who he is. Here we think of the wonders of God, of his attributes, of his nature. We contemplate the holiness of God. We ponder his grace. We respond in awe to his majesty. And we wonder anew how it can be that the God of heaven has become our Savior, that the Creator of the universe has become our friend, that the Eternal One now lives for me and bids me to live for him.

How, then, do we worship him?

Variety—with Limits

If the worship of God is the declaration of His worth, then what we do and how we do it are of exceedingly great importance. At the same time, the manner can vary markedly.

For example, consider one Easter, when I:

• On Good Friday led a congregation in a Passover Seder service, including the feast and all the wonderful liturgy. As a Christian leading Christians in the Jewish Passover, I made much of the varied ways these old traditions inform our understanding of the saving work of Jesus the Messiah. I showed how ancient symbols and songs point to the Savior. I led in the discovery of the setting for the Lord's Table in this ancient celebrative meal of God's deliverance of Israel from Egypt. In that setting, we worshiped the Lord.

• Attended a somewhat conventional Baptist Easter service in our congregation that is largely white, middle class, and filled with people who have many hurts but also much love for God and the risen Christ. In that setting, we worshiped the Lord.

• Joined our daughter and her husband, the only white couple in a black church, for a different worship experience. Where our service had been organized, clearly directed, and satisfying, this service had been planned also, but it seemed a lot of things merely happened. Yet the joy of the music, which went on for the first hour, was infectious, inescapable, wonderful. In that setting, we worshiped the Lord.

• Experienced an evening service with a musical drama our son had developed, including new compositions, arrangements, script, and narration. There, again, we worshiped the Lord—in the process of drama and song.

• Attended an Orthodox Pascha service the following Sunday for an "Eastern" Easter, with exquisite liturgy and ancient forms. In that setting, we worshiped the Lord.

Each of these experiences was unique, and each provided platforms of integrity for the true worship of God.

The more we study worship and the more we involve ourselves in the worship of God, the less parochial we become about the form worship must take. There are a variety of ways God's people come before him. We can worship the Lord in charismatic services as well as in formal, old-line denominational churches; in large assemblies and in small clusters; with all peoples and in all places; with orchestral music accompanying hymns, with rock and jazz bands accompanying choruses, and with people who allow no instrument but the human voice.

But we dare not worship in just any way. There are some places where we cannot worship the Lord. We cannot worship God where Scripture is denied, where the Savior is vilified, where truth is declared an error. For example, at my older son's college was a baccalaureate service presented by the (ostensibly) Protestant campus pastor. Where the cross once had been in the college chapel, there was now an Indian totem. Prayers were selected from the Hindu Vedas and from the Quran of Islam. Students spoke of mystical experiences with no mention of Christ, none of the Bible, none of the Trinitarian God. Then the service closed with a prayer to the "great earth mother goddess."

I may worship God in many places and in many ways. But I cannot worship God in all places and in all ways. Worship that is acceptable to God is in spirit and truth. This service in my son's once church-related college was an exercise in futility, indeed, of blasphemy.

We Must Worship

But it is not just that we may worship God. We must.

And as a leader in worship, we must participate in worship. What does the pastor communicate, who often does everything but worship God in the morning service? While the congregation is singing, the pastor may be whispering to someone nearby, or even phoning someone from a platform phone. At times the pastor has his head down— not in prayer but in a last-minute look at the notes for the sermon that is "next on the program." At times, when the congregation is in prayer, the pastor darts off the platform for hurried consultation.

This pastor is modeling a view of worship that it is merely preliminary to the main event: the pastor's sermon.

When we lead worship, we set the tone. If we treat worship as time wasted before the "real thing" begins, church will be a place where people come to listen not to act, a place to take notes about God, but not to enjoy the presence of God.

How shall we worship God? Again, we need to stand between realities: The indescribable holiness of God, and the inescapable nearness of God. God is holy beyond description (Isa. 40:25, 26). God is near beyond comprehension (Isa. 40:27, 28).

He invites us to worship him, and he bids us lead others in the celebration. Of course we are not worthy. And of course we will do it by the power of his Spirit. For here we are, poised between Miriam in the past and the angels of heaven in the future, calling forgiven sinners such as ourselves to the holy worship of the living God.

So let us worship!

—*Ronald B. Allen*

Resources

Allen, R. 1992. And I will praise him: A guide to personal worship in the Psalms. Nashville: Nelson.

Allen, R., and G. Borror. 1982. Worship: Rediscovering the missing jewel. Portland, Ore.: Multnomah.

Ortlund, A. 1975. Up with worship. Glendale, Cal.: Regal.

Webber, R. 1985. Worship is a verb. Waco, Tex.: Word.

Pastoral Care in Worship

The main point of Christian worship is, in the words of the Westminster Confession, "To glorify God and enjoy him forever." However, while we are busy glorifying and enjoying God on Sunday morning, we are also caring for people. Pastors who haphazardly plan and participate in Sunday worship are ignoring a major occasion for care of the congregation.

Caring in Worship

Too often we tend to think of pastoral care as one-to-one counseling. However, during worship, we are with more of our people than at any other occasion during the week. Most of our parishioners will know us, not in an individual counseling session, but in our leadership of worship. What sort of demeanor do we present as we lead worship? Will our people experience us as caring, warm individuals, or as cold, aloof people far removed from their daily cares?

Sometimes a pastor's leadership in worship becomes an invitation for a parishioner to approach him or her about some difficult personal problem. We therefore ought to look for occasions that will enable our worship leadership to become a prelude for pastoral care. For instance, in preaching about problems in marriage, we will want to appear not necessarily as the person who has solved all marital problems (an appearance that could be the *end* of pastoral care rather than its beginning) but rather as someone who is a fellow struggler working to be faithful as a Christian in marriage.

Seemingly little things, such as how we might hand someone a piece of bread in the Lord's Supper, the way we deal with children in a children's sermon, or the remarks we make at a wedding, will become invitations to explore these matters together in a more personal way at another time.

Speaking Through Actions

Because worship is the source of a congregation's life—its chief centering activity—we do well to wonder what signals we are sending on Sunday. Are all our sermon illustrations about middle-aged businessmen? Do all our sermon examples involve people who always solve all of their problems, who always successfully apply the principles of the Christian faith? What about those in the congregation whose lives are full of pain, error, and misfortune?

Along with our Sunday worship services, weddings and funerals provide excellent occasions not only to talk about life problems but also to act on our convictions, for life's deepest matters usually are acted upon before they are spoken of. Thus, a couple is asked to join hands in a wedding as a physical, public sign of their intentions. The congregation leads the family from the cemetery as a sign that true, painful separation has occurred in death.

I once overheard two people in conversation about the upcoming move of their pastor to another congregation. One person noted, "When our family went through a terrible crisis a couple of years ago, Joe was there to provide support and counseling. What a wonderful pastor!"

The other person said, "I disagree. During the six years that Joe has been here, our family fortunately had no major crisis or tragedy. We simply went to church on Sundays. There, we were often subjected to poorly prepared sermons and indifferently prayed prayers. We felt a lack of concern. I can honestly say that Joe was never a pastor to me."

We Protestants are big on preaching; we love to use words. Worship reminds us—through gesture, touch, sign, and symbol—that many human matters are too deep for words, too tough to be handled alone.

—*William Willimon*

Worship Leaders and Ushers

By being invited to participate as worship leaders and ushers, many believers have been given opportunity to use their spiritual gifts and experience a greater degree of participation in worship. However, worship teams do not just happen; they must be developed.

Coordinating Worship Leaders

Lay worship leaders can do much more than just participate in the order of service up to the sermon. They—and you—will benefit from involvement in all phases of worship planning and implementation.

Here are some ways to go about weekly preparation and training:

• *Teach your church's philosophy of worship.* Ground your worship leaders in your church's theology of worship, and they will be at one with you, enthusiastically supporting the purposes and goals of the worship practices you employ.

• *Plan services well in advance.* Make sure your worship leaders have Scripture lessons and sermon themes (and any other pertinent information) in sufficient time to work with you on designing the services—without feeling rushed. This simple courtesy will go far in enhancing team morale.

• *Implement a regular rehearsal time.* At a regular preservice rehearsal, each team member can review the service, become familiar with its flow, and catch your vision for its potential impact. Walkthroughs provide opportunity to observe the team in action. They also give opportunity to gently correct any problems, such as distracting mannerisms or mumbled readings.

• *Spend time together in preservice prayer.* This is an opportunity to minister to each other; it brings oneness to the group and helps the team center on the worship of God.

• *Consider using two worship teams.* Teams can alternate every six to eight weeks. This allows for greater creativity and involvement, while avoiding burnout.

Developing Competent Ushers

Frequently ushers are the first people worshipers meet when entering the church. Since they typically give newcomers their first impressions of a particular congregation, ushers need to be warm, helpful people who can make others feel at home. Ushers welcome people best by name, and if they don't know someone already, they can take the initiative to introduce themselves and ask people their names. Here are some items to keep in mind:

• *Heating and ventilation.* Ushers can help make the sanctuary a pleasant environment by knowing how to control the heating, ventilation, and air-conditioning systems. It is best to set the temperature a little cooler than normal. It keeps people alert, and crowds naturally boost a room's temperature.

• *Uniform seating.* Ushers will want to make the best use of sanctuary space, seating people evenly throughout the sanctuary. This makes it easier for people to experience *corporate* worship.

• *Meeting needs.* It is courteous to ask people their seating preference and then to lead or escort them to an appropriate row. If worshipers already seated at the aisle need to move to allow access to the middle of a row, the usher can request their help.

• *Seating latecomers.* The ushers need guidance from the worship leaders about appropriate times to seat people inconspicuously after the service begins.

• *Safety factors.* Ushers need to remain alert to special needs, especially medical emergencies. They should be briefed on how to handle first-aid cases, where to seek assistance, how to evacuate the building, and what numbers to call for emergencies.

Ushers work well in teams. If young people are assisting in this ministry, they will benefit from working with an older person.

—David Sherbino

14

Special Church Services

John Donne's statement that no person is an island can be said with equal force about the Christian congregation. Ministers and leaders are tempted to think of their own local fellowships as though they stood alone. Yet no church is to be independent of other church bodies or isolated from the community in which it is placed to serve. No church or denomination is the kingdom of God alone, nor should it attempt to be.

In every congregation's program should arise occasions when it acknowledges the church-at-large by its participation in, support of, and worship with the whole people of God. Such special services come in various forms, with their own unique difficulties and opportunities.

Ecumenical Services

To what extent should a congregation take part in interdenominational services? Almost always, with enthusiasm. Some ecumenical efforts may seem unimportant, and many are disappointing in attendance. We may feel that having our own congregational services is more productive. Nevertheless, cooperating in united efforts is a mandate upon Christians that can help fulfill our Lord's prayer "that all of them may be one . . . that the world may believe that you have sent me" (John 17:21).

Among the most appealing metaphors the Apostle Paul used for the church is the concept of the body of Christ. "There is one body and one

209

Spirit, just as you were called to the one hope that belongs to your call, one Lord, one faith, one baptism, one God and Father of us all, who is above all and through all and in all" (Eph. 4:4–6). "Just as the body is one and has many members . . . of the body . . . so it is with Christ" (1 Cor. 12:12). Each congregation has its own functions and makes its own unique contribution as a part of Christ's body. Participation in services of the church-at-large acknowledges oneness in Christ and Christian fraternity.

Some services when churches work together rather than separately seem to serve better the purpose of God's kingdom. The world needs to see that churches are not competitors but players on God's team. One of God's goals in history is to unify humanity into brotherhood and peace; the church is the laboratory for demonstrating loving relationships amid pluralism. How can humanity be unified if the church does not witness and practice loving community?

The pastor is the key person who can lead his or her people to a larger view. We need to get to know the pastors of other congregations, love them, and work with them in special ecumenical services.

Stirring up interest and attendance for an ecumenical service that is comparable to a congregation's enthusiasm for its own program can seem quite daunting. The diversity of theology and practice, the reluctance to engage in interdenominational fraternization, and each church's own events calendar tend to deny ecumenical services the support they need. All such efforts depend upon the church representatives and pastors conscientiously working together as a team. The following suggestions may help:

- *Choose only a few programs per year.* The sponsoring group, such as the ministerial association or fellowship of churches, should limit its offerings to those it can carry through with good success. It is better to do a few services well than to overcrowd already demanding schedules and fall short on quality preparation.

- *Appoint a broadly representative committee and a dynamic, well-organized chair.* Follow-through types should be in charge of planning, with subcommittees to assist in the preparation. It is important that no one denomination or church dominate, or the impression will be that the event is sponsored by one group.

- *Enlist as many congregations as possible.* Aim for broad participation by inviting those who are not members of the sponsoring group. You may find new commitment and cooperation.

- *Use many persons, from various churches, in the service itself.*

- *Do significant advance promotion.* Distribute newsletters and bulletins to the cooperating churches. Place stories and ads in the newspaper. Use public-service spots on radio and television. Utilize community bulletin boards and other local media.

Many Christian celebrations provide opportunities for ecumenical expressions. The most popular and widely observed are Holy Week services. The services may be held at luncheons in a different denominational church each day. The host church prepares a light lunch and places an offering basket on each table to defray expenses. People gather for a 25-minute service around meal tables. The worship consists of two congregational hymns, Scripture lesson, a choral or solo song, a sermonette on the day's Scripture, a closing prayer, and a benediction. Instead of rotating to several churches, the services may be held in the same church for the week. Some communities hold these services in the evenings.

Themes and resources for the week might be

Monday: Cleansing of the Temple (Matt. 21:10–14; Mark 11:15–17)

Tuesday: The Attack on the Pharisees (Matt. 23:13–39)

Wednesday: The Anointing at Bethany (John 14:1–11)

Thursday: The Upper Room and Gethsemane (Matt. 26:17–30, 36–46)

Friday: The Crucifixion (Matt. 27:27–50)

Good Friday is observed ecumenically in many communities from 12 to 3 P.M. in a centrally located church. The service amplifies the seven last words of Christ with the appropriate Scripture, congregational hymn, brief sermon, prayer, and choral rendition corroborating each of the last words. In this structure, meticulous attention to time becomes imperative. In other communities the churches' choirs and orchestras unite in presenting Haydn's "Seven Last Words" in a special service.

Some communities and churches have a continuous come-and-go Vigil of Prayer from Friday at 3:00 P M. until sunrise on Easter. Usually the vigil is broken into thirty 60-minute periods held in a chapel. In the night hours, especially, it is prudent to have extra security present for worshipers' safety.

Easter sunrise services are still popular in many cities. Most are ecumenically sponsored, held in a beautiful park setting, football stadium, parking lot, or church. The service conveys a celebratory mood with hymns of joy, Scripture readings, and prayers about the Resurrection, with a brief sermon. Sometimes a neighboring church provides breakfast, or the meal is offered outdoors following the service.

One of the most successful ecumenical services I have experienced is an Easter afterglow, held on the Sunday evening a week after Easter. Each participating church choir sang one or two Easter anthems. Between the choral renditions, brief Scripture readings and prayers were offered by the various ministers. Volunteers from each church provided pies for the following fellowship.

Some communities have an annual Fall Festival of Faith, during which a speaker of broad reputation is brought in to give a sermon on each of four evenings—and often an address each morning. The speaker represents a different denomination each year, and the services rotate among churches annually.

On World Communion Sunday—the first Sunday of October—people of every denomination respond to the call to observe Communion in their own congregations. This can be a tremendous Christian witness when the focus is upon the whole body of Christ throughout the world.

Many other ecumenical opportunities dot the Christian calendar, such as: the Universal Week of Prayer (in January); Race Relations Sunday (the Sunday nearest Lincoln's birthday); Ash Wednesday (the seventh Wednesday before Easter); Pentecost (the seventh Sunday after Easter); National Family Week (the first full week in May); Memo-

---

Celebrating the Advent Season

What do we do for Advent this year? This question would not have been heard in some churches twenty-five years ago, but today many celebrate Advent as faithfully as they do Easter.

Why this renewed interest in Advent, and how can it be celebrated appropriately?

Understanding Advent

Advent means *approach* or *coming*. When celebrating Advent we remember the three great "comings." (*Remembering* in Scripture means much more than mere recollecting; it involves celebrating and appropriating God's actions in history.) The obvious one is the remembrance of Christ's coming into the world. We celebrate the truth that Christ, the long-ago-promised Messiah, the long-expected Savior, finally came. Each year we step back twenty centuries as we participate in the pregnant hopefulness of God's people of old.

Our hoping is not just a stepping back in time. At the same moment that we join Elizabeth in anticipation, we also celebrate Christ's coming into our lives—now. We know more than Zechariah, and we now have a vision that Joseph couldn't possibly have imagined. We have a rich treasure of images of Jesus' life, death, and Resurrection, and of the coming of the Spirit. This treasure spurs us to celebrate Christ's coming into our hearts and lives every day.

There's more. Advent also encourages us to stand on tiptoe in anticipation of yet another coming: Christ is returning; he will come again! Each year our anticipation of his future coming is sharpened and heightened during the Advent season. So, Advent puts us in a spiritual time warp of past, present, and future all at once, allowing us to be in touch with the church of all ages.

rial Sunday (nearest May 30); Freedom and Democracy Sunday (the Sunday before July 4); Labor Day Sunday (the Sunday before Labor Day); Thanksgiving (the fourth Sunday of November); Advent Celebration (the fourth Sunday before Christmas).

Community Outreach Services

The church has a stake in its community's welfare, mores, problems, and solutions. Each congregation can assume responsibility to provide spiritual help to those in unique types of need.

Every community will have its own unique needs, but common opportunities include ministries at nursing homes, hospitals, prisons, jails or detention homes, and institutions for the mentally ill. The

---

How Shall We Observe Advent?

If your congregation observes the four Sundays of Advent, you will generally choose a theme for the season and deal with a subtheme each Sunday. For example, you could deal with various prophecies from Isaiah; or consider what the anticipation of a Savior meant for Mary, Joseph, Anna, and Simeon; or explore how hope, love, joy, and faith come to expression during this special season. The text, sermon, hymns, and anthems all support the theme for each Sunday.

Various events and ceremonies have become traditions in local church celebrations of Advent. For instance, many congregations regularly construct and use an Advent wreath. During the service a child or other member of the congregation lights a new candle each Sunday, and on Christmas Eve or Christmas Day, the Christ candle is lit along with the other candles. Other churches have discovered the tradition of decorating the Chrismon tree and the Jesse tree. These are usually hung with symbols emphasizing the promise of Christ's coming.

Opportunities for special services abound during the Advent-Christmas season. Here we can only suggest three time-tested favorites:

• *Lessons and carols.* This service, from a fine British tradition, is the one in which Scripture readings are alternated with carol singing by the congregation and choir.

• *Pageants and plays.* These have always been popular. Here a congregation has to decide if it wants to follow Scripture closely or perpetuate Christmas mythology, in which the three Magi share the stage with the shepherds.

• *"Amahl and the Night Visitors."* This opera is demanding but has become a wonderful tradition in some communities.

Above all, we must remain sensitive to the true spirit of Advent. Commercialism, materialism, and excessive partying surround us during the season. Each congregation and each Christian will have to find ways to transform the "shopping days till Christmas" into the Advent of Christ.

—*Harry Boonstra*

setting for services in these places is not always as conducive to worship as one might wish, unless there is a chapel. Often a makeshift altar and lectern can be arranged with some creative aesthetic improvisation. Attenders will be from many backgrounds, culturally, economically, and religiously. They may feel awkward. The relationship of preacher and congregant is a bit strained, at least initially. Nonetheless, the service is an opportunity for witness and communication.

The criminal population in America is overflowing the present institutions. What great opportunity for loving Christian outreach! Normally, chaplains on the staffs of prisons and reform schools provide one-on-one and group spiritual counseling, and conduct regular chapel services. Local jails and detention homes, however, usually depend on volunteer church people and pastors to assist.

Lent and Holy Week

Easter is the holy day on which Christians commemorate one of the great mysteries of salvation: the Resurrection of our Lord. But forty days (not including Sundays) before Easter comes the first day of Lent, Ash Wednesday. During that day's service, worshipers traditionally receive ashes on their foreheads with the admonition, "Remember that you are dust, and to dust you shall return." Public worship during Lent should remind believers of their physical and spiritual frailty.

The first day of Holy Week is the Sunday of the Passion, also called Palm Sunday. It often begins with a festive procession, with the congregation waving palm branches and singing, "All Glory, Laud, and Honor" and other appropriate hymns. Then the mood shifts with the reading of the Passion from one of the synoptic Gospels. Some churches use a dramatic setting in which various worshipers read the parts of Peter, Caiaphas, Pilate, Herod, and the mob, while the minister reads the part of Jesus. The sermon and the music for the latter part of the service should focus on the meaning of Jesus' sacrifice.

On Wednesday (or sometimes Thursday or Friday), many churches hold a service of Tenebrae (darkness). Musical Tenebrae services use Scripture lessons and hymns to recreate the events of Jesus' road to the Cross. A large candelabrum in front of the church holds one candle for each lesson. After each reading, a candle is extinguished, leaving the church increasingly dark.

Maundy Thursday focuses on the institution of the Lord's Supper, or Eucharist. In some churches, the ancient practice of foot washing is revived to commemorate Jesus' humility as he washed the disciples' feet. The word *maundy* comes from the Latin term for "commandment." On this night Jesus said, "A new commandment I give unto you, that you love one another as I have loved you"

Attitude is important in a jail setting. Those who minister need the attitude: "There but for the grace of God go I." One effective pastor addresses the inmates as "fellow sinners," people to be loved and encouraged to fulfill their spiritual potential. Often testimonies work well, as do messages with themes such as "Within Your Soul You Can Be Free," "God's Assignment for You Behind Bars," "You Are More Valuable Than You Think," "Life's Second Chance," "The Love of God," and "The Transforming Power of God."

Among groups ministering to inmates, Chuck Colson's Prison Fellowship has initiated marvelous programs. The Gideon Society, Southern Baptist churches, and many evangelical bodies have developed most helpful and effective ministries of pastoral counseling, group Bible study, and worship. Working with established ministries helps churches enter this foreign world with effectiveness.

(John 13:34). Because foot washing may make some people uncomfortable, careful planning and clear directions are required. We may point out that Peter wasn't at ease with Jesus washing his feet, either.

Churches commonly conclude this service by removing banners, crosses, lecterns, and other decorations and furnishings from the front of the church, leaving only an unadorned Lord's Table. This bareness prepares people to remember the spiritual struggle our Lord endured in Gethsemane.

On Good Friday, a lengthy midday service is traditional, stretching from noon until three, the hours when Jesus hung on the cross. This service has often included the chanting of the passion from John's Gospel. The church has long held that on this one day of the year, the Eucharist, a "sacrifice of praise and thanksgiving," is inappropriate. Likewise, the sober, reflective mood is intensified by limiting Good Friday and Holy Saturday music to the unaccompanied human voice.

On Saturday night, by the bibli-

cal reckoning of time, the Sunday of the Resurrection has arrived. At this time, the early church celebrated the first service of Easter by receiving new members, baptizing those who had been prepared, and giving them their first Communion.

A contemporary Easter vigil service can be moving and exciting. It begins in the dark, with the kindling of new fire. A series of readings from the Scriptures follows, recounting God's saving acts in history. Baptismal vows are taken, and new members received. Then all proclaim the Easter faith:

Minister: Alleluia! Christ is risen!
People: The Lord is risen indeed! Alleluia!

Then follows a celebration of the Eucharist.

On Easter morning, the service will be festive, drawing on the members' most creative worship efforts. Because Easter is one of the few days on which inactive Christians come to church, ministers should be sure the service and the sermon clearly convey the Good News.

—*David Neff*

Denominational Gatherings

Churches with common historic traditions and bound by organizational structure and covenant are obligated to work together. They need to huddle occasionally to plan strategy, receive instruction, execute plans, and offer mutual encouragement. Each church thus can look beyond its walls to give support and strength to the larger fellowship and causes. In the process the local congregation gains depth and spiritual maturity.

Several types of meetings gather people from many churches:

● *Denominational meetings.* Periodic meetings and conventions are necessary on the various levels of the denomination to make agency reports, promote program emphases, and set budgets to meet needs. The meetings also allow attenders to experience praiseful singing, inspirational preaching, and meaningful worship together.

As denominational loyalty erodes, some local churches remain completely unassociated with any responsible broader fellowship, communion, or denomination. They could benefit by finding ways to participate with others of similar belief in larger gatherings.

One of the frequent criticisms of convention services is that they tend to use the same personnel time and time again, rather than get new voices or broader participation. Care must be exercised in resisting political favoritism or yielding to personal ambitions.

Convention programming includes worship opportunities among the other legislative, informative, and business sessions. Since worship is God-directed, the time and sermon should not be used for the promotion of church business. The hymns chosen should be broadly familiar and singable, and Scripture readings need to amplify the theme of worship. To the preacher is given—as always—the task of expositing the Scripture and its relevance to the people of God.

● *Regional or district meetings.* Some areawide meetings may take up only an afternoon or evening. Usually, the assembly opens with a brief worship service that includes prelude music, welcome and call to worship, opening hymn, invocation, Scripture lesson, hymn singing, pastoral prayer, and choral music. A keynote speaker often presents a theme message.

After the business of the day, a concluding worship service—sometimes Communion—may be held, symbolically uniting all in Christ and to each other for Christian service. The assembly speaker often gives a motivational and inspirational message.

Some denominations gather denominational officials and elected representatives for area business and legislative meetings. Frequently at such gatherings, such elements as a daily Bible lecture, musical renditions, dramatic presentations, and morning or evening worship times with a sermon are common.

● *Installation of a regional minister or bishop.* What a joyful and celebrative occasion is the installation of a bishop (or the equivalent)! It happens only once in five or ten years in most denominations.

Although terminology differs among the diverse denominations, the occasions are common. The inaugural of a chosen leader is a significant chapter in any denomination and provokes interest even beyond the denomination. Therefore it needs to take place in a broadly public setting.

Included as special guests of honor should be representatives from various levels of the denomination's administrative ranks. Comparable denominational leaders, seminary administrators and faculty, the mayor of the city where the service is held, and representatives of the media also deserve invitations.

The formal service, in accord with the denomination's customary worship practices, should be joyful, triumphant, and meticulously planned. The service might include a sermon by the top executive or preacher of the denomination, appropriately grand music that incorporates instrumental and choral anthems, and congregational singing. Persons from within the denomination normally are chosen to preside, lead the worship, and introduce the candidate. Appropriate parties are designated to give charges to the newly installed leader and to the churches, and an installation prayer is an important element of the service. Interdenominational participation often is appropriate for the invocation, various Scripture readings from the Old and New Testaments, and of course fraternal greetings. It would be appropriate to televise such an auspicious service for a wider viewing. A reception in an adjacent spacious area typically follows, giving all in attendance a chance to meet the new spiritual leader.

World Conventions

The world meetings or assemblies of denominations usually are geared more toward fellowship, inspiration, and education than toward legislative tasks. Those who have the privilege of serving on the program committee of such a meeting find the planning tasks formidable. The committee needs to have from various countries representatives who will meet at least annually, and if possible, at least once in the city where the convention is to be held. The culture, music, and language of the host area need to be celebrated and respected, which may require instant-translation arrangements, interpreters, and material printed in two or more languages.

The planning group needs to choose a theme appropriate for a world meeting. They must exercise extreme care so as to give balance in participation, offending no country, race, or segment of the denomination. The delicate task of choosing speakers who are universally acceptable and understandable must be handled with care. It is important to have participants representing many countries and ethnic groups, as well as lay men and women, youth and older persons, mature clergy as well as younger, various national and world denominational leadership, and various theological segments. Since speaking slots normally are quite limited, the planning committee's task is to tap leadership that will characterize the assembly as creative and contemporary in its variety, but in good taste.

—*James L. Christensen*

Resources

Blackwood, A. 1959. Pastoral leadership. Nashville: Abingdon.

Christensen, J. 1980. The minister's church, home and community services handbook. Old Tappan, N.J.: Revell.

Leibert, J. 1965. Behind bars. Garden City, N.Y.: Doubleday.

Duck, R. 1985. Flames of the spirit: Resources based on the testimony. New York: Pilgrim.

Schaller, L. 1987. It's a different world. Nashville: Abingdon.

Weems, A. 1980. Reaching for rainbows: Resources for creative worship. Philadelphia: Westminster.

Ordination and Installation of a Minister

Depending on the form of church government, a candidate for ministry may be approved in a number of ways. In Episcopal systems, the bishop plays a significant role. In Presbyterian circles, the presbytery examines and ordains candidates recommended by the local congregations. In congregational polity, the autonomous local church initiates the action and determines who should be invited to sit on the examining council.

The trials leading up to ordination also vary. Whatever the form, it is important that the examination of the candidate be scheduled on a day apart from the ordination to keep the examination process from appearing to be no more than a formality.

In common examinations, candidates present their statement of conversion, relate their Christian experience, tell of their call to ministry, and explain their doctrinal position. Candidates are questioned on such topics as relating the Bible to life, clarifying and defending their doctrinal positions, and their position on such life-related issues as the role of women in leadership or spiritual gifts, among others. Examiners need to focus on questioning and listening to the candidate, not on championing their own pet positions.

When questioning ceases, the candidate is excused, and the examiners meet in closed session to consider recommending the candidate for ordination. The group votes to af-

firm or not affirm a recommenda-
tion. Once the proper body has
cleared the way for the candidate to
be ordained, the news should be
communicated not only to the local
church, but also to the candidate's
college and seminary, and to the
community at large.

The Ordination Service

In some denominations no set
form must be followed, although several denominations adhere closely
to standard rites. Often a brief
charge to the candidate is given, followed by a charge to the church.
The candidate may be asked to affirm ordination vows. The ordination into ministry often takes place
in the form of a dedicatory prayer,
with all ordained ministers present
laying hands on the candidate. In
some traditions, the candidate
kneels.

The people giving the two charges
and praying for the candidate are
commonly selected in accordance
with the candidate's wishes. Special music, preaching, and other elements of Christian worship enhance
the occasion.

Some churches provide a gift to
the candidate, such as a pulpit gown
or a set of commentaries. A certificate of ordination is often presented
during the service.

Installation of a Minister

The service of installation of a
minister balances joy with responsibility. It functions as a time to
cheer what the Lord has done by
providing his minister for these
people. Thus joy ought to permeate
this service that officially inaugu-
rates a pastor's new ministry.

A special message designed to
present the congregation and pastor as a team can serve as the worship focal point. Music, Scripture
readings, testimonies, and prayer
reveal the delight of this dedication. A well-designed responsive
reading between the people and the
minister being installed helps to
clarify the relationship between pastor and people.

When a church installs a minister, it should make public the expected responsibilities. The solemn
sanctity linked to functioning as a
minister of the gospel needs to be
communicated. The minister's duties to God, his family, the church,
the community, and the world can
be addressed. When the uniqueness
of the office of pastoral ministry is
highlighted, the people become informed about ministry in general,
and the specific ministry of their
new pastor.

—*Samuel Canine*

Reception of New Members

In the early church, the reception of new members was a tremen-
dously important part of worship.
Reception of confirmands climaxed
a three-year process in which the
new Christians were introduced to

the mysteries and body life of
Christ's church. A confirmand's first
Communion was celebrated after
baptism on Easter morning, and it
was a memorable experience.

It is easy, given the polity of

some churches, to receive new members by letters of transfer and to let it go at that. But it is also possible to reclaim the high spiritual experience of the early church by making the incorporation of our new members an important worship experience.

Receiving Confirmands

Robert Webber's book *Celebrating Our Faith* (HarperSanFrancisco, 1986) has an excellent section (chapter 7) on the historical background of receiving confirmands. Such a public reception, which tends to be for those in the younger years, should be an unforgettable experience that young people can take with them into their mature years. It is worth taking pains to make the occasion memorable.

Such activities as a confirmation retreat allow young people to enjoy recreation but also provide structured time for reviewing classwork and meeting with church leaders. The experience of professing their faith before the governing board in the presence of their peers can be powerful and moving. It is good to end such a retreat with a Communion service, in which the confirmands are given the chance to express what their faith means to them.

Receiving Adults

When adult members join themselves to a new congregation, their incorporation should include a reaffirmation of their baptismal vows. A study of denominational baptismal standards provides an opportunity for people unfamiliar with the congregation's traditions to become acquainted with them. This can be done in the new-member class in preparation for the day of reception.

It may be appropriate at the end of the class for the new members to remember their baptismal vows by entering the sanctuary for an incorporation ceremony. There the baptismal vows may be reaffirmed in the presence of the lay leaders of the church. Likewise, this may be done at a worship service on the Lord's Day. Such an experience can be as memorable for adults as for young people.

One way to add to the occasion is to give new members a metal cross inscribed with JESUS IS LORD. Perhaps at the last session of the new-member class, a dinner can be served in which Communion climaxes the meal. Following the meal, the pastor can lead the new members into the sanctuary, where they will repeat their membership vows.

The pastor can give a brief homily about the gift cross, pointing out that the confession "Jesus Christ is Lord" is one of the earliest Christian creeds. The vertical beam of the cross points to heaven and is anchored in the earth to remind us of God's irrevocable involvement in the affairs of humankind through the Incarnation. The horizontal beam of the cross reminds the believer that the arms of Jesus Christ are stretched out in invitation to all people.

As the new members individually reaffirm their faith through the repetition of their baptismal vows, the pastor can give them the cross and commission them to carry it as a sign of their faith in Christ. At the conclusion of such a service, the equivalent of the New Testament holy kiss may be shared as the church leaders welcome the new members with a handshake or an embrace. A shortened version of this incorporation ceremony may be repeated at worship on the Lord's Day, as the entire congregation witnesses the reaffirmation of the new members' baptismal vows, and a reception is held to welcome them.

—*Dave Philips*

The Church as a Healing Community

Several years ago, the elders of the First Presbyterian Church of Hollywood desired to develop our congregation as a healing community. As we sought Christ's guidance, we became convinced of several basic biblical truths: Christ desires to do through the church today what he did through the apostles in the book of Acts; the spiritual gift of healing is still valid; Christ alone is our Healer, who desires to meet every spiritual, psychological, physical, and interpersonal need.

In light of these affirmations, we asked ourselves several questions: How can we more creatively support what the healing professions are doing to alleviate pain and suffering? At the same time, how can we express our faith that Christ often heals directly as a result of prayer, and always offers strength, comfort, and hope to those who suffer? How can we develop a ministry of healing prayer that is consistently available as the needs of people arise?

The Broader Meaning

When we speak of healing, we do not refer to physical healing alone. In the New Testament, the word *healing* (*sozo*, the Greek root from which we get *salvation*) expresses the many aspects of wholeness we desire for all people. Christ came to save us from our sins, reconcile us to God, live in us, and make us whole people in every facet of our beings. Before we accept Christ, and even after, we acquire mental, emotional, volitional, and physical diseases that hinder us from living the abundant life fully. Since Christ is concerned about all our needs, the church's task as a healing community is to help people surrender their needs to Christ the Healer and trust him completely.

Invitations to Healing

If it seems that many people's continuing spiritual and physical needs are not being met, try an experiment on a Sunday morning: Rearrange the order of worship to allow for a ten-minute period, after the sermon and before the benediction, during which people are invited to come forward for prayer by the elders. In preparation, train your elders in the biblical meaning of healing and how to pray for the various needs of people.

On the designated Sunday, teach about the healing power of Christ and then give the invitation for people to come, kneel, and pray with the elders. Depending on the tradition of your church, you may consider anointing with oil as well (see James 5:14). You probably will find people streaming forward each week to commit their hurts and hopes to Christ, claiming his healing power.

Common Concerns

Whenever a church takes seriously Christ's commission to pray for the sick and needy, certain troublesome or confusing concerns may arise. One is that not everyone gets healed *when* we want, or in the *way* we want. This often creates a reticence to pray boldly. It's tempting to proclaim that the Lord will deal with everyone in the same way. But with such false expectations, we deny his immense originality in working with his people. An emphasis on getting results *according to our perception of what is best* puts the focus on our prayers rather than on the power and wisdom of the Lord.

In spite of these concerns, one of the most remarkable benefits of a healing ministry is what typically happens to the elders. As they witness the Lord working in mighty ways through their prayer ministry, their faith and commitment to Christ soars to new heights.

—*Lloyd John Ogilvie*

Revival Services

In his famous prayer of repentance, David pleaded: "Create in me a pure heart, O God, and renew a steadfast spirit within me. Do not cast me from your presence or take your Holy Spirit from me. Restore to me the joy of your salvation and grant me a willing spirit, to sustain me" (Ps. 51:10–12). In response to the kinds of spiritual longings that David expressed, and that believers still feel, churches have conducted revivals for several centuries.

Revival Efforts

For the most part, individual churches plan revival emphases. The church's leadership sets aside some days on the church calendar for a series of services and then enlists a preacher—either a full-time evangelist, a church-renewal exponent, or a dynamic pastor. Many churches also invite guest musicians to join the effort.

In days gone by, revival efforts sometimes lasted as long as two weeks. Only a few decades ago the typical time period dropped to about a week. Today, most revival campaigns last less than four days—say, a Sunday morning through a Wednesday evening.

The evangelist, as he or she is called (even if a pastor), preaches sermons designed primarily to reignite the faith and commitment of Christians, but also provide enough "pure gospel" to encourage the conversion of non-Christians who attend. The musicians join in the effort by singing gospel songs that touch the human spirit.

Often spirited zeal and intensity characterize these efforts. People are encouraged to be faithful in their attendance and to bring their family members, friends, fellow workers, and neighbors.

Revival Strengths

The strength of a revival effort is that it meets the need of Christians to get a second wind in their spiritual-growth journeys. Every believer seems to enter periods of dryness, when the mountaintop experiences give way to extend treks through the valley. Time and temptation take their tolls on the human spirit. People do become "weary in welldoing" (Gal. 6:9). Any means of recharging the spiritual batteries will be welcome at these times.

Participants are taught to rethink the depth of their commitments and evaluate their maturity levels. Christians rededicate their lives or reaffirm the vows they have made to the Lord at baptism. Occasionally, there are new conversions.

Revival Weaknesses

Many people have grown tired of apparent gimmicks and showy endeavors used merely to procure their bodily presence at church events. Others have become suspicious of high-pressure tactics that have occasionally been used to get people "down the aisle." And the *number* of decisions to accept Christ has some-times been considered more important than the decision-makers themselves. In this context, revival planners may put too much pressure on the leader to be "successful."

Revival Today

Until the middle of the twentieth century, revivals were nearly always synonymous with evangelistic crusades. Today, however, with the exception of isolated outbreaks of fervent community evangelism, most revivals are strictly believer centered. The word most used today is *renewal.*

Revivals, or periods of renewal emphasis, can take any number of creative forms. Church leaders should not assume that they must follow the older patterns of an evangelistic preaching service. Each church must carefully discern the needs of its members and choose renewal approaches that will best meet those needs.

Many effective renewal efforts simply put people together in small-group sharing cells. There, mutual affirmation and confession of sins reignite the fires of the believers' first love for the Lord.

—Jerry Hayner

Outdoor Worship Services

G. K. Chesterton once remarked, "The world will never lack for wonders, only wonder." A worship service in an outdoor setting is a "wonder-full" opportunity. It's a chance to do more than simply *talk* about God's glory. We can look at, listen to, touch, and even smell the wonders of his creation.

How to Use the Setting

Admittedly, there are better places for a worship service—if we mean to keep it strictly traditional—than an outdoor amphitheater surrounded by pine trees, or a campfire circle at the ocean's edge. So if we are going to gather for worship outside, we need to capitalize on the natural surroundings to let them enhance and enable a unique time of worship together.

Consider these suggestions for effective outdoor worship:

• *Draw attention to specific natural features.* Give these natural wonders a connection to your worship theme. Blue sky, clouds, stars, wind, rain, trees, flowers, mountain peaks, birds, animals, rivers, ocean waves— all these potential "distractions" can be great worship aids if you take the initiative, directing attention to them rather than futilely attempting to ignore them. Psalm 148 reminds us that all of creation is praising God in obedience. Let these representatives of creation surrounding your group of worshipers lead you, as you recall that their praise is involuntary, while humans alone in all creation have the option of praising God by choice.

• *Expect the unexpected.* Worship leaders in the outdoors must be prepared for so-called interruptions and be ready to adapt to them. Let's say it's time for prayer, and suddenly a blue jay lands in full sight of everyone, contributing a loud squawk or two. Relax. Why not greet the visitor with some words of welcome and enjoy him right along with the entire group? Perhaps you could invite comments on Jesus' words regarding sparrows, or speak of the Father's care for birds and for us.

Even if the unexpected comes in the middle of a sermon, it's best to let the event subvert the agenda while taking your own importance with a grain of salt. Flex with interruptions. If you can return to your agenda gracefully after a moment, fine. If not, rejoice in the spontaneous learning or worship opportunity at hand.

• *Involve all the senses.* In addition to *seeing* so much more than they do when in a church building, your worshipers now have the chance to employ their other senses as well. Invite them to *smell* the vanilla fragrance of sugar pine bark or a wildflower's perfume. Pass around a sea shell or pine cone and ponder the creativity behind it as you all *feel* its texture. Provide a moment of pure silence, and then ask what people *heard.*

• *Be mobile.* Some of my most rewarding moments have come as I traveled to several different locations with others in the course of an outdoor service of worship—praying with our eyes open on a mountain ridge; singing a joyous hymn as we marched through the forest; standing stalk still as snow fell on our forest glade; speaking out sentences of praise as we lay on the sand, looking up at the stars. Who said we have to stay put?

When Job finally got his audience with God, he didn't get his deep theological questions answered verbally. Instead, the Lord took him on a "grand tour of creation," as Presbyterian Pastor Earl Palmer calls it. Job was taken from the seashore to the mountain heights and shown a wide spectrum of created wonders. Being directly confronted with the infinite variety and intricate details of God's mighty handiwork proved to be an enlightening worship experience indeed.

—Sonny Salsbury

Fine Arts Festivals

By nature, we humans not only work and think; we also sing, dance, pray, tell stories, paint pictures, and celebrate. A fine arts festival gives us an opportunity to renew our appreciation for our God-given creative imaginations, to reconnect with this aspect of our human nature, and to rejoice in it. Rather than being suspicious of the imagination because it cannot be defined and controlled rationally, we can utilize the power of the arts for enhancing spiritual growth.

A Festival Format

The Sunday worship experience can be used as a hub for festival activities, a celebratory culmination of the workshop experiences that precede it. In this format, a group designs weeknight workshops to involve individuals, children, and families in hands-on artistic experiences before the festival Sunday. Here are some suggestions for workshop themes along with some tips on how to use the resulting projects in a Sunday Celebration of the Arts.

• *Family banners.* Encourage family members to work together creatively on a banner that can be hung in the sanctuary to enhance the festive environment or carried by the family in a procession of praise during the Sunday celebration.

• *Liturgical banners.* Usually larger than the family banners, these can be constructed during a Saturday or midweek workshop to further illustrate in the sanctuary the theme of the festival. Well-designed and constructed banners of either simple or elegant fabrics can be stored (roll them up) for similar events in the future or to mark seasons of the church year.

• *Prints and murals.* Children can design simple prints during the workshops. Use them for program covers and publicity as well as for display in gallery space. Children of varying ages and expertise might participate by making murals of the Creation or of the Peaceable Kingdom.

• *Drama or readers' theater.* A dramatic presentation during the worship service can teach without preaching as it focuses on ideas and images embodied in the theme of the festival. It can also build congregational interest for the future use of this medium in other worship services. Readers' theater can involve from two to ten or more people. It's important to set aside sufficient time to compile a quality, perhaps provocative, script. Sometimes readers are stationed in various positions in the sanctuary to enhance the dramatic impact.

• *Creative dance.* With dance, the medium truly is the message. We are allowed to experience the grace of the dancer as we yearn to stretch and extend ourselves to God. The dancer's free and fluid movement can help the spirit of the congregation soar in ecstatic praise to the glory of God. In some churches, workshop participants may do the performing; in others, local artists.

Tips for Effectiveness

• *Begin planning well in advance* to ensure the artistic quality (and wise integration with worship) of your fine art presentations.

• *Develop a dramatic concept and theme early in the process.* This gives the festival its required unity and helps guide the development of the program. Churches are wise to give great attention to involving as many church members as possible, both in the planning and in the performing aspects of the festival.

• *Contact visiting artists well in advance.* In order to secure visiting artists such as dramatists, photographers, poets, musicians, dancers, or speakers, you may need to sign contracts at least a year in advance.

• *Carefully work out a publicity timetable.* This helps ensure the fullest participation. Send brochures to church members as well as to interested persons and groups in the community.

• *Register potential workshop participants in advance* to allow coordinators time to prepare and to secure sufficient workshop materials.

—*Michael Stauffer*

Radio Services

Radio is a technological tool that has generally served the church well over many years. It offers Christians access to biblical exposition and offers churches the opportunity to reach out to the community with a taste of appetizing Christian worship. Radio can be a ministry for a local church.

Assessing the Benefits

There are several reasons why a local congregation would want to transmit their weekly service. First, visibility in the community is a direct benefit for the broadcasting church. Even if a listener dials by the worship in search of news or music, he or she identifies the church as one that is reaching out into the community. Second, a church whose community has a large number of shut-in or immobilized members can extend the music and the message of the sanctuary into the living room of the chronic absentee. Third,

evangelism can take place among individuals reluctant to explore issues of faith in a public forum but who are seeking God in the secrecy of their car or home. A healthy pride develops among members of a church who share their pastor with the outlying community.

Getting Started

Once a church decides to take to the air, it must twist a few dials in preparation for going public.

First, someone must contact the general manager of a local station and explain the church's desire to broadcast the service. Most stations will broadcast only one service in its entirety, so a church may need to try a different station if another church is already broadcasting.

Second, negotiate the costs for air time with the station management. A station in Alaska donates the time for a Covenant church to air its Sunday service. A station in

California charges $100 per week for an hour broadcast of a Nazarene service. A Presbyterian church in Washington pays $400 per month, which includes use of its remote transmitter. Costs depend on the size of the market, the listenership, and the policies of the station.

Third, budget for additional equipment costs. In addition to the amount the station will charge, a church must also pay the telephone company monthly to install and service a "dedicated program line." This communications loop connects the church's audio console to the radio station's studio. Costs vary, but plan on $200–$300 per month. Many churches also need to purchase better microphones and a mixing unit.

Fourth, critically review your worship service. Eliminate whatever would bore or confuse. Avoid "dead air." Electronic worship is impersonal at best, but little gestures on the part of the worship leaders can help listeners feel included. Let listeners know you are aware that they are tuned in by referring to their letters or phone calls and by using sermon illustrations that relate to them.

Fifth, determine how you will come on the air and how you will close. Unless you have a professional announcer in the church, let the announcer at the station introduce your service complete with a listing of participants, special numbers, and the title of the pastor's message.

The close of the broadcast is most critical. To avoid having the station fade the service out before the sermon is complete, designate someone to sit in the front pew with time cards to assist the pastor in bringing the message to a logical ending for the radio audience.

Sixth, identify a simple but dependable follow-up process. At least send a packet of pertinent information about your church and basic Christian beliefs to those who call or write.

—*Greg Asimakoupoulos*

Televised Services

The basic assignment of ministers of the gospel is, of course, to bear witness to Jesus Christ—that is, to fulfill the Great Commission. They can carry out that assignment in two primary ways. They may do it by direct contact with persons: witnessing to an individual, a couple, or a family, or preaching to a congregation.

A second way is to take up the tools provided by modern technology—such as television—and catapult their messages beyond the confining walls of the church sanctuary. Preachers may reach thousands or tens of thousands—perhaps even millions—of listeners and viewers through the electronic miracle of television. With any success at all, televised services will be seen by more people on a given Sunday than will attend the church in a full year.

Being Effective

Assuming that all those weighty initial decisions involving budget, personnel, and equipment have been resolved satisfactorily, here are some basic considerations for churches and their pastors who seek maximum effectiveness for their airborne worship services:

• *Define your audience.* Are you limiting your outreach to the local or regional market area? Is your purpose to stimulate church growth, or is it simply to get the gospel to the homebound and shut-ins of your community? Concentrated emphasis on purely local goals could constitute a handicap if later expansion to satellite or network broadcasting is contemplated.

• *Try to ignore production distractions.* The intrusion of cameras, lights, wiring, and technicians can at first appear to be insurmountable invasions of worship decorum. It is surprising, however, to see how soon the congregation, the choir, and all who participate in the services become oblivious to the constant low-level commotion required for professional televising. These distractions become minor indeed when compared with the vastly increased outreach and response to the gospel generated outside the church.

• *Pay meticulous attention to timing.* Impact can be crippled by a program that runs too long or that comes up short. Don't depend on five verses of a hymn to fill up time. Also refuse to crowd in announcements that will invade territory reserved for preaching.

• *Maintain a consistent screen image.* Avoid week-to-week changes in what the viewer is accustomed to seeing. Occasional breakaway shots are acceptable, but predictability is important as far as appearances of the pulpit, choir loft, and chancel area are concerned. Viewers get used to the furniture, the instruments, the vestments—and expect to find few surprises.

• *Play down denominational distinctives.* The television public may be totally unlike the congregational supporters and may include many responsive viewers who are totally ignorant of doctrinal differences. If they can be brought to Christ through the effective preaching of the gospel, they can be instructed later in a particular set of convictions.

• *Involve your viewers.* Never fail to make a direct appeal to those who are tuning in to your broadcast. Make it convenient for them to write in for helpful material, such as printed copies or videotapes of the sermon. Along with offering opportunities to share in financial support, let people know how they can share prayer requests with members of the local congregation. After all, these are the people who now make up the greater part of your total parish.

No Easy Programs

Don't expect this process to be easy. Televising services and preparing end segments is time consuming, expensive, and sometimes technically frustrating. But it is worth the effort and can prove to be one of the most visible blessings in the life of the church.

—*D. James Kennedy*

15

Special Services
in the Community

When the opportunity arises to speak out in the community or participate in special services, most pastors feel a bind. Yes, they want to be a witness, to take Christianity and its world-view out among the people. But, no, they don't want to be used by those who have no idea of what Christianity is about; nor do they want to dilute their time with peripheral matters and neglect the heart of their pastoral responsibilities. Every pastor feels this dichotomy when considering activities in the more secular realm.

For example, there was a time when I was on the fast track with the media—network news, *Time* magazine, the "Phil Donahue Show," radio talk shows—as the spokesman for a leading religious and political movement. God used the wise words of a friend, however, to make me evaluate the merit of these media opportunities and to lead me into full-time pastoral ministry much more removed from the public limelight.

As pastors, we receive invitations to speak for community or media affairs. Here are a series of questions that can help us decide which invitations to accept.

Will This Advance the Cause of Christ?

A pastor's focus is on the advancement of the cause of Christ and his gospel. Consequently, a speaking opportunity that doesn't some-

229

how advance the gospel should probably be declined.

This is where the wise admonition of a brother in Christ helped me so much. I was waiting at a small airport for my commuter flight home. My adrenaline was still in overdrive. I had flown in from New York City, where I had appeared on the "Phil Donahue Show" to defend the Boy Scouts' exclusion of an Eagle Scout who had refused to affirm belief in God. The Boy Scouts felt belief in God was a fundamental value for membership in their organization. Phil Donahue had the scout and his mother on the show. I was the only other guest.

It was high drama and, I must admit, a lot of fun. Most of the audience had been against me, which made the program all the more challenging and enjoyable. Now it was over. I was rushed to the airport and had barely caught my flight. So there I was, sitting alone, when a voice said, "Hey Ed, on your way back to Lynchburg?" It was a friend of mine, an author and Bible teacher. "Where have you been?"

"I've been on the 'Donahue Show.' "

"You're casting your pearls before swine," he replied. I was shocked and angry with his answer, but before I could defend myself he continued, "You have the gift of teaching and preaching, and that's what you ought to be doing. When you get to heaven, God won't care how many times you appeared on 'Donahue.' "

I was so caught off guard by my friend's comments that I didn't even bother to respond or argue. But his words have stayed with me.

In examining an invitation for a form of public discourse or debate, we must consider both the subject we're asked to address and the forum in which it is to be addressed. For example, I was invited to appear on the "Geraldo Rivera Show" to debate pornography. I declined. Pornography is an important moral issue; we should be concerned about it. However, I did not feel the subject and the particular forum were conducive to advancing the gospel.

I did accept an invitation to speak on pornography before a group of journalists and lawyers in Philadelphia, though. I had one hour to present my case, followed by a response from several people and then an open question-and-answer period. This format gave me the opportunity to present the gospel, referring to biblical values and relating those values to a social problem in our culture. This forum had far greater potential for advancing the cause of Christ than the TV talk show.

Of course, we shouldn't necessarily turn down all invitations to deal with matters in a public forum such as television. When the Gulf War was about to erupt, I was invited to a local television station to debate the issue of "end times" with a minister who happens to be a friend. Should I accept? I did, because Christians were being misrepresented by alarmists and fanatics who were declaring the end of the world. In this situation, I felt the cause of Christ could be advanced by presenting a more moderate and responsible position.

Will I Unnecessarily Alienate People?

The church is called to reach all kinds of people and groups, yet God is neither liberal nor conservative, Republican nor Democrat. So before accepting an invitation to pray or speak, it's good to try to determine whether our words will unnecessarily alienate any group.

Notice the word *unnecessarily*. Sometimes we *will* alienate groups. That is part of being true to our convictions. For example, I have prayed at pro-life banquets. This may alienate some pro-choice advocates, but sometimes moral values do alienate. I have been invited to pray at partisan political events, too. But I have declined all such requests. If I prayed at a Republican event, I might alienate Democrats and vice-versa. The key is to be wise in our choices so we don't alienate people without a solid biblical and moral reason.

Will I Be Censored?

America has developed a public, civil religion. This means we are encouraged to water down our religious beliefs so they are basically nonoffensive to people of different beliefs and nonbeliefs. Thus when we are invited to pray or speak, we need to find out what the boundaries are. If we are asked to water down what we will say or pray, we may decide to decline.

Several years ago I was at a dinner meeting in New York City with some Jewish rabbis and Lutheran ministers. We were standing around before dinner talking about prayer. One of the rabbis said he really gets angry when Christians pray in front of him and conclude their prayer "in Jesus' name." Some of the other rabbis agreed. This launched a discussion, rather intense at times, on whether or not Christians should refer to Jesus in front of people who do not accept him as the Messiah.

Suddenly it was time for dinner. One of the Lutheran pastors was asked to give the blessing. I expected a watered-down prayer, but I was wrong. He not only prayed for the food, he also thanked God for Jesus Christ and spoke of him in a brilliant, theologically correct way. He finished by praying "in the name of the Lord Jesus Christ." The place was silent when he finished.

I learned a lesson that night: We need not back down on what we believe, although we don't want to be obnoxious, either. If people want us to drop all reference to Jesus or the gospel, we'll likely need to count ourselves out as lecturers or pray-ers. After all, can we, in good conscience, accept an invitation that comes with such binding theological strings attached?

Is This Issue a Personal Passion?

No doubt, we will have many opportunities to comment on issues through the media or in local public forums during our years in ministry. However, it is probably best to respond only to issues that truly are our passion—things we deeply care about.

For example, I have a consuming passion to minister to people with AIDS. Our church has been involved for several years in extending love and support to people with AIDS, apart from the reason they contracted

---

Baccalaureate Services

Graduations, one of the great hinge points in life, swing students out onto society's Main Street. The elements involved in graduation play into the experience: banquets for celebration, picture-taking for memories, caps and gowns for pomp and circumstance, and a ceremony for closure.

So where does faith enter in? Some communities offer a spiritual element to the graduation process: a baccalaureate service.

Why a Baccalaureate Service?

Some think the baccalaureate service obsolete. First, they say, students are so excited and overscheduled at graduation that one more occasion seems superfluous, if not unwanted. Even if they attend baccalaureate, students may not soak up anything said. Second, with the religious diversity in many communities, what kind of service can be offered? And, third, school administrators fear tripping over the "establishment of religion" clause. Each of these objections, however, has a

counterpoint to match it.

First, any milestone needs a grand occasion to recognize it. That's why we have inaugurations, anniversary celebrations, wedding ceremonies. As Christians, furthermore, we understand the spiritual significance of events. Graduation completes a chapter in students' lives, and the following chapters loom large, if not frightening. How appropriate for people of faith to shed spiritual light on not only the accomplishment at hand but also the life ahead!

Second, although religious diversity has grown recently, most people in most communities still retain a significant—if sometimes nebulous—core of Christian values and beliefs. Voluntary baccalaureate services of a broadly Christian nature remain quite appropriate in a majority of communities.

Third, school administrations are free to *allow* baccalaureate services (even several of different faiths) if they feel *sponsoring* a service would be unwise. They have not promoted one faith over another if they allow announcements of baccalaureate

the disease. Recently, I was asked to go on a local radio talk show that is devoted exclusively to the AIDS issue. The host is HIV-positive, and the program is led and supported by many in the gay community.

My decision? I accepted the invitation with enthusiasm. First, it was a great opportunity to share the gospel and advance Christ's love and compassion. Second, I had complete freedom in what I said, including the chance to support the biblical value of monogamous, heterosexual marriage. Third, I felt the only people I might alienate were legalistic Christians. And to top it off, the issue is one of my passions.

We cannot be deeply involved in all of the issues in our communities, but we can make a difference *somewhere*. For me, that some-

---

services to accompany other graduation materials.

What To Do?

A baccalaureate isn't the easiest service to plan. It usually involves leaders of various denominations, tastes, and talents. Students will not share a common heritage or expectation. A variety of sensitivities must be taken into consideration, so here are some guidelines:

• *Be broadly Christian but not generically religious.* Christians share so much in common that it is unwise for baccalaureate planners to focus on any particulars of practice. Services can concentrate on the shared center of Christianity, the broad themes all can agree upon, such as God's love or our need for him.

At the same time, a watered-down, vaguely religious, interfaith service is ill-advised. When our country or human growth or the future of education becomes the center of the service—replacing Jesus Christ—baccalaureate services will meet no one's deeper spiritual needs.

• *Be contemporary.* To many students, religion is stuffy, trite, yes-

terday's concern. We may not want to sacrifice venerable church tradition on the altar of relevance, but music, visual elements, personal manner, and sermon content must be designed to keep students interested.

• *Be personal.* Students remember relationships long after concepts fall forgotten. The baccalaureate service is for worship, but the major recipients of the message must be the individual students. Stories in the sermon, genuine warmth from the worship leaders, and understanding acknowledgment of the students' hopes and fears—all will increase the baccalaureate's effectiveness.

• *Be focused.* Graduation's hectic schedule means minds and thoughts will be scattered. A single focus—"Life's Biggest Decision" or "You've Got a Friend"—may be remembered, whereas a generic worship service in praise of God or a service that tries to cover the full sweep of the gospel will be left scattered on the floor with the bulletins.

• *Be brief.* Match the service to the expected attention span of the congregation: about 45 minutes.

—*James D. Berkley*

where is AIDS awareness and education. Therefore, I have chosen not to speak to other issues so I can speak to AIDS in a meaningful way.

Besides focusing our community efforts, this test also allows us to be more effective. If we speak everywhere on any issue, we may come across as people whose prime interest is in getting our names before the public. When we speak on issues dear to us, however, we can speak out of our own life experiences. For instance, I can speak of my friends who have died of AIDS, of my involvement with the AIDS Resource Center, of having a person with AIDS share Christmas dinner with my family.

If we discipline ourselves to address only the issues in the larger public arena in which we (and our churches) are actively involved and deeply committed, we can speak with great power and credibility.

Military Chapel Services

Military chapel services are unique in character and composition. They are required by public law and reflect the government's acceptance of its responsibility to provide for and protect the free exercise of religion for service members. They range in size from mass gatherings of cadets and midshipmen in magnificent cathedrals to small, informal groups on hillsides in the shadow of a gun turret or dug in in the desert. Services may be highly liturgical or largely freeform. Every tradition and form of worship may be encountered. But at their core, military chapels are essentially gatherings of people—believers and unbelievers together—seeking to worship God.

A Unique Group

The group gathered for chapel may be representative of thirty or forty different denominations—maybe more—with possibly no one from the worship leader's church affiliation. The group will almost certainly include people with little or no biblical or theological knowledge, as well as mature believers, so chaplains must minister to both extremes. While the government can neither prescribe an order of worship nor dictate the content of prayers or sermons, nevertheless, the chaplain faces the challenge of finding a way to provide ministry to all members of the command, regardless of their orientation. The military chaplain is paid by the government to *serve* this community, which has a right to expect the chaplain to know and deal with their spiritual needs.

Worship leaders, when called upon to share leadership of services with chaplains of differing views and theologies, are expected to cooperate, but it is "cooperation without compromise." The chaplain is allowed to determine the extent to which he or she can participate.

Have I Prayed about This Opportunity?

The appeal of speaking to the broader public can become an almost satanic temptation. When we see ourselves on television or in print, our egos swell, and we may forget who we are: servants of Jesus. Appearing before community organizations, we may begin to believe the résumés we gave them for our introductions. That's why it is critical to pray over every invitation.

During prayer God will reveal improper motives that need confessing. It may mean declining a perfectly good invitation because we are too carnal at the time to accept it. We should accept an invitation only when we are impressed by the Holy Spirit to accept it.

When I arrived back in Lynchburg after the "Phil Donahue Show,"

While there is no requirement to compromise one's message (chaplains are protected in this regard), a chaplain may need to modify personal style or approach to tailor ministry to a particular situation.

Civilian clergy can be a great encouragement in a military chapel because they are a voice from the outside, from back home. Guest civilian speakers need not mute their message; they have considerable leeway as to what they can say, since they are not government employees. They do, however, remain a guest, ministering to military folks in *their* chapel, and their hosts may have to answer later for what they say.

A Flexible Approach

Genuine evangelism is acceptable, but proselytizing is not. The key to success is having a true servant heart toward those in one's charge. The chaplain ministering in a pluralistic setting can take nothing for granted. It's wise to use familiar hymns and to publish or project words and Scripture passages. Mere courtesy dictates caution that one not disparage other faiths or forms of religious expression.

Here are some other specific do's and don'ts:

- Be flexible in your approach and prepared to condense what you have to say on short notice.
- Be accepting of unsanctified lifestyles. Meet the military personnel where they are in their search for life's meaning. We don't want to lose an opportunity to minister because we are put off by coarse language or behavior.
- Use amplification in field ministry whenever possible. "Field noise" can prove very distracting, so it's best to keep messages short and dynamic.
- Show your congregants you love them. Since military life can be tough, we need to be tender in chapel services.
- Don't hesitate to challenge the hearers. They have chosen a challenging profession, and they can handle strong words. Call them to be salt and light in a society that has a tough mission but still has respect for a Word from the Lord.

—James Edgren

my wife, Lorna, picked me up at the airport. As we drove home, I launched into a one-way verbal barrage about the excitement of being on live, coast-to-coast television. I gave her a blow-by-blow review of everything that had happened. She was strangely silent.

As we drove up the driveway to our log cabin in the woods, she said, "That's great, but could you take the trash up to the dump?"

As I drove to the dump in my 1949 Studebaker truck (with my make-up still intact), I thought, *Christianity is not to be lived in the glare of television lights. Real Christianity is taking somebody's garbage to the dump.*

When faced with opportunities to speak on television or radio, in newspapers, or to public groups, I remember Lorna's words and ask myself, *Am I still willing to take people's garbage to the dump?*

—*Edward G. Dobson*

Hospital Chapel Services

Hospital chapel services are unique and challenging. They must be inclusive and interfaith, mostly predictable yet flexible, sometimes traditional and sometimes nontraditional, and creative. The congregation of the chapel service is as varied as the daily hospital census and the staff caring for those people. Yet the services must respond to the needs of its congregation.

Four Tips

• *Expect the unexpected.* People attending the service didn't get up leisurely on a Sunday morning, carefully dress, plan the afternoon recreation, and then drive to their regular, routine service of worship. Chapel services rarely are that neat and well-planned. Rather, ministers must learn to go with the flow.

I once welcomed about fourteen patients from the Adult Psyche Unit to a chapel service that began with a brief prayer and the singing of "Amazing Grace." As we got fully into the hymn, a middle-aged African-American woman began to sing above and beyond the group. We others stopped singing as the woman continued through all four verses, her eyes seeming to focus on scenes that only she saw. She stood up and began to sway back and forth as she sang, still gazing far away. When she ended with "as long as life endures," she sat down. Every face in the small chapel was damp with tears. The quiet seemed to hold an echo of her voice. After a few moments, I said Amen and ended the service. Anything more would have been irrelevant.

• *Keep hospital services short.* Patients cannot be off their unit for long. Staff members will not want to be away from their responsibilities for long. Families will not want to be away from their loved ones for long. Twenty to thirty minutes is a practical goal. Yet, while the service itself needs to be short, we shouldn't be surprised if some of the visitors stay to talk. We should allow the time to stay with them.

• *Offer prayer services that focus on global events.* Hospitals often employ hundreds, even thousands of people. This means that global events affect the employees, and we can be ready to attend to the needs of hospital personnel affected by outside events. For example, in my hospital we held daily noon prayer services for the duration of Operation Desert Storm. Two women whose sons were infantrymen in Saudi Arabia did not miss a single day.

• *Extend pastoral care to patients, families, and staff.* The spiritual needs of the persons attending chapel services in a hospital are immediate. Everyone attending worship services in an institutional setting is under some kind of stress. They are patients or residents themselves. They are family members of patients or residents. They are staff people, entrusted with the care of patients or residents. They find the chapel and come to the service because they *need* to be there.

Memorial Services

One service that effectively meets hospital-personnel needs is the memorial service. When a staff person loses a co-worker, often the loss is experienced as a family loss. Having a memorial service gives co-workers the opportunity to remember, to tell stories, to seek comfort from Scripture and from each other.

Perhaps the memorial service will be for one of the patients. Staff people get emotionally involved with patients, and the patients' families get attached to the staff. Since staff often cannot get to a funeral home for visitation, a hospital memorial service gives them the opportunity to talk about the patient and embrace the tasks of mourning together.

—*Ann A. Letson*

16

Balancing Tradition and Innovation

A woman visiting a liturgical service kept punctuating the sermon with "Praise the Lord!" Another woman finally turned around and said, "Excuse me, but we don't praise the Lord in the Lutheran church."

A man down the pew corrected her. "Yes we do; it's on page 19."

The conflict between form and freedom is not new, and I have experienced both sides in our congregation. Some wish we would throw out the liturgy so we could be free to "move with the Spirit." Others are tired of innovations and want to return to the good old days when they knew what was happening and could follow the bulletin play by play.

Is it possible to have the best of both worlds? Yes! Order and ardor can be happily wed. Truth is canonized, but not style. The issue is not structure or freedom, tradition or innovation, but Spirit. God has no preference for formless spiritualism or Spiritless formalism; he rejects both. Spontaneity offers no innate advantage over liturgy. Liberty is where the Spirit is, not where the preacher has thrown away his notes.

Protestants have traditionally been better workers than worshipers. Pastors may spend fifteen hours on sermon preparation and fifteen minutes throwing the service together. Yet God wants worshipers above anything else. Jesus told the Samaritan woman, "He seeketh such to worship him." If we agree, then worship must not be "the things we do before we get to the important stuff."

One glimpse into heaven reveals that it is of eternal significance.

The whole book of Leviticus was written to teach a nation how to worship, an acknowledgment that at the center of life is the worship of God. Like other Christian disciplines, worship requires balance. Here are some of the areas to handle appropriately.

Balancing Praise and Worship

Reading about the worship of Israel convinces me that God is no grouch. Dancers, singers, and instrumentalists combined to make worship a time for rejoicing: "Four thousand shall offer praises to the Lord with the instruments which I have made for praise" (1 Chron. 23:5).

One of the men in our church said, "I used to think Cecil B. De Mille was overdoing it—trumpeters on this wall, heralds on that wall, and a chorus in every corner. But after reading the Old Testament, maybe he was downplaying it! I'd love to see a service with processions, banners, colorful vestments, and antiphonal singing." David declared it legal to shout to the Lord; Pentecostals have gradually made it more acceptable.

And yet after entering his gates with thanksgiving and his courts with praise, there comes a time of needful quiet. "Know ye that the Lord is God" is best done in silence. "Be still and know that I am God."

One of the Hebrew words for worship means "falling on one's face." Prostration before God says we are seeing something of his greatness in contrast to our frailty. In worship, Isaiah's "Woe is me" is more appropriate than Peter's "It's sure good to be here."

In worship we realize that we ultimately have frightfully little to say to the Lord who inhabits eternity. In the words of the hymnwriter: "Oh, how I fear thee, living God, / With deepest, tenderest fears, / And worship thee with trembling hope / And penitential tears!"

A congregation that praises loudly without worshiping meekly has not experienced the awesome and terrible side of the Almighty. To celebrate his presence is one thing; to tremble before him, as the psalmist exhorts, is another.

Yet praise is usually the necessary prelude to worship. It is rare for people to drop to their knees after the opening prayer. The skillful leader woos the congregation into worship like the patient lover draws the beloved. The congregation is brought into the audience of God more by evoking than provoking. The leader who breaks in with a jarring "Okay, let's sing all the verses of Number 317 and real loud on the last verse" doesn't realize that instead of exhorting, it's better to enter into the experience of praise and encourage others to follow by example.

Some congregations excel in praise, complete with guitars, tambourines, and drums. But having learned to make the joyful noise, let us also practice the blessed quiet. Noisemaking seems out of place when "the Lord is in his holy temple." Clapping after every choir anthem does not distinguish between the joyful moment and the sacred one. The holy hush is just as powerful as the jubilant hallelujah.

I've found most congregations are more adept at praise than worship. Where this is the case, I have used times of planned silence. A sermon that has gripped hearts may need a moment to settle before the service moves on. We have discovered that words of confirmation and personal application often grow out of the soil of silence.

But we do not begin there. Our preludes used to be quiet organ meditation. People entered in silence and did not make a sound until the opening hymn. But starting with silence makes it harder for people to feel a kinship with one another. Too often the quietness betokens only the unholy hush of mental inactivity.

We now sing songs of praise for fifteen minutes before the service "officially" begins. This change has brought a greater spirit of celebration and camaraderie. It helps us balance praise and worship.

Balancing Structure and Spontaneity

Liturgical forms give worshipers a sense of continuity. Confessing the ancient creeds reminds us that the church is a lot bigger than we are and has been around a lot longer. Forms help establish community by creating church-family traditions, so valuable for people whose present situations change by the minute.

Liturgy gives people identity. It links them with saints around the world and down through the ages who share a common confession. It helps guard against an individual piety and a proud contemporaneity. People who tend to be dazzled (and tyrannized) by the latest model of car and computer appreciate coming to a Sunday service and finding that certain things don't change as fast.

Liturgy gives structure to worship, reminding the participants of the breadth of concerns in the hearts of the saints. You *will* have an agenda, whether it is planned years in advance or on the spot. Ritual provides a workable plan, which is often the springboard for spontaneity.

Liturgy is drama, and the better it is performed, the more beautiful worship can be. The psalmist who combined holiness and beauty ("O worship the Lord in the beauty of holiness") saw that ethics and aesthetics are friends.

Protestant worship often lacks aesthetically because it has, throughout its short history, shown more of a propensity for freedom than form. But, if actions do communicate better than words, if symbols are the language of the soul, then the forms of the faith can speak to our subconscious in ways that spoken propositions cannot.

Forms do have their liabilities, of course. We who want to worship God in the worst way often do. Rite easily moves into rote. Those active participants may learn the forms and stay disengaged throughout the whole process. The prophets denounced the priests who made rite more important than righteousness. Jesus said of the scribes, "In vain they worship me." While their lips honored God, their hearts were far from him.

Unfortunately, Spirit can be replaced by technique—doing the rite thing the right way. The state of the art then supersedes the state of the heart. Any sensitive worship leader appreciates the importance of mechanics, but when the how to's get magnified, externals have replaced internals. Nothing made Jesus angrier. Liturgy void of Spirit is brassy.

Contemporary Worship

When we are in heaven, we will be in the fullest state of rejoicing and celebrating as we behold the beauty of our Lord. Every time we come together in worship, we must work to give all people—believers and our unbelieving friends and family—a preview of that joy and enjoyment that will come from dwelling in the presence of the loving, holy, and living God.

Therefore, corporate worship, founded on God's truth, should be full of meaning, joy, and happiness. Yet if it is also to be *contemporary* worship, it must be fitted to our times and target audience. Here are six principles that can help us enhance contemporary worship.

Six Principles

• *Develop a working definition of worship,* and then measure every part, prayer, and participant against this definition. Though the Bible often describes worship, it offers little in the way of a strict definition. Nevertheless, we need a working definition that really works and that is both biblical and measurable.

For example, here are two definitions of worship that I use: (1) Developing a lifestyle of active response to the person and work of God. (2) Activities of intentional focus on the person and work of God.

• *Develop a working view of creativity.* Without a practical understanding of creativity, we'll either create for the sake of creativity, change for the sake of change, or never change for the sake of tradition. All three options likely will be recognized as purposeless and eventually prove to be ministerially disastrous.

The Bible is clear: The gospel never changes, but culture does—rapidly. So our worship forms and styles must be flexible and open to innovation if we desire to stay effective.

Consider these two working views

So, we emphasize freedom and leave the rite—right? Wrong. Freedom without form imprisons us as much as form without freedom. What the Corinthian Christians lacked in maturity, they made up with frenzy. Paul put an apostolic check on their emotional excesses and gave some structure and guidelines to their free-wheeling worship. Freedom can be human-centered, superficial, or just lazy.

From an anthropological point of view, Mary Douglas argues that "the concept of external ritual in modern western society has led to a private internalizing of religious experience. . . ." We miss the artistic, the mysterious, the subconscious, and the historical in the overly intense drive for the immediate. Enthusiasm may run high, but nervous systems cannot take that much stimulation for long.

Again, we need balance. A Spirit-inspired free prayer does more than a cold form. But, a well-crafted written prayer that expresses the

of creativity I've used for about a decade: (1) Creativity is taking a fresh look at the familiar. (2) The higher the predictability, the lower the impact.

• *Develop a real view of our world.* We are responsible to initiate worship in a real world, and our world is diverse. Therefore we must diversify—give options for the various worship styles, times, and flavors—to meet needs.

As we do, we must keep three sets of factors in mind: (1) The style of the majority ethnic group within the congregation (while remembering the minority groups), (2) the needs of the churched versus the unchurched in background, and (3) the variant expectations of believers born before and after the Second World War.

• *Disciple a contemporary worship leader.* You must *be* a contemporary worshiper to *lead* contemporary worship. Thus churches that want to include or develop contemporary worship need to embrace, disciple, and develop (or hire, if there is no skilled volunteer within the congregation) someone who can lead out of his or her natural orientation.

• *Develop a commitment to planning.* The key to planning is to focus on transitions between songs and on the flow between major sections of the service. In the age of television, "dead air" will kill a service!

• *Determine the desired outcome.* I want people to feel as if they've met with God in our worship services. You may express your outcome differently, but we must at least point toward something by which to measure success. If people are saying the outcome is being achieved, we can keep doing what we're doing. Otherwise, we need to experiment with leaders, components, and planning.

The contemporary need not throw out the traditional; they can work together and be mutually corrective. When both tradition and renewal come together in meaningful, relevant worship, we truly experience a foretaste of heaven on earth.

—*Byron Spradlin*

heart of the worshiping community does not have to be cold. Liturgy that breathes will not suffocate the saints.

A small directive can give worshipers just enough structure to set them at ease. A train on its track is going somewhere. Some might call that limiting, but those willing to be instructed make good team players. They can have their part, play their part, and know it is a part, not the whole. Theologian J. J. van Allman writes, "Liturgical beauty is a protest, not only against all aesthetic self-centeredness, but also against negligence, coarseness, casualness and in general against vulgar familiarity." Total freedom leads to heresy. Anything *doesn't* go. There are ways to approach God, and there are avenues that become dead-ends. Uzzah found that out when he touched the ark. Truth is a boundary in which the Spirit moves.

Art in Worship

Most pastors have wondered at some time: *How do I go about introducing more of the arts to enhance worship in my church?* Here are two insights and some cautions to keep in mind as you upgrade the level of artistry in your worship services.

First, church members may consider art a shallow substitute for true religion. In some churches "art is only for kids." Some Christians feel that when we grow up, we should "put away such childish things" as art. As adults, we should become serious about eternal realities and human desperation. Is it wise to talk of art when men and women are struggling with the big questions of life and seeking serious answers from the church?

Yet, most congregations recognize that at least some forms of artistic expression can work wonders for a worship service. The challenge for the skeptics is to learn that, rather than trivializing worship, art tends to broaden and deepen a service's spiritual impact. For example:

• Congregationally produced banners will enhance the foyers and even the chancel of the church to set the mood for worship themes.

• Displays of icons, old Bibles or hymnals, and murals should help broaden people's perspectives on the church's diversity and history. Using photography (including slide presentations that illustrate sermon points or special music) simply acknowledges that the greatness of God's creation is not only something to *hear* about at church. *See* the majesty of God and bow before him!

• Tableau can picture a theme silently with motionless actors during a dramatic reading. This is one of my favorite image makers. We use tableau often to present the worship theme of the day.

• Ballet and other forms of dance are often beautifully done by the young children of the church who take dance lessons. These youngsters make it possible to introduce dance into a special service in which

Worship is as much a matter of seeing as of hearing. We have so elevated the pulpit (sometimes as much as twenty feet in some post-Reformation sanctuaries) that we have created stiff-necked people who think they have worshiped if they took good sermon notes. For Israel worship was a dramatic production that invited the attendance of the majestic Lord of Hosts. The more the senses are involved—seeing, smelling, tasting, touching, hearing—the more the people of God are doing liturgy. If the form has not created such action, we have not properly used it.

One way we have sought to let the liturgy live in our church is to combine the great hymns of the church with more contemporary worship songs, often without a break in between. When they are in the same key, one can flow beautifully into the other. The hymns have a

---

adult dancers might be considered inappropriate. Those who might object to whirling women in tutus will smile with delight at young interpreters.

Second, sensitivity to taste is all-important when introducing the arts. For instance, I am not a Matisse fan. A big reason for my anti-Matisse bias lies in my inability to forget that for six months one of his paintings hung in the Metropolitan New York Gallery upside down. And nobody noticed—not even the gallery's curators.

My dislike for Matisse, however, is not a global affliction; it's just a matter of taste. A given congregation may see more art in a Waylon Jennings single than it will in a whole album of Beethoven. The key, then, to using art in worship: Know your people and never forget their taste.

Four Cautions

As you introduce the arts, keep these cautions in mind:

• Do the most professional job possible. Do not embarrass your audience with shocking or amateurish productions, lest the church abandon its interest in all artistic expression.

• Begin where people are in their tastes, not where you wish they were. I once quoted a too-long passage from *King Henry VIII* to a rural congregation. After the service, one of the members sniped: "That was so good, I almost came forward and accepted Shakespeare as my savior." I've never forgotten his rebuke.

• Offer the artistic innovation in bite-sized pieces. Taste in worship can be improved, but it is best done in gradual steps. Too much, too quickly will distort the artistic intention to the point that people won't be able to see the portrait of God that worship art ought to paint.

• Aim for the midpoint between shock and boredom. The old rarely speaks with the power of the new; the totally novel, however, can shock as much as the totally hackneyed bores. Shakespeare was not commenting on worship and the arts in *Hamlet*, but he might have been, when he said: "Be not the first by which the new is tried / Nor yet the last to lay the old aside."

—Calvin Miller

theological richness often missing in modern songs. On the other hand, the songs of today have simple Scripture texts that are quickly learned. They enable people to worship freely without props.

We also include well-known liturgical responses as a part of our informal prayer and praise services. By doing this we are telling the people we like to bring out the treasure of things both old and new.

Balancing the Timely and the Timeless

God is a progressive. While the saints are singing, "Gimme that old-time religion," the Almighty is declaring, "Behold, I do a new thing." He is not the old fogy some might picture him to be; *we* are the experts at maintaining the status quo. We routinely turn movements into monuments, institutionalizing them so we can control them.

We don't do well with change, though we desperately need it. Those trained by Jesus to be people of the Spirit rather than people of technique will be alive to the now. "The Spirit blows where it wills," and sensitive people are eager to catch the direction of the wind.

The New Testament has two Greek words for time: *chronos*, or linear time, and *kairos*, which is opportunity. Hebrews thought more in terms of *kairos* than *chronos*. The opportunity presents itself and must be seized. It is the fullness of time. All times are in God's hands. He orders the times and seasons, and his creation must be sensitive to his actions and respond appropriately.

If we are alive only to the *chronos* (and in our church, the clock is in clear view), we might get out at the scheduled time, but we fall short of God's opportunity. Sensitivity to the moment does not preclude planning, but it may prompt the minister to change direction because of some nudging from God. When God comes into the midst of his people, we should know it and be able to respond to it. To be locked in to the bulletin is to be absorbed with the menu rather than enjoying the food.

There are times in liturgical worship that cry out for free expression. That's why we often allow people to tell how God is working in their lives. To miss this is to leave worship unfulfilled.

And yet the past has volumes to say to the present. Faith is related to history. The God who acts is known because of the God who has acted. History and encounter are cousins. Remembrance and realization meet in worship. James Dobson, Christian psychologist, writes that "our generation has the idea that history first began when the Beatles hit the Palladium. Such thinking alienates us from yesterday and creates a rootless society."

The strength of the contemporary is that it speaks our language. The major liability is that it appears (and may be) shallow. It has not stood the test of time. The danger of time-dated material, however, is that it is so distant it seems unapproachable. Gregorian chants make fine songs for monks, but not for kids in Levis and sandals, or so it seems. People like one or two antiques around the house, but they don't get much use.

Can we blend the two? We try by offering a *variety of musical styles.* To throw out Bach because half the church is under thirty is to cheat the young. Those who appreciate "good" music will get it elsewhere, but few youth will ever go for Baroque unless we make use of it in our church services. Contemporary music reaches their ears. Still, there is a side of God they are less likely to know. When President Kennedy was assassinated, several radio stations abandoned their normal programming and played three days of powerful classical music. Rock 'n' roll was judged inappropriate for the situation. It could not speak what had to be said.

So we use both hymns and worship songs. Music shapes theology. Of the 287 Old Testament quotes in the New Testament, 116 come from the Psalms, the hymnbook. The theology of today's songs will shape the minds of our children. Luther said, "Music is the handmaiden of theology." His enemies said, "Our people are singing their way into Luther's theology." We need to make sure our music is saying what we want it to, and then use it generously.

We also *mix free prayers with written prayers* of the great saints. This way, people grow to appreciate "the older members of their family."

Balancing Leaders and Laity

Worship in the New Testament drew both from the sacrificial system as well as from the postexilic synagogue service. The Lord's Supper took the place of the Passover as the dramatized act of redemption. The indwelling Spirit made every believer a priest and gifted member of the body. According to New Testament theologian Ralph Martin, Pauline worship stood on three legs: the didactic, the eucharistic, and the charismatic. Word and sacrament were blended with the sovereign activity of the Spirit.

By the time of Constantine, the freedom of the Spirit had been replaced by form. An increasing division between the people and the priest left the laity with little to do but watch. They did not share in Communion, now a Mass. Long cathedrals magnified the separation.

The Reformation recovered the truth of the priesthood of all believers. The Scriptures were given to the common people, singing by all was encouraged, prayers were spoken in a language all could understand, and sermons were preached to build up the people of God. And yet how much new ground have we won since 1517? Does the Spirit blow at will in our services? Do we have a new Trinity, as some suggest—the Father, Son, and Holy Scriptures? On Sunday morning are we entertaining spectators or training participants? Is it a one-man show or a gathering of the called? A revolution in communication has indeed put the pressure on pastors to do their stuff on Sunday. Some feel guilty if they do not run a three-ring circus for people who are paying well to see a good show. God deliver us!

But we do need pastoral leadership in worship. Paul's admonition about the need for "distinct notes" (1 Cor. 14:7) came in the context of corporate worship. Tending the flock includes giving them the best we can when they are all gathered together. The more secure the leader, the more we are able to draw the people into worship and take them where the Spirit is moving.

One way I've tried to live this out is by letting the proclamation of the Word be shared by a variety of people, although I do most of it. I work with people individually and as a group to prepare them for speaking assignments. When I preach, I often use members to share testimonies as an illustration of my main point.

The Great End of Worship

How often we spend too much time with people, too little with God! We enjoy the *koinonia* in the outer court; we are less comfortable entering the Holy of Holies. We ride more on the good ship fellowship than the more important one called worship. Yet the cure of countless physical and spiritual maladies is found in approaching his Majesty.

When have we worshiped? For some, it is when people have raised their hands or clapped joyfully; for others, when they have contributed to inspired singing or heard a powerful sermon. For still others, worship is when the service has moved smoothly without any hitches in the sound system, the ushering, or the music.

For Israel, however, it was meeting with God. Being in the Presence might bring quietude or exuberance, weeping or joy, repentance or reflection. But worship meant coming to God on his terms and encountering him. And that, of course, is the reason for all our attempts at balance—to enable people to enter the presence of God to worship.

—*Paul Anderson*

Resources

Martin, R. 1964. Worship in the early church. London: Marshall, Morgan and Scott.

Martin, R. 1982. The worship of God. Grand Rapids: Eerdmans.

Ortlund, A. 1975. Up with worship. Ventura, Cal.: Regal.

Underhill, E. 1936. Worship. New York: Harper and Brothers.

Webber, R. 1985. Worship is a verb. Waco, Tex.: Word.

Webber, R. 1982. Worship old and new. Grand Rapids: Zondervan.

Symbolism in Worship

Because we are living in the television age, we have become an image-centered people more than a word-centered people. Gene Edward Veith, Jr., writes in *Reading Between the Lines* (Cornerstone) that reading "demands sustained concentration, whereas television promotes a very short attention span. Reading involves (and teaches) logical reasoning, whereas television involves (and teaches) purely emotional responses."

If Veith's analysis is correct, we in the church must work hard to communicate religious truths to contemporary society by using the powerful tools of visual symbols, the language of the eye. In other words, we must learn to show, to act out, to paint pictures of, to illuminate the sacred. Preaching and teaching can keep pace in this time-compressed, present-oriented, immediate-solution world if, in a myriad of ways, they integrate the visual. Like Christ (who was the *eikon*—the image or the visual showing forth—of the invisible God), the One who took on our fleshly symbol, we must find ways to employ the visibly material to communicate the unseen spiritual realities. We must allow beauty to show forth the great I Am; we must explore ways to resymbolize the sacred truths that so many in our society need to hear and see afresh. To do this, we must marry the image to the Word.

What Is a Symbol?

A symbol is anything that stands for something else. Acts of the body can be symbolic: kneeling in prayer can stand for an attitude of submission; hands lifted in praise can say, "I am reaching heavenward toward you, O Mighty One."

Things can be symbolic. The book of the Gospels, carried aloft in an entrance processional, stands for Christ, the Living Word. The very arrangement of worship space can be symbolic. Is the Communion table in the center of a circular sanctuary? What does that mean? Is it at the eastern end of a nave? Was it once glimpsed through a screen, or is it now hidden behind an icon-decorated partition? What are these placements saying?

People can be symbolic. For instance, I was greatly astonished, having been raised in a free church background, by the deep healing effect of my Episcopalian rector's liturgical vestments. His gentle approval of my spiritual gifts freed me to use them just when I thought I should keep them at bay. I realize now that this man, clerically garbed, stood for the institutional church—and the church was saying *yes* to me and my gifts. God used this powerful symbol to straighten a lamed leg in my inner identity.

The Old Testament prophets lived among a people dominated by graven images. Their prophetic voices—those of artists, of dramatists, of poets, of mystics—communicated the Word of the Lord by resorting to visual and spatial language. Study the visual language in Jeremiah, for instance. He used allegory, analogy, dramatic role-play. The prophets howled; they wailed; they wept; they acted; they sang. They reveled in the use of imagery, unafraid to use their visual imaginations. They spoke and acted symbolically. And in our times, in our image-dominated culture, so must we.

Symbols in worship are powerful. They can jump the defenses of the intellect. They can free the soul—to laugh, to fly upward, to heal scarred tissues of bitterness. They can startle us with silence, with the profound peace that is beyond words, that pierces us only through the act of gazing.

—*Karen Burton Mains*

Vestments

All pastors wear vestments, which are nothing more than the clothing adorning clergy, especially as they lead worship.

Those from a free-church tradition usually wear a suit or a coat and tie. By wearing the typical, usually formal dress of their culture, they emphasize the essential equality of laity and clergy, as well as the need for simplicity in worship.

Many churches, however, have found that pastor and people become preoccupied with style. The slightly bright tie or, in the case of women, a new dress, elicits undue attention, pulling people from the worship of God.

Consequently, many clergy wear special vestments, such as a robe or an alb, in worship. These vestments "hide" the individual, highlighting instead the function he or she is fulfilling. In spite of some concern about the elitism special vestments may engender, many feel that such clothing adds dignity and beauty to worship, highlighting appropriately the unique responsibility of those called to lead.

Variety in Vestments

Among the vestments clergy of various traditions wear are these:

● *Geneva robe.* Resembling an academic robe, it represents the special education required of clergy. Bands on the sleeves designate a doctorate degree, and, classically, red piping stands for theology. Now, however, colors are often merely matters of style.

In addition, some pastors also wear an *academic hood* to denote their degree and academic institution, as well as to add color to their vestments.

Although black maintains a certain simplicity, it can detract from worship as the celebration of new life. Thus robes today come in a variety of colors. The traditional black robe, though, has been the mainstay of Presbyterian and Reformed worship for centuries.

● *Collar.* Formerly the full white band around the neck was the collar of Anglicans and low-church ministers, and the black collar with an opening of white in the front, the Roman. That distinction no longer applies, but in either case, the collar is said to represent the yoke of Christ (Matt. 11).

● *Cassock.* Commonly black, this full-length, close-fitting, long-sleeved, and high-necked tunic has buttons or a zipper from neck to hem. Sometimes it is worn under an alb and chasuble during worship, sometimes alone as special clergy dress.

• *Alb.* This long, white garment is straight cut and collarless, with narrow sleeves. It has a short-buttoned frontal neck opening and reaches to the feet. For some traditions, the alb goes over the cassock and under the chasuble. For others, the simple alb tied with a cincture, is the principal liturgical dress.

• *Surplice.* It is similar to an alb and white, but fuller and shorter, made with a yoke and wide sleeves. It is worn over the cassock.

• *Girdle* or *cincture.* This long cord or white band is used as a belt for an alb or cassock. It is said to represent being girded with truth (Eph. 5).

• *Stole.* This long, narrow scarf, three to five inches in width, that hangs about the neck, reaching to the knees, comes in a variety of liturgical colors to accent the church season. It is the insignia of ordination, representing the yoke of Christ.

• *Chasuble.* It is the outer garment worn when celebrating the Eucharist. Made from a half-circle of fabric, it is usually conical in shape and envelopes the wearer like a tent (from the Latin, *casuble*). It is often intricately decorated in the color of the season with modern or traditional symbols, particularly a cross (sometimes Y-shaped).

One Use

Depending on one's tradition, other vestments may be used. Climate, tradition, symbolism, and personal preference all play a role.

Although one can find many "rules" for using them properly, in the end, there is only one guideline: to help people worship God.

—*Mark Galli*

Choral Readings

Paul writes to Timothy, "Devote yourself to the public reading of Scripture" (1 Tim. 4:13). Yet surveys conducted among church members reveal that public Scripture reading is considered one of the more boring parts of their worship services.

One way to combat the poor quality of public Scripture readings—with its characteristic last-minute preparation, poor pronunciation, and shallow interpretive understanding—is to form a standing speech choir that can develop choral readings. Though you can present many parts of the worship service (such as the Nicene Creed) in this dramatic-speaking format, Scripture particularly lends itself to natural and effective scripting.

How It Works

The following is an example of a simple Old Testament adaptation.

Prayer for His Glory
A Reading adapted from 2 Chronicles 7:14–15 for five voices: a leader and four speakers.

Leader: If my people, who are called by my name,

Voices 1 & 2: If my people, who are called by my name,

Leader: Will humble themselves and pray,

Voices 3 & 4: Will humble themselves and pray,
Leader: And turn from their wicked ways,
Voices 1, 2, 3, 4 (Stage whisper): And turn from their wicked ways,
Leader: Then will I hear from heaven and will forgive their sin.
Voices 1, 2, 3, 4 (Very deliberately, with a half-beat between each word): And / will / forgive / their / sin.
Leader: And I will heal their land,
Voices 1, 2, 3, 4 (Joyfully): And I will heal their land!
Voices 1 & 2: Humble us, O Lord, we pray.
Voice 3: Convict us of sin.
Voices 2 & 4: Give us strength and desire to turn from wrongdoing.
Voice 1: So that your face may be turned toward us.
Voice 1 & 2: Your eyes opened unto us,
Voices 1, 2, 3: Your ears attentive to us,
All: So that your glory may again visit our land. Amen.

People tend to listen more intently when a reading group presents any part of worship through the vehicle of choral reading.

Getting Started

So how do you begin?

● *Recognize talent.* Call out the gifts of those who have backgrounds in the dramatic arts or who have talents in this area. Too often these abilities are relegated to use in Christmas pageants and skits for church socials. Empower these folk to integrate their unusual skills in the worship services.

● *Start simply.* Hold to the perspective that choral-reading work in most churches is a laboratory experience. Precious little literature exists on speech-choir usage in worship; you will most likely have to create your own scripts, even your own tonal markings. To begin, employ easy responsorial forms such as the sample above. In time, the congregation and the speech group will become more accustomed to unusual spoken sound. Then experiments can be made: cascades of sound, crescendos and decrescendos, overlapping voices, contrasting pitches, antiphonal chants, dramatic interpretations. Competency and complexity will evolve naturally.

● *Work hard.* Be prepared to practice and to work hard toward improvement. A speech group is like a singing choir; each voice has unique timbre, and each individual must learn to blend his or her sound with the whole group. In practice sessions, tape the reading (through the church amplification system, if possible). Then listen to what is being spoken. Evaluate: How will this sound to the congregation? Is any section unintentionally jarring? What changes will improve the script?

Scripture readings and other sections of the worship service are never quite the same once a good choral-reading group surprises us with fresh meaning.

—Karen Burton Mains

Drama in Church

People respond positively to drama, which is the most compelling argument for its use in the church today. One could argue that drama and worship were born together or that drama was reborn in the church after it had formally died out in Rome, approximately A.D. 500. But these reasons are unconvincing. Then, too, one might assert that the primary focus of the church is to preach the Word. Indeed it is, and there are few more effective supports for this mission than the medium of drama.

Good drama captures the imagination, inducing people to drop their defenses. Through identification with characters, people can laugh at themselves or be moved by the truth they witness.

Many churches are discovering the effectiveness of short sketch material, both comic and serious. While drama can inspire worship, perhaps it is most powerful when used to augment a sermon. A contemporary sketch (five to ten minutes long) that mirrors real-life experience is an effective means by which to identify with a congregation and prepare them for the pastor's message.

Pitfalls to Avoid

When the church resorts to drama, sometimes it is used as a vehicle to preach. Dorothy Sayers, however, succinctly warns, "Playwrights are not evangelists." Drama is effective in creating points of identification with a congregation, touching people on an emotional level, and raising questions. However, drama does not preach well.

Drama poses questions; preaching provides answers. The two can work together to maximize the impact of the teaching portion of a worship service. Drama can give three-dimensional life to an abstract idea, a biblical principle, a relational dynamic, or a personal challenge.

In addition to the mistake of preaching, church drama can oftentimes be removed from reality. Church platforms may present people with stereotypic, one-dimensional characters, who too easily solve life's most perplexing problems. Such an approach prevents a congregation from confronting the real power of drama, because it does not deal honestly with life's tensions and strains. Conversely, a real-life character portrayal that presents someone in the midst of a struggle has the potential to engage and impact a congregation powerfully.

In addition to pitfalls related to content, performance problems must also be addressed. Achieving the proper pace or rhythm can be challenging. Much amateur drama production suffers from slow pacing. If such is the case, it communicates an appearance of low energy and ensures that the audience will not remain attentive.

Another problem deals with the area of movement, either too much nonspecific wandering or too little movement, which has the effect of making the drama seem static. Movement needs to be specific, motivated by character, and helpful in the telling of the story.

Getting Started

Drama suffers more than the other arts due to the difficulty in assessing ability. If one cannot sing a song or play an instrument, it is clearly evident. The craft of acting or directing well, however, can be illusive. Thus, many well-meaning church people reason that though they cannot sing or play the piano, they can do drama, but they lack the technical skill to make it work.

Unless there is a qualified person to lead the charge, a church should move carefully. God, or a congregation, will not be served by bad drama. A drama director should have a background in drama and good artistic instincts, along with people skills.

If the person has little training, the church can assist by paying tuition for a course in directing and/or acting at a nearby college. While one essentially learns to direct by doing, some basic tools upon which to build are crucial.

—*Steve Pederson*

Dance as Worship

Shout for joy; sing in praise; sound the trumpets and beat the drums, but . . . *dance?* We know it was used in both the Old and New Testament communities. But how do we begin to implement this form of expression in our worship today?

Historical Precedent

The Hebrews embraced dance as a valid form of expression before their God. Miriam danced with joy after the sea crossing (Exod. 15:20, 21) and David danced triumphantly before God when the ark of the covenant entered Jerusalem (2 Sam. 6:14). Other expressions of movement in biblical processionals are described as whirling, spinning, twisting, circling, jumping, and leaping.

Both Jesus and the apostle Paul recognized dance as a normal means of expressing joy. When he told the story of the Prodigal Son, Jesus in-

cluded the dancing and rejoicing that followed the son's return (Luke 15:25). Paul reminded early Christians that they should glorify God with their bodies as well as with their spirits (1 Cor. 6:19–20). Physical movement would also aid in effective praying: "I want men everywhere to lift up holy hands in prayer" (1 Tim. 2:8).

The apocryphal Acts of John, dated around A.D. 120, tells us that Christ and his apostles formed a circle and danced in the garden after the Last Supper. At the very least, this story shows that dance was apparently still a part of the religious expression of the early church in the second century.

By the fourth century, dance still was used in worship, but with restrictions. Greek and Gnostic dualisms influenced some of the early theologians with their "flesh as evil" thinking. Thus, Augustine vehemently opposed dancing, mime, singing, and acting.

After the Council of Toledo in the seventh century, any theatrical performance was forbidden, and dance virtually disappeared from Western civilization until the Renaissance.

Dance Variations

The word *dance* in worship today can cover a wide variety of forms, purposes, and means. It can refer to highly stylized and technical movements or to simple bodily actions. Therefore, sign language, mime, and pantomime also qualify as means of offering praise and thanks to God in worship.

Not only do these activities enhance individual or corporate worship of God, they can beautifully portray aspects of human nature for reflection and meditation before the Creator of human nature. Dance can also act as a conduit for spiritual gifts, such as prophesy and words of knowledge (1 Cor. 12:8, 10), which may be given through movement along with voice. Designated soloists or groups may perform, or the entire congregation can take part through simple arm and hand movements.

When to Use Dance?

Almost any occasion within the worship life of the community can appropriately incorporate dance. It works especially well in a prelude to worship, as a conclusion to a sermon, in celebrating a wedding, in adding interest to a Sunday school class, in enhancing a church-picnic theme.

It's best to be creative and respectful, and to recognize some of the essentials:

• *Appearance.* Dancers must be sensitive to views of the congregation. Always check costuming with the pastor; it's important not to offend by costumes that some would judge inappropriate.

• *Rehearsal.* Never perform without it. A well-prepared and well-rehearsed dance is essential.

• *Authority.* All dancers must submit to one designated leader or director, and there is no excuse for show-offs.

• *Ministry.* Be extremely sensitive to the Holy Spirit. Dance is an act of worship, not a display of personal talent. This is the time when spiritual gifts can wonderfully unfold through movement.

—*Diane J. Wawrejko*

Multimedia in Worship

Inactivity plagues many worship services. The pastor may commune with God; the choir may praise God. The congregation, however, may simply nod in agreement, or possibly in sleep. Of course, we cannot dignify such passivity as true worship. Multimedia ventures a solution: to involve mind, soul, and body in worship by using more than one medium at the same time. Recognizing that people respond to diverse stimuli, we use a variety of methods—audio tapes, videos, slide shows, films, drama, object lessons—and thereby appeal to the whole person and a wider audience.

What Can Multimedia Add?

• *Multimedia activates the five senses.* Successful communicators have discovered that sensory experience stimulates intellectual involvement. "Tell me, and I forget; show me, and I remember; involve me, and I understand." I can still recall my father's message about the blood of Jesus cleansing us from sin. I don't recall the words, but I remember his gospel "magic" that turned black water clear when he poured a red liquid into it. He captured my attention. He gave me a lasting message. He pointed me to Christ.

• *Multimedia activates people in corporate worship.* If you have ever *watched* a parade, you know how a brass band looks and sounds, but if you have ever *participated* in a brass band on parade, it was no doubt a thrilling experience that you will never forget.

God doesn't appoint pastors to worship for us so that we can simply look on and applaud. Yet the body of Christ includes an inactive segment whose gifts are rarely tapped: the artists among us. Let them praise God with multimedia.

What Are the Problems?

There are some pitfalls to watch out for when using multimedia:

• *Calling attention to the medium.* Be sure to seamlessly integrate the media with your message. Set up early and rehearse, so that you can move smoothly from one part of the service to the next. Don't say

things like: "Okay, we're going to show a really neat film now."

• *Getting objections from traditionalists.* In some settings you'll have to start slow, using multimedia only on special occasions and then letting people air their opinions about how it went. Eventually, the blessings that flow from the multimedia events should overcome serious objections to wider use.

• *Coping with equipment failure.* Keep equipment in top repair with back-ups close at hand. The more media involved, the more that can go wrong. As they say in the audiovisual business, "With a-v, it's foresight or no sight."

The New Multimedia

In the business world today, *multimedia* means text plus highfidelity sound plus color graphics plus animation, all controlled by computers. These programs offer greatly improved reliability, mass information-storage capability, and split-second access to any visual or audio segment. Quite possibly this technology presents a solution to the problem of inactivity in worship. Attend any computer convention, and you will hear buzzwords like *presentation* and *interactive*. These words suggest the missing elements in many worship services:

• *Worship should be a presentation.* Worship is the act of giving ourselves and our gifts to God. A multimedia presentation is one way that we can offer our praise as a *present* in an appropriate and artistic gift wrapping.

• *Worship should be interactive.* Just as public presentations now encourage more spontaneous giveand-take, so worship should be a two-way street. God speaks to us, and we can respond to him with a multitude of media.

Praise God in his sanctuary. Praise him with . . . multimedia.
—*Donald P. Regier*

Worship for People with Disabilities

You step up to the pulpit and launch into your sermon with a funny incident that occurred earlier in the week. As you pause, you expect appropriate laughter, but what happens next throws you off balance.

"Auuugh! Hah!" The loud gaffaw fills the worship center. Halfway down the side aisle sits a cerebral-palsied young man from the local residential center. He flings his stiff paralyzed arms, trying to stifle his laughter, but his weak throat muscles aren't much help. It's obvious: he loves your story!

I'm glad this young man is enjoying Sunday service, you think, *but will he burst out again? Can I keep my concentration? What about the attention of the congregation?*

Questions such as these crop up whenever a church begins a disability ministry. What *do* you do when a person with disabilities cannot control his behavior in church? Or is it enough to provide a sign language interpreter for deaf people — and how can you know if the interpreter is faithfully representing your message? Is it practical to immerse in baptism a person who is paralyzed?

Biblical Guidelines

These are good questions, and since disabled people are complex individuals with varying degrees of functioning capabilities, the answers are subjective. You can make wise judgments if you recall these basics:

• Jesus said, "Come to me, all you who are weary and burdened . . ." (Matt. 11:28). Remember the "all" includes "those parts of the body that seem to be weaker . . . and the parts that we think are less honorable, we treat with special honor" (1 Cor. 12:22–23).

• The preaching of God's Word is paramount in worship, for "faith comes from hearing the message, and the message is heard through the word of Christ" (Rom. 10:17).

What Can Be Done

Let's examine a few of those earlier questions in light of those guidelines.

• *How to handle the person who cannot control his or her behavior?* People with disabilities should have the privilege to worship as anyone else. The complexion of Christ's body should include people with disabilities, even if some of their actions seem distracting or distasteful. The loud or frequent outbursts of a severely disabled person, however, may become a serious distraction to the preaching of God's Word, and at that point, the needs of the congregation as a whole should be considered. In love and sensitivity, pose the honest question to the person with a handicap (or a family member) and together arrive at a creative solution.

• *How can you select a good interpreter for persons who are deaf?* Excellent resources are available for Christian interpreters who want to improve their sign skills. Make certain your people are linked with disability parachurch resources, such as Deaf Opportunity Outreach (P.O. Box 1327, Louisville, KY 40201) or Joni and Friends (P.O. Box 3333, Agoura Hills, CA 91301).

• *What about baptism by immersion?* You would be surprised at how skilled disabled people are at overcoming seemingly insurmountable barriers. It may require assistance from an elder with strong muscles, but immersion is definitely pos-sible. Ask the disabled person for advice.

Being Made Perfect

God may want to enlarge the hearts of the nondisabled members of your congregation, and he may choose to do it through people with disabilities. They remind us all that God's power "is made perfect in weakness" (2 Cor. 12:9).

The well-groomed woman sitting properly in her pew halfway down the side aisle may gain a new slant on that verse as she holds the hymnal for that cerebral-palsied young man.

—*Joni Eareckson Tada*

Architecture, Acoustics, and Lighting

Bruggink and Droppers wrote in *Christ and Architecture* (Eerdmans), "Architecture for churches is a matter of gospel. A church that is interested in proclaiming the gospel must also be interested in architecture, for year after year the architecture of the church proclaims a message that either augments the preached Word or conflicts with it."

The relative emphasis a congregation places on the basics of architecture, acoustics, and lighting will direct how it builds its church. Given that the sanctuary is primarily a place for worship (the acknowledgement of God's worth) and that growing awareness of that worth comes through a growing understanding of the Word and Sacraments, the task facing the church is to convey effectively these fundamental truths in temporal ways so as to aid and not detract from that process of understanding.

The Message of Architecture

• *Baptistries.* Churches that immerse might well be able to incorporate the splendid running-water fonts now used in Roman Catholic churches where immersion is again being emphasized.

• *Baptismal fonts.* Communions that sprinkle will need only a font, but it should at least be of such size, quality, and placement that it acts as a constant visual reminder to the congregation of their baptism into Christ.

• *Pulpits.* A large pulpit of quality, carefully placed to focus attention and enhanced by beautiful antependia or a sounding board, visually speaks of the importance and authority of the Word.

• *Tables*. Like the pulpit, the Communion table needs to be placed to both reflect the importance of the Lord's Supper and effectively service the congregation. The theology of the church will determine the extent to which it appears as a table, an altar, or a combination.

• *Seating*. Seating should reflect the fact that the congregation is the gathered people of God who live in fellowship with one another. The size of the congregation will determine what is practicable, as will the style of worship.

• *Choir*. For proper placement, consider these questions: Is the role of the choir to praise God on behalf of the congregation, to support the congregation in their singing, or to entertain? Will the placement allow their participation in the worship? Will the choir be a visual distraction relative to the primary worship emphasis on Word and Sacrament?

The Message of Acoustics

If the church room is of ideal proportions—as high as it is wide and twice as long, and finished with hard surfaces—an acoustician or electronic sound system may not be needed. When acoustical advice is needed, however, it should be sought from a qualified acoustician and not from a salesperson for electronic equipment.

While electronics may make it possible for the preacher and choir to be heard, other elements of worship such as congregational singing need to be considered. If hymnody is an important part of worship, do the room's acoustics support that function? If the congregation cannot hear itself sing, merely amplifying the song leader or choir will only make matters worse by increasing the sense of being "sung at" rather than increasing a group's sense of corporate praise.

The Message of Lighting

The psychology of lighting is of utmost importance. Dim lighting within a large Gothic structure may increase a sense of awe and reverence, whereas dim lighting in a small church may only be annoying. Some variation in levels of illumination do make it easier to concentrate on the ministry being performed, but care must be taken not to exaggerate the leaders involved lest a message of separation between themselves and the laity be communicated.

In the final analysis, unifying the body of Christ in worship is the ultimate aim.

—Donald J. Bruggink

Part III

Music

Surely music, of all our earthly pursuits, comes closest to simulating for us a taste of heaven! Yet music is one church enterprise we seem to have such a difficult time getting right.

Not only behind musicians' backs do pastors call the music department the "war department." Not only at musicians' conferences do music directors lament the state of congregational awareness of things musical. Not only in sick churches do congregations lock horns over the approved list of hymns to sing or instruments to play or musicians to play them. Music, it seems, with its direct line to the heart, also stimulates the ire and idiosyncrasies in people.

This need not be so. Heavenly strains mustn't necessarily lead to earthly strain. Ego isn't a Siamese twin to musical gifts. The knowledgeable and godly musical team can transport a congregation to the gates of splendor without dragging them through the ports of controversy.

How this is done is both a gift and a science. And the writers in the following section offer those gifted with music a periodic chart of the elements of a fine musical program. Even those who need a briefcase to carry a tune will find better ways to understand and appreciate both the music and the musicians who offer their songs to God.

17

The Purpose of Christian Music

Music and the people of God have been partners ever since God called out a people for his name. Scripture points out that it is God who truly gives a song. At Creation the stars sang together, and when the Jewish nation was born, music was placed in the hearts of God's people. The Book of Psalms, the hymnal of Israel, is located in the center of God's Word.

David, the man after God's own heart, was the "sweet singer of Israel" and calmed his sheep and his king with his harp music. The Jews were the singers of the ancient world. Even when the nation was taken into Babylonian captivity, they were asked to sing (although they had temporarily lost their song through disobedience and had left their harps hanging on the trees).

In temple worship, singing was vital to the proceedings—singers and trumpeters with one voice would lift powerful music to God, and he was pleased. Levites (the worship leaders of the nation) who were talented in music were encouraged in every way to discipline and train themselves in the craft of musical composition and performance.

The scriptural refrain "sing a new song to the Lord" has inspired believers in every generation to vital, relevant expression that will magnify the King of Kings. Musical literature is full of sacred expression that has expressed eternal truth from the soul of believers. Perhaps no vehicle of expression has more power than music to address the conscious and subconscious mind of humankind with information that will be retained.

Music is an art form that brings the intellect and emotions together uniquely. Musical texts with biblical and theological substance weld facts and feelings.

Humankind has the ability to be rational and thoughtful about eternally significant truth. A tendency to go by feelings—"How do I *feel* about this?"—accompanies most people's rationality, however, and sometimes life situations cause us to react more by how we feel than by what we know to be true. Music of theological merit uniquely informs our feelings. It communicates much of what we know of God and how we respond to God.

A nonsinging Christian is like a nonswimming fish. It is natural for the joyful heart to sing, and no song is greater than the song of the soul set free, no message greater than the fact that we have been forgiven, reconciled to God. The fact that we get good at what we practice should motivate us to rehearse our faith in song and to strive constantly to improve that song to the glory of the God who gave it.

The Language of Emotion

Music can be defined as a language of emotion. It is made up of component parts of tone (timbre) which gives the sound identity, melody (tune), harmony (simultaneous sounding of related pitches), and rhythm (or meter). The juxtaposition of these components is directly related to the innate talent and training of the composer. The art of composition has long been honored by humankind, but historically, many of the greatest artists were not recognized as significantly during life as after death.

Music exists for its own sake, (i.e., for beauty and expression of the otherwise inexpressible). It has also been found to be functional: to accompany dance, to tell a story (i.e., program music) as vocal accompaniments or dramatic accompaniment (as in musical theater and worship).

Often the "function" of music has given the particular sound an inherited meaning. A strong three pattern soon became associated with the waltz (or other dance form). A four-beat march pattern became associated with the military or parades, as in Sousa marches. A rhythm that is in four with accents on the second and fourth beats brings association with jazz or rock. Tempo added to these rhythms sets a mood from relaxed and dreamy to frenzied.

Various timbres of musical sound have become associated with function as well. A smooth, silky violin speaks of romance, a raspy saxophone of sensuous activity, the blast of a trumpet with a call to arms, and so on. Certain kinds of harmonies also have associations. Clustered dissonance represents chaos or unrest. Other altered chords speak the language of jazz. Simple straight chords say hymnic or folk music.

Listening to film scores will further clarify the matter of association. Note the music in a western, a science fiction classic, a love story, a city scene, a country setting, a lively club, a tranquil forest, a cathedral wedding, a funeral, and so on. Your imagination has probably changed musical association while simply reading this list.

Music in Church History

This matter of association has had a great influence on church music through history, and still does. Certain sounds tend to send messages based upon the activity most commonly associated with that sound. New Testament times undoubtedly produced music that sounded very Jewish, since early Christians came from a temple background.

Familiar Jewish folk music such as "Havah Nagilah" is minor, peppy, and happily melodic, with open harmonies and strong, even rhythm. This music in a "verbal" tradition has been rather consistently preserved through history and can still be heard in neighborhood synagogues.

From the early Roman church came various modes and chants that dominated the music of that church until the Reformation (1520s). All kinds of rules were developed to keep the chant "pure" and free from worldly association. Scale systems and eventually harmonic combinations were canonized and then protected for sacred use. Sacred and secular music were, for the most part, clearly distinct. Church music performance was primarily limited to the clergy.

With the Reformation came a move to give the music back to the people. German folk songs (drinking songs) were "sanctified" and brought into the church so the people could sing recognizable melodies and harmonies. These were refined and further defined and nationalized, and thus a hymnic tradition evolved in the various countries and denominations of Christians.

Great debate followed as to the kinds of music permitted for Christians and where and when music could be used. Can singing be accompanied? Can it have harmony? Who can sing the melody? Can words other than Scripture be sung? Can thoughts other than prayers be musically expressed? Who can lead the songs? Denominations split over the answers to some of these endless questions. People served jail time for singing the wrong song at the wrong time or in a wrong manner.

Music has had many limitations specifically spelled out, all in the name of pleasing God. In some situations, it became such a problem that decisions were made to eliminate it from the church altogether. Music is such a dynamic, vital vehicle for the praise of God, the teaching of his people, and the proclamation of the gospel, that the Enemy has constantly worked to neutralize it in the church.

Church Music in the U.S.

In the brief history of the United States, many traditions unique to a given time and culture have grown around church music. Early European settlers brought their country's and sect's traditions and were often protective of them. Early in our history, Africans introduced a highly developed, complex rhythm not heard before by the settlers. The combination of these cultures ultimately gave rise to spirituals, blues, jazz, and rock—the result of European melody and harmony energized and adapted by African rhythms. Regional influences became recognized in the spirituals and sacred harp of the South, the defined traditions of New England, and the functional folk influences of the West, not to mention the ethnic preferences of communities and denominations.

Performance or Offering?

Music is important to God. He clearly led David to provide organized professional musicians among the Levitical priests. God also revealed that he actively responds to the music offered to him in worship. Through music, he changed the heart of Saul in preparation for his role as the first king of Israel (1 Sam. 10:5–6), healed the impaired spirit of Saul through David's anointed playing (1 Sam. 16:23), revealed his perfect will to the prophet Elisha through the ministry of an instrumentalist (2 Kings 3:13–15), demonstrated his glory during the first worship service in Solomon's temple (2 Chron. 5:11–14), delivered a seemingly hopeless battle into Jehoshaphat's hands (2 Chron. 20:20–23), released Paul and Silas from prison and brought salvation to the family of their Roman guard (Acts 16:25–34). Should we expect less of our Father today as we offer music to him?

Is Music a Performance?

The way we design most of our worship settings evokes ideas of entertainment—fixed theater seating, creative lighting, excellent sound reinforcement, padded pews, well-qualified leaders, pleasing colors, flowers, candles, banners, stained glass. In addition, by the very nature of their medium, church musicians easily perceive themselves as performers. When they direct their music only to people, performers they are. The object of worship then becomes the music itself. But when they direct their music to God, he rightly becomes the focus. So the essential question is this: Who is the primary audience?

Try as we like, we simply cannot divorce all elements of performance from an organized, corporate worship service. Even when the pastor preaches, his or her desire is to communicate with excellence and

Various revivals and outstanding movings of the Spirit of God have contributed other unique sounds. Revivalists such as Dwight L. Moody, with musicians Ira Sankey, P. P. Bliss, and others, gave a whole new sound to the gospel. Radio, with music and preachers like Charles Fuller and the "Old-Fashioned Revival Hour," brought in chorus-choirs, quartets, and piano styles to the Christian community. The "Jesus movement" of the 1960s and 1970s added its unique brand of sound to Christian music.

Recently the recording studio, with endless possibilities for songs and styles, has flooded the market with music in the name of God. Compact disks, tapes, music videos, and magazines about Christian music represent a giant industry in modern communication. Christian television programming, which creates tastes for large segments of the Christian populace, is having a great influence on what people

---

clarity. Yes, the preacher wishes to be a prophet, empowered by the Holy Spirit, but he or she will wisely employ proven communication techniques to enhance the message. Thus, even the preacher is a performer—at least in part.

The key is to keep our focus on God, whether speaking or playing music. The goal of all worshipers is to make a suitable offering to God— an offering of excellence. The challenge to the church musician is to make this offering with integrity of heart.

How Worshipers Respond

Worshipers are to be participants, not spectators. They are to participate with their whole beings—heart, soul, mind, strength. But how can the congregation be participants when the choir or instrumentalists are the ones making a musical offering? And what is an appropriate emotional response by the congregation when music stirs them?

The obvious answer to the first question is that the congregation must often participate vicariously. This is true of many acts of worship. The answer to the second question is not so simple. In many churches, verbal responses or even applause are welcomed. In others, no outward response at all is expected.

How do we deal with these differences? Consider the issue of applause. In our biblical models, there are many appropriate acts of worship. Some of these may not be stylistically or culturally acceptable in modern settings, but they are biblical, nevertheless. Among these are speaking, singing, shouting, dancing, playing musical instruments, and— yes—clapping our hands. This act becomes applause only when it is offered as a *reward for a performance rendered*.

So the question again emerges: Who is the audience? If the musicians have correctly directed our attention to God, then perhaps applause may be gratefully offered to him—an appropriate biblical expression of emotional release, offered in his very presence.

—*C. Harry Causey*

expect to hear in church on a Sunday morning.

All of these factors have brought us to our current world of music in general, and church music in particular.

Music as an Ally

Christians of all stripes can view music as a great ally in ministry. Those committed to a rich, historical tradition of classic proportions can benefit from a good dose of openness to contemporary sounds and expressions. Those who believe today's church demands only "now" sound can gain historical perspective and a sense of the continuity of Christian music by learning their musical heritage. Youth needs what experience has taught for support and meaning. Likewise, older Christians need youth to stay vital and alive. Music is a marvelous transgenerational bridge.

Music is a tool in our hands to do the work of ministry. The church is not a museum for preservation of the arts or a showcase of creative

---

Dealing with Conflicting Musical Tastes

"I *like* what I *know*, and I *know* what I *like*." When we stop to consider the great variety of backgrounds and cultural exposure represented in any church, we begin to realize that, when it comes to taste in music, some like it hot and some like it cold. Some prefer the twang of a country-western ballad, while others crave the harmonic intrigue of a finely textured chorale. Each of these—and most forms of music in the broad range of styles between them—can have a place in corporate worship when used with discernment and creativity.

Is "Liking It" Essential?

Somehow we have nurtured the idea that we must *like* everything we hear in our churches. Could this be akin to the immature adolescent who resists an otherwise beneficial activity because "It's no fun"? Cer-tainly the criterion for our musical values should go deeper than that.

Remember the first time you ate an artichoke or any other delicious vegetable that was distasteful to you upon first bite? Perhaps now it is a unique delight to your palate. I used to tell my freshman music-appreciation students, "You don't have to *like* Stravinksy or Wagner or Schoenberg, but you do have to give them a hearing and be open-minded to those new sounds and aural combinations. Come back to them again and again and again."

The wise music minister recognizes cultural diversity and makes every effort to touch the congregation at many places in the spectrum of music understanding and appreciation. This does not mean he or she will have no personal standards; it will mean that he or she will practice art not only in *what* is performed but also in *how* it is performed.

talent. It is a vital organism of God, the bride of Christ here to carry out God's eternal plan. Music allows the people of God to join in one voice to his glory. We can sing the same words at the same time and focus on his attributes of holiness, mercy, grace, and glory. He created us to glorify himself, and music helps us do it. Music teaches the truth of God; truth sung is permanently planted in the singer's mind. It is a sure way to teach the alphabet or phonics, and just as sure a way to teach doctrine and theology. Singing it equals retaining it.

Music has also been one of the greatest means of expressing the gospel to unbelievers. Revivalists from Charles and John Wesley all the way to Billy Graham have sung the gospel and had it sung. Contemporary musicians using all the musical resources at their disposal sing the gospel to their generational peers, often with great results. Well-worded metrical texts set to the current musical sound have reached into unbelievers' hearts with conviction. Interestingly, once a musical style is used evangelistically, it has impacted tradition.

There is an artistry in the choice, placement, usage, and sensitive rendition of a simple Gaither melody or response chorus, while there can be some rather inferior renditions of Bach polyphony. Giftedness in music leadership shows through when one can utilize various styles of music in their appropriate and best-suited places in worship. When any piece of music is honed and perfected in the best of taste, it can be offered to God with joy—*soli Deo gloria*. This careful choosing and implementation of musical "tools" for just the precise task at hand in worship, and not for self-aggrandizement, is the mark of a craftsperson in the ministry of music.

Could Prevention Help?

Much future conflict can be avoided when the minister-of-music candidate enters the interviewing process, long before he or she stands at the front of the church to be formally accepted by the congregation. Serious, probing questions must be asked at this time—and answered honestly. In seeking out a music minister, or in looking for employment, we may try to avoid the embarrassment of clearly defining our likes and dislikes, our hopes and ideals, our musical tastes and fancies, only to pay the price of disillusionment in later days.

When an impasse does occur in an ongoing staff relationship, and the problem seems unable to be solved, sometimes it is best simply to realize that people are not on the same track and perhaps never will be. There would have to be too great a sacrifice of individual ideals, standards, and aspirations for the music ministry to continue to ignore this widening gulf.

Neither party or point of view need be considered invalid, yet the church and minister of music likely will benefit if plans are laid for finding more mutually compatible situations.

—Howard Stevenson

A Theology of Music

A basic theology of music may be developed by observing some of the occasions in Scripture where music appears prominently. In the worship service described in Exodus 15, several principles emerge: (1) Moses led Israel in singing to and about their exalted God (Verse 2: "The Lord is my strength and my song; he has become my salvation."). (2) Their music rehearsed the mighty, redemptive work of God, who had delivered them from the hand of a formidable enemy. (3) Their song exalted the attributes of God. He is called majestic, exalted, holy, and awesome, and he possesses unfailing love.

The text of their song is a lesson to all who would sing to and about God. Our songs should remind people of the character of God, his absolute victory over the power of sin, and the superior way he leads and guides those he has redeemed. It seems that too often songs concentrate on ourselves and our problems rather than on the Lord, who is the very essence of victorious life.

Another biblical music lesson comes from the Book of Nehemiah, in which the man of God who obediently rebuilt the walls of Jerusalem under difficult conditions dedicates those walls. He sought to carry out the festive occasion in a manner pleasing to the Lord. In 12:27 he calls out the Levites to lead in "songs of thanksgiving and with the music of cymbals, harps, and lyres." The Levites purified themselves, the people, the gates, and the wall. All who would serve the Lord in music should see to their own purity of heart and motive. It is always vital to ministry that we heed the command of God to be holy and sacrificial toward him.

Note also how carefully the musical offerings were organized and rehearsed in verses 31 and 38; the choirs proceeded in a carefully planned and orderly manner. The singers performed, led by Jezrahiah, offering sacrifices with rejoicing. The joy was so great that it was heard from far away. The musical offerings gave voice to triumphant hearts, and the entire community became newly aware of the wonder of God. A mark of biblical music ministry is the impact it makes on all who participate, both hearers and performers.

Many more lessons of theological significance may be gleaned by a study of the Psalms. Emotions ranging from tears to dancing, exclamations of fear to praise, clapping to weeping, thanksgiving to complaint were all set to music. The range of musical expression is limited only by the imagination, as we consider the incredible greatness of God and the tremendous need of humankind to relate to him.

One final Bible passage informing our theology of music comes from the pen of the Prison Apostle who sang with great power in the Philippian jail (Acts 16). Paul instructed both the Ephesian church (5:19–20) and the Colossian church (3:16) with similar words. He established a priority of variety in singing "psalms, hymns, and spiritual songs."

What exactly qualifies as each kind of music has been widely debated, but the fact remains that we should sing *psalms*, and there are 150 easily definable ones in the canon of Scripture. *Hymns* are usually regarded as being of human composure but solidly God-centered in terms of declaring his power and attributes (objective in nature). *Spiritual songs* usually are considered more subjective and based more on our experience. Some would even define them as extemporized "songs of the spirit" primarily intended for private worship. The overarching principle here is to balance our singing to include all of these in an effort to express a view of God that is fixed in his eternal Word (psalms), his immutable character (hymns), and our relational experience in knowing him (spiritual songs).

A Costly Sacrifice

There are challenges to music ministry that must be faced if we are to be effective. Hebrews 13:15 refers to our "sacrifice of praise" as "the fruit of lips that confess his name." A study of biblical sacrifice reveals the mandate to give to God the best, a costly sacrifice. This surely rules out shabby, poorly rehearsed musical offerings. This principle to serve God with our best may vary from person to person, but we and God both know when we have done our best for him.

Mankind's tendency to claim glory that belongs only to God presents musicians another challenge. The flesh has a habit of looking for human approval. Too frequently well-rehearsed and well-trained musicians seem to obstruct the view of God by communicating the notion that they are great. This puts no premium on shabbiness in the name of humility; it is intended only to remind us that God will not share his glory with another, and that he resists the proud but gives grace to the humble. The lofty goal of excellence with humility is one to which every musical servant of God should aspire.

The need for meaningful enjoyment for the believing community is valid. The danger, however, is to fill the need for fame and fortune instead of the eternal glory of God. We must constantly ask ourselves, *Why am I doing this?* and come up with a God-honoring, honest answer.

Music offers the people of God one of their most valuable assets. The worship of God—our highest priority—is powerfully served by music. With united voices we sing back to God his wonder-working power in sovereign design. One generation can declare God's power to another in song, and teach them of him. The educational power of music is undisputed. The unbeliever can be confronted with God's eternal truth effectively through music. All of ministry—worship, edification, and evangelism—has music as a willing, powerful tool.

Music has been used in these three dimensions for generations. Our task is to learn from history, align ourselves with it, contribute to it, and express God's truth, until he calls us to himself—the church triumphant, in which "the song" will continue eternally in musical terms we can't even imagine here and now.

—Gordon L. Borror

18

Planning a Music Program

Why are we here? What is our unique calling? What does God want us to accomplish? Church leaders planning a music program must first hammer out a clear, concise statement of objectives in answer to such questions, with biblical priorities and congregational expectations clearly in mind. The Bible teaches that glorifying God is the ultimate purpose of life: church life, family life, personal life. Therefore, we must come to see that music in the church exists to bring glory to God, both through direct praise and service, and through ministry to people (reaching the lost and nourishing believers). Maintaining these vertical and horizontal dimensions will help shape and clarify the musical purposes and goals of a church, regardless of its size or resources.

Once such philosophical guidelines are brought to the surface and understood, we can then grapple with the details of how to go about the work of music programming in the local church. Let's begin by considering congregational needs and expectancies.

At a basic level, humans apparently need to express their love for God in song. Throughout biblical history, God's people have been singers. The most important music in the church, then, is to be made by means of congregational voices and hearts joined in praise. The music offered to meet this need should be accessible and singable, and should represent the best of our Christian heritage of the past and the best of the new musical expressions.

Congregations have expectations as well as needs. People in our churches should expect the music to be spiritual—that it represent biblical truth delivered with spiritual and musical integrity. Those who "perform" should be prepared, both musically and spiritually, to handle the musical selections responsibly and to believe in (and seek to live by) the texts they sing. My observation is that congregations will increase the level of their valid expectations for quality music programming as they are led by a music ministry that has appropriate variety and that is sensitive to that particular community's educational, socioeconomic, and cultural experiences. All of this is done with an eye toward constantly elevating and enriching a congregation's image of God. Again, the glory of God is the issue, not the musical taste of pastor, people, or musicians. Music ministry seeks to magnify the Lord!

Assuming you are philosophically and theologically on target with your sense of purpose and mission, you are ready to tackle the "practical" side of music ministry. Here are eight key issues that typically confront pastors and people in churches of all sizes, along with some suggestions about how to approach the decisions they require.

Issue #1: Space

I once got quite a surprise when I entered a church to speak on music ministry. I walked into a spacious auditorium that would seat 700 people but had a platform area so tiny there was barely room for a pulpit and a chair. One of the members explained to me that the founding pastor wanted to be sure there would never be space for a choir because "when Lucifer fell, he fell into the choir loft, and if you want to find where trouble starts in the church, look to the choir." Ridiculous!

Effective music ministry demands sufficient space for a choir. The key is to make the space flexible. Avoid built-in risers for a choir, or rails bolted to the floor. Since our society has become progressively more visually oriented, build in ways to change the area's appearance occasionally. Consider using movable risers with stackable seating for your choir members. The surface of the risers should be hard, to reflect sound, with ten-inch steps between rows.

Try to avoid a fenced area for the choir, since such architectural barriers tend to separate those members from the rest of the congregation, inhibiting a strong sense of community. Ideally, all are participants in worship, so work to do away with the appearance that some members are the performers and others are merely the audience. For pageants, musicals, dramatic productions, and so on, the flexibility of movable risers permits many more arrangement options. Platform furniture should also be minimal and movable.

The permanent instruments, probably the piano and organ, should be placed side-by-side to facilitate the musicians' ability to hear one another and to move easily from one instrument to the other. This also eases the director's access to the accompanists by looking in one direction. If other instruments are a usual part of services, they, too, should be in close proximity to one another.

Music ministry also requires additional space in the form of rehearsal facilities, such as choir rooms and practice rooms. Dedicating space for this assures people of the ministry's significance in the church and provides an environment conducive to quality preparation. Ideally, rehearsal space should be at least as large as platform space, so rehearsals will not be totally dependent on the availability of the worship center.

Don't forget storage space. Costumes, props, lights, and other equipment easily become lost or ruined when there is no place to store them for future presentations. Also, the music library will eventually represent a large investment; proper storage space, which is accessible and organized, will go a long way toward preserving it.

Issue #2: Instruments

A music director will be concerned about the purchase and upkeep of church instruments. The most historic church music instrument is, of course, the organ. The next most obvious instrument is the piano, which is best placed on a hard surface for reflection of its sound. And today electronic keyboards of all types and price ranges have become viable options for music ministry. Historically, these keyboards grew up in pop music with studio applications, so it's wise to use sensitivity in adapting them for church services.

In addition to the typical, traditional instruments, do not overlook the orchestral instruments and those in your church who play them. Many publishers offer music for ensembles of all sizes and composition. Providing sanctuary space for orchestral players (along with church-owned stands and books for playing along with hymns and choruses) will help encourage their participation.

Many churches have almost totally abandoned traditional church instruments in an effort to make proceedings feel less churchy. For instance, they use a worship band, with a few miked singers to set the tone of contemporary celebration. Synthesizers, guitars, and drums are amplified, and the sound reflects the pop culture. There is little doubt that God can and does use a great variety of sounds and styles to communicate his message.

Issue #3: Sound

In recent years, the sound system has risen to nearly disproportionate levels of importance. Historically, church buildings were built to reverberate sound, which added to the sense of mystery in worship.

The spoken voice and music gains a heightened sense of the Spirit when there are a few sounds of ambient reverberation bouncing around the room.

Many churches now, however, are built with acoustics that more closely resemble a recording studio, which means the natural ambience is dampened by carpet, drapes, and furnishings. Though you may try to replace that naturalness electronically, the general rule is that you cannot make up for a dead building with a good sound system. If the main musical event is congregational singing, then we must design facilities to heighten the singers' acoustic environment, since we certainly can't put a microphone at every pew!

Basic to good sound is an environment that compliments natural sound. There must be at least some reflective surfaces so the church

---

Selecting and Purchasing Music

A great deal of planning usually goes into the selection, purchase, and performance of music used in worship. Wise selection of music involves a careful consideration of the text, the tune, and the available funds.

The Words

Some ministers of music rely on denominationally published suggestions of hymns and choruses that follow the lectionary. However, if the preaching in your church typically is topical or expository through extended portions of biblical texts, you likely design services around a worship theme, focusing on truth presented in the message for a particular Sunday.

The text of the hymns must then draw worshipers to the same key truth or attribute of God that the sermon and the rest of the service lifts up. The topical index and scriptural-allusions index found in many hymnals and companion books become invaluable resources as we

plan for such services.

The hymn and choral texts must say something that can be understood by the worshipers and must also be consistent with the theology of the church. Though well-known texts bring the security of the familiar, they may also cause the singer to pay little attention to what is being sung. Sometimes, a new text challenges us with a fresh look at a truth about God.

Be aware of the cultural implications of texts. Inclusive language is important to many congregations. The use of biblical feminine imagery when referring to God will go unnoticed in some churches but raise concerns in others. If we sing Psalms that speak of the clapping or raising of hands, we shouldn't be surprised if some of our congregants do just that.

The Tune

The musical score of hymns and anthems (as well as instrumental music) has tremendous power to evoke emotions and memories. For

body gathered can get an aural sense of community. If the room is so acoustically dead that music loses natural presence, the people will not sing freely or sense they are in the congregation of praise. If the musical accompaniment blares at the people, they will not hear themselves and will again lose the sense of corporate worship they should expect.

As with major instrumental purchases, seek help from those who understand sound reinforcement and who know the nature of your particular ministry. The most important considerations are speaker placement, microphone type and placement, and control-center requirements and placement. Will you need chancel microphones? How many microphones—and in what arrangement—will you need for the variety of situations likely to arise?

example, the instrumental introduction to Bach's Magnificat in D absolutely commands excitement and praise. The tunes of "Amazing Grace" and "O Store Gud"—"How Great Thou Art"—will be instantly recognized by most American Christians and bring certain emotions to the surface when played on the instruments, even before a single word is sung. The first few chords of a familiar carol will move all our thoughts to Christmas. The tune of "Jesus Loves Me" draws us to the reality of God's love for our children.

We need to be aware that these emotions will be in our congregation when we use a particular piece of music. The mood of the music can be joyful and exciting or pensive in nature, causing us to look inward, drawing us to prayer and confession. The design of the worship experience should tell us what mood we want at a particular location in the service, and the music should be selected accordingly.

The Budget

After being selected, most printed music is purchased in Christian bookstores or by phone or mail. Many churches order from discount choral music services, which typically offer a discount of 15 to 30 percent off retail. Some of these discount services have staff persons who can make suggestions about particular worship needs. Others offer a free service of drilling holes in scores to permit use in a three-ring binder.

Here are some major discount choral music companies:

- Creative Music, Austin, TX (800) 926-2424
- Kempke's Music Service, Longwood, FL (800) 753-6753
- J & J Music Service, Chickasaw, AL (800) 456-4966
- Pine Lake Music, Decatur, GA (800) 241-3667
- Christian Supply, Spartanburg, SC (800) 845-6718
- Accelerando Music Service, Odessa, TX (800) 433-4267
- Southern Baptist Music Service, Nashville, TN (800) 368-7421
- Church Music Lending Library, Normal, IL (309) 452-6710. (They'll loan music to your church for 60 days, with a small membership fee.)

—*Larry Ellis*

Good sound does not call attention to itself. Like so many aspects of ministry, if the vehicle becomes more obvious than the message being delivered, the stepping stone has become a stumbling block.

Issue #4: Lighting

Though music ministry is primarily about sound, we must be careful not to overlook its silent partner—lighting. Obviously, all participants must have sufficient light to see their hymnals, Bibles, music, and orders of service. Be certain there is sufficient candlepower where it is needed in the room. Highlighting the platform area can be a great asset to communication. Floodlighting the choir, orchestra, ensemble—or tastefully spotlighting a soloist or speaker—focuses attention where, and when, it is desired.

Obeying Copyright Law

You are planning a worship service, but the pew hymnals don't include a song you want. Someone checks a second hymnal and discovers the perfect hymn. "Let's print it in the bulletin," someone suggests. "Or, how about using an overhead?"

"Do we need permission?" wonders another.

That's a good question, because knowledge of copyright regulations is as much a part of music ministry as choosing music. Ignorance of the law is no excuse. New songs and hymns are offered to churches by composers and publishers who have made an investment to make these songs available to the public. The church should honor that investment, and determining what is and isn't legal to use is a beginning.

Basic Definitions

Simply put, we may not make copies of a copyrighted song if by doing so we are avoiding purchase of the song in its published form.

Copyright is a means whereby a song or other creation can be protected for a given time. Both international and national copyright laws protect the use of these creations. Copyrights are indicated by the copyright symbol © or the phrase, "Used by permission of . . ."

After a given number of years, a work ceases to be protected by law and enters the *public domain*. Generally speaking, if something predates this century, it is in the public domain.

Suggestions

Here are some thoughts for properly handling copyright matters:

• *Texts as well as music are creations under the protection of copyright law.* In fact, the text, the tune, and the harmonization of the tune may all be copyrighted. It is possible for three different publishers to share copyrights to a single hymn. It is also possible that just one element of a song be copyrighted while

Lighting as an art form grew up in the theater and can become incredibly complex and costly. Much has been written on just how to achieve the desired effects. This is not a suggestion to make church services into theatrical experiences, but it is a plea not to overlook another valuable asset for effective musical presentation. The lighting of any environment influences the overall mood, which, in turn, does affect the response of those involved.

Issue #5: Hymnals

Does a modern music ministry need hymnals? Yes! Through the hymnal we join hands with saints of other ages who have been through the crucible of human experience and have discovered that God *is* able. It has been well said that through the Bible, God speaks

the other parts exist in public domain.

Churches sometimes print the texts to choral music in the bulletins to enhance congregational understanding, but if the song is under copyright, permission is necessary to do so. Even out-of-print choral pieces remain protected by copyright, and permission is needed for copying.

• *Permission must be obtained for the use of transparencies or song charts.* If the song appears in the pew hymnal, the right to use it has been purchased. In such a case, publishers often grant permission at no extra charge.

• *Organists may duplicate music in order to facilitate page turns.* As long as a copy has been purchased, publishers generally do not require an organist to purchase a second copy.

• *Soloists shouldn't copy music for accompanists.* If two copies are needed for performance, two copies should be purchased.

• *You may be able to duplicate copyrighted hymns under certain circumstances.* If a choir prefers not to

mark up their hymnals, copies can be made of hymns—*if* a copy of the hymnal exists for each duplication and the choir isn't avoiding purchases by making copies. Still, permission ought to be requested.

• *Permission to copy must be printed on the copies.* Churches should print an acknowledgement as stipulated by the copyright holder. Small type may be used, and the information may be placed at the bottom of the page or the end of the printed service.

Moral and Legal

Permission is available, and it is worth the time and investment to get it. The cost for using a song one time is a phone call and a small fee, seldom exceeding ten dollars. Some publishers and groups of publishers provide annual license agreements whereby churches may use all the songs under their copyright. It is wise to keep records of copyright permissions obtained, including records of correspondence and phone calls.

—*Emily R. Brink*

to us; through the hymnal, we speak to God. The two books have been companions for generations, and whether or not it is recognized, we still need that companionship. If our hymn singing is dead, it is because we lack the leadership to bring it to life.

Many fine new hymnals are available that incorporate new as well as older songs and offer a great variety of service helps and ideas. You can get instrumental versions, concordances, companion volumes, devotional guides, and cross-indexes to help you vitalize your hymnic experiences. A local church should replace its hymnal every 10 to 15 years to stay up-to-date.

A book of hymns links the life in Christ with the truth of God. When Christians are encouraged to use their hymnals as devotional resources, they quickly recognize the spiritual wealth they have at their fingertips. If the hymnal is considered optional and left in the racks, the message is that we don't need it anymore.

Though projecting words on a screen has it advantages, those words can be difficult to read for visually impaired people who *can* see a book in their hands. Plus, if congregational singers do read music—or ever hope to learn—they must be able to see the musical notation.

I am not speaking for the *exclusive* use of the hymnal. I believe creative options are good and often beneficial. I am simply speaking against a growing tendency to ignore the wonderful resource for worship, evangelism, and edification found in the hymnal.

Issue #6: Leadership

Who will lead our music program, and how will we get people involved? This is one of the most challenging questions facing so many pastors and leadership boards. Recent awareness of the musical demands of our churches has elevated the role of worship leader/musician to new heights. Ideally, church music leaders should be called as surely as pastors, missionaries, and youth leaders. They should have the sense that they *must* serve God and that music ministry is *his* choice for them. Occasionally the pastor will find a person in the congregation who has the necessary musical skills; that person must then be discipled to employ those gifts in the local church.

The pastor and musician(s) should see themselves as players on the same team, never as competitors. Too often, communication breaks down, and these two leaders somehow begin competing for recognition in public services. My experience has taught me that I have much to learn from my pastor and other associates, and that I can teach them, too. When leadership is seen as partnership, God's glory shines through.

Once you establish your musical leadership, participation in the program must be sold to the people at large. Choirs, ensembles, and instrumentalists can be mobilized and encouraged by God-honoring, church-edifying quality in music. People love to be on board when they are convinced that what is being done is edifying, satisfying, fulfilling, and truly carrying out their beloved church's ministry priorities.

Issue #7: Planning

Many churches employ a music-program planning committee to insure that the church body has appropriate representation. This committee requires visionary leadership that is well-apprised of the overarching philosophy of music ministry. Musical styles, the number of participants, instruments employed, service-music demands, special occasions, and other concerns all bear on the planning process. Here are some areas to cover:

- *The availability of talent.* Do we have the people and talent to do what is being called for in our ministry?
- *Scheduling.* When taking a look at the calendar, ask: How many regular services require musical input? How varied will the ministry be? How many special/seasonal events will produce added demand for music ministry? Who will meet these needs?
- *Scope.* Do plans contain visionary goals that can be reached as God provides additional resources, or do they reflect only a maintenance mentality?
- *Breadth.* How are we attempting to meet the music ministry needs of the various generations? Graded choir programs have been shown to be outstanding training and involvement activities for children and youth. Service music as well as musicals should be planned for all choirs and ensembles. Interest in a church depends on the involvement of the greatest numbers of our people. What they believe in, they prepare for; what they prepare for, they attend; what they attend enthusiastically, they invite others to share.
- *Worship planning.* This, too, must be a team effort. If your church follows a liturgical plan, much of the direction is set by the seasons of the year. All could learn, including free church devotees, by looking at the church year and the reminders it provides.

Pastors and musicians do each other a large favor when they know what the other is doing. As a music leader, I appreciate it when my pastor, well in advance, gives me his sermon titles, primary Scripture references, and a broad outline of his sermon objectives. I can then keep them in mind as I make music choices to ensure that the service is coherent from beginning to end. The objective is to have a well-focused congregation, not confused sheep, when the service concludes. Any attendee should be able to articulate the main idea of the service as he or she exits.

Issue #8: Finances

The glory of God is the issue, not how much we can spend. What will it take to do the job well? One general rule of thumb is that 10 percent of the church's operating budget (*not* including salaries of music personnel) should be designated for music ministries. A ministry as public and important as music must have funding to function. The cost of instrument maintenance, special-event productions, retreats, and participant-enrichment seminars should be built into the budget from the beginning. Too many churches see the music ministry as the "entertainment division" of the church, and think that when they can't afford to be entertained, they will do without.

On occasion I have heard of churches that receive music offerings at special musical events. What comes in at this time can then be spent on the music program. This places too much of the responsibility for funding on the people already involved and committed to music ministries. Instead, *all* programs of the local church should be shared by the entire body. Where our treasure is, there our heart follows. When the whole church invests in music ministry, their collective heart is far more likely to respond to it.

To say that every church requires the same music program would be absurd. Your program may look like no one else's and yet be just right for you. In every case, however, music ministry is right when people are more interested in pleasing God than in pleasing themselves or impressing others. It is right when both spiritual and musical integrity are held in high esteem, since music and ministry were made for each other.

—Gordon L. Borror

Resources

Allen, R., and G. Borror. 1987. Worship: Rediscovering the missing jewel. Portland, Ore.: Multnomah.

Hustad, D. 1981. Jubilate! Wheaton, Ill.: Hope.

Leisch, B. 1988. People in the presence of God. Grand Rapids: Zondervan.

Lovelace, A., and W. Rice. 1976. Music and worship in the church. Nashville: Abingdon.

Mitchell, R. 1978. Ministry and music. Louisville: Westminster/John Knox.

19

Overseeing a Music Program

Music has always been at the center of the worshiping community. It is one of God's most glorious gifts, able to move people beyond the realm of mere words. Without doubt, music touches the eternal.

Many times, however, it is the center of temporal turmoil, even among God's people. Although there are moments of sublime harmony between pastors and musicians, there are also times of painful dissonance, as opinions, traditions, and egos clash.

Who is to decide the proper role of music in the church? Most ministers of music will say the responsibility is theirs. Most pastors will remind them that they still lead the church. Members of the congregation offer more opinions than Bach has cantatas.

Some congregations see music as a distant cousin to the "real" ministry of the church and basically "hire someone to do it for us," to dress up the services. As a result, services (and often the music ministry itself) become more performance than participation. The people tend to assume the roles of critics rather than worshipers. The music director produces rather than ministers, and the gap between musician and congregation only widens.

The pastor is forced to side with the congregation or the minister of music. If he or she chooses the congregation, a staff member is alienated. If he or she sides with the music director, his or her own ministry becomes more vulnerable to criticism.

Neither approach is the solution. Too often these conflicting attitudes and expectations can threaten congregational health. Must music be a continual battleground between musicians and pastors? No.

There is a better way, but it's not a quick formula to guarantee a spectacular music ministry.

A pastor can bring a strong, balanced calm to a church through hard work, patience, and skill. The following principles are characteristic of such a pastor who encourages musical excellence in his or her church.

Minister to, Not Just Through, Musicians

Musicians are real people with real needs, just as the rest of the parishioners and the pastor are real people. Obviously, ministers of music differ in age, gender, training, and abilities. They may be part-time or full-time. Their musical tastes may well be very different from those of the pastor. Yet, they almost always share one common trait: commitment.

Most music ministers see their ministry as a distinct calling, although they often struggle with the same things that hinder pastors—insecurity, feelings of inadequacy, exhaustion. They need someone they can trust. They need a pastor.

Everyone in ministry exhibits a reasonably confident leadership style by necessity. But no one should mistake the reality that few of those called by God to minister have an overblown view of their own ability and position of leadership. Indeed, deep within everyone whose vocation lies within the church is a yearning for profound and abiding friendship. In times of personal crisis especially, those called to ministry need a friend, someone who can listen. As Dietrich Bonhoeffer wrote, "Christians have forgotten that the ministry of listening has been committed to them by the One who is Himself the great listener and whose work they should share. We should listen with the ears of God that we may speak the Word of God."

No one knows whether there was a song leader in that happy, calamitous band that traveled with Jesus, but if there was, certainly he knew he could share his burdens with his Master, whom he knew would listen. This is no less true regarding the relationship between ministers of music and pastors.

One also surmises that Jesus was more than willing to share a laugh with his disciples. Ministry to colleagues means sharing glad times as well as struggles. Laughing together is a life-giving exercise.

Malcolm Muggeridge once commented that the steeple and the gargoyle of the medieval cathedral provide a healthy pattern for the Christian life: the steeple symbolizing the heart reaching for the infinite God in heaven, the laughing gargoyle reminding humanity of its earthbound limits. What a pattern for healthy co-ministry relationships! Amid the urgency of the task, the joy of shared laughter can lighten heavy loads, calm ruffled feelings, refresh weary pilgrims, and renew an eternal perspective.

Good relationships must be worked at, but the result is worth the effort. Mutual concern and joy are contagious. Congregations should be encouraged to see that their leaders not only work well together but actually enjoy being together. Listening and laughter are two gifts any pastor can offer. Musicians, like anyone else, care about ministry because they've received a ministry of care. Belonging is the foundation of all motivation.

Fix the End; Flex the Means

People tend to work better—certainly more enthusiastically—when the end is clearly established but the freedom to develop the means is fluid. As Peters and Waterman said in *In Search of Excellence*, people are motivated by a simultaneous need for both meaning and independence. Unfortunately, it's easy to try to determine the meaning for people without allowing them the corresponding independence to reach it.

For instance, one seminary graduate approached his first parish keenly aware of the inadequacies of his church and the solutions for solving them. It was a rather arrogant ignorance with a spiritual veneer. He planned great moments for the congregation, where the worship could finally be what God intended the saints to experience. He took particular care to select hymns of substance, structure, and style. No gospel fluff was allowed.

This particular young pastor, however, wasn't aware of his rather limited knowledge of hymnody, nor of his ignorance of the tastes and abilities of the congregation. These liabilities, although real, did not deter him, for it was he who knew best.

Eventually this sincere but misguided young minister was graciously reminded by his minister of music that familiarity and singability aren't sins. The musician worked with the pastor to broaden his use of the hymnal, helping him to incorporate hymns that might be less sophisticated yet that still provided excellence in worship. The pastor learned—gently—that this was an area better known by the minister of music.

Indeed, music ministers are generally more knowledgeable than pastors, and they are often more creative. We pastors often need to learn to heed their creative ideas.

Another story: One year during Advent, one minister of music decided to have the Christmas choir concert in the fellowship hall. She wanted people to invite unchurched friends who might not come to a church service but would come to a more intimate evening of music, hot cider, and cookies. The fellowship hall, however, when tightly seated, had about one-third the capacity of the sanctuary. This meant at least three performances, with tickets to regulate the crowds.

Inwardly the pastor shuddered as he thought, *Welcome to the Covenant Cabaret!* Top on his mind were the logistical and ecclesiastical headaches. When it was over, however, it was the unchurched friends who seemed to enjoy it most. Again the lesson came home: Allow freedom for individual gifts to be expressed and grow, but do it within the context of structure.

Planning is the key. The more strategy employed, the better the harmonization. Thus, regular staff meetings are a must. Regular cal-

Working with Organists and Pianists

Working with an organist or pianist means that you're working with an artist—someone who is creative, who has imaginative ways of accomplishing goals, who strives for perfection, whose work is intensely personal. How can this creativity be channeled to benefit the whole church? How can personalities in the music staff and the pastoral staff work in harmony? How can excellence be achieved by both?

What Musicians Need

Church musicians need pastoral support when facing difficult situations, whether the problem be complaints about the tempo or volume of their hymn-playing, their choice of prelude or postlude, or even disagreements among staff members. The important thing to remember is that one person's negative (or positive) comment doesn't necessarily mean that immediate, drastic changes must be made in the music program. Specifically, an organist/pianist needs the pastor or worship leader to do these things:

- Provide the hymns and service music early enough in the week (or month) so musicians have time to practice, consider free hymn accompaniments, and/or cross-reference hymn tunes to preludes, offertories, and postludes.

- Ensure that dates and times of rehearsals and services are coordinated with all musicians well in advance.

- See that the choir director provides copies of anthems to the accompanist for competent preparation prior to the scheduled performance date.

- Meet with the director of music and the organist/pianist to plan and schedule the music and to determine who will be responsible for each aspect of worship planning: Who chooses hymns? Who suggests a change of music for service music? Who will provide titles to the secretary for inclusion in the bulletin?

- Evaluate Sunday services: Was the choice of hymns appropriate?

endar reviews, both long- and short-range, anticipate seasons and special events before they spring up as surprises.

Is it possible for the pastor to give to the music minister his preaching schedule for the next six (how about three?) months? It is, and it is amazing how much this helps. The choir doesn't have the pastoral luxury of waiting for last-minute inspiration to decide what to do on Sunday. They need weeks of rehearsal time. Musicians must plan ahead even if the pastor does not. Why not work together?

Such planning not only gives direction to the music ministry but also enhances corporate worship and probably makes for better preaching. It even eases the pastor's Saturday-night nerves.

Were the hymns singable? Were there awkward moments due to poor preparation or planning? Did the ego of the musician interfere with worship in some way? In what ways did the musician encourage congregational participation?

What Pastors Can Expect

Organists/pianists have varying degrees of musical training. Some have had a few lessons; some play only by ear; some have doctorates in their instruments from major universities. Some may serve as choral directors or as overall music coordinators in their churches. Others may be responsible for working only a few hours a week. These factors, of course, help determine what to expect and how to establish channels of communication.

Remember that most organists/pianists feel fulfilled in their service to God during a worship service if: (1) the service flows smoothly, (2) there is a sense of cohesiveness between musical elements and the spoken Word, and (3) the musician is satisfied with his or her performance. Effective service planning and open communication among all the worship leaders is the key. Encourage musicians to:

- Learn new music and keep their creative and imaginative juices flowing.
- Attend professional conferences, workshops, and seminars— ideally at the church's expense.
- Join professional or denominational music organizations, such as the American Guild of Organists or the Association of Anglican Musicians, again, at the church's expense.
- Share their concerns—musical and personal—with you. This will require establishing a nonthreatening atmosphere that will slowly build in levels of trust as you learn to communicate with directness and love over the years.
- Ask questions to understand the pastor's reasons for particular aspects of the services.

Since both pastors and church musicians share in common a sense of professional pride and ownership in their ministries, mutual respect makes the best foundation for an effective working relationship.

—Joseph M. Galema

Encourage Musicians to Grow

Professional development and spiritual growth are crucial to any ministry, including music. Unless the pastor personally encourages such growth, it might not happen. Such encouragement is both direct and indirect.

First, the direct. It's good to thank the minister of music regularly for the hours spent preparing for Sunday morning, and say how much the music ministry means to the church. When musicians bring success, they need to know it.

It's easy to focus on areas of weakness, thinking that correcting faults will lead to better performance, but success is usually a more powerful motivator than failure. After affirming strengths, then we can strengthen weaknesses based on a firm foundation of accomplishment. Direct, honest encouragement pays rich dividends.

Should Church Musicians Be Paid?

Some churches believe music is a ministry to be carried out by volunteers. There always seems to be someone available who will play the organ or direct the choir in the weekly anthem. Other churches expect to pay to maintain a certain level of music performance. The music budget is quite large to make certain that this standard continues. Let's look at how Christians might argue key points on each side of the question.

Points in Favor

• The music ministry is important to our worship and outreach philosophy. Since the amount of time needed to do the work exceeds what is reasonable for a volunteer, we choose to pay a person to ensure that the ministry will stay strong.

• When we hire someone as a minister of music, we are providing leadership to equip the congregation for ministry, not just to maintain a program. Our music minister brings a significant historical perspective and vision to our worship. He or she actually is much more than a songleader, spending considerable time selecting music and planning our corporate worship.

• We are called to be stewards of God's gifts to us—music in particular. We also wish to employ a wide spectrum of music in our worship. For that reason, we feel we need leadership from people who have prepared themselves for the ministry of worship and music, just as our preaching pastor has been prepared for the ministry of the Word.

• We use many people from our church in our music ministry. However, there are some significant needs that cannot be met from within our church. Therefore, we supplement our work with professionals from outside our congregation from time to time. This actually

Encouragement can also be indirect. There are times when it is appropriate to be a music ministry ally—sometimes even an advocate—to the church board. For example, it may require pushing to increase the budget so new music can be purchased. Some may feel the choir can still sing the old songs, but these same folks never want to hear the same sermon twice.

Freshness is part of creativity, so encourage musicians to improve their craft by attending seminars, workshops, and classes at the church's expense. Why not provide money for subscriptions to professional journals and music libraries?

Then, if the musicians are paid, there's the issue of salary. Here's where the baton hits the podium. Pastors need to be willing to recommend realistic raises at annual-review time. Raises inspire pastors to do their best better, and it's no different for ministers of music.

One last form of encouragement: We should pray with and for mu-

---

strengthens our overall ministry and allows us to attract musicians into our church who might never otherwise be a part of our ministry.

Points Against

• We are a small church with a limited budget, so what is done here with music must be done through volunteers. We do provide great opportunities for those who would like to test their spiritual gifts in music.

• Our theology of spiritual gifts tells us that God provides all the resources needed to do what he calls us to do as a church. Therefore, to go outside the church to hire someone to make this happen seems to contradict our biblical understandings.

• We aren't looking for a "professional" church musician. We prefer the older hymns, and since we really like a full orchestra for the choir, we use prerecorded accompaniment sound tracks.

• Our church has other priorities that seem to override the desire

for a paid music director. For instance, we concentrate on social ministries. Because we have paid staff members in these ministries, we do not want to add a music minister's salary to the church budget.

Coda

There may be no universal answer to the question as to whether or not musicians should be paid. However, evaluating some of these ideas in light of a particular situation may assist any decisions.

In any case, if churches hope to develop and improve the celebration aspect of their worship, Christian musicians must be able to spend the time necessary to provide the leadership. Volunteers are paid only in the satisfaction of their work well done. For some people this is adequate. For others it means they cannot offer ministry to the church as they would like, because they must work other jobs to provide for their financial needs.

—Larry D. Ellis

sicians. Too many times these colleagues relate on a solely professional level. Musicians need prayer as much as anyone. It's tough ministering week by week to a media-blitzed congregation whose tastes run from Amy Grant to Giovanni Gabrielli. Musicians feel the pressure and need to know they are being prayerfully supported.

Dignify the Ministry of Music

To dignify the ministry of music, we must be willing to go public, to let the congregation know how valuable music is, to develop appreciation for the musicians. Corporate worship is a prime time to affirm the work of musicians and ministers of music.

Some churches offer a prayer of consecration at the beginning of each choir season. Some regularly refer to the anthems and solos (even to unsung accompanists) during worship. It's one thing to say "Nice anthem last Sunday" passing in the hall. It's something else to express the same on Sunday morning from the pulpit.

What of applause? While we want to avoid the entertainment complex, heartfelt applause out of adoration for God and appreciation for his gift of music can sometimes be a genuine form of public affirmation.

Congregations enjoy showing public gratitude. Surprise the music minister with an evening of recognition, and it's practically guaranteed that the ministry of music will become even better as a result. Such is the value of giving the music ministry the dignity it rightly deserves.

Even with all this, however, problems can still arise, so there remains a need for at least one more principle.

Know When to Intervene

There are times in any organization when a part runs ahead or away from the rest. This can be true of a music ministry, usually as the result of exuberance and enthusiasm. When the rivers overflow their banks, there are times the pastor has to sandbag.

Knowing when to intervene is an art that demands patience, wisdom, firmness, and love. Because people and situations are different, lists of what to do aren't always useful. Instead, it is helpful to try seeing the situation two ways: through objective and subjective relationships.

Objectively, pastors need to be concerned about the relationship of music ministry to the larger ministry of the church. Subjectively, they need to be concerned with their relationship with the minister of music. Both must be weighed to solve any problem successfully.

Private intervention is always best. When a problem arises, it's wise to talk with the music minister. Chances are a mutually satisfactory solution will be reached when the larger ministry of the church is kept in view. Two heads work better than one, and this will prevent major conflicts from developing out of single-minded and, many times, narrow perspectives. Often, early intervention can be timely and helpful.

Other times, however, intervention is a mistake. For instance, early in one pastorate, I decided to bring a different emphasis to Christmas. Instead of the annual Christmas Eve service the church was used to, I proposed a traditional Scandinavian *Julotta* service at 6 A.M. on Christmas Day.

My concerns were genuine but not well-informed. The minister of music was less than enthusiastic and pointed out that the Christmas Eve service was an opportunity for outreach; a 6 A.M. service probably was not. But I was adamant, so the plans went ahead as I instructed.

Although the service was reasonably well-attended, it was lifeless, as though everyone was being dragged along through the worship experience. The lesson learned: Worship is corporate, not just individual. The pastor's taste and prerogative may not alone be a sufficient foundation on which to build.

While wise intervention by the pastor is occasionally needed in the continuing duet with the minister of music, the ability to admit unwise interventions is also a necessity.

"Music," said one minister of music, "comes from the Chief Musician. Finding it, however, demands hard work." Hard work is required to sustain music in the life of the church. The continuing improvisation between pastors and musicians will keep on going. Simplistic solutions are not to be found. But it's better to strive for a duet, not a duel, in our service for the kingdom.

—*Garth Bolinder*

Purchasing Musical Instruments

Most churches depend on a variety of musical instruments for a number of needs. Though typically the music staff will assess needs and do the purchasing, it's best to involve a small committee of parishioners interested in music, worship, art, and education. These people represent the congregation to the visionary musicians and will help sell the purchasing plan to the rest of the congregation. A consultant, someone who can go into a room and know just what would work in that environment, can help guide this committee through the choices.

Here are the instruments you will likely consider over the years:

● *Pianos*. Try to find at least a six-foot grand for the sanctuary. The rich sound of a fine grand piano will not only be an inspiration in worship, but will encourage young musicians to want to play it. Uprights are good for other rooms in the church, where you will save money with a clean, functional style. For classroom use, secure a good electric keyboard with a built-in speaker.

• *Organs.* Pipe, electronic, or a combination? You be the judge after you've listened to a lot of different organs. The old adage that an electronic organ costs less than a pipe is no longer as true as it once was. Any organ is expensive, if it's a good one. Also, insist on the ability to interface with a computer (MIDI). Even if you don't use that capability now, one day you will.

Don't be swayed by dealer arguments about lower maintenance costs with either pipe or electric. It costs to maintain them both. The Associated Pipe Organ Builders of America (P.O. Box 155, Chicago Ridge, IL 60415; 800/473-5270) can give a lot of good advice, even if you decide to go electronic.

• *Handbells.* You can start with a two-octave set of good quality and expand to a larger set when more people and money become available. There are also less expensive handchime products available, which are easy to maintain and carry. Consult the American Guild of English Handbell Ringers, Inc. (1055 East Centerville Station Road, Dayton, OH 45459-5503; 800/878-5459) to start on the right track.

• *Carillons.* Now in digital/electronic form, carillons provide many worship enhancements and can be played from an organ or synthesizer keyboard, or can be preprogrammed

to do just about anything. Major dealers advertise in leading organ and choral journals.

• *Synthesizers.* These electronic marvels have invaded the church with good results. Since technology is constantly changing, the church musician must stay alert and up-to-date by attending workshops and seeking out those musicians who are using synthesizers successfully. Synthesizers can be expensive but so versatile and enriching.

• *Other instruments.* In some cases churches may want a harpsichord, although a real one is costly to acquire and maintain. Some find a good synthesizer substitute acceptable. Timpani are nice if a church frequently uses orchestral ensembles. Other orchestral instruments customarily are provided by their players.

• *Recycled instruments.* You can find bargains in various stages of use or abuse at any price. However, beware of the donated instrument; *do* look a gift horse in the mouth, because donated instruments can turn out to be musically worthless. By careful shopping, reading the ads, talking to other churches, and getting a second opinion, you may find a quality buy, however. Check with the Organ Clearing House for used organs (P.O. Box 104, Harrisville, NH 03450; 603/827-3055). You can find used pianos through local dealers or tuner/technicians.

In general, it's important to visit other churches—big ones, little ones. See what works. Hear what works. Ask who's happy, who's not happy, and why.

—William Phemister

Maintaining Pianos and Organs

Musical instruments contribute to vital worship and education in your church. Each one needs to be maintained in a state of readiness so that it will provide good service and enjoy long service.

Finding the Right Tuner

Every piano needs to be tuned at least once a year, and some instruments will need it two to four times per year, depending on how often they are played and how important they are to your music program. An average pipe organ will need to be tuned at least twice a year. While an electronic organ may not need tuning in the same way, certain mechanical functions require the same attention as a pipe organ, such as regulation of the action and key contacts.

In light of these regular maintenance needs, you'll need to choose carefully a professional tuner for an ongoing relationship. Ask other churches and schools for recommendations. Is your potential tuner a member of the Piano Technicians Guild? Can he or she supply names of satisfied customers? Don't make a long-term commitment to a tuner until you've tried his or her services at least once and are satisfied not only with the work but with the tuner's attitude, as well.

Always secure a contract for organ maintenance. This is fairly routine everywhere. For a pipe organ, this will include the two major tunings. The only way to budget for emergencies is to know that the organ may make unexpected demands on the church's general contingency fund. An example of this would be if the organ's blower suddenly burns out (after it goes off warranty, of course!).

A good electronic-organ builder will do a free annual checkup while the original ten-year warranty is in effect. Afterward, a maintenance contract or warranty extension should be available.

Caring for Instruments

All the people who use and benefit from the instruments, not just the professional tuner, can help maintain the instruments by observing some simple maintenance tips:

• Avoid extremes of temperature and humidity in your buildings. The tuning will go up or down depending on temperature variations. When the organ tuner comes in during midweek, the room should be at the average Sunday morning temperature: about 72 degrees. When the humidity changes dramatically, everything is affected: wood, leather, felt, metal. Thus, a humidifier may be necessary in winter, and a dehumidifier or air-conditioner in summer.

• Beware the carpet-shampoo process. Enormous amounts of moisture suddenly enter the room and invade every pore of the instrument during shampooing. Encourage the use of a process that uses less water, move the piano out of the room if possible, and get the room dried out quickly. Be sure to schedule a tuning *after*, not before, the process.

• Make sure the custodian and musicians are working together.

This applies to avoiding conflicts with vacuuming and practice times, and agreeing on the method and products to be used in cleaning the exterior of the instruments.

• Lock your valuable instruments during the week. For example, a pipe organ chamber should always be off-limits. Pipes that are reachable by little hands will be touched—and altered! Children love to bang away on piano keyboards, but we may need to channel their freedom of expression into more productive activities. Use heavy canvas or quilted covers to provide additional protection and security.

• Realize that no piano or organ can survive on tuning alone. Depending on the amount of use and the condition of the instrument, you'll need to arrange for voicing, action regulation, and cleaning every few years.

—*William Phemister*

20

Keys to Congregational Singing

Music is one key to the "heart dimension" of worship, whether people are gathered in a stadium, large church, hundred-seat sanctuary, or home Bible study. Singing has the power to help people freely express their feelings for God.

That's why an important part of the task of worship leaders is to involve the entire congregation in the ministry of music. Although the chancel choir, the soloists, and the instrumentalists are all vital contributors to the music of worship, the most important choir is made up of the men and women with untrained voices who sit in the pews.

Obstacles to Effective Singing

Whenever people gather, effective congregational singing doesn't happen automatically. Consider some obstacles:

• *A shrinking body of commonly accepted congregational song.* In some churches, unfortunately, the great heritage of hymnody, which represents the praise and prayer of the church of many generations, has been abandoned. At the same time, praise choruses, with a more transient life, have become popular. In addition, regional favorites may dominate a church's singing.

Although sacred music is currently more available than at any other time in history, congregations ironically are growing increasingly unfamiliar with the church's rich musical heritage, a heritage that could bind Christians together.

• *A spectator orientation.* Although singing can be a joyful experience, it is fast becoming a spectator sport in Western culture. Music has become something that is listened to, not something people participate in. College professors, for instance, find fewer and fewer freshmen who are trained and experienced candidates for their schools' choral offerings.

The age of Walkmans, concerts, video and audio cassettes, compact disks, FM radio, and ever-present headphones and speakers is here, and the proliferation of these spectator media begs the question: "How will the next generation ever learn to sing?"

• *A misunderstanding of the role of music in worship.* In churches, sometimes the power and efficacy of music is unconsciously belittled or underestimated. Many times music directors use music as a filler, saying such things as "Let's sing a song while the latecomers are seated" or "We have a little more time; let's sing that last stanza again." Other times music is considered merely as a warm-up act for the sermon.

When music is given this demeaning role, worship is diminished and congregational participation undermined. People won't fully participate—heartfully, soulfully—if they see the leaders treat music as an appendage to worship.

Music can reach, touch, and move people in countless ways, but often people don't ask or expect enough of the art of music. Underestimating it is like using a genie, with nearly limitless power, merely to do a few household chores.

Music is as essential to worship as the sermon is, so plenty of time should be given to it. When the congregation is singing, the pastor should be singing enthusiastically, modeling how singing should be regarded by all, not distracted or reading his or her notes.

• *A lack of time.* If a good sermon needs time to develop and drive home a point, so does authentic worship. Worship needs at least fifteen to twenty minutes to build. In order to devote that kind of time, as many nonessentials as possible need to be eliminated to provide maximum time for worship and congregational singing.

• *Poor acoustics.* Strong congregational singing requires the support and encouragement of the room itself. Ideally, the room should capture and blend voices when people sing. Unfortunately, many sanctuaries are lacking acoustically. In some sanctuaries, for instance, the quality of the sound varies from place to place and from service to service, especially when the room is only half full. Solving acoustical problems may well benefit congregational singing.

Creating a Comfort Zone

In music, as in most endeavors, there is strength in numbers. The average persons in the pews are reluctant to project their voices unless a host of other voices surround them. Since most people don't think of themselves as singers, they tend to be afraid of their voices. Although this fear can be a handicap in smaller churches, with the right leadership even this difficulty can be overcome.

One key is to create a comfort zone for the congregation, an atmosphere devoid of tension, where a spirit of warmth and friendliness pervades, where people are not embarrassed to "make a joyful noise to the Lord."

Here are some factors to consider when creating this kind of comfort zone:

- *The music director's personality.* If the song leader is friendly, warm, accessible, and confident, the congregation is more likely to respond in kind. For example, smiling often and speaking in pleasant, personal terms breaks down many barriers.

- *The proper accompaniment.* People sing more confidently when a full sound surrounds and upholds them; they won't feel they "stick out." When strong accompaniment provides an introduction that clearly establishes the tempo, intensity, and key, people sing the first lines more boldly.

Choosing the right instrument to accompany also helps. On the one hand, it would be difficult to render the strength and majesty of "A Mighty Fortress Is Our God" with a guitar, or even two or three. On the other hand, a meditative response such as "He Is Lord" would go well with the more intimate sound guitar strings produce.

- *The selection of songs.* At least in the beginning, tunes should be easy to sing and well-known to the congregation. A good hymn doesn't need much direction. A great piece, like "Holy, Holy, Holy," presents a straightforward succession of quarter notes and a simple, rhythmic construction. Within that disarming simplicity resides the beauty, strength, and majesty of the piece.

- *The key that songs are written in.* In a number of hymnals, many songs are written a step too high. After selecting a hymn, the music director should scan it for high notes and never force a congregation to sing any note higher than D or E-flat, or an octave plus one above middle C. If a song is written higher than that, the accompanist can transpose accordingly.

- *Permission for people not to participate.* For various reasons, sometimes some people hesitate to join in. In situations such as when a new song or chorus is introduced, the choir can sing it through while the people listen. During the second time, people often gain the confidence to join in, and by the third set, most of the congregation is singing.

- *A light spirit.* There are times to inject a little humor. Humor can be tricky, however, even deadly if it falls flat or is misunderstood. Sometimes music leaders try to perk up a lackluster hymn by good-naturedly chiding the congregation: "Let's smile when we sing, okay?" Or, "Think about the words." Yet, a fine line is walked whenever the congregation is scolded or lectured, even in good fun. Some people can pull it off, and some can't. Those who can't usually only dampen a congregation's desire to sing.

Instead, moving to a song that has rhythm and life can lighten the spirit of the group. A song such as "This Is the Day" can be reserved for that purpose. By having fun with a song like that one, people will loosen up and relax, and they'll sing more heartily after that.

Joy is close to every other strong emotion, and once it is unleashed through singing, people can move quickly to any other emotion on the spectrum. They can be laughing one moment and deeply moved to compassion or touched with grief the next. If a comfort zone for joyful expression in song is created, the Holy Spirit has greater freedom to move among God's people, speak to them, and change their lives.

Selecting a Hymnal

The attention being given to worship in evangelical circles today has made us all more aware of the value of congregational singing. Certainly we better appreciate the great emotional and educational benefits that flow from good hymnody. Yet hymnals wear out or grow outdated every fifteen years or so.

How do we go about selecting replacements?

What Do We Need?

It's best to find out who you are—your special identity as a worshiping congregation—before looking at any sample hymnals. What are the musical preferences of your people? What style of worship are they comfortable with (and likely to stay with for the next twenty years)? This self-defining process should not be limited to the perceptions and preferences of the present pastors and musicians, since they may not be in leadership five or six years hence. Instead, form a hymnal committee of representatives from the congregation to survey the history of Christian worship styles, of hymnody, and of your local church to determine where you fit in this broad spectrum of ways to approach worship and music.

If your denomination has an official hymnal, it deserves close inspection. Be willing, however, to look at interdenominational hymnals and those from other denominations as well as your own.

Ask pastors, musicians, and members of other churches like your own what they use and how they like it. They also may be able to pass on some wisdom gleaned from their committee's recent hymnal study. It won't take long to assemble a list of five to ten hymnals that you will want to examine. A local Christian bookstore can order copies for your committee to study in depth.

These concerns are seemingly mundane, yet they are crucial for powerful congregational singing. Hymns are sacred folk music. Therefore, hymn-leading is not a place for technical artistry but for simplicity, for enthusiasm, for involving everyone in the worship experience.

Capturing and Focusing the Mood

Many people live emotionless lives, at least on the surface. In the routine of life, few are touched at the deepest point of their spiritual selves. Music is an emotional art form, communicating much more than the message of the words. Sacred music especially taps into people's deepest spiritual and emotional levels.

A worship leader is privileged to bring inspiration to people. His or her job is to take people to emotional and spiritual heights, to show them the vistas and ranges of their faith, to lead them beyond the

---

What Should We Seek?

Let's divide the answer to what to look for into several categories for your committee:

• *Familiarity.* Certainly you will want to make sure the hymnal has the hymns your people know and love. Don't merely flip through the pages or read the index of first lines. Assemble a list of your congregation's hundred most-loved hymns, and then check to see how many are included in each hymnal.

• *Readability.* Look at the overall appearance and format to see if the words and notes are large enough to be easily read, especially by older people. Do the pages seem cluttered or is there ample white space? Have some (or many) hymns been set in a lower key to make it easier for men to sing?

• *Contemporaneity.* Have cultural issues been dealt with to your church's satisfaction? Look for how the hymnal handles matters of inclusive language ("Rise up, O men— or church?—of God"), archaic lan-

guage ("you and your" in place of "thee and thine"?), and topics of great concern to the twentieth-century church, such as life in the city, social concerns, and mercy ministries.

• *Variety.* Study both musical and textual styles. Look for a hymnal that generously represents many different styles. See if you can find recent songs, choruses, authors, and composers as well as the ancient hymns we sometimes neglect.

• *Usability.* The pastor needs a hymnal that will provide appropriate musical selections to fit with weekly preaching themes. Good scriptural and topical indices are a must. The many occasions for which hymns are to be chosen demand a hymnal with wide resources.

• *Versatility.* Many hymnals offer an extensive section of worship aids. Does your church depend heavily on printed prayers, creeds, litanies, descants, and standardized rituals? If so, you'll be wise to look for these in your next hymnal.

—*Lawrence C. Roff*

merely cerebral level of Christianity.

People bring to worship a wide range of experiences, tensions, needs, and moods. One woman carries a heavy load of sorrow, the man next to her a burden of guilt. The family in the next pew had a shattering argument on the way to church. Behind them is a man thinking about a business deal that went sour; his wife, who is planning next week's dinner party; and their teenage daughter, who is daydreaming about her boyfriend. Worship leaders must find some way to focus the minds and hearts of these individuals so that, with true unity, they may lift their praise to God.

Congregational singing is one of the best tools for accomplishing that task, and visualizing worship as a funnel helps channel that singing to a unified end. The opening of the service is like the wide mouth of the funnel, wide enough to include the emotions and experiences of everyone in the congregation, whatever they are. Therefore, the first hymns should deal with broad themes that speak of unassailable

Introducing New Music

Introducing songs begins long before a given worship service, and it requires a team approach. Most congregations are willing to try new songs in worship if two conditions are met: Songs must be introduced sensitively from a musical standpoint, and the congregation needs to understand the reason a particular song is chosen.

How to Do It

The following tips will help meet these conditions:

- *Know your hymnal well.* Treat it like a book of devotional poetry, which it is. Read the texts for personal edification as well as for worship preparation. Reflecting on the text without the music unifies the lyrics for the reader.
- *Keep a tally of songs used in worship.* One person—music director or pastor—can use a hymnal for

tallying purposes and list on a hymn's page each date it is sung. A separate list can tally songs that are not found in the pew hymnals.

- *Meet annually with worship leaders to analyze the listed songs to determine the balance of songs sung in worship.* What was the mix between old favorites and new songs? How many new songs were introduced? A healthy balance will include songs for all ages, from different times and places, and with varying levels of difficulty.

Other questions to ask:

—Were songs sung the previous year that didn't originate in North America or Europe? How many?

—How many Psalm and Scripture settings were sung?

—Were any songs sung too often, leading to overfamiliarity?

—Were any songs introduced but not learned?

- *Multiple-person staffs should*

truths, such as the power, sovereignty, immortality, and unchange-ableness of God. With each successive selection, the singing moves down the funnel, narrowing the focus more tightly to the theme or desired response of that service.

The selection of hymns has a powerful influence on the overall mood and worship experience. The array of congregational songs is like a toolbox. Just as a builder selects a hammer to drive a nail and a screwdriver to set a screw, worship leaders choose various songs for particular purposes.

Some hymns fill people with religious awe: "A Mighty Fortress Is Our God." Other hymns touch them with the love of God: "Amazing love! How can it be that Thou, my God, shouldst die for me?" Yet other hymns quiet their hearts and call them to prayer: "Take from our souls the strain and stress, and may our ordered lives confess the beauty of thy peace." And still other hymns soften their hearts and make them receptive to God's Spirit: "Just as I am, I come; I come."

---

meet regularly to plan services. Cooperation among staff members is critical for congregational acceptance of new music. It is helpful for the pastor to provide a list of scripture texts on a quarterly basis several weeks preceding a planning meeting. Other resources for the meeting might include worship-outline forms, Bibles, and various hymnals with good indexes. Participants can prepare by researching their repertoires for compatible music, along with suggestions for introducing it to the congregation. Thus the service themes will be augmented by fresh music for preludes, opening hymns, anthems, and postludes, and the congregation will benefit from a unified service.

• *Code worship leaders' hymnals with colored markers.* For instance, green might mean "go ahead and choose this hymn without fear that the congregation will stumble." Yellow could mean "caution, it's both unfamiliar and somewhat challenging. Perhaps use instruments or singers to introduce it." Red would mean "stop and plan well ahead, because this song is very challenging."

It's a good idea to introduce no more than one red song in a single service, and not one in every service. But once you decide to introduce it, don't drop it. If it's worth singing, it's worth repeating. Congregations benefit from diligent teaching and ample repetition, but then they will be able to sing with confidence.

• *Introduce new songs with the help of soloists or a choir.* When musicians who have practiced the music debut new songs once or twice before the congregation is expected to sing them, the congregation will be able to sing with more recognition when it comes their turn to join in.

Advanced planning is the key to introducing new songs to a congregation. With a little careful thought, the process can be enjoyable and edifying for everyone involved.

—*Emily R. Brink*

By the time the narrow end of the funnel is reached, deeply personal songs—songs that call for an individual response or make some deep, subjective impact—can be inserted. This would be the place for "Have Thine Own Way, Lord," "Open My Eyes That I May See," or "May the Mind of Christ My Savior." Or two or three brief praise choruses can be chosen to focus on people's love for God—"Lord, I Adore You" or "I Love You, Lord, and I Lift My Voice to Worship You"—simple, expressive, personal songs that people can offer to God without opening a hymnal.

The point of the funnel is to draw in and unify the hearts of the congregation, to focus the emotional flow of the worship experience, to prepare people for the ministry of the Word, and to allow them to express their response to God.

Congregational singing, even though it's done with hundreds of other people, can be a powerfully personal expression of worship. It can implant truths in the lives of individuals.

A Checklist for Congregational Singing

Music ministry and juggling have this in common: A lot of things have to be kept in the air at the same time. Spiritual sensitivity, personal preparation, attention to group dynamics, thoughtful song selection, and full-bodied accompaniment are just a few of the ingredients that contribute to powerful congregational singing. Here is a mental checklist to keep congregational singing effective:

• *Are the selected songs meaningful?* Every worship leader needs to have the gentle and engaging sense of an educator. When a song is introduced by briefly describing its history or giving a new perspective on the theme, singing becomes more meaningful for the congregation.

A hymnal with a good set of indexes is a definite plus, especially one with a topical index to match the song selection to the theme of the service. Hymns that refer to specific Scripture passages can be found in the Scripture-allusions index. When that passage of Scripture is read before, after, or even between verses of the hymn, the singing becomes more significant.

• *Am I enthusiastic as I direct the music?* People need to know that worship is enjoyable. A song leader's excitement is infectious.

• *Are eclectic tastes being cultivated?* Vary the choice of music. Since people speak different musical languages, people need to be given a variety of ways to express their worship. Traditional and contemporary music should never be presented as an either/or choice.

• *Am I avoiding routine?* Worship should be kept fresh and alive. Song leaders can use the metrical index to discover what familiar tunes will fit a new set of words (or vice versa). That's a great way to introduce new material and yet still have enough familiarity that people will participate.

• *Am I explaining enough but not too much?* The essence of every art is understatement. Music directors need not draw the congregation's attention to every clever seam in the program, which should appear seamless. Likewise, the people will discover many of the nuances of worship for themselves.

• *Am I remaining alert to the emotional energy of the congregation?* Song leaders should continually monitor how well they are doing at creating that all-important comfort zone, capturing and conveying the mood of the music, funneling the congregation, and drawing everyone into a unified experience of worship.

In the harmony of pitch, rhythm, and lyrics, the congregation comes together, breathes together, and feels together. There's something indescribably moving about a group of diverse individuals who offer songs to God because the Holy Spirit has united them and infectious enthusiasm engergizes them.

— *Howard Stevenson*

Resources

Allen, R., and G. Borror. 1982. Worship: Rediscovering the missing jewel. Portland, Ore.: Multnomah.

Causey, C. 1983. Open the doors to creativity in worship. Rockville, Md.: Music Revelation Press.

Hustad, D. 1980. Jubilate! Church music in the evangelical tradition. Carol Stream, Ill.: Hope.

Leafblad, B. 1977. Music, worship, and the ministry of the church. Portland, Ore.: Western Seminary Press.

Rayburn, R. 1980. O come, let us worship: Corporate worship in the evangelical church. Grand Rapids: Baker.

Schaper, R. 1984. In his presence: Appreciating your worship tradition. Nashville: Thomas Nelson.

Webber, R. 1985. Worship is a verb. Waco, Tex.: Word.

21

Directing Choral Music

W hat is the future of choral music in the church as this century ends and another begins? The Bible does not support a spectator philosophy of music ministry, although recordings and the media have produced a population of spectators.

Scripturally, worship and praise are described as corporate acts of the body of believers. There are numerous exhortations for believers to "sing to the Lord," and throughout the Old and New Testaments are references to groups of people singing and making music in thankfulness to the Lord. Paul instructs Christians to join in singing hymns, psalms, and spiritual songs.

There is no technological replacement for a singing church. Church choirs enjoy the role of leading congregations in corporate worship, and choir directors assume the task of training the choirs.

Requirements of the Director

In many churches, the choir director ranks next to the pastor in the level of training required for the job and the amount of influence and congregational contact involved in the position. Conducting is a skill mastered by some at the professional level and practiced by others at a basic level. Simply being able to play the piano or read music doesn't qualify someone to become a choir director; a gift of leadership in music needs to be discovered and nurtured.

For example, college music majors require at least a semester to learn the basic skills of conducting, and the learning seemingly never ends for those wanting to improve their skills of musicianship, teaching, communicating, and ministering effectively.

Musicianship is the most important skill a conductor needs to develop. Good musicianship includes sightreading skills, theoretical knowledge, understanding of performance practice, keyboard skills, and vocal technique. In addition, the choral director must understand and be fluent in the physical gestures necessary to conduct a choir. Another valuable aspect of musicianship is the knowledge of sacred choral literature and how it relates to Scripture and the church year.

Just as an outstanding teacher will inspire students to continue to learn, so an outstanding conductor will inspire the choir to sing more beautifully in service of the church. Rarely is a church choir an auditioned group. Typically it consists of people with varied musical backgrounds. The director's task is to teach music reading and vocal technique, while working on balance and blend in preparation for worship each week. Teaching becomes an even more essential component when working with children. The future of congregational participation in the music of the church lies in the musical training of young people.

Effective communication skills are essential in relating to the choir, as well as to the church staff and the congregation. Choir members become most disgruntled when they feel pressured by lack of time or when they haven't clearly understood what is expected of them. Publishing a schedule of anthems and services facilitates communication. While a pastor may be able to write a sermon in one week, it is often impossible for a choir to learn an anthem in one week. Therefore, the director needs to be in constant communication with the pastor to coordinate plans.

Communication with the congregation through social activies, coffee hours, new-member classes, and other contacts helps the director attract new people to the choir. Choir directors will never be able to recruit new singers if their only route on Sunday morning is from their car to the choir loft.

Choir directors can also communicate music to the congregation and encourage their participation through short introductions to anthems or hymns. Congregations today need encouragement to sing and actively participate in worship, and choir directors can boost enthusiasm by assuming more leadership in the worship service.

The choral director also functions as pastor to many church members. Taking time to pray and provide spiritual direction in the form of short explanations of hymn texts should be a regular part of every choir rehearsal. Many church choirs become natural support groups in times of grief or trial, and the directors can facilitate this support through their ministry of caring.

Technical Skills

The conductor plays a key role in the choir's performance and thus should possess the basic skills to help the choir members sing their best. Communicating through gesture is an essential component of choral conducting. The good conductor economizes movements in a way that reflects the beauty of the music and communicates necessary information to the choir.

Conductors serve as models for their singers, so their posture and breathing need to help the singers achieve effective breathing and tone production. Both feet should be planted firmly on the floor, with the body weight on the front part of the foot. The spine should be straight and the head held high but not pushed too far forward or back. Tension in the director can create tension in the singers.

To discover the correct arm position for conducting, the director can swing his or her right arm back and forth several times and finally bring it to a resting position with the hand just above the waist. The elbow will be slightly bent and close—but not tight—against the body. The palm should be facing the floor, and the fingers should be extended but relaxed. If the choir is planning a work with an orchestra, the conductor will want to use a baton.

With a gesture of preparation, the conductor tells the choir to begin singing. Many pieces start on the downbeat, and this gesture of preparation is the most commonly used. The right hand should begin just slightly above waist level and to the right of the body. The arm is swung upwards and to the left and brought down in front of the body. The direction of the gesture communicates what beat the choir should begin singing. A basic rule: The gesture of preparation is the pattern of the beat preceding the beat on which the choir enters. Only one beat is necessary, since accompanists and choirs can easily be trained to enter with just this one gesture. The size and speed of the gesture alert singers to the dynamic and tempo of the music. The conductor should breath clearly (though not loudly) with the gesture of preparation to encourage the singers to take a breath.

The conductor can execute a gestural cutoff by a circular motion signaling the choir to prepare to stop. The gestures of preparation and release are similar in that they consist of a preparatory motion and end with either an entrance of sound or a cessation.

Once the choir can be started or stopped, the conductor must know what to do with them as they sing. Conductors use standard beat patterns to communicate. One mistake is to try to gesture every note the choir is to sing (rather than the beats of the measure), which becomes nearly impossible to follow. It is better to stick with the basic patterns for conducting in one, two, three, four, and six beats to a measure. Conductors can practice in front of a mirror until the patterns become automatic. Sometimes conductors need to subdivide the beat, which they do by simply retracing several inches of the previous beat pattern for the second half of each beat.

Next comes the effective use of the left hand, which is used for expression, independent of the right hand. Exercises to help develop this independence include doing unrelated tasks like brushing hair or tracing geometric shapes with the left hand while conducting fluid, controlled beat patterns with the right.

Other skills include the gesture of syncopation (especially necessary when dealing with contemporary or pop music), articulation, fermatas, and mixed and changing meter. A good conductor is always striving to use economical but clear gestures.

Leading Children's Choirs

An excellent children's choir is capable of powerful ministry. Its music can lift our hearts in worship with simple, clear tones that are almost angelic in quality. People will come to hear their children sing when they would never darken a church door for any other reason.

Along with this unique ministry come a few major challenges: How does one select appropriate music for children? How can discipline be handled positively? And what are realistic expectations for children?

Music

Music selection provides the diet on which the health of the overall program ought to flourish. With the plethora of possibilities vying for attention, it is easy to become sidetracked with cute artwork and fancy packaging. We need to get into the music itself to determine its appropriateness. Three specific guidelines will help:

- *Does the song have significance?* Songs that are of little value textually have limited places for expression in the worship and Christian nurturing of our children. If we become preoccupied with cute songs, we run the risk of creating a perception of a cutesy purpose, obscuring the real significance of children's music ministry.

- *Does the text use too much abstract imagery to convey its meaning?* Young children think literally, not abstractly or symbolically. While songs that employ imagery may be biblical, they should be delayed until late childhood or early teen years to maximize their effectiveness.

- *What is the vocal range of the songs?* Much of the children's music that is being published today is written in the low-chest register. It is impossible to train children to sing in their head voice if the register is too low. The middle treble staff (from E to B) is a comfortable range for children.

The Rehearsal

Rehearsals provide opportunity for the greatest contact between the choir director and the choir. Rehearsal times vary, and finding the best time for most of the people is challenging. Always there are persons who express an interest in singing but are unable to attend rehearsals. The choir director must choose the time for rehearsal convenient for the most people and then be firm with an attendance policy.

For instance, should members be allowed to sing on Sunday morning if they were unable to attend the rehearsal? A director must decide, and many plan rehearsals such that occasional absenses don't hinder singers from singing. Asking choir members to record *expected*

Discipline

Because children have short attention spans, you'll want to structure a rehearsal with a variety of activities, thereby promoting good discipline. These activities need to appeal to a variety of learning styles. Visual, auditory, and kinesthetic learners all need teaching techniques that draw on their particular strengths in learning. Maximize every minute with activities that move quickly in short segments that complement and reinforce each other. This will work better than mere repetition. Repetition past a certain point is counterproductive because it anesthetizes the brain.

Try to integrate musicianship training and repertoire learning as much as possible. This creates a multitude of possibilities for diverse learning activities. Rhythm games that teach children to read, write, and create various rhythm patterns will develop young musicians' abilities to recognize the rhythms in their music. Staff-reading activities that teach note-reading skills, along with ear training, will help children follow the melodic contour of the phrases they sing. Also consider drawing or dramatizing a song to help the children convey the meanings they feel.

Expectations

The more one expects of a children's choir, the more one is likely to achieve. Goals must be high, because children have the right to be excellent. The ability to produce a beautiful unison, sing in two-part harmony, and interpret meaningfully the texts they sing would be minimum expectations. Every child's musical birthright ought to include a grasp of basic music-literacy skills and a broad exposure to many styles and types of music.

Martin Luther said, "Music is the only art of heaven given to earth and the only art of earth we take to heaven." How incredibly important that we offer music to our children with excellence and purpose! In so doing, we help them experience a little bit of heaven on earth and prepare them for the music of the ages.
—*Connie Fortunato*

absences is also helpful in planning rehearsals and Sunday anthems.

• *Preparing for the rehearsal.* Acoustic ambiance is the most important factor in choosing a rehearsal space. Choirs sing more effectively in rooms not too "dry" (where it is difficult to hear other singers) or "live" (where it is difficult to hear anything).

When new construction is considered, the choir director should be involved in acoustical design for both the rehearsal room and the sanctuary. Even chair purchases are important. Metal folding chairs are least ideal for singers, whereas chairs with flat seats and backs provide the best support and encourage good posture.

Arrange the chairs so that each singer clearly views the director and hears other singers. For example, a semicircle arrangement sets a better acoustic environment than straight rows. Other aspects of the

Leading Youth Choirs

Some of the best opportunities for evangelism, Christian education, training, and discipleship come in the context of a youth choir program. Whether working with a high school/college choir, a small chorus for junior high girls, a boy's bell choir, or other specialty groups, I've found that participating kids typically make solid spiritual commitments that result in their own personal growth and meaningful ministry to others.

The Incentive

Why would kids want to be in a youth choir? At first, for many of the kids in my group, it was because they wanted to see the country. Kids love to travel, so we planned a two-week tour each June for the senior choir. All during the school year, the trip was the carrot on a stick. If kids wanted to go on the tour, they had to meet the requirements. Happily, as the year progressed, and in the years to follow, those choir kids found other, deeper motivations related to the choir's fellowship, nurture, and continuing opportunities for service.

The Requirements

Requirements will vary with different situations. But here are the standards I've set for our high school/college choir across the years:

• *Age limit:* Be within the range of tenth grade through college senior. Having collegians in the group provides stronger leadership and greater vocal strength, and it builds in chaperones for tours.

• *Attendance:* Attend rehearsals and performances, as well as worship services, Sunday school, and weekly youth meetings—at a rate of at least 75 percent attendance. We do kids a great disservice if we let their only tie to the church be singing in a choir.

• *Reading:* Read an assigned Christian book each month from October to May.

rehearsal room that the choir director should be concerned about are adequate lighting, temperature and humidity control, blackboard and bulletin board space, and a tuned piano.

Careful analysis of the music prior to rehearsal is absolutely necessary. Decisions about breathing, cutoffs, dynamics, and phrasing should be made before presenting a piece of music to the choir. Analyzing a piece structurally is a valuable aid in planning rehearsals. Analysis also helps the director identify unison parts and potential rhythmic and harmonic difficulties. A conductor needs to go into a rehearsal knowing the music well enough to teach it to the choir.

A church choir is unique in that it performs every week. This creates special demands on the director and the choir, and care should be given to account for it. For example, some music can be

---

• *Habits:* Abstain from the use of tobacco, alcohol, and illegal drugs.

• *Personal conduct:* Act in a manner consistent with the Christian witness of the choir.

Across the years, some have questioned the attendance and reading requirements as too strict. I argue that young people are no strangers to discipline. What high school football player could get away with missing 25 percent of his practices? What coach would abide a team member who said he or she was too busy to learn the plays? Kids need to hear 1 Timothy 4:7–8, reminding them that while physical discipline is of value, spiritual discipline is profitable for all areas of their lives.

The Outreach

A choir tour can be much more than a prize for a year's participation. It should be a classroom in which equal emphasis is placed on the physical, mental, social, and spiritual development of the kids. More than just riding a bus and performing, the tour experience should include hard work, carefree play, group Bible study, solo quiet times, feasting, fasting, sleeping in homes, sleeping on church floors, journal keeping, and so on.

Back home, too, kids should have a regular schedule of participation in the community—ministering in convalescent homes, service clubs, malls, banquets, and even other churches on occasion. These outings build the choir's confidence, unity, and musical ability, while providing a loving gift to others.

The Message

Since a big part of a choir's message about God's love is communicated nonverbally, each member must learn to sing with total involvement. Videotape your choir singing, including close-ups of each member, and let members evaluate themselves and each other for expression, movement, posture. That's how your message is going to get across—at least from the platform. But still, the most important message is the one that is lived out by our youth choir members in their daily living.

—*Sonny Salsbury*

repeated from year to year, effectively lifting the burden of learning a new piece of music each week for the worship service.

The director should also choose music that is appropriate for the size and ability of the choir. For instance, a choir of 15 to 20 singers should not attempt thickly textured anthems from the nineteenth century. Directors who program Christian contemporary music can also have unrealistic expectations, thinking the choir should sound like the professional recording. It is wise to search for music that fits the capability of the choir. A good blend of old, new, easy, and difficult pieces eases the load of weekly performance. This blend also helps create a rehearsal that is varied and interesting.

• *Conducting the rehearsal.* The rehearsal time should begin with vocal warm-ups, since most of the choir members sing only twice a week. This time can also be spent in tuning, developing tone and breath control, and expanding range. Work on diction and vocal production can be achieved by practicing the hymns and songs to be sung in the worship service. This practice also helps to improve congregational singing.

The structure of the rehearsal is important both to the vocal health and to the energy level of the choir. Most of the choir members have worked a long day before an evening rehearsal and are tired. Singing with energy and good breath support can actually be an invigorating experience, but a poorly run rehearsal with little sense of direction will only add to the choir's fatigue.

It is best to plan rehearsals that begin and end with familiar pieces. Singing with confidence at the outset enables choristers to comfortably continue the warm-up process. Next it is best to work on the most difficult and least known piece in the repertoire. The rehearsal should continue with more familiar works and conclude with something that allows the choir to sense accomplishment. Most directors feel the pressure of preparing for Sunday, but careful rehearsal planning should include anthems for subsequent Sundays as well.

The actual rehearsal method for individual pieces will vary. A basic plan begins with reading a piece through in its entirety, followed by work on specific sections, and ending with a final read-through of the piece. Typically it is the middle section that demands the most attention.

This work compares to a medical diagnosis. The first run-through provides an opportunity to analyze what is right or wrong with the performance. This is followed by a prescription for correcting the error. The tenors may miss an entrance because they are not sure of their pitch. The solution is to listen for the note in the soprano line the measure before their entrance. Singing the piece once more helps to double-check for accuracy.

As a director gains experience, new and varied ways of rehearsing can be employed. It might be good to start at the end of a piece and work backwards, adding sections as they are learned. Or the director may choose to work on only five measures of one piece instead of attempting an entire read-through. Just as there are varieties of pieces included in a rehearsal, so are there varieties in rehearsal methodology.

No choir thrives on all work and no play! The choir rehearsal should also have social and spiritual components. Devotions or prayer times provide an opportunity for the choir members to share concerns. This time can also be used to emphasize the text of a piece to be rehearsed or to direct the choir in understanding how the anthems and hymns will add to the service.

Social time is also an important factor for the choir. People will sing and communicate better if they know each other. Coffee following rehearsal offers one way of providing fellowship. And the fun need not occur only outside of rehearsal, but also during it. Elements of humor and lightheartedness are great for building *esprit de corps*. Socializing may seem frivolous when there is music to be learned, but it is good to remember that choristers devote significant time to a church's music ministry, and one of their rewards is the fellowship they experience in that context. The ideal rehearsal is a mix of singing, music education, prayer, and fellowship.

On Sunday morning, careful voice warm-up, anthem review, and focus on the demands of the service are important. This may compete with other church activities but requires at least 15 to 20 minutes. This time is especially helpful for singers absent from the preceding week's rehearsal. Those persons may be asked to rehearse earlier in the morning, to be joined later by the rest of the choir. The choir should be alerted to any unusual events in the service and given instructions for processing, standing, and sitting. Difficult spots in the anthem should be practiced before a final run-through of the anthem. This saves time and gives the choir a sense of completion prior to beginning the worship experience.

Extra rehearsals may be needed at certain times of the year. Fall is a good time to have a workshop. This is the time to introduce a guest conductor or clinician to work with the choir. Use the opportunity to build basic vocal skills and lay a foundation for coming work. A read-through of coming anthems is helpful to the choir in understanding the work expected from them.

Special musical events, such as major works, cantatas, Christmas or spring concerts, and musicals, also call for extra rehearsal time. Structure these rehearsals carefully, since choir members are giving up time and need to feel it is worthwhile. Most singers are willing to give of their time if it is spent effectively.

Professional Development

One goal of a choral director is to enable the choir to sing better than it did at its last rehearsal, to make them better, more expressive singers and musicians. Because this calls for the constant motivation of others, most choral directors are interested in professional development. Churches should encourage staff members—including musicians—to seek professional development, and help financially as much as possible.

It is vital that church musicians continue to expand their horizons through education. Myriad workshops and courses are available, and denominations frequently have musical associations that sponsor national summer workshops as well as regional gatherings held geographically throughout the year. Most colleges offer courses in basic conducting.

Professional organizations offer workshops in technique, repertoire, and interpretation annually. Local churches are wise to join one of the several sacred-music organizations and encourage musicians on their staff to participate in them. Some of these organizations include:

- Chorister's Guild, 2834 W. Kingsley Rd., Garland, TX 75041
- American Choral Director's Association, P.O. Box 5310, Lawton, OK 73504
- American Choral Foundation, 130 West 56th St., New York, NY 10019
- Music Educators National Conference, 1902 Association Dr., Reston, VA 22091
- American Guild of Organists, 475 Riverside Dr., Suite 1260, New York, NY 10115
- Fellowship of United Methodist Musicians, Box 840, Nashville, TN 37202
- Presbyterian Association of Musicians, 1000 E. Morehead S., Charlotte, NC 28204
- Fellowship of American Baptist Musicians, P.O. Box 851, Valley Forge, PA 19482
- Hymn Society of America, P.O. Box 30854, Fort Worth, TX 76129
- Royal School of Church Music, Addington Palace, Croydon, Surrey CR95AD, England.

The call to be a church choir director demands a deep commitment to Christ and his church, a thorough knowledge of music, the technical skills of conducting, administrative abilities, and public-relations skills. These expectations seem daunting but should inspire churches to seek the best professionally qualified persons to lead their music ministries. The worship and spiritual life of a congregation is deeply affected by the leadership of the choir director.

—Mary Hopper

Resources

Ehmann, W., and F. Hassemann. 1981. Voice building for choirs. Chapel Hill, N.C.: Hinshaw Music.

Garretson, R. 1988. Conducting choral music, sixth ed. Englewood Cliffs, N.J.: Prentice Hall.

Heffernan, C. 1982. Choral music: Technique and artistry. Englewood Cliffs, N.J.: Prentice Hall.

Lamb, G. 1988. Choral techniques, third ed. Dubuque, Iowa: Wm. C. Brown.

Lovelace, A. and W. Rice. 1960. Music and worship in the church. Nashville: Abingdon.

22

Directing Instrumental Groups

Church musicians, by virtue of their talent and inclination, strive to offer beautiful sacrifices of praise to God through music on behalf of the whole congregation. They are, in fact, the first fruits of the congregation in worshiping God. They offer to God, but they also aid the entire congregation in worshiping him through their musical leadership.

First Chronicles 25 provides a biblical basis for supporting the use of instrumental music in the church. In the history of ancient Israel, it would appear that any and every instrument in existence was used in the service of the temple. David himself set apart some "for the ministry of prophesying, accompanied by harps, lyres and cymbals" (1 Chron. 25:1). Asaph, Heman, and Jeduthun were put in charge, probably because they were the most skilled musicians in the kingdom. They "prophesied, using the harp in thanking and praising the Lord" (vs. 3). They were prophesying (or preaching) in that, in addition to singing and playing instruments, they apparently composed both text and music. Instrumental music, then, is extremely useful and powerful in praising God.

Forming the Orchestra

A great way to begin an orchestra ministry is to create an opportunity for all of the instrumentalists in the church to gather, rehearse, and fellowship in a nonthreatening, fun environment, and then minister at a service. After meeting, working, and ministering with the instrumentalists, the director needs to establish a standard of ability based on how the group sounded and on the quality of the choir. Quality breeds quality; if the standard is set too low, the fine players will lose interest after a while, even with a high degree of dedication on everybody's part. The goals must be set high enough, but not so high as to exclude the bulk of the players. For example, violinists who want to play the first violin part should be comfortable and facile in playing beyond the third position with good intonation.

An audition/interview after this first impromptu performance should include the following: questions regarding the player's prior training and experience (especially important is the player's experience in orchestras or bands); exploration of the player's spiritual status and commitment to ministry in music; listening to a musical piece in order to determine the player's skill level. The playing part of the audition could include a prepared solo of the musician's choice, sight-reading from excerpts of the repertoire in a variety of styles, and scales done with a variety of articulations/bowings at your request.

Always try to create a strong sense of fellowship among the newly formed orchestra members. Focus their thoughts continually on ministry, since it is easy for an orchestra to wrongly feel like a second fiddle when compared to the choir, in terms of ministry potential. Plan social events, set up orchestral ministry opportunities outside the church, and create a caring and sharing atmosphere. Also, keep members accountable for good practice habits between rehearsals. Stress that "in order for our efforts to be an acceptable sacrifice to the Lord, we must be willing to pay the cost—in time and energy" (see 2 Sam. 24:24; Heb. 13:15).

Nurture and cultivate individual musicianship by encouraging soloists, organizing duets and trios, and providing ministry opportunities for them. Also, get to know the high school and junior high instrumentalists in the church. Go to their school concerts and meet their directors—and provide ministry opportunities for them at the church. For instance, consider presenting a youth recital series on selected Sunday afternoons.

As you begin to determine the financial needs of a church instrumental program, remember to include such line items as cost of printed music, honoraria for guest instrumentalists, purchase and repair of instruments, and music copying and postage costs. A single orchestration costs $25–$40; a single instrument book of complete hymnal orchestrations costs $20–$25; for a choral anthem orchestration that is not available for purchase but can be rented, the publishers typically charge $50 to $90 for four to six weeks' usage. Accompaniments to many of John Rutter's anthems, for example, fall under this category.

Buy enough string parts to have one per stand, remembering that string players can pair up and share stands. In addition to this, each string player should have his or her own part to take home for practice. In many cases, publishers will grant permission to photocopy string parts for individual-practice purposes only. You must ask permission from the publisher, however, in each case. The publisher will usually request that such photocopies be destroyed after the performance date.

Developing a Participation Philosophy

A big challenge as one forms an instrumental ensemble is weighing maximum participation against optimum quality. Two issues emerge at this point. First, should directors accept all qualified players, no matter what the resulting balance would be, or should they accept a limited number of qualified players in order to achieve a balanced ensemble according to a predetermined instrumentation plan?

I prefer a balanced ensemble, as much as possible, even if this means the exclusion of some players. The excluded players in such situations can be given other opportunities for instrumental ministry. For example, set up flute choirs and trumpet ensembles to give the extra players performance opportunities. Also, consider rotating personnel in the orchestra or band.

The reasons for building a balanced ensemble are primarily musical. A director needs to be ultimately concerned with the actual musical communication to the listeners (and the musicians must be counted among the listeners). Properly balancing instrumentation is an acoustical art that has to do with the dynamic and tonal capabilities of each instrument. For example, if an orchestra has five violins and seven trumpets, among other instruments, the violins will be drowned out by the trumpets and will begin to produce a harsh, strident sound to keep up. The result is frustration among the players and an unsatisfying experience for the listener. Ministry suffers in such cases.

The second issue to address is how to fill in the holes in instrumental balance. If you need a horn to cover a third part, for example, and rescoring is not possible, or if you feel that a string section needs some augmenting, do consider hiring extra players. Go to this step, of course, only if all other avenues of acquiring a volunteer have been unproductive.

The presence of paid players can be a real blessing for all. First of all, their presence will no doubt noticeably improve the sound of the group. Their playing will probably also challenge and inspire the other players and singers. If the paid player is a Christian—and every effort should be made to procure an instrumentalist that is like-minded to the congregation—the group gains the benefit of a fresh dimension of fellowship. Occasionally, however, you won't be able to find a

Christian musician to fill a need. In such cases, try to find a capable instrumentalist who has a reputation for integrity and reliability in the community. Working with non-Christians has a positive side, for there is the potential for such people to hear the gospel and accept the Lord Jesus as Savior while engaged in orchestra ministry.

Determining Orchestral Involvement in Worship

Options abound here. In some churches, the orchestra plays for the entire Sunday-morning service every week, plus performing in four or five special programs throughout the year. Other church orchestras play only on an occasional basis, perhaps once every month or two, and are augmented by professionals for the one or two special programs.

Orchestras that minister every week usually have a rehearsal each week, on a weeknight, for one and a half to two hours. If the church has a separate orchestra director and choir director, and if it has the facilities, it works well to rehearse the choir and orchestra on the same night. This can be done at the same time if there is an abundance of musical talent and no one participating in both groups. Consecutive rehearsals with some overlap in times allows a period for joint rehearsals. If facilities are a problem, the orchestra can rehearse in the sanctuary.

A hybrid model that works in some churches is to have a four-week revolving schedule, whereby the orchestra is split into ensembles, each ministering one Sunday out of the month, and then is combined on the fourth Sunday to form the full orchestra. In this model, the first Sunday may be played by a brass ensemble, the second by a string ensemble, the third by a woodwind ensemble, and the last by the full orchestra. The weekly rehearsal might be full orchestra for part of the time and then ensemble rehearsal for the rest of the time (or for all of the time, as needed). The monthly participation model could be an intermediate step in moving toward a weekly model, or it could have strong philosophical reasons for being the most attractive model for a particular church on a permanent basis.

One of the negative aspects of weekly participation by the orchestra is the potential for a lack of color variety and, subsequently, a limitation in expression. Many arrangements for church orchestra tend to be over-orchestrated (to compensate for the missing instruments in many churches) and come across sounding thick and loud much of the time. And if the church possesses a beautiful organ, the organ is regularly subjugated in favor of the orchestra.

Of course, sensitive directors will strive to provide variety in color and mood in situations where the orchestra ministers every week. However, a monthly or even biweekly schedule makes it possible to involve some of the following musical ministries on the other Sundays, in addition to those listed above: adult handbell choir, organ, *a cappella* pieces by the choir, and a praise band ensemble leading praise choruses. Variety is the key in music ministry.

Choosing Music

The types of service music an orchestra typically plays include the following: preludes, offertories, interludes and postludes, hymn accompaniments (with or without organ and/or piano), choir accompaniments, and vocal and instrumental solo accompaniments. Again, variety is the key, both with respect to effective ministry to the congregation and enjoyment and fulfillment on the part of the players.

Some modern hymnals now have companion orchestrations. Although most of these are not designed to stand by themselves as offertories, preludes, or postludes, they can effectively enhance congregational singing, and with a little adjusting and arranging, they can also be used to accompany soloists.

In accompanying the congregation on a hymn, it is important for the director to be sensitive to the words of each verse being sung and then to vary the orchestration accordingly. For example, on majestic first and last verses, use the full group with obbligatos and descants; on more reflective middle verses, perhaps use the strings, woodwinds, and piano, without organ or brass.

Be careful to purchase orchestrations that are not merely a scoring of the SATB parts straight out of the hymnal but also have parts that are more inventive and idiomatic for the instruments. For example, the brass should have occasional fanfare-type material or other rhythmic embellishments that can provide interesting musical links between phrases.

Some arrangements of hymns do stand alone for offertories and preludes. When using these, make sure you have all of the instruments called for, or if you do not, be sure you can adequately cover the part with another instrument or instruments. Unfortunately, some of the arrangements available are published with extremely poor readability. With such arrangements, the full score is difficult to decipher, which greatly increases the amount of time you will need to learn the score. Fortunately, the parts are usually in better condition than the score. Desktop music publishing should ameliorate this problem. Nonetheless, make legibility one of your basic criteria for selecting music.

Concerning accompaniments for the choir: If the piece is orchestrated or if there is a tape track available, chances are good that you can either purchase or rent the orchestration. Contact the publisher. In my opinion, working through the difficulties and challenges of producing a live accompaniment is far more desirable than using a tape track. In fact, if a church has committed itself to an orchestra ministry, determine not to use a tape track when the orchestra is available for playing.

You will no doubt delegate many orchestral responsibilities to an elected leadership group from within the ensemble. Certainly, a librarian is a must. The job of librarian includes transferring bowing and other markings from the conductor's score to the parts and organizing the players' folders. The librarian can also do the work of punching holes in the music and putting it in the order of performance in three-ring binders. Each player then receives a new notebook of music for each ministry period. (Note: Photocopies can be used in

---

Directing Handbell Choirs

The prime requirement for a handbell ringer is not musicianship, rhythmic ability, or ambidexterity; it is *dedication*. Handbell choirs cannot function unless every ringer is present at every concert and rehearsal. Therefore, a handbell choir director must present a quality program that will attract and retain ringers. He or she can start by aiming at goals in three broad categories.

Music Quality

A handbell choir director is in charge of an instrument that consists of separate tones controlled by separate individuals. Therefore, a director must develop: (1) a uniform ringing style and technique practiced by all members, (2) an assignment of bells to individual ringers that will ensure musical quality, (3) musical dynamics that are uniform and director controlled, and (4) special techniques of bell ringing as required by the chosen repertoire. Handbell manufacturers and the American Guild of English Handbell Ringers, Inc., (1055 East Centerville Station Road, Dayton, OH 45459-5503; 800/878-5459) provide information to assist directors with all of these tasks.

A good knowledge of music will not necessarily ensure success. A director needs to know the unique features of the instrument, the special requirements placed on the ringers, and the techniques to effectively manage a set of bells. The Guild offers training seminars and makes handbell clinicians available to assist new directors.

Trained Personnel

A bell director needs help. As a minimum, a director should appoint and train the following within the group:

● *A bell repairperson*, who, alone, is permitted to repair or adjust the handbells.

● *A table fixer* to keep tables, music stands, pads, and covers in working order.

● *A librarian* to file and retrieve the music.

● *A transportation chairperson* to arrange rides to events.

such notebooks only if there is a purchased, original part in the library for every photocopied part.)

Preparing Rehearsals

A conductor can give the ensemble only what he or she has pulled out of the score. Leonard Bernstein once spoke of the conductor's three levels of listening. First, you must have a clear concept of how the score sounds. This comes through hours of painstaking but rewarding study: analyzing the score and coming to the point where you can hear the entire score in your head as you look at it, with all

---

• *A costumer* to maintain the choir's uniform appearance.

• *Officers*, including president, secretary, treasurer, and publicity director.

The more work that is effectively delegated, the better the director. A bell choir easily breaks down into treble, tenor, and bass sections. Therefore, it is possible to have sectional rehearsals to work out difficult passages of music or to be sure bells are properly assigned. Directors may wish to train section leaders who can help by calling special rehearsals. On-the-job training allows section leaders to learn to serve as assistant bell directors, perhaps on a rotating basis.

The list of helpers could also include a bell-booster organization of outside supporters or perhaps parents of school-aged bell choirs. Volunteers from this group could handle important aspects of planning, fund-raising, and performance scheduling.

Rehearsal Technique

In general, rehearsal techniques for handbell choirs are similar to those used with any other musical organization. Yet, there are a few specific items to consider. The key is preparation. Bell assignments need to be made *before* music is played through to give the ringers adequate time for advanced study and practice.

A rehearsal will be a mirror of a performance. Ringers must be taught to be careful with bells at all times. There must be no clanging or careless horseplay with the bells. There must be no talking during rehearsals. Such rules for discipline should be firmly established and carried out.

Limbering up exercises have been developed for ringers. (Bass bell ringers required a unique set of muscle-strengthening exercises.) Improvising, by using chords and scales, decrescendos, rhythm patterns, and tempos, will develop ensemble skills.

Above all, the ringers must be kept challenged and enthused. Creative bell assignments can help accomplish that goal. Sometimes, however, simply adding bells will renew interest while keeping idle hands busy.

The ultimate goal is to teach as much as possible while creating music that lives up to the beauty of the bells themselves.

—*Edwin J. Duncan*

parts at their proper pitch, proper register, and particular timbre. Such knowledge of the score does not come by listening to recordings of the work, nor even by playing the score at the piano; your aural imagination must be developed.

The second level of listening comes during the rehearsal and performance: listening closely to what the orchestra is actually playing.

The third listening level is to compare the orchestra's rendition to the one in your head, and to bring the orchestra in line with your interpretation through conducting gestures and other rehearsal techniques. Such intense, deep listening can happen only after you have thoroughly studied the score.

Areas of study should include: the orchestration (including transpositions), the form (tonal and thematic areas), the melodic content and resultant textures, the harmonic structure, an analysis of phrase lengths and how smaller phrases combine to form larger sections, and decisions on interpretation (tempos and tempo modification, articulation, breaths, dynamic shape, climax points, etc.). Also make a practical study of the technical considerations of the players: mark string bowings, breaths for wind players, and special effects with articulation and bowing. The score should be marked for cues and dynamics.

In rehearsal, be sensitive to the frustration level and concentration level of the players by striking a balance between running through sections and stopping often to work on details. Create an environment that is nonthreatening but challenging. Set expectations and enthusiastically communicate praise and constructive criticism. Take care, too, to put yourself under the same scrutiny and admit your mistakes.

Establishing Conducting Technique

There is really no difference in the technique of conducting a band and conducting an orchestra. For very small ensembles, a conductor need not be used at all if the musicians have a good sense of inner pulse. In that case, you would simply act as a coach, helping the small ensemble to arrive at a unified interpretation in terms of phrasing, dynamic balances, and tempos.

Study with an accomplished orchestral conductor, if possible. Use a baton and strive to focus all attention and energy into the baton while conducting. Be careful, however, not to move the stick too fast, for it is useless to the players as a blur. Strive for good posture and clear, fluid conducting. Expression without clarity is also useless to the players since they will probably stop watching.

Other practical advice: Always make the preparatory beat the same tempo as the music (a common oversight of choral directors in conducting orchestras). Do not use the left hand to mirror what the right is doing. Instead, use it to cue instruments (this must be done rhythmically, with a clear preparatory beat) and to indicate dynamics. The left hand should specialize in body English; the statements it makes should be clear and unmistakable and *consistent*.

Concerning the set-up of the orchestra in the sanctuary, church orchestra directors have had to resort to some rather unorthodox arrangements of sections and players in order to make everyone fit. The two prime concerns are sight lines to the conductor (a must for all players) and the ability of each player to hear at least the other players in his or her section, if not the whole orchestra.

Though many opportunities for instrumental involvement do not call for a full-fledged orchestra program, the rewards of maintaining a church orchestra far outweigh the ongoing work and problem solving it requires. A beautiful anthem accompaniment or a stirring orchestral offertory can enhance the worship of God in indescribable ways. Powerful hymn orchestrations can inspire your congregation to hitherto unknown heights in musical expressions of praise.

—Daniel A. Sommerville

Resources

Blatter, A. 1980. Instrumentation/orchestration. New York: Longman.

Cone, E. 1968. Musical form and musical performance. New York: Norton.

Green, E. 1987. The dynamic orchestra. Engelwood Cliffs, N. J.: Prentice-Hall.

Green, E. 1981. The modern conductor. Engelwood Cliffs, N. J.: Prentice-Hall.

23

Concerts and Special Events

E xperienced church musicians know the intricacies involved in preparing and presenting musical concerts.
They know that at appointed times of the year, they are
expected to pour their efforts into highlighting certain events. Often,
however, the reasons for this expenditure of time and energy is lost in
the activity, and the question of which occasion to celebrate is complicated by a profusion of options. We need both a rationale for the
presentation of special events and a blueprint for carrying them out.

Focusing on the Goals

What is the purpose of presenting a concert (or, for that matter, the
purpose of any event of worship or anthem of praise)? Surely it is to
manifest the glory of God. True worshipers come to God as people
painfully aware of their creaturely status and of their preoccupation
with the affairs of daily living. They deeply wish to penetrate the
sphere of the Holy, to rend the veil that divides the seen from the
unseen, to enter into the very courts of heaven. How can this be accomplished? Is it by clever originality, or is there a given structure
upon which to build?

Since the days of the early church, the events in the life of Christ
have provided a solid framework for Christian worship. These events,
beyond all other facts of history, reveal the will and purposes of God.
They are, as it were, openings in the screen dividing heaven and earth,

327

portholes providing glimpses into the realm where God reigns supreme. It is therefore fitting that the great milestones of the Lord's life be used as a guide for our seasonal celebrations.

Christ's Advent and all the prophesies regarding his coming should be the focal point of worship in the weeks preceding Christmas. During the first weeks of the new year, we emphasize his Epiphany, or revelation to humanity. As Easter approaches we reflect upon the sufferings of Christ as he faced the Cross. On Resurrection Sunday, that great capstone of all history, a triumphant celebration of his victory over sin and death should culminate the season. Following Easter, a service might be centered around Pentecost, which would celebrate the coming of the Holy Spirit, the establishment of Christ's kingdom, and his promised future reign on earth.

What richness would characterize seasonal celebrations were they to center around the great events in Christian history! In contrast to these milestones, all other incidents pale in significance. National holidays might deserve a certain amount of recognition, but given the effort required to stage a seasonal event and the limited number of days in the church year, our time is better spent in celebrating the significant points of Christ's life.

In choosing a liturgy or format for the celebration of the life of our Lord, we find a wealth of material upon which to draw. We can look to the practices of the early church as a primary source for Christian structures of worship, which were derived from Old Testament practices. Here rite and ceremony played a significant role.

The basic elements of the emerging service of Christian worship were: (1) preparation for worship, (2) proclamation of the Word of God, and (3) response to the Word (Webber 1982, 117–130). In the celebration of seasonal events, we must seek to incorporate each of these components into the service. A procession, symbolic of God's people coming to worship, followed by an acknowledgment of God's presence in the form of a greeting or invocation would provide a fitting preparation. The choral or dramatic presentation of the Word, involving the verbal or sung responses of the people, would then constitute the body of the service. Here the emphasis should be upon the participants' offering up to the Lord sacrifices of worship. A spoken or sung benediction, followed by a ceremonial going out into the world, would serve to close the service.

Just as the liturgy for church services derives from rich sources, so does musical literature for special celebrations. Many works of the world's great composers grew from a personal faith in God and were created to fulfill a specific function in the church service. Congregations would be impoverished indeed were such sources ignored and compositions of the present day become the sole musical fare. We can look for the depth of expression that so many of the masterworks possess along with musical excellence. Whether we use contemporary church music or the great works of past centuries, quality work that is honoring to God should be our criteria for choosing music.

Naturally, we will want to avoid anything that would encourage the audience to settle for pure entertainment rather than for participation in worship. Any tendency toward entertaining congregations must be resisted, while we offer music that truly reveals the glory of God and involves his people in sincere praise.

Under close scrutiny, some popular music can be quite superficial, emphasizing the romantic or the emotional to the neglect of the powerful truth, integrity, and authenticity of the Christian message. Church music leaders must be firm in maintaining high artistic standards in their choice of literature. Otherwise, they may be guilty of profaning the Christian message by inadvertently allowing their services to be tainted with a secular world-view. An appropriate example to follow in this regard is that of the Levites who led the children of Israel in offering their sacrifices of praise to God. So, too, worship leaders must see themselves as priests who assist the people in bringing their worthy gifts to the Lord.

Planning the Celebration

Before an order of worship or celebration can be established, we must assess the talents of the church members. What choral forces are available, and at what level of ability? What solos and ensembles can we use for such a celebration? What instrumental capabilities do we find within the congregation? Realistic answers to these questions should lead to an appropriate choice of material and musical literature.

In the selection of a format or order of celebration, many music directors choose a ready-made, contemporary musical. This is certainly one solution, as long as the selection is honoring to God in its spiritual and artistic content. Another appropriate solution might be the development of an original presentation. This results in a program more suited to a specific congregation, allowing for a greater variety of materials and musical styles, and engaging the congregation more effectively.

Obviously, the planning process should begin well in advance of the actual celebration. If the format is an original one, work should begin at least six months before the celebration. This allows for adequate time to order and receive printed music. If the celebration involves substantial funding, the worship leader needs to make sure the amount is budgeted or that there is an approved plan for raising the funds. In writing the worship format, consider these suggestions:

- Follow fundamental patterns of biblical worship, as discussed above, making a concerted effort to involve and engage the congregation at every possible level.
- Choose music at appropriate levels of complexity and difficulty. Include music of varying styles and genre, being sure to balance the familiar with the unfamiliar.
- Maintain consistency in spiritual and artistic quality when selecting materials.
- Attempt to achieve a sense of mystery (as an aspect of the awesomeness of God) throughout the program.
- Make every effort to maintain reverence as people are being led in the worship of our holy God.
- Early in the service, allow time for the ushering in of latecomers.
- Avoid a stand-up concert format in which the "performers" are the sole participants in the service.
- Write the service in such a way that it flows in a natural and

Coordinating Special Music

In a well-rounded worship program, people want to—and should—share their musical gifts. At the same time, we want services that feel unified, engaging the entire congregation in worship.

An Appropriate Performer

A beautiful voice or instrumental talent is not the only prerequisite to being selected to sing or play a special number. Appropriate ability must also be combined with a gracious spirit and a life of faith generally recognized as above public reproach.

Some people draw attention to themselves because their musical abilities are painfully underdeveloped; others try to impress with their technical expertise. Best are those whose abilities don't get in the way of worship.

It's important to select Christian performers prudently and patiently. Observe them in private and in different public settings. Many you will know from the choir, but not all gifted soloists have the time or freedom to sing in the choir. A good fifteen to twenty minutes spent in a private interview and audition with people such as these will probably supply a sense of their musical and spiritual background.

An Appropriate Message

In both music and text, worship services should be well integrated. That means personally choosing musical selections, not just accepting any song musicians and singers might offer. Therefore, churches need soloists who have sufficient flexibility and humility to accept an assignment.

unified progression. This is another reason to begin planning early; you will then have time to edit and refine the service along the way.

Scheduling, Delegating, and Publicizing

In deference to the lay people who commit valuable time to the preparation of a specific celebration, the worship leader should make every effort to plan ahead and work out a complete rehearsal schedule well in advance, making sure to communicate the schedule to the participants in writing. Optional rehearsals may also be scheduled on an as-needed basis. It is strategic, at this point, for the worship leader to impart the vision and purpose of the celebration to the participants, so that they may acquire ownership and begin working toward a unified end. This approach has the further advantage of giving the participants a sense of partnership in the responsibilities of the worship leadership.

Yet, soloists do have something to offer. Since no one music minister can be aware of all the potential solo repertoire, it is good to give musicians and singers some freedom of choice. Ask the chosen artists to select three or four songs that speak to the theme of the service. Then discuss the songs with them and agree upon a selection.

An Appropriate Style

What makes some music special is the way it's handled and prepared. Musical artistry is not just in *what* is sung and played, but *how* it's presented. There can be unusual beauty in a simple folk song accompanied by guitar, or a lovely hymn sung by a dedicated, sensitive singer, or a five-part polyphonic motet. Each one, in its place, performed with care and craft, becomes an artistic experience.

At times the worship moment requires solemn contemplation, at others a gentle expression of joy. It's a matter of picking the right tool for the job, the right style for the right moment.

An Appropriate Response

How worshipers respond to a song can enhance, hinder, or even destroy the spirit of worship. For example, sometimes applause is appropriate in worship, especially as an expression of praise, affirmation, or celebration. Applause can be another way of saying "Amen," "Yes, I agree," "Me, too." There are other times, however, when silence is the better response.

Special music is done on behalf of the congregation, leading them to send their thoughts and praises to God. That's what makes the worship special, and that's why special care needs to be taken that it is done well.

—Howard Stevenson

If instrumentalists are available from within your congregation, they can contribute a great deal toward the celebratory atmosphere. If the instrumental resources within the congregation are inadequate for the planned service, contract other players early enough to accommodate busy schedules. If a sizable group of players will be contracted, one musician, well-placed and experienced, should contract the entire group in order to relieve the worship leader of that time-consuming task.

The proper delegation of responsibilities involves the worship leader's correct perception of people's talents. This selection process assumes a mature level of spiritual discernment. The most desirable and constructive procedure is for the majority of the tasks to be delegated to the members of the congregation as their abilities and desires indicate.

Using Electronics

As the church moves into the next millennium, technology will continue to expand, offering tools and instruments for worship that we can only begin to imagine. This is good news, because electronic devices can do wonders in helping a congregation worship with joy before the living God.

Sound Reinforcement

The key element in this new style of gospel communication is the sound system. In the past, a simple public-address (PA) system was used to amplify the speaking voice at the front of an auditorium. Today's modern sound-reinforcement (SR) systems are designed to provide the highest quality sound possible to every seat, insuring that every nuance of a spoken or musical message is communicated to the listeners.

Comparing a PA system to an SR system is like comparing a bullhorn to excellent hi-fi speakers. The PA system may be adequate if it is used only for speech, but if a church is updating its music and drama program, then it will need a quality SR system.

A good SR system has a tailored frequency response and dynamic range, providing the listener with an aurally stimulating and satisfying experience, while remaining sonically and visually "transparent." Crystal-clear high frequencies along with robust low frequencies provide clarity, definition, and added punch. Therefore, because quality sound translates into lower listening levels, the actual volume levels can be lowered.

SR equipment purchases and installations can be expensive, so churches need to shop carefully. A sound contractor's profit comes from both his expertise *and* equipment markups. A local music store often will want to cut great deals, but they may not have the expertise to do professional consulting, and the

Give great care to this selection process in order to avoid unacceptable results or personal conflicts. Remember that it is much easier to choose the right person for a task than it is to remove someone from a task after he or she has begun work. Though the personal and spiritual growth of the individual participants is significant, there is seldom an excuse for sacrificing the integrity of the public presentation for the benefit of the individual.

Delegated responsibilities might include: sound operation and recording; setting up and operating lighting; instrumental accompanying; printing flyers, invitations, programs; providing nursery care; contracting of instrumentalists; handling props, costumes, make-up; preparing the sanctuary and chancel; ushering; greeting; and providing and arranging flowers.

One excellent approach to publicity involves the effective witness

---

equipment they wish to sell may be out of date or slow moving. Thus it's important to check with other local churches for the best deal going. An old adage comes to mind here: Buyer beware!

Other Electronic Options

With the foundation laid for high-quality sound, churches can begin exploring the modern world of electronic musical instruments. Digital samplers and synthesizers are capable of providing practically any imaginable sound. With a little experimenting and layering, these instruments will add a whole new element to the worship dynamics, providing delicate, intimate solo sounds to rich, full-bodied orchestrations.

Drum machines now have controllable sound levels, too. Add MIDI drum pads, and the drum machine loses its mechanical feel, becoming a sound source that enables a human drummer to follow the changing dynamics of a worship service. With the advent of the music cas-

sette, many churches now utilize tape tracks for accompaniment purposes. In the early days, tracks were used by recording artists to provide accompaniments from their albums, saving them the expense of traveling with a band or orchestra. Now, generic tape tracks are available at most Christian bookstores, ready for the budding church artist or for the choir that wants a new sound.

When using tape tracks, these tips may prove helpful:

● Acquire a tape deck with variable speed or pitch, in case a track is slightly out of tune with your fixed-pitch instruments.

● Be sure the tapes are cued properly, and then double check them. It is embarrassing for a performer when the track starts at midsong, or the wrong version (or song) begins to play.

● Make sure the person running the sound system pays strict attention. Murphy's Law always seems to rear its ugly head when a track is playing and no one is minding the console.

—Shawn Micheal

of individual church members to their unchurched relatives and friends. One way to help this process is to provide church members with formal invitations or printed flyers for distribution. A problem with advertising in the newspaper and media is that it sometimes tends to draw Christians away from other churches. There are always plenty of church hoppers who enjoy going from one presentation to the next, and this practice seems to have little to do with building Christ's kingdom.

Rehearsing and Performing

In most seasonal celebrations, the choir plays the largest single role, which means the choir director's work in preparing the music is most critical. Here are some suggestions for developing the choral ensemble:

• Work out a schedule for *each* rehearsal (perhaps in five-minute increments), utilizing a chart and adjusting the weekly schedule as needed.

• Early in the preparation schedule, assess the vocal demands of the literature and begin conditioning the voices in the appropriate manner.

• Well in advance of the celebration, break the choir into sections to learn the notes and mark the scores.

• Explain the context of the literature selections during the rehearsals. This allows choir members to share your vision of the coming celebration and begin to understand its overall purpose.

• At each rehearsal, lead the choir in prayer for the coming celebration, and encourage them in their roles as worship leaders.

As the time of preparation draws to a close, maintain a healthy discipline along with the increasing level of excitement, anticipation, confidence, and readiness. Before the dress rehearsal, the worship leader should have all logistics worked out and be prepared to take the people step-by-step through the service. Some directors give these details in writing to the participants so they can better understand their responsibilities. A lack of planning and communication in this area will produce frustration for all involved.

In the final week, the worship leader should confirm plans with those responsible for all aspects of the presentation. Too little communication often causes unnecessary difficulties. Those individuals with leadership responsibilities should meet several days before the presentation to iron out any last-minute details and talk through the entire service, asking for further questions and clarifications. Try to schedule a brief meeting of leaders on the day of the service.

Ushering can be a source of frustration if not prepared ahead of time. To maintain a reverent environment, require that latecomers be refused admittance during Scripture readings, prayers, and musical presentations. Adequate and well-placed opportunities should be provided for admitting latecomers without disrupting the service. Crying and disruptive children can also be a source of frustration; encourage parents to make use of the nursery or the narthex. The ushers can do much to alleviate these problems.

Anything that the worship leader can do to avoid approaching the presentation in a harried manner is, of course, desirable. All physical set-up requirements should be done a day before the presentation to avoid a last-minute rush. Once the celebration is underway, the unexpected should come as no surprise to the worship leadership and should be treated as calmly as possible. The participants will undoubtedly reflect the frustrations and anxiety of the worship leader if those emotions are perceptible.

Evaluating the Event

In the first week after the service, the worship leadership should meet to evaluate the service's spiritual impact and effectiveness. All measurements of success should be based on scriptural standards of true worship. In what ways was God glorified? In what ways was God *not* glorified? A written evaluation will be helpful to those planning similar events in ensuing years.

Seasonal concerts or special celebrations can be glorious occasions because of their wonderful ability to help Christians mature in the grace and knowledge of our Lord. They can also be an effective way to introduce unbelievers to the gospel of Jesus Christ. This is best done with services that center around the presentation of God's Word, allowing for the heart-felt responses of the congregation, and that are rich in symbolic enactment of the life and work of Christ.

Customizing services to the local congregation (rather than relying on preplanned programs) and utilizing resident talent (rather than drawing on outside sources) is to be preferred. The service then will be a personal expression of a given body of believers—a congregation's distinctive offering to the Lord.

—*George H. Dupere*

Resources

Allen, R., and G. Borror. 1982. Worship: Rediscovering the missing jewel. Portland, Ore.: Multnomah.

Gaebelein, F. 1985. The Christian, the arts and truth. Portland, Ore.: Multnomah.

Hoon, P. 1971. The integrity or worship. Nashville: Abingdon.

Johansson, C. 1984. Music and ministry. Peabody, Mass.: Hendrickson.

Webber, R. 1982. Worship old and new. Grand Rapids: Zondervan.

Wiersbe, W. 1986. Real worship. Nashville: Oliver Nelson.

Part IV

The Lord's Supper

It was around the table that Cleopas and his companion first recognized Jesus, with whom they had just spent hours on the road to Emmaus. Fellowship around the Table is like that. In the simple elements of the bread and the cup, people meet Christ.

For the pastor, is there any task more sacred than leading the congregation into the presence of our Lord in Holy Communion? When so much of what a modern pastor does is determinedly mundane, it is refreshing to enter into the transcendent when inviting one's congregation to the Table of the Lord. Speaking the ancient words of institution, breaking bread and filling the cup, placing the body and blood of Christ within the grasp of mere mortals, reminding people so vividly of his sacrifice for us—this is high and holy work.

Because this is not the place to fumble—not in so sacred a responsibility—pastors want to be able to lead competently a seamless service of Communion, a service that expresses both the fullness of meaning in the sacrament and the familial personality of the congregation. Here is help in that quest.

Part IV

The Lord's Supper

24

The Purpose of the Lord's Supper

Christians have long discussed and debated the meaning of this service that all believe to be so important and central to their faith. The exceptions are the Society of Friends, who hold that all life is a sacrament and every meal is a means of grace, and the Salvation Army, who found the practice of drinking a cup of wine or juice a stumbling block to new converts.

The impressively simple words of Jesus, "Do this in remembrance of me" (Luke 22:19; 1 Cor. 11:24) have even been the occasion of much bad feeling and acrimonious falling out. Four hundred years ago Christians with equal sincerity and conviction were misunderstood, persecuted, exiled, tortured, and killed in the name of a "correct" understanding of the Lord's Supper.

Mercifully, these times have passed, and a new day of mutual understanding and tolerance has dawned. The last two generations have seen a remarkable coming together of Christians, a sharing of insights, and a cross-fertilizing of traditions that has tried to go back to a more firmly biblical understanding. Certainly we must consider what was at stake in the sixteenth-century debates, but first let us observe some movements of thought that have brought Christians to a more understanding frame of mind.

Movements Toward Tolerance

• *Sacramental theology has fruitfully explored the idea of signs.* Symbol has come to be seen as part of our general perception of reality—

339

and of the nature of Christianity. All truth is apprehended under "signs" that point to actions, which in turn Christians believe "reveal" God. Since there is no direct revelation available for us to inspect and experience, we depend on intimations of the divine presence in the form or shape of symbols. Such symbols convey meaning through word (language is a sign par excellence) and deed. The Eucharist involves both these aspects of human activity, based on what Jesus *did* and *said* in the Upper Room. Focusing on these signs tends to deemphasize the role played by the physical elements of bread and wine in themselves. These are the elements that Jesus "took" and over which he "spoke."

Thus, a remarkable meeting ground has resulted as Roman Catholic interpreters have drawn away from the notion of a physical change (implied in transubstantiation), and Protestants have explored what the elements become when the Word is spoken over them and they are received by the believing community; in some sense they have power to convey and actualize the reality—Christ's body and blood—that they point to and represent.

• *Biblical theology has offered a fuller meaning for "memorial."* Zwingli is usually thought to have refused any meaning to "This do in remembrance of me" other than the plain sense: We are bidden to recall an absent figure. Now a study of the Hebrew thought world behind *remembrance* has questioned this view. There is a dynamic sense of *memorial* that suggests life, not death. It is based on the evocative power of the memory of Israel in its worship of God. Hebrew worship was dramatic and vital, reliving the past through its creed and liturgy, and calling Yahweh's past deeds out of their "pastness" into a living present, where their saving benefits were newly appreciated and experienced.

• *Communicants have recognized the eschatological dimension of their meal together.* The Communion meal expresses a gospel that is hardly understandable except in terms of the new age that has dawned with Christ's coming. The church stands at the turning point of the ages, in the interval where the old order and the new eon intersect (1 Cor. 10:11). The Lord's Supper began its long history with the prayer call *marana tha* ("Our Lord, come," 1 Cor. 16:22; *Didache* 10:6), and both the Synoptic Gospels and Paul concur in attaching a forward-looking side to the meal: We break bread and take the cup "until he comes" (1 Cor. 11:26).

The "sign" language of Eucharistic actions (eating, drinking, communing) translates into a picture of the church's ultimate hope, so appealingly presented in Revelation 19:6–9. Meanwhile the church is reminded forcefully at the table that it is a pilgrim community, living "between the times" of the first and final advents, sustained by the pilgrims' gift of "heavenly" food and "supernatural" drink (see 1 Cor.

10:1–5 for these images, as well as John 6). Here we have no lasting city nor permanent rest (Heb. 4:8–11; 13:14).

The doctrine of the church comes directly under the influence of this point of view. It is a group united not simply by doctrinal purity, but, more profoundly, by organic spiritual fellowship. The fellowship-meal understanding of the Eucharist delivers it from a too ethereal and too otherworldly status, and roots its significance in the nature of the church as the family of God.

• *Modern Christians have realized that bread is a daily concern of millions.* The Communion service reminds the sharers that the church lives in a world where millions eke out their existence on the threshold of poverty, starvation, and malnutrition. The eucharistic bread has thus, for many Christians today, become a silent call to enter into the service of Christ, who fed the crowds in Galilee and died in loneliness and despair at Calvary.

The offertory, in which the people bring their gifts to the table/altar for consecration, conveys the truth that what is presented at the Eucharist represents human labor in the field and orchard. Daily work is brought under the aegis of divine blessing, with an indirect rebuke of our misuse of nature when we selfishly keep her bounties to ourselves and exploit those who labor in her fields and farms at poverty levels.

Shared Meanings: Passover to Present

"Our paschal lamb, Christ, has been sacrificed. Therefore let us celebrate the festival" (1 Cor. 5:7–8 NRSV). This statement, set in a context of apostolic admonition to a grievously falling community at Corinth, has the distinction of being the first recorded comment on what the church's holy meal-rite meant. The unusual feature, found in so many of Paul's allusions and enforcements, is that he is writing to a collection of men and women immersed in Greco-Roman culture who nevertheless are expected to catch his subtle undertones of meaning drawn from the Scriptures of the Jewish people.

The case in point is the Hebrew Passover, which commemorated the past deliverance of the nation and anticipated its future blessedness in the messianic age. Already ethical teachings had gathered around the Passover, with its various dishes, cups, and saucers. In particular, leaven was banned from Jewish households during the days of the feast, and a symbolic meaning was attached to the yeast. It stood for what permeates the batch of dough and makes it rise, that is, pride.

Paul exploits precisely this notion and warns against cherishing the presence of blatant evil (1 Cor. 5:6–8). At the center of his ruling, he set the celebration of the meal—the "Christian Passover"—since the lamb (Christ) has been sacrificed. Paul's christianizing procedure is clearly illustrated here. But the death of Jesus and the meal-rite that commemorates that death are boldly interpreted in Old Testament–Judaic categories, and the significance of both are drawn out.

There was ample justification for this procedure, going back to the Gospel tradition. Jesus, looking back in part to meals shared in Galilee, invested his final meal with a solemn significance taken directly from the Passover. Yet the novelty of what Jesus did in the Upper Room lay more with his words than with his deeds.

Let's consider two significant points about these words, which will help us see why there has been so much diversity of interpretation and practice related to the Lord's Supper:

• *The words spoken over the bread and the cup have come down to us in several ways.* Even when we grant this wide diversity, there is still a way in which to claim certain features as part of Jesus *ipsissima vox,* his authentic intention, even when we may be less than certain about what he actually *spoke.* Set within the paschal framework, the emphatic tones of his recorded sayings were heard as follows:

a) "This *is* my body . . . this *is* my blood." The most straightforward version we have seems to put all the stress on the verb *is.* Yet this cannot be so, since Aramaic has no verb "to be," and the copulative often has an explanatory force. Hence the rendering has to be "this stands for, represents. . . ."

The clearest Old Testament background is found in Exodus 24:1–11, with verse 8 ("This is the blood that seals the covenant which the Lord made with you") offering a striking parallel. Also, the bread-wine statements match the thought in Deuteronomy 16:3, where the old Jewish paraphrase has: "This is the bread of suffering our fathers ate in the land of Egypt." There is, in both instances, a representative identity between what *is* now on the table (both paschal and Christian) and what *was* then shared in the patriarchal story.

The dynamic equivalence gives significance to the action undertaken to make the past live again—but with some obvious distinctions. The "bread of affliction" is now transformed into Jesus' own person. The "blood of the covenant" is now that which is given to seal a new agreement.

b) "This . . . is the new covenant." The "new" covenant may be taken to be a Pauline edition, since we know how he exploited the idea of newness in his discussion (2 Cor. 3:1–16) of two contrasting ages that are opposed and exclusive. The whole discussion in 2 Corinthians 3 is based on Jeremiah 31:31–34, with its oracle of a coming new age and a fresh start made in God's relations with Israel.

At this point the Lord's Supper takes over from the model of the Last Supper in the Upper Room and adds some transforming dimensions, namely, that the "new covenant" is not merely revamped Judaism or the "old covenant" altered and improved. It speaks of a new relationship between God and the world inaugurated by the universal figure, Jesus Christ, whose people are neither Jews nor Gentiles but a "new creation" (1 Cor. 10:32; Gal. 6:16; Eph. 2:11–22).

c) "Do this in remembrance." The command "to repeat" ("Do this in remembrance of me," in Luke-Paul) may be a liturgical after-thought, but it may well claim the sanction of the Passover ritual that Jesus apparently utilized with some care and attention. The annual Passover celebration was held in memory of the departure out of Egypt, based on Exodus 12:4 ("to remind you of what I, the Lord, have done") and 13:9 ("it will remind you").

The human intent of the reminder is clear and straightforward: Lest Israel should become a forgetful and wayward people—a frequently heard complaint among the prophets—they needed a certain prodding. Such holy days were to make the people vividly aware—by a dynamic retelling and reliving of Israel's past heritage in history—of all they owed to Yahweh, the God of their fathers. The people would also reaffirm their present status as his chosen and ransomed people.

Jesus stood in this historical stream. The commission to remember him is implicit in the paschal setting and also in the promise of a future reunion in the Father's kingdom when he will be once again present with his own.

• *Paul enriched the Eucharistic words (or teaching) he had received (1 Cor. 11:23) in a number of directions.* We may itemize these:

First, *he emphasized fellowship.* By common consent the key term of Paul's understanding of social ethics and its dimension of partnership that unites believers with the Lord and with one another is *koinonia,* ordinarily translated "fellowship." The horizontal plane of *koinonia* was just as vivid as the vertical for the apostle. Indeed, his argument reasons from the "one loaf" (1 Cor. 10:17) to the unity of the "one body," the church. "One baptism, one table" (1 Cor. 12:13) are for him the ground plan of a doctrine of the church that stresses all believers' oneness in Christ. Unity-in-fellowship is an integral part of the church's life in this world, with the Eucharist its focal point.

Second, *he emphasized proclamation.* The statement in 1 Corinthians 11:26 ("*you proclaim* the Lord's death until he comes") is Paul's way of expressing the prospect of a future reuniting in the kingdom, as offered in the synoptic Gospels. Paul's choice of the word *proclaim* (*katangellein*) is interesting; it otherwise connotes the public proclaiming of the gospel (see 1 Cor. 2:1; 9:14; Rom. 1:8; Phil. 1:17–18). The apostle apparently saw no great distinction between the gospel as preached in his public evangelizing mission and the same gospel as presented to believers at the Lord's Table. The Eucharist for him was sacramental in the same way that his preaching conveyed and actualized the Word of God in human experience. Both types of proclamation rest on God's free grace and evoke the response of faith (Rom. 1:5;

1 Thess. 2:13). Both ordinances are effectual within the field of God's prior action in using earthly means (words, bread, wine) and are determined by the way they are received, believed, and applied.

The parallel is even closer when we press the question: How does the sacrament—whether of the Word or the Eucharist—actual "work"?

To attempt an answer means trying to take seriously the meaning behind the verb in the twin sentences: "This *is* the Word of God" and "This *is* my body, my blood." In both cases, literal identity or transferred qualities seem to be ruled out. Paul's words remain his, and by his words he stands self-revealed. Christ's body and blood are not

---

The Lord's Supper: How Often?

Over the centuries Christians have celebrated the Lord's Supper at different intervals. The New Testament gives no detailed instructions. If breaking bread in Acts 2:46 refers to the sacrament, the primitive church clearly practiced frequent observance, but this is debatable. Paul, in 1 Corinthians 11:20ff., seems to associate the administration with a common meal, the so-called love feast. Neither passage makes any particular frequency obligatory.

Justin Martyr's *Apology* and Hippolytus' writings in the second and early third centuries offer more detailed information. Apparently the Supper had now become an integral part of each Sunday's worship. Churches both East and West continued the weekly observance, though with increasing elaboration.

In the medieval West, however, the Supper underwent serious change with the development of the doctrine of transubstantiation and the ritual of the Mass. The weekly Mass might be compulsory, but it was clearly no longer the kind of Lord's Supper celebrated in the early church. Nonofficiants received Communion only infrequently—often no more than once a year—and had no access to the cup. The use of an unknown language further impeded congregational participation.

The sixteenth-century Reformers tried to remedy this situation. They introduced the national languages, simplified (to differing degrees) the accompanying rites, stressed again the related proclamation of the gospel, and restored the Supper's character as Communion. Securing more frequent Communion, however, defeated even Calvin in Geneva. He wanted a weekly celebration, but, opposed by entrenched medieval practice, had to settle for a quarterly administration, which became customary in many Protestant circles. The Anglicans, too, could require Communion only three times a year, one of them the traditional Easter Eucharist, which can still attract the largest congregations.

Common Alternatives

Since quarterly or weekly observance are two popular alternatives, consider some of the pros and cons

there on the table in any transubstantiated or consubstantiated form. Yet the action of God in sacramental power turns the earthly into what is savingly effective: so under God's sovereign hand Paul's words become kerygmatic, and the bread and cup become savingly the Lord's body and blood in which believers are permitted a share (1 Cor. 10:16–17).

The link-term, then, is *proclaim*, since the kerygmatic transformation turns the human into the divine. This occurs, not magically nor automatically as though it were a conjuring trick, but rather by faith, as human faith meets and matches divine grace in a grateful response

---

of each frequency of observance:

• *Quarterly observance.* Greater meaning and solemnity attach to what is less routine. With quarterly observance, opportunity arises for preparatory pastoral visitation. Communion seasons may also be times for more extended meetings for evangelism and sanctification, as in the Scottish Highlands and Islands. They provide more time, too, for self-examination and mutual reconciliation, as Paul enjoins.

Nevertheless, to treat the Supper too solemnly can frighten off less-committed members on the ground of unworthiness (too rigid "fencing of the table"). We must be careful to retain the Supper as an ordinance of grace.

• *Weekly observance.* Movements toward a more general restoration of weekly observance gained force in the nineteenth and twentieth centuries. An interesting Anglican development was the early Communion service (usually 8 A.M.), supplementing normal Morning and Evening Prayer. This allowed weekly observance but had two disadvantages: There was often no sermon, and restricted attendance limited genuine eucharistic fellowship among all the people.

To correct this situation, many

churches today have returned to the practice described by Justin. A full service of prayer, praise, and the reading and exposition of Scripture forms the setting of the Supper. The whole congregation participates in a regular, weekly administration. A difficulty, of course, is that this type of worship is not so suitable for evangelistic purposes. Those who have not yet made a Christian commitment can feel out of place when the Supper is an integral part of each worship service.

Because of these problems, many churches celebrate Communion monthly, often on the first Sunday of the month. This frequency makes Communion special but not a rare observance.

The absence of clear biblical precept or precedent means that no obligatory pattern of frequency exists for celebrating Communion. Certain things, however, are clearly desirable: integration of the Supper into the worship life of the congregation, adequate regularity, a good combination of simplicity and solemnity, and authentic congregational participation. How best to meet these goals, local churches must constantly and critically examine.

—*Geoffrey W. Bromiley*

to the gospel proclaimed alike from pulpit and table.

Third, *he emphasized the church's eternal destiny.* The eschatological sign under which the Eucharist stands reappears in Paul in the words "until he comes" (1 Cor. 11:26). The words were meant to remind the church of its destiny as a pilgrim people not yet arrived at its heavenly goal, still under the discipline of its earthly toils. The Eucharist points ahead to the ultimate homegathering of God's people, and prepares for the "banquet of the blessed" in the future messianic kingdom. The paragraphs that follow in 1 Corinthians 11:27–34 extend this theme with their notes of judgment and warning. Either take yourself in hand *now*, says Paul, or face the prospect of God's judgment—already experienced in certain unhappy scenes at Corinth—at the last day.

The Verdict of History

So far we have focused on the general agreements among Christians while showing that, because the original eucharistic words and actions have come down to us in several ways, specific Communion theologies and practices do differ. Yet, in spite of general agreements and recent moves toward tolerance, there is no denying the fierce controversies that vexed the churches in the Reformation period. It is clear that all the Reformers opposed any medieval notion that on the table the bread is miraculously transformed into the literal body of Christ. Yet they were divided among themselves. Three rival positions emerged at Marburg in A.D. 1529.

• *Luther* took his stand on the plain meaning of the Lord's word, "This is my body" and argued that Christ's presence was "in, with, or under" the element. This position has become known as *consubstantiation*, based on the idea that Christ's body is everywhere, though Luther professed not to be able to explain it. He did insist, however, on real faith to ensure the presence of God in Christ at the sacrament.

• *Zwingli*, at the opposite end, championed a purely symbolic view, insisting that the bread and cup were no more than signs or symbols. Their function was to serve as a memorial to us of God's great love in Christ.

• *Calvin's* viewpoint, represented by Bucer, took a middle line. There is a real presence, but it is not tied in with elements. Rather the bread and cup are vehicles God uses to come to us. The important thing is a "worthy reception" by faith, made possible by the activity of the Holy Spirit.

As we noted, recent years have seen a changing viewpoint on many of these matters. Roman Catholicism since Vatican II (1969) has moved away from the crassly magical or superstitious view of the sacrament. The Lutherans have defined their founder's somewhat convoluted position by discussion with both Catholic and Episcopalian scholars. The latter still adhere to Calvin's "virtualism" (as it is called), a conviction shared by Presbyterians, that stresses real sharing in Christ's sacrifice by the participants' faith. Independent churches (Congregational, Baptist, etc.) typically hold to what is called "Zwinglian memorialism," emphasizing that this fellowship meal is a reminder of Christ's great work of salvation and a time to examine ourselves for sin.

Yet all Christians confess to being in the presence of mystery at the Communion table, a mystery that nourishes and promotes faith. As Queen Elizabeth I put it:

'Twas God the Word that spake;
He tooke the bread and brake;
And what the word did make,
That I believe, and take.

—Ralph P. Martin

Resources

Marshall, I. 1980. Last Supper and the Lord's Supper. Grand Rapids: Eerdmans.

Martin, R. 1982. The worship of God: Some theological, pastoral, and practical reflections, ch. 9. Grand Rapids: Eerdmans.

Jeremias, J. 1977. The eucharistic words of Jesus. Philadelphia: Fortress.

25

Planning the Lord's Supper

Actions speak louder than words. As worship leaders, we are people not only of speech but also of action. Words are fine, as far as they go, but sometimes the most important experiences of life are too deep for words.

God knows this. In the Bible, God not only says "I love you" through the words of the prophets, the Law, and the sermons of Jesus, but God's love is also demonstrated, made visible. "And this will be a sign for you: you will find a babe wrapped in swaddling cloths and lying in a manger" (Luke 2:12). This babe in the manger is a sign of the redemption of God's people.

How fitting, in a faith noted for its incarnality, that our Lord chose to show forth his truth through an intimate meal with loving friends in the Upper Room! Jesus thus gave his followers a sacrament, an ordinance, a sign of love to share with the rest of the world. "Do this in remembrance of me," he said.

Sacraments and ordinances are everyday objects—like bread and wine, and everyday actions, like eating—that when done among God's people in worship convey God's love for them and their love for God. God uses everyday things we can understand—bread and wine—to show us a love that defies understanding.

New Theological Agreements

The most striking feature of contemporary worship renewal is the emerging consensus on the Lord's Supper. Here are some of the areas of theological agreement that have recently come into being:

349

• Recognizing the detriment of infrequent and half-hearted celebration of the Lord's Supper. Many of us now admit that by our neglect, we have violated the biblical testimony of the centrality of this act of worship. A full service of Word and Table appears to be the normative Sunday morning pattern for Christians. Recovery of robust, confident, frequent celebration of the Lord's Supper is important.

• Realizing that the theological focus of our Communion celebration has often been far too limited. We have celebrated the Lord's Supper as a funereal, doleful memorial to a departed hero rather than as the joyous Sunday Resurrection meal it is intended to be. We have remembered only Maundy Thursday and the Upper Room, and forgotten the meal at Emmaus on Sunday evening.

This meal is a sign of the presence of Christ, not his absence. This is the Lord's Supper, not Jesus' Last Supper. When we eat together, our focus is upon the whole saving work of God in Christ—birth, life, service, Passion, death, Resurrection, Ascension, and present reign—not simply upon a reenactment of the somber meal in the Upper Room.

• Admitting that often we have made the Lord's Supper into a private act of personal piety rather than the communal, familial, ecclesial act it is meant to be. The Lord's Supper sometimes has been transformed into a quiet, introspective, individual meal, with individual worshipers seeking salvation from individual sins—without communing with one another. Why would Jesus have chosen a meal with friends as a symbol of his kingdom if this were a private, lonely, individualized way of salvation? It is difficult to eat or to be saved alone. Every celebration of the Lord's Supper is an affirmation of our community in Christ and a means of forming the body around the Table.

• Remembering that the Lord's Supper means everything any meal means: love, fellowship, hunger, nourishment. These meanings are given added significance because, in this meal, we commune with the risen Christ, who joins us at the Table. People may not know what redemption, atonement, reconciliation, sanctification, and all our other big words mean, but everybody, from the youngest to the oldest, knows what a meal means. Therefore, when we celebrate this holy meal, our actions, elements, and words should make clear that this is a *meal.*

The Jewish faith has been called "symbiotic," meaning that it draws upon the experiences of everyday life for revelation. When we worship through wine and bread, when we point to human events like a meal, we are linking our faith with daily life, spirit with flesh, the heavenly with the mundane. This is an essential linkage for any relevant religion. Specifically, this means that when we celebrate this meal, we must use bread and wine in such a way that people know this act of worship is a meal. We thus link religion to everyday life.

Better Meals

Christians have celebrated the Lord's Supper in a rich variety of ways. That means pastors must adapt the foregoing practical insights to a particular church. Here are some adaptable ways to enliven celebration of the Lord's Supper:

• *Restore the Lord's Supper to its rightful place in Sunday worship.* Most of us Protestants need to work on this. Quarterly celebrations seem inadequate. In our worship life, infrequency usually breeds indifference and misunderstanding. Rather than making Communion something special, infrequent celebrations can lead a congregation to regard Communion as something optional, unusual, and dispensable.

As the Reformers knew, Word and Sacrament belong together. The Word must not only be preached; it also must be practiced. In congregations in which there has been long-term neglect of the sacraments, long-term reeducation may be needed. The best way to reeducate is through well-planned, enthusiastically led, frequent celebrations. Many of our people may not understand the Lord's Supper because they have never seen it. What they see, when they come to the Lord's Supper, is a stiff, cold, formal, make-believe meal with odd, make-believe food. Who can understand that?

One congregation gives out a bread recipe to families in the congregation. When the family bakes a loaf of bread and offers it on the table on Sunday, everyone knows what Communion means.

A wise pastor will try to fit the Lord's Supper into the pattern and style of Sunday worship of the congregation. One reason people may resist Communion is that it has been done in an awkward, foreign style other than in the worship style to which they are accustomed. For instance, if a congregation is unaccustomed to reading the service from the back of the hymnal, we shouldn't insist that they do so only on Communion Sundays. We can simply go through the service, using the worship book ourselves and having the people participate at our cues.

A pastor who served a rural area of West Virginia told me, "My congregation doesn't like to have Holy Communion." I said that that was impossible because, one, everyone not only likes to eat but needs to eat, and, two, all Christians want to be in the presence of Christ. I asked the pastor to tell me about his congregation. He told me that they were rural people with an average educational level of about eighth grade.

"That means you will not want to use printed material," I said. "Presenting them with long, written liturgies will only make them feel inadequate." We then discussed how the pastor might lead the service without having the congregation read the service from the hymnals.

While a pastor must respect the feelings and limitations of a congregation, there is no need to achieve unanimity of opinion before introducing new worship practices. Sometimes people do not know what they like until they have experienced it over a period of time. I am confident that when we introduce worship renewal with sensitivity, explaining what we are doing and why, and allowing the congregation opportunity for feedback, the act will speak for itself.

• *Utilize the new rites of your group or denomination.* Most of our older eucharistic rites, which we inherited from the Reformation, are historically and biblically lean. They represent the Reformers' attempt to reform the worship of the Middle Ages, often through inadequate information on older practice. The new rites provide for much more congregational participation, stress the visual quality of the sacraments, lift up a wider array of biblical themes, and are constructed in a much more orderly way. They use contemporary English without being faddish. Most congregations respond favorably to the use of these new resources.

• *Preach and teach on the Lord's Supper.* While the best way to renew the Lord's Supper is simply to do it well, congregations appreciate some attempt to explain the meaning of these rites. It is important to stress that the Lord's Supper is a thoroughly biblical experience, not some vestige from the Middle Ages. The Lord's Supper should be placed after the sermon in the Sunday order of worship. In this way we show that the Lord's Supper is the fitting response to the Good News. Most Protestant congregations react unfavorably if their preacher appears to be emphasizing the Lord's Supper at the expense of a full sermon. While our preaching may be a bit shorter on Communion Sundays, we should save our best sermons for these Sundays in order to underscore our belief in the linkage of Word and Table.

• *Pay close attention to the mechanics of your leadership.* If the pastor appears to be ill at ease about his or her leadership at the Table, the congregation will feel that this rite is something strange and out of the ordinary. We need to practice carefully the movements and gestures we will use in the service, preferably in front of a full-length mirror. Not a single action should be missed by the people in the back row. The breaking of the loaf and the pouring of the wine should be seen by everyone.

In worship, mechanics are mandatory. The main difference between a meal at a fast-food restaurant and a gourmet dinner is the difference in how the food is prepared and served. One system makes you feel like a cow being herded to the feed trough; another makes you feel like a human being. How do we make people feel at the Lord's Table by the way we serve them? No one should serve Communion who does not know how to hand someone a piece of bread in a gracious manner. Our actions do speak louder than our words.

Because the Lord's Supper is a meal, stand behind the Communion table, facing the people like a host at a table. Use large, substantial vessels, preferably a single chalice and a large platter or tray. Begin the service with the table cleared, and then, right before you give the prayer of thanksgiving, have the Communion vessels and the elements placed upon the table, as if you were preparing a meal. Likewise, after Communion, quickly clear the vessels and leftover food from the table. An appropriate amount of ceremony in preparing the meal helps to build a sense of expectancy in the congregation and also helps to link this rite with the meals they have known in daily life.

Sometimes, in the worship service when the Lord's Supper is celebrated, people complain that the service takes too long. If you are in a small congregation, this is usually not a problem. But where time is a factor, the length of the service is often more a matter of poorly planned and executed mechanics than of too much substance. Have someone time the various acts of your Communion service. You may be surprised how time is used. Some pastors are shocked to find they spend nearly as much time in announcements, merely reading the bulletin to the congregation, as they do in their sermon! If time is a problem, we should do what is necessary to bring Communion efficiently to a manageable time frame.

Usually, the things that take the most time are the nonessentials rather than the essentials. What are the essentials for the Lord's Supper? First, the Word must be read and proclaimed. Then, after the prayers and the offering, we move to the Service of the Table.

Four Historical Actions

There are four basic actions in the celebration of the Lord's Supper, four historical and biblical movements that have characterized our actions at the Table throughout the ages: take, thank, break, give (these are described in passages like Luke 22:17–19 and 24:30; 1 Cor. 11:23–26).

- As Jesus *took the bread and cup* at the table in the Upper Room, so do we.

- As Jesus *gave thanks* at the table, so do we. This is the prayer of thanksgiving, or prayer of consecration. At this point, some churches simply repeat the words of institution from the Scripture, which tells the story of Jesus in the Upper Room. Other churches have the pastor or leader offer a full prayer here, an extended table blessing that has these historic parts:

Thanksgiving: Prayer for God's saving acts in Creation, incarnation, and redemption.

Institution: A recollection of Jesus' words at the table in the Upper Room.

Remembrance: Thinking of Jesus' saving work, death, and resurrection.

Invocation: Asking the Holy Spirit's blessing upon us and upon our gifts of bread and wine.

Doxology: A concluding act of praise, followed by the congregation's amen.

● As Jesus *broke* the bread, so do we, often remembering the words of Paul, "When we break the bread, is it not a means of participating in the body of Christ?" (1 Cor. 10:16).

● As Jesus *gave* the bread and the cup in the Communion, so do we.

These are the essentials. Everything else is nonessential. If we have time for two anthems by the choir, fine. If we don't, eliminate them.

Methodological Considerations

Worship styles and methods certainly vary from place to place. However, keep in mind these three general guidelines as you prepare your Communion services:

● *The elements should be distributed efficiently, but in a manner that is not impersonal or rushed.* The method of distribution may be a denominational and congregational tradition. Evaluate your method and ask if improvements can be made. Remember as you are evaluating that each method of receiving Communion—the people seated in the pews, kneeling at the chancel rail, standing before the altar—says something about what you and your people believe is happening here.

A congregation might want to try various methods of receiving Communion. Our congregation sometimes kneels for the distribution during the season of Lent and stands during the season of Easter, in order that our bodily posture may be attuned to the feeling of the season.

The practice of dismissing each group of communicants that kneels at the Communion rail can be repetitious and time consuming. If your congregation kneels at the rail, simply invite the people to come and go continuously. Ask them to hold out their hands when they are ready to receive the bread and wine; then, after they commune, they may continue to kneel in prayer or they may return to their seats at their own discretion.

During the Communion, I like the old practice of having the congregation sing hymns. This helps lift the mood of the service and, by selecting hymns in accordance with the particular season of the year, we can focus the service in various ways. Sing hymns that are so familiar the congregation can sing without looking at the hymnals, songs that are related to the particular season. This will do more to change the tone of a service than anything else. It also gives people something to do while the rest of the congregation is communing.

• *Keep detailed instructions to a minimum.* Too many instructions only make people uptight and make the service much more rigid and formal than it needs to be. A simple "Come to the Lord's Table" is usually enough. Visitors may be given brief instructions, or they can simply watch how the members do it.

Ushers may be unnecessary at Communion. Sometimes ushers tend to make the service too formal and rigid with their stiff, lockstep directives. Most congregations, after they become accustomed to it, appreciate the freedom, the sense of unity, and the flow of a service in which they can move freely at their own discretion.

• *Prepare people for more meaningful participation.* Every congregation should have a continuing program of worship instruction. On a Sunday when the Lord's Supper is being celebrated, have the children's classes bake bread for the service. Your church might issue devotional materials that could be used around the family breakfast table on Communion Sundays before the family members come to church.

Every time the bread is lifted up, called holy, and then broken and given in remembrance of our Lord, the church enacts in visible, tangible, human ways the reality of his promise to us: "For where two or three are gathered in my name, there am I in the midst of them (Matt. 18:20).

—*William Willimon*

Resources

Willimon, W. 1980. Word, water, wine and bread: How worship has changed over the years. Valley Forge, Penn.: Judson.

Willimon, W. 1981. Sunday dinner: The Lord's Supper and Christian life. Nashville: Upper Room.

26

The Administration of the Lord's Supper

Nearly two thousand years ago, thirteen men met in an upper room in a Jerusalem home. They reclined on couches, conversed, and ate their meal, and then one of them, their teacher and Lord, washed the feet of the other twelve. During the course of the meal, their Lord took bread, gave it to his friends, and said, "This is my body." Distributing wine, he said, "This is my blood."

Today, three hundred people sit in pews in a church. After preaching a sermon, their pastor stands behind a table, holds up a piece of bread, and says, "The body of Christ, given for you." Then servers take the trays and distribute pieces of bread to the people. The same happens with grape juice, sipped from little plastic thimbles.

The two events have many similarities, but there are obvious differences, too. With the passing of time through the centuries, churches have developed a variety of ways to administer the Supper while maintaining a central focus and a common meaning. While the theology behind these variations is important, here we will focus more on the event itself, the administration of the Supper.

The Type of Bread and Wine

Not all churches use the same food and drink for the Supper. Most Protestant churches do use bread. This may be store-bought or home-made, white or brown. Some churches insist on unleavened bread;

some use crackers. Episcopal and Lutheran churches have traditionally used wafers, but many of those congregations, too, are changing to bread.

At the original Supper, Jesus and his disciples apparently used *ordinary* bread, presumably wholesome bread prepared in someone's kitchen. Perhaps our bread at the Supper should be ordinary bread, too—the kind of bread we might find on our breakfast tables. For mission churches this issue can provide the grist for an interesting theological debate, since some cultures do not consume bread and red juice or wine at all. May they use some other staple food, such as potatoes or white coconut juice?

The fruit of the vine also comes in different forms. Most Bible scholars agree that the beverage at the original Supper was fermented wine—the common table beverage of the day—although it was probably not as high in alcohol content as most modern wines. Throughout most of church history, wine was the beverage used for the Supper, and many churches today continue to use wine.

Many other churches, especially evangelical churches in North America, use grape juice, either because they believe one ought not to cause temptation for parishioners with alcohol problems or because they hold to a general prohibition against the use of any alcoholic beverage. Some congregations offer *both* wine and juice; others use nonalcoholic wine.

The Preparation of the Elements

How are the elements to be prepared? Most churches cut the bread into cubed pieces and put them on plates, for ease of distribution. Other churches do not cut the loaf, but pass it among the members of the congregation, having each person break a piece from the loaf. Even those churches that cut the bread often have a whole loaf on the table to show that in the Supper they use ordinary bread, not a special Communion bread.

Churches also use various kinds of containers for holding and pouring the juice/wine. Again, through most of church history, congregations have used a common cup, which was passed among the members. Today the Roman Catholic, Episcopal, and Lutheran churches still use the common cup. However, since the beginning of this century, because of the concern about influenza (recently supplemented by the fear of AIDS), most evangelical churches use small, individual cups.

The delivery of the bread and juice/wine to the table can be done either before or during the service. There is no prescribed arrangement of the elements on the table, although generally the plates and cups or trays are to be arranged in such a way that the pastor can easily reach the elements, both for the breaking and pouring, and for beginning the distribution to the congregation.

Some churches bring the elements to the table during the service, usually as a part of the general offering of the congregation. This custom may recall the practice of the early church, when the Supper was in the context of a common meal, with all the members contributing to the meal.

Some congregations cover the elements prior to the time of Communion. There seems to be no symbolic value in such covering, since in our home meals we normally do not cover the food, except to prevent staleness. Since Christ is to nurture us in the meal, perhaps it is more appropriate to anticipate the feast by showing the elements.

The Table and Its Utensils

Some churches use the word *altar*, while some refer to the Communion *table*. For Protestant churches the word *table* is usually preferable. *Altar* generally suggests sacrifice, and Protestant theology has rejected the teaching that Christ's body is being resacrificed in Communion. The word *table* suggests the original setting of a common meal.

Many of the boxy pieces of furniture supplied by the religious supply houses do look more like altars than dining room tables. Congregations whose theology of Communion calls for it to be strictly a symbolic fellowship meal will want their Communion table to look like a table. Chairs or benches around the table further enhance the notion that this is a place for eating and drinking, not for sacrifice.

The near-universal inscription supplied by the furniture suppliers is not particularly helpful. Do THIS IN REMEMBRANCE OF ME is indeed a Scripture quotation, but it tells only part of the Lord's Supper story— only the looking-back part. Our celebration of the Supper should also proclaim that we commune with a resurrected Lord, who reigns in our hearts and our churches. The Supper anticipates our participation in the Supper of the Lamb. Remembrance, yes. But those words should not dominate our celebration.

The silver or silver-plated Communion set is probably the most common in Protestant churches. It looks dignified and wears well. However, churches may also wish to consider other options. Many Christian potters have fashioned wonderful plates and chalices for Communion ware. Such pottery is symbolically appropriate for the Lord's meal, and the purchase supports Christian artisans.

The location of the table will be determined to a great degree by the architecture of the church and by its theology of the Lord's Supper. If the sacraments are an integral part of the congregation's worship, the table should have more visibility than it often has. In Protestant churches the pulpit is often so dominant that the table is dwarfed. If the table cannot be seen when the congregation is seated, does such invisibility indicate that Communion is not considered an integral part of the church's worship? To counteract this problem, a congregation may wish to place the Communion table on the same level as the pulpit.

The Eating and Drinking

From about the thirteenth century until Vatican II, the Roman Catholic church offered the bread to the congregation but did not permit them to drink the wine. However, most of Christendom has taught that both the bread and juice/wine is to be consumed by all the members. But there still are a number of differences among various churches in the distribution, posture, and the actual eating and drinking.

• *Sitting in the pews.* In many North American mainline and evangelical churches, the members partake of Communion while sitting in

Preparing People to Partake

"Do this in remembrance of me." How do we help people prepare themselves so that they do, in fact, remember Jesus Christ as they eat the bread and drink from the cup? Each of our traditions will structure the event differently as well as articulate the mystery differently. Yet there are a number of things all of us can consider doing to help make Communion an authentic meeting with the risen Lord.

• If Communion is being served during the regular Lord's Day service, we can, in the opening remarks or call to worship, center the service around the Table. The text of the call to worship can refer to Christ's invitation: "Come unto me." Or in the opening remarks we can say, "Welcome to worship around the Table of the Lord Jesus Christ. May he find joy in the way we worship today." As people then go through the other acts of worship, they become more consciously aware of the bread and cup.

• We can choose hymns and choruses that focus on Christ's self-offering. So many songs proclaim the gospel of his death on the cross and the outpouring of his love. I try to pick hymns that not only speak *of* him but also give people a way to speak *to* him. In this way people gradually become aware of his presence as the service moves toward Communion.

• We can plan a time for corporate confession of sin. This prayer may be the regular Lord's Day prayer or a special, more extensive prayer. When people enter the room and see the elements, they are more open to self-examination. The confession should help folks identify

the pews. The pastor stands behind the table and addresses the congregation with the words of institution and invitation. The pastor then takes the loaf, breaks it, and pours the juice/wine from a pitcher into a chalice (even though the chalice is often not used for distribution). Then the servers (elders, deacons, or ushers, depending on the denomination) take the plates with bread and the trays with small cups to distribute the elements among the people.

In some churches the bread and juice/wine are consumed as soon as they are received; in others the congregation waits until all have been served and the pastor says, "Take, eat . . ." or "Take, drink . . ." During the distribution the congregation may sing a hymn, the choir may sing, the organist may play, or someone may read Scripture. Or the time may be reserved for quiet meditation.

Although the custom of remaining in the pews is a rather late development in church history, it has several advantages. The elements can be served in a reasonable length of time, which is important in large congregations. Also, this kind of serving tends to preserve a

---

strained and broken relationships and think about ways they may be hiding from or resisting the One who was sacrificed on their behalf.

• We can choose or compose liturgical readings that articulate Christ's offer of himself and our call to respond. Resources with such material abound. Occasionally, we can have the people recite the words of institution, either in unison or responsively with the worship leader.

• Periodically, we can offer fresh, careful expositions of the Communion texts. The sermon might raise and address the theological and practical questions people are asking. We need not shy away from the tough ones: To what does "this" refer when Jesus says, "*This* is my body"? Is the risen Jesus present in the Supper in a way that he is not present at other times of worship? What does it mean to "judge the body rightly" (1 Cor. 11:25)? What does Paul mean when he says people "drink judgment to themselves" if they do not partake in a worthy manner (1 Cor. 11:27)? How do different Christians interpret the Communion event?

We can craft the sermon so that it ends by naturally leading people to the Communion table. What more appropriate response to most sermons than to take in one's hand the signs and seals of the promise in the gospel?

• We can prepare ourselves. This is perhaps the most important way we help people. They can sense whether or not we are authentically engaged in the event. People will respond to our wonder, our humility before God's grace, our contrition, our affection for Christ, our desire to deepen our commitment. It need not be expressed in words. People simply pick it up. So, like John the Baptist, may we find a variety of creative ways to say, "Look, the Lamb of God who takes away the sin of the world!"

—*Darrell Johnson*

sense of decorum, without the hustle and bustle that often accompanies other modes of distribution. Finally, distribution in the pews allows ample time for quiet meditation.

Pew Communion does have some disadvantages. If the original Lord's Supper was in the context of a regular meal, there is little in pew distribution that suggests a meal. Neither in first-century Palestine nor in our culture do people sit in pews when they eat together.

Coupled with the absence of mealtime symbolism is the absence of interpersonal communion or fellowship. Each member looks at the backs of the heads of other members. The Lord's Supper thus becomes a time of private, individual contemplation, rather than a time of celebrating together the common faith of the congregation.

It may be that with pew Communion, private meditation and the

---

Communion for Shut-ins

Jesus did not stand in front of a congregation parceled out into pews when he served the first Communion; he sat at table in a small room. As servers of Communion in an intimate setting, we, too, need to be sensitive to the proximity of giver and receiver, and to what that closeness demands practically and what it means spiritually.

Practical Considerations

When taking Communion to a shut-in, we need to give advanced notice. We all know how "the pastor coming to call" can affect parishioners. They feel the need to tidy up, to be dressed just right, and so on.

When we are bringing Communion, readiness will seem even more important. What can seem routine to us is definitely not routine when the sacraments come to the home instead of the parishioner coming to the altar. So, we give advanced notice, and if we are going to a nursing home, we check the schedule to make sure our parishioner will be available.

Here are some other practical considerations to keep in mind:

• Take the elements in a portable carrying case. There are a variety of Communion sets on the market that travel well.

• In a hospital or nursing home, always introduce yourself to the nurse, state your purpose, and ask if your parishioner can receive Communion. We must not assume an awake, alert patient is medically allowed to take anything by mouth.

• Be ready to have the patient change his or her mind upon your arrival. In a hospital or nursing home especially, we may not know the person. Factors such as being a woman, a Protestant, or any kind of minister that does not fit their expectation may not be understood. Once we have been accepted, though, we can invite any family members present to join in the sacrament.

concern for decorum have overshadowed the celebratory meal of genuine Communion, of which we get a glimpse in the early church: "They broke bread in their homes and ate together with glad and sincere hearts, praising God" (Acts 2:46b–47a).

The other ways of partaking of the meal all involve leaving the pew and "going up" for Communion. This mode involves some physical activity, and such coming forward is a fitting use of the body in worship, something sorely lacking in much Protestant worship. While the congregation walks to the front and then back to the pews, they may sing familiar hymns, the choir may sing, or the organ (or other musical instruments) may play. All the ways of coming forward cause more movement and commotion than serving in the pews does. Many churches would be reluctant to consider such movement, but, again,

---

• Take a cloth or special linens to help establish the Table. We can look around the room as we enter and make initial conversation. We need to choose a place to set out the elements in a way that is respectful and gives us and the parishioner a minimum of awkwardness.

• Help the patient get comfortable. I have never taken Communion to a patient who did not somehow want to arrange him or herself in an attitude of respectful receiving. But remember, sometimes what appears awkward to us is required body placement for a medical reason. Any rearrangement should be facilitated with care and ease so as not to further injure (or embarrass) the patient.

• After the initial social interchange, we can move into affirmation of the person's request for shut-in Communion, or let a moment of comfortable silence help shift the mood toward the actual service.

• Touch the person during prayer. This Communion is much more intimate and person-centered than in a congregation.

• Remember the vulnerability of a patient's immune system in a hospital. We need to wash our hands well between visits and wear a mask if we have cold (or don't go). Communion vessels need thorough washing between room visits.

Pastoral Concerns

The pastoral nature of the visit continues when the service is over. In the intimate setting of living room, bedroom, or hospital room, the sharing of Communion brings to the surface feelings that do not usually arise in the pew. The presence of Christ, regardless of how that presence is interpreted theologically, often is active in a meaningful way during these visits.

The truth of Jesus' promise to be in the midst of even two who gather in his name becomes especially powerful. We need to give ourselves and our parishioners time for this reality of Christ's presence to comfort and nurture. The intimacy of the setting can offer a spiritual intimacy that adds new meaning to cherished truths.

—Ann A. Letson

one may ask if decorum and quiet ought to be such a prominent consideration.

• *Kneeling.* The kneeling posture (either around the table or at the rail/balustrade) was the common way of receiving the elements during the Middle Ages. This posture may have come about as part of the veneration of the elements. As the doctrine of transubstantiation developed, the church increasingly came to view the bread and wine as mysterious and holy substances and taught that the actual body and blood of Christ ought to receive special adoration.

The Protestant Reformation, therefore, often frowned on the kneeling posture; some Reformers felt it would be difficult to separate such kneeling from improper veneration. In some early Reformed churches, the congregation did kneel around the table, but this practice was generally discouraged. This reluctance about kneeling has continued in most Protestant churches, although it is the common posture in Episcopal and Lutheran churches.

The principal motivation today for the kneeling posture is to express devout reverence. Whatever one's theology about the presence of the Lord during the Supper, this certainly is a solemn occasion, and devout kneeling effectively expresses reverence. The drawback here, again, is that kneeling at the rail hardly suggests a common meal. As with sitting in the pews, kneeling Communion tends to emphasize private devotion only.

• *Walking.* Another mode of Communion practiced in many Roman Catholic and some Protestant churches today is "walking Communion." The communicant comes forward and receives the bread from the pastor or another server and then the juice/wine from the next server. This method has the virtue of efficiency; it serves a large number of people in a short time. The drawback, once again, is that there is no meal symbolism (other than fast-food service!) here. Moreover, since the participant hardly stands still, chewing the bread while walking, this does not appear to promote a thoughtful Communion.

• *Standing.* A variation on walking Communion is the standing posture. Here people walk to the front, where they form a circle (from ten to thirty people, depending on the space available). They remain in this circle until all have been served both elements. This method has the advantage of people remaining in the circle for a comfortable length of time and being able to look at fellow worshipers. Communion is symbolized by being joined in the circle. A variation of this configuration is to have the congregation gather in a large circle around the perimeter of the sanctuary.

• *Sitting at tables.* A final way of coming forward is to have the people sit at large tables in the front of the sanctuary. This was the custom for several centuries among Scottish Presbyterians and the Dutch Reformed (and is still practiced in many churches in the Netherlands today). This custom probably comes closest to symbolizing a table fellowship, and if the congregation is small, the method has much to commend it. The reason many churches discontinued the practice was a logistical one: to serve a large congregation at tables took an inordinate amount of time.

In addition to the modes described here, there are many other practices and variations. Some congregations gather for the Lord's Supper in their fellowship room and conduct the whole service with the congregation sitting at tables. Others gather their chairs in a large circle to conduct the Communion service.

The Distribution of the Elements

Usually when congregations kneel at the rail, the minister and other servers give the bread or wafer to the communicant, placing it either in the hand or in the mouth. The server says, "The body of Christ for you; the blood of Christ for you." The juice/wine is drunk either from small cups or from the common cup.

An alternative to the separate eating and drinking is the intinction mode of partaking. The communicants hold the bread until they are offered the cup, and then dip the bread in the wine and eat the soaked bread. The walking, standing, or sitting Communion may all follow that same procedure.

A variation on this distribution is the passing of a loaf or part of a loaf. The loaf is passed from one member to the other, and each breaks off a piece, saying and receiving words such as: "The body of Christ, the Bread of Heaven . . . the blood of Christ, the Cup of Salvation." The same passing of the elements by the communicants is done with the common cup or tray of individual cups.

Nearly all the variant modes of the Lord's Supper conclude with a prayer or song of thanksgiving. Some traditions also include a special offering for the poor at the conclusion of the Supper.

What is done with any remaining food and drink? Since Protestant traditions teach that the substance of the elements does not change, there is nothing inherently holy about the bread and juice/wine. Yet, the Supper is a solemn feast in which we are reminded in a special way of God's great love and of Christ's presence among his people. We, therefore, approach the Table reverently and treat the elements with care.

Unused juice or wine usually can be poured back into the bottles and used for a future Supper. In most liturgical churches, the leftover wine is either drunk by the minister and/or other celebrants or poured into the ground after the service. The old custom of distributing the remaining bread to the poor is always appropriate, or it can be used by one of the families of the church. Some congregations dispose of the bread on the church lawn for the feeding of birds, an appropriate gesture indicating care and concern for all of God's creatures. In other traditions the bread is burned.

The Common Meaning

The review above indicates a great number of variations of practice in celebrating the Lord's Supper. Such variations need not be a cause for concern. Even though Scripture provides us general guidelines for Christian worship, specific worship traditions and forms naturally arise in the history of each church and denomination. Yet a common core of meaning can guide all churches.

Among the many interpretations and meanings of the Lord's Supper, one overarching theme remains the same: In Holy Communion the church, as a body, celebrates Christ—past, present, and future. We look back in remembrance on his Passion and death; we experience Christ's presence as the resurrected Lord, active in our lives; and we anticipate being at table with him in the new heaven and new earth. Our varied styles and modes seek to capture this communal celebration of our union with the Lord.

—Harry Boonstra

Resources

Barclay, W. 1967. The Lord's Supper. Nashville: Abingdon.

Heron, A. 1983. Table and tradition. Philadelphia: Westminster.

Marty, M. 1980. The Lord's Supper. Philadelphia: Fortress.

Rogness, A. 1982. Table of the Lord. Minneapolis: Augsburg.

Tappert, T. 1961. The Lord's Supper: Past and present practices. Philadelphia: Fortress.

Watkins, K. 1977. The feast of joy: The Lord's Supper in free churches. St. Louis: Bethany.

Part V

Baptism

A baptism is a happy occasion. After all, it marks the entrance of a new member into the family of faith. It so joyously makes public a profession of faith in our Lord Jesus Christ. It announces a victory for righteousness and belief.

Yet, even as baptismal candidates often anticipate the actual event with a touch of apprehension, so it is with many pastors. There's the matter of getting into a potentially embarrassing situation. What pastor can't relate an anecdote of a baptism gone awry? And those who sprinkle don't get by without difficulty just because they don't step into the water, as anyone who handles babies can attest.

And then the problem of which way to baptize troubles some pastors. Baptismal practices have often become the waters that divide Christian from Christian, rather than unite the one body of Christ in one sacrament.

And how do we make baptism meaningful for all who participate, especially for those who receive baptism?

The articles in this section probably won't unite all of Christendom around a single practice of baptism, but they will help inform and improve the practice of those who want to perform baptism in ways that express its magnificent meaning.

27

The Purpose of Baptism

Christian baptism is a divinely instituted washing with water in the name of Father, Son, and Holy Spirit. It signifies God's work of forgiveness and regeneration, provides entrance into the community of God's people, and gives evidence of repentance, faith, and discipleship.

Christians give and receive baptism because Christ himself was baptized (Matt. 3:13ff.), gave baptism at the hands of the disciples (John 3:22; 4:2), and issued a command to baptize (Matt. 28:19), which found an obedient response in the New Testament churches (Acts 2:38, 41; 8:38; 9:18; 1 Cor. 1:14–16).

History of Baptism

● *Old Testament precedent.* Models for baptism might be found in the common religious use of washings enjoined in the Old Testament law. Jewish proselyte baptism could also have served as a precedent, though only immediate converts received this and not successive generations. The baptism of John (Matt. 3:1ff.) offered the most direct model. By accepting John's baptism, Christ himself forged an obvious link to the church's practice. Both the baptism of John and that of Christ involved water, a demand for repentance, and the promise of forgiveness. An obvious difference is that John's seems not to have been planned as an ongoing observance. John himself indicated an even more important distinction, namely, that he baptized only with water, whereas the One mightier than he would baptize with the Holy Spirit (Matt. 3:11).

369

• *Early Christian practice.* In the missionary situation of the New Testament, the first baptisms naturally involved people who responded in faith and repentance. We learn from Acts that this would commonly happen to whole households (10:24, 44ff.; 16:15, 33); whether these included children, the texts neither affirm nor deny. For many decades the baptism of converts continued to be the common rule as the church expanded through the Roman Empire and across its borders.

A formal baptismal service developed by the early third century. It involved a profession of repentance, faith, and obedience in answer to questions. Next came anointings, a descent into the water, immersion or affusion three times in the triune name, and putting on new clothing on ascent from the water. Milk and honey might be given to the newly baptized, along with ten coins, symbolizing the Ten Commandments. One early work, the *Didache,* says that the water should preferably be cold and running. Full catechetical preparation preceded baptism. A fast—forerunner of the Lenten fast—climaxed the course; baptism followed on Easter Eve. Special baptisms were arranged in cases of serious sickness.

• *Medieval practice.* Adult converts continued to receive baptism as missions covered Germany, Britain, East Europe, Scandinavia, Russia, parts of Asia and Africa, and later the Americas. Yet, in evangelized lands, infant baptism became the rule. Origen, in the third century, had claimed that this practice derived from the apostles. In harking back to circumcision, some laws even enjoined baptism on the eighth day (or at least by the thirtieth) after birth.

Ceremonial elaboration marked medieval baptisms—the use of salt, oil and spittle; exorcism; a white robe; the sign of the cross. Belief in baptism's absolute necessity to infant salvation meant that emergency baptism might be given at any time by any believer or even a pagan. A special limbo, symbolized by an unconsecrated section of the churchyard, was supposedly reserved for infants dying without baptism. Ancient customs included a Devil's door near the font, by which the expelled demon might depart. The desire of some wealthier parents for baptisms in milk eventually received censure, as did the exclusion from the water of a boy's right arm (to permit fighting and killing without contradiction).

• *Reformation and modern practice.* The Reformers pruned the ceremonies that overburdened medieval baptism. Zwingli at first retained the white robe, and the Anglicans clung to the sign of the cross, despite Puritan objections. The Puritans preferred basins to fonts, and the Swiss Anabaptists at first poured water from a jug. An immersion in the Rhine evoked admiration, but the issue of immersion did not immediately arise. The quantity of water seemed to be immaterial as long as recipients were under it.

Some Reformers wanted parents as sponsors instead of godparents, who originally took over if parents fell victim to death or persecution. Emergency baptisms came under criticism (especially by midwives), since the necessity of baptism was not considered absolute but a matter of precept.

Radical Reformers brought deeper divisions. Extremists, followed by Quakers and the Salvation Army, dropped baptism altogether as an external rite. Most radicals rejected infant baptism, since infants cannot meet the demand for personal profession. Baptists took up this view and added their conviction that by nature, linguistically, biblically, and theologically, baptism requires full immersion. These major differences of understanding and practice still divide Protestant churches and continue to separate them liturgically from Roman Catholics and the Eastern Orthodox.

Meaning of Baptism

What, precisely, does this ceremony mean? The link with circumcision in the New Testament (see Col. 2:10ff.) gives us an initial clue. Baptism has the significance of a covenant sign. As the Lord's Supper has replaced the Passover, so baptism has replaced circumcision. Now that Christ has fulfilled the covenant of grace by the once-for-all shedding of his blood (Mark 14:24; 1 Cor. 11:25), two signs *without* blood look back to this fulfillment, as two signs *with* blood formerly pointed forward to it. In a special way, therefore, baptism is a sign of covenant fulfillment in Christ. As a covenant sign, then, baptism symbolizes at least:

• *The washing away of sin*. It is a sign of sin's remission or forgiveness, in virtue of Christ's reconciling work (cf. Acts 22:16). A close connection exists here between sign and signification, for water has the primary use and property of cleansing. The point of baptism, of course, is not bodily cleansing (1 Pet. 3:21). The external washing denotes the inner cleansing that enables us to answer with a clear conscience to God and neighbor.

• *The death of the old life*. Water drowns as well as washes. Descent under the baptismal water, whether by immersion, affusion, or sprinkling, has, then, the signification of death. The forgiveness that God graciously grants in Christ carries with it the death of the old life by participation in the death of Christ. Paul makes this point clearly in Romans 6:3ff. The Old Testament types quoted in the New Testament, the flood in 1 Peter 3:20 and the Red Sea passage in 1 Corinthians 10:2, offer graphic illustration. The old world of sin and bondage perish; a new world and a new life begin.

• *A rising to new life*. Water is also life-giving. Rightly, Christ called himself the One who gives the water of life (John 4:10ff.). The waters of the flood and the Red Sea slay, but they also save (cf. 1 Pet. 3:20). By water and the Spirit comes the birth to new and eternal life (John 3:5). As believers go down into the baptismal water for the ending of the old life, so they rise up out of the water to newness of life by participation in the life of the risen Christ (Rom. 6:4ff.). Thus baptism signifies regeneration as well as remission.

In its message of death and life as a sign of the fulfilled covenant, baptism points us plainly to the vicarious death and resurrection of Christ into which we must be incorporated for both remission and regeneration. Christ, himself, called his vicarious ministry both a cup that he must drink and a baptism that he must be baptized with (Mark 10:39). The basic message of baptism, then, is the gospel itself, the Good News that Christ suffered the baptism of blood as well as water, that he died and also rose again for us. Were it not for this baptism of Christ, there could be no meaningful baptism for us, no matter what profession of faith we bring or mode we use.

- *The ministry of the Holy Spirit.* Baptism also signifies the minis-

---

Baptism or Dedication?

Soon after the birth of their children, committed Christian parents face the question: baptize or dedicate? For many parents, it is an agonizing question, especially if they are aware of the complex debates that have taken place throughout church history. Therefore, new parents often look to their pastors to help them work through the issues for themselves.

Common Themes

It helps to begin with what both positions hold in common. Both affirm the special place children of believers have in the heart of the living God: "The promise is for you *and your children* . . ." (Acts 2:39). Both affirm the special advantage children of believers have over other children. They are born into and raised within a community of faith, where Jesus Christ is loved and obeyed, where his Word is preached, and where people pray for them. Both positions affirm that the living Lord is at work in the hearts and minds of these children long before they are aware of it, and both acknowledge that the parents' work has only just begun when the rite is concluded. The dedicated children must be nurtured to the point where they can choose to receive baptism for themselves; the baptized children must be helped to own the vows already made for them by responding personally to their Lord.

Different Views

The differences come when we ask: What is the relationship between the gift of the Holy Spirit and water baptism? If parents view the rite and gift as occurring simultaneously, they will want to baptize the child immediately.

try of the Holy Spirit giving us the new life in Christ. In the New Testament, indeed, the word for *baptism* in its full range denotes both the baptism of water (the sign) and the baptism of the Spirit (the thing signified). The new birth is birth, not of water alone, but also of the Spirit, as we see from John 3:5–8. The Spirit is the One who convicts of sin (John 16:8), leads us to Christ (John 16:14), and gives us new life in him. Baptism bears witness no less to the Spirit's work *in* us than to Christ's work *for* us. By this work in us we participate in the work for us.

• *The nature of the Christian life.* This life is one of ongoing death and resurrection, of daily dying to sin and rising again to righteousness (Col. 3:5–10), of putting off the old nature and putting on the new (Eph. 4:22–24). A process of mortification and renewal in Christ succeeds the first entry into Christ's death and resurrection as the Spirit does the work of sanctification. In this sense baptism has meaning for the whole of the Christian life. As Luther used to say, the old Adam (or

---

If parents believe the Holy Spirit is given apart from the rite, they may wonder, *What is the primary emphasis of the sign of water?* If it is primarily a sign of the believer's faith, parents will likely want to reserve the sign until the child is old enough to actually exercise personal faith. If the water indicates the sovereign call of the Lord, which by necessity precedes the exercise of human faith, parents will feel free to have the sign given before the child can choose, declaring that the gracious Lord always moves toward us before we move toward him.

The decision often turns upon one's understanding of the dynamics of the New Covenant. Are the dynamics similar to those of the Old Covenant? Or are there significant differences? If the former view is held, parents may argue that since male children under the Old Covenant received the sign (circumcision) as infants, under the New Covenant, children, both male and female, should also receive the sign (water) as infants. If the latter view is held, parents may believe that under the New Covenant, the sign is now given only to those who are able to exercise faith, since faith is the key human element of the New Covenant.

In either infant baptism or dedication, parents are saying something like this: "Child, we love you. Therefore, we are intentionally placing you in the hands of the living God, who gave his Son for you as Savior and Lord. You will find the fullness of life in following him."

And in either infant baptism or dedication, God is saying something like this: "My child, I love you. Therefore, I have given my Son for you as Savior and Lord. You will find the fullness of life in following him. My Spirit will help you respond to his call."

Thus, the words of Jesus can rightly be said upon either act: "Let the little children come to me . . . for the kingdom of God belongs to such as these" (Mark 10:14).

—*Darrell Johnson*

Eve) in us dies hard; it is dead, yet unwilling to lie down. Death throes afflict us as long as we remain on earth. The death of which baptism speaks must be a daily death; the renewing, a daily renewing.

• *The believer's assurance.* Baptism, with the Lord's Supper (1 Cor. 11:26), has a meaning that reaches to the end of earthly life. By physical death, or translation, our present life must literally end and our entry into the fullness of new life follow. Only when we die and receive in Christ the resurrection of the dead will baptism have no further meaning. For only then, when there is no more death, when the last enemy has been destroyed (1 Cor. 15:26, 54–56), will the sign of death and resurrection lose its point and relevance. Until then, however, it is for us a sign of reassurance and hope.

• *The active elements of faith: repentance and commitment.* Finally, baptism speaks to us of our own movement in this participation. Go-

---

Modes of Baptism

In secular America, where consumer tastes so often determine Christian styles, "Receive the baptism of your choice" seems to be growing in popularity. Such user-friendly offers make it difficult for pastors to face honestly certain basic concerns about the theology and form of baptism. Not to face them squarely, however, involves risk.

Two Risks

In *Introduction to Christian Worship* (Abingdon), James F. White points to these concerns:

First, since baptism has always been associated with initiation into the Christian church, we must not put *evangelism* at risk by treating baptism lightly. Strangers who call the church office to have the baby "done," or periodic visitors who want a "walk-in" baptism, must be informed about the deep Christian meaning of baptism. This usually calls for a pastoral visit or counseling session, and if the parents are unbe-

lieving, the pastor must say no to their wishes. Concerned to make the gospel as attractive as possible, we may find it hard to say no to anyone. However, during these conversations we also have a rare opportunity to make the gospel clear to the couple or single parent.

Second, we ought to be concerned about the *sign-value* of the initiatory rite. Baptism is Christian initiation, and, like other initiations, this one does not rest on words alone. Actions are basic to conveying its meaning. We must not risk confusing people about something so important. Rather, we must seriously consider what the form of initiation communicates within a particular tradition: Saving grace imparted to the soul? The covenant promise extended to an infant? Personal witness of the acceptance of Christ?

Two Convictions

Generally speaking, two firm beliefs regarding the mode of baptism

ing under the water signifies the repentance that is death to the old life. Coming up from the water signifies the faith and obedience that characterize the new life. Baptism has the force of a profession, a reminder, and a summons. As the baptized we have the sign of our own participation in Christ's work by the Spirit's ministry. Participation means personal commitment corresponding to the covenant sign and openly expressed to the world. The commitment, however, is for life and not just for the moment.

Effects of Baptism

Does baptism really *do* anything, and if so, how? At one extreme have been those who regard it merely as an external sign. They administer it because the Lord commanded it, tradition commends it,

prevail among Christians: (1) Immersion alone is the biblical and normative mode, and (2) the mode is a matter of indifference, so sprinkling or pouring serves as well as immersion.

Christian history and archaeology indicate that baptism by immersion was probably the prevailing mode until the Protestant Reformation. Old baptistries throughout Europe reveal the widespread practice of immersion. Records in the late Middle Ages, however, indicate that sprinkling was permitted as a substitute for immersion in cases of dire necessity, such as a candidate's sickness. About the fourteenth century, the Roman Catholic church introduced the choice between sprinkling and immersion, and two centuries later most Protestant bodies followed this practice after some initial resistance.

During the seventeenth century, when the sprinkling of infants was growing in popularity, immersionists, like the Baptists, insisted that lowering the body under water and raising it again was not only the original Christian practice but also the clearest sign of personal faith in the death, burial, and resurrection of the Lord. The amount of water, they insisted, does have symbolic significance (and, therefore, babies do not qualify).

Christians in modern times who practice sprinkling or pouring usually counter that the amount of water is not significant for sign-value. It is adequate to sprinkle a few drops or pour a cupful to indicate the spiritual washing of the soul, either as a spiritual birth or a sign of God's covenant promise to save. To insist on immersion as the only valid mode is to depopulate the church of most of its finest sons and daughters.

James White summarizes the debate this way: "If one's only concern is validity, then a teaspoonful of water is enough. But if one's concern is to communicate the life-giving flood in which God acts, then a tubful communicates better." Above all, pastors should avoid making baptism "an act of Christian cuteness; the center is God, not the baby."

—*Bruce L. Shelley*

and meaning attaches to it. At the other extreme, many want to ascribe to baptism, when correctly administered, the automatic effecting of what it signifies, unless an obstacle such as unbelief or insincerity impedes its working, which is impossible in the case of infants. Early thinkers used to say that as God used dust at the first creation, he uses water at the second.

Between the extremes a moderate view finds a variety of baptismal effects and benefits. Baptism always serves, for example, as a public initiation and reception into the visible company of God's people. It sets the baptized openly in the sphere of prayer, preaching, and pastoral care, which is the sphere of God's own gracious operation by these appointed means. Recognizing the baptized as members, the community of faith grants them the benefits of its ministry and incorporates them at the same time into this ministry.

Baptism publicly identifies the baptized with Christ and his people. This is an especially momentous step in a missionary or evangelistic situation in which it can have serious consequences socially, economically, or politically. It loses its more dramatic character in the case of infants, who cannot as yet make their own declaration of faith and commitment. And it may, indeed, have little or no meaning at all when Christianity becomes a national religion, and baptism acquires a conventional character, perhaps with superstitious associations. The church certainly needs the scriptural witness against this type of practice.

Baptism acts, too, as a proclamation of the gospel. It depicts what Christ did for us and what we are to do by participating in his saving action. It has the force, then, that we ascribe to God's Word. As a visible or enacted Word, it supplements and illustrates the audible Word that accomplishes what God himself purposes (Isa. 55:11).

In this regard, baptism has as its main function the confirming rather than the generating of faith. Faith comes by hearing, and hearing by the preached or audible Word (Rom. 10:17). Paul as an evangelist saw it as his primary task to preach, not to baptize (1 Cor. 1:17). Baptism as a sign and pledge reinforces and assures us of the truth of God's gracious work in Christ. Hence Luther in times of doubt could tell himself (and the Devil!): "I am baptized! Christ did indeed die and rise again for me, and I by faith participate in this death and resurrection."

Finally, baptism also summons the baptized to lifelong discipleship as daily mortification and renewal. Here, as always, it has its effect through its meaning and not its mere performance. We do not repeat baptism, but as we attend the baptism of others we see again the scope of our renewing and the implications of our commitment. Baptism is thus an aid to sanctification. Indeed, it also strengthens us in hope as it points beyond daily dying and rising again to the final death and resurrection when, fully cleansed and sanctified (Jude 24), we enter into the fullness of Christ's saving work.

Can baptism have any of these effects for infants? Opponents of infant baptism see no effects that might not be had without it. Proponents advance the benefits of public incorporation into the sphere of prayer and proclamation, the signified application of Christ's vicarious work, the summons to the complementary response, the invoked assistance of the Holy Spirit, and the beginning of his regenerative and sanctifying work, which he may well bring to rapid completion in the case of infants who die before they can make personal professions of faith.

Responsibilities of the Baptizer

In offering baptism, churches provide a significant ministry that Christ himself instituted. At the same time they incur serious responsibility for a proper administration that goes beyond correct external performance.

• A *first* responsibility is to give ample pastoral preparation to the candidates or parents (and sponsors). The early church set an example here with its catechetical courses. New Testament converts might be baptized more quickly (Acts 2:41, etc.), but they had an Old Testament grounding that we cannot take for granted today. All who seek baptism should know what it is and what it means. Older candidates must see the seriousness of the step, and parents should understand the implications for themselves and their children.

• A *second* responsibility is to ensure, as far as possible, that the candidates or parents (and sponsors) have the faith in Christ that they profess. No one but God knows the inner heart, so we inevitably have to accept what people say. Yet we ought not to do so without careful questioning and scrutiny.

• A *third* responsibility is to administer baptism in a congregational setting with prayer, praise, and the reading and proclamation of God's Word (which explains baptism and which baptism, itself, dramatizes). At times the main readings and text might carry a baptismal reference, but in some, the audible and visible Word simply supplement each other.

• A *fourth* responsibility is to engage the prayer and concern of members on behalf of the baptized. Publicly accepted new members need prayer, integration into the Christian family, spiritual grounding, help with problems and difficulties, and the warm atmosphere of simple Christian fellowship.

• A *fifth* responsibility is to see in each baptism a chance to recall all the baptized to baptism's meaning and their own baptismal commitment, so that baptism may continue to do its work. During this time we can remind all church members of Christ's vicarious baptism, confirming their reception as God's children, calling them to sanctification, and referring them to the final resurrection with Christ beyond death and the grave.

• A *sixth* and last responsibility is to follow up the baptized, not merely with general prayer and concern, but also with specific pastoral action. This might take the form of further instruction, visitation, counseling, and integration into programs and projects. Infant baptism, in particular, demands regular contact with the parents, nursery facilities to make their attendance possible, a developing program of instruction for the children, and an opportunity for the children's personal profession and commitment at the appropriate time.

Baptism, like any other liturgical act, can easily become a formality if the churches shirk their responsibilities. When they take them seriously, however, then, under the Holy Spirit, baptism may take on its full meaning and thus be an effective means of God's working.

—*Geoffrey W. Bromiley*

Resources

Barth, K. 1969. Church dogmatics. Vol. 4. Edinburgh: T. and T. Clark.

Bromiley, G. W. et al. 1984. Baptism. In *Evangelical Dictionary of Theology*, 112–122. Grand Rapids: Baker.

Bromiley, G. W. et al. 1979. Baptism. In *International Standard Bible Encyclopedia*, vol.1, 410–429. Grand Rapids: Eerdmans.

Calvin, J. 1960. Institutes IV, xiv–xvi. Philadelphia: Westminster.

Oepke, A. 1964. Bapto. In *Theological Dictionary of the New Testament*, vol. 1, 529–546. Grand Rapids: Eerdmans.

Baptism: Private or in Worship?

Where should a baptism take place? Must it be done in corporate worship, or may it find its place in a private ceremony for family and friends? Those who accept baptism as an ordinance typically understand it as a *visible witness* to the regeneration that has already taken place in the believer. Thus, they see no salvific efficacy in the symbolic act, perceive no need of infants being baptized as an instrument leading to salvation, and would therefore argue for baptism as a public testimony of faith and commitment.

On the other hand, those who accept baptism as a sacrament do view it as efficacious: It washes away sin, confers membership in the Christian community, and ultimately results in salvation for those who continue in the faith. In this view, baptism should be administered as soon as possible after the birth of a child. A private ceremony, then, would seem quite acceptable for this purpose.

Historical Precedent

The practice of private baptism appeared during the Middle Ages. Though the change spread slowly, the separation of private baptism and public confirmation was more or less complete by the beginning of the thirteenth century. In Italy bishops resided in every city of significance and were thus able to perform both baptism and confirmation at the same time and in the same place. Over time, the geographical spread of Christianity made it impossible for bishops to live near and care for the needs of the entire population. At the same time, Augustine's theology of original sin stimulated a fear in parents that their unbaptized infants would be excluded from the kingdom should they die. As a result, Christian parents wanted their infants to receive the sign of entrance into covenant relationship with God as soon as possible. Confirmation would follow years later when, a bishop being present, the mature child would publicly profess the faith and enter into full church membership. Thus, private baptism became the normative practice of the church.

The Reformation witnessed a return of the baptismal rite to the public setting. Calvin, for example, insisted that the baptism of infants be a fully congregational event (White 1980, 67). In more recent years, Protestants have become more aware of the importance of the public acts of the Lord's Supper and baptism. They have begun to view the sacraments (or ordinances) as possessing horizontal (human to human) significance as well as vertical (human to God). Public baptisms are therefore becoming the norm among these denominations.

Some contemporary sacramental baptizers also argue for public baptism. This results from a renewed recognition that baptism is a necessary public "declaration of repentance, faith, the grace of God, the coming of the kingdom and the welcome of the church" (Green 1987, 97; White 1980, 82).

Personal Preference

If one distinguishes between baptism (entrance into covenant relation with God) and confirmation (public confession of Christ and reception into the church), then private baptisms are certainly acceptable. For those who view baptism as a personal testimony either to entrance into the covenant or to acceptance of Christ, baptism logically should be done before a worshiping congregation.

Those who hold the latter position, however, may consider exceptions to the general rule of public baptisms. An individual confined to a hospital or a soldier home for only a day or two before going on to some distant assignment may desire a private baptism with family and friends. In such cases the minister must determine whether or not the circumstances warrant an exception to the rule that he or she generally holds.

—*Timothy S. Warren*

References

Green, M. 1987. Baptism. Downers Grove, Ill.: InterVarsity.

White, J. 1980. Christian worship. Nashville: Abingdon.

28

Preparing People for Baptism

In baptism, God acts through water and the Word to enlarge the family of God and to redeem its members through their identification with the crucified and risen Lord. Baptism signifies our adoption by God and by the family of God, the church. Through baptism, we are assigned a place and a task in the kingdom, we are named as God's own, and we are ordained as members of "a chosen people, a royal priesthood, a holy nation, a people belonging to God, that [we] may declare the praises of him who called [us] out of darkness into his wonderful light" (I Pet. 2:9).

Christ's disciples are those who stand under the mandate given to God's people to "make disciples . . . baptizing . . . teaching" (Matt. 28:19–20). Baptism is nothing less than the church's faithfulness to Jesus' command to "make disciples" by initiating them into the church through baptism.

As we work to prepare people for baptism, we should note that, while the New Testament tells us almost nothing about *how* we are to baptize (the method of baptism) or even the qualifications of *whom* we are to baptize (the right age, the proper belief, or the status of the recipient of baptism), the New Testament does say much about the rich meanings conveyed by baptism. At various places within the New Testament, baptism is spoken of as a sign of forgiveness of sins, rebirth, purification, death, resurrection, adoption, and light. In short, baptism means to us what the gospel means, and thus signifies the radical, revolutionary event through which the risen Christ has "qualified [us] to share in the inheritance of the saints . . . rescued us

381

from the dominion of darkness and brought us to the kingdom of the Son he loves, in whom we have redemption, the forgiveness of sins" (Col. 1:12–14). Baptism is a dramatic sign that marks the beginning of a transformation process that is for us Christians both death and life: "We were therefore buried with him through baptism into death in order that, just as Christ was raised from the dead through the glory of the Father, we too may live a new life" (Rom. 6:4).

How can we prepare people for more meaningful participation in baptism so that this vivid act of God and the church can be all that it is meant to be?

Baptism as the Culmination of Instruction

No person should be baptized who has not been thoroughly instructed in the biblical and historical meanings of baptism. We make a mockery of baptism when we baptize those who have not been personally taught about its rich meaning. People may have had a deep, life-changing religious experience, but have they had the experience of Christian faith? Through baptismal instruction, we enable people to speak about their unique experiences of God's grace working in their lives. However, we set those experiences next to the church's experience of baptism. Our personal experience of God's grace is thereby deepened, and we find new meaning through reflection on the foundational experience in which all believers partake.

Such reflection and instruction may be accomplished through a series of meetings with the pastor. In those meetings we make it clear that in baptism we are busy "making disciples." Candidates must know they will be asked publicly to affirm their allegiance to Jesus Christ and his church. We would not want to mislead anyone about the significance of that act. We would not want to make that allegiance appear easier or less costly than it really is. During the time of baptismal instruction, we have an opportunity to lift up the cost of discipleship and to allow the candidate to ponder if he or she is ready to pay the price of servanthood.

As we do these things, we'll generate plenty of questions about baptism and its meaning. Those questions themselves can help us as we think about how to structure our baptismal instruction. They become the makings of a modern, man-on-the-street type of catechism—with questions and possible responses like these:

• *Why do I need to be baptized? Can't I just say that I give my life to Christ?*

One of the early church fathers was once asked, "Does God need baptism to save us?"

"No," he replied, "but God knows that we, creatures as we are, need visible, tangible evidence of his love for us." God deals with us in ways we can understand—through the everyday, essential, life-giving reality of water; through the everyday, life-giving reality of this congregation of his people. We don't believe that serving Jesus is a private affair. It takes the support, correction, and encouragement of other people—the church. It takes putting your faith into practice in public, visible, witness, just as you do in baptism.

I could have answered your question by saying that you need to be baptized because Jesus was and because Jesus told us to baptize. That response is okay, too. I've tried to answer on the basis of the needs of human nature and on the basis of what Christian discipleship actually means.

- *What does baptism really mean?*

It means just about anything that water means. What does water mean to you—refreshment, birth, cleansing, death? In the New Testament baptism has all these rich meanings. It is our way of making clear that, to be a Christian, one must submit to new birth, cleansing, and death so that the life of the Spirit may blossom within.

- *How old does one need to be in order to be baptized?*

Different churches have different views on this. An essential part of baptism is public, visible response. We are to "repent and believe the gospel." Some churches wait until a person is old enough to make such a confession of faith for himself or herself. Other churches baptize the children of Christian parents, having the parents pledge to raise the child as a Christian, and having the church pledge to help them.

The debate over what age is best for baptism is really best framed as a significant question that Christians answer differently: How are people best formed as Christians?

- *What if I'm not sure about all of the beliefs of this church?*

Baptism is a public sign that God has acted in your life in a life-changing way, and that you want to commit your life to Christ and his church. You and I, as your pastor, must decide when the time is right for your baptism. Just remember, baptism is the *beginning* of your walk with Christ, not the end of it. Expect to keep growing in your faith. I am not troubled that you are not yet sure about *everything* related to the Christian faith; few of us are, even years after our baptism. However, I want to be sure that you have enough information and faith to be ready to begin your walk with Christ.

Baptism as Pastoral Action that Teaches

One of the most important aspects of baptismal instruction is the way we do the act of baptism in itself. God's gift of water should be lifted up in all its vivid beauty. Water should be seen, heard, and experienced. Where a congregation baptizes by immersion, this should not be a problem. In congregations that baptize by sprinkling or pouring, perhaps a pitcher of water could be presented at the beginning of a baptism. Then, with some drama, water can be poured from the pitcher into the baptismal bowl or font.

Baptism has many rich meanings, but the beginning of these meanings is the meaning of water itself. Our daily, mundane human experience of water is the beginning of our experience of God's grace in baptism. As Augustine once said, water is water. However, water set next to the Word of God is baptism.

In preaching or teaching about baptism, the pastor is speaking to three main groups within the church. He or she speaks to the persons

---

Infant Baptisms and Dedications

Pastors of all stripes are called to welcome little children. Whether through baptism or dedication, such occasions can have eternal consequences.

Jesus and the Children

Whether in infant baptism or dedication, pastors can reflect God's concern and love for children, applying some of the following considerations:

• *Know the child's name.* As basic as this might sound, it indicates the pastor's attitude and involvement. It shows care to become familiar with—even to memorize—the children's names.

• *Consider the logistics of the service.* Many pastors include children early in the worship service. This spares anxious parents the trial of trying to keep down the din as the noontime feeding and nap approaches.

• *Set a caring tone.* The pastor's attitude sets the tone for the involved families, the congregation, and the infants. With so many things

occurring, it's easy to telegraph busyness or preoccupation. A smiling face, a gentle voice, and a firm yet tender embrace tell children of Jesus' love.

Jesus and the Parents

Let the little children come to Jesus, but insist their parents bring them. Baptisms and dedications are opportunities for family ministry. Sensitive preparation of parents is both a theological and a practical necessity.

While it may not be possible to cultivate a deep relationship with every set of parents, make efforts to integrate parents into the baptism or dedication process. Personal contact with parents helps them understand the significance of what they are desiring for their child.

When parents come to the pastor with their concerns for the spiritual welfare of their infant, it is a great opportunity to counsel them about the true meaning of the gospel, repentance, forgiveness, and a life of obedience.

who are being baptized at this service. The sermon will be an opportunity to speak directly to them about the significance of this event for their Christian lives. The pastor also speaks to those in the church who are preparing for, awaiting, or considering baptism. The baptismal sermon will say, in effect, to these people, "Here is what the church will do and say to you when it comes time for you to be baptized."

The pastor should remember that he or she is also speaking to those who have already been baptized. For them, the baptismal sermon will be a continuing exploration of the significance of this event for their growth in discipleship. Martin Luther once said that one of the most

---

Teaching and Witness

Jesus pointed to children and said they illustrate the values of God's kingdom. Children are windows to heaven. Baptisms and dedications especially offer marvelous opportunities for teaching and witness. Here are some creative ideas:

• The parents can select appropriate Scripture passages to be read.

• A person other than the pastor can pray for the child and family. Many times this person will be a family friend or a relative. It can also give godparents more than a superficial role in the spiritual nurture of the child.

• Special music can be used. Choirs can sing in preparation. So can soloists or ensembles. Even gifted musicians can compose songs to be sung during the ceremony. Sometimes a parent, relative, or family friend can write poetry or prose to be used in the ceremony.

Faith in a Faithless World

Both baptism and dedication boldly declare to the world two foundational truths about the human condition:

First, all are sinners who need to be washed. Regardless of the innocent beauty of children, they also need redemption. Jesus invited the little children to come because he knew they needed him.

Second, when they came, he welcomed them with open arms. Baptism and dedication not only declare people's utter helplessness and need, but they also point to Jesus Christ as the only "name under heaven given among men by which we must be saved" (Acts 4:12).

Pastoral words spoken and ministry given during the moments of baptism or dedication carry unusual weight. The infants are recipients, but so are their parents. And the people in the congregation not only hear the *story* but also become part of it as they bring children to Christ.

When we ask the congregation to join in the nurture of the children before them, we give Christians a glorious privilege. It is no longer a child or family alone against the world. God's people are united—pilgrims together—passing on the faith to the next generation.

— *Garth Bolinder*

important things Christians can do is to remember their baptism. It is a great comfort, in times of difficulty and hardship in our lives, to continue to go back to our baptism, to bask in the lifelong assurance that this act gives us as Christians.

In some congregations, the pastor invites all the children to gather around the font when there is a baptism. In a few clear words, the pastor describes the significance of baptism to the children. Adults listening in on this talk with children are also receiving baptismal instruction.

Baptism as an Act of Initiation

Baptism is spoken of, particularly in the Roman Catholic Church, as "Christian Initiation." In baptism, we are initiating people into the church, the body of Christ. In the early church, baptism instruction before this initiation event lasted for as long as three years. Today's church could certainly learn from such a practice as it seeks to avoid

---

Preparations for Adult Baptisms

Baptism is near the heart of our faith. We present it as significant, but we must not allow it to separate Christians into groups of resentment or condescension. It must not become the "water that divides us," but the water that witnesses to our commitment to Christ.

Objections to Overcome

Adults who come to Christ often object to baptism for three reasons:

First, there persists the feeling that baptism is for children. Being baptized as an adult is a psychological stumbling block that is a widespread problem, and it takes work to overcome it.

Second, since baptism is normally performed in public, many people are afraid and ask if they can be baptized in a private ceremony. Part of their fear is that they are unfamiliar with the rite.

Third, some people have to overcome their vanity. Baptism is, admittedly, an undignified experience, especially for those who are immersed. It is helpful to remember they are not carnal converts who are making theological complaints; they are objecting because of their self-image and natural self-esteem.

The best and most honest way to overcome these objections is to bring them out into the open. We can tell new converts that fear is understandable. Everybody faces it. But there's more: to respond out of vanity when they have just given their entire lives to Christ is inconsistent.

Steps to Baptism

Gentleness, patience, and thorough explanations smooth the passage from conversion to baptism.

creating "stillborn Christians"—people who have received an initial birth into the Christian faith but who never take fire and live as active, committed disciples of Christ.

In larger congregations where there are many baptisms, and even in smaller congregations, pastors might consider training a group of lay people to be baptismal sponsors. These people—credible Christians who have been trained in the biblical, theological, and historical bases of baptism—would know something about the history of this particular congregation and its expectations of its new members. Candidates for baptism could be given to these baptismal sponsors for instruction over a period of time in preparation for their baptism. Standing with the candidate on the day of his or her baptism, sponsors would signify the care and responsibility that the entire congregation has for sustaining new Christians in the faith. After baptism, they might serve as a new Christian's mentor for the first months of the newly baptized person's membership within the congregation.

A small educational guide to baptism might be devised by the con-

---

The first step is to be open about baptismal practices. Converts must see all aspects of their relationship with their newfound Lord, beginning with public profession of faith in Christ—and baptism.

The second step is to keep the converts well informed about the arrangements. Letters can spell out when and where to meet the pastor before the service and what to bring (including towels, dry undergarments, and hair dryers).

The third step is to remember everyone's right to dignity. In both the men's and women's dressing rooms, partitions should be provided to keep anyone from having to undress in front of others.

The fourth step is to brief participants several minutes before the service. Explain how to enter the baptistry and leave it and the importance of using the handrails. It is helpful to read aloud each candidate's name in the order they will be baptized and introduce people assisting with the service. Tell candidates exactly what you will say and what they will say. They also need to know how you will hold them during the rite and how you will call them to the water and send them from it.

End the briefing with group prayer. This prayer celebrates the importance of what they are doing and points to the spiritual meaning of the event. It can also allay some of the natural fears of those about to be baptized. Prayer brings a sense of community to the group. It is difficult to feel alone while praying with others who are going through the same feelings of fear and inadequacy.

The last step: remember that the event is an act of worship. It reminds people who have undergone the water that they are to serve one another in love and welcome all into the arms of Christ.

— *Calvin Miller*

gregation. This guide could be given to people who visit the church or inquire about the possibility of baptism. Such a pamphlet would also be a signal to inquirers regarding how seriously the congregation takes its baptismal responsibilities.

In congregations that baptize infants, someone in the congregation could be designated to visit in homes of newborn children. A visit by this person could include both an expression of the congregation's joy at the birth of this new child and an initial discussion about the possibility of baptism.

Baptism as an Act of the Congregation

It should be clear from the preceding suggestions for baptismal preparation that baptism is an act of the entire congregation, not just something the minister does. If baptism initiates us into the family of God, none of us can be loner Christians. In other words, Christianity was never meant to be a home-correspondence course in salvation. Rather, baptism signifies that, to be a Christian, one must be adopted, nurtured, loved, challenged, and guided by a family. We call that family the church.

Baptismal preparation is most effective when it is made clear that it is an act of the whole congregation, involving many different people. One congregation insists that people preparing for baptism go through a mandatory, five-week course of instruction. This course, guided but not exclusively led by the pastor, consists of a series of meetings in which various members of the congregation present the denomination's history and theology, tell about the local congregation's history and ministry programs, and respond to inquirers' questions. Of course, in such a group, the baptismal candidate is not only being instructed, but also has an opportunity to be with other new Christians in conversation and reflection. This congregation therefore sees its baptismal-instruction classes as a means of forming new adult groups within the church. At the end of the five-week period, the inquirers have become a sharing, caring group. After their baptism they may wish to continue as an adult class or fellowship group. Thus, new groups of Christians are continually given birth within that congregation.

Because Christian salvation is such a communal affair, no one should be baptized apart from the presence of the church. The church really does not do private baptisms. Even in cases of emergency, or when someone is baptized in the hospital, a pastor should attempt to involve other members of the congregation, at least as representatives of the whole congregation.

Since meaningful participation in baptism begins with a congregation in which baptism is viewed as a central act of the whole church, the pastor's own commitment to baptism will be a cue for the congregation's attitude. What are the pastor's own feelings toward this act of worship? When baptism occurs, is it hurriedly done, haphazardly prepared, wedged into an already-full service? Or is it evident that the pastor is heavily invested in this act, has carefully prepared for it, and enters into it with great enthusiasm and expectation? Every time a pastor performs baptism, he or she is busy teaching the congregation about its meaning and significance.

Because there can be much mystification and misunderstanding in regard to baptism, today's pastors should consider preaching a sermon about baptism every time a baptism occurs in the congregation. There are so many rich biblical images related to baptism that finding a biblical text should not be difficult. Central Christian themes such as conversion, growth into faith, the grace of God, and the necessity of forgiveness are all critically related to baptism.

The best setting for baptism is in the regular Sunday service of the congregation. Thereby we witness to the public, communal character of our faith, and participants are given an opportunity to renew personal memories of baptism.

In churches that follow the liturgical year, various Christian seasons are designated as excellent times for baptism. *Easter* is the historic festival of baptism, providing a powerful linkage between Christ's death and resurrection and our own. *Pentecost* prods the congregation to reflect on the gift of the Holy Spirit at baptism. *All Saints' Day* helps us recognize baptism as our entrance into, and sharing with, the communion of all saints.

Baptism as a Personal Event

While baptism is a communal affair of the whole church, it is also a deeply personal marker of God's work in the individual's spiritual life. At baptism, candidates ought to be encouraged to testify to their faith at this moment and to thank members of the congregation for important spiritual guidance during the period of preparation.

Because baptism is a sign of our assumption of our Christian responsibility, the lay leadership of the congregation might publicly assign the newly baptized person some responsibility or office to fulfill within the congregation, something directly related to that person's known gifts. In baptism, we are ordained to share in Christ's priesthood to the world. The rite of baptism should be as active as we expect this new Christian's life to be in Christ.

Historically, certain gifts have been given to the newly baptized person as a sign of the significance of baptism. A large candle ("You are the light of the world. Let your light shine . . .") is given by many congregations to the candidate. When children are baptized, other children in the congregation might give this person a baptismal banner that displays the child's name and date of baptism. The pastor might write a letter to the newly baptized child or infant, which could be opened on the tenth anniversary of the child's baptism and serve as an important remembrance of the event. Some of the newly baptized receive a tape recording of the baptism, with encouragement to listen to it on baptismal anniversaries.

Baptism is nothing less than the birth and creation of the church, created anew in each generation by the loving, powerful act of God. What sort of church shall we be? Will contemporary disciples understand the cost of discipleship and be willing and equipped to pay that cost? These are baptismal questions. They point to the importance of examining how well we make disciples through water and the Word.

—*William H. Willimon*

Resources

Kavanagh, A. 1978. The shape of baptism: The rite of Christian initiation. New York: Pueblo.

Stookey, L. 1977. Baptism: Christ's act in the church. Nashville: Abingdon.

Willimon, W. 1980. Remember who you are: Baptism and the Christian life. Nashville: Upper Room.

Willimon, W. 1984. Handbook on preaching and leading worship. Louisville: John Knox.

Difficult Requests for Baptism

What do we do with requests for baptisms that do not fall within our churches' normative practices? How do we maintain our integrity and teach our biblical understandings of baptism while at the same time ministering effectively to persons or families who care little about our theological nuances?

Perhaps the potential candidates simply wish to proclaim their faith through baptism in ways they have seen their friends doing. But what does the Baptist or Disciple do when requested to baptize an infant? What does the Presbyterian do when called upon to rebaptize? What does the Quaker do when requested to baptize *at all*?

Three important principles can guide us when facing a difficult baptism request: be pastoral; be true to established church policies; be imaginative.

Being Pastoral

To be pastoral requires us to listen closely to what is actually being requested, to be sensitive to the personal issues behind the bare request. The anxious parents who want their baby baptized immediately may be genuinely alarmed because of preconceptions about salvation and original sin that they bring from another tradition. They may bear certain beliefs and attitudes that have been imposed upon them by parents or other family members.

Such people do not need to hear unequivocally that "your request would be impossible, because we just don't do that!" Instead, a caring, pastoral response would be to invite the couple to talk about the church's tradition and practice and to help them see how and why it was developed. With a little fuller theological understanding, most people will recognize evident errors in reasoning and will modify their requests to be more in line with accepted church practice.

Being True to Tradition

To be true to one's tradition still requires, however, that we make clear to the requesting persons what our particular church believes about baptism. The most effective way to do this is to teach the church's practice whenever baptism is observed. Thus, each time we perform a baptism, we can take a few moments to remind the congregation about what baptism is, why it is done, and what is required for receiving it. In this way, the whole church will have its practice reinforced continually. In churches in which members are given a choice about when to be baptized, for example, pastors can explain the option of believers' baptism whenever an infant baptism is administered, and vice versa. This method reminds worshipers that both practices are part of Reformed history and tradition.

Being Imaginative

To be imaginative means listening carefully to hear beyond people's requests to the issues they care about. The person requesting re-baptism is expressing a desire to make a public confession of faith as an adult. Let him or her participate, with others, in a service of renewal of baptismal vows. The parents with a newborn may need to assure the child's grandparents that their grandchild has been presented to God in a service at the church. If baptism is not in order, perhaps their need could be met with a dedication service or a service of thanksgiving for the birth of a child (as found in the *Book of Common Prayer*, The Episcopal Church, 1979).

Regardless of how clearly we have formulated our beliefs about baptism, our certainty of doctrinal correctness must never blind us to—or shield us from—the needs of people. We are not called to do things that compromise our beliefs. Yet, we are required to work with those who come to us in order to unfold the truth, and perhaps discover what creative means God will provide for applying it.

—Larry D. Ballenger

29

Performing Baptisms

A baptism service can be both an uplifting worship experience for the congregation and a powerful witness to God's reality for visitors. But such a service doesn't just happen. Participants must prayerfully prepare themselves, knowing that performing baptism is more than a ritual. It's a celebration of new faith and a proclamation of the gospel of Jesus Christ.

The logistics of a baptismal service go far beyond just bringing people and water together. Here are some principles for planning and conducting baptismal services.

Understand the Purpose

Baptism starts long before the pastor steps into the water or approaches the baptismal font. It is an integral part of a larger event: the baptismal service. Therefore we begin preparing by refreshing ourselves as to the purpose of the service. Knowing the purpose enables us to plan the details of the service so we can reach our objectives. There are at least five things I want to accomplish in a baptismal service:

● *Initiation.* Baptism is the "official" beginning of the Christian life. Of course, from the human standpoint, salvation takes place in the moment of repentance and personal faith. But since baptism could be considered the "coming out ceremony," it ought to be significant for each candidate. The event should be a benchmark the new convert can point to in times of doubt. It can serve as an anchor in times of temptation.

If we tell people we are going on a diet, that means that from that moment, we are being watched. The public announcement keeps us on our guard. Baptism serves the same function. It's a public declaration of faith that says, "I want everyone to know I've signed up to follow Jesus. Watch me and help me grow."

• *Celebration.* I want to give the congregation an opportunity to celebrate with the angels over those who have been converted. Baptismal services let the church family know what God is doing. This is particularly true in settings where people are rarely asked to respond to a public invitation or altar call. A baptismal service says, "God really is at work in our church."

Water baptism is a public event. It would be a shame to focus so heavily on the actual baptizing that we neglect to lead the congregation in celebrating the joyous event. We want to strive to make it something significant.

• *Instruction.* People should learn during a baptismal service. A wealth of biblical teaching surrounds New Testament baptism, and the service is a prime opportunity for biblical instruction. In addition to the usual baptismal texts, such as John the Baptist's baptizing (Matt. 3:1–12), Jesus' baptism (Matt. 3:13–17), and the many examples of the disciples' immersing new converts in Acts, there are other significant passages. Romans 6:3–7 explains how our baptism is an identification with Jesus' death, burial, and resurrection. Throughout the New Testament, baptism is associated with certain Old Testament events and practices: the flood (1 Pet. 3:20b, 21), circumcision (Col. 2:11, 12), and the crossing of the Red Sea (1 Cor. 10:1, 2). As we delve into these Scriptures, baptismal services become a meaningful time of instruction for our congregations.

• *Proclamation.* Non-Christians are likely to be present at baptismal services. Since these people have seen a live demonstration of faith by their friends and relatives, we can give them a clear statement of the gospel to explain what the newly baptized have done.

• *Invitation.* After finishing the actual baptizing, we may want to give an invitation to the congregation to respond. This is a strategic moment for non-Christians, because the Holy Spirit's ministry of conviction is often strong at this moment. People have heard the call of the gospel, and we can invite them to become followers of Jesus.

Prepare the Candidates for Baptism

We can prepare candidates for baptism by making sure each one knows what will happen and feels comfortable with each step. At the top of the list is making sure there is a true understanding of repentance and faith. It's important to determine that each person has a personal assurance of salvation.

Special preparation classes offer an opportunity to set people at ease. Fears are common, particularly in adults who are new to the Christian community. These fears must be lifted up and faced.

Our church provides a checklist of information for baptismal candidates, with practical suggestions and clear statements about what will be expected of them. The checklist includes items the candidate should bring: towel, change of underwear, bathing suit. Churches that don't use baptismal gowns need to suggest the type of clothes to be worn. I advise women not to wear clothes that will be see-through when wet or that are too tight-fitting. (I also warn about wearing wigs. It's quite a sight to see a full head of hair go under the water and an escaped wig come floating up!) I ask women to take it easy on the make-up; it's better to look a little plain before baptism than to be streaked with mascara afterward.

It's good to assure candidates to consider the people in the congregation as fans in the stands, cheering them on in what they are doing. I remind people that they will be sopping wet, but that this is a minor embarrassment compared to the disgrace that Jesus went through in public for us at Calvary.

Some people can handle the other fears but still harbor a deep-seated fear of being submerged in water. We can try to build a level of trust between ourselves and the fearful candidates by assuring them they can trust us to look after them. When they are entering the tank, we can go part way up the steps to hold their hands as they descend the stairs. A chance to calm themselves before proceeding with the actual baptism also helps.

We use two techniques to set people at ease. First, we show a video of an actual baptism service. Second, we walk them through the process. We take them onto the platform where they will give their statement of personal faith; we show them the changing rooms and the baptismal tank. I've never actually rehearsed baptizing someone, though I'm aware of those who have done it to show extremely fearful people that everything will be all right.

The week prior to the baptismal service, we should send a notice to the candidates, reminding them of the service. We find it useful not only to confirm the date and time, but also to remind the candidates of what to bring and where to meet prior to the service.

Despite all our efforts to prepare candidates, people may still be confused or ill-prepared. So thirty minutes prior to the service, it's good to meet with the candidates once again. We can give final instructions as to where they will sit during the service (we like them to sit together, not with their families), walk through the order of service so they can anticipate being called, and, most importantly, pray together, asking God to make the service significant both for them and for the guests they have invited.

Do encourage candidates to invite guests—friends and relatives. A baptismal service can be an evangelistic event. New Christians have a legitimate opportunity to invite their non-Christian friends to witness their baptisms. Therefore, we can encourage candidates to invite their friends by providing printed invitations to the service. These invitations can be signed by the candidate and distributed freely among friends.

Help Candidates Prepare Their Testimonies

The testimony of the candidate is a significant part of the baptismal service. After being embarrassed on a few occasions, I have learned to take great care in assisting candidates in preparing their

---

The Role of Godparents

Godparenting may be the least understood job in Christianity. Some parents select sponsors in baptism to honor family members or friends; others look for responsible parent-types just in case something happens to themselves. Few parents, however, have well-formed expectations about what godparents should do for their child, and godparents themselves are often confused about their responsibilities. Yet, through careful education and preparation, godparents can serve as a vital link between the candidate's Christian family and the community of faith into which he or she is to be baptized.

Guides for Godparents

When a parent requests an infant or child baptism, it's wise to arrange a meeting with the parents and godparents to discuss the meaning of baptism and the responsibilities of Christian parenting and godparenting. During that time, three responsibilities of godparenting can be explained:

• *Godparents represent the church* as new members are initiated into the Christian faith. As far back as the Middle Ages, young men and women had a series of three sponsors during the period of their initiation into the church—one for their period of instruction, a second for their baptism, and a third for their confirmation. At each occasion, it was the godparent who presented the candidate to the church for consideration as a member.

Today, as those who stand for the church at baptism, godparents maintain a vital interest in the spiritual vitality of the candidate's family life. Their continuing concern helps provide a spiritual atmosphere in which the child is raised. Even if godparents live at a distance, this can be accomplished by daily prayer for the godchild and his or her family, regular contact through letters and visits, and gifts of age-appropriate Christian books and music.

testimonies by providing guidelines about what to include in their confessions of faith. Here are some guidelines for what to cover in a testimony:

- Briefly describe in a candid and clear way what your life was like before you accepted Christ. Did you give much thought to God or the church at that time? When and where did you come to understand that you were a sinner in the sight of God?

- Describe how you came to place your faith in Jesus for salvation. How did the Lord speak to you? Was it through a friend or a church service?

- In your own words, express thanks to God for sending Jesus to be your Savior and for dying on the cross. Thank the Lord for his faithfulness in forgiving your sins.

In these ways, godparents have the privilege of making a child's baptismal or confirmation anniversary a special occasion. Thus, a godparent brings the life of faith to the Christian family as a friend and representative of the greater church.

- *Godparents guarantee the Christian education of the baptized.* In the past, some branches of the Christian church have traditionally charged godparents with specific tasks related to the candidate's education in the Christian faith and life. In some churches, this simply meant insuring that the child knew the Ten Commandments and the Lord's Prayer. In other churches, it meant providing the candidate with the information necessary for confirmation preparation.

In our time, godparents are rarely a child's primary educator, but the sponsor can maintain a lively interest in the candidate's Christian education. This, of course, assumes that the godparents themselves possess a level of spiritual maturity, enabling them to offer the gift of self to enrich the child's spiritual development. Resources for this responsibility are extensive, and the abundance of material available to godparents through churches and Christian bookstores can make sharing the substance of the faith with a godchild a rewarding and exciting calling.

- *Godparents serve as lifelong mentors, helpers, and friends.* When asked if they are willing to stand as sponsors in baptism, potential godparents should consider seriously whether they are capable of making a lifetime commitment to another human being. As representatives of the family of believers in Jesus Christ, they must expect to be available to their godchildren for counsel, encouragement, and companionship.

In our time, the concept of spiritual friendship, of companionship on the faith journey, has become extremely popular. Rather than being a new concept, this is, in fact, an old idea, grounded in a vision of the wonderful relationship children can have with their godparents, their first friends in the faith.

—*Douglas G. Scott*

- Tell how your life has changed since you received the gift of eternal life. Highlight some of the good things God has done in your life since you have been converted. Be specific.
- Declare your determination to follow Jesus Christ and your willingness to serve him throughout your life.

Candidates need a time frame to work with, and it's best to have them write out the story of what God has done for them. Writing it out makes sure the basics are covered and helps people overcome their nervousness when standing in front of the congregation. Candidates may want to memorize their stories, if possible.

Candidates can give their public confessions of faith in at least two ways. They can give their statements directly from the baptismal tank just prior to the actual baptism. This is probably the most frequently followed practice. However, we've discovered that having the

The Congregation's Role in Baptism

Along with its other profound personal meanings, baptism marks a person's incorporation into a community of faith. Thus, a baptism service should have a full communal flavor, rather than being just something a cleric "bestows" upon a candidate. Congregations need to be aware of, and clearly demonstrate, their promised supportive role.

Encouraging Involvement

- *Involve your congregation in practical, supportive roles.* For example, consider having members of the congregation introduce the baptismal candidates to their fellow members. An infant can be carried down the aisle and handed to a member of the congregation while a vow of support is read to the child. The congregation can sing hymns appropriate to baptism and then welcome newly baptized adults to a reception following the service.

Long-time members can learn about newer members through special interviews in the church newsletter.

- *Welcome children's participation.* Invite children to come up to sing "Jesus Loves Me" to an infant. Or ask them to make cards in Sunday school that would welcome newly baptized children. Involve children in worship; avoid consigning them totally to adult-proof Sunday school rooms until they "pass" confirmation class. Note: To involve the children, you may have to challenge some of your members' ingrained attitudes about children and worship.
- *Remind your congregation of the educational task related to baptism.* Make it clear that congregations can help nurture the newly baptized by supporting the church's Christian education program. (Yet, don't give in to the temptation to ask for teaching volunteers right after the vow of support is spoken to the newly baptized child or adult. This might ap-

testimonies given from the pulpit, prior to the candidate entering the baptismal tank, brings the candidates closer to the people, and the statement of faith seems to have greater impact. If the candidates give their testimonies from the pulpit, they will need time to change for baptism.

We need to be prepared to step in and help when, through nervousness, candidates stumble in their testimonies. We can ask leading questions that bring out the person's commitment to follow Jesus Christ. Sometimes the answers in such situations can catch us off guard, however. I asked one fellow if the Lord had made a difference in his life. His answer, straight from the baptismal tank (and straight from his heart) was: "He sure has! He's made a *hell* of a difference in my life!"

The Lord used the crudeness of this new believer's vocabulary as a

---

pear to be practical but is not considered sporting.)

• *As you welcome new members, indicate where they were baptized.* People will see the linkage among Christian congregations created by vows of support taken in one setting and continuing to be fulfilled elsewhere. Baptismal vows transcend local ministries. Congregations will more readily respond to their responsibilities to support a new member when they recognize that this "new" person was made part of God's larger church perhaps years ago.

• *Encourage your congregation to be newcomer friendly during and after baptisms.* Congregational warmth and friendliness needs to extend not just a few Sundays at first, but for the entire assimilation process, which can take years. Choose an elder or deacon to welcome newly baptized adults into some of the activities of the church, inviting them into adult Bible studies and Sunday school classes. Then other congregational members can quickly take over in the welcoming process.

Baptized into a Family

In *Christianity Rediscovered,* Father Vincent Donovan told about his years of evangelism among the Masai people of Africa. At one point, he met with a village elder, spending considerable time with the old man sorting out those who sporadically attended services, those who didn't seem to be growing in the faith, and those who showed little evidence of genuine conversion.

The old man's response illumines the communal nature of baptism: "Padri," he said, "why are you trying to break us up and separate us? . . . Of course, there have been the lazy ones, but they have been helped by those with much energy. There have been the stupid ones, but they have been helped by the intelligent. There have been ones of little faith, but they have been helped by those with much faith. From the first day you came, I have spoken for these people, and I speak for them now. We have reached the place where we can say, 'We believe.' "

—*Cinda Gorman*

fresh reminder to our staid congregation that God was saving needy people through our ministries. When this man came up out of the water, a strong current of praise flowed from the congregation.

Prepare Yourself

Not only do we prepare our candidates for baptism, we must also get ourselves ready for the service. This starts with the spiritual discipline of prayer and includes cultivating a proper attitude, reminding ourselves that baptism is more than a routine; it's a time for rejoicing. It's obeying a command. Here is a checklist of some key preparation tasks:

• *Compose a list of the candidates.* Make sure you have a list of the candidates in the order they are to be baptized. Peruse the list to confirm that you can correctly pronounce each name. Try to recall personal details about the individuals. I tape the list where I can read it clearly in the baptismal tank. I want to make sure I get the names right.

• *Check the accuracy of names.* This is important. One pastoral friend of mine had a call on the Saturday evening before a baptismal service from a recently converted couple. The woman indicated that the pastor should probably use her maiden name, as they were not actually married but were living together under common law.

• *Get baptismal clothing in order.* Since the Bible doesn't tell us exactly what to wear, many traditions have developed. Some ministers use clothing that can get wet. Others wear a tailored gown over a bathing suit. Some like to wear fishermen's hip waders under their gowns.

One important feature in baptismal gowns is weights in the hem. Simple fishing weights placed in the hem will keep the gown from floating to the top of the tank and causing embarrassment.

• *Arrange for support staff.* Ministers need helpers to assist people in and out of the baptismal tank. These helpers should be both men and women. I make sure they are physically healthy, mature people who are not afraid of touch.

Know the Process of Baptizing

I have yet to meet a pastor who did not enjoy baptizing new believers. The most common practice, for those who immerse, is for the pastor to enter the baptismal tank with the drapes for the baptistry still closed. When the drapes are opened, the pastor normally addresses the people, makes some introductory comments, and introduces the first candidate. This requires having a microphone for the pastor and candidates to speak into. Touching an improperly grounded microphone can give a person quite a jolt, so it's safer not to touch the microphone and to warn candidates not to touch it, either.

Here is how I baptize: I have the candidate cross her hands over her chest, and I place my right hand over her nose. I place my left hand around the candidate's back, just below the shoulders, so I can gracefully lift the person back up out of the water.

Some pastors have the candidate hold her own nose. Either way can be satisfactory. I've simply discovered that holding the crossed arms under my right arm (which is holding the nose) puts me in control. There's no way arms can fly up and knock my glasses into the water. There is no struggling as the immersion takes place. On a few occasions, when a nervous candidate has frozen as the baptism was about to take place, I've been known to use my right foot to knock his feet out from under him. The candidate soon goes under the water, grateful for my discreet assistance.

I try to baptize people as close to the front of the tank as possible. This ensures the most visibility for the congregation. Since I'm right-handed, I get the candidate to stand as far to the right side of the tank as possible. I make sure there's enough room to baptize the person without bumping his head against the other end of the tank. When I've thought there wasn't enough room, I have suggested that the candidate bend his knees as he is submerged.

The baptismal formula varies slightly from pastor to pastor, but many include Jesus' Trinitarian formula from Matthew 28:19, such as: "[Name], upon your confession of faith in Jesus Christ as Savior and Lord, and your determination to live for him for the rest of your life, I now baptize you in the name of the Father and of the Son and of the Holy Spirit."

When the candidate emerges from the water, I give her a moment to get composed and then direct her out of the tank. Make sure a woman's gown has not clung to a leg or that there is any immodesty as she leaves the tank. A slight tug at the hem of the baptismal gown as it comes out of the water is not seen by the congregation but can save considerable embarrassment.

It's always a thrill to baptize couples and even entire families. We may want to bring the family into the tank together. It's a beautiful sight for the congregation and a great opportunity to make a brief statement about the Christian family. As the actual baptism takes place, those waiting to be baptized can stand behind us at the back of the tank.

Unique situations call for ingenuity, tact, and special care. For the elderly, movement into and around the tank must not be rushed, or the shock can be jarring. Frail or handicapped people need to be handled with gentleness and respect. Often their greatest fear is getting in and out of the tank. I resolve this by having them enter the tank with me while the drapes are still closed and having them leave the tank with me after the drapes are closed.

There's certainly nothing wrong with having others in the tank to assist us. Congregations today are sensitive and appreciative and will rejoice with the individual in such situations. The key to such situations is to set the congregation at ease by letting them know we have thought through what we are going to do; we are not panicking or rushing through the baptism.

Keep Accurate Records

Denominations vary greatly as to how they keep baptismal records, yet we will probably want to do three basic things. First, give to each person a baptismal certificate signed by the pastor. Second, list the newly baptized persons' names in the monthly newsletter so that everyone in the congregation can recognize their special event. (I used to publish these names in advance but stopped doing it when people failed to show up for baptism, often because of sickness.) Third, carefully add the baptismal information to church records.

Some churches have an official baptismal register; others just add the information to their computer's data base. The information is valuable to have on hand when the person considers membership or transfers to another city or church.

—*Calvin C. Ratz*

Baptism Follow-up

I once bought an ungerminated redwood tree in a Dixie cup. It was just a seed, but in a couple of thousand years it would be a giant, like the other coastal redwoods that made 300-foot arches above me in Muir Woods. I looked up at the huge trees, glanced down at the Dixie cup, and doubted. Could something this small become something that large—ever?

"Just keep it wet, and it will grow," advised the sales lady.

Immersed in God

Keep them wet—good advice for seedling redwoods and fledgling Christians. An easy mistake to make with new Christians is to lead them to see baptism only in its most obvious and shallow definition. In effect, we sometimes read Acts 2:38 ("Repent and get wet, and you will be saved") without the balancing truths that flow from passages such as Mark 10:35–38. There James and John ask, "May we sit on your right hand and left hand when you come into your kingdom?"

In his response, Jesus reminds them that the seating schedule of heaven is not like picking a seat in the lodge or orchestra; it is a matter of baptism, and baptism is not *only* something that happens with water, according to Jesus. It starts there—as an act of obedience—but baptism continues as a process, a way of life. It is the living-out of all that Christ requires, never asking, "Why me?" Baptism is a constant call to service that always probes, "Why *not* me?"

So before new converts are baptized, we must lead them to see that they are not merely getting wet with obedience; they must remain immersed in the purposes of God. Baptism does not conclude God's requirements of us, but rather initiates us into daily obedience forever.

Involved in Church

Some newly baptized persons, as soon as they dry off, find themselves uninvolved in the life of the church. By involvement I don't mean plugging them into a committee or administrative structure (cool assimilation), but helping them enter into the Bible-study/evangelism/ministry/outreach organisms of the church (warm assimilation). I use *cool* to designate those activities or structures that use people's time for institutionalized service: money management, building maintenance, and program flow. I use *warm assimilation* to indicate the groups and structures that will enlarge and enhance a person's view of Christ and his call to discipleship and ministry with others.

Churches should be baptizing new believers. Yet only those churches that remain wet with a large definition of the word *baptism* will develop classes, structures, and assimilation techniques that keep the new convert immersed in Christ's daily call. Every great church does this. Other churches practice only low-impact evangelism, counting converts that may never count for much.

Often, at the conclusion of my baptism services, I quote Psalm 1: "Blessed is the man who does not walk in the counsel of the wicked. . . . He is like a tree planted by streams of water, which yields its fruit in season and whose leaf does not wither. Whatever he does prospers." While they are still wet with the physical waters of one-time obedience, I want new converts to see their connection with the water that nourishes ongoing spiritual growth.

If we who shepherd sheep not only get our converts immersed in his purposes but also keep them immersed in his will, they can grow by grace into such titans of faith that they will "turn the world upside down" (Acts 17:6).

—Calvin Miller

30

Confirmation

Confirmation class has been defined as "that time of the week when the pastor questions his call to ministry."

I remember my father, a pastor, grumbling that "these kids want to attend catechism class about as much as they want to sit in school." I never appreciated my father's feelings until I became a pastor and, sitting in the middle of a confirmation classroom, began to consider seriously my aptitude for selling insurance. Not that the time was a complete loss. I learned a great deal—that the epistles were the wives of the apostles, for example, or that Martin Luther King, Jr., was Martin Luther's brother.

Frustrations like these led my church to a new confirmation process, from the first parents' orientation meeting to the close of the confirmation service. After overseeing the new program for twelve years, I am still amazed how a few key principles transformed what could have been a downer into a delight.

Get Them Early

A vital confirmation experience begins long before that Sunday in late spring when the nervous confirmands stand before the congregation. That's why we start early with years of classroom instruction. But many churches may not start early enough.

Most teenagers are convinced that confirmation is a bad idea. The only way a pastor has half a chance is to reach kids before they become teenagers and hear from their peers, "Aw, confirmation is a bummer." So we go after kids in the fourth grade. The children proceed through three years of instruction during fourth, fifth, and sixth grades and then have a year of transition and service in their seventh-grade year, with confirmation that spring.

Too early? You should see how eager these fourth graders are. They tug on your arm in August and announce, "I get to start confirmation this year." For them, confirmation means honor, not boredom.

For example, when my son Andrew started the confirmation process, he and I went to the orientation meeting and sat with the other fourth graders and parents. The lay people who led our program passed out the workbooks the youngsters would be using during the year and walked them through a few sample assignments. A good amount of each lesson was mechanical: underlining key statements in the biblical text, marking symbols to show contrasts, identifying the passage's main idea. My son, looking it over, blurted out, "Hey, this is going to be fun!"

Fourth graders' hearts are usually still tender toward the gospel. They have had fewer years of indoctrination in a worldly system of thought that resists spiritual penetration. They are less influenced by peers, who in a few years might try telling them that religion is nowhere. And they are equipped to handle the spiritual concepts we teach.

We sometimes tend to underestimate the abilities of these older children, rather than overestimate them. They may be more ready to grapple with truth than we are to challenge them with it.

Go Beyond Teaching to Training

While teaching informs, training forms. Our best teaching means little if we don't train children to live what they learn. We want them not only to know Bible truths, but also to live Bible lives. So we need to spend as much time on application as we do on information.

In one unit, the students wrote a play on the miracles of Jesus and then presented it in a convalescent home. For a lesson on prejudice, students interviewed the local newspaper editor about where prejudice is at work in our community and asked our church president about prejudice in our church. Following a lesson on service, classes have washed windows for church members and sometimes have cleaned my office.

Training also means we establish a relationship with students. One way to do that is for students and teachers to meet for dinner before class. If talking about the lesson during dinner is considered off-limits, conversations will turn toward what went on in school, skateboarding, fun times they've had lately, and other topics of interest to the children.

A confirmation class, while training, also is teaching, so a church cannot violate sound educational principles and hope to succeed. To refine teaching skills, our confirmation teachers go through a four-session course. We try to pair each beginning teacher with a seasoned one. This gives the less experienced person a valuable apprenticeship, lightens the workload of each person, and keeps the class going even when one teacher must be absent. Two teachers in the classroom also assure fewer problems keeping classes quiet and orderly.

Teachers are wise to use lecture sparingly and to incorporate drama, games, word exercises, songs, and other more innovative approaches. For example, we had one student put the life of Abraham into a rhyming story. For a lesson on heaven, a class threw a Heavenly Festival, including a time of worship and angel food cake for refreshments. The goal is not to entertain, but to teach the vitally important subject matter as winsomely as we can.

Keep Them Involved

Many congregations struggle with how to integrate students into the youth group and the life of the church following their years of instruction. Some families have inherited the understanding that the confirmation service ends the child's obligation to the church, and that must be counteracted in every way possible.

One way to thwart the tendency to usher children out of the church with confirmation is to insert a year of transition and service after the children complete their studies and before they are confirmed. During this year the kids are supported in their regular involvement in worship and youth activities, and they are encouraged to be engaged in service projects. For example, we've had young people baby-sit for new member classes, clean the building, and set up tables and movie projectors for church events.

Confirmation ought to serve as the launching pad for service in the congregation, and it is exciting to see that expectation pay off. Before the confirmation service one spring, I had a young man come up to me and say he couldn't wait for confirmation, because he wanted to be doing more in the congregation.

Work with the Parents

A confirmation program can be rigorous, and parents usually breathe a deep sigh of relief when the three years are over, but they can feel good about being part of a job well done. One couple from my church, whose three young-adult boys still talk about their confirmation experience, smiled as they told me, "We huffed and puffed our way through catechism."

Martin Luther wrote the *Small Catechism* to help parents teach their children the key points of Christian doctrine. A church's role is not to supersede parents in this primary role, but to assist them. That can be made clear at an orientation meeting, when leaders ask parents to work with their children on the lessons. One suggestion is for families to use the lessons for their family devotions.

Parents can also be drawn into the interview process preceding the formal confirmation service. Sometimes the pastor takes this responsibility to interview students to determine if they are ready to be confirmed. But who knows children better than their parents?

Once I interviewed a young person prior to confirmation and afterward told him I had some concerns about his readiness. Later his parents, who had another son in the program, came to see me. "If you had said this about our other son," they said, "we would agree. But we know our boys, and this one is more ready than the other. He's quiet and not as articulate, but he has a genuine faith."

So now I have parents interview their children first and then give me a brief written report that I may use as material in my own interview with the child the following month. I write a letter to the parents and suggest questions they may want to use in their personal conference with the child. The questions range widely but focus on the child's growing commitment to Christ. For example, one question I often suggest is, "When have you felt closest to God?"

Many parents have told me this conversation is one of the most meaningful they've had with their children. They also tell me it's not easy. One strong supporter of our program admitted, "That was hard work." Hard work it may be, but it is good work that involves the parents in the confirmation process.

Parents also can take a significant role in the confirmation service itself. They can be invited to come forward and participate in the prayers that accompany the laying on of hands. Then the parents and confirmands can be the first group to be served Communion.

Add the Personal Touch

Soon before Confirmation Sunday (I use the Saturday before), it's good to meet with the parents and the children. This meeting has three goals: To prepare the parents and confirmands to feel as comfortable as possible during the service, to make sure they understand what's happening, and to add a personal touch, to seal one's pastoral contact with them.

This is a good time to review "Why confirmation?" and explain how this ceremony is not an end but a beginning, parallel to Jesus beginning his ministry after his confirmation at the Jordan. The pastor can reiterate what the youth are confirming—their faith in Jesus

Christ, that they will live in the covenant of their baptism. The children can be encouraged to expect the Holy Spirit will do some confirming as well, as we pray in the service, "Father in heaven, for Jesus' sake, stir up in your child the gift of your Holy Spirit; confirm his faith, guide his life, empower him in his serving, give him patience in suffering, and bring him to everlasting life." This meeting also provides an excellent opportunity to walk the children and parents through the service, so they will know what is coming.

I have found this day before confirmation a good time to invite all the kids to my house for lunch following the meeting with their parents. I take time to talk with each one to refresh my memory about interests, hobbies, and family situations.

The next day, when the confirmands come forward during the service, this information makes great material to introduce each one personally: "This is Ryan Hoffman. Ryan really enjoys skateboarding. Ryan feels God may be calling him to be a missionary. Let's pray for him in that regard." Each child can share a portion of Scripture that has been especially meaningful to him or her. Such personalization allows the congregation to get to know the young person better.

Another personal touch comes when parents are invited to come forward to join in the prayers that accompany the laying on of hands. It's so moving to hear parents pray for their children. Sometimes parents will say a few words to their son or daughter during this time. I recall one father saying to his daughter, "You have been such a fine, obedient girl. We really love you and believe God has a special plan for you." Last year one child's grandmother came forward to pray for her grandson. We were all deeply touched by her prayer.

I've found that these personal touches in the prayers, Scriptures, and prophetic words are what people remember most.

Weigh the Trade-offs

This approach to confirmation comes with a price. For my church, for example, building a strong confirmation program meant gathering a crew of adults to be teachers, cooks for the weekly supper, administrators, table hostesses, and so on. The price was the loss of our strong choir. When we began our new program, the choir dropped out of existence.

A church has to weigh the trade-offs. We feel the gains in our situation outweigh the losses. The team-teaching approach means we have trained dozens of teachers in the process of training our youth. The biblical literacy of our congregation has risen considerably. Relationships among young people and adults remain vital. In fact, young people tell me their favorite activity is our annual family retreat.

The students have more confidence reading the Scriptures; they are not intimidated by obscure minor prophets. They have discovered the Bible speaks to their lives and helps them with the other children in the program.

Confirmation may cause some pastors to question their calling, but with the right approach, I've found it actually confirms mine.

—Paul Anderson

Resources

Hendricks, H. 1987. Teaching to change lives. Portland, Ore.: Multnomah.

Jungkuntz, T. 1983. Confirmation and the charismata. Lanham, Md.: University Press of America.

Tappert, T., ed. 1991. Luther's small catechism and explanation. St. Louis: Concordia.

Wangerin, W., ed. 1967. When God chose man. St. Louis: Concordia.

Part VI

Weddings

S tanding tall at the head of the aisle, service book re-
assuringly in hand, a pastor watches the bride enter to
join hands with her beloved. Then, just an arm's length
away, the service plays out in all its tender power. The pastor enjoys
the best vantage point for one of life's most important episodes: the
union of husband and wife in holy matrimony.

Of course with the privilege comes a great deal of responsibility. It
is the pastor who steadfastly directs the planning and calmly guides
the nervous wedding party through the worship service that unites
two into one. The pastor remembers how to do the right things at the
proper time. It's the pastor who steps in when the unexpected happens, who navigates the unknowns with knowing grace, who helps
maintain the *Christian* nature of what could turn into a circus.

To do this well, the pastor needs a deep well of knowledge and
practice from which to draw. And even those who have united their
share of couples still learn from each new experience. Here, pastoral
writers share the fruits of their study and the experience accumulated
from years of officiating at weddings.

31

The Purpose of a Marriage Ceremony

Is the wedding ceremony truly a worship service in which we approach the presence of God reverently? Or is it merely a showcase for the bride and her family? What should be taking place in a wedding ceremony? What is its proper purpose and mood?

The following words provide the classic context for such an occasion:

> We have come together today in the presence of God to unite this man and this woman in holy marriage, which is instituted by God, blessed by our Lord Jesus Christ, and to be held in honor among all men. Let us therefore reverently remember that God has established and sanctified marriage for the welfare and happiness of mankind.

It is commonly held that the marriage ceremony is to be a worship service. We come together as a community to worship God through the union of the couple in marriage "reverently and in the fear of God." But what is the role of the community of God in the wedding ceremony, and why do we consider the wedding ceremony a service of worship? There are at least two reasons why it might be properly considered so, both of which support the concept that marriage is a reflection or an image of a spiritual reality.

● *Marriage is instituted by God.* Some of the questions generally asked of couples in premarital counseling are these: Why did you come to the church to be married? Why didn't you go to the justice of the peace and have him perform the ceremony?

The answers often center around the recognition that weddings are

413

not simply civil ceremonies but involve something more. There is an innate realization that marriage belongs to God and therefore should take place in a church and be performed by a minister.

In fact, marriage does belong to God. Its institution is found in the first chapters of Genesis: "The Lord God said, 'It is not good for the man to be alone. I will make him a helper suitable for him' " (Gen. 2:18). Only several verses later are stated these familiar words, "For this reason a man will leave his father and mother and be united to his wife, and they will become one flesh" (Gen. 2:24).

Marriage did not evolve as some arbitrary social convention. It was instituted by God for mankind's welfare, and because of its origin, marriage must be taken seriously. It should not be haphazardly entered nor, by the same token, should individuals lightly consider "dividing that which God has united together."

Since marriage is instituted by God, it must also be understood on his terms. God considers marriage as a permanent (Matt. 19:6) and monogamous (Gen. 2:24) relationship. By creating one man and one woman and joining them into "one flesh," God from the beginning intended marriage to be lasting.

Since God instituted marriage, and the wedding ceremony reflects his plan, the sacred process of coming before him to unite two persons is fitting. Wedding participants should focus upon him and desire to appropriate his perspective of the event. Because the very nature of the wedding ceremony revolves around God and his design for his creation, its chief aim should be to glorify him.

 • *Marriage is an image of God's relationship to his people.* A second way to understand the wedding ceremony as a worship service is through the biblical imagery of Christ's relationship to his bride, the church. When we comb our hair in the morning, we see in the mirror an image that accurately reflects ourself. Likewise, marriage mirrors what is true in the spiritual realm. Because of the special relationship that exists between a man and a woman in marriage, God uses the same imagery to illustrate the special relationship he established with Israel (Isa. 61:10; 62:5; Hos. 2:19–20) and through Christ with his church (Eph. 5:23–32).

Reflections of Biblical Tradition

Old Testament wedding ceremonies consisted of two main parts. The betrothal period traditionally came first, following a rather detailed process of arranging the marriage. The traditional time for the betrothal period was one year.

An integral part of the betrothal period was the signing of the marriage contract. It recorded all the obligations the husband would undertake toward his bride-to-be. Specifically, it spelled out financial, sexual, and other obligations to be met by both parties during the marriage. Its extensive wording was developed to protect the wife in particular, so that the husband could not easily divorce her.

When the Bible speaks of Mary being betrothed to Joseph, it is referring to this first part of the wedding ceremony (Matt. 1:18). One of the important parts of the marriage contract was the stipulation of virginity. If a bride ceased to be a virgin, a bill of divorce was written. This was the source of Joseph's concern when he was told that Mary was expecting a child.

After a year had passed for the couple, the second part of the marriage process (the wedding ceremony as we know it today) began with a procession (Gen. 31:27; Judg. 14:4–11; Jer. 7:34). According to tradition, the bridegroom dressed in festive attire and then, accompanied by his friends and relatives, proceeded to the home of the bride. The bride awaited the arrival of the groom and also dressed in festive garments. Her friends, family, and attendants anxiously awaited the arrival of the groom and celebrated in grand fashion upon their reunion (Jer. 7:34; 16:9; Matt. 25:1–12).

The groom then escorted his bride, along with their friends and family, to his home, where the ceremony was completed. The veiled bride was led to a private inner chamber where the presentation of the couple was made by the bride's father, the marriage vows were exchanged, and the documents were signed. This last act denoted that the actual marriage had taken place.

The guests anxiously awaited the appearance of the groom and his bride for the marriage feast, whereupon great celebration (Gen. 29:22; Matt. 9:15; 22:1–14; John 2:1–10) lasted anywhere from a day to a week. Finally, the bridal pair was led to the bridal chamber, and the marriage was consummated (Sevener 1988).

The Preservation of Imagery

Much of today's wedding ceremony remains amazingly close to the traditional ceremony from biblical history. While there have been minor changes, the basic structure has remained intact.

Although the New Testament frequently uses wedding imagery, it offers little detail about the proceedings of an actual wedding ceremony. Neither are the early church fathers helpful in this regard. Additionally, the early church apparently allowed existing wedding customs of the day to persist alongside the new meaning the Christian gospel presented to marriage. For instance, Roman wedding customs contained the betrothal vows, the joining of hands, a sacrifice at the family altar, a banquet, and the marriage-bed rites. The ceremony also began at the home of the bride and concluded at the couple's new residence.

The early church's initial role in weddings began simply as an encouragement to Christians to marry Christians. Its influence upon the ceremony itself increased over time, perhaps, at first, due to necessity. When Rome fell, the keeping of wedding records fell to the church. (Often the only literate person in a village was the clergyman!) The marriage records helped to provide proof of such things as the legitimacy of children and the right to inheritances. Ordinary citizens—Christian and non-Christian—required written wedding certificates, and the clergy became the logical witnesses and record keepers for this important event.

In time Christian traditions began to dominate the wedding ceremony. Christian blessings substituted for those of pagan deities, and the Lord's Supper was celebrated in place of the Roman sacrifice at the family altar. The full wedding service did not take place com-

---

Divorce and Remarriage

The church has a difficult task in responding to the growing problem of divorce and remarriage. On the one hand, we encourage and applaud lifelong commitment. On the other hand, we extend grace and acceptance to those whose marriages have fallen apart. We offer divorce-recovery workshops, support groups for single parents, and help for the children of fractured families. Yet at times, these two obligations seem in conflict.

Because the Bible apparently teaches two grounds for divorce—infidelity (Matt. 5:32) and the case in which a nonbeliever divorces a believer (1 Cor. 7:15)—many pastors make judgments on a case-to-case basis when asked to marry people who have been through a divorce.

Making Decisions

The following questions can help us arrive at a reasonable level of comfort in performing marriage ceremonies in such situations.

• *Was there biblical justification for the divorce?* This is the fundamental question. We must respond to people and their circumstances through the grid of what we believe the Scriptures say. If a divorce was on grounds other than the scriptural ones, many of us will tactfully decline to do the requested ceremony. This does not mean we condemn and shun the people if they do get married. But the couple needs to know why we cannot in good conscience do the ceremony.

• *When did the divorce occur?* Were the potential partners believers when they divorced their previous spouses? Were they unbelievers? Believers have a higher obligation to keep their marriages together. For instance, while I would not remarry believers who divorced on nonscriptural grounds, I might marry people who divorced for other reasons if their divorce occurred before they came to Christ. In salva-

pletely within the church building until the time of the Reformation. Until that time the ceremony usually was conducted on the church steps, the place of legal transactions, "in the sight of God" (White 1980).

Imagery's Meaning

Things related to the spiritual realm, past and future, are beautifully depicted in the traditional wedding ceremony, graphically communicating God's love for us. The bride represents all believers—the church—and the groom depicts Jesus, the Savior. The relationship between the bride and groom wonderfully demonstrates God's covenant relationship with his people. And just as the bride presented to the groom gifts given her by her father, so shall we, as believers, pres-

---

tion "the old has gone, the new has come" (2 Cor. 5:17b).

• *Is there hope for reconciliation?* Even if the divorce was granted on biblical grounds, it's good to explore whether there is still hope for reconciliation. Sometimes there is no hope. For example, the former partner may already be remarried. But if the former spouse has not remarried, it's important to encourage the person to work toward reconciliation.

Gauging the possibility of reconciliation is a judgment call. When I am reasonably convinced there is no hope for getting back together, I may consider doing the ceremony.

• *Has there been adequate time for healing?* Divorce tends to destroy a person emotionally, spiritually, and sometimes even physically.

If someone had biblical grounds for divorce and there is no hope of reconciliation, we will want to explore whether he or she has worked through the shattering personal consequences of the divorce. We need to find out whether people are in the process of emotional and spiri-

tual healing before they enter a new relationship.

For example, if a woman started dating her prospective spouse during the marital separation and prior to the divorce, I would think it unwise to proceed with the new wedding ceremony. Also, if a couple has not gone through extensive premarital counseling and taken positive steps toward emotional stability, even if they had biblical grounds for divorce, I would likely not do the ceremony.

No Easy Decisions

The biggest frustration in dealing with these issues is that there are often many shades of gray in each situation, while we look for pure black and white. So when making a judgment call in typically confusing circumstances, it is best to ask ourselves one last personal question: *Will I do this ceremony with a clear conscience?* If we have reservations, even if everything else lines up, we should decline.

—*Edward G. Dobson*

ent our gifts, provided by God our Father, to the groom, Jesus Christ.

Traditionally, once the wedding ceremony ended, a great feast was held. Likewise, when the bride (the believers who comprise the church) and the Groom (Jesus Christ) are joined together, there will be a great celebration biblically referred to as the Feast of the Lamb:

> Hallelujah!
> For our Lord God Almighty reigns.
> Let us rejoice and be glad
> and give him glory!
> For the wedding of the Lamb has come,
> and his bride has made herself ready.
> Fine linen, bright and clean,
> was given her to wear.
> Then the angel said to me, "Write: 'Blessed are those who are invited to the wedding supper of the Lamb!' " (Rev. 19:7–9)

Dealing with Matters of Etiquette

Etiquette is simply morality in action, expressing Jesus' command to love our neighbor. As we guide a couple in planning their wedding, we can focus on this spirit of love, avoiding arguments about petty details of protocol and procedure. Here are guidelines to help us do that.

Who Is in Charge?

Since a Christian wedding is a Christian service of worship, the minister, rather than a bridal consultant, is in charge of the service. In the first interview, we can let the couple know that it is our role to direct both the rehearsal and wedding.

Knowing who is in charge solves myriad potential problems and conflicts related to etiquette. For example, consider the seating of parents. When parents of the bride or groom have been divorced, former marriage partners may not wish to sit side-by-side. After discussing this matter with the wedding couple, the minister in charge can direct adjustments to the traditional seating arrangements, such as seating parents in two rows, rather than one.

Planning and Rehearsing

Planning is the most important aspect of putting etiquette into action, since it provides time to think through the options and implications of such things as seating arrangements, processions, and receiving lines for the wedding reception—before the wedding actually occurs. It's good to go over the complete ceremony with the couple in the church, home, or other location for the wedding, determining their stance on each question of procedure and etiquette. Some ministers use a legal pad to plot each step in the wedding process.

As Christians we are awaiting the procession of the Groom as he comes to escort his bride to the home he has prepared. In the meantime, the church is preparing itself and "dressing in its most festive of garments." We are dressing in deeds of righteousness and purity, utilizing the gifts God has given us as part of the wedding contract in order to present them to the groom when he returns.

A Christian Wedding

In *Christian* weddings, God's plan should be emphasized. We need to highlight the spiritual imagery of the wedding ceremony to make a Christian ceremony distinct from what else exists today in secularized ceremonies.

There are four essential elements of the traditional wedding ceremony that ought to be retained today in some fashion. Having survived the centuries and withstood the test of time, the following can

---

The wedding might be thought of as a drama consisting of three acts: processional, wedding ritual itself, and recessional. One rehearsal method begins with all members of the wedding party in the places they will occupy at the end of the service right before the *recessional*. Following a recessional practice, the wedding party processes in and goes through an abbreviated ritual before recessing once again. This process should be repeated until the whole ceremony goes smoothly. By rehearsing this way, each issue of etiquette or protocol can be dealt with as it arises in the unfolding of the action.

It's important, however, that the activities of the rehearsal be based on the prior decisions made in discussions with the wedding couple. Never leave any such decisions for the actual rehearsal, for members of the wedding party will invariably dispute matters of etiquette based on "the way it was done at So-and-so's wedding."

Allowing for Differences

Two families may be meeting for the first time at their children's wedding, bringing vastly different traditions to the event. Therefore, we need to remind ourselves that there is no right or wrong way to do many of the wedding procedures, only appropriate and desirable customs. For example, although it is traditional for the bride to process on the arm of her father, brother, or other male relative, it is entirely appropriate for the bride to process alone if that is her wish.

Christian weddings are to be grace-filled events, not legalistic affairs. Because we are all imperfect, even the most carefully planned wedding can have glitches and mistakes. However, in the context of Christian worship—an environment of joy and confidence—we can let everyone know that human error cannot thwart the grace and purposes of God.

—*Perry H. Biddle, Jr.*

be readily endorsed by worship leaders today.

• *A marriage involves the consent and the intent of the will between a man and a woman.* It is a binding covenant—not a license—between one man and one woman. It is unfortunate in this day that the vows sometimes become viewed as a contract rather than a covenant between the couple. A contract deals with impersonal matters in which the action of God is not apparent, while a covenant recognizes God's action and is based on the lifelong ideals of mutual love and fidelity.

• *Marriage is strengthened in the presence of parental recognition and support.* Marriage was ratified by the parents in biblical times (Gen. 21:1; 34:4–6; 38:6; Josh. 15:16; Judg. 14:2–3; 1 Sam. 17:25; 18:20–27; Eph. 6:27), and that remains the preferred model today. The giving away of the bride by the father not only carries with it great imagery but also demonstrates the recognition and support of the parents toward the marriage.

• *The presence of witnesses is important to the wedding ceremony.* Just as marriage ceremonies historically implied the legal ratification of vows before the public, today's ceremony should also include witnesses. Not only does the congregation witness a legal ceremony, they also demonstrate their acceptance and support of the newly formed marriage covenant. Witnesses are also important in observing the signing of the marriage license (Gen. 29:25–26; 34:12).

• *Physical consummation of the marriage is expected after the exchange of vows.* Physical union has been one objective of marriage since its inception. God clearly planned for a man and woman to marry and "become one flesh" (Gen. 2:24). Holding to this sequence of events is no small challenge in light of our culture's permissive attitude toward sexual relationships. The wedding couple comes before God and the community of believers who witness and sanction the vows they make to one another. *Then* their union is consummated in the bridal chamber.

The biblical model for the wedding ceremony offers helpful insight to understanding the wedding ceremony as a worship service. As the community of God comes together in obedience to him to witness the wedding vows, it is saying, "This is right and good and is what God desires." Marriage fulfills our creative destiny. In Genesis God's people are commanded to leave their parents and cleave to their mates. A man and woman joined together in marriage obediently reenact God's divine order. Whenever we participate in a wedding ceremony, even if only as witnesses of the event, we affirm God's good plan.

The wedding ceremony as a worship service glorifies God's creative pattern. We come as a worshipping community to witness the uniting of two persons and express our gratefulness to God. God initiated the pattern; we simply reenact it.

The mood of a wedding ceremony should be one of great awe and wonder as we respond to God's revealed truth, which is reflected and made visible in marriage. The joy of the service should not be centered upon the bride or groom, but rather upon God, who established this precious model and its accompanying imagery.

—Douglas M. Cecil

References
Hutton, S. 1968. Minister's marriage manual. Grand Rapids: Baker.
Sevener, H. 1984. The Jewish wedding ceremony. *The Chosen People* 4.
White, J. 1980. Introduction to Christian worship. Nashville: Abingdon Press.

32

Planning a Wedding Ceremony

Much of what happens in a wedding today has roots in ancient customs and practices. In the early centuries, marriage was mainly a civil affair in which a man and a woman united by making certain vows in public. The role of the church at first was simply to bless these vows. In the Middle Ages, however, the social order began to break down, and marriage was not considered so important. In response, the church developed a fuller liturgical expression of the wedding ceremony. What had taken place primarily outside the church building was brought inside.

It is not simply the perpetuation of customs, however, that is at the heart of the wedding ceremony. For Christians, the ceremony is an enactment of faith, a celebration of divine promises in the midst of a covenant community. In a word, the marriage ceremony is worship. While this fact should be obvious, it is easily overlooked. When planning the ceremony, the pastor and couple should view everything through the lens of faith, seeing the primary purpose of the wedding as being the worship of God in gratitude for his gift of marriage.

The general pattern for a Christian wedding was established early on and persists today. There are essentially three parts to the standard ceremony: the betrothal, the vows, and the blessing.

The Betrothal

This part of the service originally took place outside the church building altogether. In time, some of the actions of the betrothal were brought to the front steps of the church. In modern weddings some hint of this history remains in that the first part of the service is often conducted on the floor level, and then the wedding party moves up into the chancel area for the vows and blessing.

• *Publishing the banns.* The word *banns* comes from an Anglo-Saxon word meaning "to summon by proclaiming" and simply means the proclamation or announcement of a proposed marriage. The banns may be given in church, although today it more commonly comes in the form of newspaper announcements. This is the time of the engagement to be married. Some weeks or months before the marriage ceremony, the couple announces their intent and makes implicit commitments to proceed toward marriage. Invitations to the wedding are part of publishing the banns, as family, friends, and sometimes a whole congregation are notified of the time and place of the marriage.

• *The entrance.* The type of entrance procedure is usually conditioned by custom. Tradition has it, for example, that bride and groom will enter from different directions, reflecting an ancient practice of the bride leaving her home, and the groom his, to meet elsewhere to contract the marriage. The bride being escorted by her father carries connotations of the father "giving away" his daughter. But the bride may choose to be escorted by both her parents, or enter singly.

It may even be appropriate for the bride and groom to enter together. They and their families may gather with the other members of the congregation for worship as they ordinarily would. Or, the bride and groom might enter accompanied by special music after all others have gathered, or during the singing of the first hymn. When the bride and groom come in together, they clearly indicate that they have come jointly to enter into a mutual covenant.

• *Call to worship.* The ceremony proper begins with sentences from Scripture (or other appropriate words) to remind those gathered that their purpose is to worship God. The call to worship may be in responsive form, a dialogue between the pastor and congregation. This involves the congregation, which helps set the tone for the service.

The call to worship need not be lengthy. It may be a simple statement such as: "God is love, and those who abide in love abide in God, and God abides in them" (1 John 4:16). This may be followed by a hymn that praises God as worthy of our worship. All music in the service should focus on God's love. It is not human love that is extolled in weddings, but the divine love, of which human love is but a pale reflection.

• *Statement on the meaning of marriage.* Early in the service, the minister briefly, but clearly, explains the Christian understanding of marriage. His or her statement begins with an announcement of the purpose of the service, namely to witness the union of two people (who should be mentioned by name at this point) and to support them with prayers for God's blessing.

The statement goes on to stress the richness of marriage. Marriage is a relationship of mutual caring and commitment between a man and a woman. It is necessary to the well-being of society, because it creates families in which children are nurtured. Marriage has a mystical dimension, for two lives become one, reflecting the mystical union of Christ and the church. Since marriage is a gift from God, those who are married seek God's will for their life together.

The statement stresses that marriage is blessed by Christ's presence, even as he was present at the wedding at Cana. Marriage is sustained by the power of the Holy Spirit and requires persistent prayer by the man and woman and their families. The statement may conclude with a brief prayer calling upon God, by the power of the Holy Spirit, to bless the couple (by name) and to empower them to live fully and faithfully in this relationship.

• *Declarations of intent.* Originally, these statements were made much earlier than the ceremony itself, as part of the betrothal. Now they are incorporated into the ceremony. They are most often phrased in the form of a question so the bride or groom answers simply, "I do" or "I will."

The questions follow closely what has gone before, the statement on the gift of marriage informing their wording. Having heard what Christian marriage means, the bride and groom are asked if they want to enter into this relationship. It is not a question of whether they want to be married, but whether they want to be married *on these Christian terms.* If both people are baptized, the questions may be asked with reference to that fact—whether they intend to live out their marriage as a fulfillment of their calling as Christians.

• *Affirmations from family members.* In some contemporary wedding ceremonies, the bride is given away by her father. Usually the question is asked, "Who gives this woman [or name] to be married to this man [or name]?" And the customary answer from the father is, "I do" or "Her mother and I do." This practice comes from ancient times and other places, and has lost much of propriety today. We now recognize that the bride is not the property of the father to be given away. Marriages are not arranged by families in our society, but by mutual consent of the bride and groom.

With this in mind, a different liturgical act can be substituted for the giving of the bride—namely affirmations from the families. The parents and other family members of the bride and groom are asked to stand and answer a question regarding their blessing of the couple (by name) and their promise to do whatever they can to support them in the marriage relationship during the years to come.

• *Affirmations from the congregation.* The congregation as a whole may then be invited to stand and answer a similar question regarding its personal promises to be supportive to the couple throughout their married life. This is a powerful way to involve the whole congregation in the ceremony. A hymn of praise may be sung (such as "For the Beauty of the Earth"), or other special music offered, as a way of signalling the transition from the betrothal to the vows.

The Vows

What has come before was preparation. Now the focus of the service is on the exchange of vows, the essential act of the wedding.

• *Scripture and sermon.* Immediately before the vows are exchanged, it is appropriate to have one or more readings from Scripture, again emphasizing that the marriage of the two people is made possible by God's gift of love and that obedience to God is the foundation of the marriage relationship. People other than the pastor may be called

---

Writing Vows

Many years ago I uttered words that pledged my love and fidelity to my wife, Patty. Back then, the idea of writing our vows would have been a unique thought. Today, however, some couples are creating their own alternatives to the traditional vows. How can we, as pastors, help couples in the process of deciding on appropriate vows? How do we help them make the vows meaningful while maintaining the integrity of the Christian wedding ceremony?

• First, we can remind the couple that the vows are the heart of the ceremony. They are the reason the community of God has gathered —to hear the couple's expression of mutual love and commitment to each other and to affirm the couple's commitment as well as God's plan for them.

• Second, the couple needs to hear the difference between a covenant and a contract. Marriage vows are a binding covenant between a man and a woman in the sight of God, while contracts deal with impersonal matters in which God's involvement is not apparent. Contracts rarely include love. A covenant, on the other hand, is based on the lifelong ideal of mutual love and commitment, not on the technicalities of a legal contract.

Vows, therefore, should include elements that stress mutual fidelity, exclusiveness, and commitment. Escape clauses such as, ". . . as long as we both shall *love*" have no place in a lifelong covenant. A covenant leaves no room for the possibility of separation or divorce; the two become one.

• Third, we can work with the couple to enhance the expression of their unique personalities. As a couple seeks to write vows, they desire to express their love and devotion to one another in a refreshing and

upon to read. Often members of the bride's and groom's families or other close friends will do this.

It may be desirable for the pastor to preach a brief sermon. The sermon will be directed not only to the couple, but also to the congregation. It expounds the Scripture just read in light of some aspect of the couple's situation. The couple themselves may have suggestions for the preacher, stressing some aspect of the statement on the gift of marriage. If the bride and groom are from different Christian traditions, such as Protestant and Roman Catholic, a theme of unity and how love overcomes barriers is certainly appropriate.

• *The exchange of vows.* At this point the couple may move to a different location (into the chancel, for example) to give visual emphasis to the fact that this is the primary part of the service. The couple should face one another when making their vows, joining their right hands (a traditional sign of making agreements or covenants). They may either join right hands throughout both vows, or the one

---

personal way. Our job is to help the couple accomplish this goal.

For instance, we might provide a number of examples of previously used vows to stimulate their thoughts. Speaking their vows into a tape recorder and then working with a transcript of that recorded message often makes the vows warm, real, and personal. Singing or memorizing the vows can also make the service more meaningful. We also can stress that there is nothing wrong with reading vows or using the "repeat after the me" method for those too nervous to rely on memory.

• Fourth, we should review the vows with the couple to make sure the important elements are expressed with dignity and clarity. The couple needs to understand that the pastor retains the last word on what is and is not acceptable. The vows need to be warm, personal, and contemporary, but also theologically sound. This pledge of a lifelong covenant between a man and a woman, with no escape clauses, should be expressed as intimately and as forcefully as possible.

• Fifth, as pastors, we're wise to make sure we are prepared for any unexpected developments in the exchange of vows. Though the couple plans to express their vows from memory, it's still important to carry a copy of the text to help out in those moments when the memories may lapse. Unless the couple strenuously objects, we should practice the exchange of vows during the rehearsal. Practice makes perfect.

We work with couples to plan their wedding ceremony. And when a couple creates an intimate expression of love and commitment to each other, it not only helps make the ceremony more personal, it also highlights God's unique design for each marriage. As that design is fully realized, the community that has gathered to witness the union will respond with praise to the One who made it all possible.

—*Douglas M. Cecil*

speaking the vows may take the hand of the other. The couple should be instructed to speak their vows loudly enough for all to hear.

The bride and groom make promises to each other, in the presence of their families and friends, and in the presence of God. The promises of the bride and groom are made in the context of the promises already made by their families and the congregation, and especially by God.

The vows exchanged by the bride and groom often take the traditional forms found in most liturgies, Protestant and Roman Catholic. Even civil ceremonies have borrowed traditional religious vows. The bride and groom, however, with guidance from the pastor, may wish to write their own vows. The pastor can guide the couple in examining traditional vows for their content and assist them in expressing in their own words the promises they will make.

Since the commitment made between the bride and groom is mu-

The Wedding Sermon

Some ministers may downplay the importance of the wedding message because it will be eclipsed by the emotions of the moment. They believe the couple isn't listening, can't concentrate, and won't remember what is said.

Another perspective, however, considers this an important opportunity to make an impact for the gospel. More people, churched and unchurched, are present and paying attention than on many other occasions.

Also, many couples now use a VCR to make this the most intensive media event of their lives. They will review the ceremony time and again, with the message sending deep roots into their lives.

What the Message Says

The effective message will tap into the emotions of the moment and communicate the truths of eter-

nity. It will be both biblical and personal. A generic wedding message is neither fair nor adequate. We should preach a message that is personal to the couple and affirms those who have come to support them. This type of message requires the prior context of a relationship with the couple.

The first premarital counseling session provides the ideal time to get acquainted. We can find out how the couple met and what they most value in marriage. What do they hope will be the message of their wedding service? If they could say one thing to those gathered, what would they say?

If they are openly committed as Christians, we can explore what spiritual message they want communicated in the sermon. Do they have any favorite Scriptures (such as life verses) or other passages they've selected as the basis for their marriage commitment?

tual, the wording of their vows should be similar, if not precisely the same. Their promise to one another is a sign of God's promise. The wording of the vows expresses an absolute covenant, not just a promise kept for as long as it is convenient to do so. We realize that it is only by the grace and power of God that the total commitment of wedding vows can be fulfilled, day by day.

In making their vows to one another, the bride and groom have three choices. They can memorize them, read them, or repeat them line by line after the pastor. If the couple memorizes their vows, they are able to speak directly to each other without visual or audible assistance. Yet memorization is difficult for some people and is made more difficult by the emotion of a marriage service. The couple may choose to read the vows from the service book or a printed page held by the pastor before each one as they face each other, but this prevents them from having direct eye contact throughout the vows. Re-

---

How the Message Develops

The sermon can arise from three main sources. The first source is the couple themselves. As we spend even a minimal amount of time with a couple, we will notice their qualities and their professional pursuits. For example, I married a couple who were accountants. My message was entitled "The Mathematics of Marriage." Based on Genesis 2:24— "and the two shall become one"— the sermon spoke of unity in the home, as one plus one equals *one* in Christ.

We can also build from a couple's primary interests. One couple was interested in backpacking and mountain climbing. I preached on "The Three-Fold Cord of Marriage," based on Ecclesiastes 4:10–13. The image of climbing communicated the adventure of marriage, which requires that the couple be tied together by the strands of faith, of hope, and of love.

A second source for the message is the ritual and ceremonial elements of the wedding service itself.

Many fresh messages can be written by paraphrasing the wedding vows. In a sermon titled "Faithful Attraction," I paraphrased the traditional vows with the following three points: "for better or worse" I will walk with you through the good times and bad times; "for richer or poorer" I will value the most important things in life; and "in sickness and in health" I will be with you when you need me most.

A third source of inspiration arises from well-known portions of Scripture. With 1 Corinthians 13 or Colossians 3:12–17, for instance, we might focus on a few specific words, going more in depth as it fits the couple and their life situation. Less can be more if we savor but one verse. The trilogy of faith, hope, and love are especially applicable to a wedding sermon.

The repetition of basic themes at a wedding is inevitable, but we must try to keep our messages fresh. Even in those situations in which we don't know the couple well, we can offer a special word.

—*Douglas J. Rumford*

peating after the pastor, line by line, frees the couple from the burdens of memory and the intrusion of the printed page, but it does involve some awkwardness, too. If the latter practice is followed, as it often is, the pastor should not try to whisper or otherwise hide the fact that the couple are repeating each line as they hear it.

• *The exchange of rings or other symbols.* The giving of a ring to the woman was originally a symbol of her marital responsibility for household goods. Often today two rings are exchanged, which more appropriately signifies the mutuality of marital responsibility. Other symbolic gifts, such as coins or food, may be exchanged at this point in the service with appropriate changes in the liturgical language.

The rings may be received by the pastor at the same time and held in one hand. The pastor might want to interpret for the couple and the congregation something about what they symbolize. They are tangible expressions of promises made and will serve as reminders of a commitment to mutual faithfulness throughout their life together. The act of exchanging is itself a symbol of the giving and receiving that will characterize their life together from this point on.

As the pastor holds the rings, he or she can say a blessing. It should be clear that the rings are symbolic of the marriage covenant, and the blessing is not so much of the rings as it is of the relationship.

In giving the rings, the bride and groom usually state to each other that they are giving the rings as signs of the covenant they have made. If only one ring is given, the recipient may respond with a statement of acceptance, again stressing that marriage is a mutual relationship. If both are baptized Christians, the traditional Trinitarian formula ("In the name of the Father, and of the Son, and of the Holy Spirit") may be added to their words; if either one is not Christian, then neither should say it.

Where one or both of the parties has been married before and there are children of the previous marriage present, it is appropriate to acknowledge their place in the new family created by this marriage. The bride and groom may share special gifts with those children at this time.

An additional symbol of the union of two lives is the lighting of a single candle by the bride and groom. This becomes an enactment of the wedding vows for all to see. The bride and groom may begin by lighting their separate candles from a Christ-candle, signifying that they are dependent on God's love as revealed in Christ.

The Blessing

This part of the service concludes the entire rite with prayers, the authoritative announcement that the marriage has happened, and the sending of the couple and the congregation on their way.

• *The wedding prayer.* This prayer highlights the Christian nature of the wedding service. Having made their vows, confirming them with the exchange of gifts, the couple now kneels before God to receive God's blessing.

The pastor offers specific petitions for the bride and groom. The prayer asks that the couple be of mutual strength and comfort in their life together, that they live in the unity of God's Spirit, that they learn to share God's forgiveness with one another, and that their mutual love will overflow in love to the world around them.

Prayer should also be included for all in the congregation to be strengthened by God's love and, for those who are married, to have their promises renewed. Freeform prayer can be invited here, asking those in the congregation to share aloud their prayers for the bride and groom. The wedding prayer can end with the Lord's Prayer. It may be sung, but is better said by the whole congregation, because it permits full participation.

• *Announcement of marriage.* The pastor makes a public announcement that the bride and groom are husband and wife by virtue of the vows they have made. The pastor may hold the couple's right hands as a visible way of signifying this union. Another tradition is for the pastor to wrap one side of his or her stole around the couple's joined right hands. The traditional words of Jesus, based on Mark 10:9, may be said either by the pastor or by the congregation in unison.

Because the pastor is also a functionary of the state in marriages, there may be a reference in the announcement that the couple is now married in accord with the laws of the state as well as in the eyes of the church membership. While this is a service of worship, it has legal implications as well.

• *Celebrating the Lord's Supper.* If the Lord's Supper is to be celebrated, it should include the whole congregation. The pastor makes arrangements for this with the governing board of the church and then serves the sacrament as it customarily is done in that church. The full order for the Lord's Supper should be followed, including the invitation to the Lord's Table, the great prayer of thanksgiving, the words of institution, the Communion of the people, and the prayer following Communion. The service may then end with a Communion hymn, such as "Jesus, Thou Joy of Loving Hearts."

• *Charge and benediction.* A final word is given by way of a charge to the couple, followed by a benediction. The charge is a reminder to the couple that they have made their vows before God and are to live out their commitments in the context of their Christian discipleship. The pastor pronounces the benediction, not on the couple alone, but on the entire congregation as well. This sends the people out with God's blessing on commitments made and renewed, with assurance of God's power to enable the people to keep them.

● *Recessional.* The wedding party leaves the sanctuary to the accompaniment of instrumental music, or as the congregation sings a hymn.

—*Donald Wilson Stake*

Resources

Davies, J. G., ed. 1986. The new Westminster dictionary of liturgy and worship. Philadelphia: Westminster.

Office of Worship for the Presbyterian Church (U.S.A.) and the Cumberland Presbyterian Church. 1986. Christian marriage: The worship of God. Philadelphia: Westminster.

Wedding Music

As couples begin to think seriously about their weddings, questions about music inevitably arise. What songs may be sung in a Christian wedding? Must they use one of the traditional marches for the processional and recessional, or is other music available and appropriate? Since a Christian wedding is a sacred service reflecting a scriptural view of love and marriage, how can they convey that sacred theme through music?

Many churches attempt to answer these questions by providing the couple with a written wedding policy. The church organist then consults with the couple well before the wedding to assist them in choosing the finest music possible. Of course, the organist's expertise, repertoire, and individual tastes will influence the choice of wedding music.

Here are some basic criteria for choosing wedding music:

● Appropriateness for a service of worship.

● Church policies, norms, theology, and liturgy.

● Skill level of musicians, including soloists.

● Time of year or period on the church calendar.

● Architecture and acoustics.

● Media of performance and instrument to be used.

● Budget allotment.

Music Selections

● *The processional.* The organ processional needn't be a march but should be festive, majestic, and bright. Church musicians sometimes suggest the following pieces of music as alternatives to the traditional marches:

"Trumpet Voluntary in D (Prince of Denmark's March)," by Jeremiah Clarke.

"Trumpet Tune in D," by Henry Purcell.

"Trumpet Voluntary in D," by John Stanley.

"Hymn to Joy," by Ludwig van Beethoven.

"Canon in D," by Johann Pachelbel.

"Jesu, Joy of Man's Desiring," by J. S. Bach.

"Rigaudon," by Andre Campra.

"Prelude to a *Te Deum*," by Marc Antoine Charpentier.

"Rondeau (*Sinfonies de Fanfares*)," by Jean Joseph Mouret.

Is it appropriate to use "Here Comes the Bride" as the processional? Wagner's own granddaughter said she would be afraid to get married to this traditional "Bridal Chorus," since the marriage of Lohengrin and Elsa didn't last long. Layers of modern emotional attachments, however, have removed this traditional piece far from its original —and rather suspect—connotations.

• *The recessional.* This should be joyful and dignified, perhaps including several pieces of varying degrees of volume. Any processional listed above may also serve as a recessional, with the addition of one or more of these:

"Hornpipe (*Water Music*)," by George F. Handel.

"The Rejoicing (*Fireworks Music*)," by George F. Handel.

"Psalm 19," by Benedetto Marcello.

"Toccata (*Symphony V*)," by Charles-Marie Widor.

• *Congregational hymns.* Hymns that reflect God's love and joy bring an added sense of celebration to the wedding. Do keep in mind the size of the congregation when deciding whether to include hymn singing. Possible places for hymns during the service include: processional or recessional, before or between Scripture readings, as the couple moves to the altar, and during Communion. Here are some suggestions, with tune names in parentheses:

"Praise to the Lord, the Almighty" (*Lobe den Herren*).

"Praise, My Soul, the King of Heaven" (*Lauda anima*).

"Joyful, Joyful, We Adore Thee" (*Hymn to Joy*).

"Now Thank We All Our God" (*Nun danket*).

"The King of Love My Shepherd Is" (*St. Columba*).

"Love Divine, All Loves Excelling (*Hyfrydol* or *Beecher*).

• *Vocal solos.* All solos should be based on sacred texts. Schedule a separate consultation with the soloist, with the music selections subject to final approval by the pastor or organist. Each church should establish, publicize, and abide by a set standard procedures for approving solos.

As we make decisions, however, we must be sensitive to family traditions and people's feelings. Weddings are highly emotional experiences. Each situation is unique and requires special consideration. We want everyone present at the wedding to celebrate through the music the joy that comes from God's love.

—*Joseph M. Galema*

Wedding Innovations

"Can we include the song, 'Take Me Out to the Ball Game' in our wedding?" The question did not catch me off guard. By that time in my ministry, I had been asked to make many changes to the traditional wedding ceremony, from "Can we have the wedding at the rodeo?" to "Can another couple be married at the same time?"

Certainly weddings ought to have a personal—even unique—flavor, because God has made each of us with different tastes. Yet, as soon as we begin to explore the innovative possibilities, we have to match them up against some theological criteria to see if they really are appropriate for a Christian blessing of marriage.

Four Checkpoints

Here are some questions to consider as wedding innovations are suggested:

• *Does the addition glorify God and uphold the grace of the gospel?* Since God initiated marriage, he should at least have center stage. The ceremony is a time to worship him for who he is, what he has created, and what he has called us to do and be in marriage.

• *Does the innovation encourage and uphold the values of Christian family?* God's intent for marriage was to put a man into relationship with a woman so they might support one another, encourage each other, and help one another in the task of raising children. This commitment to family should be a factor in deciding what is to be a part of the wedding service.

• *Does the innovation help us see the God-given uniqueness of the bride and groom?* God, in his creativity, makes each person different, and that uniqueness should be celebrated. If an innovation will help the gathered worshipers reflect upon the special way God created the newly married couple, then it bears consideration.

• *Does the innovation remind us of the value of friends?* Friends are the people God has commanded us to love and serve. The body of Christ exists to give us encouragement and to give us that opportunity to serve. Friendships enhance marriage and can be included in the ceremo-

ny in many appropriate, innovative roles.

These four questions help us decide if an innovation should be included in the wedding service. They can help us determine if, for example, the desired location allows us to draw attention to God's creation, or if the requested music would elevate the kind of family love God intends for marriage (even if the original singer might have had something else in mind).

Hard Calls

I did once marry a couple in the middle of a rodeo arena after the rodeo was over. The reason? Rodeo was their life, and the people in the stands were their friends. I spoke of the glory of God and salvation in Jesus Christ, and raised examples of God's infinite love in all of life. After the kiss, the couple mounted horses and literally rode off into the sunset. God was glorified in the words of the ceremony, the family was encouraged, and friends were given the place of honor.

By the way, "Take Me Out to the Ball Game" did fit as the recessional of a wedding for a professional baseball player. As the bride and groom turned to face their friends, without the groom expecting it, the organist began to play. God was glorified in the beaming smiles that brightened his house.

While Christian weddings need to be Christian in character, they need not be stuffy or mindlessly traditional. The little touches a pastor and bridal couple include in the wedding service can point to the variety of ways people reflect God's glory.

—*Edd Breeden*

The Blessing of a Civil Marriage

The blessing of a civil marriage is a Christian worship service that takes place after a couple has been married by a judge, justice of the peace, or other civil authority. It may follow the civil service by a few days, months, or years. Its purpose is to recognize the meaning of Christian marriage and to ask God's blessing on a couple previously married in a civil service. The blessing ceremony should follow only when a minister is convinced a couple is prepared for Christian marriage and both partners are sincere about wanting God's blessing—and influence—in their marriage.

Preparation Sessions

Ministers will want to lead the couple in a series of interviews to prepare them for understanding Christian marriage. Many ministers provide reading materials on Christian marriage to give couples opportunity to read together as they raise the critical issues of Christlike attitudes and behaviors in the marriage relationship. It is good to survey key Scripture passages dealing with marriage, particularly Paul's words in Ephesians 5:21–6:4.

One of the problems in requiring counseling is a feeling by the couple that since they are already married, they do not need to go through marriage preparation with the minister. Or they may feel that having their marriage blessed is a kind of magic formula that will appease family members and bring their marriage good luck without any effort on their part.

In response ministers can emphasize that marriage is a *process* of growth, and the blessing is a way of asking for God's complete entry into that process. The blessing represents a brand new start. Recommending a marriage-enrichment or marriage-encounter program can also help them in this growth.

Practical Considerations

The blessing ceremony may be as simple or as formal as the couple wants, but the following suggestions are advised:

- *Determine the present marital status first.* Experienced pastors have learned not to take this for granted; they always ask to see a copy of the legal marriage certificate before the ceremony takes place. This check assures that the couple really is married, not merely wanting to appear married to avoid legal commitments. It also determines that the couple is not a same-sex couple seeking to avoid the legal aspects of a civil service.
- *Clarify your purpose.* State at the beginning of the blessing ceremony that the couple has been married earlier by a civil authority. Let the couple decide if they want the time and place of the earlier marriage to be stated.
- *Include the children.* If the couple has children from previous marriages, or from their own, those children should be included in the service. At an appropriate time, you may recognize them, and be sure to include them in the prayer asking God's blessing on the marriage.

• *Ask the bride not to wear a veil.*
Wearing the veil has traditionally
been a symbol of being married for
the first time.

The blessing of a civil service can
have deep meaning for all concerned, especially for family and
friends who were not present at the
civil ceremony. It can be a time of
joy and celebration, as the couple
publicly affirms the importance of
Christian faith in their marriage.
                    —*Perry H. Biddle, Jr.*

The Renewal of Marriage Vows

The renewal of vows most often
takes place as part of an anniversary
celebration. It is appropriate for the
church to provide a liturgical means
to celebrate the anniversary of such
an event because of the deep religious significance of Christian marriage. Preparation and planning for
the celebration provides a rare pastoral opportunity.

Preparation for the Service

It's necessary to meet with the
couple at least once in order to plan
the service. Sometimes the couple
has saved the text of their original
wedding ceremony, but it is best to
develop a new service. Even if elements or wording from the original
are preserved, the couple ought to
make the service meaningful for the
present rather than simply recreate
a quaint ritual from the past.

The service for the renewal of
marriage vows serves a different
purpose from that of the wedding
ceremony. It marks not the beginning but the midpoint of a growing
relationship. The couple remembers
the past as a way of making a new
commitment for the future. Yet,
we'll want to provide much the same
counsel in the planning of the service as is given to a prospective bride
and groom. The theological content
of the meaning of marriage will be
the same.

Structure of the Service

While a service for the renewal of
marriage vows may be simpler than
a full wedding, it follows the same
pattern. The service is appropriately held in the church sanctuary and
may include a celebration of the
Lord's Supper. Some portions must
be changed to stress the renewal aspect of the service, while others remain essentially the same. Here are
items that need to be changed for a
renewal service:

• *Entrance.* The couple enters together after other guests have been
seated. Those who attended them at
their wedding may be present to
stand with them again, or family
members may stand and take places
nearby. A call to worship begins the
service, and a hymn may be sung.

• *Statement on the meaning of
marriage.* The purpose of the service
requires a clear statement, followed
by mention of the qualities of Christian marriage as exemplified in the
divine gifts of love to the couple in
their marriage.

• *Declarations of intent.* The husband and wife declare that in light
of the meaning of marriage just expounded, they wish to renew their

commitments of love to one another.

• *Affirmations of family and friends.* It is particularly poignant to have children of the marriage affirm their parents' love and pledge to support them in their future relationship. Friends' support will be similarly valued.

• *Renewal of vows.* The vows should be reworded to indicate that they are being renewed.

• *Exchange of symbols.* While wedding rings are not exchanged, other gifts might appropriately be given, symbolizing the renewal of commitments. For example, a corsage and boutonniere might be given as signs of renewed commitments, or jewelry with inscriptions appropriate to the occasion.

• *Wedding prayer.* This prayer will include specific thanksgivings for past blessings of love and claim God's promises for the future.

• *Charge and blessing.* Instead of giving an announcement of marriage, the pastor charges the couple to uphold their renewed commitment and follows with the blessing. If the Lord's Supper ensues, the benediction comes afterward.

It is most appropriate to celebrate the renewal of vows as a part of Christian worship. A dinner party or reception following the service then finds its context in a recognition of God's grace as it is seen in the continuing and growing mutual love of the couple.

—*Donald Wilson Stake*

33

Performing Wedding Ceremonies

F̲ew experiences in life compare to the privilege of joining two people in Christian marriage. To be invited to
witness so closely such an intensely moving experience,
to watch a strong man actually quake in excitement as his beloved
walks down the aisle, to see the tear form in a bride's eye as she speaks
her vows to her husband, to be an instrument used in a wonder-full
process of joining two lives into one—this perquisite of pastoring is
truly blessed.

Granted, there are times when we may feel used by a couple—
impersonally "booked," like the limo and the strolling guitar player,
as part of a wedding package. Sometimes we're made to feel like necessary but excess baggage in the gaudy affair. Some couples consume
hours and days of our time, with never a thank-you (much less a decent honorarium) in return. But these times are few, and most often
the sense of being exploited is avoidable.

Participating with a couple in their wedding should be enjoyable,
worthwhile, exciting. It usually can, when we keep a few thoughts in
place regarding our roles and expectations.

Understanding the Pastor's Roles

We juggle several responsibilities simultaneously when we perform wedding ceremonies, and the responsibilities generally relate to
the roles we play, such as:

- *Priest*. Any justice of the peace can perform a ceremony of sorts,

439

but as Christian ministers, we carry the mantle of priestly responsibility, mediating between the mundane and the magnificent. Since Christian weddings take place within the structure of Christian worship, pastors officiating at a wedding also bear the weighty responsibility of leading the people of God in the worship of God. No amount of flowers and rice and pageantry should sway us from conducting the rites of worship rightly.

Prayer and blessing offer us grand opportunities to touch both the bridal couple and the entire gathered congregation with the fatherly love of our heavenly Father. What we join together in the ceremony, God seals in heaven. Where we show love and grace, God is seen to be loving and gracious. When we speak the benediction, God acts in lives.

In the wedding ceremony, we stand in for God. It is a high honor, a solemn responsibility.

• *Master of ceremonies.* The pastor, in many ways, serves as a combination host and master of ceremonies at the church. It is the pastor who gathers the people, speaks the words of welcome, sets the tone for the occasion, and moves everyone through the ceremony.

The ability to mix graciously with the wedding guests, to impart a sense of well-being to critically nervous participants, and to orchestrate a seamless ceremony serves a pastor well. The bride may have the spotlight, but the pastor is the director, on whom the responsibility rests for an excellent service.

• *Ambassador.* Many people attend weddings who wouldn't normally frequent a church. To them, the pastor officiating at the wedding represents every pastor, or even *God*, for that matter. If the pastor is competent, warm, likable, they may reconsider negative stereotypes or consider returning to church.

As pastors, we, for a few brief moments, have the people in sway. We can build bridges or erect walls, depending on how we play the role of ambassador. What we want people to hear and see in us is a credible witness to the gospel, so that they eventually will hear and see the goodness of the gospel.

• *Sergeant at arms.* While the other roles are positive, this one isn't as much fun. Yet somebody has to retain command of the wedding occasion. When we don't do it, into the vacuum step rowdy fraternity brothers, a self-important photographer, nose-out-of-joint relatives, or any number of other parties eminently unqualified for worship leadership.

Most often tactful yet resolute diplomatic efforts win the day. The bottom line: We must maintain the upper hand—be it ever so velvet-gloved—at weddings, or we will regret the abdication of authority when the day dissolves into chaos.

Making Preparations

In the time leading up to the ceremony, our responsibility is to make sure all is prepared. This task divides into three areas of accountability:

• *Making people ready.* Adequate premarital counseling is a foremost responsibility. It's important to know the couple as people, and for them to know and respect us. We probably wouldn't feel right stepping into such a momentous occasion in a couple's life without becoming at least a small part of their lives prior to the ceremony. And they need from counseling all the strength and resources possible to make a go of their marriage.

People also become prepared through the wedding rehearsal. Although some pastors leave the rehearsal for wedding coordinators to conduct, many feel the rehearsal offers not only an opportunity to walk through the choreography of the next day, but also to establish a relationship with the wedding party and to help make the occasion memorable. The rehearsal, often light in tone, helps people to relax and feel confident about their parts in the big ceremony to follow. As we instruct people about the ceremony and direct their movements, we prepare them to participate more fully in worship at the wedding, since they've been through it before and don't have to be apprehensive about any unknowns. Repetition is the best preparation.

• *Making the church ready.* Although most of us don't get caught up in placing flowers and choosing the color of ribbons, we do need to administer the church staff and facilities in such a way that the wedding proceeds without problems. Such factors as doors unlocked when the flowers and attendants arrive, the temperature of the room adjusted appropriately, furnishings properly in place, sound system working flawlessly, and custodians and wedding hostesses trained to work as a team all add to a smooth wedding. Many aspects of a wedding elude our administrative control, but those elements we can manage, we should.

• *Making ourselves ready.* Of course we will want to be certain about our part of the wedding ceremony. Everyone looks to us to know what is supposed to happen, and so we do well to be well-versed in the ceremony and the attendant arrangements. Many pastors have memorized their standard wedding service yet carry a copy with them to avoid the terror of a sudden memory lapse. Even if we don't memorize the service, we'll want to rehearse it thoroughly and repeatedly to add to the poise of our presentation.

But beyond our exterior provisions is the interior preparation needed to produce the proper attitude. For instance, I want to be sure I'm feeling kindly toward the couple. If I feel put off by them, I'm apt to show it in subtle yet telling ways. I also need to block out any sense of being harried or anxious, so that the wedding ceremony itself *feels* like the single most important thing I could be doing at that time. I like to remember the congregation—probably filled with broken, hurting people—and their need for a positive word about love and relationships in Christ.

Our attitude as we enter and conduct the service plays a major role in how it is perceived by the bride and groom and by the rest in attendance. Therefore, a preparatory attitude check is in order.

Managing the Mood

Two overwhelming feelings should dominate the mood of a wedding: solemnity and joy. When either is left out, a wedding suffers.

The Wedding Rehearsal

The rehearsal can be both a mine field of unexpected hazards and a gold mine of opportunity for sharing Christ's love and speaking what God intends for his children.

Setting the Tone

Job number one is setting the tone of the rehearsal and diplomatically establishing the fact that you as the pastor are in control of the proceedings. One way to smooth that process is to take time during the last premarital counseling session to decide about the order of the processional, the seating of the family, and the details of the service. Then at the rehearsal, no one has to be asked for an opinion or to make a decision about these things, thus avoiding time-consuming discussions in which everyone tries to participate in the decision making.

Many pastors find it helpful to commence the rehearsal with everyone seated in the front of the sanctuary for a preliminary talk. They set the tone by describing some of the reasons the couple has chosen to hold their wedding in a church rather than simply have it ratified as a legal contract before a judge.

This preliminary talk can serve many purposes, not the least of which is sharing some of the gospel in a low-key way. Sometimes wedding participants have given little thought to the meaning of a Christian marriage. It may never have occurred to them that God has been the primary matchmaker in the lives of the couple, or that the ceremony is pleasing and important to God, or that God's blessing is the deciding factor in the success of the marriage. Often talking about these deeper meanings has a profound effect on the wedding party.

Doing a Walk-through

After helping the wedding party understand the meaning of what

By solemnity I don't mean sadness or furrowed brow. It is more the sense of grand and weighty majesty. A wedding ceremony—with the sovereign God present, earnest and sobering vows being made, a future being set, and the business of worship to attend to—is no light matter. Something enormous—something very good yet very awesome—is taking place as two people join their lives into one for a lifetime. This is no light and frothy matter, no matter how frilly the dresses; this is consequential business, holy matrimony.

Thus, the very mood of the ceremony needs to reflect the solemnity. We accomplish this in a number of ways. First, people dress up for the occasion. We wear our best, look our best, do our best. We want the visual element to complement the momentous reality of the occasion.

Second, we employ pageantry to gain the feel of circumstance. We don't just saunter into the room; we process, and we do it to grand

---

they are doing, it's time for the walk-through.

One good way to begin is by calling participants out of their seats one at a time and placing each in the spot he or she will stand at the end of the processional. Adhesive dots placed on the floor for each of the attendants to stand on simplifies the process.

When everyone has been thus placed, the minister proceeds through the ceremony from that point. Some explain each step and its meaning along the way. Some speak all the words of the actual ceremony. Others use just enough of the words to make certain the bride and groom recognize them the next day and know the correct responses.

The walk-through should be thorough enough that the wedding party can concentrate on their more important duties of prayer and support for the bridal couple on the following day, rather than worry whether they are walking properly or standing or moving at the right time.

A reminder that you will be there to coach anyone who forgets what to do will help calm their nerves and allow them to participate more fully in the service.

Ending the Rehearsal

Wedding rehearsals often end with several simultaneous conversations as the final details are attended to — candles, flowers, rides to the rehearsal dinner, times of arrival the next day. By that point it's difficult to recapture people's attention. That's why, while one still has the floor for a moment, a final statement in prayer is both appropriate and helpful.

If it has been a good rehearsal, prayer solidifies the bonds among the pastor, the wedding party, and the two families. If tensions remain between the families or between the couple and their parents, prayer provides an opportunity to help people transcend the minor details and focus on the eternal meaning of what soon will happen.

— *Nancy Becker*

and uplifting music. We don't just gather in a cluster, peering over shoulders; we seat people in an orderly fashion, and we stand with the wedding party in a festive array. The choreography of the service signals that this is something out of the ordinary, something worth the extra effort and attention.

Third, and more subtle, is personal bearing. As ministers, even the way we move and stand can impart weight and significance to the assembly. Bearing gets communicated by posture, by the dignity of our movements, by the attentiveness and energy of our presence, by the expressions on our face. As we stand at the head of the church when the ceremony begins, often joined by a nervous groom and flustered groomsmen, we can bestow dignity to the service purely by presence—not a haughty standoffishness or self-importance, but rather a composed, courtly, gracious nobility.

The Role of Wedding Hostess

Who is the wedding hostess? Though the answer may differ in various churches, the hostess is usually a woman in the congregation whom the pastor has recruited (and often, trained) to assist in the execution of well-organized weddings. She carries out her role as a liaison between the church staff and the wedding families and their vendors. It is her duty to see that the wedding proceeds smoothly and in concert with the worshipful, holy nature of a Christian ceremony.

Here are the specific tasks of the wedding hostess, summarized under three categories:

General Tasks

• Meet with the bride and her mother at least three times prior to the wedding.

• Provide a personal orientation, for the bride and her mother, to the church's facilities and wedding guidelines.

• Help the bride complete an application to be married at the church. This application should be formulated in advance to help the hostess secure all the data she will need to fulfill her mandate.

• Set up a meeting with the organist at least thirty days prior to the wedding to determine music requirements and fees.

• Send a letter to the florist and photographer regarding church guidelines within which their services should be rendered.

• Collect appropriate fees prior to the wedding and forward them to the church office for distribution.

Rehearsal Tasks

• Arrive at the church thirty minutes before the rehearsal to assure all arrangements are in order.

• Gather the wedding party at the front of the church to begin the rehearsal on time.

• Assist the pastor in arranging the wedding party members for their places in the ceremony.

Finally, the words we speak will greatly influence people's perception of the import of a wedding. The rich, historic words of ceremonies passed down to us have stood the test of time. They "feel" like a wedding. Yet warm, heart-felt, contemporary words—not exactly casual, yet personal and appropriate—can impart a more modern sense to the service.

More important than the era of the language, given that it is theologically appropriate, is the way it is expressed. Do we just rattle it off as paragraphs to pronounce, or do we speak it from the heart with earnest care? Do we pronounce the words fully and richly for all to hear, or do we throw them out perfunctorily?

While solemnity is appropriate to a high and holy occasion, it can drag us under by its own weight without equally appropriate joy to boost us. Along with birth and conversion, is there anything more

---

- Organize and direct the wedding party at the rear of the church for the second phase of the rehearsal.
- Meet the wedding party in the narthex after the rehearsal to review procedures and answer questions.
- Arrange and rehearse the seating of the parents and be especially alert to the special needs of divorced and remarried parents.
- Notify the organist of the signal to indicate the playing of the wedding march.
- Apprise the wedding party of the location of dressing rooms.
- Instruct the wedding party of any specific church regulations (such as no smoking).
- Be sure the wedding party is aware of the arrival time on the wedding day.

Wedding Tasks

- Arrive at the church at least one hour before the wedding.
- Have a supply of breath mints, hair pins, safety pins, hair brushes or combs, and other items that are frequently forgotten by wedding participants under pressure.

- Speak to the photographer to be sure he or she understands the church's guidelines regarding picture taking during the ceremony.
- Speak to the audio and video operators to be sure they perform their tasks within church guidelines.
- Facilitate the execution of all plans practiced at the rehearsal.
- Check the dressing rooms after the wedding for remaining personal items.
- Organize the reception line or other means of exit for the bridal party.
- If the pastor requests it, be prepared to direct the activities at the reception. (It is best, however, to recruit an assistant hostess for such an activity.)

These guidelines are suggestive, not exhaustive, and are meant to be used as the starting point in a hostess-training program. As pastor and hostess work together through several weddings, they can refine and adapt the role and tasks of the hostess according to their particular needs.

—Howard Eyrich

innately joyful than a wedding? Out of self-giving love—preceded by God's providence and modeled on God's fatherly love—two people are pledging their lives to each other for good. This is a happy occasion!

Joyful, however, does not mean giddy. When rich joy is allowed to degenerate into sloppy sentimentalism or inane frivolity, we trade happiness for silliness. A wedding deserves better. This grand pageant of loving commitment demands nothing less than radiant joy, fueled by the love of God and stoked with tender care. This joy can be communicated through the service in several ways.

Music is a good start. The proper choice of wedding music can lift the occasion to emotional heights. Let the music be grandly joyous. Let it draw from people the feeling that God's love is magnificent, and the love of husband and wife is something to be celebrated.

Faces probably communicate joy better than any other single medium. When we officiate at a wedding, our faces should beam with joy. As we strive to make dignity incarnate, we can also personify warmth and exuberant love. A pastor's smile will draw a terrified bridesmaid or the bride herself down that long, scary aisle purely by charisma. A look of tender happiness can communicate to the bride and groom how much this wedding service means to all the rest of the people gathered in the church.

At the wedding rehearsal, we need to officially grant the wedding party enthusiastic permission to smile during the wedding, because they may not feel it's appropriate. They look to us to set the tone, because, after all, we know the turf. Our warm smiles can spark theirs. (While we encourage smiles, it's usually a good idea to say a few words about pranks and other frivolities, which downgrade joy to hilarity and simply don't fit the dignity of the occasion.)

Joy is also telegraphed through the warmth and excitement of the pastor. When pastors appear semi-bored or perfunctory in their responsibilities, a ceremony can feel listless, inappropriately routine. But if we have an energy level in our voice and bearing, if there is warmth in our eye, everyone picks it up. The message needs to be, "Wow! This is a happy time! Let's take a deep breath and experience it fully."

It shouldn't be hard to impart a sense of joy to a wedding. In most cases it is like adding color to a sunset. Yet the joy we propagate can be a deeper joy, informed by the realities of God's providence and generated by a genuine affection for the people in our care.

Communicating the Christian Nature of Marriage

In performing a marriage, we want to communicate a number of truths:

- *The prevenient love of God.* While human love with all its attractions often has center stage at a wedding, a pastor wanting to lead a *Christian* wedding will work to bring attention to the great Matchmaker who caused all this to happen. From the early Genesis accounts until today, God has been the social director of life. He invented love. He models love. He gives love. And he gives us someone to love specially as a husband or wife.

We need to speak the fact that God precedes all that happens at a wedding ceremony. We must give God his due on a day when flowers and rice have too much ado.

- *The Christian nature of marriage.* Not much of what people know about marriage these days is Christian. In the ceremony we lead, two people aren't getting hitched for as long as it appears reasonably convenient. No, we call two people before the throne of God and into the midst of witnesses most important to them, and we ask them to make vows that will subjugate their own wills to another for the rest of their lives. This aspect of marriage blessed by God cannot be overstated in the wedding service, since it is all but lost in conventional wisdom.

- *The support of the church.* Only two people make vows, but their families and their church—their Christian family—stand behind them. Their marriage is of importance to the church and to the fiber of society itself. We need to impress on the bride and groom that they have a Third Party involved from the start, and they have a supportive cast of pastor and Christian friends surrounding them.

- *The continuity of care.* This marriage service only begins an odyssey. Much unknown territory lies ahead, and couples will experience difficulty and peril. We can let them know in the ceremony that they don't need to travel alone, any more than they are alone at the time of the ceremony itself. Wherever they go, the church is there first.

I make it a point to tell the couple that my marriage ceremonies carry a warranty, and they can bring the marriage in for maintenance at any time. In fact, the church has franchises all over the country, so even if they no longer live nearby, they can use the warranty at any location.

Working Damage Control

Much can go wrong at a wedding ceremony, and the likelihood is that *something* will go wrong. We hope it is minor, and we plan to make sure major problems do not arise. With people well instructed and plans intelligently formed, most weddings can go off without major hitches.

Little problems, however, can actually add texture to a wedding— the hastily pinned tuxedo cuff, the flower girl who sits down halfway down the aisle, the stammered "I do." We even grow to remember such departures fondly in retrospect.

Also, some things a perfectionist pastor might consider a problem don't begin to worry the wedding party. If everybody isn't quite ready at the appointed hour, the world won't stop turning. If no one indicates to the congregation when they should exit and they cut off the groom's parents, the wedding isn't ruined.

Those brides and grooms who want a flawless wedding often plan and work to make it run like clockwork. Those who don't especially care often get as much perfection as they desire. While we pastors want to perform our responsibilities with professional care, we don't need to worry if all is not done perfectly by others. In fact, an over-zealous perfectionism can cast a pall on an otherwise satisfactory wedding.

Some factors of the service do bear our consideration as worship leaders:

• *Dress.* Today we cannot assume the propriety of wedding gowns and bridesmaid's dresses. Early in the premarital counseling and planning stages, we need to bring up discretely the matter of women's apparel appropriate to Christian worship. Most churches discourage low necklines, open backs, and transparent bodices.

• *Alcohol.* We need to set a firm policy about the consumption of alcohol on church property, discuss it with the wedding party, and enforce it when necessary. Many churches outlaw it completely, and pastors often instruct members of the wedding party to refrain from alcohol prior to the service the day of the wedding. We are not out of line if we refuse to allow a person to participate in the ceremony if this reasonable request is violated.

• *Photography.* Churches wanting to maintain the decorum of worship often restrict flash photography during the service. We are wise to instruct photographers to shoot the wedding discretely from the extreme back of the church or the balcony, using ambient light.

When we lead the worship service in which a couple is married, we bear the responsibility of control. Most of the time, there is little call for us to wield raw authority, but sometimes we must do just that in order to maintain a sense of worship and propriety. Law and grace may both enter into our consideration, but where law applies, we are the final arbiters. An uncooperative photographer can be barred from future weddings, or a drunk usher can be refused the opportunity to participate. In fact, we can, when all else fails, refuse to take part in a travesty, and the wedding will not take place. Of course, this is a drastic solution most of us should never have to invoke.

The major factor leading to a smooth and happy wedding is our relationship with the bride and groom. As we get to know them pastorally, as we counsel them prior to the wedding, as we work with them to plan a memorable ceremony, and as we interact with them at the rehearsal and wedding, we are pastoring them. It is such a privilege that the responsibilities pale in comparison.

—*James D. Berkley*

Resources
Biddle, P. 1987. Abingdon marriage manual, rev. ed. Nashville: Abingdon.
Presbyterian Church (U.S.A.). 1986. Christian marriage. Philadelphia: Westminster.
White, J. 1980. Introduction to Christian worship. Nashville: Abingdon.

The Role of Wedding Musicians

In addition to the bride and groom, many people contribute to making the wedding special. Not the least of these support people are the musicians: the organist, the soloists, and the other instrumentalists. Although a bride and groom may have certain ideas about music choices and personnel, they should be encouraged to discuss their wishes not only with the presiding pastor, but also with the organist and other musicians, whose experience in music and in wedding ceremonies will be helpful.

Music Choices

To help the couple think clearly about their choices of music, the officiating pastor needs to emphasize that the wedding ceremony is a sacred service, a time of worship. The service also dedicates a new family that all hope will flourish in the strength of two lives now joined together as one. If this is truly the celebrants' point of view, it will have a profound effect on their choice of worship music for the wedding. Selections from the latest musicals or from the pop charts will be strangely foreign to such a setting.

Church musicians, by encouraging the couple to do a careful study of text and concept, can usually guide them in making choices that lift up genuine love and commitment. By drawing in the church music leaders, it is possible to give the couple a preview of the music, to let them hear melody and text in combination, and, thus, to gain valuable insights as to what is being said and sung in the various musical elements of the service.

Because music frequently comes closest to expressing the deepest and most heartfelt emotions of the wedding day, melody and text should express the couple's devotion to each other and to God in the clearest, most profound terms.

Musician Choices

It is not uncommon, unfortunately, for those who perform wedding music to be friends or relatives of the bride or groom—and that is their *only* qualification for musical performance. The distraction resulting from an unsure voice, a problem in melodic intonation, or other irritating sounds can be embarrassing and painful.

We need to strongly counsel couples to choose talented individuals who may or may not be family members. There are other ways relatives or close friends can serve the bride and groom for such an auspicious occasion. The musicians in any wedding should be those who, by virtue of their training and experience, can add to and complement a joyful and excellent ceremony. An inferior and obviously incompetent musical rendition will only draw attention to a second-rate singer or instrumentalist instead of heightening the drama of a beautiful wedding.

A couple may choose to be married without any music at all, as happens in many strictly secular settings. Or they might naively diminish the highest ideals of relationship and family love with an extremely poor choice of text and music.

But ideally, the best, most spiritually significant music will leave a lasting impression of God's goodness and blessing upon family, friends, and the couple.

—*Howie Stevenson*

34

Handling Wedding Details

Good administration is one characteristic of effective ministry, because time well-spent in planning and record keeping frees pastors to do more ministry in the long run. Since weddings are full of administrative tasks, when we do these tasks well, we have had a greater ministry.

Wedding administration falls into three main categories: taking care of our legal obligations to the state, overseeing the work of the church, and being the professional minister.

Taking Care of Legal Obligations

• *Asking licensing questions.* All states, as well as counties and even some cities, have marriage laws. It is prudent to determine the local laws wherever one plans to perform a wedding. The county clerk or the office of marriage licenses is the first place to inquire. Pastors can call the county office that handles marriage licenses and ask the person in that office if he or she has time to answer some questions. Here are some pertinent questions to ask:

—Who can legally perform a wedding in this county?

—What do I have to do to register with you so I can perform weddings? (In some states, such as California, nothing is required. Other states may require an official copy of ordination papers.)

—Would you explain to me the licensing process, such as what the bride and groom need to do, how much it costs, and how long the license remains effective? (There is a time limit on most licenses within which the wedding must take place.)

—Do you have more than one type of license? Could you please explain the differences to me? (In my county, one of the two types of license requires blood tests and witnesses; the other doesn't.)

—After the ceremony is over, who is responsible to mail the license, the couple or the pastor? How many days before this needs to be done?

—How do people obtain an official copy of their license after the wedding? How much does this cost?

A marriage license is a legal document and thus cannot have any corrections on it, so it is important to fill it out carefully and completely. It's not pleasant to make mistakes by rushing and then have to go to the clerk's office to file another copy, paying the costs to do so.

• *Knowing licensing tasks.* The pastor functions as a servant of the state in this matter and is responsible to carry out the marriage and licensing process in keeping with the laws—which need to be known. The license needs to be obtained by the couple before a ceremony can be performed since it signifies clearance from the state that the two people are of age and legal to marry, according to the state. A license sets the pastor free from concerns about the legality of the marriage.

The license should be given to the pastor before the wedding can be performed. Savvy pastors encourage the couple to bring it to the rehearsal along with the various fees, so the administrative tasks can be taken care of before the wedding day.

Since a license requires meticulous attention, it's wise to fill it out ahead of the wedding service. Although the responsibility can be delegated, many pastors like to handle this task personally, making a copy for their own records.

Sometimes a decorative copy of the marriage license is included in the packet from the state. Couples enjoy a filled-in copy as a keepsake, although these are not official documents. If someone in the church writes in calligraphy, it is a nice touch to fill out the decorative copy in such an ornamental style.

Typically the best man and the maid of honor sign the licenses as witnesses. In some states the bride and groom also must sign the license, and in other states this is handled at the clerk's office.

Meeting the county filing requirements means not letting the license get lost on one's desk, since some states expect the document to be returned within four days of the ceremony. It also is important for pastors to keep a record of the wedding, with names, date, and license number to guard against the nuisance of a license being lost in the mail. This may not be known for many years—until the couple goes to the clerk and asks for an official copy of the license. At that point, the county office does not know whether the license was used or just discarded. In these cases, the pastor may be called in to sign an affidavit that the marriage took place between these two people on a particular date.

Overseeing the Work of the Church

● *Setting official policies.* Many pastors develop specific wedding policies to oversee the difficult weddings or to know how to answer people when they ask about variations in the services provided. If weddings are rare, the trouble of putting together a wedding manual may not be necessary. If, however, a pastor conducts several weddings a year, a written wedding policy is advisable.

To write one, it's wise first to consult with the people who will be involved in the wedding process: the worship committee, musicians, secretary, custodian, wedding coordinator, other staff pastors, and any church group that might be willing to cater receptions, if asked. Place in writing all things that might be a question or concern. From there a rough draft can be made available for group revision. Since a policy rarely answers all the questions and concerns that arise, churches can expect to revise even the best policies on a regular basis.

Copies of the policy should be made for each group member and for future wedding couples to receive at the onset of counseling and planning. Often the secretary can hand out a copy at the first contact, or the pastor gives it out at the initial interview.

Here are some questions couples often ask, which a policy statement will need to address:

—"Do you perform weddings for nonmembers or just for members of your congregation?" If pastors are willing to perform nonmember weddings, are there any special considerations? (For example, nonmembers may pay more and be required to use a designated pastor).

—"What is the meaning of marriage to you and your denomination?" Clearly state your theology so the couple knows up front what they can expect.

—"Do you require counseling before marriage, and how many sessions?" Who is responsible for setting up the sessions, you or them? What consequences will there be if they don't come to the sessions?

—"Do you provide a wedding coordinator?" Should the coordinator (or hostess) be paid by the church or by the couple—or at all? What service can the coordinator offer the couple, and what are the limits of the coordinator's job description? For instance, if a couple expects the coordinator to pour tea at the reception, is this part of the responsibilities?

—"Do you have limits on what kind of music may be played at the wedding?" Churches should state their answer to this clearly. Some churches even have a list of acceptable songs to choose from, vocal and instrumental. Some churches also prefer to control who can play the organ or piano.

—"What are your rules for the use of flowers?" For example: Is it okay for the flower girl to sprinkle rose petals on the floor in front of the bride? Who is going to clean up? Is the wedding party expected to leave the flowers for the Sunday worship service? Often they will, and it's kind to acknowledge in the bulletin where the flowers came from.

—"Will there be limitations placed on the photographer?" Picture-taking, either by a professional or a friend, needs to have a certain amount of control. Do you have a problem with people taking pictures during the service? Do you have a concern about a photographer walking in front of guests during the service? Rules need to be clear from the start.

—"What are your guidelines for use of candles and other decorations?" Plans for use of candles, bows, and runners need to be monitored. Do you mind if the candles drip wax on your carpet? Is it okay

Working with Photographers and Florists

Pastor, photographer, and florist each have goals and expectations for the wedding ceremony. Sometimes these goals clash. The pastor and the church board can smooth the way by developing a clear policy that promotes the goals of each of these professionals as they work together. Here are some items to consider in developing such a policy:

Setting the Policy

• *For photographers.* Ministers generally agree that photography should not distract the participants from concentrating on the ceremony. A policy prohibiting flash pictures during the ceremony is common. Most churches permit the photographer to take flash pictures of the members of the wedding party as they walk down the aisle, but then ask that the photographer stop taking pictures until after the benediction. Some allow the photographer to take nonflash pictures during the

ceremony from the back of the sanctuary or the balcony.

Since an aggressive video photographer can be very distracting, the church policy should direct where videocameras can be set up and whether operators may move about during the ceremony. Most ministers prefer that the video camera be stationed in one inconspicuous spot, though some churches allow an unattended, stationary video recorder in or near the chancel.

• *For florists.* What might damage the sanctuary furnishings? Most churches allow attachments such as ribbons or threads to hold decorations in place but do not permit tape or wire, which could damage the finish of wooden pews.

The time of day when the florist can gain entry to the church should be agreed upon in advance. If there is a custodian or a wedding hostess, your policy should give instructions on how to arrange with them for unlocking church doors.

with you if the people use tape to attach bows to the pews? What about nails?

—"Can the wedding party bring a bottle of wine into the church building while they are dressing?" What is your recourse if you find this to be the case even after you have stated a policy against it?

—"What will be the role of the pastor?" Sometimes couples want to use the building and import their pastor or friend to perform the wedding ceremony itself. Is this allowed? Who will be in charge of the building if the pastor is not present? If one of the pastors of the church has to participate, how will that person feel about being a token minister at a wedding where he or she knows no one?

—"Will we be charged for the services of the custodian?" Who pays—the church or the couple? How much? Will this be required for

---

Aisle runners are usually a nuisance to install and often become rumpled as they are used. But if flower petals are to be dropped and then walked upon, a church might want to use the aisle runner as protection for the carpet. When there is to be an aisle runner, make it clear that the florist installs it and prepares it for unfurling, rather than leaving that job—and a handful of straight pins—to the pastor.

Who is in charge of the flowers after the ceremony? Sometimes the florist moves the flowers to the reception. Sometimes the family decides to leave them for the next day's worship service. This should be determined in advance to prevent confusion and hurt feelings.

Some other issues to consider: Does the florist supply the candles? Can artificial arrangements be used? Can flowers be put in front of the cross, or on the Communion table?

Communicating the Policy

Many churches develop a printed statement of the church's expecta-tions of photographers and florists to give to bridal couples. But even the wedding guests may need to be informed about the policy to prevent amateur photographers among them from snapping flash pictures during the ceremony.

A portable sign in the narthex—perhaps done in needlepoint or calligraphy—can announce: THE BRIDE AND GROOM REQUEST THAT THERE BE NO FLASH PHOTOGRAPHS DURING THE CEREMONY.

For clear communication, meet with the florist and the photographer as they arrive at the rehearsal or as early as possible on the wedding day. They are professionals and usually are easy to work with. Yet, in dealing with those few who are uncooperative, many pastors have found it helpful to voice the reminder that they have many opportunities during the year to recommend (or *not* recommend) florists and photographers to bridal couples! That thought alone can quickly douse the flames of conflict and secure surprising cooperation.

—*Nancy D. Becker*

every wedding? What services will it include?

—"What are the total costs involved?" A policy should lay out all the costs so the couple can see them before they make any commitment. What is the cost for the building? Will a reception at the church cost more? Will there be a difference for a member or a nonmember? Who pays the wedding coordinator, the organist, and the soloist—and how much? Also included might be the expected honorarium for the pastor, which will probably be different for members and nonmembers. If a church group is willing to cater the reception, the policy should include what they offer, along with the various prices.

• *Keeping official church records.* Some denominations require that specific marriage records be kept by ministers. It may be as simple as keeping a copy of completed marriage licenses in a file, or writing names, date, and license number in a permanent record book.

Since honorariums are considered by the irs to be income, it is

---

Rehearsal Dinners and Receptions

If "weddings are magnets for mishap," as writer Robert Fulgham says, then rehearsal dinners are mine fields for mayhem. When else does someone willingly invite a dozen or more people—many of whom often don't know each other—to spend several high-tension hours together?

We may want to politely duck out of as many of these occasions as we can, but actually they can be fruitful opportunities to minister.

Ministering Socially

True ministry can happen at wedding occasions; we simply need to seize the opportunities. For instance, at one rehearsal dinner I was seated next to a distant cousin of the groom and told: "Reverend, Mike needs all the help he can get. Try to talk some sense into him, will ya?" With an introduction like that, the conversation could only go downhill, or so I thought. Actually, Mike was a free-spirited guy who had a wonderful story to tell, but his family hadn't listened. I did, and with a few leading questions, I began to build a bridge to Mike.

As we capitalize on opportunities like these, we may begin to appreciate rehearsal dinners and wedding receptions as occasions for ministry. When else does someone like Mike drift into church? Talking with the Mikes of the world can give us a wonderful chance to show non-churched people that pastors are okay kinds of people and churches may have some value after all.

Conversation Guidelines

From gospel stories about Jesus being "at table," we can learn from his example:

• *Jesus, even as a guest, adopted the role of host.* In Luke 7:36–50, Jesus was invited to dinner with the

important for pastors to keep records of wedding honorariums. This money usually is reported on Form 1040 Schedule C under business income.

● *Determining fair payment for the use of church facilities.* Deciding on the amount to charge for the building requires consideration of at least two factors: First, what do other churches in town charge? Second, what does it actually cost the church per hour to open the building and operate utilities at full capacity? Because churches are not profit-making corporations, they run the risk of being questioned if they begin to operate a money-making business through facilities that are tax exempt for the purposes of worship. Even though churches consider weddings worship, that may not be true in the eyes of the state.

A reception at the church usually requires an additional fee to pay the cost of extended use of the facilities. (Churches need to state clear-

---

Pharisees. Plenty of hidden agendas were at work, and yet Jesus kept focused on why he was there. That's an important priority. We may be at wedding festivities by invitation, but in truth we are there to share the love of God with whomever we happen to meet.

One way to do that well is to play the host by telling ourselves that we must help make those around us feel comfortable. We step out of the role of a guest looking to be served and become—as hosts—people sensitive to the needs of others.

● *Jesus typically put aside his agenda.* Another table account comes from Luke 19, the story of Zacchaeus. No doubt Zacchaeus was nervous inviting Jesus to his home. Would Jesus berate him, condemn him, scold him for his cheating ways? Luke writes, "Zacchaeus received Jesus joyfully." Why? Because Jesus put aside his own agenda to really hear the troubled little man. Jesus met Zacchaeus on his own turf and disarmed him with love. Jesus didn't ask him to immediate-

ly repent; instead, he befriended the lonely man, who, in turn, adjusted his lifestyle.

● *Jesus rarely asked a question that could be answered yes or no.* Rather than asking, "Do you live near here?" we can ask, "Where do you live?" Or rather than "Are you a friend of the groom?" ask, "How long have you known the bride or the groom?" Rather than asking, "Do you go to church?" ask, "Where do you do most of your socializing?" Asking about where people fellowship allows them to say they are members of a nonchristian group.

After a minute or two of this kind of conversation, we've received enough information to direct the conversation toward the other person, and we've shared enough about ourselves to make him or her feel comfortable. At wedding receptions and rehearsal dinners, there is no need to get into heavy theological discussions. These are great opportunities to build a bridge, not construct a wall.

—Don Maddox

ly the policy on the consumption of alcohol on church premises. Many churches are comfortable with people finding other places for their reception because of a no-alcohol policy.)

Serving Professionally

● *Overseeing the wedding details.* The following things need to be taken care of in order for the wedding to go smoothly. Depending upon the size of the church and the number of staff, these tasks may be divided among pastor, secretary, wedding coordinator, and custodian. Here is a suggested breakdown of tasks for the three supporting staff members involved, assuming some churches may need to divide the responsibilities among fewer people:

—Secretary:

1. Sets up the initial interview with the pastor.

2. Marks the date on the church calendar to avoid any double bookings or conflicts in building use.

3. Notifies the wedding coordinator and others of the planned wedding date.

4. Collects a deposit and the information form, if applicable. Sends copies of the information form to others involved.

5. Stocks copies of the church policy for distribution as needed.

6. Makes sure the church receives all payments.

—Wedding Coordinator:

1. Talks over all arrangements with the bride before the wedding, answering questions about colors, flowers, policies, what the church has available, and what needs to be rented.

2. Specifies when to open the building on the day of the wedding for flowers, for the bride to dress, and for photographs.

3. Notifies the organist as to the date and time of the rehearsal and the wedding.

4. Instructs the wedding party at the rehearsal on the details of the wedding ceremony, especially if the pastor is not present. The coordinator also helps the candlelighters, ushers, flower girl, and ring bearer understand their parts in the wedding service.

5. Arranges for the building to be opened for flowers, decorations, photos, and the wedding party on the day of the wedding. If needed, the coordinator will find the safety pins, iron, mirrors, and other items that are required. The coordinator oversees the dressing, the arrangements in the sanctuary, the ushering, and the entrance of the bridesmaids and the bride herself.

—Custodian:

1. Cleans up the facility in preparation for the wedding.

2. Opens the doors at the stated time.

3. Makes sure the furniture is in the proper place in the sanctuary,

including a kneeling bench and candelabra. If the church uses colored paraments, white is the appropriate color for a wedding day. The custodian usually changes these unless that job is specifically given to someone else.

4. Cleans the facility after the wedding, preparing the sanctuary and other rooms for the next event, typically Sunday worship.

5. Locks the church building when all have left.

● *Accepting honoraria.* "Receive for services, $25"—so reads the Monopoly card, and so goes the payment pastors receive for weddings. People know little more of what to expect without being told. Therefore, to avoid misunderstandings, it's important for pastors to determine how much they think they should receive for a wedding and state it clearly, without apologizing for it. The IRS, after all, requires pastors to claim it as income on tax returns.

The amount ought to be discussed with the church board for the sake of understanding. Some churches publish the expected honorarium as part of the official wedding policy. The amount for members often is substantially lower that nonmembers, although membership doesn't necessarily entitle people to pay nothing.

Pastors have a tendency to try to be loving and thus avoid questions about an honorarium. Consequently, they at times feel used and end up resentful. It's better to proclaim the love and grace of God in our concern for couples, our words to them and others, and the service we perform for them. The message of the gospel is free, but the performance of a wedding is work, no matter how much fun it is.

● *Administrating well.* If we watch the details early on, make it clear up front what we expect from the couple, and clearly state what they can expect from us, we will find ourselves much freer to minister to them and their friends. Ministry, after all, is the goal of our good administration.

—Edd Breeden

Part VII

Funerals

Death.

Final. Irrevocable. Unchangeable.

It demands resolute, powerful assurances that only Christianity offers and which pastors are particularly well-placed to provide. At a time of death, the survivors need a pastor, perhaps as strongly as at any other point of life.

The need is deep and varied. Initial shock calls for care. Difficult decisions require counsel. Funeral services demand planning. Grief must be worked through. The pieces of life need careful reassembling and repair. And there are personalities to work with: the mourning family, of course, but also funeral directors, cemetery personnel, and musicians.

While it's nice to be needed, it's even better to be able to provide for the need with a quiet confidence born of informed experience. Pastors accumulate that experience over years by doing, and then observing the lessons learned from that doing. Yet one benefit of collegial ministry is that pastors can learn from one another. In the following pages, pastors offer their examined practice of funeral ministry, that all might better honor the dead, care for the living, and point toward the immortal.

35

The Purpose of Funerals

C hristians view death as a mystery that cannot be fully comprehended. Yet, the Christian memorial service, with its biblical underpinnings, can render significant hope, comfort, and support to those who grieve. The funeral service, perhaps more than any other Christian function, calls for deep levels of wisdom and caring from both minister and congregation.

Reasons for Funeral Services

Why should there be a funeral? Most Christian ministers view the funeral in terms of the comfort and peace it brings the survivors. They also see it as a ceremony emphasizing the hope of a future life. The funeral service has several specific purposes, directed primarily to the living:

• *To remember the deceased with appreciation.* For family and friends, the funeral is a celebration of the life that has been lived among them. Fifty years ago seminary theological departments advocated formal, standardized funeral services and discouraged eulogies or characterizations of the deceased. The minister was urged to use the denomination's worship book or funeral manual with prescribed Scriptures, prayers, and hymns, and a brief meditation. Personal references to the deceased were clearly discouraged.

Today, however, the move is to make the service more personal. When it is appropriate, many ministers desire to voice appreciation for the person's life, celebrating areas of Christian faithfulness and characterizing the person's personality.

• *To demonstrate loving support to the living.* Members of the entire clan and cherished friends come together to convey love, understanding, and sympathy to those closely affected by the death. Those in attendance say, "We belong to one family of God. Your loss is our loss. Your grief is our grief. We stand beside you with loving concern. We promise our support and love. We want to help you cope."

The old Greeks, in whose language our New Testament was written, discovered that if one really cared about the circumstances of another, he or she might enter vicariously into that person's experience. They called this idea *sympathos*, meaning "with suffering," from which comes our word *sympathy*. By means of sympathy we enter into the minds and hearts of those who suffer, to share their sorrow.

• *To provide a means of healing.* The grief syndrome inevitably takes people emotionally through the journey of disbelief, rebellion, numbness, anger, loneliness, hostility, and guilt, finally moving to acceptance and assimilation. For some, the healing is more rapid than for others. Not always are the feelings in the same sequence. Nevertheless, the process has to be faced, each emotion dealt with satisfactorily. Though the funeral service highlights the stark reality of death, it can work as an antidote to the frayed nerves, emptiness, and loneliness immediately experienced.

The funeral service includes biblical assurances, pastoral prayers for forgiveness, and petitions and intercessions for strength. The Holy Spirit, the divine Comforter, brings mourners the "peace of God, which transcends all understanding" (Phil. 4:7). There is healing in faith, hope, and love.

• *To celebrate and reaffirm faith in God and eternal life.* The Christian funeral calls us to trust in the divine wisdom that brought human life into existence and whose love will guide and provide its future destiny. A man whose son died of cancer said, "I do not know how people can face death without God. I know I could not." As the Psalmist testified, "God is our refuge and strength, an ever-present help in trouble. Therefore we will not fear" (Ps. 46:1–2a). The funeral service affirms God's everlastingness, his invisible friendship, his love and forgiveness, his empathy, assurance, and power.

• *To respectfully dispose of the body.* This body once contained a loved human being. The physical body gave expression to a human spirit through the voice, the eyes, the gestures. The body has served its sacramental purpose, being a temple of God's Spirit, housing the personality of the individual, which in the life to come receives a new, appropriate means of expression and relationship. The funeral will certainly emphasize that the remains are not the person; they are like the cocoon from which a butterfly emerges. Nevertheless, as the outward, visible sign of the personality, the body is disposed of with dignity and reverence.

Historical Roots

It is said that of all the "animals" of earth, only the human being buries its dead. Historically, people disposed of dead bodies through four methods that relate to the components of ancient chemistry: air, water, fire, and earth. Customs have varied with different cultures and times, from burial at sea to cremation to disposal by air (the Zoroastrians, for instance, lay the corpse in a place where birds of prey strip the bones clean).

● *Semitic customs during Old Testament times.* Both Jews and Arabs rejected the elaborate, tomb-centered, pyramid burials of the Egyptians. They disapproved of giving offerings to the dead and consulting with the spirits (see Deut. 18:11; 26:14). They also disapproved of cremation. Abraham was the first in the biblical record to arrange for a corpse disposal. After the death of his wife Sarah, he purchased the cave of Machpelah so he could bury her body (Gen. 23). Burial was immediate because of the hot climate, and there was no embalming.

The Semitic people did demand decent and respectful burial. Yet it was simple, with no coffin or casket, the body being placed in an unpretentious grave or cave. A competent funeral orator usually delivered a eulogy at the home, at the graveside, or while a procession bore the body to the grave. A funeral feast probably was held at the tomb on the day of burial.

The ancient Israelite burial was characterized by highly emotional mourning lasting for a week or so. Lamentation included tearing clothes, disfiguring faces, wearing sackcloth garments, shaving the head, and covering it with ashes or dust. Sometimes families employed professional mourners who would carry out these expressions of grief on their behalf.

● *Customs during New Testament times.* Jewish customs remained virtually unchanged throughout New Testament times. Although some Jews were coming to believe in an afterlife and in resurrection, there is little to indicate this in the traditional Jewish burial ceremony. (The Sadducees rejected belief in personal immortality. The Pharisees, however, did believe in some form of a resurrection doctrine.)

The Greeks believed in the immortality of the soul. They both buried and cremated their dead, though cremation was most common. According to Plato, the human was not only a body (*soma*) but also a spirit (*pneuma*). The spirit, by its very nature, was thought to be indestructible by the forces that kill the body. After death the soul would therefore live apart from the body.

Wealthy Romans typically received cremation, while commoners were buried in graves and tombs. Monuments and markers often bore epitaphs, such as: "I was, I am not, I do not care" and "What I have eaten and what I have drunk is all that belongs to me." Such are typical expressions of the materialism, hedonism, and cynicism that prevailed in the ancient Roman empire. The flippant words convey disbelief in a beyond-the-grave existence.

Then Jesus came! He brought the glory of a redemptive interpretation of death and the grave. Death is a painful human experience that will one day be wiped out, but it is not the extinction of personality or the expiration of all the value of a person. It is the passing from this domain into a continuing existence of joy and growth. Jesus' own Resurrection was God's vindication and assurance of these truths to all who would believe. Thus, the Christian contribution was utterly different from the vague mysticism of the Greeks, the hopeless cynicism of the Romans, and the confusion of the Jews. It gave a new meaning to death. The funeral lost its usual sadness and gloom, and became a celebration of entrance into an eternal dwelling place (John 14).

During the early centuries of Christianity, the mode of Jesus' burial was the standard for church members. The value of the body after death had, in some ways, been reverently diminished. Christians continued the Jewish customs of simplicity in corpse preparation, modest display, and ordinary burial places.

The modern American funeral. The unpretentious European methods for body disposal were adopted in North America from colonial times until the latter part of the nineteenth century. At that time, changes in treatment of the corpse and other funeral practices became uniquely American.

The present-day funeral customs in the United States were influenced by the popularization of new embalming techniques (begun by Thomas Holmes during the Civil War) and by the preserving of President Lincoln's body for three weeks of viewing. Other important developments sparked change: rectangular, appealingly decorated caskets made of metal and wood replaced the bare, wooden coffin; the name *undertaker* changed to *funeral director;* the National Funeral Director's Association organized in the 1880s. Increased cosmetic skills in restoring youthful contours, concealing disfigurements, and restoring dead corpses to an almost lifelike natural look refined American care for the deceased.

The downside is that all of this, including beautifully landscaped cemeteries, vaults to encase and seal the casket, and expensive limousines for the service, have added dramatically to the cost of American funerals. The bereaved can succumb to the idea that their love for the deceased is gauged by the elaborateness of the funeral provided.

Specifically Christian traditions and rituals vary, but it is customary to have a relatively brief service, usually not exceeding 20 minutes. When the funeral is held in the church, some ministers use an abbreviated format of a regular Sunday worship service, with congregational singing and choral music (which extends the time somewhat). Black churches customarily have a longer service, with multiple prayers, several eulogies, much singing, and a long funeral oration.

The committal service held at the place of interment is customarily brief in the Protestant tradition.

Theology and the Funeral

Job, in the biblical book that bears his name, asks the question that has haunted people from time immemorial: "If a man dies, will he live again?" (Job 14:14). Christianity has responded with a resounding *yes!* The basic consolation for those in bereavement is belief in eternal life and in the continuity of human personality.

• *Christian belief is rooted in the historic Resurrection of Jesus.* On the third day after death, Jesus was raised by the power of God. This dramatic, compelling, and revolutionary occurrence was verified by postmortem witnesses on eleven different occasions and by five hundred people on one particular day. It was Jesus' Resurrection in a glorified body that was recognizable and relational. Paul, the greatest interpreter of the Christian faith, effectively discounted the various attempts to explain away the empty tomb and testified that Jesus appeared to him personally.

The early Christians did not regard the Resurrection as just an intriguing postscript to Jesus' life; it was the very foundation for their faith. It was central to the gospel. "If Christ has not been raised," said Paul, "our preaching is useless and so is your faith" (1 Cor. 15:14). Paul connects Jesus' Resurrection to the general resurrection of Christians, those who have been "raised with Christ" (Col. 3:1). Christ is "the firstfruits of those who have fallen asleep" (1 Cor. 15:20), and he "will transform our lowly bodies so that they will be like his glorious body" (Phil. 3:21). Jesus himself said, "I am the resurrection and the life. He who believes in me will live, even though he dies; and whoever lives and believes in me will never die" (John 11:25–26a). He also announced, "Because I live, you also will live" (John 14:19b).

• *Christian belief emphasizes resurrection rather than immortality.* Christians often speak about "the immortality of the soul," which was a Greek Platonic concept. Some may even believe that beyond death only some vague spiritual aspect of our nature survives in a primarily unconscious state. Yet the prospect of losing self-consciousness and individuality seems to war with our deepest sentiments about the nature of human beings.

Fortunately, Christianity teaches—and verifies through the experience of Jesus—resurrection! This bodily resurrection is more than the immortality of the Greeks. It affirms the continuity of personal, conscious life. It affirms a biblical continuity of body and spirit. It affirms that we will recognize people and extend our acquaintances and experiences beyond the grave. We will be *ourselves* in the life to come even more than we are now.

Contemporary Funeral Innovations

• *Memorial services.* The memorial service is the major innovation to the traditional funeral. Every funeral is a memorial service in a sense, but not every memorial service is a funeral. The distinction is this: In the memorial service, a casket is not present. The body has already been disposed of in burial or cremation, privately, with family and close friends. After interment, the memorial service celebrates the life that was lived.

Cremation or Burial?

Two Christian leaders lose a mother in death, but each chooses a different means of disposal of the body. One opts for cremation, the other for burial. The choices—both by pastors—illustrate how Christians hold different opinions on this delicate issue.

While most people prefer burial, there has been a marked increase in cremations. Religious groups that previously opposed cremation because of its pagan associations now tolerate it within limits. Also, the geographical separation of families in a mobile society adds further shipment costs to the already-high costs of burials, increasing the number of cremations.

This trend raises questions for Christian leaders as they minister to the bereaved: Is burial the only biblical option for a Christian? Isn't cremation a more ecological and less costly way to dispose of the body? What do Scripture and Christian tradition say?

Bible and Tradition

The Bible is blurry at best on burial versus cremation. The Old Testament nowhere explicitly forbids cremation. In Amos 2:1, judgment is proclaimed against Moab for burning the body of the king, but this is given in the context of a series of sins. The bodies of King Saul and his sons (1 Sam. 31) were cremated after their deaths, although this seems to be an isolated case. Essentially, the Old Testament is silent on funerals, although it is clear the Israelites generally buried their dead.

The New Testament focuses attention on attitudes toward death and the promise of eternal life. In 1 Corinthians 13:3, the Apostle mentions giving his body to the flames, but this seems to be a reference to martyrdom rather than to cremation. Thus, following Hebrew tradition, the early church generally adopted burial as the accepted Chris-

For the funeral service, the casket with the corpse is present for the service, followed by the procession to the burial place and the committal service. Or cremation may follow days or weeks later. Increasing numbers of Protestant churches use the memorial service, preserving most of the elements of the funeral service but without the casket present.

- *Contemporary music and readings.* Some churches use contemporary innovations in funerals, especially for youth, reflecting the cultural tastes of their peers. Such services often use contemporary music, played on musical instruments other than the organ or piano. The service may include contemporary religious songs, selected readings from modern poets and writers, and group sharing of memories and feelings about the deceased.

- *Night services.* Some memorial and funeral services are now held

---

tian method. This was based on the doctrine of the Resurrection and reflected the fact that Jesus' body was buried. Since many early church writers and leaders saw cremation as an outgrowth of pagan ritual, they considered it incompatible with Christian faith.

Pros and Cons

Persecutors of the church often had the bodies of martyrs burned and their ashes scattered in the wind or on a river in an effort to discourage belief in the Resurrection. Some theologians thus reason that since God will resurrect the cremated bodies of martyrs, he will do the same for believers choosing to be cremated. Those favoring cremation also emphasize that a buried body decomposes to its base elements, and that cremation only hastens what is an inevitable process.

In modern society, cremation has the advantage of being more economical. The average cost for burial runs four to five times the cost of cremation, which brings up concern

for stewardship. Cremation also saves space, an added consideration in light of the scarcity of land, especially in urban areas. In addition, some psychologists argue that a clean incineration of a corpse is therapeutic for the mourners because it emphasizes separation rather than the illusion that the deceased is "just sleeping."

On the other hand, burial has been and still is the accepted practice of the majority of Christians. For many, it better symbolizes the hope of resurrection and the promise of eternal life. In addition, burial acknowledges the sanctity of the human body and follows the example of how Christ's body was handled after his death (Matt. 27:58–59).

The best course in considering the disposition of the body is to encourage sensible choices made according to biblical principles. It seems best that the decision be made by the family based on the desires of the deceased and the beliefs and traditions of the family, as well as the costs involved.

—*Scott Wenig*

at night. This allows working friends with demanding work schedules to attend more easily. In such cases a private burial service would be conducted during the daytime hours.

• *Colorful dress.* Black was once considered mandatory for mourners and clergy. Today, family and friends may choose to wear bright, colorful, cheerful clothes to emphasize the celebration of a life lived. Religious leaders may vest themselves in white or in suits other than black, to symbolize the joy of resurrection.

• *Family participation.* In some cases members of the family serve as pallbearers, give short tributes, read Scriptures, or offer vocal music. Of course, ministers must exercise caution in having immediate family members participate, because the emotional strain may cause loss of composure and make it more difficult for everyone.

• *Graveside only.* Some people prefer only a committal service for their dead. Perhaps the deceased has outlived his or her contemporaries, and there are few relatives or friends able to attend a funeral. Or a long-lingering illness and confinement has put the person out of social circulation. Sometimes family and friends are far removed, and deep friendships have not been made. Perhaps the burial is in a former place of residence, where one is no longer widely known. Some people may be quite alone, perhaps have no children and few living relatives. Also, having a graveside-only service can be a way to save money, which, if the death followed a prolonged sickness, may be important.

• *De-emphasis of elaborate floral displays.* Granted the importance of floral gifts by friends, there is a distinct trend toward giving equivalent memorial gifts in honor of the deceased to charities designated by the family. The deceased's family then receives notification of the gift and donor. This can be a wise stewardship consideration when one remembers how temporal flowers are. The family will designate its favorite charities.

—*James Christensen*

Resources

Christensen, J. 1967. A complete funeral manual. Old Tappan, N.J.: Revell.

Engram, S. 1990. Mortal matters. Kansas City, Mo.: Andrews & McMeel.

Grollman, E. 1974. Concerning death: A practical guide for the living. Boston: Beacon.

Leca, A. 1976. The Egyptian way of death. Garden City, N.Y.: Doubleday.

Manning, D. 1985. Comforting those who grieve. San Francisco: Harper & Row.

Mitford, J. 1963. The American way of death. New York: Simon & Schuster.

Phipps, W. 1987. Death: Confronting the reality. Atlanta: John Knox.

36

Planning Funeral Services

In Ecclesiastes the venerable preacher opined that "the day of death [is] better than the day of birth" and it is "better to go to a house of mourning than go to a house of feasting" (Eccles. 7:1–2). I hope someday to ask Solomon about his logic. Perhaps he felt compelled to make us swallow the indigestible fact of our mortality. Yet, few would question Solomon's sagacity on this point: "There is a time for every matter under the sun."

Though a minister may have already established certain procedures for responding to the time of mourning, crucial questions still inevitably arise in his or her mind when the death call comes. Let's consider some of them.

Do I Know My Pastoral Goals?

Here are some general tasks to keep in mind as we approach funeral planning and enter into relationship with those who mourn:

• *Acknowledge God's presence and offer praise.* A funeral service (the body is present) or a memorial service (the body is not present) is essentially a worship service. Some people may not feel like worshiping in the presence of death, but true worship acknowledges the rule of God in every event in life, even death. David eulogized Saul and Jonathan in 2 Samuel 1:17ff, extolling their extraordinary exploits, versifying his profound love, and inviting others to weep. David taught his men this tribute, possibly setting it to music. But examine David's eulogy for what it lacks: worship. We certainly can't fault him, because he included that missing component in nearly all his other writings. He mastered its use, but forgot it here.

Worship, a primary element in funeral services, is what separates the ordinary weeping and lamentation like David's from a correctly conducted funeral service that centers on God and his full authority in creation. Christian funeral services, like all worship services, give proper praise to the Creator.

- *Affirm death's power and help mourners face it.* A second goal in funeral services is to help the mourners face death's reality. This is best done by acknowledging death's power (as Paul repeatedly did in 1 Corinthians 15, for instance), and by reasserting life's brevity.

Death deeply gashes the psyches of the survivors. They wander in shock and numbness, not understanding the severity of their injuries. Assisting them to pretend noninjury can be as harmful as failing to stanch the flow of blood from a flesh wound. Untreated injury to the psyche causes immeasurable emotional damage. Thus, therapy requires that we talk openly of death and lead mourners to the brink of the grave, not hasten away in denial. This can't all be accomplished in a funeral service. Acceptance comes in stages. But the service can help build the foundation for openness and proper therapy.

The model for this approach comes directly from Scripture. In John 11, while discussing Lazarus's death, Jesus at first made references to his sleep because he planned to raise him. Seeing, however, the misunderstanding building in the disciples' minds, Jesus "told them plainly, 'Lazarus is dead' " (John 11:14). He minced no words, engaged no euphemisms.

Because many hearers at funerals know nothing of Jesus' resurrection power, they need to be told in biblical language of life's brevity: "All flesh is as grass." I attempt to reaffirm this concept with some vernacular form of the statement, for example: "Our watches may have quartz movements, but the wearers are only clay. We all face this moment. We all die."

David expressed this openly in Psalm 39:4–5: "Show me, Lord, my life's end and the number of my days; let me know how fleeting is my life. You have made my days a mere handbreadth; the span of my years is as nothing before you. Each man's life is but a breath."

- *Assist the mourners to remember the deceased and overcome regret.* Rarely does guilt or regret not complicate the grief process. It cripples. It sets in faster than rigor mortis. We help the grief process along when we assist the mourners to remember their loved one without wallowing in regret. Using the gash analogy again, guilt and regret become complicating cuts and infection in the death-wounded psyche. The minister must disinfect and bind.

An elderly gentleman in our church nursed his wife for years as Alzheimer's disease took her through stages varying from forgetfulness to lunacy to passive sedateness. He never left her alone, except for an occasional break provided by a friend or professional nurse. She beat him at times, wandered out of the house naked, became totally incontinent. He cleaned up after her and took the abuse, all the while remembering her love.

One morning he led her to the front porch so they could take a brief outing. She stutter-stepped obediently behind. Repeating a procedure established by months of routine, he gently placed her hand on a porch rail so she could steady herself as he locked the front door behind them. As soon as he turned, she crumpled to the ground, fracturing her hip. In the hospital she developed pneumonia, which took her life in about ten days.

Ordinary logic says, "He nursed her faithfully for many years. She could not recover from her illness. She was no good to anyone. It's better that her suffering end." But guilt got to my friend. He saw only his error in allowing her to fall. He rehearsed the incident repeatedly, and only after two years did the pain shows signs of subsiding.

The Lord provides therapy for this, too. In our words and deeds at funerals, we let people know that everyone senses guilt in the context of death. It helps to relate some experiences of our own to let them know we've been there. We might even confess our own feelings of guilt in respect to the deceased. Thank God that we can point those who grieve to the grace of Jesus, who forgives when we confess to him (1 John 1:9)!

● *Deal with the "big question" and offer hope.* We deal with the big, unresolved question in the minds of our hearers by stages. The question, of course, is: "What can *I* do about this frightening, awesome specter called death?"

After we remind our hearers of God's authority, of death's reality, and of Jesus' forgiveness, we deal with that big question. Few dwell on it long, though it haunts most survivors immediately upon hearing of the death of their loved one. Actually, the question attacks the psyche with many different assaults: *Will death strike me now, too? Why did I survive? How can I prepare myself for it? Or escape it?*

At this point we tell people of the need to respond to the Good News of Jesus' visitation to our planet and the death-blasting power of his Resurrection. We assist grieving people to see their need to prepare themselves for the inevitable moment of death by coming to terms with Jesus and experiencing the power of his death, burial, and Resurrection on their behalf.

I rely on this same, basic, four-goal understanding of my pastoral role whether I am dealing with Christians or non-Christians, young or old. I don't believe God granted me the prerogative to declare with certainty the eternal future of anyone. Jeremiah proclaimed the heart "deceitful above all things and beyond cure" (17:9). The Lord alone fully searches hearts and minds.

Does the Service Develop Appropriate Tension?

Funerals and memorial services provide us with the chance to present the only hope of resolving the universal tension inflicted by death. It takes wisdom to utilize these occasions effectively to promote the Good News of Jesus. All elements of the service should be employed properly to use this tension advantageously. Therefore, I find it better to reserve comments regarding resurrection and heaven for the close of the service. Injury and hurt must be acknowledged by confronting death and reminiscing about the deceased. Before suturing the wound, we must disinfect it of guilt.

A natural tension can develop in the service that will remain unresolved until the close. All good movies, dramas, and, yes, even sermons develop an issue, raising important questions that do not get fully answered until the close. The longer you hold the tension, the

---

The Eulogy

To eulogize, literally, is to speak or write a "good word." A funeral eulogy, then, is a formal, commendatory statement in praise of the deceased.

Our difficulties with the place of the eulogy in a Christian funeral stem from the Bible's silence about how to conduct a funeral service. Therefore, we must look to general theological principles, church traditions, and personal preferences in deciding what we will do.

Three Opinions

Christians maintain basically three positions regarding the use of eulogies:

● *No eulogies.* Some do not eulogize at all. They point out that all believers are equal in God's sight and should be treated as equals by the church. Thus, some ministers say nothing at all about the deceased in the funeral service. They feel that using a eulogy moves the service from the objective to the subjective, that it tends to glorify the person, when God is the One to be glorified in worship. "All men are equal, as all pennies are equal," said G. K. Chesterton, "because the only value in any of them is that they bear the image of the king."

● *Long eulogies.* Other ministers use long eulogies, making them the major part of a memorial service. These ministers reason that a *memorial* service should be exactly that—a time to remember and honor the one who has died. Though all people are equal before God, people have not all lived or served equally. Some were more committed to Christ, more involved in their communities, more devoted to their families and their churches. Focusing on the good qualities of the deceased can help bereaved family members and friends who need comfort.

● *Brief eulogies.* A third position

more you keep attention. Once the hearers know how the presentation will end, they are tempted to go to sleep. But the only one asleep at our services should be the deceased! We destroy the tension if we state too quickly, "There is nothing to fear. Aunt Suzie is looking down right now from her heavenly mansion."

Most services utilize elements of worship used on other occasions: music, Scripture reading, preaching, and prayer. The type and format may vary somewhat according to liturgy, ethnic tradition, local custom, and family preference. I usually follow this basic format, with occasional variations:

(1) Opening remarks, including a statement of why the congregation is assembled.

(2) Reading of obituary information.

(3) Song. (More or fewer songs may be included according to family preference.)

---

advocates devoting a brief part of the funeral service, perhaps three or four minutes, to the eulogy before focusing the rest of the service on God and the Christian hope. Here, the eulogy commends the traits God cultivated in the deceased and emphasizes God's goodness and gifts to the individual. In this view, each funeral service should contain a gracious word about the deceased for the sake of the living.

Considerations

As we make decisions about the eulogy, here are points to keep in mind:

● The way we treat our dead reveals our view of life. The more we value the living, the more tender and compassionate we are with the dead. Joseph of Arimathea gave a grave for our Lord. Women who loved him brought spices to anoint his dead body. As the British statesman Gladstone once said, "Show me the way in which a nation cares for its dead, and I will measure with mathematical exactness the tender sympathies of people, their respect for the laws of the land, and their loyalty to high ideals."

● Death is not like a factory gate through which people go in crowds. It is more like a turnstile through which they go one-by-one. The person being buried is unique and special. Some effort, even if small, should be made to make the funeral service personal.

● "Death is not the separation of two hearts, but the tearing apart of one heart." This statement by Fulton J. Sheen reminds us that death invariably leaves behind people who need healing. Jesus wept at the grave of a loved one.

● Christian funeral services have more than one purpose. They are an opportunity to affirm the dignity and worth of every individual, to comfort the broken-hearted, to proclaim our Christian hope.

A decision about the use of a eulogy should be consistent with each of these goals.

—*Paul W. Powell*

(4) Scripture reading.
(5) Prayer.
(6) Song.
(7) Eulogy/sermon.
(8) Prayer.

In some cultures, numerous friends eulogize the deceased. Some customs practically dictate elaborate ceremonies, featuring several different soloists or groups of musicians. Many denominations require definite ritual. More formal ceremonies include processionals, recessionals, and various kinds of mood music.

In any tradition, however, care can be taken that everything lend itself to the creation and resolution of the tension I've described. How do music, prayers, and Scripture help with the tension development? Ask that the sadder music be performed first and songs of victory be used at the close. In the prayers at the beginning of the service, voice the aching emptiness, the sense of separation, and the evident silence

---

The Funeral Sermon

Because funerals are by definition emotional experiences, some people feel that preaching at such a time constitutes an invasion of personal grief and private emotion. No doubt insensitive and inappropriate sermonizing can be offensive and counterproductive. On the other hand, a sensitively presented sermon based on carefully selected material can prove most helpful.

Why a Sermon?

Any pastor who has stood with a bereaved family beside a casket, listening to the well-meaning remarks of friends and relatives, is aware of the alarming mixture of superstition, speculation, and sentimentality with which people respond to bereavement. The funeral sermon can give people the opportunity simply to hear what the Bible says on the most significant subject of death.

A second reason for having the funeral sermon is to direct people's attention toward God when many of them may be more open than at other times. We might say, "You may be surprised to know that the Bible says, 'It is better to go to a house of mourning than to go to a house of feasting' (Eccles. 7:2). The reason for this is that festivals *divert* our attention, while funerals *direct* our attention—toward the God from whom we come, through whom we survive, and to whom we go. So let's think about him for a few minutes."

A third reason, of course, is to bring words of comfort and encouragement to those who have been bereaved.

What to Include

We should raise, and in some way answer, at least three questions in a funeral sermon: (1) What does death

of God experienced by mourners. In the same way, use Scriptures at the beginning that emphasize the brevity of life. Work toward achieving a mood that naturally occurs in the initial stages of grief. This isn't manipulation. Rather, it is an attempt to create a more natural setting and atmosphere for those in grief.

Should I Encourage the Tears?

It's healthy to cry. Grief therapists recommend that weeping and mourning be induced as a key part of the healing process. Time spent reminiscing with the family serves that end. First, if we sit with the family to gather information about the deceased, their recollections often make them cry. We want that to happen. Second, when we share those vignettes in the eulogy, people likely will cry again. We want that, too. Third, when friends, neighbors, and loved ones publicly share their reminiscences at the service, it enables them to voice their

---

mean to the deceased? (2) What does it mean to the bereaved? (3) What does it mean to the rest of us?

If the deceased was a believer, it is most helpful to sketch out briefly the believer's hope in Christ, using such expressions as "absent from the body, present with the Lord," or, "I will dwell in the house of the Lord forever," or, "To me, to live is Christ and to die is gain."

The second question has to do with helping the bereaved make the adjustments required by the death. These will vary dramatically, depending upon the circumstances. The trauma suffered by a young mother of two, widowed when her policeman husband was gunned down, is quite different from that of a family whose mother has died of cancer at the age of 85. There will be grief in both instances but not with equal intensity.

So we might say to the young widow, "Cindy, none of us can fully appreciate what you are feeling at this time . . ." and turning to her children, "Tammy and Billy, look around the room and see all the people who loved your daddy and love you, too. They will help you all they can."

The third question gives an opportunity to encourage the believers present to reevaluate their own lives in light of eternity and to instruct any unbelievers on important biblical truths. We might mention that their deceased friend is like Abel in that "he still speaks even though he is dead" (Heb. 11:4), and then remind them of the eternal truths for which their friend stood.

What Manner?

We should be as warm and personable as we are able; firm in our articulation of biblical truth; and as natural, conversational, and empathetic as possible, to avoid sounding sermonic. We can offer to talk personally to anyone who would like to discuss further our words or beliefs.

—Stuart Briscoe

apprehensions and promotes healthy tears. After that, they can more naturally and readily accept the message of hope and Good News.

Job's tragedy provides a model for the natural process I refer to. After the sudden, violent loss of his children and the onset of his own sickness, he sat weeping. His friends arrived. They did the right thing for seven days: they said nothing. But then they berated, accused, and blamed him for his tragedy, and they preached at him.

Reading their speeches, we may find ourselves in familiar territory. Their scathing words resemble sermons most of us have heard. The theology is sound, but it simply is misapplied. The context of death and suffering calls for minuscule amounts of preaching.

What if Job's friends had tried to console him? Would that have been better? That depends on the type of consolation offered. Had Job's friends patted him on the back saying, "There, there; God loves you. Everything's going to be all right," they'd have offended him just as badly. We can't afford to minimize the injury others feel.

Here's what I'm emphasizing about consolation: Persons experiencing grief need time and opportunity to express their hurt and bitterness as Job did. Job's friends didn't want to give him permission to do that. When we let mourners express their anguish, it compares to the removal of foreign matter and infection from a wound. God seems remote in those moments. Job repeatedly asked God why he (God) would not answer him. The Lord understood Job's need to do that. Job's friends didn't.

As we counsel and console families, we must permit them to express their anguish. A good funeral service takes the mourners through the stages of grief and lets them know it's all right to express anguish as David did in Psalm 22:1: "My God, My God, why have you forsaken me?" After that, we assist them to reminisce by personalizing the eulogy.

Should I Offer a Eulogy?

The word *eulogy* literally means "good word." We say some good words (but honest words!) about the dead one's life.

At times the family may request no eulogy. This happens for a variety of reasons. A widow of a deceased member of our church asked me not to say anything about him. No one in church knew it, but he was a true scoundrel. His scandalous behavior truly embarrassed her. The request for no eulogy may result because the family has limited income and feels costs can be held down if not much is requested of the minister. Other times family members are not sure they can deal with the pain they imagine the eulogy will create. Funeral directors on occasion inform ministers of the family's preference. At times no one gives ministers a choice in the matter.

The minister is expected to conform to the family's wishes. When speaking with the family, we can share what we would like to do, explaining the need as we see it. But sometimes we simply must accede. Unfortunately, there may be no way to avoid the occasional failure to meet the family's (often unexpressed) expectations.

For example, I was asked many years ago to do a brief wedding ceremony for a friend of a friend. By telephone, the groom told me he wanted only the essentials. They already had been wed in a foreign country and needed a minimal ceremony to comply with California law. A judge informed me that state law required only three basic questions. Strictly conforming to law, I followed the groom's request to the letter and declared them husband and wife. At the close of the ceremony, the bride burst into tears and pleaded, "Is that all?" She said she didn't "feel married." Perhaps we need to say enough at funerals for the deceased to "feel buried!"

Matching the ceremony to the occasion requires prayer and experience. It's important to follow the family's wishes. The formats of some traditions may call for the eulogy and sermon to be done separately. Separating them need not interfere with the tension and contrast we try to build into the service. The sermon simply needs to be at the close.

Where Will the Service Be Held?

Different settings require different advanced preparations. Do funeral chapels or church buildings provide a more proper setting for the service? In urban areas, unless some liturgical requirement demands it, a strong case can be made for holding services at a chapel on the cemetery grounds for logistics' sake. No one enjoys the heart-pounding panic experienced while tailgating in processions on high-speed freeways.

On the other hand, if we see our task as one of enabling people to confront death, funeral chapels may only add to the unreality of the death scene. They stand removed from everything experienced in actual life. The deceased probably spent at least a little time in the church building.

We might expect to see in the future a trend toward funeral services in a more natural setting, outside of funeral homes and church buildings, as we presently witness with wedding ceremonies. That isn't necessarily bad. Death needs to be reinstalled into life. Perhaps someone will promote the reinstitution of death watches by family members, including the washing of the corpse, in the same way natural childbirth has been popularized in our society. Whatever the setting, our task is to assist the mourners through the stages of grief, pointing them to the recuperative power of Jesus, God's Son.

Should the Casket Be Open?

One of the most strongly debated funeral issues centers on whether the corpse should be seen at the service. Some argue that it is cruel and painful to keep the casket lid open. Those not wanting to face the corpse are likely the ones not wanting to confront death in general (and their own in particular).

If the family insists on closing the casket prior to the service, we probably do well not to argue the point. If they ask for advice, we can let them know how the open casket helps them accept the reality of the loss. Unless the remains are badly decomposed or disfigured, all the family members, including children, generally will benefit from viewing their loved one.

Mortuaries usually allow viewing times prior to the service, and we can encourage families to use these. The visible presence of the corpse at services creates a powerful foil in contrast to the resurrection body, which Paul describes in 1 Corinthians 15. Nothing compares to the weakness, dishonor, and perishable nature of a dead body. It lies in vivid, stark contrast to the immortal, spiritual body that the Man of Heaven grants us.

—Robert Blair

Resources

Blair, R. 1990. The minister's funeral handbook. Grand Rapids: Baker.

Boettinger, H. 1969. Moving mountains. New York: Collier.

Christensen, J. 1985. Difficult funeral services. Old Tappan, N.J.: Revell.

Kübler-Ross, E. 1975. Death. Englewood Cliffs, N.J.: Prentice-Hall.

Kübler-Ross, E. 1969. On death and dying. New York: Macmillan.

Music for Funerals

Not so many years ago, the liturgical color for a service on behalf of the dead was black or purple. The service itself was almost always called a funeral service. Today most churches use white as the liturgical color, and the service may be called a "witness to the Resurrection." These changes, while they may not have permeated secular society, are significant for the church. The emphasis is no longer on the sorrow of the occasion, but on the Resurrection of our Lord Jesus Christ, which we as Christians share in together.

Funeral music should reflect this change in emphasis, making use of hymns that emphasize the Resurrection and God's eternal purposes. A few years ago, for example, I attended a memorial service in which all the hymns were Easter hymns.

The atmosphere was triumphant and uplifting rather than depressing and funereal.

Organ Music

Organ music for such services should be in character with the rest of the service. Composers such as Bach, Pachelbel, Buxtehude, and Brahms wrote music that can complement the worship aspect of the service. While not written specifically for a funeral, contemplative works such as Messiaen's "Eternal Purposes" or Langlais's "Song of Peace" are in keeping with the mood of such a service.

At the conclusion of the service, it is appropriate to play triumphant organ music in keeping with our remembrance of Christ's resurrection power. The final section of the first movement of Mendelssohn's "Sonata III" can be effective at this point, too. If it has not already been sung, playing the Vaughan Williams "For All the Saints" is also good. I have even, upon request, played the *Toccata* from Widor's "Symphony V" to conclude a funeral service.

Vocal Music

When it comes to solo vocal music or choral music for a funeral, the choices become more problematic. This is because such music includes texts. If a church has a policy about what types of words are suitable for public worship, this simplifies the problem greatly. For instance, some churches use texts only from the Bible or hymnal. Though this admittedly eliminates some interesting texts, it also rules out a certain shallowness that can characterize some contemporary music.

Two vocal solos that seem particularly appropriate to funeral or memorial services are Dvorak's "God Is My Shepherd," and Handel's "I Know My Redeemer Liveth." Choral works that complement memorial-service themes are the Handel or Beethoven "Hallelujah Chorus" and the fourth movement of Brahms's German Requiem, "How Lovely Is Thy Dwelling Place." The Billings "Easter Anthem" is equally appropriate. The Vaughan Williams setting of Psalm 84, "O How Amiable," ends with the familiar hymn, "O God, Our Help in Ages Past," which gives strength and comfort to the family of the deceased.

Congregational Music

Of all the arts associated with the church, music speaks most directly to the worshiper. For this reason, the choice of music for a funeral is very important. It sets the mood of the service and makes the task of the minister either easier or more difficult, depending on what music is selected.

Here are some hymns that give strength and comfort to the family and worshipers:

"A Mighty Fortress Is Our God"
"Amazing Grace"
"All Hail the Power of Jesus' Name"
"For All the Saints"
"God Moves in a Mysterious Way"
"He Who Would Valiant Be"
"How Firm a Foundation"
"Jesus Christ Is Risen Today"
"O God, Our Help in Ages Past"
"O What Their Joy"
"The Strife Is O'er"

—*Richard M. Peek*

The Committal Service

As he hung on the cross, Jesus said, "Father, into your hands I commit my spirit" (Luke 23:46). A pastor can lead the grieving at the grave to follow Jesus' example by releasing a loved one into the hands of the heavenly Father. This is the primary focus of the committal service.

Practical Considerations

Upon arrival at the cemetery, the minister meets the pallbearers as they prepare to carry the casket to the grave, and then leads the procession of pallbearers and family to the place of burial, walking at the head of the casket. As the friends and family gather, they should be encouraged to come as close as possible so they can hear.

Unless there has not been an earlier memorial service, the actual burial service usually is brief. (I explain my intentions to the family prior to the funeral so they are not caught off guard by how quickly the service is concluded.) Standing at the grave site is not the place for long biblical dissertations, lengthy prayers, or musical programs. The emotions of most mourners at this point are too intense for that.

Following the closing prayer, it's good to greet the immediate family members and briefly assure them of our love and support. A sensitive touch can say more than words at this time. Then we may leave. If the family wants to linger for a few moments, they may, but it is family time. Since our part is over, we may graciously slip away to the car.

The Service

The main ingredients of the committal service are the reading of suitable verses of Scripture, words of committal, and a prayer. Liturgical churches will have set forms, and others often use biblical passages such as 1 Corinthians 15 and 1 Thessalonians 4 to point the grieving away from the bleakness of burial toward the certain joy of the Resurrection.

The words of committal for a believer might include: "Since it has pleased our heavenly Father, in his wisdom, to take unto himself our beloved [name], we therefore commit his/her body to the ground, looking for the blessed hope and glorious appearing of our great God and Savior, Jesus Christ, who shall change the body of our humiliation and fashion it anew in the likeness of his own body of glory by the working of his mighty power . . ."

If the deceased is not known to be a believer, it's more appropriate to use words such as: "We commit the body of [name] to the ground; his/her spirit we leave in the hands of a merciful God. May the living learn the lessons of this day and experience the comfort of Jesus Christ, who said, 'I am the resurrection and the life. He who believes in me will live, even though he dies; and whoever lives and believes in me will never die.' "

A closing prayer offers thanks to God for the life of the deceased and for the hope of being reunited at the coming of the Lord, and includes a request that those who mourn will sense the presence of God in the days ahead. If there are sufficient people, we may choose to invite everyone to sing a verse of a familiar hymn. Other groups may want to repeat the Lord's Prayer together.

The key is to remember that this is a *committal* service—committing the body to the ground. The service powerfully marks the end of an earthly relationship. Much more than that, it commits a soul into the hands of God.

—Calvin C. Ratz

Military Rites

Each of the armed services provides guidance to its chaplains on specific details relating to the conduct of military funerals. The nation renders appropriate honors to its military members who die either in active duty or in retirement, and the procedures involved are prescribed in detail.

What to Expect

While the religious service is a part of the military funeral, no particular format is prescribed. Chaplains and civilian clergy have full freedom in the selection of music and Scripture readings, and in sermon and prayer content. The officiating chaplain or other clergy usually precedes the remains in procession into the chapel and follows the casket in recession. Military pall bearers usually retire from the chapel during the service itself.

At the cemetery, a ceremonial guard forms, and the military pall bearers bring the casket to the grave. The person officiating then conducts the graveside service. Upon its completion (and depending upon the rank of the deceased) either a volley of muskets or rifles or a salute of cannons is fired. A bugler plays taps, and the United States

flag draping the coffin is then folded and presented by the chaplain or clergy to the next-of-kin. This presentation completes the ceremony, and the honor guard and pall bearers retire.

The military funeral is a simple yet dignified expression of honor. There are no rites involved that conflict with or demean Christian burial.

Special Occasions

Military memorial services are similar to other memorial services in that they allow clergy to act without restriction, except in two instances:

• *Memorial ceremonies.* A memorial ceremony by definition is conducted for a military unit in formation, under orders, or under arms. Since members have been directed to participate, the chaplain or clergyperson participating must be sensitive to the rights of nonreligious service members and those of other religious persuasions, taking care not to offend them. This is only fair, since the clergyperson is not in charge of the formation and thus cannot properly dismiss those who might be offended.

• *Unit memorial services.* Even if

the service is conducted in a chapel, if the unit or organization is present *as a whole* or has been directed to attend, the chaplain or civilian clergyperson should explain the Christian character of the service and provide an opportunity for dissent-ers to depart without embarrassment.

Sensitivity to religious rights is an essential element in the chaplain and civilian clergyperson's role in military-related burials.

—James A. Edgren

Pastoral Responsibilities for Funerals

T he British preacher Alexander Maclaren once said about his ministry, "If I had to do it over, I would minister more to broken hearts."

Ministry during the time of grief is a ministry to broken hearts. How a pastor practically handles the issue of death can establish a lifelong relationship with the bereaved. Well-handled funerals also can endear pastors to their congregation and community. The pastor's challenge is to make a funeral service one that is uplifting, comforting, and fitting.

Preparing Oneself

Funerals, with their attendant responsibilities, need not take a pastor by surprise. Here are some ways to be prepared personally to minister in such circumstances.

• *Build a file.* Begin now to build a file on death, grief, funerals, and other difficult situations. As you have the opportunity to attend funeral services or read articles that apply to particular death-related situations, add them to the file. Also clip helpful quotes, poems, or sayings that would be appropriate for funeral services.

Look for resources to provide information helpful to such occurrences as the death of an infant or a young child, or notes on how you might handle a death involving a murder or suicide. The more information we can accumulate concerning these special situations, the more we will be prepared for them when they come.

• *Investigate the local customs.* One way to do this is to interview local funeral and cemetery directors. Find out about state laws, such as the requirements concerning embalming, autopsies, cremation, caskets, and vaults. Ask about local funeral customs. Do people traditionally view the body the day before the funeral? What are the local customs concerning wakes and open caskets? What about costs? Ask about death certificates and the costs of caskets, vaults, grave plots, headstones, and the opening and closing of the grave.

Finally, it's wise to observe a local funeral service, since we cannot assume customs are uniform everywhere. The more we know about local customs and laws, the better equipped we will be to counsel the family during its time of need.

• *Prepare personally for death.* Most of us need to come to terms with the impending reality of our own death. We can study the Word of God as it pertains to death, grief, and the Resurrection. We must determine our personal approach to cremation, counseling the terminally ill, and donating organs. When faced with a grieving family looking for guidance, it is essential that these major issues already be thoroughly processed in our own minds. Howard Hendricks says that, "A mist in the pulpit is a fog in the pew." Nothing can be more true when counseling a grieving family. Therefore we must have a handle on our own convictions concerning death before we are called to counsel others who are struggling.

One effective stimulant for this theological reflection is to cultivate close relationships with our people before death strikes. Then as death comes, we witness firsthand the stages of the grief process as we learn how to effectively minister to those who are bereaved. Knowing the stages of grief and the appropriate ministry response to those stages is extremely helpful in understanding the wide range of emotions we encounter.

Preparing the Congregation

• *Prepare people for the realities of death before it occurs.* We need to preach and teach on some of the passages that relate to death, dying, grief, and hope. Thoughtful exposition of Scripture can help a family unknowingly prepare for the traumatic time of death. Passages such as John 12 or John 14, 1 Corinthians 15, or 1 Thessalonians 4 are parts of the Bible we need to make familiar to our people.

Church libraries also can make available books on death, grief, and recovery. A well-educated congregation not only will be able to help during the time of a parishioner's bereavement, but it also will better understand death when it occurs in the body of Christ.

• *Know your people.* If we are intentional in our care for the terminally ill, we begin a ministry with the family weeks or months before death becomes reality. This time we spend with the ill and aged before a death pays rich dividends as we minister at the time of bereavement. Part of the time can be spent helping people prepare for their death. Some of the most meaningful funerals are those where the deceased have played a part in planning the service.

Preparing the Terminally Ill

While our time ministering to the terminally ill will be of immense aid later when preparing the funeral, our responsibilities concerning death actually begin before death. And this ministry of caring also promises to be a rich and rewarding time for us, since some of the most fulfilled persons are those with terminal illnesses.

• *Discern the spiritual condition of the terminally ill and minister to their need.* The many physical needs of the terminally ill tend to overshadow their spiritual needs, so we need to talk with them about faith, hope, and assurance. We can be honest and open about life, death, and the person's condition. Oddly enough, those who have worked through the grief process to a place where they can accept their illness often are capable of ministering to us!

• *Do not neglect the families of the terminally ill.* The loved ones are also working through the illness and prospect of death. We need to surround them with a supporting group of believers sure to be available during the darkest hours.

Taking the First Steps

When actual notification of the death arrives, we have a number of tasks ahead of us.

• *Go to the grieving family.* We ought to go immediately and express our sympathy. This is not the time for theological dissertations or discussions; it is a time to sit and listen, forgetting our watches. It's usually wise to be slow to speak. An expression of sorrow such as, "I am so sorry" or "I came because I care for you" is appropriate and all that is needed at that time. Our mere presence with the grieving family at this time is a ministry. Experienced pastors know they best express themselves through little things like a hug or warm handshake.

We can encourage the family to talk through their experience by simply asking, "Can you tell me what happened?" I like to encourage the expression of happy memories but also allow the privilege of expressing grief. We shouldn't be afraid to "weep with those who weep."

At the appropriate time it's good to help the family think through the next logistical steps. They will need to contact a funeral home and plan the service. It is not our responsibility single-handedly to plan the funeral, but rather to offer support as they think through what needs to be done. Our task is to enable rational thinking during a time of crises.

Many pastors arrange to meet the family at the funeral home to complete the funeral plans. They offer to provide help by organizing the congregation to provide meals, transportation, and child care.

When friends and family gather to communicate their love to the immediate family, we can help this group form a natural support group. We may want to solicit specific forms of support for the family, such as care for house pets or transportation of an aged relative.

At this first contact, it's best to stay long enough to ensure that things are under control. After identifying the support group that has gathered to help, we might read an appropriate (short) passage of Scripture and offer prayer to share the hope found in God. Encouragement like, "It is often during our times of greatest weakness that God grants us his greatest strength," gives needed assurance. Since during this time the family is processing many emotions, our talent for great biblical exposition probably will not be necessary.

● *Meet with the family to plan the service.* When we meet with the family at the funeral home, a number of decisions need to be made. Given the traumatic nature of the occasion, it is an ideal time for pastoral comfort and guidance. The funeral director gathers personal information and handles the business portion of the funeral. The pastor's primary task is to support the wishes of the family.

Often pastors are consulted on decisions that are made at this time. Since we are somewhat removed from the situation and can see things more theologically and less emotionally, we can help the family explore their options and provide helpful comments as appropriate. We must, however, avoid overstepping our bounds of authority. This is not a time to inject our personal tastes and biases. For instance, we may prefer that the family not purchase the most expensive casket, but they, not we, will ultimately live with the decision.

This is often the time to gather information helpful in providing the best possible service to the family. We need to address: location and time of the service; visitation hours; prayer service for the family before the funeral; number of ministers conducting the service and their respective roles; music—soloists, congregational singing, and hymns; obituary notice; the eulogy; testimony by friends and family; time, place, and nature of interment (Will it involve a military service?); the possibility of a second memorial service in another town; time and location of meals for the family; what to do with memorial gifts; other ways the church can reach out to the family; and means of contacting principal parties.

Two other items bear discussion: When will the body be viewed? I encourage the family to open the casket before the service and close it permanently prior to the service. Also, will fraternal orders expect to be a part of the service? If so, I encourage that the rites be performed before the service prior to the casket's arrival at the church.

After meeting with the family, we need to contact the funeral director to make final plans. We're wise to be sure he understands our expectations as well as the wishes of the family. In ideal circumstances we may be able to share with him our perspective on death.

The Funeral Service

One kind gesture is to arrive at the funeral service promptly, long before anybody has an opportunity to worry. Once we are there, we again are presented with a number of responsibilities.

• *Ministry before the service.* When at the place of the funeral, it's good to meet with the family prior to the service and assure them of your presence and support during this difficult period. Then we can wait for the start of the service in whatever quiet spot works best. But wherever we go to collect our thoughts, we need to make sure the funeral director knows where to find us to begin the service.

• *Ministry during the service.* The funeral service typically begins with an organ prelude or vocal solo. Following the prelude the presiding minister typically offers an opening sentence, a verse of Scripture, and a prayer, followed by special music or congregational singing and the reading of Scripture designed to comfort and encourage the bereaved. An obituary or eulogy often precedes the message.

Usually we want to keep the message relatively brief. Most ministers agree that fifteen minutes is appropriate. We need once again to recognize that family and friends are functioning on an emotional rather than intellectual level, so we should frame our remarks accordingly.

The benediction concludes the service. In some parts of the country, a viewing is customary at this point. If this is the case, often the pastor moves to the head of the casket while those in attendance file by as they exit. Traditionally, the minister remains with the casket and accompanies it to the hearse.

• *Ministry at the graveside.* We need to determine whether to ride to the cemetery with the funeral director or drive. One advantage in riding with the funeral director is that we arrive punctually at the cemetery at the right grave site.

At the cemetery the minister usually walks at the front of the procession as the casket moves from the hearse to the graveside. A slow, dignified pace allows the pallbearers and pastor to avoid falls on unsteady footing.

The committal at the graveside should be simple. It's traditional to speak from the head of the casket. Many services begin with a Scripture reading and include the reading of the words of committal, a prayer, and a benediction.

As the funeral director dismisses the assembly, it's good to offer your personal condolence to the family. This simple gesture of lending your prayer support will be appreciated.

Ministry after the Funeral

We will probably want to contact the family the day following the funeral to make ourselves available to counsel them. We need to prepare them for the grief process, which normally lasts fifteen to eighteen

---

Working with Funeral Directors

Pastors get to know funeral directors by doing funerals. A partnership is formed in the ministry of comfort. For a good working relationship, cooperation is the key.

Expectations

A funeral director has the right to expect a pastor to:
- Be a competent comforter, understanding the grieving process.
- Place the grieving family's needs first.
- Have the confidence of one's theology to be able to handle difficult situations with tact and kindness.
- Be present while the family makes funeral arrangements, if requested by the family.
- Cooperate with the director in planning the service, music, and occasions for fellowship;
- Conduct the funeral with sensitivity and dignity.
- Be candid about honorarium expectations.
- Help the grieving family following the public services.

In turn, a pastor has the right to expect the funeral director to:
- Treat those in sorrow as persons.
- Guide the family through necessary decisions and provide clear explanations.
- Respect the beliefs of the family and their church.
- Be direct in discussing costs and methods of payment.
- Invite the pastor to be present at the family visitation.
- Intervene in difficult moments.
- Handle details such as sending flowers to the home or church.
- Ensure that paperwork, such as death certificates, forms for veteran's benefits, and the cemetery plot deed, is properly processed.

Whether the funeral is held in the funeral home or the church, most funeral directors respect the authority of the pastor in structuring the service. Music should be planned with family members and specific requests honored whenever possible. The pastor's responsibility also

months. Especially through the first year, there will be anniversaries of special occasions, holidays, and birthdays during which the family will experience great loss. It's good to note those dates and plan to contact the family, especially on the anniversary of the death. A phone call to let the family know we are thinking of them will be appreciated.

Another way to help the family is to write a letter recounting happy memories of the deceased. We can offer positive alternatives for the family to consider to help deal with their grief, such as support groups, reading material, or grief-recovery conferences. As caring pastors, we need to be especially attentive to the needs of the spouse of the deceased as he or she goes through great transitions.

---

includes addressing the spiritual needs and questions of family and friends. When convenient, a copy of the liturgy can be given to the funeral director preceding the service.

The start and conclusion of the graveside service are the funeral director's duty. He choreographs people's movements, including the seating of guests, the directing of pall bearers, moving the casket to the hearse, guiding the procession to the grave, and overseeing the burial.

Discussions

These questions should be asked of the funeral director:
• Will the casket be open during the service?
• Will the church be used for a luncheon after the funeral, and who will extend the invitation?
• Is the church expected to provide the meal?
• Are there special family situations to consider?

The pastor needs to take the lead in explaining any church policies when the funeral is at the church. Any information that helps the logistics—such as the best doors to accommodate the casket—will be appreciated by the funeral director.

Pastors are often invited to ride to the cemetery with the funeral director. This allows time to think about the graveside service and get to know the director. It also affords an opportunity to jointly evaluate the family's needs. If it is appropriate, this is an opportune moment to compliment a funeral director who has served the bereaved family well.

Funeral homes often host seminars on grief-related issues or sponsor grief-support groups. Some church classes on death and dying will include a tour of a funeral home and a discussion of actual costs. In such ways, pastors and funeral directors work together to help families, both participating in ways they know best.

In conducting a funeral, the pastor and funeral director are supporting agents. Their joint ministry is to comfort people with broken hearts. They can reach that goal through professional cooperation, personal concern, and the power of Jesus Christ.

—*David W. Wiersbe*

Personal Notes

It's important to record the funeral in one's personal and church records. Someone may request this information at some future time, or we may be called upon to do another funeral for the same family and wouldn't want the sermon to appear to be a duplicate.

It's good to be prepared for questions regarding an honorarium. Some funeral homes routinely include this as part of the funeral expense. If so, we will want to speak with the funeral director about what we consider appropriate. If the issue is handled directly with the family, we need not be hesitant in sharing what we normally receive for our services. At the same time, we can be free to graciously waive an honorarium or apply it to a memorial to the deceased.

Ministry to those who are experiencing grief can be a valuable experience. Being well prepared will pay rich dividends. The family, as well as the congregation and the community, are watching to see how a person of God responds to difficult situations. Our sensitive, comforting, and compassionate responses reflect God's compassion and care. Isaiah 40:1 reads, "Comfort, comfort my people, says your God." Our calling uniquely qualifies us to offer that comfort to those with broken hearts.

—Douglas M. Cecil

Resources

Blair, R. 1990. The minister's funeral handbook. Grand Rapids: Baker Book House.

Justice, W. 1982. When death comes. Nashville: Broadman Press.

Wiersbe, W., and D. Wiersbe. 1985. Comforting the bereaved. Chicago: Moody Press.

38

Handling the Hard Deaths

Death comes through many doors. For some, it slips through the door marked "merciful healer" and liberates a person from pain, illness, and a worn-out body. In these cases, death makes sense; it's easy to see how death fits naturally into the cycle of life. Any death certainly produces grief in those who survive. A natural death following a long, full life, however, tempers grief's pain with the achievement of a life well-lived and a smooth transition from one life to another.

Then there are times when death bursts through the door marked "obscene intruder." It comes as a vicious thief who robs the victim and family of health, happiness, and much of the abundant life Christ taught was God's intention. These deaths are untimely—suicides, accidents, murders, terminal illnesses, or stillbirths. These deaths take babies, children, young adults, and those in middle age. These deaths make no sense; they frustrate any attempt to provide tidy answers when hurting people ask, "Why?" These are the hard cases.

What Makes Hard Cases Hard

Of all the funeral services ministers perform, the ones remembered most are the hard cases.

Funerals for suicides, for example, are difficult not only because of the grief that is heavily laced with guilt, but also because of the societal and ecclesiastical attitudes toward death by one's own hand. How are we, as pastors, to handle the funeral of a suicide if we are taught—and believe—that to kill oneself is a sin?

493

What can we say when we perform, as I once did, a funeral for a young man who seems to have everything going for him? This man was an accomplished professional chef, he had a good marriage, and he was expecting a baby soon. Like Richard Corey in Edwin Arlington Robinson's poem, however, this outwardly successful man had found something in himself with which he could not live. One fall evening he took his brother's deer rifle to a stand of trees outside of town and shot himself. As it happened, the brother who owned the rifle arrived at the scene just in time to hear the gunshot.

Deaths caused by automobile accidents shock people with their untimeliness. Often a sense of unfairness shackles the loved ones. For instance, the bitterness was almost palpable at the funeral service of a popular young police officer from our town who was killed one summer night when his car flipped and hit a telephone pole. Since the officer was so well-liked, the funeral was huge, and as I talked to people at the service, I detected less an asking of why it happened than a basic rage *that* it had happened.

Increasingly we give pastoral care to families of people who have succumbed to AIDS. From the most recent information, AIDS will continue to claim many lives. Since many victims of AIDS are homosexual males, at these funerals we encounter deep negative feelings toward the homosexual lifestyle. Add the fear of AIDS among the general population and the double burden parents often carry, adjusting not only to their child's death but also to the newfound knowledge of his sexual orientation, and the combination makes for a truly hard case. It's not unusual in an AIDS-related funeral situation to do as much counseling with the parents regarding homosexuality as one does concerning death.

Funerals for babies and children confront us most graphically with unfulfilled dreams, dashed hopes, and unrequited love. How difficult it is to stand next to a tiny white casket and try to comfort a desolate family at the funeral of a stillborn infant!

The Challenge of the Hard Cases

Few ministerial duties provide as great a challenge and opportunity as these funerals. In a hard case, the funeral becomes more than a ritualized leave-taking from the deceased. When funerals are done effectively, the bereaved can experience firsthand a sense of God's care and concern. This caring cuts through the worst pain and provides the strength to withstand it. People can feel free to be angry with God, secure in the knowledge their anger will not drive God away. They can express their feelings, knowing they will survive the pain. Ultimately, those who experience the most difficult grief may emerge stronger in their faith with the aid of good pastoral care; that is, of course, if the job is done well.

For all the good things we can do for families in the hard cases, however, we can do just as many bad—and avoiding the bad is the challenge. Poorly given, ministry can have a definite counterproductive effect on those in grief, actually damaging the emotions and spirit. The bereaved may feel estranged from God and the church family just when closeness and nurture is needed most.

When grieving people perceive any insincerity on the part of the pastor, they tend to think that since the minister doesn't care, God must not either. The grief process may thus be arrested for a considerable length of time, and symptoms of grief such as anger, guilt, and a sense of loneliness may be intensified.

For instance, not long ago the director of our community mental health agency asked me to talk with a young staff member whose father had died two months previously. The director told me that in reaction to his grief, the man was making work difficult for clients and the rest of the staff.

I talked with the young man and found he was distressed about the anger he was venting on everyone. He revealed that the minister who served the family during his father's illness and funeral seemed more concerned about the details of the will and the settlement of the estate than about the pain of the family members. No doubt this young man was angry about other things as well, but his anger increased as he perceived the awkward ministry to the family as a lack of caring.

What to Avoid

In difficult funerals, effective ministry becomes clear when we consider what we should avoided:

• *Resist being the "answer man."* A mystique surrounds pastoral work, much as in the field of medicine. We spend years of preparation and more years of practice to answer life's most basic and imponderable questions. It feels good to have people seek us out for answers.

When we are confronted with a hard case, however, there are no easy answers. Nothing we can say or do will bring back a dead son or reverse a car accident. No answer we give will make a suicide easy to think about.

Once I read a sermon a fellow minister had delivered at the funeral of an AIDS victim. The thrust of the message was that this untimely and tragic death was perfectly understandable—it was God's punishment for the victim's lifestyle. I wondered: Was this "answer" to the question of why this young man had to die really helpful to the family and friends left behind?

We cannot fix painful situations by providing answers to questions that are unanswerable.

• *Don't treat this as "just part of my job."* Difficult death situations demand special treatment, added vulnerability, and "heart."

Some time ago I sat with the family of a dying woman. Prior to the event that caused our hurried summons to the hospital, she had been proceeding along a normal postoperative course of recovery. Then a weak spot in her aorta ruptured. As her blood pressure dropped dramatically and her pulse faded, her family and I sat silently in the waiting room. Our feelings of shock and helplessness bound us together.

With us sat another minister called at the daughter's request to lend emotional and spiritual support to her. Instead, he fidgeted in his chair and glanced frequently at his wrist watch. When the woman finally died, the daughter, disgusted despite her grief, told the minister he could leave. When the clergyman compounded his mistake by offering to stay longer, the daughter icily informed him that wouldn't be necessary. It was a long time before that woman returned to church.

The minister probably cared, but he behaved as he did because he was feeling as uncomfortable as the rest of us. What should he have

---

Funerals for Strangers and Nonbelievers

Periodically we are asked to conduct funeral services for people we have never met. The request may come from funeral directors acting on behalf of unchurched families, or perhaps from church families who have lost an unchurched loved one. Accepting such assignments and ministering to the people concerned is commendable, but we must make it clear that the service will be based on biblical principles and that we will not pretend to speak personally about the deceased.

Personal Words

We should arrange to spend time with the family prior to the funeral, both to minister to them and to learn something about the deceased. While we will be unable to make firsthand observations concerning the deceased, we can certainly quote reliable sources if the information will honor the deceased and comfort the bereaved.

In some instances it might be appropriate to invite a responsible person to speak briefly about the life of the deceased, although it's wise to ask to go over the proposed talk before the funeral. This part of the service can be introduced by saying, "Unfortunately, I did not have the privilege of knowing our friend Bill, but I am aware that all of you did, and so you have the advantage over me. It would be rather odd if I, not knowing him, were to speak to those who did know him, so I have invited Bill's college roommate, Henry, to say a few words . . ."

Helping the Living

Having paid respects to the deceased, we need not feel compelled

done? Acknowledge his discomfort at the outset, and let the rest of us support him while he supported us.

● *At the funeral, don't give a canned presentation.* Recently I took an informal survey of funeral directors to check their perceptions of clergy effectiveness in problem funeral situations. To say the least, their responses were discouraging.

One funeral director told me, "It seems as if most of the ministers come with a service that's cut-and-dried no matter what the cause of death. For every service they use the same Bible passages, the same prayers, and the same messages. It's almost as if they don't care." Virtually all the other funeral directors echoed the same sentiment.

If such is the case, what must the families be feeling? Do they think we are there just to perform a perfunctory service, an empty ritual? Since grief's pains magnify people's feelings, probably they who need us most—those in the hard cases—feel angrier, guiltier, and lonelier when we minister superficially.

If in the funeral of a suicide victim, the minister makes no mention of the suicide, hardly refers to the deceased by name, and reads the

---

further to address specifics concerning the person's life; a funeral service is for the benefit of the living rather than the dead. This being the case, we can speak gently but firmly about the fact that life is a gift from God to be enjoyed fully and to be lived wisely and well, according to God's instructions. Failure to do so leads to estrangement from God and resultant spiritual maladies, but there is the hope of forgiveness and a new start because of Christ's work for us. We can emphasize the uncertainty of life and the inevitability of death, while building in words of encouragement to nourish one's spiritual life in the light of eternity.

In my experience of this type of funeral, people are responsive to a "talk" rather than a sermon. They are warmed by a sense of caring and understanding and are perfectly open to be instructed, comforted, and challenged. For instance, on numerous occasions total strangers have said to me after a funeral,

"Thanks, Reverend. You gave me a bit of hope."

I usually have felt free to say, "If I gave you hope by telling you lies, I am a scoundrel. But I didn't; it was the *truth*. So let me encourage you to respond to the truth and find hope in Christ."

If we have no reason to believe the deceased was a believer, it would be wrong to state that he or she was, or even to leave that impression. In truth, we cannot know categorically a person's spiritual condition at the moment of death, so we need make no pronouncement on this matter. We can, however, speak with authority to those who are still alive, and this should be the emphasis of any of our funeral services.

I have found funeral services of this nature both valuable and rewarding. The important thing is to be gracious, honest, and caring. People will respond.

—*Stuart Briscoe*

rest of the service out of a book, people feel as if they are being led to the table but denied permission to eat. A canned funeral service that takes no consideration of the unique circumstances of the death will seldom be helpful to people hurting in a hard case.

We may want to resort to canned services because of our discomfort; the prepared, impersonal service appears an easy way out of the situation. We become far more effective in handling the hard cases, however, when we allow ourselves to grieve along with the bereaved.

The best thing we can do as we prepare for each difficult funeral service is to ask ourselves what it is that gives us the most courage and strength, given the way we feel about the situation. It is as true in ministry as in anything else: We work best with what we know and have ourselves experienced.

What We Can Do

So what can we do?

The funeral service is the place where we can define the boundaries of grief. We acknowledge the loss of the deceased, we recognize the feelings we experience as a result of the loss, and we offer hope that this most terrible time will pass and we will be able to affirm life as good once again. With those thoughts in mind, there are several things we can do:

• *Tailor the service to the family at hand.* The message that worked for the loved ones of the "church grandpa" will be ineffective for the family of the child who succumbed to leukemia. When preparing the service, we need to keep the family and circumstances in mind. If possible, we should get to know something about the deceased and his or her family prior to the service. How the person died will determine, more than anything, the cut of the funeral service as we tailor it to the needs of those attending.

• *Mention the cause of death.* It frustrates a family when a pastor talks all around the cause of death without addressing it directly. In some cases, the circumstances will be obvious, as in the death of a child. In other cases, part of our effectiveness lies in enabling the survivors to admit "John was killed in a car wreck" or "John was murdered," or even "John killed himself." Mentioning the cause of death gives everyone present the chance to start recovering from grief from a more-or-less common starting point.

Of course, sensitivity and care need to be exercised, and plans discussed with the family ahead of time. Given strong emotional attachments to concepts like suicide and AIDS, it is essential we discover the most tactful yet honest way to present the cause of death. In the case of the AIDS victim, I obtained the consent of the family before reading as a part of the obituary that he had died of Acquired Immune Deficiency Syndrome (that was honest, yet not so scary sounding as AIDS).

• *Acknowledge that this is an abnormal time.* This openness helps the survivors place their unpleasant feelings into perspective. Often, a grieving person will feel as if he or she is losing touch with reality. Surviving spouses say things such as, "I feel like I'm losing my mind. I won't be able to function normally ever again. I can't think straight, and I can't remember a single thing."

Our honest acknowledgment can help the bereaved see that this situation is something we do not normally encounter; it is a time for unusual feelings and reactions. There is good reason to feel spiritually and emotionally out of kilter when the one we've known and loved dies suddenly and tragically.

This acknowledgment also offers the hope that feelings will return to normal once the worst of the grief is overcome. That in itself can be a great comfort to people who are thrown into a spiritual vertigo by a tragic death.

• *Allow for honest ventilation of feelings.* In the case of a murder, suicide, child death, or other difficult situation, certainly there should be anger. Often guilt or other feelings will manifest themselves. By reminding people that these signs are neither mental instability nor a lack of faith, we can provide a place from which the bereaved can begin working back to where things are normal and life is good.

• *Emphasize God's presence.* Even though grieving people may be angry at God to the point of rage, God's love is still important to them. The effective pastor is the one who can help the bereaved through Scripture and prayer to know that God is present, not as the oppressor but as the Comforter on the side of the oppressed. While we may not know why a fatal accident happened, or why a child contracted leukemia, or why a woman killed herself, we do know that God is present and on our side.

In addition to lifting up God's presence through the promises of Scripture, we may also point to God's presence as we find it in caring family members and friends. I have seen friends surround widows and others at the cemetery and infuse those hurting people with their strength through touches, hugs, firm clasps of the hand, and other expressions of caring. This kind of comfort is the most effective thing to pass along to family members and friends of hard cases.

As pastors, we are physicians of the spirit. We bring talents, training, and special gifts to the hard grief cases, just as doctors take their talents and skills into difficult medical cases. An openness to the guidance of the Holy Spirit, the sensitive use of the pastoral skills we possess, and a willingness to share the grief journey of those we serve can place us in partnership with God—who truly brings forth miracles in the hard cases.

—Roger F. Miller